Antiquity

Greeks and Romans in Context

Frederick G. Naerebout and Henk W. Singor

WILEY Blackwell

This English edition first published 2014
© 2014 John Wiley & Sons, Inc.

Originally published in Dutch as Frederick G. Naerebout and Henk W. Singor, *De Oudheid: Grieken en Romeinen in de context van de wereldgeschiedenis*. Amsterdam: Ambo | Anthos, 2008.

Edition history: Ambo | Anthos (Dutch editions: 1e, 1995; 2e, 2001; 3e, 2008)

Translated from the Dutch by Frederick G. Naerebout and Henk W. Singor. This is an authorised translation from the Dutch language edition published by Ambo | Anthos. Responsibility for the accuracy of the translation rests solely with John Wiley & Sons, Inc. and is not the responsibility of Ambo | Anthos. No part of this book may be reproduced in any form without the written permission of the original copyright holder, Ambo | Anthos.

Registered Office
John Wiley & Sons Ltd, The Atrium, Southern Gate, Chichester, West Sussex, PO19 8SQ, UK

Editorial Offices
350 Main Street, Malden, MA 02148-5020, USA
9600 Garsington Road, Oxford, OX4 2DQ, UK
The Atrium, Southern Gate, Chichester, West Sussex, PO19 8SQ, UK

For details of our global editorial offices, for customer services, and for information about how to apply for permission to reuse the copyright material in this book please see our website at www.wiley.com/wiley-blackwell.

The right of Frederick G. Naerebout and Henk W. Singor to be identified as the authors of this work has been asserted in accordance with the UK Copyright, Designs and Patents Act 1988.

Library of Congress Cataloging-in-Publication Data
Hardback   9781444351385
Paperback   9781444351392

Naerebout, F. G.
   [Oudheid. English]
   Antiquity : Greeks and Romans in context / F.G. Naerebout and H.W. Singor. – 1
        pages cm
   Translation of: De oudheid.
      Includes bibliographical references and index.
   ISBN 978-1-4443-5138-5 (hardback) – ISBN 978-1-4443-5139-2 (paper) 1. Civilization, Classical. I. Singor, H. W. II. Title.
   DE59.N3413 2014
   938–dc23   2013028405

A catalogue record for this book is available from the British Library.

Cover image: Syria, Palmyra Ruins. © Ocean/Corbis.
Cover design by Nicki Averill

Set in 10/13pt Minion by Laserwords Private Limited, Chennai, India
Printed in Malaysia by Ho Printing (M) Sdn Bhd

1 2014

Antiquity

Contents

List of Figures ix
List of Maps xi
Preface xiii

Part I Introduction **1**

1.1 Sources and Chronology 3
 Sources *3*
 Chronology *7*

1.2 The Ecology of History 11
 Physical Geography *11*
 Agriculture and the Pre-Industrial Economy *13*
 Demography *20*

Part II Before 900 BC **25**

2.1 Prehistory 27
 Paleolithic *27*
 Neolithic *32*

2.2 Early Civilizations in Eurasia 36
 The Rise of Distinct Civilizations *36*
 Peoples and Languages *41*
 Western Asia and Egypt in the Bronze Age *45*
 The Aegean and Southern Europe in the Bronze Age *52*

Part III 900−500 BC **59**

3.1 A Historical Outline 61
 Eurasian Communities *61*
 The Greek World *71*
 Italy and Western Europe *86*

3.2 The Social Fabric 93
 Economic Life *93*
 Social Hierarchy *97*
 Political Organization *102*

3.3   Daily Life and Mentality   109
        The Individual and Society   *109*
        Men and Women   *113*
        Religion, Philosophy, and Scholarship   *117*

Part IV   500–300 BC   **129**

4.1   A Historical Outline   131
        Eurasian Communities   *131*
        The Greek World   *139*
        Italy and the West   *149*

4.2   The Social Fabric   152
        Economic Life   *152*
        Social Hierarchy   *159*
        Political Organization   *163*

4.3   Daily Life and Mentality   169
        The Individual and Society   *169*
        Men and Women   *175*
        Religion, Philosophy, and Scholarship   *178*

Part V   300 BC–1 AD   **189**

5.1   A Historical Outline   191
        Eurasian Communities   *191*
        The Greek World   *200*
        Italy and the West   *221*

5.2   The Social Fabric   241
        Economic Life   *241*
        The Social Hierarchy   *252*
        Political Organization   *262*

5.3   Daily Life and Mentality   269
        The Individual and Society   *269*
        Men and Women   *277*
        Religion, Philosophy, and Scholarship   *279*

Part VI   1 AD–500 AD   **291**

6.1   A Historical Outline   293
        Eurasian Communities   *293*
        The Roman Empire   *298*
        The Greek East and the Latin West   *308*

6.2   The Social Fabric   314
        Economic Life   *314*
        Social Hierarchy   *321*
        Political Organization   *327*

6.3 Daily Life and Mentality 333
The Individual and Society 333
Men and Women 341
Religion, Philosophy, and Scholarship 343

Part VII   After 500 AD **367**

7   The 6th Century and Later 369
Eurasian Communities 369
The Byzantine East 378
The Christian Church 382
Islam 387
The Ancient Heritage 390

Appendices 395
Classical Athens 396
The Classical Roman Republic 397
Imperial Rome: The Principate 398
Imperial Rome: The Dominate 399
Hellenistic Rulers 400
Roman Emperors 402
Philosophers 403
Scholars and Scientists 405
Poets and Prose Writers 407
Christian Authors 409

CHRONOLOGY 411

Suggestions for Further Reading 419

Index 433

List of Figures

Fig. 1   Roman road at the Welsh–English border (1st c. AD).   5
Fig. 2   The dendrochronological method.   9
Fig. 3   A Sumerian frieze showing dairy production (c. 2600–2350 BC).   15
Fig. 4   The face of the Tollund Man, an Iron Age bog body from Denmark.   21
Fig. 5   Worm eggs from the intestines of the Lindow Man, a British bog body.   32
Fig. 6   Chinese burial site with traces of a chariot (c. 1300 BC).   39
Fig. 7   Stele with the Code of Hammurabi (1728–1686 BC).   49
Fig. 8   Mycenaean body armor (15th–14th c. BC).   54
Fig. 9   An inscribed bronze vase, China (9th c. BC).   64
Fig. 10   A relief from Nineveh depicting Assurbanipal in his pleasure
          garden (7th c. BC).   67
Fig. 11   The so-called Dipylon vase from Athens (c. 735–725 BC).   75
Fig. 12   A Roman copy and a contemporary depiction of the Athenian sculpture
          group of the Tyrannicides (originally c. 475 BC).   81
Fig. 13   Vase in the form of a cock (c. 650–600 BC).   92
Fig. 14   The Narmer Palette from Egypt (c. 3100 BC).   102
Fig. 15   Outside of an Athenian cup with a *gumnasion* scene (early 5th c. BC).   110
Fig. 16   A *kouros* and *kore* from Attica (c. 550 BC) and the so-called
          Getty Kouros (6th c. BC?).   118
Fig. 17   The outside of an Athenian amphora and an Athenian *oinochoe*:
          battle scenes with Greek hoplites and Persians (c. 480–460 BC).   124
Fig. 18   An Etruscan helmet dedicated to Zeus of Olympia by the
          Syracusans (474 BC).   139
Fig. 19   Ostraca found in the Athenian Agora (5th c. BC).   142
Fig. 20   Philip II? Fragments of a skull from Vergina (4th c. BC) and a facial
          reconstruction based on those fragments.   148
Fig. 21   Ancient terracing in Attica.   157
Fig. 22   Stele with an Athenian decree (408/407 BC).   165
Fig. 23   Athenian reliefs with two groups of dancers (323 BC).   174
Fig. 24   Inside of an Athenian cup with the god Dionysus as seafarer (c. 530 BC).   181

Fig. 25 Copies of the statue of Athena Parthenos from the Parthenon on the
         Athenian Acropolis (originally 447–438 BC).   185
Fig. 26 Coins of Greco-Bactrian and Greco-Indian kings (3rd–2nd c. BC).   198
Fig. 27 Building block with the dedication of the temple of Athena at
         Priene (4th c. BC).   202
Fig. 28 Roman copy of the statue of the goddess Tyche as the city goddess
         of Antioch (originally c. 300 BC).   213
Fig. 29 Carthaginian coins with war elephants (3rd c. BC).   226
Fig. 30 The so-called relief of Domitius Ahenobarbus (1st c. BC)   231
Fig. 31 Delos and Hatra (2nd–1st c. BC).   245
Fig. 32 Slaves in Hellenistic art (3rd–1st c. BC).   250
Fig. 33 Relief in situ at the Horus temple at Edfu, in Greek Apollonopolis Magna,
         from about 130 BC.   253
Fig. 34 Sculptures from the Buddhist monastery at Tepe Shotor, Afghanistan
         (3rd–4th c. AD).   270
Fig. 35 A model of the acropolis of Pergamon as it looked in the first half of
         the 2nd c. BC.   275
Fig. 36 Stele from Petra with the goddess Atargatis (1st c. AD) and the head of an
         Atargatis statue from Armenia Minor (2nd c. BC).   280
Fig. 37 Stele of a Cretan dream interpreter from Sakkara in Egypt (3rd–2nd c. BC). 285
Fig. 38 The so-called Lyon Tabulae inscribed with a speech by the emperor
         Claudius (1st c. AD).   299
Fig. 39 The Roman city of Timgad in Algeria (2nd–4th c. AD).   311
Fig. 40 Stamps on *terra sigillata*, naming producers, and a *terra sigillata* plate
         inscribed with the oven load of a pottery (1st–2nd c. AD).   317
Fig. 41 Grave stele of Regina, from South Shields on Hadrian's Wall
         (2nd–3rd c. AD).   324
Fig. 42 A wooden tablet from the Roman fort at Vindolanda, containing an army
         strength report (2nd c. BC).   335
Fig. 43 Graffito of a gladiator from Pompeii (before 79 AD) and gravestone of the
         gladiator Apollonius, from Asia Minor (late imperial period).   339
Fig. 44 Altars for the goddess Nehalennia, from the Scheldt river in the
         Netherlands (3rd c. AD).   334
Fig. 45 A wall painting from the synagogue at Dura Europos (245 AD).   350
Fig. 46 The Nag-Hammadi Codices (4th c. AD).   360
Fig. 47 Sculpture of a foreigner on horseback, China (7th–9th c. AD).   370
Fig. 48 Mosaic from Ravenna with the Emperor Justinian (6th c. AD).   385

List of Maps

Map 1   Colonization of the world by *Homo sapiens*.   28
Map 2   Languages in Eurasia, 2nd–1st millennium.   43
Map 3   The Near East and Egypt, 3rd–1st millennium.   46
Map 4   The Aegean world, c. 1600–c. 1100 BC.   56
Map 5   Eurasia, 10th–5th c. BC.   62
Map 6   Greece, 8th–6th c. BC.   74
Map 7   Western Mediterranean, 8th–4th c. BC.   87
Map 8   Eurasia, 5th–4th c. BC.   132
Map 9   Greece, 5th c. BC.   140
Map 10   The Cleisthenic organization of Attica.   143
Map 11   Athens, 5th–4th c. BC.   153
Map 12   The southern half of the Athenian plain.   154
Map 13   Eurasia, 3rd–1st c. BC.   192
Map 14   The Hellenistic world, 4th–3rd c. BC.   208
Map 15   The Second Punic War, 218–201 BC.   224
Map 16   The Roman Empire, 3rd–1st c. BC.   239
Map 17   Eurasia, 1st–6th c. AD.   294
Map 18   The Roman Empire, 1st c. AD.   300
Map 19   The Roman Empire, 2nd–3rd c. AD.   304
Map 20   The Roman Empire, 4th c. AD.   309
Map 21   Rome, 1st–2nd c. AD.   318
Map 22   Imperial Rome and its environs   319
Map 23   The Germanic states, c. 525 AD   374
Map 24   The Germanic states, c. 575 AD   375
Map 25   The Eastern Roman Empire, 6th c. AD   379
Map 26   Religions in Eurasia, 7th–8th c. AD   383
Map 27   The Islamic world, c. 750 AD   388
Map 28   The world, c. 800 AD   393

Preface

We wrote this book with a wide audience in mind. It is aimed primarily at undergraduates who in the course of their studies are confronted with the Greco-Roman world. However, all others who for whatever reasons are interested in the ancient world can find here a reasonably comprehensive one-volume overview.

When this book was first published in Dutch in 1995, the question arose: why another general account of ancient history? There were many textbooks available, but not any Dutch-language textbooks that were quite comparable. Anyhow, it became a success, and almost 20 years on, it is still in print. Now it has been translated into English, and again one will ask: why? We feel our enterprise has a number of distinguishing features compared to other such currently available accounts. First, we have tried not to be too concise—which is often the case nowadays—without going to the other extreme. The result is a book that is both a suitable introduction to its subject, and a basic work of reference that one can come back to whenever the need arises. Second, we have also attempted to combine a fairly traditional chronological account with a quite extensive coverage of several subjects taken from social and economic history and the history of mentalities that came to the fore in the 1970s and that are still central to present-day research in the field. Third, we have not confined antiquity to Greco-Roman history, but have tried to show something of the wider temporal and spatial framework in which this history is embedded; that is, on a time scale from early prehistory to well into the Middle Ages, and ranging across all of Eurasia and North Africa.

Although this book has a broad scope, the Greco-Roman world of between 1000 BC and 500 AD holds center stage. This one and a half millennium is discussed in four parts: the Archaic period (1000–500 BC), the Classical period (500–336 BC), the Hellenistic period (336–30 BC), and the Roman imperial period (30 BC–500 AD). These four parts are arranged in a strict chronological order: we have avoided the time-honored but utterly misleading division of Greek and Roman history into two individual accounts. Also, all four parts consist of the same number of chapters, which have identical titles in each of the four parts in order to stimulate a comparative approach to their contents. This core of the book is flanked by two parts that provide an overview of early prehistory down to 1000 BC, and of the 6th century AD and beyond. These six parts are preceded by an introductory account of sources and methods, and of the material foundations of the ancient world from an ecological, demographic, and economic standpoint.

The book contains images, maps, diagrams, tables, a chronological chart, and suggestions for further reading. We speak of images, not illustrations, because these are not merely illustrative, but, together with their captions, intended as a source of information in their own right. The maps, diagrams, tables, charts, detailed index, and the bibliographical material enhance the suitability of this book as a work of reference.

This textbook is the work of just two authors. We are only too aware of the almost insurmountable problems involved in writing a book of this kind. Nobody can master the sources or the literature, not even for a small part of the history that is dealt with here. Still, we both feel that a team of specialists would not be a good choice to write a general and synthetic account such as our book seeks to provide. We would rather have some unity of vision and of style, with all its faults. Once in a while, someone has to attempt the impossible.

Having a co-author was a great help. But two authors are two human beings with their own individual histories. Even though we have critically examined each other's texts and both accept responsibility for the entire content of the book, we have decided not to remove all traces of individuality. Below we have indicated who is responsible for what chapter.

A final word about the history of the present text: six years after its first publication, it was fully revised, in 2001. In 2008, we again revised the full text. In part, these revisions were in response to comments by the book's users, and in part they were an attempt to keep it up to date. Of course, this is a textbook, which implies that we have always been quite conservative: you are not likely to find last week's new insights here. Developments in the field will trickle down into our text with a delay of a couple of years, when the dust has settled and it seems that the new findings have come to stay. For the English translation— each of us translated his own part of the book—we have based ourselves on the 2012 16th printing of the Dutch edition. We have made corrections and slight revisions and rearrangements where this seemed necessary.

Part I Naerebout
Part II
Chapter 2.1 Naerebout & Singor (Neolithic)
Chapter 2.2 Singor
Part III Singor
Part IV Naerebout
Part V
Chapter 5.1 Singor
Chapter 5.2 Singor
Chapter 5.3 Naerebout
Part VI
Chapter 6.1 Naerebout
Chapter 6.2 Naerebout
Chapter 6.3 Singor
Part VII
Naerebout & Singor (Eurasia, Byzantium, Christianity)

Leiden 11 June 2013
Frederick G. Naerebout and Henk W. Singor

PART I

INTRODUCTION

Chapter 1.1

Sources and Chronology

Sources

The diversity of sources

Without sources, there is no history. The human memory cannot be trusted, and it has a limited range. To memorize the past, humanity is in need of an external memory. This external memory is provided by the sources. Almost everything can function as a source, whether it is intended as such or not. Thus, sources consist of not only writings, but of all relics of human behavior, even if this behavior was not intended to produce a source of some kind. We should even include phenomena that have occurred independent of human interference, such as a layer of soil deposited by flooding water; all can be used to inform us about the circumstances of life at some moment of time. To come to grips with this extremely diverse material, we had best categorize the sources. The most common classification is that of written and unwritten sources.

Written sources

Written sources are the results of the application of a human script. This category can be subdivided into primary sources, that is, sources that are the immediate result of past actions (documents), and secondary sources, that is, sources that have been mediated, have gone through some filter such as a historian's selection and arrangement (literary sources). The opposition between primary and secondary sources is not absolute but relative: whether a source is considered primary or secondary depends on the questions asked. For example, if one is interested in the social and economic dimensions of slavery in the ancient Greek world, plays in which slaves figure are a secondary source, as opposed to primary sources such as so-called manumission decrees, texts drawn up when a slave was granted his or her freedom. But if one is interested in how Athenians of the 5th century or the 4th century imagined slaves or slavery, those same plays, written and watched by contemporary Athenians, have turned into primary sources. And this would certainly be

Antiquity: Greeks and Romans in Context, First Edition. Frederick G. Naerebout and Henk W. Singor.
© 2014 John Wiley & Sons, Inc. Published 2014 by John Wiley & Sons, Inc.

the case if one chooses not Athenian slavery but Athenian drama as the object of one's research.

The ancient world has left us a wide range of written sources. First, we have countless inscriptions, also called epigraphic sources: all texts cut into a carrier of some sort, usually stone, ceramics, or metal. Many texts written with ink or paint on hard surfaces or laid out in mosaic are also classified as epigraphic material, although these are strictly speaking not inscriptions. Inscriptions have been produced by every society that was able to write. They range from the codification of laws to shopping lists, from epitaphs to obscene graffiti. Inscriptions can be archival texts, for example, many of the inscribed clay tablets of the ancient Near East; or texts put up in some public space, for example, many of the hieroglyphic texts of ancient Egypt; or texts put to some more specific use, for example, the inscriptions on so-called oracle bones used in large quantities in ancient China. The Greek and subsequently the Roman culture displayed a most remarkable propensity to make public texts of many different kinds by having these inscribed and put up for all to see. Thus, for the study of classical Greece, the Hellenistic world, and the Roman Empire, epigraphy is a very important source indeed: we have thousands upon thousands of texts, and new ones are found all the time.

Written sources other than inscriptions from the ancient world are rare: papyrus, parchment, paper, and other perishable materials, as bamboo or silk, have only seldom been preserved. In the Mediterranean world, papyrus was the most common kind of writing material, as was paper in China from the 2nd century AD. Alas, most texts written down on these carriers have been lost, the only exception being Egypt, where papyri have been preserved in large numbers owing to the desert conditions prevailing in most of the country.

Many written sources have not been preserved in ancient texts, but have been handed down to us: the writings of most ancient poets, philosophers, historians, orators, and so on, have survived by being copied, usually repeatedly. For the millennium between the epic poetry ascribed to Homer, of which the version that has come down to us should probably be dated to the second half of the 8th century BC, and 200 AD, we have now over 20 million words of over 1600 authors, and by far the largest part of this huge amount of texts is known to us from medieval manuscript sources. Still, this large corpus is only a small part of Greek literature, as we know from references or small fragments. With Latin texts it is not different.

The modern historian, of course, relies heavily on the works of ancient historians that have managed to survive. There we find the ancients reflecting on their own history and society. But other written sources can be as important, or, depending on the subject, even much more so. Literally every text that has survived, in its original form or via tradition can be put to some purpose in studying the ancient world.

Unwritten sources

This category of sources, negatively defined as everything that is not a written source, can also be subdivided. First, there are objects: everything surviving from the past, from complete buildings to the smallest find. These objects need not be human-made, such

Figure 1   Roman road at the Welsh–English border (1st c. AD.) Roman surveyors and engineers have left their mark on the European landscape, in the form of roads, bridges, aqueducts, and field systems. On this aerial photograph, we can see the road known as Watling Street West, which runs south (the direction we are looking at) from Wroxeter, Roman Viroconium Cornoviorum, along the Welsh–English border. The road is still in use, and with its hedgerows is easily the most conspicuous feature of this landscape. It runs between the hills and marshland, along the valley floor. In the far distance, it bends toward the so-called Church Stretton Gap. The road may have been built as part of the Roman effort to subdue Wales between 43 and 77. Photo: Cambridge University Collection of Aerial Photography

as tools, jewelry, or coins. Also, biological matter, from a complete skeleton down to carbonized seeds or fossilized pollen, should be included. Architectural features are the most obvious immovable objects, but many other immovable objects or even particular characteristics of such objects can be relevant, from a discolored patch of soil or a crop mark as indicative of some past occurrence, to complete landscapes or infrastructures. These sources are all the subject of archaeology, assisted by a range of scientific disciplines such as air photography, cartography, and even surveying by satellite.

Second, there are images made by humans, of course objects too, but still easily distinguished as falling in a category of their own. Images or representations are unwritten sources, but are more closely related to texts than are other objects. Texts are also, in a sense, images made by humans of their surroundings, their fellow creatures, or themselves. Images should be approached with care: never can they be used as if they convey the same kind of verity that we find in documentary photography. Works of imagination would actually be a better word to describe many of the images that have come down to us. In order to interpret the images produced during some past period, one has to have some acquaintance with the procedures governing portrayal during that period. Even if we have such knowledge of a period's image making, many questions surrounding the use of images as sources will remain unanswered.

Generally speaking, unwritten sources will never be allowed to monopolize research, unless there is no alternative (obviously, this is the case when dealing with a community that is without writing; also, there are scripts that as yet have not been deciphered). However, unwritten evidence can complete, nuance, or correct the views based on the written sources. In that way, unwritten sources are without doubt of the utmost importance. However, interpreting, for example, the remains of a wall is not always an easy task, and interpreting the image painted on a wall or a pot might very well be much more difficult still. The written sources, primary or secondary, will always be fundamental to any *historical* account.

Using the sources

As we just saw, there is no end to what can be used as a source in historical inquiry. This ensures an almost unlimited supply of source material. Still, we should not forget that for many questions that can be asked, the situation is not nearly as favorable as this general picture suggests. Sources are not distributed evenly across periods, areas, and subjects; nor are all sources equally useful. Not only can appearances be deceptive, but human-made sources can also be produced in order to deceive (interesting in itself, but then one has to recognize such instances first). There are no easy ways around this problem; thus, it is a mistake to consider, for instance, that inscriptions are always more reliable than literary texts. Every source has to be carefully scrutinized as to what it can actually contribute. A source is like a telescope, or a magnifying glass: without it we cannot see anything, but it sits between the observer and the observed and distorts whatever there is to see.

In the end, we are left with many questions to which none of the sources available provide any answer. Then one can sit and wait until new relevant sources will be found, or, more realistically, try to come up with some hypothetical answer: what seems to be at a given moment the best, most consistent explanation. Theory, model making and comparison by way of sources from other periods and places will usually play an important part in the formulation of any such hypothetical answer.

Someone eager to learn about the past will most of the time not immediately turn to the relevant sources, but will make use of modern literature that is based directly or indirectly on source material. If one is after some information concerning the early Roman Empire, one does not nowadays read the Roman historian Tacitus, but will seek this information in some work of reference or, if the need arises, in more specialist publications. This also holds good for the present-day historian, who, even when he or she might have been inspired by reading some sources, will not usually embark upon a study of all possibly relevant sources, but will first read modern scholarly works in order to be better able to formulate questions, to get acquainted with a wider context, or possibly to build some model to guide further research. Of course, the subject selected and the kind of information wanted determine at what moment one will one turn from the modern literature to the sources: treading relatively unknown paths, one will be forced to turn to the sources fairly soon. However, serious scholarship almost always necessitates going back to the sources sooner or later. In dealing with antiquity, these will often be published sources, such as text editions or excavation reports. This does not mean that the ancient historian need only pick up the sources in order to get the required information. It might be possible to quickly falsify the work of some other historian, but usually the sources, whether published or not, have to be interpreted in a painstaking process. This implies that although every piece of historical scholarship ultimately depends on the sources available, the relationship between the sources on the one hand and the publications based on those sources is hardly ever simple and straightforward: the necessary act of interpretation always interferes.

Chronology

Relative and absolute dating

In order to use sources in writing history, they have to be dated. And when dealing with written sources, also the occurrences reported in the source need themselves to be dated. In dating, we should distinguish between relative and absolute dating, even if these two methods of dating cannot be separated. Relative dating provides the age of something relative to something else: A is older, as old, or younger than B. Absolute dating provides something with an age relative to some fixed point: A is *x* units of time before or after point P on the total time scale. An actual example of relative dating is the stratigraphic principle in archaeology. In a greatly simplified form, this states that if layer x is covered by layer y, layer x is the older of the two layers; finds from layer x are thus older than finds from layer y (if they have not moved from their original position). An example of absolute dating is, for example, the dating of layer x some time after 54 AD, because among the finds from layer x is a coin struck during the reign of the emperor Nero, who succeeded to the throne in 54 AD. "After 54" is an absolute date, because the Christian era is based on a fixed point in the time scale. Though absolute, "after 54" is not precise: the archaeologist or historian has to try to take everything into account; in the case of a coin among other artifacts, that coin could have remained in circulation or could have been hoarded for long periods.

Ways of reckoning time

The preceding example of absolute dating begs the question: how do we actually know that Nero became emperor in 54 AD? In using the absolute chronology commonly used in historical scholarship and in large parts of the world, with the fixed point put at the supposed year of Christ's birth, we tend to forget that both past and present know of several other absolute chronologies. Thus, before the 6th century AD, the specific Christian way of reckoning time did not yet exist. To convert the many different chronologies, absolute, but also relative, to one another is no easy task. One has to ask what, in a particular time reckoning, was the duration of whatever basic unit was employed, how this was subdivided, where the beginning of every unit or of longer cycles was located, and how units were named or numbered. Some examples might illustrate the remarkable complexity of this problem.

In ancient Egypt, a year was 12 months of 30 days each, with five festival days added. This year of 365 days gets out of pace with the sun, but the Egyptians did not use leap years. The years were counted from the succession of the reigning monarch. In Mesopotamia, many local calendars were in use, with different solutions to keep lunar months and solar years in track. The Assyrians named every year after the magistrates who oversaw the time reckoning (they are called eponymous magistrates, "magistrates who give their name"). The Babylonians originally numbered the years in a single sequence, but later they gave every year an individual name derived from some particular occasions. From the 16th century BC, we find regnal years in common use in Mesopotamia. Greece originally did not count years, but generations of variable duration; or the regnal years of the Persian monarch were referred to. In the 5th century, the tradition of naming of years after eponymous magistrates or monarchs established itself, and happily we have some lists of names that enable us to at least date texts or occurrences relatively. In Rome, the annual consuls were the eponymous magistrates, and later the regnal years of the emperors were used.

We also find systems comparable to the Christian chronology, using a fixed point: the so-called eras. To reckon time effectively in any such system, one needs a regular year, with leap years to stay in sync with the sun. Hellenistic rulers copied this from the Babylonians as the basis of their eras. Later, in 46 BC, Julius Caesar reformed the Roman calendar; this so-called Julian calendar was an improved version of the Egyptian solar calendar, with one leap day inserted every four years. An important era was the Seleucid era, with its fixed point in, to put it in our terms, 312 BC, which was widely used in the Near East, until well into the middle ages, and by the Syriac Church even to the present day. But in Hellenistic and Roman times, there were several other eras in use in monarchies and in individual cities. Roman historians reckoned from the founding of the city of Rome, in 753 BC. The Greeks had a time-honored era: the Olympiads. The Olympics were a festival in Olympia that was held every fourth year and which was important enough to serve as the basis for a Panhellenic chronology. The Olympics run from 776 BC in our terms (776 BC is Ol. 1.1, that is. the first year of the first Olympiad). Already in ancient Greece, the Olympiads were synchronized with lists of rulers and eponymics.

The Christian chronology was created in the 6th century. The monk Dionysius computed the future dates of Easter, which were based on the Jewish lunar calendar, but had to be fitted in with the Julian solar calendar. In the 6th century, the Diocletian era, which began with the first year of the reign of the emperor Diocletian, 284 AD, was still in common use, but Dionysius did not want to head his Easter table with a reference to a heathen emperor who persecuted the Christians. Instead, he computed the date of Christ's birth and re-baptized the year 248 of the Diocletian era as the year 532 "after the incarnation of Our Lord." Thus, a Christian era was born, adopted in the Byzantine Empire in the 6th century, and in the 8th century all over Christian Europe. Now dates expressed in the Diocletian era or in Olympiads could be converted into dates before or after Christ's birth, the last year before Christ (1 BC) being immediately followed by the first year after Christ (1 AD).

In order to check whether our conversions of other dates into the Christian chronology are correct, we need information on events that are astronomically absolute and can be expressed unambiguously in the Christian chronology. Thus, an eclipse mentioned by an 8th-century Assyrian governor must have taken place on the 10th of June, 763 BC, and another eclipse reported by the Greek historian Thucydides can be dated to the 3rd of August, 431 BC. And so on and so forth. Now we are left with some certain dates. However, this does not mean that all our problems have been solved: the struggle to reconcile different methods of reckoning time, which began in antiquity, is still under way.

Science-based dating

When dealing with objects, an absolute dating can often be arrived at by using scientific methods, among which the best known is radiocarbon dating. This is based on the fact that in the atmosphere there is both ^{12}C (carbon-12, non-radioactive carbon) and ^{14}C (carbon-14, a radioactive isotope formed under the influence of cosmic rays). Both types of carbon occur in the CO_2 (carbon dioxide) present in the atmosphere and dissolved in water. CO_2 is absorbed by living creatures, and thus the entire biosphere contains ^{14}C. If an organism dies, the absorption of carbon dioxide stops. The levels of carbon are not replenished. The radioactive isotope goes on decaying at the immutable rate at which all ^{14}C is decaying all the time, but the amount of ^{12}C remains constant. In organic material, one can measure how much ^{14}C is left, and as of course the rate of decay, the half-life, of the isotope is known, one can establish the age of the sample being studied; that is,

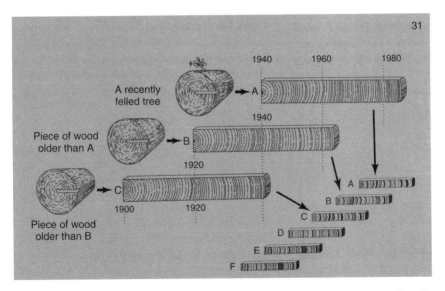

Figure 2 The dendrochronological method. The dendrochronological method is based on a comparison of year ring patterns in different pieces of wood. If there is a match, such pieces can be fitted into an overlapping sequence. If within a certain area there is enough wood available from trees with overlapping life spans, it will be possible to obtain a reference chronology stretching back for centuries.

if we correct (calibrate) for a number of systematic errors, especially variations in the amount of ^{14}C present in the atmosphere. The result is a dating in years BP ("before present," understood to be 1950; remember, we need a fixed point for absolute dating). The importance of radiocarbon dating can hardly be overrated: before it arrived on the scene, many archaeological finds were dated only relatively. However, the dates procured are not very precise; there is a wide margin of error.

Radiocarbon dating is supplemented by other techniques, among which the most important is dendrochronology: the study of tree-ring dating. Seasonal variation in the growth of trees leads to observable annual rings. The width of these rings varies under the influence of climate. The resulting patterns of wide and narrow rings are unique. Thus, pieces of the wood of trees felled at different dates can be compared and matched in order to create an overlapping series of tree rings ranging from the present back to as far as a continuous series of timbers can be established. In some parts of Europe, this continuous series now stretches back for 9000 years, which means that every piece of well-preserved wood, not older than 9000 years and of the same or a comparable species, can be dated with exactitude. This is not just a revolutionary way of providing dates that are absolute and exact; dendrochronology has also helped to calibrate the radiocarbon results, and generates data to be used in the research into past climate.

The range of science-based dating techniques is growing all the time. Many are designed for dating prehistoric evidence. Important for historical times is thermoluminescence, which enables one to establish when an inorganic object (that cannot be dated by radiocarbon) was heated to over 300°C for the last time, as, for example, dating when a piece of ceramic was fired.

Chapter 1.2

The Ecology of History

A number of material factors are of evident importance in deciding the course of history, such as climate and soil, the organization of agriculture and economic life in general, and demography. Of course, these factors do not determine history: a specific soil, climate, or population density does not necessarily lead to predictable results. Still, material factors can be called the "basics" of history: they determine what, under given circumstances, is possible and what is not; they create preconditions for and impose restraints on human life. Thus, every culture has been in many respects the expression of the ways in which some group of human beings managed to adapt to the ecosystem in which they happened to be living, which might also be described as ecological anthropology.

Physical Geography

Climatic and geological change

Paleoclimatology is the study of past climates: the plural form, climates, expresses the fact that climate is not unchanging, even although change has been slow on a human time scale. Methods such as the reconstruction of the variable extension of glaciers, or the measuring of tree rings, enable us to say something about long-term climatic change. From 10,000 BC, that is, after the end of the fourth Ice Age, there was a period of rising temperatures that caused the borders between different climatic and vegetation zones to move apart and toward the poles. This was a slow process: in 4000 BC, for example, the Mediterranean was still a cooler and wetter place than it is nowadays. Apart from this type of change on the very long term, there also occur fluctuations of shorter duration: 1300 to 450 BC was a relatively cold, and 450 BC to 700 AD a relatively warm period.

Similar to climate, Earth's crust is changing continuously. The rising temperatures after 10,000 BC melted most continental ice. The subsequent rise of sea levels meant a slow but drastic change of the continents' coastlines. Also, geological processes as erosion or

Antiquity: Greeks and Romans in Context, First Edition. Frederick G. Naerebout and Henk W. Singor.
© 2014 John Wiley & Sons, Inc. Published 2014 by John Wiley & Sons, Inc.

sedimentation can change a landscape beyond recognition, in a long-drawn-out evolution, in an overnight disaster, or anything between those two extremes. In this context, one should certainly mention seismic and volcanic activity, both caused by the drift of the tectonic plates that form Earth's crust. Especially along the edges where plates collide, earthquakes occur frequently, and active volcanoes are found: this is the case in the Mediterranean, around the Arabian peninsula, along the southern rim of the Himalayas, along the coastline of all of East and Southeast Asia, and along the western rim of both Americas. Except for earthquakes and volcanic eruptions, there also occur destructive flood waves, tsunamis, when certain kinds of earthquakes have their epicenter somewhere in the sea. Often, such natural disasters leave traces in geological, archaeological, and historical sources. Examples of large-scale disasters that keep many scholars occupied are the explosion of the island of Thera or Santorini in the second millennium BC (the exact dating of this giant eruption is strongly debated; it is important because it provides a means of calibrating our chronology of that period); and the eruption of the Vesuvius in 79 AD, when pumice, ashes, and other volcanic matter buried the towns of Pompeii and Herculaneum, a disaster that provided posterity with unique insights into Roman town life.

Vegetation zones and climate zones

In the past 5000 years, there can be distinguished three natural vegetation zones in Eurasia and the Mediterranean. These were not always in exactly the same place: climatic fluctuations led to temporary changes in the exact location of these zones. Thus, the limit of viticulture was situated further north than in the recent past during the aforementioned warm interval between 450 BC and 700 AD. But the general picture has remained quite stable for five millennia, until present-day global warming has set things moving. It should be stressed that we are talking of natural vegetation: this natural vegetation cover has in many places been largely or completely replaced by crops and pasturage, or otherwise destroyed by human interference. This profound alteration of the landscape had already started in the ancient world.

The first zone, to the north of the limit for viticulture (around 40 degrees north latitude, in Europe only 50 degrees) has, from north to south, tundra, boreal coniferous forests (taiga), mixed forests and deciduous broadleaf forests, steppe and (semi-)desert, and at the higher altitudes, specific mountainous vegetation. Northern, western, and central Europe are mainly forest areas, except for a bit of tundra in the extreme north. The climate here is humid, from the sub-Arctic climes in the north, by way of the marine climes of the west to the continental climes of the center. Central Asia has extensive steppe areas, stretching all the way from Hungary in the west to Manchuria in the east; toward the north, this shades into desert, which in its turn gives way to taiga and Arctic tundra. In the south of this area, the climate is cold and (semi-)arid, and in the north it is sub-Arctic: humid with long, severe winters. Eastern Siberia and northeastern China form an intermediate zone with mixed forests and broadleaf forests: they have a humid continental climate with cold winters and warm summers.

The second zone lies between the limits of viticulture and the Tropic of Cancer (at 23.5 degrees north latitude) and is characterized by Mediterranean vegetation, steppe, desert, and mountainous vegetation. Southern Europe and northern Africa have a specific Mediterranean climate: warm dry summers and mild humid winters. The typical Mediterranean vegetation, with evergreen broadleaf trees and shrubs as the most conspicuous feature, is found all around the Mediterranean, although in parts of northern Africa the desert nowadays reaches the sea. The desertification of the Sahara region is a comparatively recent phenomenon: northern Africa started drying out from about 5000 BC, but only in the third millennium did traffic across the Sahara begin to be impeded by the desert. Slowly, but surely, northern Africa became isolated from sub-Saharan Africa. Ever since, the desert has been encroaching. Egypt, the Near East, and the Arabic peninsula are largely desert and steppe, and have a desert climate. Only the river valleys of the Nile, Euphrates, and Tigris, and a number of oases are the exceptions: alluvial instead of desert soils and plenty of water. From Anatolia in the west to the Punjab in the east stretch mountain ranges and upland plateaus, with steppe and desert vegetation, and again mountain vegetation on the higher slopes. Further to the east we find the mountains of Afghanistan and the Himalayas. The climate varies from a warm and dry continental one to a tundra climate in most of the Himalayas. In China, the north consists of plains and regions with loess soils, with a steppe or desert vegetation and a climate to match. The south is mountainous, with forest cover, and a humid and warm subtropical climate.

The third zone to the south of the Tropic of Cancer is characterized by subtropical and tropical vegetation. The main landmass is the Indian subcontinent, with the alluvial plains of the Indus, Ganges, and Brahmaputra, and to the south plains and uplands. The annual rainfall increases from west to east, with the exception of the western rim of the subcontinent. The vegetation varies from desert immediately to the east of the Indus to tropical monsoon forests in the delta of the Ganges. The southern subcontinent has tropical rainforests on its west coast and in Sri Lanka; otherwise, there is dry tropical forest and savannah. The climate also runs the gamut from desert to tropical. Southeast Asia is an area with mainly tropical rainforest and monsoon forests. The climate there is tropical, except for the subtropical north.

Agriculture and the Pre-Industrial Economy

Carrying capacity

Agriculture is the manipulating of living organisms, both plants and animals, by humans in order to safeguard their food supply. An important concept in judging the impact of agriculture is carrying capacity, that is, the maximum population density at which the balance between the environment and the human population can be maintained. The technology humans use to acquire food and other raw produce is an important factor in determining the carrying capacity: when the necessities of life are satisfied by hunting and gathering, the carrying capacity is relatively small. One could also say that the territory that a group needs for its survival is comparatively large. The population densities we have to think of when dealing with hunter-gatherers are 0.1 persons per square kilometer (247 acres) or less, down to as little as 0.01. But with agriculture playing an important part in the food supply, densities can rise to 4 or 5 persons per square kilometer. In a fully developed agricultural economy, this can be as high as 30. This is the average density across a whole area, of which usually only a part is cultivated, and of which not every part will be equally fertile. These figures are still relatively low densities: what one can expect of the carrying capacity of an agriculture that is technologically primitive. On different grounds, a population of 50 to 80 million has been proposed for the Roman Empire at its largest extent, from Scotland to the Euphrates. That figure tallies quite well with the carrying capacity as supposed above.

The rise of agriculture

As the account on carrying capacity shows, agriculture enables a community to feed a larger number of people on the same territory. But what could have been the reason to increase the carrying capacity in the first place? On this, there are several different hypotheses. One, held by many, presupposes scarcity. That is, within a given area, either the population is growing, or natural resources are dwindling. Agriculture then is a way to combat scarcity. Another interesting hypothesis presupposes the wish to produce a surplus as an insurance against lean years. This, however, causes the population to increase, and if there is nowhere for this extra population to go, the population density increases. Before long, there is no turning back: the choice is between carrying on with agriculture or starvation.

Whether agriculture arises out of scarcity or an attempt to avoid scarcity, it can only do so in favorable climatic and geographical circumstances. In the climatic and vegetation belts in the north (tundra, taiga, or desert), small groups go on hunting and gathering, with the possible addition of some stock breeding. As already indicated in the preceding text, Central Asia and Iran have a very limited agricultural potential, and thus a very limited carrying capacity. In the steppes of Central Asia, nomads took to extensive cattle breeding. It is only on the margins of the Eurasian continent that agriculture can flourish. In the Near East, about 8000 BC, at the end of a long drawn-out process, a number of plants and animals have become domesticated, especially wheat, barley, sheep, and goats. From 6500 BC, agriculture makes headway in Europe and in what is now West Pakistan; in 5000 BC, millet is cultivated in Northern China (along the Huang He or Yellow River) and rice in Southern China and East Asia. These dates are, it should be noted, provisional: all the time new archaeological discoveries push back the earliest dates of agriculture in Asia. Possibly, we are dealing here with developments independent of what happened in the Near East. That is certainly the case in New Guinea, where an independent horticulture develops from around 7000 BC. Africa enters into the story rather late: from the 3rd millennium BC onward, millet and sorghum are cultivated. Central America and South America are a world apart: from the 7th millennium BC onward, products such as beans, peppers, potatoes, manioc, and maize are domesticated; cattle breeding, however, always remained relatively unimportant. In due course, the specific New World agriculture would give rise to complex cultures independent of Eurasian or African developments.

Figure 3 A Sumerian frieze showing dairy production (c. 2600–2350 BC). This Sumerian frieze of limestone inlaid with bitumen and copper, from a sanctuary at Tell Ubaid, near Ur, now in the British Museum, has been dated to between 2600 and 2350, and thus is the oldest known depiction of the milking of cows (on the right-hand side) and what probably is the churning of butter (on the left). Dairy production, the spinning of wool and the usage of animals as draft or pack animals and as mounts are the most important outcomes of the so-called secondary products revolution. Photo: © The Trustees of the British Museum

Domestication is not a single event: it is an ongoing process. Vines and olives, for example, were domesticated in Syria and Egypt in about 3000 BC. Newly domesticated animals and plants go on dispersing: thus, the cultivation of vines and olives reaches Greece in about 2500 BC, and enables the characteristically Mediterranean polyculture of grain, vines, and olives to develop. Also, the so-called secondary products revolution, which followed the original domestication, was as important as the domestication itself. During this secondary products revolution, in fact not so much a revolution as a slow evolution, ever more secondary products were extracted from domesticated animals and plants, such as dairy products, wool, hair, and linen, and animals were put to work as draft animals in front of sledges, carts and plows, and as mounts or beasts of burden.

Thanks to agriculture, sedentary societies arose on the periphery of the huge Eurasian continent: in Europe, in the Near East, in India and Pakistan, and in East and Southeast Asia. These sedentary societies, quickly developing into states, were largely dependent on farmers. The northernmost parts of Eurasia were too sparsely populated to allow for state formation, and the Central Asian heartland became, as was stated earlier, the realm of pre-Mongolian stock-raising nomads. Different climatic zones give rise to different societies: two basic economic systems can be distinguished, that of the cattle-herding nomads who mainly exploit the natural resources in a certain area and then move on, and that of the farmers who invest in the land they work, by weeding, plowing, manuring and so on, and thus tend to stay put. Both systems usually exist symbiotically side by side. Nevertheless, there is also endemic conflict between the haves of the periphery and the have-nots of the center. In these conflicts, the peoples of Central Asia sometimes prevailed, as when in the last half of the second millennium BC, groups that were later to be called Iranians and Indo-Aryans turned to the south and established themselves in Iran and India. Also, from about 1200 BC, Mongolian nomads, and in the first centuries AD, the Turks, played an important part. But usually the successes obtained by the invaders from Central Asia were short-lived, as the communities of farmers on the periphery were so populous: the invaders were almost always absorbed by the groups they tried to subject.

Agricultural yields

An enlarged carrying capacity does not imply abundance. On the one hand, the increased food production is offset by a growing population (demographic growth may even have preceded the introduction of agriculture, as was suggested earlier). On the other hand, agriculture in the ancient world can increase the carrying capacity only ever so much. The yields we may expect in ancient agriculture, especially in arable farming, must have been very much lower than those obtained today with the introduction of modern systematic plant breeding and the use of fertilizers. In order to estimate how much lower the yields were, we need detailed information on soil, climate, crops, crop rotation, and fallow. The influence of soil and climate is obvious; even microclimates and microenvironments can make all the difference—but if we want to say anything at all, we will have to generalize. Some plants can stand heat and drought better than others: thus, we find more barley and less wheat in Mediterranean farming. However, yields also differ per species: for instance, different types of wheat have stalks with different numbers of grains. We have to know whether fields were left fallow, and how often: there can be a two-field or a three-field system. Such a system can also encompass crop rotation: a field is not left to rest, but is sown with, for instance, legumes, a crop that restores the nitrogen levels of the soil. In general, we want to know about the number of different crops being farmed; in the ancient world, arable farming was mostly polyculture. There will have been grain, but also viticulture, olive trees, fruit trees, vegetables, and fodder crops. The techniques in use and how much labor was available per unit of land also influence yields.

What we want to get at is the yield per plant, and the yield per unit area of land under cultivation: the number of seeds sown, and the number of seeds harvested, per plant and per hectare. With the sparse information in our sources and with the comparative evidence adduced by the historians of agriculture, we can start figuring—a decent guesstimate is all we can hope for. In the case of barley, rye, and wheat, the ratio of seeds sown to seeds harvested is supposed to have been very low: 1:3 to 1:5. And one should not forget that one third to one fifth of the harvest has to be set aside as seeds for sowing. For the drier parts of the Mediterranean, it has been estimated that the yields from one hectare under grain could support a single individual for one year, if we accept the FAO (Food and Agriculture Organization) figures for the amount of calories a human needs to stay healthy and functioning, and if we accept that in antiquity three-quarters of these calories came from the consumption of grains (that assumption seems reasonably secure). The daily needs are likely to be somewhat overestimated, the yields to be somewhat underestimated. The fact that despite this one hectare can feed one person is quite reassuring, because what we know of landholdings shows these yields to be at subsistence level or over.

Reality was of course very different from the earlier guesstimates: it has already been stressed that the productivity of one piece of land may be very different from that of another piece of land the same size, even if they are situated in the same region. And this certainly holds good when we look at the bigger picture: thus, irrigated arable land, as in Mesopotamia and Egypt, had far larger yields. Some places may have had multiple harvests. Also, as already stated earlier, most farmers will have practiced polyculture: they did have other crops besides grain. And then there is also animal husbandry and fishery.

The importance of livestock differed from one region to the other. In the Near East, outside the river valleys, sheep and goats were quite essential, whereas along the Nile and the Mesopotamian rivers, cattle was of greater importance. But in all sedentary agricultural communities, livestock was secondary compared to the basic food supply from arable farming. In southern Europe, animal husbandry was less important than in the Near East. Goats, sheep, and pigs—the last-named being the main source of meat—were most prominent among domestic animals. The eating of flesh was a relative rarity, although we have to take hunting and the breeding of domestic fowl into account as well. It was goats and sheep that not only produced wool and hair, and horns and hides, but also milk and cheese, never cows. Cattle were important for plowing or for drawing ox carts. In Italy, animal husbandry may have been slightly more important, especially in the north, where there was more pasturage. This certainly holds good for north-western Europe, where pigs and cattle were much more common than in the Mediterranean world.

Quantification is not possible, but it is certain that agriculture in the modern Western world is a completely different business. In the ancient world, it was mostly small-scale, and all labor was manual labor, at most assisted by oxen or donkeys as draft animals. Implements were mainly hoes, mattocks, plows, sickles, and mill stones. Poor farmers, but also those working fields on steep slopes, had to use the hoe and had to prepare the soil for sowing with their manual labor alone; the richer farmer might have possessed a pair of oxen to draw his plow: he could work a larger plot. But even the farm large enough to employ slaves was a relatively simple affair.

Environmental consequences of agriculture

Agriculture increases the carrying capacity, but this increase comes at a price. It has already been stated that humans have often replaced the natural vegetation with crops and pasturage. Even when we disregard the large-scale developments in the 19th and 20th centuries, especially the extension of arable land into steppe and desert areas by way of irrigation and the use of fertilizer, we can still say that the landscape of Eurasia is in large parts human-made. Of course, this differs from region to region: thus, large parts of Central Asia and of the taiga forests remained to some extent untouched. But elsewhere, humans modified their environment, almost always in harmful ways.

A decreasing complexity of an ecosystem, for instance, a decreasing number of plants or animals, usually implies an increasing instability of the system. Even attempts to improve soil quality, such as fertilizing, can have such effects, but one should think above all of deforestation in order to clear land for cultivation or pasturage (permanently or for so-called shifting cultivation), or to obtain wood or charcoal. Overgrazing can stop a forest from regenerating. Deforestation and overgrazing can lead to soil erosion by wind and water, and this in turn can deregulate water systems, and so on. There are other mechanisms of soil degradation as well: drainage leading to oxidation and settling, as in peat bogs in northern Europe, or salinization because of irrigation as along the Tigris, Euphrates, and Nile. Desertification or flooding can be the ultimate consequences.

Not all environmental damage should be laid at the door of agriculture. Humankind has always been introducing pollutants into the environment. In the context of the ancient world, one should not only think of the smoke of heating and cooking fires, waste water, and refuse, but also about the by-products of mining and smelting. Lead was a by-product of silver mining and silver extraction, and mercury and arsenic were used in certain manufactures. An increase in the levels of atmospheric lead during the Roman Empire is visible in measurements taken from drill cores of polar ice or of lake sediments.

Exchange

Extremely simple communities with subsistence farming only are relatively rare. In the context of the ancient world, one will have to think almost exclusively of peasants: farmers who feed themselves and produce a surplus. A surplus implies exchange. Exchange is also implied in the fact that there is no place on Earth that once a certain level of production and consumption has been reached can do without raw materials or semi-manufactured goods brought in from the outside. Exchange can, of course, take many forms. In a peasant economy, the surplus can be brought onto a market, or it can be gathered in by some center of religious and/or political power in order to be redistributed.

The existence of exchange is important not only from an economic point of view, but also because exchange is a form of interaction. During this interaction, not only are objects or living creatures moved from place to place, but ideas are also transferred. This movement of organisms, goods, and ideas, called *diffusion*, is one of the more important among exogenous stimuli for change that a society can be subject to (others are warfare and migration; examples of endogenous stimuli are demographic change or invention).

The nature of ancient economies

Exchange lies at the basis of every economic network. We spoke of the exchange of an agricultural surplus. Every general account of the economy of the pre-industrial days should start from the notion that agriculture was by far the most important sector of the economy (it still is, if we do not want to starve, but its contribution to the gross product has decreased enormously in industrial and post-industrial societies). Mining and quarrying could be locally important. Manufacture, trade, and services were always marginal compared to agriculture. But not only were the relative sizes of the economic sectors different, economic thought also differed. Although most of the time making a profit was considered a proper thing to do, this should not lead us to believe that a modern economic rationality was always employed in order to do so. In pre-modern economic thinking, essential concepts of our economic discourse, such as investment, depreciation, amortization, or profit maximization, were all lacking. And it is not only the vocabulary that is lacking: they did not always act in ways that we would consider to make good economic sense. Thus to calculate rationally, for example, by taking into account (!) amortization, is a recent development. This does not imply, of course, that ancient individuals were incapable of rational thought. Only, they never got round to thinking some things that were only thought of at some later date.

The preceding need not lead to an unduly primitivist view of the pre-industrial economy. The agrarian sector did produce for the market, and the manufactures and trade may have been relatively unimportant, but were crucial for developing monetary economies. The Roman Empire in the first centuries AD is an interesting example of such a monetary economy. Neither should we deny economic life in antiquity all dynamism: we can again point to Rome, which in the 2nd and 3rd centuries had a dynamic and flourishing economy. We can see evidence of this from the number of shipwrecks, the number of coins, or the environmental pollution due to Roman industry, as already mentioned. But the dynamism was restricted in scope: growth (and shrinkage) of the economy took place within very narrow limits. Demography and technology were the main barriers to continued growth, but other factors also played their part. For a start, in every pre-modern economy, the purchasing power was small. The basic necessities swallowed up most or all income, so the supply easily outpaced the demand. Also, there was but little incentive to invest: the near-subsistence levels at which small farmers, craftsmen, and tradesmen lived meant that any profits in fat years tended to be saved for the lean years likely to come, rather than be invested in some dangerous experiment: "money not spent is money earned" and "waste not, want not" were the guiding principles. The rich, who did not need to worry so much, tended to spend their money on consumption rather than investment, because of the importance in ancient societies of conspicuous consumption. Of course, this generated demand, but the rich were few. Non-consumptive expenditure by the rich was usually on the purchase of land: wealth was commonly expressed as land holding in a society in which agriculture was the dominant economic sector.

An impediment to trade was the almost complete absence of deposit money, bonds, bills of exchange, checks, promissory notes, money orders, or whatever would help traders avoid carrying about large sums of money. In the Mesopotamian world and later in Egypt, some moves were made in this direction, but they turned out to be dead ends. One could also say that the restricted amount of money (money in the ancient world is largely precious metal) put a brake on economic growth. Money creation by banks was non-existent; there was no such thing as a central bank either: governments had a marginal role in the economy. They did not try to steer the economy, probably because the notion that one could do so was not there, as one might conclude from the fact that all imports and exports tended to be taxed indiscriminately.

Debatable—and much debated—is the role of a supposed "ancient economic mentality." Agricultural norms and values remained dominant; as just stated, land ownership was considered the most proper form of ownership: the more land, the better. To farm one's own land as one's ancestors had been doing for centuries was an ideal that held good for all of the ancient world, even if the rich did not really dirty their hands and had others farm their land for them. At the top of society, we find a land-owning leisure class. Next we have independent farmers, then tenant farmers and all forms of dependent labor: tradesmen, craftsmen, day laborers, all the way down to slaves. It might surprise one to find tradesmen and craftsmen, and all those who work independently for their own account, listed here as dependent labor: but that is how men who need patrons or customers in order to survive were regarded in the ancient world. That the rich were willing to indulge in trade themselves, possibly by way of middlemen, did nothing to change the low esteem in which the trader was held by the elite. The modern notion of industry and trade as the moving forces behind economic growth was lacking; even economic growth, speaking macro-economically, was not something anyone was consciously aware of. There was a prevailing acquisitive mentality, as opposed to the modern productive mentality. This may have hampered technological progress: even where theoretical knowledge was available, technology lagged behind. This has been explained by the number of slaves or other dependent labor: if there is enough cheap labor available, the need for technology to replace labor does not arise. Although this may have been a contributing factor, it cannot be the whole story: there were many periods and places in the ancient world characterized by no, or only a few, slaves, and we should not forget that slaves were expensive, both in terms of their purchase and upkeep. But there were no breakthroughs in technology there either. An unwillingness to change seems to have been the main factor.

If the mentality had been different, some of the aforementioned barriers would have remained in place, as indeed they did until the Industrial Revolution, and the scientific revolutions of the 19th and 20th centuries. There is a technological ceiling: the knowledge of the properties of materials was too rudimentary, so some developments were impossible. Take, for instance, transport, which was slow and expensive, and would largely remain so until the steam engine and the internal combustion engine brought about a revolution indeed. For the Roman world, it has been calculated that, depending on local circumstances, the relationship between the costs of sea, river, and land transport was 1:5:25. That does not mean land transport was too expensive: the cost depended on the kind of goods, their value, the distance over which they had to be transported, and the kind of road. But transport of a bulk commodity such as grain over land would have pushed up its price above what was considered reasonable, which was the price of the grain when it was transported by water. In agriculture, the technological ceiling is evident as well: until the arrival of modern irrigation, fertilizing, and breeding, a large increase in productivity was impossible. Agricultural production could be increased by bringing more land under cultivation (the total productivity goes up), or by a change in strategy, such as intensification (the productivity per hectare goes up). But when all available land was under cultivation, and if all strategies had been employed, the rise in productivity stopped.

Demography

Limits to growth

The limits put on agricultural productivity, together with the incidence of diseases against which humankind had no defense, also imposed strict limits on demographic growth. Of course, without agriculture there could be hardly any growth at all. It was the development of agriculture that formed the precondition for a long and sustained growth of the human population. An increase in carrying capacity because of some new agricultural technology, the introduction of a new crop, or a change in the climate could keep up growth—for the time being. But a rise in productivity was strictly limited, as we have just seen, so demographic growth was limited too. The disease pool that is always there, but which among agriculturalists was enlarged because of diseases transferred from domestic animals to humans, also kept growth within bounds—even more so when vulnerability increased because of the close mutual contacts within larger groups of humans that followed from a sedentary way of life. Of course, within a human group, immunity against certain diseases caused by bacteria or viruses will slowly grow—such diseases disappear or live on as relatively harmless childhood illnesses. But there will also be new diseases coming in, either by mutating pathogens, or by contact with other human groups where some previously unknown diseases were endemic. Until the invention of modern antibiotics, humans were at the mercy of disease, again and again. Famine and disease imposed a natural demographic ceiling. A few cities could for some period of time outgrow their hinterland, because of their riches and power, and could become extremely populous despite the fact that in such closely packed cities mortality was high—but this only because there was somewhere else a structural surplus of food and of people with which those cities were fed continuously.

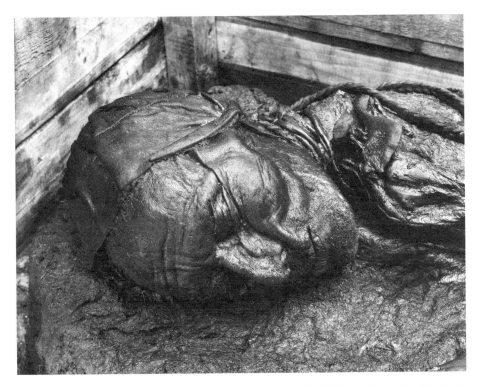

Figure 4   The face of the Tollund Man, an Iron Age bog body from Denmark. Bog bodies are human remains found in what once were peat bogs, where the conditions for the preservation of specific kinds of organic material, such as soft body tissue, are exceptionally good. Even internal organs of bodies lost in the bog may be preserved, enabling us, for instance, to establish the composition of the last meal eaten by an individual, the presence of parasites and the general state of health. The extremely well-preserved body known as the Tollund Man was found in 1950 in Jutland, Denmark; only the head has survived (and can now be seen with a reconstruction of the body in the Silkeborg Museum). The Tollund Man suffered a violent death: he had been strangled before being deposited in the bog. Many bog bodies dated to the Bronze or Iron Age are of individuals who had been executed, whether as a punishment or as a sacrifice (the one does not necessarily exclude the other) is a matter of much dispute. Photo: National Museum of Denmark

Reconstruction of a population

The history of human populations is the subject of historic demography. Ancient sources offer but very few statistically useful figures. Demography provides us with the mathematical tools and historic demography with the comparative material that enable us to arrive at some demographic reconstructions. Every population answers to some general rules. Even if our sparse sources barely allow us to describe any ancient population in some detail, we can at least indicate within which parameters those populations will have developed. Exactitude is beyond bounds: human fertility and life expectancy are influenced by many factors, such as the environment, food and water supply, hygiene and the prevalence of disease, housing, the duration of breast feeding, the norms or laws concerning marriage age, birth control, abortion and infanticide, and so on. For most times and places, the sources do not inform us about some or all of these factors. Also, migration is always a distorting factor when a population is reconstructed on the basis of supposedly general patterns, at least when one is interested in the size and the development of the population of an individual region or settlement. The same applies to the relatively short-term effects of war, famine, epidemic disease, and natural disasters.

Assuming that the societies of antiquity are comparable to other pre-industrial societies—and there is no reason to think otherwise—a high mortality rate of about 40 per thousand would have been compensated by a high birth rate (about 40 to 45 per thousand). The annual growth of the population would then have been between 0% and 0.5%. A growth rate of 0.5% is quite considerable: if this continues year after year, the cumulative effect means that a population will double in 140 years. It seems likely that for most of the time the ancient world did not keep up such growth rates for long.

If the preceding pattern is about right, it follows that almost a third of all children will die during their first year, and over half of all children before reaching the age of 15. Of every 100 newborn, 40 could expect to reach the age of 25, and 25 the age of 50. The high mortality rates should thus be in large part attributed to infant mortality. The life expectancy at birth is a mere 25 years, but the life expectancy at age 5 is 40 years. The age division of ancient societies must have looked like a pyramid with a wide base and narrow top: 40% to 45% of the population was under the age of 18, and the mean age was between 25 and 30. This was no ageing population, which of course does not mean that the ancient world did not have any experience with old age: in antiquity, some people became old or even very old; but the old were a very small minority in a world teeming with children.

The high mortality in the early years ensures that half or more of the newborn will never reach sexual maturity. If a population wants to reproduce under such conditions, every woman who does reach her fertile period should have five or six pregnancies. If we combine this fact and the supposition that in most pre-industrial societies breast feeding continued for long after birth, up to three years, during which time the mother could not become pregnant, we are forced to conclude that the age of marriage for girls was very low to take maximum advantage of the reproductive years. Indeed, ages of 12 to 18 years are mentioned in the sources from several different societies. A mean of five or six pregnancies is then possible (which does not mean that people have families consisting of five or six children: we have to subtract infant mortality).

The high mortality rates in antiquity meant that there was enormous social pressure on individuals to marry and produce children. To beget and bear children was the duty of every member of the community, advocated as the greatest blessing that the gods could bestow on humankind. It is no surprise that movements or ideologies that propagate celibacy and childlessness were unknown, until such a movement arose in India sometime before 500 BC. But also there the ideals preached never caught on with the population at large. When comparable ideas appeared later in the Mediterranean world, these met with strong resistance, as utterly foreign to ancient civil culture. In the early first millennium BC, asceticism was not preached anywhere. Indeed, religion was in large part occupied with ensuring the fertility of humans, beast, and crops.

PART II

BEFORE 900 BC

Chapter 2.1

Prehistory

Paleolithic

Human origins

Human beings probably originated in Africa. Four to five million years ago, Australopithecus roamed the savannahs of East Africa. This "apeman of the south" was a hominid. Around 2 million years ago, again in Africa, there appeared *Homo habilis*, "the handyman," and around 1.7 million years ago *Homo erectus*, "the man walking erect." Possibly *Homo habilis* and certainly *Homo erectus* can be considered as direct forebears of modern humans: they walked upright, were mainly right-handed, produced stone tools, and had harnessed fire. Whether they possessed articulate speech is uncertain. Because of the stone tools used and produced by early humans, we designate the extremely long period from the very first usage of stone tools down to about 10,000 BC as the Paleolithic, the Old Stone Age.

From 1 million years ago, *Homo erectus* colonized all of Africa, and large parts of Europe and Asia. Modern humans, or *Homo sapiens*, evolved from *Homo erectus* about 200,000 years ago. It is debated whether this happened independently in evolutionary processes in Africa, Asia, and Europe, or whether this was a development unique to Africa, from whence *Homo sapiens* some 100,000 years ago colonized the other continents in a second wave of migration out of Africa. If the last is correct, *Homo sapiens* must have everywhere pushed aside older types of humans, possibly because of some evolutionary asset such as superior language abilities. Anyhow, "modern" humans and less evolved types of humans such as the Neanderthal lived side by side in Europe and Asia for some 100,000 years, from 130,000 to 30,000 years ago. In the end, the *Homo sapiens* survived, and the other humans died out. To the arguments from skeletal evidence and tools have been added genetic ones: geneticists argued backward from part of the modern human DNA, both the Y chromosome that is exchanged between father and son, and the so-called mitochondrial DNA that is inherited in the female line only. This shows that the most recent common ancestor of the males and females of the human species lived sometime between 100,000 and 160,000 years ago, in sub-Saharan Africa. Those advocating a multi-regional evolution are not convinced. But whether humans colonized the world once or twice from Africa, when around 10,000 years

Antiquity: Greeks and Romans in Context, First Edition. Frederick G. Naerebout and Henk W. Singor.
© 2014 John Wiley & Sons, Inc. Published 2014 by John Wiley & Sons, Inc.

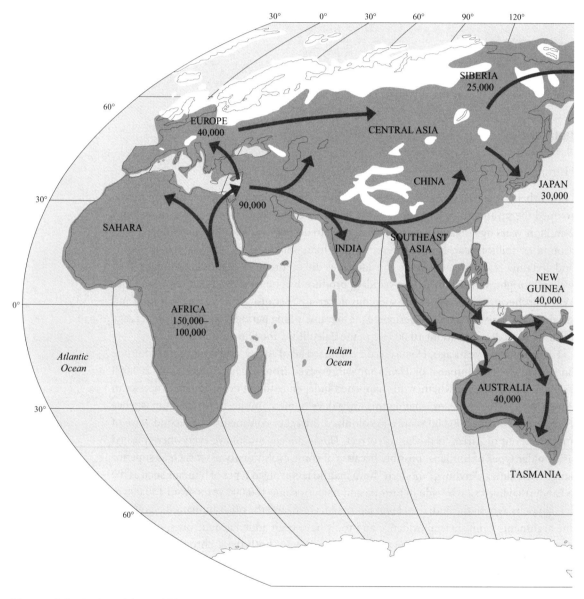

Map 1   Colonization of the world by *Homo sapiens*

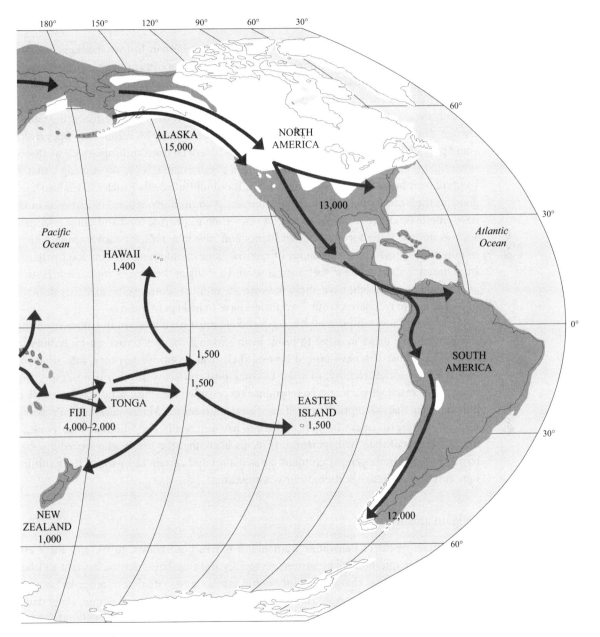

Map 1 (*Continued*)

ago the Ice Age was coming to an end, and with it the Paleolithic, modern humans were to be found across our planet, except for the Arctic regions, the big deserts, and Polynesia.

Economy and society

All through the Paleolithic, which constitutes 99% of human history, humans lived in small, more or less nomadic communities of hunter-gatherers, in anthropological terms: in bands, egalitarian groups of fewer than 100 individuals. The carrying capacity of a territory is strictly limited for hunters-gatherers: the land can feed only so many people. This is certainly the case for the sub-Arctic lowland zone of northwestern Europe during the fourth Ice Age, during the Late Paleolithic, when the lands between the Meuse and the Oder rivers could provide for an estimated 1200 people. Models derived from anthropology may throw some light on the life of Paleolithic bands from about 30,000 to 40,000 years ago, that is bands of members of the genus *Homo sapiens*. It is doubtful whether such models also hold good for the Neanderthal and other early humans. A community of hunters-gatherers must have employed clever strategies to survive: they tried to provide food and other essentials such as animal skins for clothing and tents and raw materials for tool making with a minimum of effort and a minimum of risk. We know something of their food patterns from the analysis of refuse at their campsites and a study of the wear of tools. Factors such as food taboos that might have interfered with the rational choices being made are difficult or impossible to reconstruct, but nevertheless have to be kept in mind.

Mobility was most important: hunter-gatherers must have been on the move from the one camp to the other in order to profit from seasonal changes across several ecological zones. They must also have ranged beyond their own economic territory, into what we may call their social territory, in order to come into contact with other bands, especially to exchange marriage partners. To reproduce successfully, the single band was too small: a human group that can reproduce itself must be at least some 175 individuals large. Probably the females were the ones who were exchanged between bands, and who were incorporated into the bands of their male partners. It seems likely that the bands who shared a social territory were a homogenous group as far as dialect and certain elements of their culture were concerned, though scattered across a huge area.

Religion and art

The spiritual world of Paleolithic humankind is largely unknown to us, and there are definitely more questions than answers, especially since we have become hesitant to label any archeological find that we cannot readily explain as a "ritual" or "religious" object. There have been several attempts to relate religious ideas and behaviors of much later dates to some Paleolithic origin: especially animal sacrifice and all rituals connected to that have been supposed to go back to the world view of Paleolithic hunters, but one would be hard put to adduce any proof for that notion. Of course, it seems that there are no human societies without some forms of ritualization and symbolization, and it is likely this was no different in the Stone Age. But recognizing these in the archeological record will remain something of a challenge. The use of red ocher in graves of a Late Paleolithic date must point to some symbol of life, but whether this is a life after death is unknown. The provision of food for the dead might be a better indication of this, but it is not attested: the Paleolithic people did not know of ceramics as a way to store food. Thus, we end up by saying that death was already marked in Paleolithic times as perhaps the most important rite of passage in a human life, and was associated with some rituals, but we cannot really go beyond that.

From around 30,000 years ago, humans have been making "works of art." Maybe we had better speak of representations. Even though we nowadays tend to look upon these creations as "prehistoric art," we should not conclude that their makers were moved primarily by esthetic considerations. Esthetics will have played some part, but many of these works of art are located in places where they could hardly be seen by their creators, let alone by others admiring their work. This especially holds good for cave art, such as the famous wall decorations in the caves of Lascaux in France or Altamira in Spain, and paintings on rock faces in the open air. We also have movable objects, such as engravings in bone and ivory, and statuettes, many of the type of "Venus figures," richly endowed motherly beings. A religious context seems likely for all or most of this art. With the cave art deep down in almost inaccessible caves, and certainly not in inhabited grottos, to interpret this as some kind of hunting magic seems plausible: there are many animals depicted, and these are usually the species that we know were hunted by Late Paleolithic humans. They are shown wounded or trapped, or mating, or with young. Were these images intended to secure success for the hunters, to pacify the spirits of the animals killed and slaughtered, or to ensure the fertility of the animals and thus the future food supply? We cannot know for certain. We also have imagery of humans dressed up in animal skins: gods or other supernatural beings, or human shaman-like individuals. With the Venus figures, a link with fertility seems fairly evident, also considering the fact that we have representations of breasts or pudenda only. But whether we have to think of "mother goddesses" is again impossible to establish.

The end of the Paleolithic

A large part of the Paleolithic was coterminous with the Ice Ages, interspersed by the warmer so-called interglacials (in fact we should not speak of "Ice Ages" but of glacials, that is periods of extensive ice cover across large parts of Earth; but colloquially these are referred to as "Ice Ages"). The fourth Ice Age came to an end some 12,000 years ago. From there down to about 9000 years ago, in Western Europe down to 5,500 years ago, was a transitional period during which populations increased in size and the bands of hunters-gatherers tended to be become sedentary. With the withdrawal of the ice, flora and fauna entered a new phase, and the carrying capacity was much enhanced. One could also say that the economic and social territories shrank. Mobility decreased, and nomadism was in part replaced by sedentary living. This transitional period is often labeled as the Mesolithic (the Middle Stone Age). The Mesolithic is the era in which tools become smaller, more refined, and more specialized. But, of course, the true importance of the period lies in the slow evolution toward a completely new phase of human culture, the phase characterized by sedentary communities that practice agriculture.

Neolithic

Beginning of the Neolithic in the Near East

Around 10,000 BC, in Eurasia, the ice of the last Ice Age gradually began to withdraw toward the North Pole and to the higher regions of the Alps and the great Asian mountain chains. Although it would take another few thousand years for the icecaps to reach the size they had in the 20th century AD, the process of a gradual warming of the climate paved the way for important changes. Slowly the sea level rose, so that between 10,000 and 5,000 BC, England and the continent of Europe, and Denmark and Sweden, to mention just a few examples, became separated from each other. Behind the retreating ice, the zones of vegetation moved up to the north. In the Mediterranean regions and especially in the Near East, the typically Mediterranean climate settled in after around 10,000 BC, a climate with warm and dry summers and with the rainfall mainly limited to the cooler winter periods, although the contrast between summer and winter temperatures in the period between roughly 10,000 and 4,000 BC was much sharper than it is today. Under the regime of extreme changes in temperature between the seasons, with a pronounced and long dry period in the summer months, there developed a great variety of plants that would not survive longer than one year. Various sorts of eatable grasses, in particular a primitive variety of wheat, belonged to these species of vegetation. Since the natural occurrence of such crops was the necessary condition for the transition to agriculture, the Near East provided the environment required for a change in human culture that was to have far-reaching consequences.

For the first time, this change took place in the Near East, and for the next few thousand years, all innovations in the vast western half of Eurasia would arise mainly in this region and find their way from here to the Mediterranean and Europe. The explanation for the primacy of the Near East can be found in the special development of this region after the

Figure 5   Worm eggs from the intestines of the Lindow Man, a British bog body. Microscopic images of two worm eggs, enlarged x1000, from the intestines of the Lindow Man, a bog body found in 1984 in Lindow Moss in Cheshire, England. The body dates from the Late Bronze Age or the Iron Age—conflicting C14 dates for the body and the surrounding peat make it impossible to more precise. The worm egg on the left is *Ascaris lumbricoides*, and that on the right is *Trichuris trichuria*. Both are common intestinal parasites, but in Europe between the Iron Age and the Early Middle Ages worm infections are supposed to have been quite general and extremely severe. Human infection with *Ascaris lumbricoides* is thought to have resulted from the domestication of the pig. Photos: York University

end of the last Ice Age. It was here that groups of hunter-gatherers for the first time took up a partially sedentary way of life that made the discovery of edible grasses possible. At first, these were merely gathered, but the next step was cultivation: it was discovered that the grains could be sown, so that after some time at the same spot a larger amount of these could be gathered or harvested. To this must have been added fairly early the experience that by selecting and sowing certain varieties the quality of the harvest could be enhanced. With this, agriculture proper was born. This step was taken, possibly at a number of places during roughly the same time period, that is, the period between around 10,000 to 8,000 BC, in the hilly stretch of lands of the so-called Fertile Crescent that runs from modern-day Israel across Lebanon, Syria, and northern Iraq into Iran. It is not clear, however, whether the pressure of an increased population forced the first experiments with an additional food source, or that the addition of grains to the existing food source began as a "luxury" that developed into a necessity when the population had as a consequence increased. With this, a far-reaching cultural and economic change, the Neolithic or New Stone Age, began. Originally, this era in prehistory had received its name from a new phase in the working of stone instruments, characterized by polished instead of unpolished stone utensils, but the real criterion for the beginning of the Neolithic is the domestication of certain plants and the transition to a sedentary way of life.

Almost contemporaneously with the appearance of the first agrarian settlements, as we have seen, the process of domestication of some animal species began. Presumably, already in the Late Paleolithic, dogs had become the companions of the human hunters. Hunter-gatherers already manipulated nature to some extent: for example, they mostly spared the females and the young of their prey in order to ensure a steady supply of the animals in a certain area, or they tried to lure their prey by felling trees in order to produce forest clearings attractive to big game. The Neolithic way of life, however, opened up the possibility of a human-enforced adaptation of certain animal species to living in close proximity with and dependence on humans. By crossbreeding animals with the qualities desired and by thorough-breeding on these qualities, Neolithic farmers created the first domestic animals. Exact dates are hard to give, but probably somewhere between 10,000 and 5,000 BC in the Near East, successively sheep and goats, pigs and cattle became domesticated. In the late fourth millennium BC, somewhere in the steppes of southern Russia or Central Asia, the horse would be added to these, initially only for the consumption of its meat.

The introduction of animal breeding meant a significant extension of the economic base of Neolithic life because of the provision of meat, wool, hide, and milk, and the use of cows and later of horses as draft animals and pack animals. As a result, Neolithic groups of people acquired important advantages over the rest of the human species, also in a demographic sense, for the breeding of small and large animals contributed to the food supply and hence to the overall growth in population of these groups. At the same time, the transition to agriculture and herding was accompanied by the spread of new diseases caused by microparasites to which humans as hunters had not been exposed to such an extent before. In all probability, the Neolithic transition must initially even have weakened the population groups involved, but in the long run it must have given them, in contrast with the groups of hunters outside their territory, a certain immunity against many of these diseases. Moreover, the higher density of population in an agricultural society caused certain diseases to become endemic in that population. In the gradual extension of the areas of Neolithic culture, therefore, diseases must have played their role, however hard it is for us to qualify, let alone to quantify that role. That extension must have been the result of various contributing factors: population growth, erosion of the soil used for agriculture forcing people to move to other grounds within a few years, and probably also the adoption of the Neolithic way of life by peripheral human groups. Often, however, contacts between Neolithic people and groups still living in a Paleolithic hunting culture must have been fatal for the latter: not only numerically but also physically, they more often than not must have succumbed to the carriers of both a new culture and new diseases.

Spread of Neolithic cultures

The spread of Neolithic culture from its origins in the Near East was a gradual and steady process. Initially, in the 10th and 9th millennia BC, agriculture was restricted to the Fertile Crescent stretching from Israel into Iran, although it cannot be excluded that already in this period much farther to the east in various places an independent development toward agriculture had taken off. For the rest, however, in vast areas the Paleolithic lived on. In the course of the 7th millennium BC, the agricultural way of life spread via Anatolia (modern-day Turkey) to Greece and the Balkans, and in the 6th millennium along the river valleys of the Danube and the Rhine further to Western Europe. By the 5th millennium BC, the whole of Europe south of the line Oslo–Stockholm had become acquainted with agriculture. The cold regions north and northeast of that line remained for a long time inhospitable areas where the ancestors of Laps, Finns, and various Siberian peoples maintained their Paleolithic hunter cultures relatively unscathed.

In another direction, Neolithic culture already in the 7th millennium BC spread to northern Africa, but here the gradual drying up of the climate and the formation of the Sahara desert presented a growing barrier. In tropical Africa, agriculture and cattle breeding presumably spread only slowly in a long process starting from Egypt south to eastern Africa and beyond. To the east, Neolithic culture reached Iran and the Indus valley. There, the first agricultural settlements arose in the 5th millennium BC, at the latest. Further to the east, in India and Southeast Asia, a possibly independent development began, in which the gathering of plants and various tropical fruits and crops lead to a semi-sedentary way of life and where in the 4th millennium BC, if not earlier, the transition to rice growing was made. From here, at a later stage, the growing of rice would spread to southern China. It is still not clear whether the cultivation of grain in the loess areas of northern China had been an autonomous development as well, or that it derived, ultimately, from the Neolithic heartland in the Near East. The beginnings of this culture are as yet insufficiently dated, but there are indications that here too an independent development took place that possibly was as old as the one in the Near East. In any case, the appearance of agricultural societies in the whole of Eurasia caused the areas of older, Paleolithic cultures to gradually shrink toward the Siberian north or to inaccessible jungle areas or isolated islands off the coasts of the continent.

Complex societies and Megalithic cultures

Between the old world of the Paleolithic and the new one of the Neolithic there were gradual transitions nearly everywhere. Usually, the transition was a prolonged process and not a sudden revolution. It was, moreover, a process that did not stop at the domestication of plants and animals but created its own dynamics that led to a series of changes and innovations. How complex all these developments may have been can be illustrated by the case of pottery. In near-eastern cultures, ceramic pottery appeared at the latest in the course of the 7th millennium BC. In the 6th millennium BC, the potter's oven was known here. In Southeast Asia, the production of ceramic pottery hardly started later, whereas in northeastern China, Korea, and Japan, pottery probably had already made its appearance even before the transition to agriculture had taken place; recent discoveries in southern China even suggest ceramic pottery going back a few thousand years into the Paleolithic.

Some settlements already at an early stage possessed buildings or large wooden constructions for the creation of which sizable groups of people must have contributed their labor. This points to a more complex organization of these communities, but we know practically nothing of the forms such organizations might have taken. There are as yet no indications of a distinction between an elite and the rest of society. Presumably, many Neolithic societies had one or more particular persons who were entrusted with certain religious functions or who were considered to have some sort of special knowledge, and presumably such a role might often have been combined with authority in other respects as well. Female figurines in the tradition of the Venus-figures of the Late Paleolithic probably point to fertility cults. In Anatolia, at least from the 7th millennium BC, a cult of a Great Goddess connected with natural vegetation and wild animals can be discerned. There and at other places in the Near East and in Mediterranean areas, traces of a bull cult can be detected as well, possibly again in connection with fertility. We may assume that in the first millennia of the Neolithic, religion, that is, religious thought and acts, must have been shaped at least as strongly as in the Paleolithic by the new fundamentals of life, expressing itself in fertility rites for humans, animals, and crops, in the observation of the seasons and the heavens with an eye to sowing and harvesting, in funeral rites, and so on. It is hardly a surprise that the oldest large buildings in stone, often constructed of big slaps—hence: megaliths, that is "big stones," and megalithic culture—must in one way or another have served the purposes of religion. One may think here of the rows of stones and stone circles in Western Europe (5th to 3rd millennium BC), of the grave tombs of megaliths in the coastal areas of Western Europe, as well as of the pyramids and temples of huge polished blocks of stone in Egypt and, albeit much later, in some pre-Columbian cultures of the Americas.

Chapter 2.2

Early Civilizations in Eurasia

The Rise of Distinct Civilizations

The earliest civilization in Mesopotamia

The spread of agriculture was a necessary condition for the rise of more complex societies. For a civilization of some complexity to arise, a greater concentration of population and a more structured social organization are required. Such civilizations could originate in a few exceptional regions where the natural environment demanded a high degree of communal organization and at the same time promised high rewards in the form of exceptionally rich harvests. In or close to Eurasia, that was the case in the river basins of the Euphrates and Tigris, of the Nile, the Indus, and the Huanghe.

In the course of the 6th millennium BC, the inhabitants of the stretches of land along the middle and lower Tigris and Euphrates began to use these soils for agriculture. This was the land, in present-day Iraq, that the Greeks would later call Mesopotamia, that is: land between the rivers. Perhaps this was the work of immigrants who had come here for the same reasons as other Neolithic groups who, tempted to bring into cultivation new lands because of a relative overpopulation in their places of origin, had spread their Neolithic way of life from one place to another. In southern Mesopotamia, where there is practically no rainfall and where only the rivers provide water, this cultivation required a communal effort to dig canals and construct dikes in order to maximize the use of the water supply. Here, larger settlements arose than were possible in the hilly and mountainous areas of the surrounding regions, because the land thus irrigated and put to cultivation yielded harvests that could feed many more people while at the same time requiring the collective labor of far greater numbers.

Each of the settlements in southern Mesopotamia appears to have had at least one large sanctuary, presumably serving as a center of religious and political organization. The settlement and its surrounding fields constituted a small "state." We get the impression that between these states, strips of land were purposely left uncultivated as no-man's land serving as frontier zones. Thus, toward the end of the 4th millennium BC, Mesopotamia must have known a few dozens of such mini-states. The temples and the walls around the

Antiquity: Greeks and Romans in Context, First Edition. Frederick G. Naerebout and Henk W. Singor.
© 2014 John Wiley & Sons, Inc. Published 2014 by John Wiley & Sons, Inc.

settlements were made of sun-baked brick covered with a layer of oven-baked tiles. We may call these settlements the oldest cities known, and hence we may speak, from around 3000 BC on, of the first urban civilization.

Inventions: The beginning of the Bronze Age

From the very beginning, people in Mesopotamia were acquainted not only with the use of polished stone utensils but also with the use of copper for knives and for beads and other ornaments. This, the earliest phase of metallurgy, had originated in the 7th millennium in the use of the potter's oven for the production of ceramic pottery in northern Iraq, Iran, and Anatolia and would in the 5th and 4th millennia spread all over the Near East and large parts of Europe. It is possible, however, that in the Balkans copper metallurgy arose independently, as it would later in East and Southeast Asia. As a relatively soft metal, copper remained of limited use until in the later 4th millennium it was discovered that by applying an admixture of tin, a harder, albeit sometimes brittle metal was acquired that could well be used for various tools and weapons. It is unknown where the first ever bronze was produced, but the oldest bronze objects known in western Asia stem from southern Mesopotamia. Here, the Bronze Age began around 3000 BC. It is a period in prehistory and ancient history that, like the Neolithic, began in different regions at different times.

Roughly at the same time or just a little earlier, in the later part of the 4th millennium BC, another invention made its appearance here as a result of a—for us—rather obscure development: the use of script. These two great inventions, as well as others, were in a sense the result of the big step that had been the genesis of the first urban civilization. For it was the cities that provided the required concentration of population that in its turn made possible an ongoing specialization of labor, creating the space and leisure for innovations and inventions. After the great Neolithic change, it was this urbanization that led to the rise of more complex civilizations.

The origins of Egyptian civilization

Circumstances comparable to those in Mesopotamia explain to a large extent the rise of civilization in Egypt. In the course of the 5th millennium BC, Neolithic groups from North Africa and the eastern Mediterranean coastlands settled in the delta of the Nile and along the river's edges in Egypt. Here too, a large population could arise thanks to the exceptionally high yields in the cultivated strips of land. Relative to the Near East, Egypt for some time remained, so to say, the receiving and junior party. Not only had the knowledge of agriculture come, ultimately, from the Fertile Crescent, as would later the knowledge of copper and bronze, but early Egyptian architecture also suggests some derivation from Mesopotamia. The Egyptian hieroglyphic script appears around 3000 BC, rather suddenly and in an already developed form; its antecedents are unknown but most probably indigenous. In any case, contacts with the Near East in the 3rd millennium seem to have become more difficult, perhaps as a result of further desertification, especially in the Sinai, and from then on Egyptian civilization developed for a long time in relative isolation. Cities, comparable to those in Mesopotamia, did not appear here, the population went on living in villages. On the other hand, not long after the beginning of the 3rd millennium the country was unified politically, an event that doubtless had been furthered by the existence of the one river on which all inhabitants depended. As a consequence, Egyptian civilization developed mainly around the person of the king, who governed the whole country, and around a religion in which that king played a central role. Bronze remained unknown here for a rather long time, but the working of stone was since the 3rd millennium BC in the typically Egyptian form of a late Neolithic copper culture brought to great finesse and used for the erection of temples and grave monuments in the service of religion and kingship.

The first complex civilizations in South Asia

In the Indus valley, after the first Neolithic settlements in the early 3rd millennium BC, a civilization arose that in the light of the excavated remains of houses, granaries, and fortification walls can clearly be called urban. The building material was sun- and oven-baked clay, as it was in Mesopotamia. The short specimens of writing, found mainly on seals from the 3rd millennium BC, are as yet undeciphered. This region must have been connected commercially along the coast of Iran and through the Persian Gulf with Mesopotamia as well as with other cultures across land routes to the north and northwest. To this were added influences from farther east, from where the knowledge of rice growing must have reached the Indus area. In its turn, this Indus civilization doubtless bequeathed a legacy, especially, we may assume, in the realm of religion, to other and later Indian civilizations. But as long as the script of the Indus valley remains undeciphered, much will rest uncertain. In the early 2nd millennium BC, this civilization decayed and its remains would finally be destroyed around 1500 BC. Probably, a major role in this was played by the immigrants who would later be known as Indo-Aryans, arriving in the Indian subcontinent from the northwest, possibly in a steady infiltration of small groups in the course of the 2nd millennium BC.

In Southeast Asia, in the course of the 4th millennium BC, the first sedentary societies had appeared based on the growing of rice. Bronze production of a surprisingly high level made its appearance here rather suddenly around 1500 BC. A connection with the metallurgy of the Near East seems out of the question. But the step toward an urban civilization was not made here for another 1500 years or more.

The beginning of civilization in China

In northern China, in the middle basin of the Huanghe (or Yellow River), there arose a civilization with a whole set of characteristics of its own. Its origins are as yet not very clear, but there is no doubt that this was the cradle of Chinese civilization. A Neolithic phase characterized by habitation in villages and the growing of barley, wheat, and other cereals, was followed, again rather suddenly, around 1500 BC by a highly developed Bronze Age culture. The bronze was used for ritual kettles, gongs, bells, and vessels, as well as for arms and chariots. The latter, drawn by horses, point to contacts with the steppe regions to the west. Presumably, horses and chariots had been introduced into China by people from

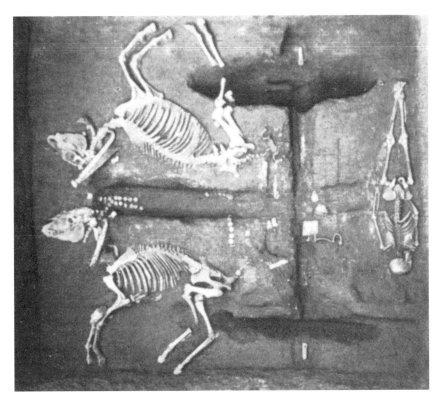

Figure 6 Chinese burial site with traces of a chariot (c. 1300 BC). A grave site with two horse skeletons, a human skeleton, and the traces of a wooden chariot, now disintegrated except for some metal fittings. This grave is part of the royal tombs near modern Anyang, where the last capital city of the Shang Dynasty was situated. The tombs are generally dated to around 1300 BC. Thus, this would be one of the earliest examples of the chariot in China—its shape seems to point to a Central Asian origin. The human skeleton would be a charioteer, sacrificed together with the horses to follow his master in death. Human sacrifice was not at all uncommon during the Shang Dynasty. Photo: Topfoto

Central Asia. The origin of bronze working, however, remains unknown but seems to have been an autonomous development rather than an importation from elsewhere. In any case, this Bronze Age culture from the start constituted an integral part of Chinese civilization. According to Chinese tradition, it was the dynasty of the Shang that ruled here from around 1500 to around 1100 BC. Their territory along the Huanghe became the base for a steady expansion of the Chinese civilization, peacefully by the cultivation of ever more stretches of land cleared from its original forests, and also by means of military conquest—a pattern that would be a feature of Chinese history for the next 3000 years.

Many ingredients of Chinese civilization were already there in the era of the Shang: foremost the town, developed as a royal residence, rectangularly laid out and walled; further, the sharp distinction within society between an elite of the larger landowners and chariot fighters around the king on the one hand, and the mass of the peasant population on the other. The latter for a long time kept its Neolithic way of life, tilling the soil in a primitive way without knowledge of the plow, whereas the use of bronze in the hands of the elite remained mainly limited to the spheres of warfare and religion. At the same time, the peasant population could always be called up to help rein in the river. For the Huanghe meanders through the northern plain and would, without human interference, constantly change its bed. Therefore, even more than in the other river basins—Nile, Tigris and Euphrates, and Indus—a massive input of labor by an obedient population was required in order to prevent calamities or restore damage by strengthening dikes or building new ones. Other factors in their turn must have contributed to what would remain the typically Chinese organization of society for a long time to come. Among these, ancestor worship should be mentioned together with the accompanying authority of the elders and the eldest in the community, and hence of those who more or less professionally maintained contact with the ancestors, like the heads of families and clans and ultimately the king himself. The worship of gods and of forces of nature also played a part here, especially where the fixed rituals of the calendar were concerned. The Chinese script also made its appearance under the Shang; originally a pictographic script, it quickly developed into a form that was the direct ancestor of the modern Chinese characters. Apparently, its use was in this period limited to religious purposes, especially oracles. In general, many achievements of Chinese civilization would for a long time remain restricted to the elites of the court and of the army—for instance, the use of silk, discovered in this period and already in its early phase developed to a high degree of technical refinement.

Toward the end of the 2nd millennium BC, the power of the Shang kings began to wane, presumably as a result of a growing independence of the larger landowners and army commanders. In Chinese tradition, the last king of the Shang is represented as a degenerate monster whose deposition by a western "duke" therefore fulfilled the will of Heaven. It was said that "the Mandate of Heaven" had passed from the Shang to a new dynasty, the Zhou, and that version of events would become the accepted explanation for every change of dynasty that henceforth was to occur in the long history of China.

Complex civilizations and their peripheries

Under the Shang, the process of sinification of northern China began, a process that would be continued in the following centuries over Central and South China. But the influence of a great civilization does not remain limited to its direct political sphere. In the case of China, we may speak of a wide and growing periphery that came into China's cultural sphere, and that would ultimately encompass a large part of East Asia. The same phenomenon—a core region, where a complex civilization had arisen, and a large periphery—occurred elsewhere as well. The Indus civilization in the 2nd millennium BC clearly influenced the sedentary communities of the Ganges valley until, after the arrival of Indo-Aryan groups, the center of gravity of Indian civilization would shift to the Ganges valley in the 1st millennium BC, later to move further southward. Likewise, Egyptian civilization from its beginning exerted a strong influence on the Sudan to the south and on the eastern Mediterranean coastlands to the north. In the latter, the periphery of Egyptian civilization met with that of Mesopotamia.

To some extent, Mesopotamia, the region of the first complex civilization, drew the whole of the Near East into its cultural periphery and it exerted influences that went even beyond the Near East, especially in a western direction. Those influences manifested themselves in a number of areas. We may think here of the technique of bronze working, of the use of a script, of various religious customs and ideas, including complex mythological stories. But that influence can also be discerned in the techniques of agriculture and horticulture, even if these by themselves were not always of strictly Mesopotamian origin. Here, irrigation may be mentioned, as well as various crops, plants, and trees with, for instance, the accompanying art of grafting, that would spread westward from the Near East, among them also the vine. Until well into the 1st millennium BC, Mesopotamia would thus be a cultural leader that was followed directly or indirectly by large parts of western Eurasia.

Peoples and Languages

Migration

Humans are excellent at changing their habitat and adapting to new circumstances. Therefore, migration is a phenomenon of all times. For instance, when the natural environment changed, as a consequence of a change in climate, either humans had to change their way of life or they moved on to elsewhere. As we have seen, after the fourth and last Ice Age, Paleolithic hunters moved northward with the retreating ice. A wide zone of a temperate climate thereby opened up for the first Neolithic agriculturalists: starting from the Near East, people, animals, and crops colonized the whole of South and Central Europe. The history of the Neolithic is practically everywhere the history of a steady expansion of areas inhabited and cultivated by these early farmers and at the same time the history of an ongoing shrinkage of the wild areas where groups of hunter-gatherers survived. That expansion must often have been accompanied by the migrations of particular groups, resulting in a mixture of old and new inhabitants in certain areas, or in the expulsion or extermination of the "primitive" hunters by the "modern" farmers and herdsmen in others. And migrations did not stop with the arrival of a sedentary population. Exhaustion of the soil because of simple and destructive agricultural methods—as, for example, the slash-and-burn techniques of clearing forest grounds—as well as the pressures of a relative overpopulation time and again pushed new groups of people to move on. In addition to this, there developed along the edges of certain agricultural zones forms of nomadism where the owners of herds of sheep and goats lived in a form of symbiosis with the agricultural settlements with which they would exchange their products. Such symbiosis would often lead to an enlarged food supply, which in its turn would lead to population growth among the herdsmen, until a critical point was reached that forced them to plunder and sometimes to conquer the neighboring agrarian regions. This was especially true of fertile and densely populated agrarian areas that were easily accessible, as were the river basins where the early Bronze Age civilizations had arisen. Immigration here often took place in the shape of conquests by foreign invaders who, however, in the course of time, regularly merged with the much more numerous local populations and so mostly lost their original nomadic habits.

Languages and peoples in the Near East: The Semites

Only from the time that written documents are available do we know anything for certain about the movements of ethnic groups and language groups in Eurasia. For the preceding period, we have to be content with reconstructions on the basis of later situations and backward projection from there, in combination with archeological material that is not always straightforward in its significance. We call the people who created the first urban civilization in Mesopotamia Sumerians, for they themselves in their written documents call their land Sumer. Their language is not related to any other language known to us. In contrast, the land of Akkad (Agade) bordering Sumer to the north was inhabited from around 3000 BC by speakers of a Semitic language, Akkadian, who had adopted the script of their Sumerian neighbors. These Akkadians probably originated in the desert and semi-desert areas of Syria and northern Arabia, from where in the course of time various Semitic peoples, herdsmen in origin, would emerge and disperse all over the Near East. They constituted a single language family that in the preceding millennia had become separated from its near relative, the family of the Hamitic languages—to which the Egyptians and the Berber peoples of northern Africa belonged. The Semitic migrations began around 3000 BC with the settlement of Akkadians in Mesopotamia; later in the 3rd and 2nd millennia, there followed the Amorites, who likewise infiltrated in and settled all over Mesopotamia; in the later 2nd and early 1st millennium BC, it would be the Aramaeans who would penetrate into Mesopotamia, Syria, and Palestine.

The Indo-European language group

To the east, the north, and the west of the Near East, comparable phenomena occurred. Here, in all probability in the areas of southern Russia and Central Asia around the Caspian Sea, was the cradle of the Indo-Europeans, another large family of languages. A recent theory based on computer modeling suggests Anatolia as the region of origin of the Indo-Europeans, but all solid historical and linguistic evidence still points to the steppe areas just mentioned. They were acquainted with agriculture and were cattle breeders. Moreover, in the 4th millennium BC, they had begun domesticating the horse, although that animal presumably did not play an important role in the first stages of their expansion, which must have begun around 3000 BC. Before the end of the 3rd millennium BC, Indo-European groups reached northern Mesopotamia and Anatolia. In the latter case, it was the ancestors of the people later known as the Hittites who infiltrated that region from across the Caucasus. Roughly in the same period, about 2000 BC, the first speakers of an Indo-European language must have moved from southern Russia and the Balkans—if not partly, perhaps, from Anatolia in the east—into Greece, where from a mixture of Indo-European and indigenous elements the Greek language would emerge.

Presumably in Mesopotamia, and not long after 2000 BC, an important invention was made by people acquainted with horses—whether Indo-Europeans or indigenous groups or both—and transmitted to other horse-breeding groups: the chariot. The Sumerians had already known a rather heavy cart with massive wheels drawn by asses. This was transformed

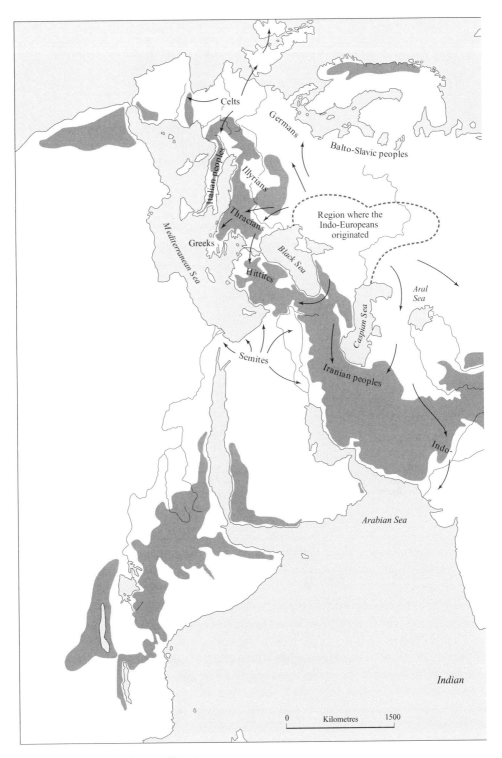

Map 2 Languages in Eurasia, 2nd–1st millennium

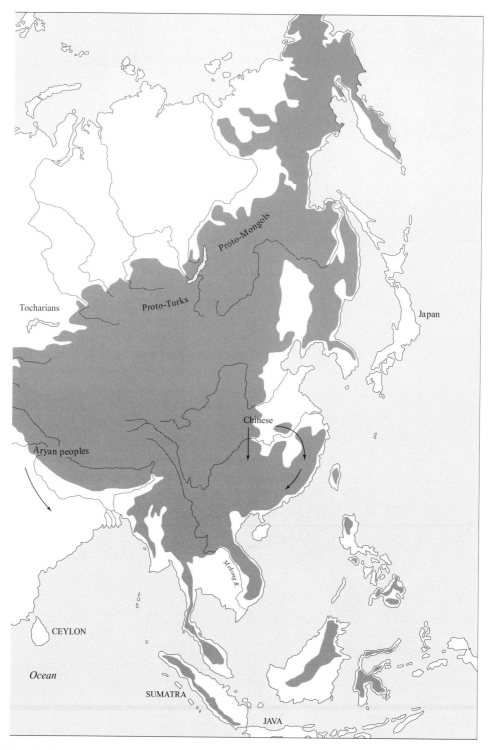

Tocharians

Proto-Mongols

Proto-Turks

Japan

Chinese

Aryan peoples

Mekong R.

CEYLON

Ocean

SUMATRA

JAVA

Map 2 (*Continued*)

into a light chariot with two spoked wheels drawn by horses. In the Near East, the chariot became the foremost attribute of Indo-European warlike groups. Their migrations now often took the shape of conquest by small war bands. In that form, probably, Indo-Iranian and Indo-Aryan groups penetrated and settled in Iran and from around 1500 BC in the Indus valley. In Central Asia, more isolated Indo-European groups had expanded eastward with their horses, and it was presumably from them that not long before 1500 BC the Chinese had acquired their knowledge of horses and chariots. More to the west, the chariot made its appearance in Greece around 1600 BC. Toward the end of the 2nd and in the course of the 1st millennium BC, Indo-European peoples would spread over practically the whole of Europe. The most important linguistic subgroups there were the Italic peoples in Italy, the Illyrians in the western Balkans, the ancestors of the Celts in Central and Western Europe, and the ancestors of the Germanic peoples around the Baltic, and those of the Baltic and Slavonic peoples in the northeast of Europe. Only the Basques, the Estonians, the Lapps, and Finns would to the present day preserve their pre-Indo-European languages. Everywhere else the indigenous populations must have mixed with Indo-European-speaking immigrants and gradually have taken over their languages. That the language of a dominant minority in the end becomes the language of the people at large is a widely occurring phenomenon. Remnants of the pre-Indo-European languages can be found in various regions of Europe, mainly in geographical and topographical names.

Language groups and peoples in Asia

Elsewhere in Eurasia, such movements of linguistic groups and peoples also occurred, although we do not know very much in any specific detail. In South and in East Asia, certain ethnic and linguistic groups clearly expanded, as did the Indians (the Indo-Aryans), at first across the Ganges valley and then to the south of the subcontinent, and the Chinese from their core region along the middle Huanghe. Older, and sometimes culturally less advanced, peoples were either assimilated to the newcomers or reduced to forms of semi-slavery or serfdom, if not simply expelled. The latter circumstance probably explains, at least in part, the movements of Austrasian and Malay groups from the mainland of Southeast Asia to the islands off the continent toward the southeast. To the west and the north of China in the course of the 2nd millennium, language families of nomad peoples arose: Iranian speakers in the west, and proto-Turkish speakers as well as Mongolian peoples more to the north.

Western Asia and Egypt in the Bronze Age

Mesopotamia: The Sumerian cities

The cities that had emerged in southern Mesopotamia in the later 4th millennium BC long remained separate states, although they did not differ significantly from each other in language, population, and political organization. Everywhere in these Sumerian city-states, the temple of the main god of the city initially played a central role. The servants of the god

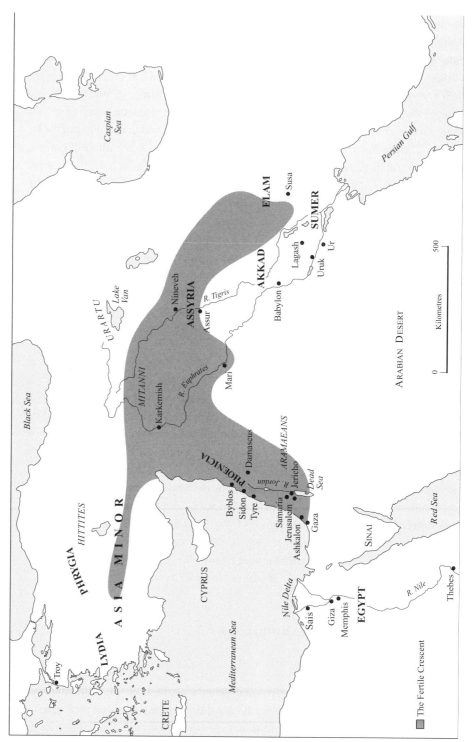

Map 3 The Near East and Egypt, 3rd–1st millennium

(his priests) oversaw the collective activities of the population and organized the storage and distribution of the produce of the land. It is not clear, however, whether the fields and gardens were originally collective property, or whether they at least in part had been in private hands from the beginning. In any case, private property developed strongly in the 3rd millennium BC and must have been the norm, according to our sources, from around 2300 BC on. The main priest of the main god of the city may have developed into a "king" in some places, but this cannot have been a general rule, for already at an early stage non-priestly persons, such as the commander of the citizens at arms, could assume kingly powers as well. Certainly, the monarchy in these Sumerian cities seems to have been an ancient institution. In the 3rd millennium BC, the royal palace became the center of the city's political organization, next to or combined with the temple. It is important to note that in the relationship between the king and the world of the gods, the king retained some priestly functions and presented himself as the first and most beloved servant of the god. In Mesopotamia, the king was not, at least certainly not as a rule, a god in human form. On the contrary, the idea that the gods are far elevated above the world of men always remained strong in Mesopotamia and in fact in the whole Near East.

In the 3rd millennium BC, the Sumerian cities lived in a state of constant rivalry among themselves. We are informed of wars from which now this city-state, now another, emerged as a hegemonic power among its surrounding neighbors. Important power centers were, for instance, Uruk, Lagash, and Ur. Shortly after 2400 BC, a warlike king of Uruk succeeded in acquiring a short-lived hegemony over all of South and Central Mesopotamia. It was the first attempt in history that we know of to build with the use of force an "empire" that encompassed practically the whole known and "civilized" world. "King of all," or "King of the four regions of the world" would since remain the titles expressing the pretense of ruling the world, titles to which many a king in Mesopotamia would henceforth aspire. This first Sumerian empire was soon destroyed and supplanted by the first Semitic empire of Akkad under the famous king Sargon, who around 2375 BC conquered the whole of Mesopotamia and even for a moment reached the shore of the Mediterranean Sea. But after a few generations, this empire too met its end, caused by the incursions of warlike peoples from the mountainous regions to the north of Mesopotamia. Following this, the Sumerians for a last time, under the leadership of the city of Ur, exerted their power over at least the south and probably the whole of Mesopotamia. Toward 2000 BC, that empire in its turn came to an end, in part as a consequence of the infiltrations of new Semitic groups, this time the Amorites. Thereafter, the language of the Sumerians disappeared as a spoken language, although it would remain in use as the language of learning for religious and some other writings.

Script and religion

The fact that in Mesopotamia since the late 4th millennium BC a script had been in use is of the greatest historical importance. According to a widely accepted definition, the appearance of a script and of written documents signifies the end of prehistory and the beginning of history proper. Thanks to the written documents from Mesopotamia, we for the first time become acquainted with names of peoples, cities, kings, and gods, and for the first time we get some idea of the thoughts and aspirations of the people with whom history began. Initially, their script was pictographic but it developed rapidly into a syllabic script of roughly 600 characters, each of which in principle represented one syllable. After the specific form of these characters, impressions made by a reed shaft in soft clay and described as cunei or "nails," it is now called cuneiform. The clay tablets could be baked when it was deemed important to store these texts, or else they could be reused after a while. Many tablets have been preserved for us as an unforeseen result of fires that destroyed temples and palaces. The original purpose of the use of a script had presumably been its application in the administration of the temples—but actually we know nothing for certain here. What we do know is that it did not take very long for the cuneiform script to be used for less strictly mundane purposes: the writing down of religious hymns and prayers, political treaties, laws, etc. What we may call historiography did not appear until very much later, but lists of the names of kings of various hegemonial cities were preserved, and perhaps around 2000 BC some form of chronicle writing developed. The succession of kingdoms, hegemonies, and dynasties in a sense stimulated a certain historical consciousness. Connected to this was a sense of the powerlessness of humans compared with the all-powerful gods who were unpredictable beings, always demanding obedience and reverence and meting out punishment in the form of the downfall of cities or catastrophes such as great floods of the rivers for any form of disobedience and even for no disobedience at all, out of pure whim. Such ideas would have a long history and exert no small influence on other cultures that became acquainted with Mesopotamian literature.

Even though the temple must have lost its function as a political center of the city in the 3rd millennium, becoming intricately connected with the palace and the kingship, still the temple would put its stamp on daily life in Mesopotamia for a very long period. Built on an artificial hill of at least three and ideally seven platforms, the *ziggurat*, the sacred building, literally towered above the houses of the people. Sacrificial festivals and other rituals marked important moments in the year, such as the New Year's festival in spring. The calendar was naturally religious in character. Numbers connected with the observation of heaven and the reckoning of time acquired a symbolic and often sacred character: 12 (for the months of the year and the signs of the zodiac), 60 (counting was in a combination of decimal (base 10) and sexagecimal (base 60) systems, that is still with us in the 60 minutes of the hour and the 360 degrees of the circle), and 7 (after the 7 known "planets," among which also sun and moon were reckoned). The symbolism of these numbers as well as a basic knowledge of mathematics and astronomy are part of the cultural legacy of Mesopotamia from which many peoples would ultimately profit.

Babylon and Hammurabi

In the 1st half of the 2nd millennium BC, the center of gravity moved northward, and it was the city of Babylon in Central Mesopotamia that under an Amorite dynasty for the first time acquired hegemony over the lands of Sumer and Akkad. Its king Hammurabi (around 1700 BC) became especially renowned; he ordered an extensive law code to be set up, known to us from a famous inscription. Hammurabi's laws are not the oldest ones known, for we

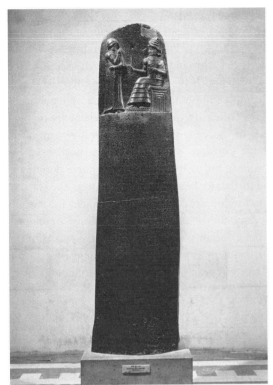 

Figure 7 Stele with the Code of Hammurabi (1728–1686 BC). A stele of black basalt, found in Susa, the old capital of Elam, now in the Louvre in Paris, and carrying the Code of Hammurabi. Not long after the end of Hammurabi's reign, Babylon was captured and plundered by the Elamites, and on that occasion this copy of the Code of Hammurabi must have been carried to Susa. Part of the cuneiform text was removed, but comparison with other copies enables us to reconstruct most of the code, which comprises almost 300 laws. The relief on the Louvre stele shows the Babylonian king standing in front of the enthroned sun god Shamash. In Mesopotamia (and later in the Greco-Roman world), the all-seeing sun was associated with the idea of justice. The god is depicted as a king, and the king as his humble servant. Photo: De Agostini/SuperStock

possess parts of the legal codes of some Sumerian kings from the 3rd millennium BC. In comparison with these older law codes, there is in some respects even a certain regression in Hammurabi's code. For instance, the laws of Hammurabi prescribe corporal punishments and acknowledge the principle of "an eye for an eye, and a tooth for a tooth," whereas for many such cases in Sumerian law fines had been deemed sufficient. But Hammurabi's law code is the most detailed and presents the historian with a lot of information on social and economic life in Mesopotamia in his times, especially, the many rules on selling and buying, renting, leasing and borrowing, inheritance, and so on. Private property and individual freedom of action were not a given in this period, for in near-contemporary Mari on the middle Euphrates, the economy was centralized, with the royal palace, like the temple in the older Sumerian cities, dictating the various tasks of a large part of the population and regulating and distributing the products of agriculture and handicrafts.

The empire of Hammurabi did not last long. Babylonian power came to an end through new incursions of mountainous peoples from the northeast and invasions of the Elamites, a pre-Indo-European people in Southwest Iran from the area surrounding the city of Susa, whose civilization had developed parallel with and roughly over the same period as the civilizations of Sumer and Akkad, with which there were great similarities. From around 1600 BC, a period began in which South and Central Mesopotamia were politically surpassed by neighboring powers that had often derived important elements of their civilization from southern Mesopotamia: in the east, the Elamites already mentioned; to the north, along the Tigris, the Semitic kingdom of Assyria; to the northwest, the kingdom of Mitanni, where an Indo-European aristocracy of chariot-fighters dominated an indigenous population of Hurrites; and further to the northwest in Anatolia, the Hittites, mainly Indo-European but with an admixture of Hurrites, ruling over older inhabitants of the region. Between these kingdoms, a system of "international relations" developed, with political coalitions and concerns about a "balance of power." Soon, Egypt too for the first time got involved in this international system as a result of its ongoing efforts from around 1500 BC to control the eastern Mediterranean coastlands of Palestine, Phoenicia, and Syria.

Egypt

Shortly after 3000 BC, Egypt had already become a unitary state ruled by a king, the pharaoh. The names of the kings survived in lists composed in the "sacred script" (the literal meaning of the Greek term "hieroglyphics") that was developed about the same time. The texts on the inner walls of the pharaoh's funeral chamber were written in this script. Much later, after Egypt had been conquered by Macedonians and Greeks, these royal names would be grouped into dynasties of succeeding royal houses, 30 in all. Under the first two dynasties, the unification of the land was consolidated, with the kings residing at the southern point of the delta. With the 3rd dynasty, the first great period of Egyptian history began, lasting from around 2750 BC to the beginning of the 7th dynasty at around 2250 BC. In this period, known as the Old Kingdom, Memphis in northern Egypt was the royal residence. Not far from Memphis, were erected enormous solid monuments, the pyramids, which resembled artificial hills of stone and deep inside housed the funeral chambers of the kings. The three largest near Gizeh on the edge of modern Cairo belonged to the pharaohs of the 4th dynasty, the pinnacle of the Old Kingdom. In that period, Egyptians already undertook expeditions to Nubia (along the Nile south of Egypt), to the Sinai, and Palestine. Contacts with the farther Near East, however, seem to have been rare. Egypt was a country largely turned inward with a civilization that was in many respects unique.

In Egypt, unlike Mesopotamia, the king was considered to be a god in human form. He and the other gods guaranteed, so to say, the well-being of the people that was so dependent upon the one river that alone seemed to make life possible here. Already at an early stage, the Egyptian priests developed a calendar, a solar calendar of 365 days, in order to accurately fix and predict the yearly flooding of the Nile. The Sun would always remain one of the high gods of the Egyptian pantheon, and the reigning pharaoh would be considered his son. In the Old Kingdom, only the soul of the king was thought to ascend to heaven for eternal life after his death, the king's body being mummified because preservation of the body was deemed necessary for the soul's journey. In a later period, even the souls of ministers and other notables of the land were thought to ascend to heaven. In the 2nd millennium BC, in principle, every deceased person could hope for the soul's immortality as long as he or she was, albeit often in a rudimentary fashion, mummified and provided with the correct sacred texts (the so-called Book of the Dead). Pyramids were only built during the Old Kingdom. In later periods, the kings and notables were buried in funeral chambers cut into the rocks along the Nile valley, while the commoners were simply buried in the desert sand.

The Egyptian gods seemed directly associated with life in the long and narrow stretches of land on both sides of the river. The fertility of the Nile's sediments made extremely rich harvests possible. The population lived scattered over villages, and even the residences of the kings could hardly be called cities. Already at an early stage, the government of the pharaohs developed a bureaucracy of officials whose task it was to oversee the delivery of goods and the payment of taxes in kind to the temples and to the palace. At the same time, they oversaw the work for the community that the peasant population was required to provide in connection with the irrigation of the fields during the annual flooding of the river, or with the building of public works, such as the pyramids in the Old Kingdom and the palaces and frontier fortifications in later times. These officials were rewarded and thereby bound to the throne by grants of land. In the long run, however, this led to a certain undermining of royal authority because some powerful ministers acquired so much land that at the local level they could behave like independent potentates. This to some extent explains the weakening of central authority in Egypt that occurred periodically and every time was followed by a period of renewed centralization. For when effective royal authority was limited to a part of the country, or when two or more kings reigned simultaneously in different parts of the land, civil war and total chaos threatened to thoroughly disrupt the order of life in this peasant society regulated by the natural tempo of the Nile. Usually, a local potentate after a while succeeded in forcefully subjecting his competitors and re-establishing unity under a new dynasty. In this way, periods of unity and a flourishing of culture were interrupted by periods of disunity and decay. The Old Kingdom was at around 2250 BC followed by such an interim period, after which at around 2100 BC local potentates from Thebes in Upper Egypt established the Middle Kingdom comprising the 11th and 12th dynasties. In its turn, this flourishing kingdom gave way to another period, lasting from roughly 1750 to 1550 BC, of renewed disintegration that was made worse by the arrival of immigrants from the Near East, who founded a separate kingdom in the delta. These newcomers, called the Hyksos in our sources, had come under the influence of Indo-European groups and introduced the horse and the chariot into Egypt.

International politics in the 2nd millennium BC

For a second time, it was a prince from Thebes in the south who united the country under a new dynasty, the 18th, expelled the Hyksos, and ushered in a period in which Egypt in its turn was to become involved in the great political events that occurred in the Near

East. Now the period of the New Kingdom began, which would last from around 1550 BC to around 1100 BC, the period of the 18th to 20th dynasties that in many respects was the pinnacle of ancient Egyptian history. Time and again, Egyptian armies marched into Palestine, Phoenicia, and Syria in order to take possession of the coastlands for the pharaoh, especially the Lebanon with its cedar forests, Egypt itself being very poor in wood. Despite considerable successes and masses of booty and captives being brought back to Egypt, the kings of the New Kingdom never completely succeeded in subjugating both Palestine and Syria. They met with too much resistance, especially from the Hittites, who had since about 1600 BC developed into one of the strongest military powers of the Near East. From their core region in Anatolia, they extended their dominion over large parts of northern Mesopotamia and Syria. After a few large battles around 1300 BC, Egyptians and Hittites agreed to delineate their respective spheres of influence, which henceforth bordered each other in the south of Syria. Thus, for some time there was a precarious balance of power during this last phase of the Bronze Age in the Near East between Babylonia, Assyria (which had in the meantime conquered the kingdom of Mitanni), Egypt, and the kingdom of the Hittites. These states maintained standing squadrons of chariots and a relatively costly and professional military class. Bronze and horses, next to rare sorts of wood and timber for building as well as for chariot making, were the most coveted articles that every kingdom strove to acquire either by exchange, as plunder, or as gifts. Not least because of these articles, the kingdoms maintained a network of diplomatic relations among themselves, sometimes strengthened by royal weddings with foreign princesses. At the same time, these Late Bronze Age kingdoms were vulnerable: if the central leadership from the royal palace failed, and if relations with the other kingdoms were for a long time interrupted, the whole edifice of state could come down. Such a catastrophe, brought about by migrating groups across the eastern half of the Mediterranean, indeed occurred at various places around 1200 BC. About that time, the great Hittite kingdom disappeared, while in Egypt, which had managed to ward off invaders from Libya, from Palestine, and from the sea to its north, a new period of decay set in after the glories of the New Kingdom. Thus, the world of the Bronze Age in these regions came to an end in the final decades of the 2nd millennium BC.

The Aegean and Southern Europe in the Bronze Age

The Minoan civilization

When at around 6000 BC agriculture became known in Greece, a Neolithic culture did develop here as well. Its heartland gradually moved from the north (Thessaly) to the south (the Peloponnese) of the country. It was a world of small and simple village communities, based on the growing of barley and the breeding of pigs and sheep. The influence of the Near East, where agriculture and animal breeding had started off much earlier, is unmistakable. But we know very little about life in these oldest peasant societies of Europe. Around or just after 3000 BC, however, a new cultural phase began, again most probably as a result of impulses from the Near East: the Bronze Age.

During the Bronze Age, it was mainly the south of Greece that led the way. On the island of Crete, there arose the Minoan civilization, named by modern scholars after the legendary king Minos of the later Greek saga. Here, influenced by the Near East and possibly by North Africa, a particular civilization developed, based on grain and sheep, to which were added, after around 2000 BC, olive trees and viticulture. The island must have reached a relatively high stage of economic development and wealth thanks to the export of wool and products based on olive-oil like aromatic balms and perfumes, and of high-quality ceramics. Of the organization of society, however, we know much less. Presumably, the wealth created by trade benefited a Cretan elite. Impressive remains of palace-like structures—their exact purpose is still debated—have been excavated at various places, among which Knossos and Phaistos are perhaps the best known. They must have constituted some sort of political and religious centers for the people of the surrounding countryside and are not towns or cities in the sense of urban concentrations of population. What does look like very small "towns" with houses of two floors along narrow streets have been discovered in Gournia in eastern Crete and on the island of Thera (modern Santorini), dating from the early 2nd millennium BC. Remarkably, fortification walls around the Cretan settlements are lacking, which is often taken to imply that the inhabitants did not fear attackers and must consequently have dominated the surrounding seas, but this again is not at all certain. The many small objects of art, like seals, gems and rings that have been discovered, often are decorated with clearly religious scenes, in which goddesses seem to play a dominant role. In addition, the bull seems to have had a function in cultic performances, while the bull's horns and the double ax (maybe the instrument with which the animal would be slaughtered for sacrifice) functioned as religious markers or symbols.

Dating from the time of its highest development, around 2000 to around 1700 BC, we have clay tablets from Crete written with a peculiar script. This must have been a syllabic script, called Linear A by modern scholars, in which the palace administration was carried out. In this respect, Knossos and other palaces in Crete presumably resembled the "palace economies" in the Near East, like Mari, and possibly they had even derived much of their organizational features from there, just as they derived the olive, the vine, and the art of bronze working from the Near East. Linear A has not been deciphered, but it is certain that the language behind it cannot have been Greek. Greeks arrived on the island, from the mainland, only after the Minoan civilization had passed its prime. It is possible that the enormous volcanic explosion that sometime around 1650 BC had destroyed the island of Thera also caused the collapse of the Minoan civilization in Crete, but it must be stressed that much is still uncertain regarding these events. The eruption did end the flourishing Cycladic civilization on the islands of the middle Aegean Sea, which in the late 3rd and early 2nd millennia BC had developed there under strong influences from Crete. In the 16th and/or the 15th centuries BC, Crete itself fell victim to invaders from the mainland, most probably the first Greek-speakers on the island, who conquered Knossos and maintained a Late Minoan Culture there under Greek domination. The Cretan script in use for the administration was adapted to the new language, Greek, and became the Linear B that has been deciphered as the oldest script denoting Greek. In this last phase of the Bronze Age, Crete formed part of the Greek world that had its center of gravity on the Peloponnese.

The Mycenaean civilization

The Bronze Age on the Greek mainland is called the period of Helladic culture by archeologists, which means the culture of Hellas, which is the name of present-day Greece, but it was not necessarily a *Greek* culture. In the 3rd millennium and the first half of the 2nd millennium BC, this culture underwent strong influences from Minoan Crete. On the basis of archeological evidence, it is generally (but by far not universally) assumed that the first speakers of what would become the Greek language infiltrated the country from around 2000 BC on. We have to think of small groups penetrating farther and farther to the south and not of a massive invasion of a conquering people. These Indo-European immigrants must have adopted many elements of the indigenous culture—the Greek language is rich with words from pre-Greek languages—and at the same time endowed these with their own character. That character found its expression foremost in the last and clearly most "Greek" phase of the Bronze Age: the so-called Mycenaean civilization (around 1600 to 1100 BC)

The Mycenaean civilization is named after one of its main centers: Mycenae in the northeastern Peloponnese. Fortifications with thick defensive walls of often huge blocks of stone and rich graves for elite people with arms and armor as grave goods testify to the martial character of a society in which a king in a fortified palace ruled over the surrounding country. Materially, much derived from Crete, but the bronze or bronze-clad

Figure 8 Mycenaean body armor (15th–14th c. BC). A bronze suit of armor, found in a grave at Dendra, not far from Tiryns, one of the main centers of the Mycenaean world, now in the Museum of Navplion. It dates from the 15th or 14th century. It is extremely heavy and must have seriously hampered all movement. However, the discovery of fragments of comparable armor elsewhere shows that such suits of body armor were actually worn in the Mycenaean period. Its possible role in battle is uncertain. It is likely that the owner of such a suit of armor traveled in a chariot. Probably only the elite that had chariots at their disposal (or an even smaller group among those) could afford such body armor. To do battle, the armored man descended from his chariot, possibly to fight a duel with an equally armed champion of the enemy. Photo: akg-images/De Agostini Picture Library

armor of the elite warriors and the horse-drawn chariots were newly introduced. Close by Mycenae, a fortified palace was in use at Tiryns. More such palaces have been discovered in Boeotia (Thebes and Orchomenos), in Attica (Athens), in southern Thessaly (Iolkos), in Messenia (Pylos, but that unfortified), while recently traces of such a palace fortress have been detected in Laconia as well (and the Mycenaean invaders of Crete erected their fortress at Knossos). Presumably, the best explanation for the situation, at least in the last phase of the Mycenaean civilization, is the existence of a sort of high king at Mycenae to whom various lords in other areas—but not necessarily all of these—owed allegiance. Everywhere, we may assume, the local population was subject to these lords in their fortified palaces, although, again, we do not know very much about the social relations and organizations in the Mycenaean world. In Knossos and Pylos, a relatively large number of clay tablets with Linear B texts have been found—to which may be added a few from elsewhere in Greece—that have been preserved for us by the destruction by fire of these places. In the oldest Greek known, various administrative records are thus preserved, such as deliveries to and from the palace, or to and from surrounding villages, gifts to sanctuaries, and so on. There emerges a picture of a complex and regimented society centered around the royal palace not only politically but also economically, a "palace economy" of the Minoan and Near Eastern type. The richness, especially in golden objects like ornaments, drinking cups, and death masks, is surprising in a country that was itself rather poor. One is inclined to think of plunder from overseas raids, although Mycenaean Greece might also have taken over much of the trade in wool and aromatic substances from Crete. In any case, there were clear overseas connections with the west coast of Asia Minor, with the Syrian and Phoenician coasts, the island of Cyprus, Egypt, and with southern Italy and Sicily. In the last stage of the Mycenaean civilization, this even led to Mycenaean settlements on Cyprus and at some places in Asia Minor.

The fall of the Mycenaean civilization: New migrations

Not long before 1200 BC, the city of Troy on the shore of the Dardanelles (the ancient Hellespont) in the northwest of Asia Minor was destroyed by attackers from the Mycenaean world, an event that would live on in Greek saga. But shortly afterward, around 1200 BC, the decline and fall of the Mycenaean civilization itself set in, a process that has as yet not been completely explained. Perhaps the limited agricultural base—barley, a primitive sort of wheat, and wild olives—had made its society vulnerable in times of population increase; certainly, this Late Bronze Age world was vulnerable in its network of outward relations for the supply of copper and tin, of wood and horses, while the whole apparatus of fortified palaces, servants, and a professional military probably made it top-heavy. It is also possible that tensions and conflicts between the Greek or Mycenaean population and the pre-Greek or at least pre-Mycenaean population undermined society and political order. Moreover, what happened in Greece cannot have been isolated from events elsewhere: the fall of some great Late Bronze Age kingdoms in the Near East and Egypt. Invaders from the north most probably played a part in this, but the exact course of events remains obscure. In any case, around 1200 BC, some Mycenaean centers such as Thebes and Pylos were destroyed, while at the same time

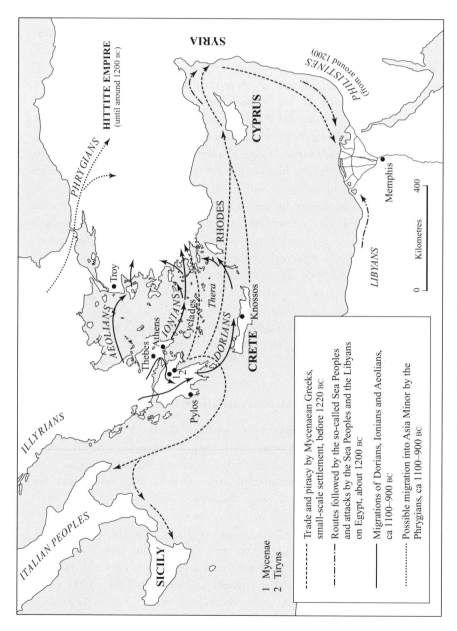

Map 4 The Aegean world, c. 1600–c. 1100 BC

ILLYRIANS

ITALIAN PEOPLES

SICILY

Pylos

Thebes
Athens

AEOLIANS

Troy

PHRYGIANS

IONIANS

S.DORIANS

Cyclades

Thera

RHODES

CRETE Knossos

CYPRUS

SYRIA

HITTITE EMPIRE
(until around 1200 BC)

PHILISTINES
(from around 1200)

LIBYANS

Memphis

1 Mycenae
2 Tiryns

0   400

Kilometres

---------- Trade and piracy by Mycenaean Greeks,
            small-scale settlement, before 1220 BC

– ·· – ·· – Routes followed by the so-called Sea Peoples
            and attacks by the Sea Peoples and the Libyans
            on Egypt, about 1200 BC

―――― Migrations of Dorians, Ionians and Aeolians,
            ca 1100–900 BC

·········· Possible migration into Asia Minor by the
            Phrygians, ca 1100–900 BC

Egypt was threatened by attacks on both its land borders and from the sea (by the so-called Sea Peoples, mentioned thus in Egyptian documents) and the once mighty Hittite empire fell, never to rise again. Many historians assume that in Greece the invaders responsible for the destructions moved on, in part together with the Sea Peoples just mentioned, to Egypt and hence, perhaps, to Sicily and Sardinia, while refugees from the Mycenaean areas fled to Asia Minor and Cyprus. In the country, now greatly impoverished, some Mycenaean centers such as the fortress of Mycenae itself and for an even longer period the fortress of Tiryns would continue to exist. According to this reconstruction, the last remnants of the Mycenaean civilization disappeared only in the years 1100–1050 BC. By the latter date, the Bronze Age in Greece had finally ended.

When the 2nd millennium BC came to an end, Greece was in a sorry state. With the Mycenaean palaces, the whole political superstructure as well as the palace-organized economy had disappeared. The Mycenaean Linear B script too was no longer in use in Greece—among Mycenaean colonists on Cyprus, it would live on for a few centuries—so that mainland Greece fell back into prehistory for a while. The population had sharply declined. Politically, the country must now have been divided up into countless mini "states." In this demographic and political vacuum, new Greek speakers from beyond the northern and northwestern borders of the former Mycenaean world moved in, speakers of the so-called Northwest-Greek dialects, among whom the Dorians were the most important group. Most probably—for this too is a reconstruction that is not shared by all experts, albeit widely accepted by many—Dorian groups established themselves in large parts of southern Greece, often as warlike conquerors subjugating the local inhabitants (mostly former Mycenaean Greeks). Because the Dorians had lived outside the orbit of Mycenaean civilization, their arrival strengthened the tendencies toward more primitive political and economic relationships in Greece around 1000 BC. Memories of the Mycenaean world, however, lingered on. Many gods and goddesses of the later Greek pantheon derive from that world (being mentioned in Linear B texts), while important Mycenaean palace-fortresses would live on in legend and saga, material for great poems in a later age.

Italy and Western Europe in the Bronze Age

At the time in which in Greece the Mycenaean civilization arose and flourished, various Indo-European-speaking groups spread from Central Europe to the south and the west. About the exact circumstances of these migrations, or of their size in population terms, we know practically nothing. For later history, however, they are important in as much as the newcomers in the long run succeeded in imposing their languages, with very few exceptions, on the existing pre-Indo-European populations. As a result, nearly the whole of Europe became a region of Indo-European languages. In Italy, we speak of the Italic peoples who settled there in the course of the 2nd millennium BC and who would become the ancestors of the Italic peoples known from historical sources in the 1st millennium BC, among whom would be the Romans.

The older Neolithic population groups in Central and Western Europe were already acquainted with simple forms of agriculture, and perhaps the Indo-European newcomers introduced improved techniques. Probably they brought a more intensive form of cattle breeding with them, and certainly they introduced the horse. With that, their arrival generally meant an improvement of material culture and presumably more complex or more hierarchical social organizations as well, although again very little is known in detail about this. In this connection also the technique of bronze working could spread further until around 1600 BC the whole of Europe, apart from Scandinavia and the northeast, were acquainted with this form of metallurgy, with which the Neolithic period finally came to an end.

PART III

900–500 BC

Chapter 3.1

A Historical Outline

Eurasian Communities

Around the year 1000 BC, the greater part of the world still lived in the prehistorical era. The combination of a more or less developed form of agriculture, urbanized settlements, the use of metal, and the knowledge of a script existed as yet only in a few relatively small areas: in the Near East and Egypt, in northern China, and in northern India (but there still without a script). Outside Eurasia, cultures in modern-day Mexico and Peru developed their own metallurgy, a sophisticated architecture in stone, and a specialized agriculture. The rest of the world was inhabited by Neolithic farmers and herdsmen, or by hunters and hunter-gatherers, the latter spread over vast and sparsely populated areas. In the 1st millennium BC, however, the expansion of more complex cultures with their cities, metals, and scripts, which had already begun in the Bronze Age, would continue at a quicker pace. Not only would the core regions of these cultures expand further, but also various peoples in their peripheries would under their influence develop their own but related cultures. Thus, Korea and Japan in the 1st millennium BC, under Chinese influence, laid the foundations of what would become their own civilizations, while the Chinese civilization itself expanded from the basin of the Yellow River, especially in the southern direction. On the other side of the continent, Greek culture embarked on a phase of strong expansion across practically the whole of the Mediterranean world.

China

China was in theory a unitary state ruled since around 1100 BC by the dynasty of the Zhou, but in fact it consisted of a number of various more or less autonomous regions under "vassals" of the Zhou kings. When the residence of these kings was moved eastward to Luoyang in 770 BC, it signified the beginning of a period called the Eastern Zhou, in which central authority was left with only a ritual and ideological significance. A certain sense of a common Chinese identity was thus kept alive, while for all practical purposes the country fell apart into independent states. The structures of these states resembled those of the first Chinese empire: strongly patriarchal and hierarchical and with a strong tendency

Antiquity: Greeks and Romans in Context, First Edition. Frederick G. Naerebout and Henk W. Singor.
© 2014 John Wiley & Sons, Inc. Published 2014 by John Wiley & Sons, Inc.

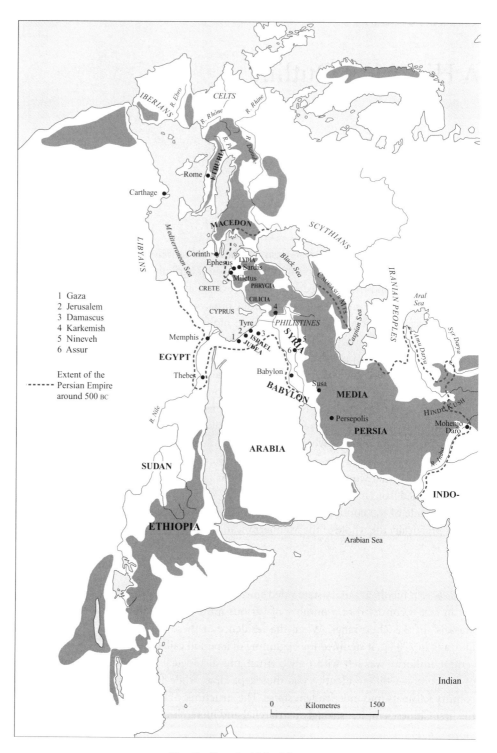

1 Gaza
2 Jerusalem
3 Damascus
4 Karkemish
5 Nineveh
6 Assur

Extent of the
Persian Empire
around 500 BC

Map 5   Eurasia, 10th–5th c. BC

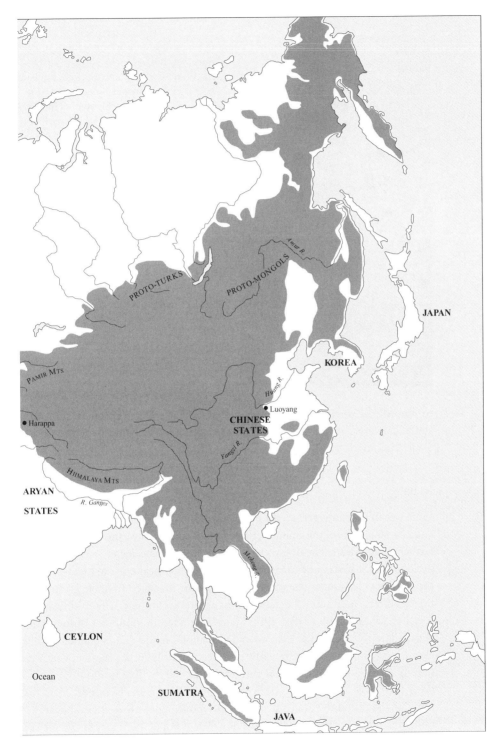

PROTO-TURKS

PROTO-MONGOLS

Amur R.

JAPAN

PAMIR Mts.

Hyong R.

KOREA

● Harappa

● Luoyang

CHINESE
STATES

Yangzi R.

HIMALAYA Mts.

ARYAN

R. Ganges

STATES

Mekong R.

CEYLON

Ocean

SUMATRA

JAVA

Map 5   (*Continued*)

Figure 9   An inscribed bronze vase, China (9th c. BC). This is a large bronze vase, almost 60 cm tall, known as a *hu*, which was used for ritual purposes. It dates to the 9th century (the Dynasty of the Western Zhou), and was found in Shaanxi. Is now is in the provincial museum of Xi'an. It is decorated with the highly stylized image of a dragon and an inscription that translates as follows: "On the day *geng wu* of the 5th month, Tong Zong, who lives in the western palace, gave to his vassal Ji Fu six bags of aromatic herbs, four slave families, and ten *jun* of metal. In recognition of this generous gift, Ji Fu had this costly *hu* cast, and it is his hope that his sons and grandsons will keep this forever, as a special treasure." Photo: akg-images/De Agostini Picture Library

to subordinate the individual to the interests of the collective. The rivalries between these states, however, in no way hindered the continued expansion of the area of Chinese civilization to the south as well as to the northeast.

India

India was in the same period not politically unified at all but divided into numerous states and city-states. From the Ganges valley, Indian culture nevertheless penetrated farther and farther to the south. The origins of the later Hindu caste society have to be sought in this period. At first it was unclear who occupied the top of the social hierarchy: the priests or the warriors and kings. The priests or Brahmans managed by their greater knowledge of the sacrificial rituals and the accompanying prayers to gradually gain a stronger grip on social and political life. These rituals had been fixed in a number of long poems dealing with religious "knowledge," the so-called *Vedas*, a name that is etymologically related to "knowing." Initially orally transmitted since about 1500 BC, these poems were put into writing at an unknown date, but certainly after 500 BC. Exposition of and meditation on these texts gave rise to a mystical philosophy, again initially in oral form. At the same time, in the 6th and 5th centuries, ascetic movements made their appearance, possibly under the influence of the indigenous non-Aryan population, that taught an ideal of world renunciation and would inspire new and important religious movements after around 500 BC.

The steppe nomads

The great centers of cultural radiation—northern China, northern India, and the Near East together with the eastern Mediterranean—were separated from each other by deserts and mountain chains, while to the north they were hemmed in by a broad zone of forests and steppes that stretched from the Atlantic to the Pacific. Around the beginning of the 1st millennium BC, in this steppe area there occurred an economic and social change that was to profoundly influence the history of the continent: the emergence of horse nomadism. The utilization of the horse for riding, unlike its use as a draft-animal for chariots that was already known in the 2nd millennium B.C, conferred a new mobility on peoples who depended for their livelihood on their horses and herds of sheep. This made them practically self-sufficient, while their new mobility allowed them to acquire more goods, by plunder or extortion and also by commercial exchange, from the sedentary inhabitants of the agricultural areas. In this way, a period of confrontation and symbiosis between two worlds began that was to last far into the European Middle Ages. The symbiosis was important for all concerned, but the impact of the opposition between these two worlds was mainly negative. The agrarian and urbanized societies never succeeded in eliminating the dangers posed by the nomads, despite numerous punitive expeditions and payment of subsidies. In their turn, the nomads could periodically plunder the areas of sedentary culture but were unable to permanently subjugate them without giving up their own nomadic way of life. This situation ultimately prevented the expansion of urbanized cultures to the north and created for many centuries a barrier to overland contacts between the worlds of China, India, the Near East, and Europe. The agricultural areas would time and again suffer the often-destructive incursions of successive invasions from the steppes by peoples of Iranian, Turkish, or Mongolian descent, with as a consequence sometimes unexpected twists and turns in their history. The interrelationships between various nomad peoples created a largely homogeneous culture between the Danube in the west and the Amur in the east, characterized by the rich graves of warrior-chieftains, a predilection for abundant ornamentation with various animal motifs, as well as, perhaps, by the dominance of shamanism in religious matters.

Western Eurasia

Conditions in Central and Western Europe differed greatly from those in the steppes. In a region that was then heavily forested, the expansion of various Indo-European peoples continued from the 2nd millennium BC. In the first few centuries after 1000 BC, it was especially the ancestors of the later Celts who spread to the West and Southwest as far as Spain and the British Isles. In these years, the use of iron, which had been derived from the older civilizations in the eastern Mediterranean, especially in Anatolia, became well known in Italy and the Alps region, and spread from there since the 7th century BC to the whole of Western Europe. Here, the so-called Halstatt culture (named after an archaeological site in Austria) arose, characterized, among other things, by fortified hilltop settlements (in German: *Herrensitze)*. Perhaps, the use of iron, like the use of bronze in an earlier period, deepened an already existing social divide between the warriors and their leaders on the one hand and the mass of the peasant population on the other, stimulating an appetite for plunder and conquests in those who possessed the metal weapons.

In expanding over Europe, peoples such as the Celts and the Illyrians would in its southern regions come into contact with the urbanized civilizations on the shores of the Mediterranean Sea. Unlike the nomads of the Eurasian steppes, these Indo-European groups mainly wanted places for themselves to settle in within this—for them—alluring Mediterranean world. On their part, the Mediterranean urban civilizations would ultimately absorb many of their European neighbors, because these essentially were sedentary societies too, not differing greatly in their basic social structures. But in the first half of the 1st millennium BC, these developments were still to come. In that period, urbanized culture was still limited to a few Mediterranean regions. In the first two or three centuries after 1000 BC, the Phoenicians from present-day Lebanon explored the coasts of the Mediterranean as far as Spain and established trading posts at various spots. Their colony Carthage, founded in the 9th century BC on the north coast of Africa, would in the following centuries even develop into a great commercial and political power. Meanwhile, the Greek world, after its decline as a consequence of the fall of the Mycenaean civilization, experienced from around 900 BC a steady revival under the influence of the Near East. As a result, an urban and literate society appeared in Greece in this period. In the 7th and 6th centuries BC, partly under Greek influences, such a society took root among the Etruscans in Central Italy as well. Brought by Phoenician, Carthaginian, Etruscan, and Greek traders, bronze objects, luxury ceramics, wine, and other articles from the "civilized" urban world found their way to the chieftains in the interior of Central and Western Europe in exchange for silver, tin, or slaves. As a consequence, the differences in wealth and prestige within these European societies increased, while princes and their retinues of warriors were motivated to attempt further plundering raids, especially in a southerly direction.

The Near East after the Bronze Age

Toward the end of the 2nd millennium BC, the great Bronze Age states of the Near East had disappeared or were greatly reduced in power. Nevertheless, until well into the 1st millennium BC, the region would remain culturally ahead of all the rest of western Eurasia. New peoples and new states made their appearance in the centuries around 1000 BC. From the once great Hittite empire in northern Syria, some Neo-Hittite princedoms emerged, such as Karkemish on the Euphrates, whereas former core Hittite lands in Anatolia fell into the hands of the Phrygians, who had presumably crossed into Asia Minor from Europe. In the same period, around 1200–1000 BC, Semitic Aramaeans from the Arabian-Syrian desert penetrated into Mesopotamia and the Syrian-Palestinian areas. Despite the fact that the states founded by them would in the end all lose their independence, the Aramaeans would prove to be an important influence in the Near East. The dispersal of this people over various parts of the Near East would make their language an international medium, a lingua franca for commerce and administration in the whole area. This was made possible by the rise from the 9th century onward of some great empires that would politically unite an ever-greater part—and in the end, even the whole—of the Near East and Egypt: the empires of, successively, the Assyrians, the Babylonians, and the Medes and Persians.

Assyria and the Assyrian Empire

Since the 2nd millennium BC, both Babylonia and Assyria had fought for hegemony in Mesopotamia. Unlike Babylonia to the south, Assyria was not dependent on artificial irrigation, and perhaps because of this it had a peasant population that could easily be mobilized for military campaigns far from home. In any case, already in the last centuries of the 2nd millennium BC, Assyria acquired the reputation of a bellicose and aggressive state. Around 900 BC, it embarked on a period of expansion that would make it the strongest power in the Near East and finally the first "world empire" in history. Almost every year, its kings led their armies north, south, east, or west. The defeated had to pay tribute, so that these regular expeditions secured the transport on a grand scale of all sorts of products from a wide periphery to the Assyrian heartland on either side of the Tigris. Refusal to pay tribute was treated as a rebellion and mercilessly punished by the destruction of cities and the extermination or deportation of all the inhabitants of cities. The military technology of this period—chariots; since the 9th century, cavalry; as well as various siege engines—enabled the Assyrians to carry on their campaigns over great distances. Gradually, these campaigns changed into conquering expeditions, meant to permanently hold the subjugated lands. The conquered peoples henceforth not only had to pay tribute but to provide recruits for the Assyrian army as well. The army as a result

Figure 10 A relief from Nineveh depicting Assurbanipal in his pleasure garden (7th c. BC). Under the rule of Assurbanipal, mid-7th century BC, the Assyrian Empire reached its apogee. This relief from Nineveh, now in the British Museum, shows Assurbanipal in a pleasure garden. The king is seen lying on a beautifully decorated couch under a pergola of vines. Mesopotamian kings spent lavishly on gardens and parks, and sources mention exotic plants and animals that were brought from far and wide to their capital cities. The king's consort is seated at his feet, there are slaves with fans on either end, to the left one can see food being brought in, and at the far left there is a harp player. The king will be pleased, because he has a good view of the head of one of his enemies hanging from the top branches of the tree in front of the harpist. It was common for male members of the elite to recline on couches in the Near East; this habit had already spread in the 7th century BC by way of Asia Minor to the Greek world. Assurbanipal's consort is in a chair: we will see this in the Greek world too: men used to recline, but women, children, and servants sat up. Photo: The Art Archive/Alamy

changed from a yearly mobilized peasant militia into a professional standing army, raised largely from non-Assyrian peoples. Ideologically, the victories and conquests of Assyria were justified by the kings as so many offerings for the high god Assur, whose devout and humble servants these kings professed themselves to be.

Yet, in the brutal division between the oppressors and the oppressed, the Assyrian Empire carried the within it the seeds of its own eventual downfall. It always had to be on the alert for uprisings anywhere, especially in Babylonia—which, proud of its own ancient history, repeatedly rebelled—and of possible coalitions of its enemies across the borders. Under King Assurbanipal in the 7th century BC, Assyria reached the zenith of its power with the simultaneous submission of—though for a short time—Egypt, the Phrygians in Anatolia, the mountainous state of Urartu around Lake Van in present-day eastern Turkey, and Elam with its capital Susa in southwestern Iran. Probably, the effort proved too great, for by the second half of the 7th century, all these countries were again independent or in open rebellion, while a new power threatened Assyria from the east: the Medes. Ultimately, it was a coalition of the Medes and the Babylonians that in 612 BC conquered the Assyrian capital Nineveh and brought about the total demise of this state just a few years later.

Egypt, Israel, and Phoenicia

Egypt had survived the attacks of the so-called Sea Peoples around 1200 BC but had since strongly declined in power. Shortly before 1000 BC, it even broke apart into a northern and a southern part. Following this, Libyan mercenary chiefs, Nubian and Ethiopian princes, and the high priests of the god Amun succeeded each other as dominant powers in the land until the Assyrian conquest. Despite all this, a sense of unity was maintained during this period by the idea of a sort of theocracy of Amun, as if the god himself governed the land and the various kings were merely his subordinates. It was also a period in which all kinds of magical religious beliefs and practices spread, and the worship of cats, crocodiles, monkeys, and other sacred animals became very popular. The subjugation by Assyria was short-lived, around 690–670 BC. A new dynasty, the 26th, arose from the resistance to these foreign overlords that from its seat in Sais in the Nile delta would transform Egypt once more into a great power.

The Canaanites, inhabitants of present-day Israel and South Syria, in the last years of the 2nd millennium BC were forced to cede parts of their country to the Aramaeans. Of the many Aramaean principalities that sprang up, the kingdom of Damascus in South Syria would prove to be the strongest. In the same period, the Philistines, who had arrived together with the Sea Peoples from the area of the Aegean Sea, settled along the coast from Gaza to Ashkelon. The indigenous Canaanites managed to maintain their independence only in the coastal cities of modern-day Lebanon. There, in the 1st millennium BC, Tyre, Sidon, and Byblos created a new and flourishing civilization. It was their inhabitants, whom the Greeks called Phoenicians, who as seafarers in the beginning of the 1st millennium BC dominated a large part of the Mediterranean and spread Near Eastern culture westward by founding, as has been mentioned earlier, Carthage and other colonies.

In this politically fragmented but culturally highly developed eastern border of the Mediterranean, a new kind of script developed: the alphabet. Already from the

2nd millennium BC we have examples of a form of alphabetic writing in inscriptions from the Sinai and in texts on clay tablets from northern Syria, while shortly before 1000 BC the alphabet as a script of 22 signs, most of them being consonants, was known in Byblos. In comparison with Egyptian hieroglyphs or with the Mesopotamian cuneiform script, an alphabetic script was far easier to read and to write, and would ultimately revolutionize written communication. From its presumably West Semitic origins, the alphabet spread rapidly in various closely related forms like the Aramaic, the Hebrew, and the Phoenician. From the latter, at some time between 900 and 750 BC, the Greeks would derive, with just a few adaptations, their form of the alphabet. People wrote on wood, stone, ceramic, leather, metal, or, in the Egyptian tradition, on papyrus. And it was in the shape of easily transported papyrus scrolls that the book began to spread throughout these parts of the world. Although books would for a long time to come remain the precious property of only a few, and although the writers were at first mainly scribes in the service of temple or palace, the appearance of the book would in the end have unforeseen consequences. Books written in an alphabetic script circulated more widely, and their contents had a more profound influence than any text written in the older scripts.

The history of the Israelites provides an example of the influence that religious ideas could exert when put into writing. The stories about the history of the Israelites as told in the Hebrew Bible—that is, the Old Testament of the Christians, written down, presumably not before the 4th century BC—are largely legendary. It is certain, however, that in the 9th and 8th centuries BC there existed two small states, Israel and Judah, of which the former was undoubtedly the more important. But whether they had split off from a previous unitary state that had been the realm of King David and his son and successor Solomon is still debated. In fact, even more strongly debated is the whole of Israelite history before these kings: the time of the so-called Judges, and before that the period of Moses and of the exodus of the people from Egypt. This oldest period of the history of Israel, which traditionally began with the patriarchs Abraham, Isaac, and Jacob, is from a historical point of view unknown. Of the greatest importance, however, was the idea of the Covenant, that is, the mutual bond between a people and its god that found expression in the vicissitudes of the Israelite nation as told in their legendary and semi-historical records. It was an idea that was not unknown elsewhere in the Near East but was most consequentially worked out in Israel. The god of Israel was supposed to have already promised the land to Abraham, to have given laws to Moses, and to have promised that in the future he would always come to the help of his people. When calamities, such as the attacks by other peoples, occurred, these were interpreted as divine punishments for acts of disobedience by the people. That, too, was in the Near East not a completely new idea, but among the Israelites it was time and again formulated anew by the prophets, who in both Israel and Judah reminded kings and priests of the Covenant, foretelling disaster or happiness as divine punishment or reward. From the late 8th century BC, many prophecies were put into writing, and from then on they could be consulted and re-read in future situations as texts of warning or consolation. To this was added another idea that, again, had some parallels in neighboring states: the notion of a high god or the tendency to consider one god to be supreme, to whom all other gods, including the gods of neighboring peoples, were inferior. Among the Israelites this even led to the suppression of the cults of gods other than their

Yahweh. The Yahweh-alone-movement was well under way, but had not yet achieved its goals when in 722 BC the state of Israel was destroyed by the Assyrians and the elite of its population deported to Assyria, there to disappear, absorbed no doubt by the other populations of Mesopotamia.

In the little state around Jerusalem, where Israelites of the tribes of Judah (hence, Jews) and Benjamin lived, the movement just mentioned continued after 722 BC. The worship of Yahweh alone, and that too only in his one temple in Jerusalem, became here, in part again as a consequence of the preaching of prophets, the norm. To this was added a growing set of rules and prescriptions concerning daily life that were attributed to the legendary lawgiver Moses. After the fall of Assyria, however, this small state of Judah in its turn got involved in the power politics of the Near East. When the Neo-Babylonian Empire at around 600 BC followed the example of the Assyrians and extended its power to the west, Judah was threatened, beaten into submission, and after an audacious attempt at resistance in 587 BC wiped off the map by the conquest and destruction of Jerusalem. Again, the elite of the conquered nation were deported, this time to Babylon. However, in this case the exiles preserved their religious and national identity. In Babylon, all sorts of religious customs and rules, and probably various prophecies and other traditions, were put into writing and became the basis for the later Hebrew Bible. At the same time, Jewish religion developed into a pure monotheism, that is, the existence of other gods was denied in favor of the one Yahweh as the sole God, the creator of the world and the director of human history. World history, it was believed, occurred solely for the benefit of the followers of this one God. When the Persians under King Cyrus conquered Babylon (539 BC) and allowed the Jews to return to Jerusalem, this was interpreted as God's intervention. Likewise, it was held that He would in the future intervene again and bring His chosen people to unheard of wealth and power. That happy situation would be brought about by a new king or the "Anointed One" (Hebrew: *hammasiach*, "the Messiah"). Thus, when in the course of the 5th and 4th centuries BC the temple in Jerusalem was rebuilt, there developed under the generally mild sovereignty of the Persian king, of whose empire the land of Judah had become a part, a remarkable religion centered around the worship of one God in one temple and inspired by a number of sacred books (law codes and prophecies). It was a religion that tied its followers to a whole range of holy prescriptions and rules of life (principally, food regulations, circumcision, and the Sabbath as the day of rest on the seventh day of the week) and strengthened them in the expectation of a great future that would be brought about by God Himself. This was a set of ideas that would have a profound influence in subsequent centuries, ultimately shaping to a large extent Christianity and Islam.

The Neo-Babylonian Empire, the Medes, and the Persians

In the years following the fall of Nineveh (612 BC), a couple of states fought each other for hegemony in the Near East. While the Medes extended their power over the whole of Iran and the mountain ranges to the north of Mesopotamia, the so-called Neo-Babylonian Empire consolidated its rule over Mesopotamia, and Egypt under the 26th dynasty enjoyed for the last time a period of political independence and influence on its neighbors. The eastern borderlands of the Mediterranean formed the bone of contention between Egypt and the Neo-Babylonian kingdom. In the armies of both states served groups of mercenaries from the west of Asia Minor, among whom were Greeks, an indication of the ever closer contacts between the Aegean world, the Near East and Egypt since the 8th and 7th centuries BC. The Babylonians were victorious over the Egyptians and seemed poised to become the successors of the Assyrians. Under the reign of Nebuchadnezzar, the king who as a prince had conquered Jerusalem in 587 BC, Babylon for a short time became the center of the world, an impressive city with enormous city walls, temples, palaces, and its famous "hanging gardens" on the palace rooftops. But the power of Babylonia was not to last long.

Shortly before 550 BC, in the vast territory under the dominion of the Medes a shift of power took place that transferred the kingship to a new dynasty from another Iranian people, the Persians. Cyrus, from the family of the Achaemenids, became the new king under circumstances that are not very clear to us. What we do know is that Cyrus embarked on a systematic policy of expansion. Around 545 BC, he conquered Lydia, which at this time under its king Croesus comprised the west of Asia Minor and was strongly influenced by Greek culture. The Greek cities on the coast also fell one by one under Persian dominion. A few years later, he attacked Babylon and put an end to the kingdom of Nebuchadnezzar's successors in 539 BC. Next, he extended Persian power to the extreme northeast of Iran, where he was killed in combat with Central Asian nomads. His successor, Cambyses, continued the series of conquests with an invasion of Egypt, resulting in the incorporation of this country as well into the Persian Empire. In this manner, the Persians achieved for the first time the political unification of Egypt, the Near East, and Iran. In fact, large parts of the urbanized and sedentary world of western Eurasia and northern Africa were now brought together in one empire. Under Cambyses' successor, Darius I, it was divided into 20 satrapies in which the population, although in many respects retaining some degree of independence, had to acknowledge Persian sovereignty and pay taxes to the king. To the north, the empire bordered on the territories of the Iranian steppe nomads of Central Asia and South Russia that the Greeks called the Scythians. An expedition against them under King Darius failed. In the east, the river Indus became the border of the empire, where high mountain ranges and deserts in present-day Afghanistan and Pakistan sealed the empire off from most of the Indian world. Likewise, Arabia to the south was an inhospitable desert region. Further expansion seemed feasible only toward the west, and this westward expansion would be achieved by the same king Darius around 500 BC in a clash between the Persian Empire and the world of the Greek mini-states.

The Greek World

In the period between 1000 and 500 BC, the foundations of the Greek civilization were laid. This civilization would flourish in the following centuries and leave its mark on a large area of the Mediterranean region as well as the Near East. Before around 500 BC, however, it was the Greeks who were at the receiving end and underwent strong influences from abroad, especially from the Near East. This period is usually divided into the time of the Dark Age (1000–750 BC) and the Archaic period (750–500 BC). The Dark Age got its name from the scarcity of sources for the period, which makes this period "dark" for modern historians, while at the same time, the little that we know seems to point to a state of political organization and of general culture, at least on a material level, that was at a low ebb: a dark period in that sense as well.

The so-called Dark Age

After the demise of the Mycenaean civilization, the population of Greece must have declined sharply, for the number of graveyards and settlements as well as their extent was much reduced. Moreover, the general level of culture of the Dark Age was poor: there was very little built in stone, ceramic pottery was decorated in a non-figurative, geometric style, and the use of a script had disappeared; the exception was metallurgy, where the use of iron—in swords and spear points, for example—spread.

Greece, impoverished and reduced in population, must have been politically fragmented into small communities that were often just clusters of huts, the inhabitants of which would in times of danger take refuge on a nearby hilltop. Power was in the hands of men who were often called *basileis* (singular: *basileus*), a term that originated in the Mycenaean society of Pylos, where it had denoted a village head or district head or the head of a group of workers. In the Dark Age in Greece, it acquired the meaning of "strongman" or "powerful lord." When there was only one *basileus* in a given community, the term could be translated as "king," but sometimes there were various *basileis* at one place. In any case, the "kinglets" in their mini-states had always to reckon with other gentlemen—who usually formed a sort of "council" together with the "king" or "kings"—and with the assembly of all free men, who carried arms and who could cheer the king and thereby approve his decisions, or show their disapproval by remaining silent. It would be rash, however, to speak of a primitive democracy, for the balance of power would always have favored the minority of gentlemen or kings who possessed a little more land or cattle than the common people and who could afford iron swords and spears, and sometimes horses. Here and there, a *basileus* must even have had a chariot, which he would have mainly used for riding to the field of battle, where he would usually have dismounted to fight on foot. The horse was a possession that lent its owner great prestige and recalled the times of the Mycenaean kings and their chariot warriors. The memory of that Mycenaean world was both preserved and embellished by traveling singer-poets with their orally transmitted stories in verse about the heroes of the past.

Gradually, in the 9th century BC, the population of Greece must have increased again. Perhaps the migration of various groups from European Greece across the Aegean Sea to the west coast of Asia Minor was at least partially due to population growth. In any case, around 900 BC and during the 9th century, several Greek-speaking groups from the European mainland settled in most of the Asian coastal areas and on the near-by islands: speakers of the so-called Aeolian dialect in the northern part and on the island of Lesbos, Ionians originating from Central and South Greece in the central part and on the islands of Chios and Samos, and Dorians in the southern part and on the islands of Kos and Samos. These Dorians belonged to the same group of immigrants who after the fall of the Mycenaean world had moved into Greece from the northwest and had subjugated most of the Peloponnese and the island of Crete. Thus, along the coast of Asia Minor and on the bigger islands off the shore, there arose many settlements, several of which would develop into important cities, mainly Ionian, such as Miletus and Ephesus. This migration also stimulated—if it was not to some extent a part of it—further exploration: toward the end of the 9th century BC Greeks visited the harbor towns of Syria, Phoenicia, and Cyprus. On Cyprus, Greek colonists had already settled in the wake of the fall of the Mycenaean civilization, but contacts with the motherland after around 1000 BC had initially been very rare. All these renewed contacts with Asia Minor, Cyprus, and the Near East would prove to be of great importance. The Greek world was now no longer isolated but in a position to renew itself both materially and spiritually, so that by 750 BC the Dark Age came to an end.

Contacts with the Near East and the beginning of the Archaic period

The term Archaic period (750–500 BC) was borrowed from a period in the history of Greek art that art historians in the 18th century called "archaic," that is, pristine and not yet at the height of its potential, which once attained was called the classical stage of art. The term has been adopted by general historians for the period in which the Greek world for the first time becomes clearly recognizable and in which the beginnings can be discerned of many traits that would come to full fruition in the following centuries. From around 800 BC, the contacts that had been made with harbors in the Near East, especially by Greeks from Euboea and other islands in the Aegean Sea, resulted in a series of innovations in the Greek world: improvements in the technique of bronze and iron working; a new style of pottery painting, where already in the 8th century small figures of men and animals had made their appearance between the geometric patterns and where not long before 700 BC images of plants and trees, animals and humans, derived from or inspired by Near Eastern examples, became common; free-standing cult statues and open air altars for burnt sacrifices; mythological stories, religious customs, and ideas; folk stories and epic motifs; and, perhaps the most important innovation, the adoption of the art of writing in the new alphabetic script taken over from the Phoenicians.

It is unknown when exactly the Greeks developed their own alphabetic scripts, but the oldest inscriptions known thus far date from the first half of the 8th century BC. It is certain that knowledge of the new art was disseminated rapidly and that several local varieties of the Greek alphabet arose. It was shortly before 700 BC that somewhere in Ionia, whether on the island of Chios or on the mainland, an unknown poet (traditionally known as Homer), using as raw material the orally transmitted poetry about the legendary war of Greek heroes and *basileis* against the city of Troy in Asia Minor, composed his magisterial epic the *Iliad*. It is possible that he used the new art of writing to record his creation, although this is still debated by modern experts. In any case, soon after its composition, the *Iliad* must certainly have been put into writing, which, in fact, marked the birth of Greek literature. Homer's *Iliad* as well as the *Odyssey*—also attributed to him but perhaps the work of a slightly later poet—are next to the archaeological record the most important sources for our knowledge of Greek society and civilization in the later Dark Age and early Archaic period. For although these epics as a result of oral transmission over a long period do contain some very old elements reflecting the Mycenaean world, most of the speeches and descriptions in them refer indirectly to the world of 8th-century and sometimes even early 7th-century Greece.

The Greek *polis*

From the Homeric epics, a picture of an aristocratic society can be distilled. Aristocratic lords, obsessed with matters of reputation and honor, dominate social and political life. The *basileus*, in fact, is not much more than the first among equals; the assembly of the people does exist but is in practice powerless. Yet, something else is present as well: a community in the form of a burgeoning "state" with an accompanying sense of community. We get the impression that in the time of Homer, this was still in a nascent phase. The Greeks called that state a *polis*. It was a small piece of territory—for instance, a mountain valley, a coastal

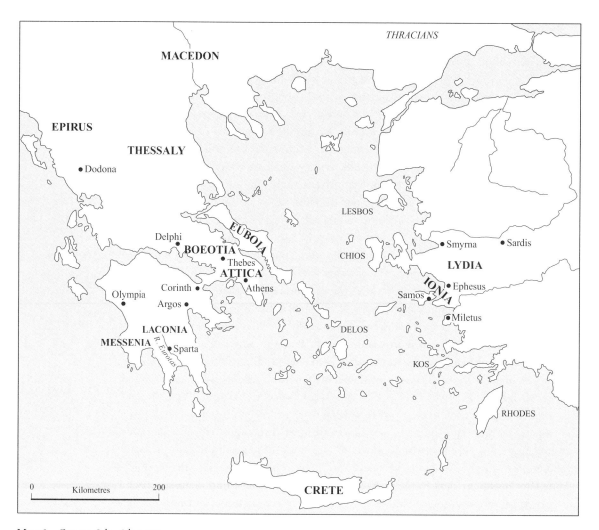

Map 6   Greece, 8th–6th c. BC

Figure 11   The so-called Dipylon vase from Athens (c. 735–725 BC). An 8th-century vase, in the so-called Geometric style, found in the cemetery at the Dipylon Gate of Athens, now in the National Museum there. A text running round the body of the vase has been scratched into the baked clay. This is one of the oldest known alphabetic Greek inscriptions of more than a few letters. The text, running from right to left, says: "He who performs best of all dancers, for him this vase [is the prize]." The words interpreted as "this vase" are doubtful, and toward the end the text trails off in apparently disconnected letters. But that this was a prize in a dance contest, and that it was marked as such in writing, seems certain enough. Photo: © The Art Archive/Alamy; Drawing © F.G. Naerebout

plain, an island, or only a part of such an area—whose inhabitants considered themselves autonomous and handled their own affairs. That is, they practiced their own "politics" in a "political" space where both the *demos* or "the people"—all the free men who together constituted the *polis*—assembled and the aristocrats lived and held their councils. That nucleus would often develop into a city or something resembling a city, and in that case we may translate *polis* as "city-state." This development took place mainly in the southern and eastern parts of mainland Greece, whereas in the west and northwest of the country many areas would remain without a *polis* organization for a long time to come. It is even possible that the *polis* emerged first in the 8th century among the Greek colonists in Sicily and South Italy and from there reached the motherland from where these colonists had departed in the first place.

Politics in a narrow sense was in the Archaic period mainly an aristocratic affair. In most of the small states, kingship had disappeared. In its place, magistrates had made their appearance. They were selected annually from among the more prominent members of society, and could have different titles in different *poleis* (plural of *polis*). In some places, there were magistrates who retained the title of *basileus* (king), but they usually had priestly duties. The aristocrats derived their dominant position from their prestige and (relative) wealth. The latter manifested itself among other things in the possession of horses and from around 700 BC also in the possession of the then new sets of arms and armor consisting of bronze cuirasses and bronze helmets, bronze-clad shields, and iron-headed spears and swords. With that weaponry they fought on foot, soon in small formations of similarly equipped warriors. The Greek term for such a formation in line was *phalanx*. Certainly, initially these weapons must have been costly, so that the emergence of *phalanx* tactics of heavily armed groups could even have contributed to the dominance of an aristocratic elite over the mass of the population who could not afford such equipment. Not before the later 6th century BC, larger phalanxes appeared in which also an important part of the non-aristocratic population participated as *hoplites*, as the heavily armed infantrymen were henceforth called, after the *hoplon*, the shield.

Several *poleis* tended to expand their territories at the cost of their smaller neighbors. Thus, in the Archaic period, a few relatively large *poleis* came to the fore: on the Peloponnese, Argos, Corinth, and Sparta; in Central Greece, Athens and Thebes; in Ionia, Samos, Miletus, and Ephesus; and in Sicily, Syracuse, and Akragas.

Population growth, colonization, and overseas commerce

The rise of *poleis* such as the ones mentioned in the preceding subsection can be seen against the background of a population growth that after its beginnings in the 9th century BC accelerated in the 8th century. That population growth stimulated both emigration of Greeks away from the motherland and expansion over adjacent lightly populated areas or weaker communities—thereby contributing to armed conflict between neighboring *poleis*. Thus, Sparta subjugated the whole region of Laconia and in the late 8th century BC started the wars that would lead to the annexation of neighboring Messenia. Argos extended its power over the area of the Argolid, while Athens unified the peninsula of Attica into one *polis*. The emigration to regions outside Greece inaugurated the so-called Archaic Colonization movement. A "colony" in this context means an overseas but independent settlement, not a subdued region held in subordination to a "motherland." From the second half of the 8th century until well into the 6th century BC, Greek colonies were founded on various shores of the Mediterranean and Black seas. The best known of these were Syracuse and Akragas, already mentioned, as well as Katane, the oldest colony in Sicily; in South Italy, Tarentum and Neapolis; in present-day South France, Massalia; on the north coast of Africa in modern Libya, Cyrene; and on the Bosporus, Byzantium.

These colonies as a rule adopted various institutions and cults, as well as their dialect and their alphabet, from their mother cities, but politically they were, as stated in the preceding text, independent *poleis* from the start. The oldest colonies had primarily been trading posts, but soon agrarian settlements dominated, and many colonies were founded at locations that had excellent soil for grain or viticulture in the vicinity. Thus, this Greek colonization movement can also be seen as part of a broader movement of migration of peoples and crops from east to west in the course of the 1st millennium BC. Greeks consciously contributed to the spread of improved grains (wheat), the cultivated olive, and the vine to the western basin of the Mediterranean. The emergence of these daughter cities no doubt stimulated commerce as well. Soon, grains from Sicily and the south of Russia were exported to Greece proper, while bronze vessels, luxury ceramics, and wine went from the motherland to the colonies. There, the Greeks often passed these products on to chieftains and princes in the hinterland, Scythians, Celts, and others, who in this way developed a taste for Greek products. Ceramics, especially, can be of relevance in this respect for modern archeologists in their efforts to reconstruct contacts between Greeks and non-Greeks by way of migration and trade.

Internal Relations within the *poleis*

The colonization movement and the impulse to commerce resulting from it; the growing contacts, both peaceful and violent, between the various *poleis*; the increasing significance of the alphabetic script and hence of written documents such as laws and decisions of the *polis* community, which since the later 7th century BC were usually inscribed on stone: all these influenced relations within and between the many small states of the Greek world. At the very least, social relations within a community became more complex and differences in property and wealth more pronounced. Nearly everywhere, the elite tried to maintain or to enhance its standing by acquiring the new luxury goods that after around 700 BC reached Greece from the East. At the same time, manual labor became more and more despised in these circles and was stigmatized by association with those who were un-free. The majority of the citizens, however, had no choice other than to work with their hands, and were often dependent on the aristocrats. In some states, a narrow circle of aristocrats or richer citizens—wealth and aristocratic birth as a rule went hand in hand—monopolized all power, as happened in Corinth in the first half of the 7th century BC. In other states, such as Athens in the second half of the 7th century BC, rich landowners even made a mockery of the very idea of the *polis* as a "community" of free citizens by their extortions and enslavement of poor citizens. In other states, aristocrats and other citizens joined hands against a subjugated population that was forced to work the fields of their masters, whereby the aristocrats had to rein in ostentatious displays of luxury, and the common citizens, on the other hand, adopted some aristocratic attitudes, such as a scorn for manual labor. This was the case in Sparta and in many small states on the island of Crete—not by coincidence, areas where Dorian immigrants had subjugated indigenous populations. In the latter cases, internal tensions were resolved at the expense of some section of the population separated from the citizenry and deprived of their rights. In the cases of Corinth and Athens—and comparable situations must have existed elsewhere—the internal tensions led to internal conflicts. These conflicts in their turn sometimes stimulated the exodus of a section of the citizenry to found a new colony elsewhere.

Turannoi

The conflicts within the *poleis* were to a large extent exacerbated by rivalries and personal ambitions within aristocratic circles. The result was that here and there "bigmen" seized power by force and established a form of monarchy that the Greeks called *turannis*. The term was borrowed from the Lydians in western Asia Minor and pointed to a sort of monarchy that had been established illegally. The ruler himself was called *turannos* ("tyrant"), and the fact that the Greeks used these foreign terms suggests that they already saw in this phenomenon something that was essentially foreign to the character of the *polis* as a community of citizens. We do not have a clear idea about how these *turannoi* gained their positions of power, but the scanty evidence we have points to military coups. As a rule, the *turannos* was supported in this by a group of aristocratic friends and other supporters, often from outside his own state, and often by groups of mercenaries as well—the latter a new phenomenon in the 7th century BC. Around 650 BC, the ruling aristocracy in Corinth was expelled by a certain Cypselus, who established his own *turannis* in the process. His son Periander ruled around 600 BC as one of the most famous *turannoi* of Greece. In those days, the term *turannos* did not have a pejorative connotation. Many a *turannos* was popular, at any rate with the non-aristocratic population, because he curried their favor with, for instance, programs of land distribution, turning popular sentiment against his aristocratic rivals. Some *turannoi* stimulated a certain patriotism and organized or re-organized cults and festivals on a "national" platform. After two or three generations, however, the *turannoi* as a rule had not much more to offer to the common people, and then the traditional aversion against a "monarchical" regime led in many cases to their final expulsion. Seen in retrospect, the phenomenon of the Archaic *turannis* undermined the position of the traditional aristocracies and thereby in some *poleis* even paved the way for a later democratic government.

Developments in Athens in the 7th and 6th centuries BC

Athens was the prime example of a *turannis* paving the way for a democracy. We have the impression that in the 7th century BC. Athens lagged a little behind many other states, such as Corinth, but toward 600 BC a development took place here that would eventually give this *polis* an advantage over the rest of Greece. Around 620 BC in Athens, the criminal code was for the first time put into writing by a certain Dracon—in a later period, his laws had the reputation of being "draconian"—which implied a weakening of aristocratic power, because now for the first time the "state" to some extent limited the often endless feuds between aristocratic families and at the same time restricted the freedom of action of aristocratic judges. Yet, tensions in Athens remained strong because here the richer landowners could sell their insolvent debtors into slavery outside Attica. Many Athenians had become the debtors of the richer landowners by pledging their land as security against their loans and, presumably, failing this, their own persons, with the looming risk of being sold abroad in the end. This situation seemed to present an opportunity for a seizure of power by a would-be *turannos* who could find support in the mass of discontented citizens.

Probably to prevent this, around 590 BC a generally respected and distinguished magistrate called Solon was given extraordinary powers in order to reorganize the *polis*.

Solon's measures were mainly the following: first, Athenian citizens who had been sold abroad were as far as possible brought back, and borrowing with one's own person as security was henceforth forbidden. Also, the worst forms of the dependency of poor peasants on richer landowners came to an end, although we do not know the exact measures that Solon took to accomplish this. But the result of his reforms in this field is certain: all Athenian citizens were henceforth free in the eyes of the law, but many of them remained very poor, because a redistribution of land, a remedy that some *turannoi* had resorted to, was not permitted by Solon. In the political reorganization of Athens, he strengthened the role of the assembly of the people and undermined to some extent the position of the aristocracy. Traditionally, the population of Attica consisted of three orders or "classes": the *hippeis* or "knights," literally, those who owned horses; the *zeugitai* or "plowmen" (i.e., the owners of a yoke with two oxen, the possession of which separated the not so poor from the poor); and the *thetes*, a word meaning something like "servants" or "landless laborers." Solon now introduced a system according to which nobody would automatically, on the basis of birth, belong to one of these classes; henceforth, one would be assigned to one of the classes on the basis of property assessment. Property was measured in annual yields of grain. Moreover, from the *hippeis* Solon separated a new class of rich citizens, the highest in this system, called the *pentakosiomedimnoi* ("500-bushel-men," who harvested at least 500 *medimnoi* or bushels of grain each year). In many respects, this organization remains rather obscure to us; the property assessments recorded for the other classes, 300 bushels for the *hippeis*, 200 or 150 for the *zeugitai*, are dubious, to say the least. Nevertheless, the thrust of Solon's reforms is clear. The political rights of the citizen population were now closely bound up with membership of one of these property classes. From the two highest classes, the yearly magistrates or *archontes* were selected, while the former *archontes* became members for life of the Areopagus, a council named after the *Areios pagos*, the hill of Ares, a small hill at the foot of the Acropolis, the main fortress hill and religious center of the city. The assembly of all the citizens would elect the *archontes* and would also function as the supreme court of appeal if necessary, sitting in judgment of the *archontes* themselves. With this, the lower classes acquired more political influence than they ever had, although the reins of power were still with the elite. At the same time, the economic problems of a large part of the population remained. Solon's work of reform had not been all-encompassing; nevertheless, one can discern in it the basis of Athens' later democracy.

After Solon had renounced his extraordinary powers—a gesture that earned him the lasting reputation of being a wise and disinterested man—it soon turned out that the internal problems of Athens had not all been solved. Rival aristocratic factions opposed each other, among whom was Pisistratus, a man who was popular among the poorer citizens. Around 560 BC, he tasted power for the first time by seizing the Acropolis with a group of followers—that is, according to the tradition told one century later, the details of which are hard to verify. Resistance from the other aristocrats led to his expulsion. After a short second stint in power—again, according to tradition—he finally succeeded shortly after 550 BC with the military support of friends and mercenaries from outside

Athens in defeating his opponents and establishing his *turannis* permanently. According to a later tradition, Pisistratus was a mild ruler who as far as possible left existing laws and the existing "constitution" untouched. Presumably, he reorganized some of the state cults, such as that of Dionysus and of the city goddess Athena. In their turn, these cults with their accompanying festivals would be a great stimulus for athletic competitions and the arts. Not only a certain pan-Athenian feeling but also a certain pride in the new glory of Athens were thereby enhanced, although it remains unclear to what extent this was a conscious policy of Pisistratus. For the mass of smallholders and landless citizens, his rule was, presumably, advantageous in that he supported them with loans and probably also distributed land among them. Attica underwent a partial transformation: it became a land of small and medium landowners who apart from barley and wheat now also grew olives and grapes. The olive oil must at least partially have been destined for export. With this olive oil and with the development of a high-quality ceramic industry, there opened up some space in Athenian society for commerce and for the emergence of people who no longer earned their livelihood with agriculture—however small this group, it would always remain an important part of the citizen population of Athens.

In all probability, the authority of the Athenian *turannos* rested on the support of professional hoplites: mercenaries from outside Athens, but, presumably, also poorer Athenian citizens who had been equipped at the expense of the *turannos* and served him personally. Aristocratic opponents had fled or were exiled. In the course of time many reconciled themselves with the monarchical regime and returned. But under Hippias, who after the death of his father Pisistratus continued the *turannis*, an opposition movement of aristocrats built up. This movement gathered strength when after a few years Hippias' brother was murdered, albeit not for political but for purely personal reasons. The two perpetrators, who had themselves been killed, were celebrated by Athenian exiles—as they would be later by the Athenian democracy—as "tyrannicides" or "tyrant-slayers" and national heroes. Hippias' rule thereupon became more oppressive, and he managed to disarm the citizens. Aristocratic exiles then pressured Sparta to mount a military invasion in Attica. In 510 BC, Hippias under Spartan pressure had to leave Athens, and found refuge with the Persians in Asia Minor. With that, the period of the *turannis* in Athens came to an end.

Disappearance of the *turannoi*: Influence of the hoplites

The fall of the Athenian *turannoi* was symptomatic. Nowhere in the Greek motherland after around 500 BC did "tyrants" manage to hold on to power. It was different in Asia Minor or in the world of the Greek colonies, but there as a rule *turannoi* succeeded in remaining in power only with the help of mercenary armies and the support of powerful foreign friends, for example, in Asia Minor, the Persians. In the Greek motherland, the *turannis* remained an aberration, an exception to the rule of the *polis*. After a while, the *turannoi* met with resistance everywhere, and in the second half of the 6th century BC that resistance could often reckon on the support of Sparta. In many cities, after the expulsion of the *turannoi*, aristocracies returned to power, as happened, for instance, in Corinth in the middle of the 6th century BC. In Athens, however, history took

(a)   (b)

Figure 12   A Roman copy and a contemporary depiction of the Athenian sculpture group of the Tyrannicides (originally c. 475 BC). To the left, a Roman copy of the sculptural group of Harmodius and Aristogiton, the men who in 514 BC killed the brother of the Athenian tyrant Hippias. The background to this assassination may not have been political at all, but in 5th-century Athens, Harmodius and Aristogiton came to be honored as *turannoktonoi*, "tyrant slayers," heroes of Athens' democracy. The original sculptures were bronzes of about 475 BC, which have been lost, as have so many Greek originals. The large industry of Roman days devoted to turning out numerous copies of famous statuary for philhellenic Roman patrons helps us to visualize many lost works of art. How this group was originally displayed can be seen in 5th-century Athenian vase paintings, as in the Panathenaic prize amphora (an amphora that, filled with olive oil, was once a prize in the Panathenaic Games) shown on the right. On one of its sides, the amphora carries the image of the goddess Athena in full panoply; the shield she holds up carries the tyrant slayers as its device. In democratic Athens, this choice was very deliberate: to show the city's goddess in this way says something about the popularity of the *turannoktonoi*. Photos: a) Photoservice Electa/Universal Images Group/SuperStock; b) © The Trustees of the British Museum

another turn. Admittedly, there too in 510 BC conflicts immediately broke out between rival aristocratic lords and their supporters, but the period of the *turannoi* had profoundly changed the social structure of the *polis*. For the *zeugitai* had in the meantime developed into a "middle class" of small landowners with a new sense of self-esteem. Among them were also those Athenians who had served the *turannoi* as hoplites. Both politically and militarily, they could now influence the political balance to a greater degree than had been possible before the *turannis*. One of the ambitious Athenian aristocrats in the struggle for power in 510 BC and the next few years understood this: Cleisthenes, who became archont (*archon*) in 508/507 BC, allied himself with the people (the *demos*) of Athens and thereby succeeded in ousting his main rival. When the latter again invoked the help of the Spartan king, that king also, together with his Athenian friends, was driven from the city of Athens by the *demos*. We may infer from these events that under Cleisthenes the class of the *zeugitai*, which must have been many times larger than the elite, indeed had begun to equip themselves as hoplites. From then on, the non-aristocratic *demos* had become the decisive power in Athenian society and politics. Cleisthenes, after getting rid of his rivals, therefore, could not in his turn establish his own "monarchy" but on the contrary was obliged to reorganize the Athenian state in such a way that henceforth the *demos* would really rule the *polis* of Athens. With that, a new period in Athenian history began: that of democracy.

In this development, Athens was ahead of other *poleis*, for elsewhere in Greece democracies made their appearance only later. But everywhere in Greece the *demos* had toward the end of the 6th century BC gained in self-respect. Even in those states in which aristocracies still ruled or had returned to power, it was found necessary to induct all those who were able to pay for the hoplite equipment into the citizen armies, so that the ruling aristocracies were forced to look after the interests of these "middle" groups of free citizens a little better than they had been used to doing. At the same time, and because of this, warfare between the city-states in the second half of the 6th century BC changed and became more serious in character. Armies became larger now than the elitist war bands of a former period and battles costlier. Power politics between the more important *poleis* became more serious as a consequence. In this constellation of affairs, Sparta emerged as the state that for the time being seemed to eclipse the others militarily.

Sparta

Sparta originated in the 10th century BC as a group of villages in the center of Laconia near the river Eurotas. Presumably from the very start, the Spartans had subjugated the population of the surrounding countryside and reduced them to a state akin to serfdom. These *heilotes*, helots, as they were called, were forced to work the fields of the Spartans, who alone were citizens of the *polis* Sparta. At the latest since the middle of the 6th century BC, the Spartans practiced a form of communal life that to some extent was characteristic of several Dorian communities, especially on the island of Crete. But in Sparta we encounter an extreme version of this communal life, which featured collective upbringing of the boys and young men of the community, organized in year classes and age groups, with an emphasis on toughening them and building up their endurance of pain, hunger, and so on. Adult men congregated in clubs or messes organized for warfare, hunting, and eating together. In Sparta too, from the late 8th century BC, there had been tensions between the richer and poorer members of society. Possibly in connection with this, Sparta started wars of conquest and annexed neighboring Messenia in the course of the 7th century. The Messenians became helots in their turn, and their land was distributed among the Spartans. From then on, the Spartans, a group of a few thousand adult men, formed an elite among a far larger population of helots, against which the Spartans always remained on their guard. They called themselves Peers or Equals (*homoioi*), and paid much attention to their collectivist ways of life that turned the citizen into a sort of professional soldier, since the practice of any manual labor was formally forbidden. Relative to other Greek states, Sparta thereby acquired a military advantage, certainly after all Spartan citizens had become hoplites in the early 6th century BC, if not before. Small autonomous communities in the mountains around Sparta and on the coasts of Laconia and Messenia were demoted to the status of *perioikoi*, that is, "dwellers-around," who in time of war had to provide troops for the Spartan army and in general lived under a form of Spartan sovereignty. The larger *poleis* in the Peloponnese were, with the exception of Argos, in the course of the 6th century BC subjugated by Sparta in the so-called Peloponnesian League. As the leader of that alliance, Sparta could count on contingents of Corinth and other Peloponnesian cities for any military campaigns outside the Peloponnese, which made her, shortly before 500 BC, the most powerful state in the Greek world.

Central and Northern Greece; The Western Greeks

In Boeotia in Central Greece, Thebes toward the end of the 6th century BC managed to force the smaller *poleis* in her neighborhood into an alliance under her leadership and thereby dominated this area. Farther to the north, in Thessaly, *polis* organizations had not yet developed. This was a region where aristocratic landowners ruled over a serf population and did not for some time stimulate any urban development. Likewise, in the mountainous to the northwest and north of the country, even more "primitive" tribal organizations were the rule, and settled urbanized centers were lacking. This was also the case in Macedon in the north, where kings still ruled. There, during the Archaic period and for long afterward, the society known to Homer seemed to live on with a *basileus*, warlike nobles, and a vociferous but powerless warrior assembly. In the Greek colonies, however, *poleis* flourished—indeed, as was suggested above, the *polis* organization may have emerged there even ahead of the motherland. It was probably owing to rapid population growth in what were practically "virgin" territories—which, when brought under cultivation, could feed many people—that the Greek cities, in Sicily especially, already in the 6th century BC greatly enhanced their power at the expense of the indigenous populations. There, in several states, *turannoi* emerged. Elsewhere in the west, in the 6th century BC, Carthaginians and Etruscans hindered Greek expansion, expelled the Greeks from the coasts of Corsica and Spain, and after around 500 BC excluded them from a large part of the western Mediterranean.

The Greeks in Asia Minor and the Persian Empire

In Asia Minor, it were especially the Ionian city-states that flourished in the late 7th and 6th centuries BC. Contacts with the Asian hinterland, where the kingdom of Lydia extended its power, as well as overseas contacts with Cyprus and the Syro-Phoenician coast, seem to have familiarized the Ionian elites with luxury goods such as stone-built houses, couches, and purple-dyed textiles earlier than their counterparts elsewhere, while at the same time stimulating the first budding of philosophy and science in the 6th century BC. Usually, aristocracies ruled these cities, although *turannoi* were not unknown here too. From around

600 BC, the kings of Lydia embarked on a policy of systematic subjugation of the various Greek *poleis* on the coast, a goal that was achieved by around 560 BC. In their internal life, though, the Greek cities did not undergo much change as a result; they henceforth had to provide soldiers for the armies of the kings at Sardis, who on their part were very much impressed by Greek civilization and in general took a benign attitude toward their Greek subjects.

Beyond Lydia, further to the east, in the 6th century a new power emerged: the Persians. Shortly after the middle of the century, the last king of Lydia, the proverbially rich Croesus, was defeated and captured by the Persian king Cyrus, a turn of events that made a deep impression on the Greek world. A little later, the Greek cities on the coast and on the offshore islands also came under Persian domination. Persian rule was no doubt more oppressive than Lydian rule had been, for the Persians demanded both tribute and the provision of men and ships in times of war. Thus, for their campaign against Egypt, which they conquered in 525 BC, the Persians had a large fleet built and manned by their Phoenician and Greek subjects. In this way, in the service of the Persian king, many eastern Greeks became directly involved in the power politics of the empire. In their turn, the Persians as a rule put their trust in *turannoi*, who with their support could maintain themselves in the Greek cities. Those *turannoi* naturally had to obey the Persian satrap in Sardis, and ultimately the Great King in Susa. As a result, the Greek scorn for *turannoi* that had developed in the later 6th century easily acquired an anti-Persian character. This, together with the intrigues of certain Greek politicians in the Ionian cities that we now can no longer follow in detail, led to the Ionian Revolt (500–494 BC). The insurgents for a while got hold of the Persian navy in the region and in this way managed to dominate for some time all the coastal waters from Byzantium to Cyprus, which had revolted as well. Remarkably, they also sought help from the Greek *poleis* in Europe, invoking a certain pan-Hellenic ("all-Greek") sentiment against a common non-Greek enemy. The strongest state, Sparta, refused to send troops so far from home. Only Athens sent a small squadron, which, however, returned after the first setbacks for the insurgents. Persia, in the meantime, equipped a second and partially new fleet while attacking the Greek cities from land. A lack of cooperation between the various contingents coupled with inexperience in the handling of large fleets probably explains the heavy defeat suffered by the insurgents in a sea battle not far from Miletus in 494 BC. After that, the revolt collapsed. The cities were taken one by one and again brought under Persian domination, but Miletus, as a punishment for its leading role in the revolt, was destroyed and its population deported to Mesopotamia. As a consequence, Ionia was no longer one of the leading players in the Greek world: both politically and culturally, the center of gravity now moved to the states in Europe. The rise of Persia as the domineering power in the eastern Mediterranean and the outcome of the Ionian revolt had underscored the importance of naval power, and the city of Athens especially was to draw lessons from this. In order to punish those who had helped the insurgents, according to the official message coming out from Persia, the Great King now set his mind to attacking the Greeks in the motherland, thereby extending the empire further west. That conflict would cause another decisive turn in the history of the Greeks.

Significance of the Archaic period

The Archaic period was the time when Greek civilization, so to speak, was born. The inheritance of the Mycenaean world, and of even older Bronze Age and Neolithic cultures in Greece; the traditions of other Greek population groups, such as the Dorians, who had emerged only after the fall of the Mycenaean world; certainly the strong influences from the Near East which had reached Greece during the Dark Age and the early Archaic period—all these ingredients contributed to the rise of Greek civilization. This was a civilization that despite its inherited traditions and borrowings from older and other cultures was a completely new phenomenon that in its turn was going to leave its mark on a large part of Europe and the Near East. It was in the Archaic period that the *polis* developed as the typically Greek state, the foundation on which democracy could arise.

Economic life was enriched in the Archaic period by the invention of money. The invention was in fact made in Lydia in the late 7th century BC: small pieces of *elektron*, electrum, a natural alloy of gold and silver, were stamped on one side with a mark stating and guaranteeing their weight and hence their value. The purpose of the invention was possibly to pay mercenary soldiers, Greeks among them. Around 600 BC, Greek cities such as Ephesus and Miletus minted their own "coins": pieces of silver with the stamp or emblem of the city. In the course of the 6th century, many Greek *poleis* in Europe, among them Athens, adopted the same custom: while still under the *turannis*, Athens started minting coins with the owl of the goddess Athena for an emblem. Coinage in this way also became an expression of the autonomy of a *polis*. Whereas in Lydia the circulation of the first coins had been extremely limited, in Greece in the 6th century, coinage was much more widely employed. Before long, smaller bronze coins meant for small transactions were minted. With this, the economy certainly did not become fully monetized as yet, for barter would always remain important throughout antiquity, but the introduction of coinage nevertheless greatly stimulated commercial activity.

Unmistakably, in the 7th and 6th centuries BC there was more wealth in Greece than there had been in the preceding period, though it was far from equally distributed. Material culture had evidently improved. Since the late 8th century BC, some *poleis* began to build temples in stone for the more important city gods, and in the 7th century they began to embellish sacred spaces with free-standing sculpture, while the art of painting, in murals and on pottery, flourished throughout the Archaic period. Religious festivals developed into occasions for the performance of music, dance and poetry. Some sanctuaries functioned as oracles and attracted visitors from far afield, especially Delphi in Central Greece, with its oracle of Apollo. Also, games with competitions in wrestling, boxing, athletics, music, and dancing (activities typical for the aristocratic elites in the Archaic period), which were dedicated to the gods and connected with religious festivals, attracted participants and audiences from many *poleis*. That was especially true of the games held at the sanctuary of Zeus in Olympia on the Peloponnese. Such events stimulated contacts between Greek states and enhanced a certain all-Greek or Panhellenic sentiment. That sentiment would be invoked by those states that in the beginning of the 5th century BC were determined to defend themselves against the coming Persian attack.

Italy and Western Europe

As in Greece, in Italy too in the first half of the 1st millennium BC a transition took place to an urbanized civilization with knowledge of an alphabetic script. But it occurred later than in the Greek world and was for the time being limited to only a few areas. The Italian peninsula was inhabited by various peoples who had settled there in the course of the 2nd millennium BC and had partially mixed with the older Neolithic populations. The more important among these peoples were the speakers of closely related Indo-European dialects, the Italic peoples, as they are called by modern scholars. Among them various subgroups can be distinguished, especially the Latins in the area of Latium on the coast of Central Italy southeast of the Tiber, the Umbrians in the Apennine region of Central Italy, and the Samnites in the mountainous inland regions of the south. Apart from them, and constituting a linguistic category of their own, were the Etruscans in present-day Tuscany. Presumably, the first Etruscans had settled here from somewhere in the Aegean region, possibly from western Asia Minor, in the 12th or 11th century BC, and had probably mixed with indigenous groups; as a separate nation, they emerged in the 8th century BC. In the centuries after the turn of the millennium, migrations continued: some Italic groups probably crossed over into Sicily (if not already in the later 2nd millennium BC); the Carthaginians established posts on the western side of Sicily and on Sardinia; Celts occupied parts of northern Italy; peoples related to the Illyrians colonized parts of the eastern coastal regions; and since around 750 BC, Greeks settled on the coasts of Sicily and southern Italy.

The migrations from the east to Italy fit the pattern of an east–west movement of peoples, animals, and crops that had characterized the Mediterranean from the start of the Neolithic. Probably, the Etruscans introduced the knowledge of iron and iron working; the Greeks brought with them, among many other things, their version of the alphabet. The transition to an urbanized culture took place both in the Etruscan and in the Greek territories. In that process, the Greeks as a rule presented the models that were followed by the Etruscans.

The Etruscans

Around 700 BC, the Etruscans adopted and adapted one of the local variants of the Greek alphabet used by the Greeks in the south of Italy. The Etruscan texts that have been preserved—mostly very short texts in inscriptions—have largely defied translation, so that the Etruscan language still remains unknown to us. It certainly was not an Indo-European language, and the Etruscans, therefore, should be classified as one of the pre–Indo-European population groups in Europe and the Mediterranean area surviving into historic times. In their turn, many Italic peoples would adopt both the alphabet and the accoutrements of urban life from the Etruscans.

The Etruscan cities showed some similarities with those of the Geeks but were clearly distinct from most of the Greek cities in that they were based on a class system of freemen and serfs. They had ruling elites consisting of Etruscans proper and subjugated populations consisting mostly of the descendants of the indigenous peoples in their territories. It is

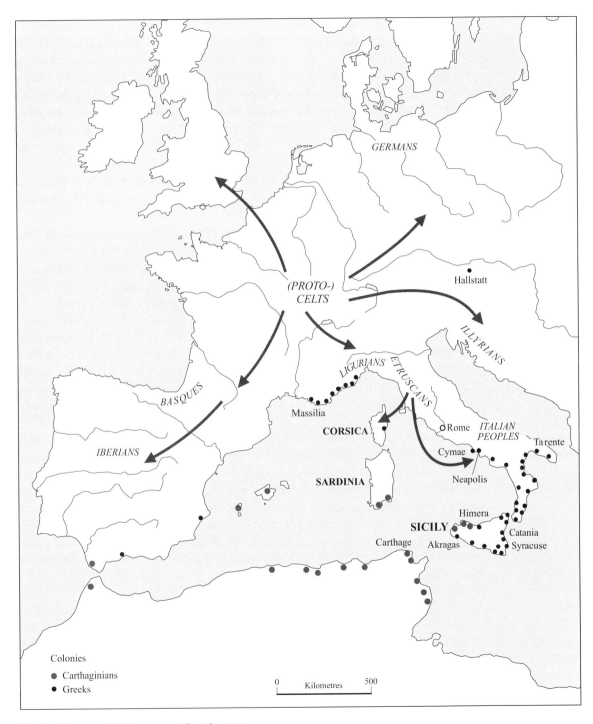

Map 7   Western Mediterranean, 8th–4th c. BC

quite possible, though, that the situation differed from city to city, since our knowledge of Etruscan political organization is fairly limited. As far as we can see, the Etruscan cities were in the period up to around 500 BC ruled by kings. Among themselves, the Etruscan cities maintained some relations of a religious character that were expressed in the reverence of a common sanctuary, but politically each city was independent. This period is mainly known from grave finds: weapons and ceramic pottery. The latter would from the 7th century BC onward be influenced by Greek pottery painting and would come to resemble its Greek models fairly closely. Since the 6th century BC, impressive and often splendidly decorated funeral chambers were built for the Etruscan aristocracies, a custom that would be practiced until well into the 3rd century BC. Their lively mural paintings give us some glimpses of Etruscan life and of Etruscan ideas on death and the after-life. In any case, the latter must have played an important role in Etruscan religion, in which Greek influences and wholesale adoptions of Greek gods and myths are clearly visible. In contrast, the stress in Etruscan religion on divination, that is, the art of foretelling the will of the gods from various signs such as the liver of the sacrificial victim or the spot struck by lightning, was probably a more typically Etruscan feature that can possibly be traced back, at least in part, to Asia Minor.

Warfare must always have been at the heart of Etruscan politics. In the 6th century BC, they adopted from the Greeks the heavy equipment and the tactics of the hoplite *phalanx* and embarked on a period of considerable expansion. Various cities succeeded in extending their power at the expense of Italic populations or in establishing daughter cities. As a result, in the 6th century, a large part of the Po valley became Etruscan territory, as did the fertile plain of Campania around the Gulf of Naples. That expansion brought the Etruscans into conflict with the Greeks and would also provoke a reaction from the Latins in coastal Central Italy.

Of the Italic peoples, many herded goats and sheep besides practicing a rather simple agriculture. This was especially true of the Samnites and related groups in Central and South Italy. It provided them with a certain mobility and offered an incentive for constant expansion in search of new pastures or fields for cultivation at the expense of the inhabitants of the small coastal plains. In the 6th century BC, the expansion of these peoples was to some extent halted by the Etruscan expansion. The region of Latium, situated between Etruria proper (modern Tuscany north of the Tiber) and Etruscan-dominated Campania, must in that century also have fallen under some form of Etruscan dominance. That is the background to the emergence of the city of Rome.

The origins of Rome

Rome was propitiously located on the left bank of the Tiber not far from the sea and on the crossroads of a route west-east along the Tiber into Central Italy and north-south from Etruria to Latium. Here, in the 10th century BC, the first settlements made their appearance on a couple of hills surrounding a swampy valley. The inhabitants were Latins and other Italic speaking people from the mountainous inland areas to the north. The dialect of the Latins must have been dominant, so that Latin would become the language of Rome. In later times, the Romans had their stories about the origin and the early history of the city:

stories of the twin brothers Romulus and Remus, of the seven kings of Rome (of whom Romulus had been the first), and of all sorts of heroic exploits of individual Romans in their struggles against the Etruscans and other surrounding peoples. Of all those stories, however, only a tiny bit can be said to be historical. In any case, the date that the Romans themselves later gave for the foundation of the city—in modern reckoning, 753 BC—is both too late, for the site had been inhabited already since the 10th century, and too early, for only around 600 BC did Rome became a real city.

The earliest social and political structures of Rome

The first Rome—presumably not yet called by that name—was a small group of villages consisting of simple huts of wattle and daub. It has often been assumed that these villages were originally all separate "mini-states," but it seems more plausible that from the start, or in any case from very early on, they formed one political community. Something can be presumed about its organization from institutions and terminology that was preserved in later times. Thus, we know that this community was ruled by a king or *rex*. It is quite possible, but not certain, that this *rex* at the beginning had mainly priestly or sacrificial tasks to fulfill and did not have much secular power. What we further know for sure is that the society of this very early Rome must have been organized around the heads of families. Every *paterfamilias* had in principle unlimited authority over his wife, children, and other dependents such as slaves, irrespective of their age. Between the *patres* (the "fathers") there existed ties of relationship, real or imagined, on which the institute of the *gens* (plural: *gentes*) was based. A *gens* was a group of families that all had the same family name and were considered to be related in the male line. Members of a *gens* were supposed to support each other in a form of family solidarity. All *gentes* together constituted the Roman people or *populus Romanus*. Presumably, from the start this also included those people who were neither totally free nor slaves but "clients" (Latin: *clientes*), who were bound to a *paterfamilias* in a relationship of dependency "as of a father" (Latin: *patronus*). Perhaps the first *clientes* were a sort of landless peasants leasing their fields from their *patroni*; in later times, when they certainly were Roman citizens, they were supposed to help their patrons by voting for him, for his candidates, or for his proposals in the assembly of the people, and by paying respect to him and honoring him in various ways, in exchange for his protection and help, for instance, when they were in trouble with the law or materially in times of bad harvests, and the like. This mutual bond, called *clientela* or *patronatus*, was very strong and was considered by all involved as a moral obligation, hence the alternative name *fides* or "loyalty" for this institution. It was one of the most important elements in the make-up of Roman society and would always remain so.

Probably, this oldest Rome had already its *comitia*, the assembly of the people, an institution that in those early days possibly had not much more to do than cheer a new *rex* now and then, and perhaps vote on those questions that the king and the aristocrats chose to submit to her. For the king, in any case, did not "rule" alone. The oldest heads of families or the heads of the most distinguished families—the former were not necessarily the same as the latter, although it is quite possible that what began as an assembly of the eldest became in the course of time an assembly of the most distinguished—constituted a council: the senate or *senatus* (literally, "council of the eldest"). Its members, in any case, could be called *patres*, from which later the term *patricii*, "patricians," would be derived to denote the aristocracy in Roman society. In the first few centuries, though, that society remained rather simple, though gradually increasing in area and population. The various settlements on the hills near the Tiber literally grew together, and there are some finds from the 7th century BC, among them the remains of a chariot, that indicate a differentiation in property and wealth between an elite—perhaps the chariot belonged to the king—and the rest of society. The group of villages, however, was not yet a city, let alone a center of power for the surrounding areas. That was to change with the arrival of the Etruscans around 625 BC.

Etruscan Rome (around 625–500 BC)

Roman tradition knew of a man named Tarquinius who came from Etruria to Rome and there became king. He was supposed to have commenced the building of the temple for the main deity, Jupiter, on the smallest of the hills of Rome, the Capitol. The name Tarquinius is indeed Etruscan, and the core of the legend is most probably true: that the kingship of Rome passed into the hands of Etruscans and that henceforth Etruscans imprinted their mark on what was to be the city of Rome. An important change was the draining and paving of the central valley between the hills of the Capitol in the west, the Palatine in the south, and the Quirinal in the north, transforming the area into the central place or forum of the city: the Forum Romanum. The Capitol became part fortress and refuge in times of emergency and part sacred space for temples, foremost among them the temple of Jupiter. The other hills were for habitation; probably, some streets were already paved, and a first earthen wall was built around the city. With this, Rome in the course of the 6th century BC became a city in outward appearance too. It is practically certain that the name Roma was given to this city by the Etruscans. Its meaning is unknown.

These developments must have been accompanied by political and social changes, the details of which are, again, very uncertain. Presumably, the Etruscan kings in the 6th century BC gave Rome a more effective organization, both politically and militarily. The introduction of hoplite equipment and phalanx tactics created a division within the citizenry: those who could afford such equipment were obliged to fight in times of war and in anticipation thereof to mobilize yearly a force of 3000 heavy infantry, the so-called *legio* or "levy." Next to these, the aristocrats had every year to field a squadron of 300 cavalry. The poorer citizens, who had insufficient property, as a rule did not have to fight and lost in practice any vote they might have had in the assembly of the people. The whole *populus Romanus* was divided into three parts or *tribus*. Perhaps the term *tribus* meant originally "one third," but it is traditionally translated as "tribe." Possibly, the *tribus* already existed before the Etruscan influence asserted itself, but in the 6th century this organization acquired real importance. For instance, the heavy infantry was divided into three subdivisions of 1000 men each, commanded by a *tribunus*. One belonged to a particular *tribus* on the basis of birth. In the later part of the 6th century BC, however, another organization was created apart from the traditional *tribus*. The city of Rome was now subdivided into four new *tribus*, which were territorial entities, while the surrounding countryside was divided into a steadily increasing number of rural *tribus* or "districts." They served as administrative units for the levying of a rudimentary tax (*tributum*) and for the recruiting of the infantrymen by the *tribuni* (plural; that remained the title for the highest military officers, derived from the original three *tribus*, which must now have lost most of their meaning). Roman tradition ascribed the new organization to Servius Tullius, the second Etruscan king in Rome. He is credited with dividing the citizens into at least two property classes: those who were liable for service in the *legio* and those who were exempt from military service. But there is much uncertainty and therefore controversy about the supposed reforms of Servius Tullius. What we can accept, however, is that the authority of the Etruscan kings was in the end resented by the older Roman aristocracy. Plausibly, the Etruscans had transformed the traditional kingship into a more powerful political institution. A number of *insignia* that would later in Rome symbolize the highest political power are of Etruscan origin, such as the *fasces*, bundles of reeds around an axe, carried by special servants, the *lictores*, in front of the king (and after the disappearance of the kingship, in front of the higher magistrates); or the exclusive right of the commander in chief (initially the king, later a magistrate) to enter the city on a special chariot at the head of his victorious army in a parade, the so-called *triumphus*.

The end of Roman kingship

The last Etruscan king in Rome was according to tradition called Tarquinius Superbus, that is, Tarquin the Proud, a name that characterizes him as a man of ambition and important achievements—for instance, he is credited with having completed the building of the great temple of Jupiter on the Capitol—but also as a tyrant. Certainly, in legend he was portrayed as such, and it was his tyrannical behavior, it was said, that led a group of Roman aristocrats to mount a coup, expel the tyrant, and abolish the kingship altogether, thus founding the Roman Republic. But we do not know what really happened. We may assume, though, that the last Etruscan king was driven out of Rome in a rebellion of Roman aristocrats against a regime that in their view had become too much of an autocracy.

Roman tradition dates the expulsion of Tarquinius Superbus in the year 510 BC, making it contemporaneous with the expulsion of the *turannos* Hippias from Athens. In later times, at least, a clear parallel was seen between the two events. In reality, the end of Roman kingship must have occurred a little later, at around 506 BC (according to some historians, it was even considerably later, at around 475 BC; the chronology of this period is still debated). Together with the change of power in Rome, the Etruscans also lost their grip on other regions. Around 500 BC, they lost their influence in Latium, and after a defeat against a Greek force, they were driven from Campania. In Rome, the Etruscans left a clear heritage: apart from the *insignia* of royalty already mentioned, which after the fall of the monarchy would be transferred to the highest magistrates of the republic, we may point to various religious customs, especially the art of interpretation of the livers of sacrificial victims and other signs of the divine will, and to the Etruscan alphabet that was adopted by the Romans and became the so-called Latin alphabet (which is the same as our modern alphabet).

The West of the Mediterranean

Further to the west, the Carthaginians in the 6th century BC extended their influence over the coasts of North Africa, western Sicily, part of Sardinia, and the southern tip of Spain. In cooperation with the Etruscans, they halted further Greek expansion in a western direction. They had not been able to prevent, however, the establishment of Massalia and other Greek colonies on the southern coast of present-day France.

Figure 13   Vase in the form of a cock (c. 650–600 BC). A small bird-shaped bottle of a kind of black ceramic ware called Bucchero, found in Viterbo, in Etruscan territory. It dates from the second half of the 6th century BC. An abecedarium is written across the breast of this cockerel. The shapes of the Greek letters derive ultimately from the island of Euboea that lies off the east coast of the Greek mainland. During the Archaic period, this island sent out many colonists to Southern Italy. Examples such as this abecedarium, which we have from the 7th century onward, show how the Greek alphabet was adopted in Etruria, ultimately to form the basis of their own alphabet, from which, by way of Rome, our alphabet is derived as well. The bottle in now in the Metropolitan Museum in New York. Photo: The Metropolitan Museum of Art/Art Resource/Scala, Florence

Chapter 3.2

The Social Fabric

Economic Life

Agriculture

Agriculture was practiced from the Neolithic period onward, but in the Near East time and again innovations were introduced that with some delay would find their way westward to the Mediterranean world. The 1st millennium BC, especially the first half of that millennium, was of great importance in this regard. It was in that period that an improved species of wheat reached Greece and a little later Italy; that the vine spread as far as the south of modern-day France; and that the cultivated olive began its triumphant conquest of practically all the coastal areas of the Mediterranean, to become a mainstay of agriculture in many regions. It was also the period in which various fruit trees as well as the art of grafting reached the Mediterranean lands from the Near East, especially from Mesopotamia and the mountainous regions to its north. The new food sources enabled the demographic recovery of Greece in the 9th and 8th centuries BC and help explain the relatively strong population growth of Italy—a more fertile country than Greece—in the course of the 1st millennium BC, from which the Greek colonies, the Etruscan cities, and the Italic peoples would all profit.

The techniques of agriculture were traditionally rather simple, and there were no major improvements in this period. This meant that higher production could only be achieved by extending the area of cultivation; hence, the growth of settlements and cultivated fields in areas that had been sparsely populated before, such as many parts of Attica around the center of Athens; and hence the migration of Greeks to various new *poleis* outside the motherland in the Archaic period. Work on the fields was performed either by the farmer-landowner himself or by peasant-renters or serfs dependent on him. As far as we know, this was the case everywhere in the Near East and the Mediterranean. In the short periods each year in which much of the work was concentrated, especially in the harvest period, extra labor was often hired, or the work was divided between all family members and neighbors that could be mobilized. In general, however, agriculture was not very labor intensive, which made it unprofitable to have slaves to do the work. Slavery on a large scale

Antiquity: Greeks and Romans in Context, First Edition. Frederick G. Naerebout and Henk W. Singor.
© 2014 John Wiley & Sons, Inc. Published 2014 by John Wiley & Sons, Inc.

was unknown in agriculture. Yet there were large landowners: certainly, the kings, high officials, and military officers, presumably some private individuals too, in Egypt and in the Near East, but their properties were scattered over various unconnected parcels worked by renters or serfs. Large estates of continuous fields or pastures worked by slave gangs, such as would appear in a later period, for all practical purposes did not exist.

Perhaps cattle breeding and meat consumption in Greece were more important in the Dark Age than in later periods: in the epics of Homer, at least, meat eating is presented as a normal diet. The rise in population in the 8th century BC would have led to the transformation of pasturage into agricultural fields and thus to the marginalization of cattle breeding. In any case, since the Archaic period, cattle breeding was often literally pushed to the margins of the *polis* territories, where sheep and goats roamed the uncultivated areas that as a rule were considered communal property. Cows and oxen were used to haul plows and carts; cattle were not raised for milk, and only very rarely for meat production. Fish, such as tuna, on the other hand, were a common and relatively cheap source of food. Poultry would arrive in Greece from Asia only in the 6th century BC. In relatively sparsely populated areas, game would provide extra meat. Horses everywhere belonged only to the wealthier citizens or kings; their possession lent the owners great prestige, but horses were hardly of much practical use outside warfare, sports, and hunting. Because of the amount of fodder they consumed, ownership of horses was a parasitic luxury in a basically weak agrarian economy.

Agriculture, wealth, and poverty

The possession of agricultural land was the main form of wealth in Greece, as in every place where agriculture was the backbone of the economy. Equal property rights did not exist, not even in the colonies where, presumably, when they were founded, the areas available for cultivation had been divided into equal parcels among the settlers. As a consequence of divided legacies or concentrations of legacies in the hands of single heirs, the custom of dowry, and no doubt other practices, inequality of landed property must as a rule have arisen fairly soon. Especially the rules of inheritance—which could also vary according to whether or not daughters could inherit as well as sons—often led to the division of fields and parcels into tiny pieces of land. The average farmer in Greece always worked a couple of fields, which might not always be situated in close proximity to each other. A rich man owned more such small parcels than a poor man, and naturally did not work them himself. Thus, to grow rich or to become poor was often a matter of being a single heir or having to share one's inheritance with others, combined with profitable or unprofitable marriages. Selling and buying land was considered shameful in many *poleis*, and even banned by law in some, at least in the Archaic period.

By these mechanisms, in this period some families climbed the social ladder, while others fell into poverty, though those who were rich already could more easily maintain their status than a poor man could acquire riches. That had partly to do with the nature of non-agricultural sources of income.

Craft and industry

Craft and industry in Greece in this period were just as small scale in organization as agriculture. Potters, smiths, leatherworkers, stone cutters, and other craftsmen normally worked in small workplaces, owned by the craftsmen themselves. They were assisted by family members and maybe a few slaves. Some sculptors became famous exhibiting their work—statues of gods and goddesses, athletes and priestesses—in religious centers such as the island of Delos and in places such as Delphi and Olympia, where also small figurines of bronze or lead were offered for sale to visitors who could dedicate these at these sanctuaries. This would explain the stylistic similarities and mutual influences that can be discerned in these objects of art and craft. Many of the other crafts were "house industries" in the hands of women: wool working, spinning, and weaving, although some textiles such as the expensive purple-dyed materials must have been produced in more or less industrial workplaces (fulling and dyeing were strenuous work, done by men). In the larger cities of the Near East such as Babylon or Nineveh, greater specialization in crafts and professions was possible than in Greece. Technically, the industries of pottery, sculpture in stone and marble, and bronze working by the 6th century BC had all reached a peak that in subsequent periods would hardly be surpassed. In each *polis*, though, only a small number of persons could have derived their livelihood from sources of income other than agriculture: a smith, a carpenter, a potter, a stone cutter. Even less frequently would one have encountered someone like a singer-poet who dramatized the great epics and who, like the oracle-monger/healer/magician, often traveled from one *polis* to another.

Commerce

Commerce in Greece was practiced by everybody who had an opportunity to do so: the landowner who brought his surplus to the local market, and the craftsman who received his customers in his workplace. The trader, someone who would buy products and sell them for a profit, was a rarity, though not completely unknown. In the Dark Age, one only ventured abroad when armed and in company with others; hence, the "trader" in those days was usually a large landowner or aristocrat who could afford to equip a ship with 20 or more oarsmen. Such persons were adventurers, pirates, or traders as circumstances allowed. Bronze, iron, precious metals, Near Eastern luxury goods such as ivory, purple textiles, and costly vessels: such were the items, apart from male and female slaves, that were bought and sold, or pillaged. In the Archaic period, Greek overseas commerce may have become a little less brutal—although piracy would always remain a more or less respectable profession—but only a wealthy man could equip a ship. It was not necessary, though, for the owner to board, let alone to command it himself, for he could leave the navigation and even the entire enterprise to a fellow citizen or a subordinate.

We may fairly assume that the colonization movements of the Greeks must have stimulated overseas commerce between the mother cities and the colonies, but in the absence of meaningful quantitative data, it is hard to assess the contribution of commerce to the total economy. Presumably, that contribution before around 500 BC in the Greek world was considerably less than, for instance, in Mesopotamia, and certainly less than in Phoenicia. The Phoenicians were the great merchants of the Near East, trading in products of their own, such as cedarwood, purple textiles, as well as those of others, such as metals, Egyptian papyrus, and linen. Their colony, Carthage, assumed this role in the western Mediterranean, characterized by strong monopolistic traits and partially successful attempts to maintain their monopolies with military force. Warfare was always an important factor in the economy throughout antiquity, for military enterprises often were a direct form of enrichment. That was true not only of the campaigns of the Assyrian kings in the Near East, but also of the near-permanent warfare between so many of the Greek *poleis*, where war booty often must have been the second-most important source of surplus wealth after agriculture. The connection between warfare and the economy is clear from the fact that, as stated before, the first coinage to be used was probably payment for the mercenaries in the service of the Lydian kings. Among those mercenaries there were Greek adventurers who would have introduced the idea of money to the Greek world. In the course of the 6th century, most of the *poleis* began to mint their own coins, both of silver and of bronze. Undoubtedly, that must have stimulated commercial activities, both at home and overseas.

The Greek *poleis* were certainly not all engaged in commerce at the same level. In the 7th and a large part of the 6th century BC, the city of Corinth was commercially at the forefront. Corinthian pottery has been found at many places of the Mediterranean, especially in its western parts. In the course of the 6th century BC, however, it was supplanted by black-figure Athenian ceramics (motifs were applied with a slip that turned black during firing, while the background was left the color of the clay). This black-figure pottery was, similar to the Corinthian ware, luxury pottery produced for overseas export by specialized potters. It is estimated that toward the end of the 6th century in Athens, all in all about 200 persons could have been involved in its production. With this, the ceramic industry in Athens, together with some other crafts such as bronze working and wool working, did indeed provide some non-agricultural employment, but relative to the whole of the Athenian economy it must still have been a modest contribution. Shortly before the end of the 6th century, black-figure pottery gave way to red-figure pottery (now the motifs on the vases remained the color of the clay, while the background was filled in with the slip, and in firing turned black) that in its turn became a great export success. We should not forget, though, that this was luxury ware: the pottery used daily by common people was always locally produced and cheap.

Presumably, grain started to be imported into Greece from Sicily and from the Greek colonies on the northern coasts of the Black Sea from the 6th century BC. But it is not known whether these imports occurred regularly enough for some of the Greek *poleis* to become dependent on imported grain. Probably that was not the case yet, and the imports of grain in this period were relatively negligible. From Greece there developed some export trade in wine and olive oil to non-Greek areas such as the coasts of southern France and Spain as well as the northern coasts of the Black Sea.

Social Hierarchy

An agrarian society

In many areas around the Mediterranean Sea, those who worked the fields lived with their families in villages or small towns, not in isolated farmsteads. The reason may have been the scarcity of water sources, which forced groups of people to share what available water there was. In any case, such "agricultural towns" and their surrounding territories formed strong economic units, the inhabitants of the town living off the land outside that they owned and either worked themselves or had worked for them by renters or serfs. This was the pattern in Greece, in large parts of Italy, and also in Syria, Palestine, and in other regions of the Near East. Beyond the grain fields of the community, there was a zone of uncultivated countryside left for sheep and goats to graze in and where sometimes hunting could take place. There one would find undisturbed nature, in contrast to the cultivated areas, always inhospitable and potentially dangerous, the abode of herdsmen, robbers, tramps, and all sorts of "weird" people, those literally on the margins of society. In Greece, it was only small groups or even individuals who were thus characterized, but in the Near East and North Africa complete tribes with their livestock moved around in the border zones between the agricultural areas and the deserts. Barter, robbery, raids, and pillage usually made up what contacts they had with the sedentary populations. They were the outsiders in societies dominated by the inhabitants of villages or agricultural towns.

In that agrarian world, society was divided along several lines. There was, first, the division between men and women: only men had a voice in the affairs of the community, and only they could vote in an assembly wherever there was such an institution. In the past, it was sometimes thought that in antiquity or in prehistory there had been societies ruled by women or where women at least would have played a dominant role, but any evidence for that is lacking—even the custom of some peoples of giving their children the family names of the mothers or letting inheritances pass along the female line are not the "relics" of such a supposed "matriarchal" society. A second division was between members of the group and all outsiders, to which belonged not only the marginalized people mentioned in the preceding text, but also foreigners from another town or city, and slaves. The foreigner on a visit could normally expect temporary hospitality but would only very seldom be permanently accepted into the community. Slaves would remain outsiders too, at least in Greece.

Slavery

Slaves were "un-free" individuals who were the personal property of their owners and could be bought, sold, or set free at will by their owner. Slaves were captured in war or slave raids, or sold to slave traders by kidnappers or sometimes as young children by their own parents, or were born in slavery to slave parents, although the latter possibility was in all likelihood rare. Of the early forms of slavery in the Near East and the Mediterranean world, much is still unknown. Presumably, the number of slaves was relatively low in comparison with later periods of antiquity. That may have been because in small-scale agriculture, slavery did not substantially enhance production, because there was not enough work for them. In crafts and commerce, though, slaves could be employed. However, as long as the level of these activities remained relatively modest in the Greek world, the overall utility of slaves remained limited. Consequently, the possession of slaves in Greece in this period was mainly a status symbol: both male and female slaves worked in the households of the rich as personal servants. Probably, this was true also of Egypt and the Near East, although there the numbers of slaves possessed by a rich man could be much higher, while the Persian kings and their satraps certainly employed great numbers of these un-free persons, a few of whom by their close proximity to the ruler could sometimes wield great influence behind the scenes. In Greece, before the 5th century BC, slavery was not widespread, but the possession of slaves as status symbols must have contributed to the development of a mentality that associated manual labor with slavery and coupled the notion of a free citizen with the ideal of not having to work for one's livelihood. That mentality naturally was more pronounced in those who possessed slaves, but to some extent these ideas filtered down to the whole of the free population.

Groups intermediate between slavery and freedom

The line separating slavery and freedom in the Archaic period was not always clear. For instance, in Greece, there were groups in society that were not regarded as slaves officially, but were de facto slaves who were not accepted into the community of the *polis*. Thus, Sparta had its subjugated population of helots: they had to till the plots of land assigned to individual Spartans and surrender a large part of the produce to them; they had no freedom of movement, being bound to their masters and to the fields they had to work. Yet, individual Spartans could not freely dispose of "their" helots as if they were slaves, for example, by selling them or setting them free, for it was only the state that could give them their freedom. Thus, the helots were slaves of the Spartan *polis*, of which they could not be citizens. Somewhat comparable situations existed in Crete, where the Dorians had established many small states that were usually, as in Sparta, based on a clear demarcation between citizen-warriors on the one hand and an indigenous subject population on the other. The latter worked the fields of the citizens but had presumably a slightly better position in society than the helots in Sparta. In Thessaly, in the beginning of the 1st millennium BC, an aristocracy emerged that had more or less divided the peasant population among themselves; we hear of large numbers of serfs belonging to individual noblemen. Their exact status is hard to delineate, but it seems that the serfs here were more closely bound to their overlords, whereas in Crete and especially in Sparta they were primarily subject to the collectivity of the *polis*. Traces of comparable institutions have been found in various other Greek states, but the details are mostly unknown to us. In all these cases, however, the affected people had been living in a certain area for some time before being subjugated by the citizens or the elites of *poleis* founded in their midst, and although they were not formally treated as slaves, they were reduced to a position of serfdom and were never adopted into the communities of the *poleis*. In Italy, we may think of the city-states of the Etruscans, where, as far as we know, the indigenous Italic populations lived in a state of serfdom. Greek colonies in Sicily, such as Syracuse, and presumably many Greek cities on the coasts of the Black Sea, had also reduced the indigenous populations in the vicinity to a form of serfdom, if not downright slavery.

Citizens with inferior status

The cases referred to in the preceding text concerned population groups that although not formally slaves, were kept apart from the citizen-community and lived in conditions that closely resembled slavery. But in many societies of the Archaic period, it was also quite normal for some citizens who were considered members of the *polis*, the state, the people, or some other recognized collectivity to nevertheless live in complete dependence and submission to richer or more powerful members of the same community; thus, in practice, they were un-free. Many, if not the majority of the population in most states of the Near East and in Egypt must have lived in these conditions. Certainly, in Egypt, the greater part of the peasant population lived in complete dependence on local potentates who, whether in the name of the king or not, compelled them to provide various goods and services, thereby in practice binding the population to the soil. In Mesopotamia, there existed all sorts of rent or lease arrangements for longer periods that in practice turned the renter into a slave during the period concerned; sometimes, in legal documents, he was even called a slave, although his temporary condition was different from that of a "real" slave. In Greece too, renters were considered persons who were not totally free and were therefore accepted only as second-class citizens in the emerging *poleis*. We know that at around 600 BC in Athens, poor peasants had to surrender one-sixth of their produce to rich landowners, probably as a form of interest on what they had borrowed with their land as security. When Solon put an end to this, he presented it as a liberation, just as he had liberated other citizens who had borrowed by pledging their own persons as security and fallen into debt slavery. Early Rome had its *clientes*: persons completely dependent on their *patronus*, and originally perhaps their renters; but even if this was not the case, they had to obey their lord "as a father" in exchange for his protection. This kind of strong dependency between members of the same political community as we find with the Roman *clientela* was unknown in Greece, at least in the form of a generally recognized and respected institution, and this may in part explain why in Greece at the end of the Archaic period—and even more so in the subsequent period—the idea of equality among all citizens could re-assert itself, but not in Rome.

The *fulai* in Greece

Characteristic of the Greek *polis* as a community of citizens was the institution of the *fule*. The term is usually translated as "tribe"; it denoted an organization to which one belonged by birth. The Dorian *poleis* of Greece were always subdivided into three *fulai*. Elsewhere that number could vary; in Athens, for instance, it was four. In origin, perhaps, the function of these *fulai* may have been primarily military, but already in the Archaic period they were also organizations through which the citizens participated in the religious festivals and ceremonies of the community. Because all citizens, rich and poor, belonged to the *fulai*, these institutions to some extent strengthened a communal sentiment. Thus, they could also acquire political functions, for instance, in the selection of groups of citizens rotating in councils or commissions—in the democracies after around 500 BC, that function of the *fulai* would become more important. In Rome, on the other hand, the *tribus* had much less importance. The original three were in the course of the 6th century BC supplanted by local or territorial districts, also named *tribus*, their purpose being the levying of taxes and the levying of soldiers. They lacked a religious function, so that the *tribus* never became "living" institutions that could enhance feelings of community or even equality.

Primitive forms of egalitarianism

In Rome, any sense of community was primarily fostered by the institutions of the *clientela* and the *gens*, the former based on the relations of dependency between the poor and the rich, and the weak and the powerful; the latter based on the solidarity between related families. The Greek *polis* had hardly any organizations that could be compared with these. This seems to be a fundamental difference that has been explained, sometimes, by the assumption that the *polis* was rooted in a form of society in the Dark Age in which not property or birth but people's age was the organizing principle, hence the term *age class society*. In such a society, all members born in the same year undergo a collective form of upbringing or training, after which they are adopted into the community; rights and obligations depend on the age of the person, and in general, authority lies with the elderly. In the early 20th century AD, various African societies still followed such a pattern. Whether it was once common in Greece, however, is hard to prove. But to a large extent, this pattern can indeed be discerned in Crete, and especially in Sparta. Thus, in Sparta all boys from the age of 7 were raised collectively—an upbringing that inflicted deliberate hardships: the famous Spartan education—and organized into age or year groups. The adult men in Sparta formed messes called *sussitia* consisting of small groups of men—not family members—of various ages, of which the oldest again was the leader, who had to dine together on a daily basis and also, sleeping in one tent, formed the smallest units in the army. Typically, they called themselves the *homoioi* or Peers. In Sparta, this social organization existed at least since the 6th century BC, although our sources describing it mostly date from later times. Presumably, the Spartan organization had deliberately strengthened the features of equality, collectivity, and frugality in the 6th or even 5th centuries BC, lending Spartan society also an air of artificiality, by which it set itself clearly apart from other *poleis*. However, Spartan social organization probably was rooted in age-class traditions going back to the Dark Age. That is presumably true for Crete as well, but whether other Greek *poleis* had comparable origins remains unknown, because the evidence is lacking. Yet, it is striking that the Greek *polis*, notwithstanding all divisions of wealth and prestige among its citizens, was based on a relatively strong sense of community and equality: an underlying egalitarianism that in a subsequent period would give rise to the first democracy in history.

Rich and poor: Property classes among the citizenry

As yet, in the Archaic period, there certainly was no democracy in the true sense of the word. On the contrary, this period seems to have been characterized by a growing inequality in property and status. Property, or the lack of it, became more than ever the criterion by which one's place in society was measured. Growing divisions in wealth within the *polis* since roughly the 8th century BC—resulting, among other things, from the renewed contacts between Greece and the Near East—must have put an end to any "equality," wherever that may have existed, except in places where the power of collectivity managed to suppress individual manifestations of wealth. That was, again, the case in Sparta, where in the later Archaic period—and for a long time afterward—various forms of luxury were officially forbidden and where the equality of all the citizens became, at least officially, an equality in frugality. In practice, in Sparta too some citizens were richer than others, but they could hardly show off their wealth except by breeding horses, for in the *sussitia* all citizens ate the same food and were clad in the same simple manner, while any displays of luxury in houses, either internal or external, were forbidden. In other states, the growing differences in wealth between the citizens in the Archaic period led to new subdivisions of the citizenry apart from the *fulai*, divisions that were based solely on their property. Thus, in Athens, as we have seen, Solon changed an existing division of three groups by birth into a division based on property, measuring the latter by bushels of grain and adding a top class of "500-bushel-men" set apart from the *hippeis* or Knights. The citizens belonging to these two upper classes had more political rights and influence than those of the two lower classes.

Comparable subdivisions of the citizens can be seen in other city-states as well. In Rome, a census was introduced in connection with the organization of the hoplite army in the 6th century: those who were called up for the *legio* and therefore must have had enough property to afford the necessary equipment were wealthier than those who were not called up. In Greece also, in the later 6th century BC, the spread of hoplite equipment and phalanx tactics in various *poleis* led to the enrollment of citizens into hoplite armies on the basis of their wealth. Often, this entailed a certain division between full or first-rate citizenship for those who served in the army and a lesser or second-rate citizenship for those who could not. Nearly everywhere, membership of councils and the tenure of magistracies remained the prerogative of citizens "of the first class." Thus, the rise of hoplite warfare contributed to the tendency of assigning rights and obligations to the citizens on the basis of property. On the other hand, the hoplite class grew so large—in the 5th century, it would be at least 40% of the free population—that the existence of the citizen-hoplites hindered the emergence of smaller and closed aristocracies. At the same time, the underlying sense of equality of all citizens could find expression in the organizations of the *fulai* and in religious festivities of the entire community in which everybody could participate. The rich and the aristocrats exhibited their supremacy on the occasions of parades and games by literally riding or sitting in front of the other citizens, but this was only natural: only they in the Archaic period held the high magistracies and only they enjoyed the leisure to devote themselves fully to sports or cultural activities. Thus, the Archaic period especially was the period in Greek history in which the rich and the aristocrats enjoyed an unabashed preeminence in society without, however, completely excluding the poor.

Political Organization

The monarchies of Egypt and the Near East

In Egypt and the Near East, the highest authority was usually vested in a king, while lower functionaries derived their authority from him. In his turn, the king as a rule derived his authority from some form of selection by the gods. This was the case in, for example, China, where the so-called Mandate of Heaven bestowed absolute power on the king as long as he maintained his position; a successful conqueror or rebel who expelled him

Figure 14 The Narmer Palette from Egypt (c. 3100 BC). The so-called Narmer Palette, preserved in the Egyptian Museum in Cairo, is a 63-cm-tall stone plaque with relief sculptures on both sides. These show the power of the pharaoh in a graphic manner. The pharaoh in question is called Narmer: the hieroglyphs for that name are on both sides at the top, between the heads of the horned goddess Hathor. Narmer must have reigned immediately before the First Dynasty (about 3100 BC). To the right, we see him wearing the crown of Upper Egypt, wielding a club, with a defeated enemy at his feet. This enemy is called Wash. The scene above the head of Wash seems to indicate that the king (in the shape of the falcon god Horus) has conquered the Nile delta (symbolized by the papyrus stalks). Behind Narmer there is a servant carrying his sandals, and at the bottom register there are two more defeated enemies. On the other side of the Palette, we see Narmer again, now wearing the crown of Lower Egypt, who proceeded by standard bearers has come to inspect his decapitated enemies, neatly laid out in two rows. In the bottom register, the king in the shape of a bull tramples his enemy and crashes through a city wall. The middle register has two mythical creatures (whose necks intertwine to form a small basin for cosmetics; hence, "palette"). They might stand for Upper and Lower Egypt now united under a single ruler. Photo: Ivy Close Images/Alamy

proved thereby that the Mandate of Heaven had passed from an unworthy person to a new ruler. There is undoubtedly a connection between the notion of such a divine foundation of absolute monarchy and a strictly hierarchical structure of society that rested, ultimately, upon a peasant population that was coerced into delivering the necessary goods and labor. Egypt provides probably the closest parallel to China. Here too, it was a vastly underprivileged peasant population that had to support a social pyramid of functionaries and ministers, above whom towered the king as a living god on earth. For the pharaoh was seen as an incarnation of Ra, the sun god, or of Amun, the high god equated with Ra, which lent his orders the aura of divine sanction. In the Near East, kingship usually lacked such an explicitly expressed divine character. In Mesopotamia, since the time of the Sumerians, the king was considered to be the first "servant" of the deity, his "beloved son" on Earth, but not himself divine, a representation of kingship that was also cultivated by the Persians. In practice, however, it did not make much difference whether the king was seen as divine in his own person or as an especially elected person with a unique relationship with the gods, for in both cases his absolute power could invoke the divine will.

Matters could become a little more complicated when, for example, high priests mediated that special relationship with the gods. In such a situation, there existed a delicate balance between the king, whose power often rested on his function as commander of the army, and the priests, who guarded the customs and laws guaranteed by the gods. This was the case, for instance, among the Israelites, especially in the small kingdom of Judah, and presumably among more peoples in the region of Palestine and Syria. It was also the situation prevalent in India, where in many small kingdoms in the north of the country, the kings were increasingly circumscribed in their ability to rule by the priests, who developed into a powerful caste that was ultimately recognized as the highest in society. In a few places in India, the kings even disappeared, to be replaced by aristocracies of warriors and priests. Elsewhere in Asia, the republic was a phenomenon that was practically unknown, except among the Phoenicians, some of whose city-states were probably governed by aristocratic councils rather than kings. In any case, the Phoenician colony of Carthage was such an aristocratic republic. But these are exceptions to the rule: we may conclude that practically everywhere in the civilized world, monarchy was the norm, and it generally provided the most effective form of government. Certainly, where large territorial states emerged that demanded a strong central government, monarchy, and especially absolute monarchy in which the ruler's authority was in one way or another sanctioned by the gods, was in fact the only form of government that could hold such realms together. That was true of the Assyrian and the Neo-Babylonian kingdoms, and it was possibly even truer of the vast Persian empire. In the eyes of educated Asians, the Greek *polis*, therefore, seemed something abnormal and even primitive.

The Greek *polis*

In the emerging *poleis* of Dark Age Greece, here and there a person with the title of *basileus* held a monarchical position, but he was always first among equals, that is, among other aristocrats, and was never an absolute monarch. In course of time, when the aristocratic elites became richer and more powerful, this ancient kingship disappeared practically everywhere. Only in Sparta, which preserved some older institutions, did kingship survive—and there, in the remarkable form of a double kingship in which two kings from two different families always reigned side by side. But even in Sparta, the kings did not have very much more authority than to command the army. In other places, we hear sometimes of an annually chosen *basileus*, a magistrate with certain priestly functions. Magistrates were persons who had been chosen for a fixed term, usually one year, to perform certain government functions for the community. The Greek *polis* was a form of political organization that was characterized by a cooperative collective of magistrates, the council, and the assembly of the people.

The assembly of the people had very ancient roots, almost certainly going back to assemblies of warriors, that is, of all able-bodied and armed men of the community. Such warrior assemblies were not unknown among other peoples, both among Semitic peoples in the Near East—at least, the oldest history of the Israelites provides some glimpses of that institution—and among various Indo-European peoples, such as Italic and Germanic tribes. In many cases, this ancient warrior assembly disappeared in the course of time, certainly when the people involved came to inhabit an ever larger territory. In Greece, the epics of Homer refer to such assemblies of men at arms. They did not have much power: the men could not do very much more than shout approval or disapproval of decisions made by the aristocratic lords—and in cases of disapproval, it is not clear that the latter acted on public sentiment. In Sparta, in any case, it was laid down in a rudimentary "constitution" of the 7th century BC that when the assembly of the people voted "the wrong way," it was the kings and the council who made the final decision. Still, the mere fact that practically everywhere in Greece an assembly of the people was preserved in one form or another would prove to be of great significance. The preservation of people's assemblies was, of course, made easier by the small size of the *poleis*: these were "states" where the political center that made the decisions was practically always at walking distance. In the Archaic period, the powers of the assembly became more formalized, mainly where the election of magistrates was concerned. The growth in power of the aristocracies that monopolized the magistracies did indeed threaten the position of the assemblies, but a formal abolishment of the assembly seldom, if ever, occurred. There was, however, a tendency to limit access to the people's assembly to those citizens in possession of a certain minimum property: since the 6th century BC, those who could afford hoplite equipment. In some city-states, this must have been introduced as a formal requirement. In Athens, on the other had, since Solon, the assembly of the people was open to even the poorest citizens, the *thetes*, and this would facilitate the emergence, toward the end of the 6th century BC, of a real democracy.

Every year, in the *poleis*, magistrates were chosen to perform functions such as army commanders, judges, and priests of certain important deities of the city. There were not that many functions to perform, and the number of magistrates, therefore, always remained small. In Athens, they were called *archontes*, and there were nine in all, although only three of them had administrative tasks to perform. One of them gave his name to the year; the list of such so-called eponymous archons came to be used for dating events in the past and would thus provide a chronological base for later historiography. Possibly already in the 6th century BC, that list was put into writing in the form of an inscription in stone—in any case, such an inscription existed in the later 5th century BC—and that was a decision that in many ways was typical of the Greek *polis*. Already in the second half of the 7th century BC, some decisions of the *polis* were preserved in writing. The oldest epigraphic document of such a decision that has come down to us is the decision of a small *polis* in Crete at around 630 BC concerning the election of magistrates, laying down the rule that one could not hold the same magistracy twice within ten years. After Solon had acquired the authority to introduce far-reaching reforms in Athens around 590 BC, his enactments were written down on wooden tablets that were preserved on the Acropolis. In this manner, an important principle was realized: the laws of the community should be written laws that could be looked up and verified, so that the decisions of magistrates could be examined in the light of the laws. Thereby, not only was the subjectivity of magisterial decisions limited to some degree, but also the idea was fostered that the laws might be fixed in writing but could also be amended; that, in principle, laws were not unchangeable and that new laws could replace older ones, in short, that the organization of the *polis* was not something established for eternity but could be shaped by the *politai*, the citizens, themselves. Thus, ultimately, "politics" came into being. In the Archaic period, that remained rudimentary at best, but its foundation was nonetheless laid in the *poleis* of that period.

Whereas the magistrates mostly held their positions for one year and the assemblies of the people usually met only a few times in a year at the most, the various councils in the Greek states were more permanent governing bodies. As a rule, membership was for life. In the Archaic period, their composition was usually aristocratic in that only persons of some prestige were admitted to them. In Athens, this meant that after Solon, ex-archons, who were always citizens belonging to one of the two highest property classes, automatically became members of the council called *Areopagus*. In Sparta, it was 28 citizens aged over 60 and enjoying enough public esteem to be chosen by acclamation—hence its name *gerousia* or "council of elders"—that together with the two kings formed a permanent council of 30. In other *poleis*, the councils were of a more or less similar composition: their members were former magistrates and/or of a certain minimum age. These councils often functioned in an informal way, but in some cases it was laid down that decisions of the assembly of the people should first have the approval of the council, while the council also acted sometimes as a court in serious cases such as high treason. In fact, the power of the council in an aristocracy was always considerable; since the short-tenured magistrates came from the same social background as the councilors and were looking forward to becoming members of the council themselves, they did not often oppose the wishes of the latter.

Thus, in the archaic *poleis* the aristocracy retained its political power by its dominance of the magistracies and the councils. Yet, in the 6th century BC, in some *poleis* the idea was voiced that the *demos*, meaning the "common people" as opposed to the aristocracy, should have more of a say in politics. Sometimes, the powers of the people's assembly were indeed expanded, and/or a new council was introduced, democratically selected from among all citizens or at least from a much larger segment of the population than the aristocratic councils were. These councils had hundreds of citizens as members, often selected on the basis of the *fulai*, and were much larger than most aristocratic councils. Perhaps Athens, since the time of Solon, had such a council of 400—a hundred from each *fule*—but this is uncertain. In any case, even with such a council, Athens still was not a full democracy. Very little is unknown about early forms of democracy in other states. When Athens in 508/7 BC received a truly democratic constitution, it was indeed based on both an extension of the powers of the assembly and on the introduction of a new and large council side by side with the existing *Areopagus*.

The period of aristocratic dominance in the Greek *poleis* was also characterized by the phenomenon of the *turannis*. The *turannoi* were ambitious aristocrats who by using force managed to arrogate power to themselves and thus turned their fellow aristocrats into their political enemies. In order to maintain their position, the *turannoi* employed mercenary soldiers from abroad and presumably also equipped some members of the lower classes of their own states as soldiers. Moreover, they often sought political support from the non-aristocratic segments of their population. As a result, they generally undermined the grip of the aristocracy on politics and society. The *turannis* was in the Greek context an abnormal form of monarchy that as a rule lasted only a couple of years or decades. After the expulsion of the "tyrants," practically everywhere the aristocrats returned to power. But they had henceforth to reckon with a *demos* that had acquired new strength, especially because the spread of hoplite tactics made it advisable to accept citizens into the army who could afford hoplite equipment, so that toward the end of the 6th century BC, a large part of the *demos* was politically much more empowered than it had ever been. Several *poleis* in this way developed into moderate oligarchies, that is, literally, constitutions in which only "few" ruled. It was a form of government that could be distinguished from an aristocracy in that the ruling few were selected not on the basis of birth or prestige, but exclusively on the basis of property. In such oligarchies, the actual citizenship, and with it admittance to the people's assembly, was reserved for those who could serve as hoplites. In Athens, on the other hand, the fall of the *turannis* of Hippias, the son and successor of Pisistratus, in 510 BC led after a short power struggle between aristocratic factions not to an oligarchy but to the introduction of democracy.

Etruscans, Italians, and Rome

In Italy, the Etruscan cities during the Archaic period were, as far as we know, ruled by kings. It is possible that those kings wielded more effective power than a *basileus* in Dark Age Greece had possessed. But we have also to reckon with the possibility that these Etruscan kings in the 7th and 6th centuries BC imitated the Greek *turannoi* and ruled in a more authoritarian fashion than before. At any rate, after some generations they too met resistance from aristocratic circles in their cities, and in the late 6th and 5th centuries they, like the Greek "tyrants," gave way to aristocratic republics. Assemblies of the people did not exist here, nor did they emerge when the Etruscans adopted hoplite tactics. The Italic peoples, on the other hand, were acquainted with such assemblies—or rather, warrior assemblies—as well as with councils. Besides, in many places, there was a form of kingship that must have resembled the rule of a *basileus* in Dark Age Greece, although the kingship in Italy may have had a stronger religious and priestly character. Thus, early Rome had a *rex*, a council of elders or *senatus*, and an assembly of the citizens in arms. In all probability, under Etruscan rule, the authority of the kings of Rome was strengthened, a development that would in the end lead to the expulsion of the kings from the city by the Roman aristocrats. Then, according to tradition in 510 BC, Rome too acquired the constitution of a republic in which annually appointed magistrates took over the most important tasks of the former kings.

Peoples in West and Central Europe

The triad of king, council, and assembly of the people was characteristic of Greece in the Dark Age and of the Italic peoples until about 500 BC. Very little is known about the social and political organization of peoples elsewhere in Europe in this early period. It is certain, though, that nowhere in Europe in this period were there territorial states with a distinct political center and governed at the local level by functionaries and servants acting in the name of, or appointed by, a monarch, such as the states of Asia and Egypt. In western and central Europe, not only were the material foundations for such developed states—such as urban centers and a script—lacking, but also several peoples and tribes were still on the move, expanding at the expense of others, or migrating to new areas of settlement, sometimes over great distances. As a consequence, men who possessed arms and were able to fight were considered free, whereas others, in practice often the peasant populations of conquered territories, were seen as more or less un-free, serfs, or subjects of the men with arms. The assemblies of these warriors, even in the guise of people's or tribal assemblies, did not produce a primitive democracy, since the traditional supremacy of the leaders and aristocrats was well entrenched. That supremacy manifested itself sometimes in strong bonds of dependency of groups of warriors on an aristocratic chief, relationships that bore some resemblance with the Roman *clientela*, but went much further in that they demanded unconditional loyalty—even unto death—of the warriors to their leader. Perhaps, similar organizations of warrior bands had existed also in Dark Age Greece and in Archaic Italy, but with the development of *polis* and the city-state there, they had disappeared. Among Celts and Germanic peoples, as well as among a few others in Europe, on the other hand, these organizations remained in existence for a longer time. On the one hand, they stimulated migration movements and military expansion, whereas on the other hand they hindered the emergence of stronger political structures and more durable states.

A connection between political and military organizations

Thus, there was a certain interconnectedness between the internal political development and the military organization of a community. In Greece, among the peoples of Italy, and in large parts of Europe, there was a clear tendency to consider only the warriors as full members of the community. In Greece and Italy, though, this tendency was fully realized only in some places, for instance, in Sparta and a few other *poleis* where all citizens were hoplites. In many Greek states, the warrior assemblies developed into people's assemblies. But it was only in Greece that the idea of an equality in principle of all citizens on this basis could establish itself and could, toward the end of the Archaic period, even give rise to democracy. In Rome and elsewhere, such notions were more than adequately countered by the much stronger bonds of *clientela* and of personal loyalty to a chief. Still, nearly everywhere in Europe as a rule, the ability to fight together with one's neighbors or kinsmen made a man truly a member of a community. Conversely, military service was, from the Greek *polis* to the Celtic tribe, an obligation as well as a right of those who called themselves free. The world of large territorial states and monarchies in Egypt and Asia was very different from this. There, warfare was in the hands of a relatively small and professional elite that during a military campaign could form the core of large conscript militias raised from a subject population. This was, with many variations, the case from China to the Persian Empire. The royal court maintained some specialized troops, since the 2nd millennium BC charioteers, and since the early 1st millennium, cavalry as well as royal bodyguards. But however costly that professional core army might be—and certainly the cost of maintaining the horses was levied, ultimately, from the peasant population—in times of war, it had to be supplemented with recruits, mainly again from the peasant populations. But however large some armies for some particular campaigns might have been, they always constituted but a small percentage of the total population. The mass of the people was essentially disarmed, for as a rule the drafted recruits received their arms from the royal arsenals and returned them at the end of a campaign. A Greek citizen, on the other hand, kept his spear and his shield at home and only a "tyrant" could try to disarm the citizens. In Greek eyes, therefore, all those subject to the Great King of Persia were, in fact, no more than slaves.

Chapter 3.3

Daily Life and Mentality

The Individual and Society

The main forms of collective entertainment

Social life in Greece was mainly a man's business: dinner parties and literary circles were, a few exceptions notwithstanding, all-male affairs, just as clubs and all sorts of collective entertainment were predominantly the preserve of men. Of the social life of the vast majority of the people hardly anything is known. We are, paradoxically, comparatively well informed about some very exceptional societies such as Sparta. But there are parallels between the various cultures: in broad outlines, the social life of all or most male members of a given community or of just its elite was based on the pleasures of collective hunting, collective and competitive sports or play, collectively staging a plundering raid outside the territory of one's community, and, finally, eating, drinking, and singing—or listening to songs—together. There was in these forms of collective entertainment, moreover, a clear distinction between the highly developed states of Asia and Egypt on the one hand and the cultures of Europe on the other. In the former, hunting was in practice a privilege of the kings and the elites, while raiding and plundering by the common people was subject to severe limitations as well: in fact, the kings reserved these pleasures for themselves too. Of communal meals, outside the sphere of religion, we hear very little in these states, except again among the elites and at the royal courts. Several forms of sport and play were undoubtedly indulged in by most people, but our knowledge of these entertainments is very limited. In contrast, among European peoples, and certainly in the more "primitive" parts of Europe, all these forms of entertainment were open to all free men of the community, that is, all those who could afford some weapons. This was, among the Iberians, the Celts, and the ancestors of the Germanic peoples, a world of male clubs and warrior bands, often but not always led by more "aristocratic" leaders, who fought, hunted, and feasted together. In essence, this was the background of the situation in Greece as well.

Greek sagas and the epics of Homer show us the heroes in small bands on the hunt, in warlike or adventurous enterprises, or feasting together around the hearth of the *basileus*.

Antiquity: Greeks and Romans in Context, First Edition. Frederick G. Naerebout and Henk W. Singor.
© 2014 John Wiley & Sons, Inc. Published 2014 by John Wiley & Sons, Inc.

Further, they are seen practicing all sorts of sports, such as athletics, wrestling, boxing, and disk throwing. Sporting competitions were often held on the occasion of some hero's cremation, in which case they can be considered as being held in honor of the dead man, but they were staged on other occasions as well. In Homer, it looks as if only aristocrats participated, but in reality, in the Dark Age other men too must have taken part in such games, in hunts and in raids, albeit more incidentally, whereas these activities must have been the normal pastime for aristocrats. In Sparta, such a life remained even in later times the norm for all free members of society—but that exceptional society considered itself an aristocracy with respect to the mass of subjugated helots who had to perform all the labor. In Sparta, social life was based on the *sussitia*: the messes or clubs of the Peers, who ate together and who formed the smallest units in the army. Here, sports were clearly part of the collective upbringing of the young and therefore a matter involving the state. Elsewhere in Archaic Greece, however, sports and communal meals were primarily the domain of the aristocracies. In the territories of densely populated *poleis*, hunting became

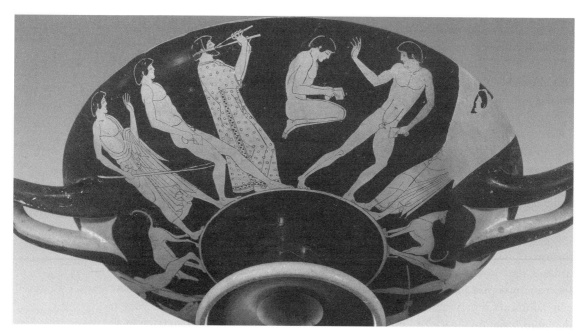

Figure 15   Outside of an Athenian cup with a *gumnasion* scene (early 5th c. BC). The painter Douris decorated and signed this Athenian red-figure *kulix*, a cup for drinking wine, in early 5th-century Athens. It now is in the Antikenmuseum in Basle. What we see on the outside of the cup is a typical *gumnasion* scene, with three young men practicing the long jump, part of the pentathlon. They move to the rhythm of a tune played on the *aulos*, an oboe-like instrument. On the left, there is another man carrying a forked stick, which identifies him as the trainer. All three jumpers carry weights in their hands. These so-called *halteres*, made of stone or bronze, and weighing about 2.5 kg each, were used to increase the impetus of the jump and thus extend its length. How the jump was performed is not exactly known, and despite the fact that we have a jumper in full flight, his technique cannot be deduced from this image. The *gumnasion* is an important institution of the polis, as was the *sumposion*, where this cup was to be used. The *gumnasion* as an ideal is what the painter has tried to express; he certainly did not aim for a realistic depiction of a sports event. Photo: Antikenmuseum Basel und Sammlung Ludwig/A. Voegelin

less important, while private raiding and plundering more or less vanished when warfare had become more and more a community affair.

Games in Greece: The *gumnasion*

Games in Archaic Greece had always had a sacred character. One of their purposes had been, as stated in the preceding text, to honor a dead nobleman; the atmosphere surrounding the games was in any case ceremonial, and they were always connected with some sanctuary or religious festival. In another respect, the games almost functioned as substitutes for warfare, and the victors were feted by their home cities as if they had won battles in a war. It is no coincidence that the growth of a certain sense of common "Greekness" in the Archaic period went hand in hand with the rise of games at a couple of sanctuaries that were open to participants from the entire Greek world. The most important of these sanctuaries was that of Zeus at Olympia in the Peloponnese. During the Olympic Games, a sacred armistice was proclaimed, for warfare was, as it were, temporarily replaced by another sort of competition; at least, this was the ideal. The Olympic Games were held every fourth year (fifth according to the Greek method of counting), their regular recurrence eventually leading to a method of reckoning time in terms of Olympiads. According to tradition, the first games were held in 776 BC, a date that should be more or less correct, although the exact beginning is still disputed. It is certain that they did begin rather small with only a foot race, but soon a chariot race must have been added, and in the 7th and 6th centuries BC both the number of participants from various Greek *poleis* and the number of different sporting events steadily grew, with wrestling, jumping, disk throwing, boxing, and others being added to the program. The prestige won by the victors was enormous, although formally they received only an olive crown as their prize—but already before the Classical period, the home cities of the winners would often supplement these honorary prizes with substantial sums of money. Apart from Olympia, Delphi and Corinth could boast famous Panhellenic games, but every *polis* of some importance had its special festival at which sports games would be held—in Athens, for instance, the festival of the Panathenaea, in honor of the city goddess Athena, was celebrated annually, and every fourth ("fifth") year with especially great splendor.

In the past, historians often assumed that the frequent sporting competitions among the Greeks were typical of the Greek mentality, an indicator of a culture that was more competitive than other cultures. That the Greeks, and especially the aristocrats, had a very competitive mindset is beyond doubt, but a similar or very comparable mentality can be observed in many cultures. However, the competitiveness in Archaic Greece, perhaps as a result of the overall aristocratic dominance in society, was able to stamp its mark on a wide segment of Greek culture, not just in the field of sports. What is certain is that this competitiveness in general, and in particular in the field of sports and athletics, was responsible for the origin of an important phenomenon in Greek culture: the *gumnasion*. The *gumnasion* was a place for physical exercise. During the course of the 6th century, several *poleis* introduced public spaces for the use of citizens, usually consisting of a square, open-air, sand-covered field for practicing various sports, especially wrestling. The performing area was sometimes surrounded by arcades, resting rooms, facilities for massaging and oiling, for changing clothes, etc. Citizens who did not have a suitable place for physical exercise at home could come here for their training. As a result, sports no longer was the exclusive domain of the aristocrats, but common citizens too were now able to devote themselves to such pastimes. Thus, the state became directly involved in the physical regimen of its citizens and the training and education of the young, for it was especially the younger citizens that frequented these *gumnasia*. In a later period, artistic and intellectual subjects would be taught there as well, so that for a very long time the *gumnasion* would exert an enormous influence on the education of the Greek *politai*, the citizens of a *polis*.

The *sumposion*

Among the aristocracies of Archaic Greece, that other near-universal form of entertainment for male clubs or warrior bands, the common meal, also developed into a specifically Greek institution the *sumposion*. A *sumposion*, literally a drinking party, usually began after dinner and was accompanied by songs, poetry, storytelling, jokes, and riddles, and enlivened by the presence of attractive young servants, both male and female. The parties would often end in drunkenness and licentious behavior, sometimes in quarrels, fights, and long-lingering feuds, but at the same time provided the breeding ground for a completely new form of literature. This was the world of lyric poetry, a form of poetry in which the experiences of the poet himself or of his public took center stage. This poetry was not about the traditional, heroic stories that the epic dealt with, but about the deeds and emotions of living persons. The subject could well be of a political nature—for instance, in exhortations to one's fellow citizens to remain steadfast in a coming battle—but more often they were strictly personal: love poetry, erotic verse, and drinking songs. In the 7th century BC, the fashion of lying down at dinner instead of sitting reached Greece from the Near East, so that men learned to eat and to drink lying on couches, leaning on their left elbow. This fashion quickly spread over nearly the whole Greek world and Italy. Henceforth, a civilized man would lie down at dinner, whereas women and children, slaves and barbarians, had to sit on chairs or stools. Children, the sons of aristocratic fathers in particular, were often allowed to be present at the *sumposia* of the adults, for their talk and entertainment, as long as drunkenness had not set in, were considered to have didactic value.

Literature and literacy

Greek civilization was for an important part built on the twin institutions of the *gumnasion* and the *sumposion*, which both developed in the Archaic period and can be considered as the way in which Greek aristocrats gave form to a kind of interaction that is characteristic of social life in many "primitive" warrior societies. It was in the Archaic period that Greece acquired its own literature. The epics of Homer were recited everywhere and would eventually eclipse all other epics about the same sagas. The work of the poet Hesiod from

Boeotia (around 700 BC) continued in the epic tradition, but it was quite different in its subject matter: a large didactic poem on husbandry called *Works and Days*, as well as a no less didactic poem on the origins and family relations of the many gods, goddesses, nymphs, and mythological beings called the *Theogony*. Hesiod was a well-to-do farmer, not an aristocrat, which makes his work for this period exceptional and very interesting. But it was the lyric poets of the 7th and 6th centuries BC who created really new poetry. In their poems, they were no longer bound to traditional meters like the epic hexameter but freely chose new ones or developed their own meters. They worked for aristocratic patrons, often for "tyrants," and were often aristocrats themselves; some of them worked for the *polis* community and wrote, for instance, choral poetry that had to be performed by choirs of singer-dancers at religious festivals.

The Archaic period was when the alphabet spread among the Greeks, and Greek culture became literate to some extent. But the use of the alphabet was still very limited. Texts could be inscribed on objects that were dedicated in sanctuaries, and laws and decisions of the *polis* could be inscribed in stone and erected at public places, but such documents were still relatively rare in the Archaic period. Gravestones and cenotaphs sometimes bore inscriptions but not invariably so. We may speak of a literacy that very slowly emerged. Only exceptional individuals possessed manuscripts in the shape of papyrus scrolls or pieces of animal skin: the professional singers who recited the epics; the lyric poets and their tyrant patrons; and some seers or oracle-mongers who tried to sell their sacred knowledge to tyrants or city councils. Books were always very expensive; sometimes they were left in temples for safe-keeping or acquired at the city's expense and then deposited in a sanctuary. In the latter case, they contained oracles and their explanations or divine advice on the occurrences of certain signs that could be consulted by the state in times of real or perceived danger. The art of reading and writing was certainly not common in this period, although we may assume that the numbers of illiterates among the free citizens gradually dropped. Even the Spartan collective upbringing provided some instruction in reading, writing, and counting, all on a no doubt elementary level—singing, dancing, and music were considered much more important. Of public education in the other *poleis*, though, we actually learn only in later periods. Certainly, every form of education provided or organized by the state must have been very simple, all forms of "higher" education remaining private and hence only affordable by the elites.

Men and Women

Demographics

Generally, in the period 900–500 BC, in most parts of Eurasia a regime of natural fertility prevailed. People did not try to limit their number of children and had families as large as the carrying capacity of their surroundings would permit. In a rather fertile but underpopulated area the population could rise quickly, only to stagnate when the limits of food production were reached. Presumably, in the fertile river valleys of Mesopotamia and

Egypt those limits had been reached already long before 900 BC and populations there had stabilized on the relatively high level that the local carrying capacity would permit. But in less developed areas, especially in southern Europe, in the early 1st millennium B.C. there were still possibilities for rapid population growth. This explains the increase in population in Greece especially in the 8th century BC, as well as the rapid development of Greek colonies from what were initially small settlements to important, and in some cases quite large cities such as the Greek colonies in Sicily. It also explains the increasing importance of Italy, which, beginning in the Archaic period, would develop into one of the most populous regions of the Mediterranean. When the material circumstances did not allow any further extension of the population, growth diminished and eventually halted automatically as a result of impoverishment and the accompanying higher mortality, especially of children, or by the emigration of the surplus numbers of the newborn. The latter phenomenon was common in Greece and Italy. Since the 8th century, the population in Greece grew very slowly, but there was a steady outflow of small groups and individuals settling in the new *poleis* along the shores of the Mediterranean and Black Sea or offering their services as mercenary soldiers in the great empires of the Near East and Egypt. In Italy, population growth stimulated the early expansion of the Italic peoples, an expansion that would be continued in subsequent centuries in the shape of the Roman conquests and the rising Roman Empire. Elsewhere too, the demographic factor was ultimately the driving force behind important historical processes, for example, in the case of the constant expansion of the Chinese states over north, central, and then south China, enormous areas that eventually became parts of a more or less homogenous state.

Of population numbers, we know very little. The *poleis* of Archaic Greece were doubtless very small, varying from a few hundred to a few thousand citizens. The whole of Greece south of Thessaly around 500 BC had presumably 1.5 million inhabitants at the most, and the whole of Egypt hardly more than 6 million. Large cities only existed in the Near East and in China, but their size is, again, difficult to estimate. Probably, Babylon in the 6th century BC had between 50,000 and 100,000 inhabitants, but these are tentative figures. It is, however, certain that practically everywhere along the Mediterranean Sea—at least along its European shores—the population in the period 900–500 BC rose considerably.

The Spartan model and the role of pederasty

In Sparta, girls married at around the age of 18 or even a little later, and the boys certainly not before their 20th year, most often between the ages of 25 and 30. This had everything to do with the social organization of Sparta and her system of age classes with collectively imposed obligations on the young and regulation of the private lives of citizens. An unforeseen effect of this system was probably that in Sparta in the Archaic period, in contrast to the rest of Greece, the citizen population did not rise and perhaps had already begun to decline very slowly. The unusually high age of marriage may have had the consequence that the average number of 5.8 live births per woman, which we think were required to sustain population levels in a pre-modern society such as ancient Greece, could not always be attained.

Sparta is an example of a community with a social organization that in the long run handicapped its demographic development. If, as has been presumed sometimes, Dark

Age Greek communities other than Sparta also adhered to the model of an age class society, their populations should probably have stagnated as well, until in the 9th and 8th centuries BC primitive egalitarian structure broke down owing to rising inequalities in property and wealth. Such inequalities caused lineage and property to become more important than marriageable age, and consequently communities permitted marriages at a younger age. This in its turn led to rising birth rates everywhere, except where the age class society was maintained at any cost, as was the case in Sparta. This is, however, a modern reconstruction and is by no means historically proven. But it is a reconstruction that to some extent offers a logical connection between the fragments of historical data that we have. It is a model that, moreover, offers an explanation for the fact that, again in historical Sparta and in Dorian Crete, homosexual relations between boys and unmarried young men were recognized by the state and even encouraged. Perhaps, this "institutionalized" homosexuality also had some roots in ancient initiation practices for boys at puberty, but in historical times it certainly served as a sexual substitute for postponed marriage. In other Greek states, homosexual relations—the normal Greek term was *paiderasteia* or pederasty—were common as well, but as far as we know they were not institutionalized in the way they were in Sparta (and among the aristocracies of Dorian Crete). In Athens and other cities, since the 6th century BC at the latest, pederasty played an important role in the lives of the aristocratic elites (of the common people we know in general much less in this and other respects). For elite men (not women!), a late age of marriage—the age of 30 was often seen as normal—played a part here too, but probably more important was the idealization of the young male body, fostered by the common practice of athletics in the nude. For boys of free citizen status, the age at which pederastic relationships were allowed was 18 in Athens and most probably elsewhere too—a Greek pederast should not be seen as a pedophile (although slave boys were never protected by the law). In addition, a certain admiration for and hence imitation of Spartan customs probably accounts for the popularity of pederasty in aristocratic circles in the classical age as well. In any case, since the Archaic age, pederasty remained an accepted phenomenon in Greek culture and was often idealized in poetry, philosophy, and art, in marked contrast to many other cultures in Eurasia.

Marriage and the core family

The rules and customs of marriage varied greatly across Eurasia, but from China to Western Europe monogamy was the rule, and polygamy was only allowed in exceptional cases. Likewise, it was mostly the woman who came to live with her husband or with the family of her husband, not the other way round. Dowries were known, as were bride sums. The latter had to be paid by the bridegroom or his father to the father of the bride, and the former consisted of money or goods that the bride brought with her into the marriage and to which her husband mostly obtained property rights. In the course of the 1st millennium BC, the system of dowries generally prevailed in Greece as well as in the Near East. As a consequence, the economic implications of marriage became more important, with a growing tendency for the rich to marry among themselves. This undermined the power of the community to determine or at least influence the choice and age of marriage partners. In Sparta therefore, dowries were for a long time forbidden—but eventually they would become common there too. In general, in Greece in the Archaic age we find at the most some faint traces of direct interference of the community in the marriage customs of the citizens, marriage having for all practical purposes become exclusively a matter of negotiation between the interested parties: the candidate bridegroom (and his parents) and the parents of the bride. We may speak, then, of the core family of which the man was the head, and not of a clan-like organization in which husband–wife relations were under the leadership of a patriarchal head, as was the case, probably, with the original *gens* in archaic Roman society.

Separate spheres of living

In many Eurasian societies, the married woman "disappeared," so to speak, into her family; to the outside world, she was represented by her husband, and a woman was not usually seen outside the family home. But in some regions and among some peoples, women had a much more independent position—although never fully equal to that of men. That seems, for example, to have been the case among some peoples in Southeast Asia and among Celts and Germans and their ancestors in Northwest Europe. In the Greek world, a difference can be observed in this respect between Sparta and Dorian Greece on the one hand and the rest of the country, but especially Athens, about which we know the most, on the other. In the more "primitive" and more collectively regulated society of Sparta, the position of women vis-à-vis men was in fact better than was the case in more "individualized" Athens. In Sparta, for a long time, dowries were forbidden; marriages could be arranged by the kings; daughters enjoyed inheritance rights (albeit half of a son's inheritance); girls married on average a little later, at an age that did not imperil their health, at a time when early marriage was the norm elsewhere, for instance, in Athens; girls participated in public choirs and dances and in athletic competitions; and married women often ruled the households in the absence of their husbands, who spent most of their time with their companions in the common messes. In Athens, in contrast, girls and women always were under some form of tutelage, whether of the father, the husband, a son, a brother, or another male family relation; she could not legally inherit and had not, strictly speaking, any possessions of her own, and in all her dealings with the outside world she always was dependent on her husband or her legal tutor (in practice, though, often ways could be found that gave a woman more independence and even property of her own, but that would always remain precarious from a legal point of view).

Thus, in Greece, social life was mainly centered around men. Only at religious festivals with their processions, games, sacrifices, and feasts in the open air could respectable women appear in public. Naturally, there were many differences in this between various regions and also between classes of the population. Among the very poor, there always was a certain equality between men and women, since they often did the same work and lived in such simple dwellings that a separation of spheres between them was physically impossible. Among the elites, women often exerted great influence and enjoyed some independence, although never legally, while decency demanded that there too, for instance, the married woman did not participate in the meals or *sumposia* to which her husband invited his friends. In Greece, such dinner parties and literary soirees with few exceptions were male affairs, as were club life and all sorts of collective entertainment. This situation was, if anything, even more pronounced among non-Greek peoples in Egypt and in most parts of Asia. Only the so-called barbarian peoples of Europe, some societies far away in Asia, and the Dorian Greeks of Crete and Sparta offered women a little more freedom, though even there women were always restricted by what was in essence a male world.

Religion, Philosophy, and Scholarship

Religion in the Greek *polis*

In the ancient world, religion pervaded all aspects of life, and it is difficult, therefore, to isolate religion as a separate phenomenon. Moreover, in all ancient cultures, religion was not primarily a private matter; the community or the state was also involved. In a Greek *polis* religion entered into every aspect of *polis* life. Archeologically, we can link the rise of the *polis* to the appearance of large stone temples in the late 8th and 7th centuries BC that required not a little effort and cooperation by the community to build. The construction of sanctuaries and the maintenance of rituals were matters of the *polis* community and therefore came under the ambit of "politics." Certain magistrates performed priestly functions and were charged with the organization of religious festivities. Ancient Greece did not have a professional priesthood. Most tasks that were elsewhere in the hands of professional priests were in Greece performed, often for limited periods, by elected citizens—and sometimes their wives—who could thus be considered "amateurs." The erection of stone temples in their characteristically Greek form started in the late 8th century and was closely connected with the overall revival of Greece in that period, partly under the influence of contacts with the Near East. The Greek stone temple retained some memory of its wooden predecessor, especially in the row or rows of columns that probably once were trunks supporting the roof and enclosing the inner sanctum or *cella*. The statue of the godhead was placed in the latter. In front of the temple, under the open sky, an altar was erected. Such altars, as well as the custom of sacrificing animals to the gods by slaughtering and burning them—that is to say: in practice, only a very small part was burned, and the rest was eaten by humans—almost certainly were borrowed from the Near East. The statues of gods and goddesses—probably were also inspired by Near Eastern or Egyptian religious sculpture. The goddess Aphrodite certainly had her origin in the Near East and arrived among the Greeks via the island of Cyprus. Likewise, the idea of a family of gods headed by a high god, and of succeeding generations of gods, the concept of an underworld where the shades of the dead dwelt, and several mythological images and stories such as can be found in the epics of Homer and Hesiod, must have been derived, ultimately, from Mesopotamia.

In the life of the *polis*, religion manifested itself primarily in annual ceremonies and festivities. These were often connected with the agrarian calendar, for instance, the festivals and rituals of spring and late summer before sowing or after harvesting. Rituals were then

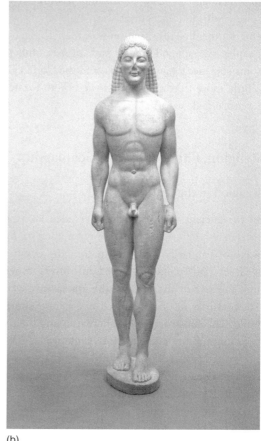

(a)   (b)

Figure 16 A *kouros* and *kore* from Attica (c. 550 BC) and the so-called Getty Kouros (6th c. BC?). *Kouroi* and *korai*, "young men" and "young women, maidens," is the name we give to a particular kind of statue produced in Archaic Greece between the late 7th and early 5th centuries. The statues of naked men and clothed women, ranging from much less than life-size to much more than life-size, were dedicated to the gods in sanctuaries, or were erected at burial sites as grave markers. They are idealized depictions of mortals; only in a few rare instances can it be argued that a divine being was intended. To the left, we see a *kouros* and a *kore* as found in Attica in 1972; they now are in the National Museum in Athens. The two statues, dated to about 550 BC, were already damaged in antiquity itself and were deliberately buried. A statue base signed by the sculptor, Aristion of Paros, that was found earlier could now be shown to belong to the *kore*. To the right, we have a frontal view of the so-called Getty Kouros. This *kouros*, of unknown provenance, was bought in 1985 by the Getty Museum of Malibu, California. According to some, this is a superb example of 6th-century BC sculpture, whereas according to others it is a superb modern fake, which however betrays itself by certain peculiarities, which to the first group of critics are proof of its authenticity. Here we are confronted with the difference between an object excavated by legitimate archaeologists, which gives the best chance of establishing authenticity, dating, and much more, and an object without any provenance or context, deriving from the antiques trade (and often illegally excavated and smuggled abroad). Any object can be aesthetically satisfying, but if it lacks a context, there is only ever so much that it can contribute to our knowledge of the past. Photo: a) from "Greek Sculpture: The Archaic Period." By permission of Professor Sir John Boardman and Thames and Hudson; b) The J. Paul Getty Museum, Villa Collection, Malibu, California

often performed and sacrifices made in honor of the great goddess of the grain, Demeter, but Dionysus, god of the wine, had his own festivals too. Other rituals probably were connected with the upbringing of the young—a few might retain remnants of older initiation rites—or the adoption of the young men into the community of adult citizens. Artemis and Apollo had their roles to play here, especially in Sparta. Athena was often worshiped as the goddess who protected the whole community—and was therefore represented fully armed—and the festival in her honor would express the solidarity and sense of community of the whole *polis*. But that was true of most *polis*-organized cults, which in a sense validated the social and political order. The functions of the various gods and goddesses, though, never were sharply distinguished from each other, for most gods could be active in various fields that nearly always overlapped, while personal characteristics attributed to the gods could also vary from one city to another.

The communal and public character of religion in Greece has had an enormous influence on the development of Greek civilization in general and on art and literature in particular. Not only did temple building stimulate further architectural endeavors, but the habit of placing votive offerings in sanctuaries inspired a burgeoning sculptural art. Typical for the Archaic period were the statues of girls in long garments (priestesses, servants of the godhead?) or *korai*, and those of young men in the nude (athletes, Apollo himself?) or *kouroi*, that were placed in or around sanctuaries. Hymns sung by choirs in honor of the gods were composed by famous poets in the 7th and 6th centuries BC. Traditionally, some choirs were dressed up and masked: they could perform humorous songs in burlesque style, from which in the 6th century BC possibly Greek comedy (from *komos*, that is, people singing and dancing in a file) would originate. But they could also sing about more serious themes that were clad in stories from myth or saga. In such performances in Athens in the 6th century BC, a far-reaching innovation was introduced when opposite the choir at the festival of Dionysus one "answerer" (Greek: *hupokrites*) was placed, so that the story could be told in an interplay between this actor and the choir. Perhaps in the 6th century too, but certainly in the early 5th century BC, a second actor was added; now both actors could hold a dialogue on which the choir could comment. With this, Greek tragedy (*tragoidia*, literally: a goat's song, but the etymology is not clear) was born. It would reach the height of its development in the decades after 480 BC, when finally a third actor would be added.

Some sanctuaries and festivals won a reputation that spread far beyond the local community. We only have to think of the games at Olympia mentioned earlier or of the fame even outside Greece of Apollo's sanctuary at Delphi. There, Apollo was the oracle-god whose advice was sought by states and private persons alike. An older woman was the god's medium: when sitting on a sacred tripod she fell into a trance, and her wildutterances were translated by a special priest, the *prophetes*, into understandable sayings. Delphi grew into a Panhellenic sanctuary, where votive offerings from many parts of the Greek world and even further away (such as the ones sent by the kings of Lydia) came to be placed in special treasuries. Delphi thereby became involved in Greek politics: the oracle and its priests could exert real political influence, while certain *poleis* could use the Delphic god for their own propaganda.

Greek ideas on death and the cult of heroes

Notions of death and the hereafter varied greatly, and not infrequently different and even opposing ideas would exist side by side, but in general in this period there was no belief in life after death, or at least no life comparable to one's earthly life. The grave was literally the last resting place, and whenever the rites at the cremation or funeral had been properly performed, the shade or ghost of the dead was supposed to be content. Only if that proper treatment had been lacking, a restless ghost would haunt the living and wander tormented by its unhappiness. Therefore, the correct treatment of the dead was everywhere an obligation of the family as well as the community. Already quite early, in Mesopotamia, the notion of an underworld can be found, a place where all the shades were assembled and ruled over by a terrifying pair of god and goddess. Greek ideas of the realm of the dead were certainly influenced by these older notions. In Greece, Hades was the name both of the realm of the dead and of the god ruling there. The shades were thought to exist there without any consciousness, although some particularly wicked criminals were eternally punished, which supposed at least some sort of consciousness on their part. At the same time, the shades also existed in their graves, which were entrances to the common underworld. Only a few great heroes of the sagas were believed to be actually living on consciously, with their own earthly bodies or with new ones, in some faraway place (similar ideas prevailed in Egypt). In Greece, in the Dark Age and in the Archaic period, another form of existence after death concerned the so-called heroes: their spirits or ghosts remaining in their graves could be restored to consciousness by special sacrifices or even spontaneously regain consciousness. Their ability to perform all sorts of deeds for the good—rarely to the detriment—of the community transformed them into demigods. *Heros* had originally, in the epics of Homer, meant a living hero, but from around 700 BC the term denoted the dead "heroes" of the past and was applied to the spirits or ghosts just mentioned, that somehow still "lived" in their graves, because these dead were supposed to have been like the epic heroes while still on Earth. Practically every *polis* had one or more such local heroes. The rise of their cult is characteristic of the Archaic period. Certainly, this hero cult contributed to a sense of community among the inhabitants of a *polis* territory.

Anthropomorphism, polytheism, and monotheism

Religion everywhere was so very much a matter of the community that, for instance, in the Near East, the gods were primarily gods of a certain state, and the organization of their cults and the building of their temples were affairs of the state. In times of war, it was not uncommon to try to lure the gods of the enemy to one's side with promises or threats, and when a city had been taken it was not rare for the statues of its gods to be transported in triumph to the city of the victors. Thus, the worship of a god could be connected with the rise and fall of a certain state or a certain people. All peoples in this period practiced what was later called polytheism, that is, the worship of "many gods." Only the Israelites, as far as we know, developed in the two or three centuries before 500 BC a religion in which only one god, Yahweh, was worshiped, who came to be seen gradually as the Lord and creator of the whole world. The Jews of Jerusalem could hold on to their religion even after their country had been taken and their city destroyed by the Babylonians, because Yahweh as a universal god transcended such events. His majesty would even be enhanced when in the years after 500 BC the notion arose that He was the only god there was and that all the gods of other peoples were at best delusions, or perhaps beings subordinate to Yahweh, or even demons. This exclusive worship of one god—we speak of monotheism when the very existence of other gods is denied—was unique to the Israelites or Jews. The religions of other states or peoples never were exclusive in that sense, for polytheism was always elastic and capable of absorbing new gods. The universe was full of gods, and people who were used to worship certain gods in their home cities were completely willing to honor or worship the gods of other cities whenever they were abroad.

In the Near East, there was in general a great distance between gods and men, whereas in the Greek world that distance was smaller. The gods of Mesopotamia, for instance, were unfathomable powers, high above humans, who demanded absolute obedience and could, nevertheless, send sudden catastrophes for no apparent reason. Yahweh too displayed similar features, certainly in the early phases of the Israelite religion. The Greek gods, in contrast, are more human: they are powerful, but not all-powerful, and they have all sorts of human characteristics. These human characteristics were emphasized by the human forms in which the Greeks imagined their gods and goddesses. They are represented in human form in statues and other works of art, and are thought to appear in that form to humans, in one's dreams or when awake. Other religions had forms of anthropomorphism (that is, the possession of human shapes) as well, but seldom in such a pronounced way. In Egypt, for instance, many gods had also animal shapes and were often represented with animal heads, whereas in Mesopotamia and Syria the gods often had wings and could be hybrid, sometimes monstrous figures, while the Israelite/Jewish Yahweh could not be pictured at all.

Developments in Jewish and Iranian religion

In the course of the 1st millennium BC in the Near East, a certain reaction developed against the traditional notions of the gods. This reaction mostly was fostered by ethical considerations: the concepts of justice and goodness demanded the existence of gods that were at least in some cases or in theory absolutely just or good, and thus above human shortcomings. Perhaps this ethical reaction was inspired by major historical events, when several states and peoples appeared to have had no help at all from the gods that they had so faithfully worshiped but were annihilated in the violent wars and upheavals caused by Assyrians, Babylonians, Medes, and Persians. Clearly, the evolution of the Jewish religion toward an ethical monotheism—in which Yahweh was the Lord of history who would in the end reward his people and punish all sinners—cannot be seen separate from the vicissitudes of the Jewish people in these centuries. Elsewhere in the Near East too, some gods acquired the characters of champions of the good, whereas others developed the features of devils. Of great influence in this respect was the religion of Iran, which in this period developed into a strongly ethical theological system, attributed to a legendary founder, Zarathustra (Greek: Zoroaster), who was probably a historical figure sometime in the first half of the 1st millennium BC. In this theology, the highest god was Ahura Mazda (or Ormuzd), Lord of Heaven, the god of light, who was in permanent conflict with the power of darkness, Ahriman. Humans were supposed to assist Ahura Mazda with morally just behavior in his struggle so that in the future Ahriman would finally be defeated. All the other gods were as helper gods and lesser powers distributed over the two opposing camps. Thus, the world of both gods and men was ordered along the principles of good and evil. These ideas would prove to have a great influence on the later religious developments in the Near East and the Mediterranean area.

A Greek development: The Orphics

In Greece before 500 BC, ideas such as those mentioned in the last paragraph hardly arose. In the 6th century BC, however, there emerged a strain of religion that laid great stress on a pure and immaculate life as a prerequisite for the immortal existence of the soul after the death of the body, in a sort of paradise under the earth or among the planets and the stars of heaven. If that was not possible, then at least a happy rebirth on Earth could be hoped for. These ideas were new in that time. Their adherents invoked the mythical singer Orpheus, who was said to have gone to the underworld in order to fetch his beloved Eurydice back to life, and who had, albeit alone, come back to the realm of the living, having overcome death in that way; hence the name Orphics. New in this was the concept of an immortal soul, which was understood to be equal to one's intellect and consciousness, whereas the emotions were thought of as the mortal and perishable part of the *psuche*. New also was the fact that these Orphics formed private associations that were outside the religious mainstream of the *polis*. Holy "books" and oracles attributed to Orpheus circulated among them. In subsequent centuries, such private movements or associations would play a major role in the spread of new religions and new forms of religiosity. In the 6th century, however, the Orphics probably were still a small group in various Greek states, particularly the Greek colonies in the south of Italy. For the vast majority of the Greeks, the traditional gods and goddesses with all their human attractions and failings probably still sufficed.

Greek influences in Italy: Ancient Roman ideas

It was the anthropomorphic gods of the Greeks that would exert the greatest influence on the religion of peoples to the west. In Italy, the Etruscans adopted a large part of the Greek pantheon, including many myths and sagas. Much the same can be said of the Italic peoples, although their adoption of Greeks gods and myths generally occurred a little later, mostly in the two centuries after 500 BC. In comparison with Greek religion, the original religion of the Italic peoples was no doubt more "primitive" in the sense that the divine powers were not or not in a very concrete way, thought of as divine personalities. The best known of these Italic peoples, the Romans, originally revered impersonal forces of nature, but their main deity was the Indo-European sky and weather god, Jupiter, manifesting himself in the bright sky but also in clouds, thunder, and lightning, the same god known as Zeus among the Greeks. We know even less of the religions of the many "barbaric" peoples in the rest of Europe, but they certainly resembled the old Italic religions more than those of the Greeks.

Greeks and barbarians

Humans are animals living in groups—a *zoön politikon* or a "*polis* creature," as the philosopher Aristotle would say in the 4th century BC. Hence, humans are inclined to judge others by the norms of their own group. The outsider is easily labeled strange, often inferior, and sometimes even non-human. In antiquity, foreign peoples were generally considered to be as human as one's own group, but they were also considered natural enemies. Whereas warfare in the Archaic age between neighboring or affiliated communities in Greece was often somewhat restricted, such limitations were not acknowledged when the opponents were total strangers. Such people could be ambushed, kidnapped, carried off as slaves, or even exterminated. Typically, the term *hostis* in ancient Rome denoted both "stranger" and "enemy." Since foreign peoples were regarded as enemies by default, a lone foreigner had to beg for hospitality by invoking the gods who guaranteed the safety of strangers.

In Greece, during the Dark Age, various communities must have been rather isolated. Whoever ventured abroad needed friends elsewhere to give him shelter and protection. Raiders from the land or sea could at any moment fall upon a settlement and enslave its population. In the Archaic period, many *poleis* seem to have established so many reciprocal relations, usually by so-called guest friendships or by marriages between aristocratic families, that the citizens of these *poleis* did not see each other any longer as strangers or enemies. In these cases, when war occurred between two such *poleis*, it was mostly of a limited character: to enslave, let alone to exterminate the defeated party, or even to completely destroy its settlement and rural area was generally frowned upon and a rare occurrence during the Archaic period. This sentiment gradually spread over much of Greece and was fostered by ideas of Panhellenic affinities and strengthened by common cults, festivals, and cultural traditions, such as the epics of Homer that were known to all Greeks.

At the same time, Greeks began to feel a sense of distance between themselves and non-Greeks. Initially, the term *barbaroi* denoted only those people whose language the Greeks did not understand, without any connotations of superiority on their part. In Asia Minor and Cyprus, during the Dark Age and the Archaic period, Greeks and non-Greeks could even coexist and cooperate in the same communities. But with the emergence of a Panhellenic sentiment, the sense of distance grew. Participation in the Olympic games, for instance, was expressly forbidden for all non-Greeks. The relations between Greeks and the subjugated indigenous populations in Sicily or along the coasts of the Black Sea further contributed to the rise of a certain feeling of Greek superiority. The emergence of the Persian Empire in the 6th century BC, of which many Greeks in Asia Minor and on Cyprus became subjects, must

(a)   (b)

Figure 17   The outside of an Athenian amphora and an Athenian *oinochoe*: battle scenes with Greek hoplites and Persians (c. 480–460 BC). To the left is an Athenian red-figure amphora of about 480 BC, now in the Metropolitan Museum in New York, and to the right a red-figure *oinochoe*, a wine jug, of about 460 BC, now in the Museum of Fine Arts in Boston. Both vases carry battle scenes, with a Greek hoplite confronting a Persian archer. One of the hoplites is shown nude, which is probably an example of so-called "heroic nudity," and not a realist depiction—but certainly making for a maximum contrast with the body suit of his barbarian opponent. The weapons of both parties also underline the contrast: the Greeks wield spears, the Persians fight with broadswords, and probably preferably with bow and arrows. The background to these images is the warfare between Greeks and Persians in the first quarter of the 5th century BC, even though the imagery seems to be based more on pre-existing models used to depict Greeks battling Amazons than on observation of the actual battlefield. The barbarians are fighting a losing battle: the Persians are no match for the Greeks, or for the Athenians in particular. But they are not portrayed as caricatures or monsters; the vase painters seem rather interested in foreign dress, hairstyles, and weaponry. All in all, these images are an intriguing example of curiosity and disdain keeping each other in balance. Photos: a) The Metropolitan Museum of Art/Art Resource/Scala, Florence; b) Museum of Fine Arts, Boston, Massachusetts, USA/Francis Bartlett Donation/The Bridgeman Art Library

have tempered such sentiments to some extent. But shortly after 500 BC, the great victories of the Greeks in the Persian Wars would stimulate a feeling of utter superiority. As a result, in the 5th century BC, the term *barbaroi* for many Greeks would carry the negative connotation of cultural (and military) inferiority.

Hecataeus and the beginnings of Greek geography

The emergence of the Persian Empire had consequences as well for the Greek view of the world. It inspired a view that saw the known world divided between east and west, or Asia and Europe. The man who thus split the known world into two continents was Hecataeus of Miletus (second half of the 6th century). What was later to be considered a third continent was called "Libue" by Hecataeus and presumably considered a part of "Asie." Hecataeus' ideas were taken over by others, and the opposition between the Persian Empire and the Greeks resulted in a permanent division of Eurasia into two continents. This geographical division, therefore, was from the start associated with a cultural and political opposition between the two. Hecataeus outlined his ideas in a book (now lost) that was probably called *Description of the Whole World*. It was one of the very first Greek books in prose.

In the Dark Age and in the early Archaic period, the Greek view of the world had been simpler and limited mainly to Greece and its immediate vicinity; the world beyond was inhabited by strange peoples and creatures of myths and fables. Moreover, the world in the time of Homer had been a simple flat surface, a big "pancake" surrounded by the waters of Okeanos, the world-ocean. Above, there was the dome of heaven with the stars and the planets, and below Earth there were the realms of Hades and the rest of the underworld. In essence, this view of the world and of the universe did not differ very much from the representations of the cosmos in ancient Egypt and Mesopotamia. By the time of Hecataeus, Greek knowledge of the actual world had increased substantially, but in essence the view of the world as a whole had not developed. There still existed fabulous peoples, but now they lived farther away, toward the edges of Earth: the wise and blessed Ethiopians in the south, the pious and wealthy Hyperboreans in the far north beyond the Scythians, and the just and long-lived Indians in the extreme east. But apart from these happy peoples, there were also cannibals and ogres, and all sorts of barbarians, and Amazons somewhere in the east. Here, we may assume the work of an imagination that wished to see ideas realized that were suppressed in contemporary Greek society, as well as the influence of a tradition that had preserved names and images that were not firmly fixed so that they could become located and relocated over time. However, for the first time we can detect a desire to know and to research. In the time of Hecataeus, a certain Scylax from western Asia Minor, in the service of the Persian king Darius, explored the course of the Kabul River and then sailed down the Indus, which marked the eastern border of the king's realm, from where he reached Egypt through the Arabian Gulf and the Red Sea. He wrote a short book about his exploits, which was almost certainly consulted by Hecataeus, who himself must have traveled in the eastern Mediterranean. Thus, a scientific method was born: to assemble facts both by first-hand experience and by information gathered from others, including reading what someone else had written on a subject, and then to organize all these facts/"facts" in an all-encompassing framework. With Hecataeus, this method presented itself, albeit in a rudimentary form, for the first time.

The Milesian philosophers: Heraclitus and Xenophanes

Heraclitus had added to his description a map of the world. With that he improved upon the work of an older compatriot of his, Anaximander, who was also said to have made a world map. Anaximander of Miletus also gave a remarkable overview of the development of life on Earth, which in his opinion had started in the seas and had known at least three main stages: fishes, land animals, and humans. He acquired his greatest fame, though, with his philosophical system. According to Anaximander, the cosmos as a whole had originated from and could be reduced to something which he called the Indefinite or the Unlimited. Perhaps he meant by this that the whole universe was in essence one kind of matter of an undefinable quality. Anaximander was one of the first Greek philosophers, when philosophy and "science" were still one and the same. Later Greek philosophers would call their early predecessors of the 6th and 5th centuries BC "natural philosophers" or "pre-Socratics" for their attempts to explain the origin and essence of the world in physical terms, whereas Socrates toward the end of the 5th century BC would mainly focus his philosophical enquiries on the theory of knowledge and on ethical questions.

Early Greek philosophy was "science," not yet in the modern sense of that term, but still a methodical enquiry, unhampered by preconceived beliefs. Elsewhere too, philosophical insights concerning humans and the world were sometimes formulated, but then often confined to mystical utterances in a religious context, as for instance in India, or limited in their intellectual scope and in the freedom of thinking by worldly and/or spiritual authorities, as for instance in China, or by a wish to be socially acceptable and not to offend established religion. In contrast, in Ionia in the 6th century BC there was a large measure of intellectual freedom. Perhaps, Ionia, after its incorporation in the Persian Empire, was a region where to a much greater extent than elsewhere in the Greek world, information could be collected about different lands and peoples and about the knowledge that other peoples had acquired, such as the astronomical observations of the Babylonians. Perhaps too, the traditional ways of thinking had been undermined here more strongly than elsewhere because of the rapid political changes in Asia Minor resulting in the loss of political independence of the Greek cities. A really satisfactory explanation, however, is hard to give for the sudden appearance here in the 6th century BC of thinkers such as Anaximander; his predecessor Thales of Miletus, who was said to have explained the origin and essence of the world by water, but of whom we know even less; and others. In any case, the new way of thinking can be defined as an attempt to describe and to explain the world in a rational manner, without recourse to religion and myth, and to reduce the totality of empirical reality to one or a few "elements." The earliest philosophers were in search of one last cause or first principle with which in their view it should be possible to explain the whole cosmos.

In the second half of the 6th century BC, a third Milesian after Thales and Anaximander, a certain Anaximenes, in his turn posited another primordial material or first principle: air. Essentially, air is everywhere; it can condense to water, and even further to solid matter or "earth," or it can rarify into fire. Thus, Anaximenes could explain what would later be called the four basic elements of all organic and inorganic material—earth, water, air, and fire—from one principle. Moreover, for the first time in Greek philosophy, humans received their place in this cosmology (i.e., "explanation of the cosmos"), for humans' *psuche*, in which both thought-consciousness and emotions were located, was "breath," or "air." "Just as our *psuche*, being air controls us, so do *pneuma* (spirit) and air encompass the whole cosmos," he must have said.

Toward the end of the 6th century, in the city of Ephesus, the philosopher Heraclitus wrote a book full of profound but often obscure sayings. His thoughts seem to have resembled those of the Milesians to some extent but were also different in some fundamental ways. According to Heraclitus, fire, being the finest form of matter, was the ultimate substance of the world. The human *psuche* too is fire, since a body without *psuche* is cold. All things decay and in the end return into the primordial "fire." For anything to remain permanently the same is impossible: everything is constantly changing and in transition, and all things are bound up with their opposites. Therefore one could not say, as the Milesian philosophers apparently said, that the world or the human "is" in a certain way; strictly speaking, one cannot even say that something "is," for the wise man knows that everything is always in a flux and in transition to something else.

A little older than Heraclitus was the poet Xenophanes. In his poems, he mocked not only the anthropomorphic representations of the gods and the mythological explanations of the world current among his contemporaries, but also the "rational" explanations of the cosmos offered by the first philosophers. For according to Xenophanes, our perceptions based on the senses are always deceiving us. Definite knowledge, therefore, was impossible for humans and the privilege only of "the godhead." The latter, being one, in a sense encompassed the whole cosmos, which in its turn implied that all being ultimately was "one."

Pythagoras and the Pythagoreans

Pythagoras of the island of Samos went his own peculiar way. Having migrated to the south of Italy sometime before 500 BC, he founded a school and a living community with his aristocratic disciples in the city of Kroton. Their aim was to acquire *sofia* or wisdom, for according to Pythagoras and his followers only wisdom could bring humans to inner harmony, guaranteeing the rebirth of their *psuche* in a human body, or even better. Pythagoras was convinced that the soul was immortal and that it originally came from the realm of the gods—and that after death it would migrate into another body, with those who had lived immoral or criminal lives being reborn as animals. A morally elevated life would lead to rebirth in human form, but only wisdom could bring about the liberation from this cycle of earthly existences and make the soul after death return to the heavenly sphere of its origins. This conception of reincarnation was new in the Greek world of the later 6th century BC. Only the Orphics entertained some comparable ideas; their movement and the one founded by Pythagoras—his following developed rapidly into a sect—often overlapped. The idea that bad people could come back in another life as animals was also known in Egypt, while reincarnation was one of the fundamental religious conceptions in India since roughly the 6th century BC, but any possible connections with the thinking of Pythagoras and his school remain utterly obscure. The whole idea, though, of an immortal soul coming from the world of the gods and destined, in the case of "wise" persons, to return thither, would prove to be of great influence on later Greek philosophical and religious thought.

Typical for Pythagoras, who combined science with mysticism and various superstitions, was the idea that a pure life, that is, a frugal life with many taboos, was a precondition for attaining wisdom. In that respect too, his movement strongly resembled that of the Orphics. The content of wisdom that was pursued—from this pursuit of wisdom a new word was born: *filosofos*, that is, "he who pursues wisdom"—mainly concerned knowledge of the regular arrangements of the cosmos. For Pythagoras, this meant primarily mathematics, and mathematics would together with medicine and music remain the most important subjects of his school. The famous proposition of Pythagoras may indeed have been formulated by the master himself, although this is not certain. Knowledge of the regularities of the universe would lead to the realization that the entire cosmos was arranged harmoniously; knowledge of this cosmic harmony would automatically lead to harmony and purity of the soul. All these ideas were developed and put into writing by disciples and followers of Pythagoras (who himself left no writings) and would deeply influence later philosophers, most of all Plato.

PART IV

500–300 BC

Chapter 4.1

A Historical Outline

Eurasian Communities

China

In China, the 5th and 4th centuries BC form part of the period of the Eastern Zhou dynasty (770–256 BC). These were centuries of growing disintegration, in which the kings of the Zhou dynasty no longer wielded any real power and were reduced to fulfilling a mere religious–ceremonial role. The Zhou Empire had fragmented into several independent kingdoms that were constantly struggling for dominance. After 480 BC, this fragmentation of power was at its height, during a chaotic era known as "the Warring States." But despite constant warfare, China was flourishing during this period. There was strong demographic growth, the amount of arable land was extended, and cultivation was intensified by increasing irrigation among other things, trade was on the increase and so was urbanization, the use of iron became common, copper coinage was introduced, and cultural life blossomed too. In the different states, the government was based on law. As far as we know, the 5th-century written laws were the first of their kind in China. The states also reorganized their armies. A large army of conscripted farmers replaced the aristocratic army of the previous centuries, and cavalry was introduced in imitation of the nomads on the western and northern borders. And despite all internecine strife, the Chinese states saw a chance to expand their territory. The sinification of areas to the south, in the valley of the Yangtze, and on the western and northern borders went steadily on.

The 5th and 4th centuries BC are important in China's intellectual history, and thus in the intellectual history of all of East Asia. This was the era in which Confucianism took shape. Confucianism would end up as the central and universal philosophic tradition of China, Korea, Japan, and the northern parts of Southeast Asia. It is named after Kongfuzi, Master Kong, a political philosopher better known in the West as Confucius (551–479 BC). Confucius' ideas are supposed to be laid down in the *Lunyu* (literally "Conversations" or "Select Pronouncements," usually titled the *Analects*); in fact, this is an effort at compilation of the 3rd century, and we cannot be sure how much of its content can be safely ascribed to Confucius himself. What we can reconstruct of Confucius' thought shows that he saw the

Antiquity: Greeks and Romans in Context, First Edition. Frederick G. Naerebout and Henk W. Singor.
© 2014 John Wiley & Sons, Inc. Published 2014 by John Wiley & Sons, Inc.

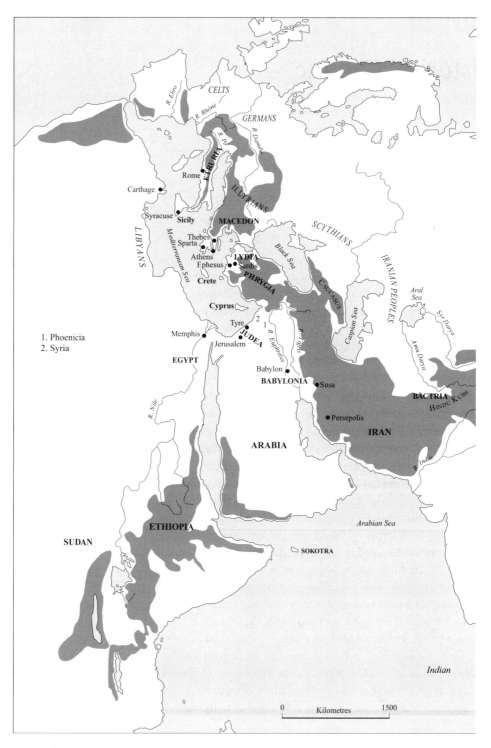

Map 8 Eurasia, 5th–4th c. BC

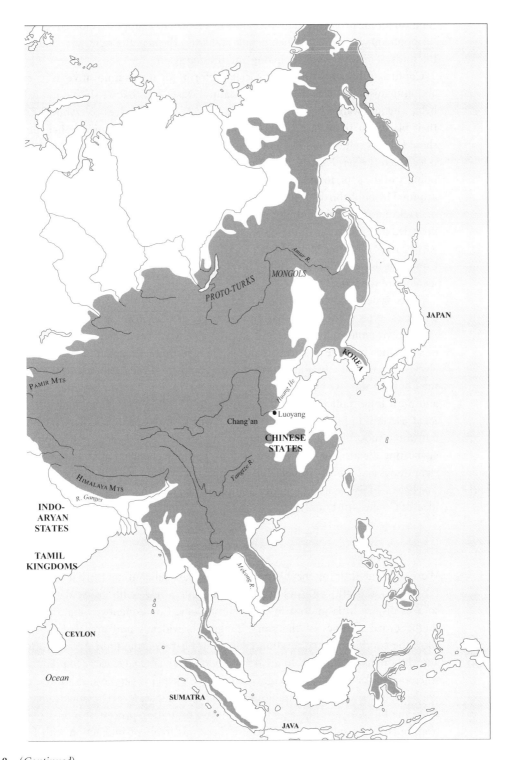

Map 8 (*Continued*)

solution for the problems of his own days in a return to a supposed Golden Age dating back to about 500 years before, when people still knew the *dao*, the right way. Study, especially the study of history, would help one find the *dao* again.

Confucian thought stimulated societal reform, for it was innovative in its rationalism and humanism: it states that the supernatural exists, but that we should not call on it for help; when we want a better world, we have to create it ourselves. Everybody should know their place, but those in a position of authority should never misuse their power. They should always remember the humanity of every fellow human being, because a good ruler is a righteous ruler. Perhaps most important is Confucius' novel explanation of nobility as nobility of the soul, to be acquired by study, integrity, and honesty, rather than something acquired by noble birth. The warfare and misery of his own days he explained as the result of a lack of nobility, true nobility, among the rulers. This emphasis on profane human ethics provided new ideals for Chinese society. Many followers and interpreters, of whom Meng Ke or Mengzi (Master Meng, Mencius, 372–289 BC) was the most important, popularized Confucius' ideas, and at the end of the 3rd century BC, Confucianism became the official ideology of the state.

Other widely known traditions of East Asia, which also originated in the 6th and 5th centuries, even if their roots lay further back, are Legalism and Taoism. Legalism is a rationalistic philosophy of statecraft, arguing that whatever a ruler does in order to enlarge or strengthen his state and army is always the right thing. Pragmatic considerations should always lead the way. In addition to this pragmatism of the legalists and the moralism of the Confucianists, we find the primitivism of the Taoists. Taoism is named after the oldest and most important text of this tradition, the *Daodejing, the Holy Book of the Virtuous Road*, ascribed to Laozi ("the Old Master"), who is supposed to have lived in about 500 BC, but who is most likely a legendary figure. Taoism or Tao is a vague philosophic amalgam, advocating the ideal of leaving things alone, banning change, not attempting to think the right things and act accordingly, but attempting to refrain from thinking and from acting. The *dao* of Taoism is a metaphysical individualistic notion, opposed to the *dao* as the social ideal of Confucianist thought.

India

We know but little of the history of the Indian subcontinent. That also holds good for the 5th and 4th centuries BC. There are only a few radiocarbon dates, and written sources display little interest in exact chronology. Consequently, we are forced to stick to the broad outlines of the story. Linguistic evidence and archaeology combine to show the continuing acculturation taking place between the Indo-Aryan groups and the autochthonous inhabitants. In the north, Indo-Aryan languages came to predominate, but when one looks at culture at large, old and new elements can be seen to fuse into a new synthesis. In the south, comparable events occurred, but the local Dravidian languages stood up to the Indo-Aryan languages better. The acculturation process also took in influences from outside the subcontinent, because there was frequent interaction with Iran—from the 6th century BC onward more specifically the Persian Empire—with Central Asia by way of the northwest, and with Southeast Asia, especially Burma, by way of the northeast.

Acculturation resulted in an Indian subcontinent that culturally speaking was relatively homogeneous: the many contacts over land and especially along the coasts brought about cultural unification. One of the instruments of this unification was Brahmanic religion, named after the priests, the Brahmans. The Indo-Aryans had brought this religion with them, and in India it subsequently developed into what later was to be known as Hinduism. Cultural unification, however, did not imply any form of political unity. Along the Ganges, a number of states developed in a long-drawn out process, but none of these managed to overcome their neighbors. Not until the late 4th century BC did a hegemonic state arise, when the so-called Maurya dynasty began building an empire.

It is suspected that the dynamics of contact between Indo-Aryan and Dravidian groups has also played a part in the growth of the caste system, a phenomenon about whose early history nothing is known with certainty. The Indo-Aryans divided their society into three layers: the priests, the *brahmana*; the warriors, the *kshatriya*; and the farmers, the *vaishya*. Whether these were hereditary, endogamous groups, as were the later castes, is not clear. It appears that after the Indo-Aryans settled in the Indian subcontinent, a fourth category was added: the *dasa*, the conquered, later also known as the *shudra*, the servants. This fourth group included those members of the autochthonous inhabitants who were seen as a part, an inferior part but a part all the same, of Indo-Aryan society. Autochthonous people, however, who were not or but little influenced by Indo-Aryan culture were considered to be outside the pale of society altogether. These four layers, the so-called *varna*, were further subdivided into a complicated system of social hierarchies, with everybody finding a place in one of the numerous *jata*, a concept that much later (by the Portuguese) was translated as "caste."

Culturally, the 5th and 4th centuries were important for India. In this "classic period," the cities along the Ganges were the most important centers, but other parts of the subcontinent shared, more or less, in the cultural dynamics. By the end of the 6th century and early 5th century BC, iron had come into use all over the subcontinent, and cities, trade, and irrigation agriculture were flourishing. Indicative of the growth of interregional exchange is the introduction, in the 5th or 4th century BC, of silver and copper coinage, based on Persian coins that circulated in the northwest (present-day Pakistan). Alphabets were derived, in the same period, from Aramaic examples, again under Persian influence. Alphabetic writing helped intellectual life to expand. Exegesis of Brahmanic writings, especially the *Vedas*, gave rise to a range of specialist scholarship: astronomy, geometry, and most importantly, an advanced linguistics.

This period of socioeconomic and cultural change was also a period of religious ferment: several religious movements and sects began competing with orthodox Brahmanism. Brahmanism was a ritualistic religion: honoring the gods involved extensive rituals, especially sacrificial ones. The holy texts, including the aforementioned *Vedas*, the most ancient ones, provided the rules for these rituals. Wandering preachers now threw doubt on Vedic learning and advocated, among other things, an asceticism that went back to pre-Vedic, probably pre-Indo-Aryan patterns of thought. Of these new movements, Buddhism would turn out to be the most important.

There is no agreement about when the founder of Buddhism, the *Buddha* ("Enlightened") Siddhartha Gautama, lived, but nowadays many scholars accept the period 480–400 BC as reasonable. Central in the teachings of Siddhartha Gautama and his followers are "the four truths": our earthly life is miserable; the cause of this misery is desire; we can end misery by banishing all desire; in order to banish desire, we should follow the "eightfold path," which comprises a set of rules for right living. Buddhism denies the necessity for any ritual and worship, and teaches that one can escape the supposed cycle of rebirth by one's own efforts. It was acknowledged that not everybody would be able to follow the eightfold path, and thus the distinction between monastics and laymen came into being. Buddhism was also a missionary religion, and in the centuries to come would spread across large parts of Asia.

The Persian Empire

The Persian Empire arose in the mid-6th century when Cyrus, the first Persian king, seized power in the kingdom of the Medes. The Persians had done very well since then. In a short time, they built an empire that reached from the Aegean to the Indus and from the Danube to the Red Sea. It was the largest empire that the world had seen. During the reign of Darius I (521–486 BC), a usurper born of a branch of the royal family, the Persian lands were consolidated. Darius also wished to enlarge his empire, rounding off its borders, in India, to the east of the Caspian Sea, in Armenia, Northern Africa, and in the Aegean. It was in this last-mentioned area that Persians and Greeks were to clash with each other over Persian expansionism.

Darius was a great organizer, and attempted to knit the heterogeneous collection of peoples who inhabited his empire into some kind of unity. To this end, he promulgated new laws that were a return to the laws of Hammurabi, created a uniform government, standardized weights and measures, and reformed the coinage. Even the Old Persian script, a syllabary making use of cuneiform, is supposed to have been created expressly for the use of Darius, who wanted his official inscriptions to be composed in writing comparable to Assyrian and Babylonian examples. However, the increasing use of Aramaic as the lingua franca for the whole empire was in the end of much greater importance. The building of a new capital, Persepolis, can be considered a symbol of the many changes taking place under Darius. The king was also a follower of Zoroaster, and favored Zoroaster's dualistic teachings without rejecting other religions. The growth of Persian dualism fits into a general trend, in which traditional religions that were exclusive to certain areas or towns were coming to be replaced by teachings of universal scope, such as Babylonian astrology and Jewish monotheism.

The immense Persian Empire was divided into provinces, over 20 so-called satrapies governed by satraps, literally "protectors of the kingdom." Cyrus had been the first to copy the Assyrian practice of turning conquered areas into provinces. Darius continued this policy. The satrapies had to pay tribute, which Darius converted from an irregular tax into a regular, yearly levy. The center kept a measure of control over the outlying areas by stationing in every satrapy civil and military magistrates who were answerable to the king, and by annually sending out inspectors. But otherwise the satraps were relatively autonomous rulers who recognized the overlordship of the Persian king.

The Scythians

Darius' military expeditions to the north brought the Persians into conflict with the Scythians, the name now given to a large collection of nomadic and half-nomadic tribes in the area between the Danube and the Don, and immediately to the east of the Caspian Sea. In the southeast, Scythian territory touched that of the Sarmatians, like the Scythians an Iranian people, living mainly between the Black Sea and the Caspian Sea and to the east of the Don. In the southwest, the neighbors of the Scythians were the Thracians, whose domain centered on modern Bulgaria. Stimulated by contacts with the Greek world, especially the Greek colonies on the Black Sea, the Scythian tribes had evolved into primitive states with a hereditary monarchy. The states were in the process of absorbing each other and turning into ever-larger units. Darius' warfare at the end of the 6th century gave this process a strong impetus, and in the 4th century a strong and unified Scythian kingdom stretched from the lower reaches of the Danube to the Crimea.

Greeks and Carthaginians

In about 500 BC, we can consider the following areas as Greek areas, that is, either areas where Greek *poleis* had been established or where Greek was spoken as the main language: the whole of the Greek peninsula from the kingdom of Macedon in the north to the Spartan territories on the Peloponnese, the islands of the eastern Mediterranean, the coast of Asia Minor, and the colonies on the coasts of the Black Sea, in the Cyrenaica, in Sicily and in the south of Italy, on the south coast of France, and on the east coast of Spain. These areas did not have any kind of political unity, but the independence of several of the numerous little states was relative. Thus, the Greeks of Asia Minor, Cyprus, and the Cyrenaica were at least nominally subjects of the Persian Empire. But the Greeks had other parties to contend with, above all the Carthaginians and the Etruscans.

The cities in Phoenicia were under Persian rule, but had managed to retain some independence under their own kings. Phoenicia was an area of great cultural importance, but the Phoenician colony Carthage became even more important than the motherland. The Persians, who for their fleet were partly dependent on the Phoenicians, never managed to get a foothold in Carthage. In 500 BC, Carthage, founded by Tyre, was already three centuries old, and had been gaining power in the western Mediterranean, with bases on the African coast, in Spain, on Sicily, Sardinia, and the smaller islands. Carthaginian trade routes spread out onto the Atlantic coasts of Europe and Africa. There is in existence a Greek translation of the account of an expedition along the African coast down to Sierra Leone, by the Carthaginian king and seafarer Hanno (about 450 BC). Carthage did not remain the sole power in the western Mediterranean, however, because the Greeks extended their colonizing efforts into Carthaginian territory. In the 6th century, this already led to open warfare, with Carthage gaining Etruscan support. In the 5th and 4th centuries BC, Sicily became the main theater of battle between Carthaginians and Greeks.

The Italic peninsula, Celts and other peoples in the West

The Italic peninsula in the 5th and 4th centuries BC is a confusing patchwork of many ethnic and political entities. The early Roman Republic was as yet a small and unassuming community in the midst of several other Italic peoples, the Etruscans, the Greeks, and the Carthaginians. Apparently it was with Carthage that the young republic concluded its first treaties. Later, Rome and Carthage would get involved in a struggle for life and death, but at this stage Rome was preoccupied with other opponents. It got drawn into conflict with several Italic peoples, among whom were also their direct neighbors, the Latins; with the Etruscans; and from around 400 BC with the Celts, who had invaded the Italic peninsula and were pushing south. The Celts were an especially dangerous enemy: early in the 4th century BC, on one of their raids, they even managed to occupy Rome. This and other setbacks were, however, temporary, and did not stop Rome from conquering in the 4th century BC, in rapid succession, large parts of Italy.

To the west and north of the Alps, the Celts were the most important presence. What actually should be understood by the designation "Celt" is not very clear. Only the period of the so-called Latène culture (about 480–15 BC), a cultural complex stretching from France to Bohemia, can be said to be Celtic with certainty. Now, the Latène culture is not completely different from the preceding Hallstatt culture (from about 750 BC), and one may judge this to be a case of cultural continuity. Discontinuities, however, are evident as well. Thus, we cannot call Hallstatt Celtic just like that. We are speaking of the Hallstatt cultural complex that is only known from archaeological finds, and which is difficult to pin down regarding ethnicity or language.

Already in the Hallstatt period, social differentiation is quite marked, as can be seen from the rich burials that have been discovered. From the 6th to the end of the 4th century BC, men, women, and even children (which indicates hereditary status) of the social layer that dominated society militarily, politically, economically, and possibly also religiously, were buried with costly grave goods, including items imported from the Mediterranean. The main status symbols of this aristocracy were four-wheeled carts and two-wheeled chariots, the chariots being especially in evidence during the Latène period. Local power was established in hilltop strongholds, so-called *Herrensitze* or *Fürstensitze*, where trade and crafts were also concentrated. There is unmistakably much Greek-Etruscan and Greek influence, arriving from across the Alps and along the valley of the Rhône, respectively. The *Gefolgschaft*, a group of warriors bound by ties of patronage to an aristocrat, can safely be expected to occur already in the early period, even if it is documented only for a much later date. Celtic society had non-farming members, craftsmen and warriors, and both groups were employed by patrons. The presence of Celtic mercenaries in the Mediterranean world from 400 BC onward fits this picture. And also the expansion of the Latène-Celts toward the south and east during the 4th and 3rd centuries BC has been linked to the phenomenon of the *Gefolgschaft*.

Even when Celtic power was at its height, not all of Western and Central Europe was Celtic. On the Iberian peninsula, we had Iberians and Basques; in the south of France and on Corsica, there lived Ligurians; in the Alps were many different tribes; and from Central Germany up into southern Scandinavia could be found Germanic tribes.

The Greek World

The Greeks against Persia and Carthage

For the Greeks, the early 5th century BC was the period of their battle against Persia and Carthage. After the Ionian Rising (500–494 BC), the Persian king Darius turned his attention to the northern coast of the Aegean. In 492 BC, Thrace and Macedon were turned into Persian territory. But Darius' attempt to bring the entire Greek peninsula under Persian hegemony and punish Athens for the help which they had offered to the

Figure 18 An Etruscan helmet dedicated to Zeus of Olympia by the Syracusans (474 BC). This bronze helmet was found in the sanctuary of Olympia, and is now in the local museum. In the 6th and early 5th century BC, Carthaginians and Etruscans cooperated in order to halt Greek expansion in the Western Mediterranean. A couple of Greek victories thwarted this alliance: first, in 480, the Syracusans crushed the Carthaginians in the sea battle of Himera, on the Sicilian coast, and next, in 474, the Etruscans in the battle of Cyme, on the Italian coast near Naples. Hieron, the tyrant of Syracuse, dedicated some of the booty to Zeus in his sanctuary in Olympia, as was the Greek custom: part of the spoils of war were dedicated to the gods, to honor and thank them, but also to advertise one's victories to the large numbers of people who visited large Panhellenic sanctuaries such as Olympia. Inscriptions helped to spread the message. The text on this helmet says: "Hieron, son of Deinomenes, and the Syracusans [have dedicated this helmet] to Zeus, from Cyme, [captured] from the Etruscans." Photo: © The Trustees of the British Museum

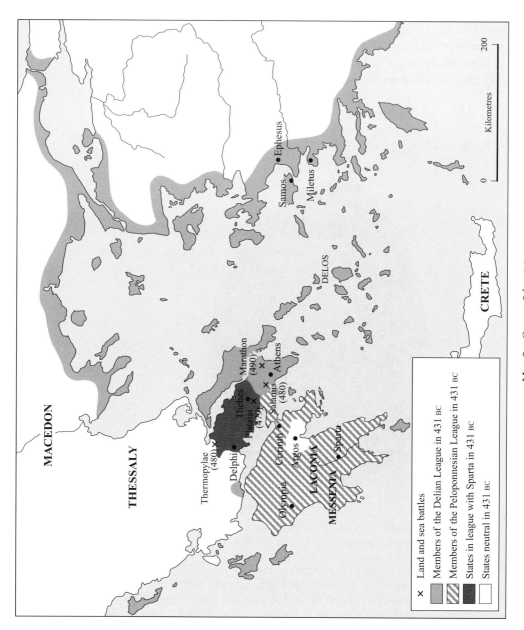

Map 9 Greece, 5th c. BC

MACEDON

THESSALY

Thermopylae (480) ×

Delphi

Thebes
Plataiai (479) ×

Marathon (490) ×
× Athens
Salamis (480) ×

Corinth

Olympia

Argos

LACONIA

Sparta

MESSENIA

Samos
Ephesus

Miletus

DELOS

CRETE

Kilometres
0   200

× Land and sea battles

Members of the Delian League in 431 BC

Members of the Peloponnesian League in 431 BC

States in league with Sparta in 431 BC

States neutral in 431 BC

Greeks of Asia Minor ended in failure. After landing on the Attic coast, a Persian army was crushingly defeated in the battle of Marathon (490 BC). This victory of the Athenian hoplites showed that the Greeks were not going to give in without a struggle, and that the heavily armed Greek phalanx was superior when fielded against an enemy army consisting largely of lightly armed soldiers.

The Greek gained a breathing space of a decade. When it became clear that the Persians, now under their King Xerxes, would mount a large-scale attack aimed at conquering all of Greece, the Greeks tried to form to a defensive alliance. Almost all of the Peloponnese, that is, Sparta and its allies, Athens, and a number of states in Central Greece joined this alliance. In 480 BC, the Persians attacked by way of Thrace and were gaining ground. Troops of the Greek alliance, led by the Spartan king Leonidas, tried to halt the Persian advance at the pass of Thermopylae, the narrow entrance to Central Greece between the mountains and the sea. But this line of defense quickly fell because of treason, and the Persians could advance to the south without encountering much opposition. They captured Athens, from which the population had been evacuated, and destroyed the Acropolis with its temple of Athena.

The tables were turned at the sea battle of Salamis, a decisive victory for the Athenians. The decisive role was played by the Athenian war fleet. This consisted of 200 ships of the *trieres*, or trireme type, that is, a warship with three rows of oarsmen above each other. The trireme was in fact a ram vessel, with the large number of rowers providing the speed needed to successfully ram and sink the opposing ship in battle. Boarding the enemy vessel was also a possibility, as the trireme also carried a number of soldiers on board. It testifies to the strategic insight of the Athenian politician Themistocles that in the years before the Persian invasion he had urged his fellow citizens to build a strong fleet, to be financed from the profits of silver mining in the south of Attica. The phalanx of hoplites showed its superiority once more: in the spring following Salamis, the Persians, who had wintered in Greece, were beaten in the battle of Plataeae, where a Greek coalition led by Pausanias, regent in Sparta, turned out to be too strong for the Persian forces. Meanwhile, Carthage had opened a second front on Sicily, but in 480 BC the Greeks prevailed against that enemy too, in the battle of Himera.

After Salamis and Plataeae, the Persian policy became much more restrained, and subsequent aggression was initiated by the Greeks, but without much success. In the west, Carthage remained a dangerous opponent, even after Himera, but for the time being the Greeks had gained the upper hand. The Etruscans were defeated in 474 BC by the fleet of Syracuse in the battle of Cyme off the coast of southern Italy. This Etruscan defeat gave Rome the opportunity of attacking the Etruscan hegemony in Central and Northern Italy. But Rome still had a long way to go. The Greek successes in the first quarter of the 5th century BC benefited Athens above all others, by giving it the chance to establish their hegemony across the Aegean. Sparta, on the other hand, afraid that Spartan power on the Peloponnese might be weakened by too many adventures abroad, withdrew in isolation. That the Spartan fears were not groundless is shown by the large rebellion of the helots in the years between 464 and 459 BC.

The Athenian democracy

When tyranny came to an end in 510 BC, the aristocrat Cleisthenes, who had played an important part in the struggle against Hippias, came into conflict with his fellow aristocrats. This was nothing uncommon, but it was unusual for Cleisthenes to turn for support to the *demos* in the way he did. The historian Herodotus puts it like this: "Cleisthenes added the *demos* to the number of his supporters." Cleisthenes did so by championing the political emancipation of the Athenian *demos*, an emancipation that had been instigated by Solon and Pisistratus before him. The events of the years between 510 and 508/7 BC cannot be reconstructed, but we can be certain that Cleisthenes initiated a program of political reforms that resulted in the shifting of the center of power to the *demos*, especially to the large group of the *zeugitai*. The military importance that the *zeugitai* gained as hoplites would have played its part. A newly formed body, the annual Council of 500, was the focal point of the arrangements. This council, or *boule*, was composed of 10 groups of 50 men,

Figure 19 Ostraca found in the Athenian Agora (5th c. BC). The potshards illustrated here date from the 5th century BC and were found on the Agora in Athens (they now are kept in the Agora Museum). They are so-called ostraca (*ostrakon* is the Greek word for potshard), which were used for the ostracism. In the years between 487 and 417 BC at least nine ostracisms were held in Athens. For an ostracism, the citizens came together in their assembly, with a quorum of 6000, and voted in a secret ballot that determined which Athenian had to be banished for a period of ten years, because he was becoming too powerful and a threat to Athenian democracy. Excavations have brought to light thousands of ostraca, carrying about 70 different names of Athenians, some known from other sources, and some not. On the shards illustrated here we read, clockwise from top left (the names are given here transcribed from the Greek and not Latinized, so that one may compare them with the writing on the ostraca): Aristeides, son of Lusimachos; Kimon, son of Miltiades; Themistokles, son of Neokles from the deme of Frearrioi; and Perikles, son of Xanthippos. Aristides was indeed ostracized in 482, Themistocles sometime around 470, and Cimon in 461. Pericles was never banished, but his father Xanthippus was ostracized in 485/484. Photo: American School of Classical Studies at Athens: Agora Excavations

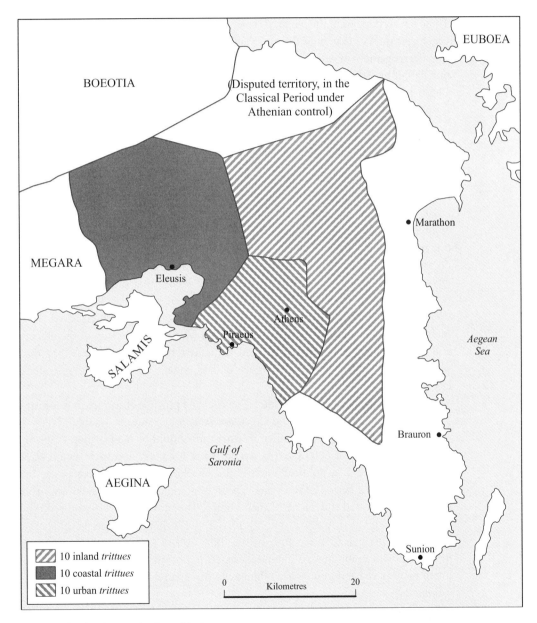

Map 10 The Cleisthenic organization of Attica

Legend within map:

- 10 inland *trittues*
- 10 coastal *trittues*
- 10 urban *trittues*

each group of 50 carefully selected to represent all of the Athenian *polis*. The same principle was applied to the army, composed of 10 units.

So, for the purpose of the *boule* and the army, the Athenian citizenry had to be divided into ten sections, in such a way that every section was, so to speak, the *polis* in miniature. These ten sections were the ten *fulai* on which the Cleisthenic system was based. The word *Cleisthenic* implies that all of this was Cleisthenes' brainchild, but it is in fact possible that this rearrangement of Athenian political and social life only took shape in the course of the first half of the 5th century BC. But we cannot trace the developments in any detail, and as Cleisthenes apparently was the one who set it all in motion, it seems justified to continue to speak of the Cleisthenic reform and the Cleisthenic system.

In order to create the ten Cleisthenic *fulai*, all local communities in Attica, the so-called demes (*demoi*, singular *demos*; here we will use the anglicized forms "deme" and "demes," in order to avoid any confusion with *demos*, "the people"), were grouped in 30 areas. Of these 30 areas, the so-called *trittues*, 10 were city *trittues*, 10 were coastal *trittues*, and another 10 were inland *trittues*. From each of these three categories, city, coast, and inland, one *trittus* was taken, and the three *trittues* selected in this way were combined into a single *fule* (three *trittues* to every *fule*: *trittus* means "third part"). In this way, ten *fulai* were created, which were artificial constructions that had nothing to do with the four *fulai* which existed before Cleisthenes. Every *fule* was composed of a city, a coast, and an inland *trittus*, three sets of demes that did not border each other (sometimes two *trittues* of a *fule* bordered each other, but never did all three). In every Cleisthenic *fule*, the Athenian citizens were mixed together, which achieved the goal of making every *fule* representative of the *polis* as a whole. Membership of the deme, *trittus*, and *fule* was hereditary. This conflicted with their territorial character, but the intent was to keep the size of each *fule* more or less equal, even if people migrated to the city.

At the same time, or somewhat later, the so-called practice of ostracism was introduced. The word "ostracism" is from the Greek *ostrakon*, which means "shard." Every year the citizens of Athens voted on whether an ostracism should be held or not. If the vote was positive, a quorum of 6000 citizens would come together, and each would scratch on a shard the name of a politically active citizen whom one would like to see banished from Athens for a period of ten years. Those who could not write could acquire a "pre-scratched" shard with the name of their choice. The individual who acquired the largest number of votes had to leave the city for ten years; hence, our usage of the verb "to ostracize." Although in the course of the fifth century BC ostracism became a weapon in the hands of ambitious political leaders seeking to oust their opponents, the original intent must have been to safeguard the young Athenian democracy by expelling potential *turannoi*.

Toward the end of the 6th century BC in Athens, power had shifted from the elite to the collective. *Demos* now takes on the meaning of "the whole of the citizenry," and not merely "the non-aristocratic people." This *demos* wielded *kratos*, the power to rule. In the course of the 5th century BC, Athenian democracy was radicalized, and the remaining powers of the aristocracy dwindled. In 487 BC, it was decided that the most important magistrates, the *archontes*, would no longer be selected, but would be chosen by lot. The archonship lost some of its power in the process, and with it the Areopagus, the council peopled by ex-archons. In 462 BC, almost all jurisdiction was transferred from the Areopagus to the new jury courts, and the supervision over Athens' magistrates to the Council of 500. Around the middle of the century, the archonship was opened up to people of the third census class, and the radical democracy culminated in pay for magistrates, *bouleutai*, and jury members. In the early 4th century BC, assembly pay was even extended to the *ekklesia*. Such fees made it possible for all citizens, also those who could not miss a day's work, to participate in the running of the *polis*. In other words: the poorest among the citizens, the *thetes*, were empowered to be politically active. This has been seen as the logical outcome of the importance of these *thetes* as Athens' mariners: it was the *thetes* who manned the fleet that was so important to Athens.

The Athenian Empire

The fleet ensured Athens' hegemony in the Aegean. In the aftermath of the Persian Wars, in 478/477 BC, a defensive and offensive league had been established, the so-called Delian League, because its headquarters and treasury were located on the island of Delos. Athens was the most important founding member. Many of the numerous other members paid a yearly sum into the common treasury, from which funds Athens maintained a fleet; there were only a few members who themselves contributed ships and sailors. In the course of the 5th century BC, this alliance developed into the Athenian Empire. The members became de facto subjects of Athens. Illustrative of this state of affairs is the transfer of the treasury from Delos to Athens, sometime before 450 BC, and also the continued existence of the League when it had become redundant, after a permanent peace with Persia was negotiated, from the middle of the century onward. Athens started behaving toward the league's members as an imperial power: members who wanted to leave the league or otherwise showed themselves uncooperative were coerced into submission, if necessary by brute force. Any *polis* that proved disloyal toward Athens was punished by having *klerouchiai* founded on its territory. A *klerouchia* is a piece of land that is confiscated and assigned to a *klerouchos*, an Athenian colonist. *Klerouchoi*, though settled outside Athens, remained Athenian citizens, and if they really went to live on their *klerouchiai*, they more or less functioned as an Athenian garrison. In this way, Athens had a permanent military presence throughout the region.

Despite these *klerouchiai*, we should not think of the Athenian Empire in terms of conquering territory and increasing the area and the number of inhabitants of the *polis*. It is all about hegemonic power: Athens strives to have other *poleis* submit to Athenian leadership, not to abolish them. Indeed, the citizenship of the increasingly rich and powerful Athens was a closely guarded privilege, if possible to be reserved for fewer, not more men. This fits in with the fact that Athens hardly interfered in the internal affairs of its subject *poleis*. For instance, the spread of democracy was not something that Athens actively propagated. Their pragmatic stance shows that hegemony was primarily a matter of economics. The tribute paid by the league members was not only used to build a fleet (which, of course, served Athens' interest more than anybody else's), but also paid for building projects in Athens, and helped to cover the costs of democracy with its pay for those who actively participated. Also, trade was deflected toward Athens' harbor, Piraeus; the *thetes* enjoyed a steady income from rowing the fleet; landless citizens got *klerouchiai*. But it would be wrong to see Athens' imperialism as being only about money: it was also quite honorable to bend other *poleis* to your will.

The conflict between Athens and Sparta

The political and military power of the Athenians, and their role as a cultural powerhouse that went with it, did not go down well with other *poleis*, which saw their independence threatened. Obviously, the state of affairs within the Delian League exacerbated such fears. Also, the presence and radicalization of democracy put Athens on a collision course with oligarchic and conservative *poleis*, especially Sparta. The closed society of Sparta, living in self-inflicted isolation and stagnation and expending all its energy on maintaining its military might, was diametrically opposed to Athens, an open society, expansive and self-confident. Sparta distrusted this dynamic society that had already carved out such a huge empire for itself. In retrospect, it seems inevitable that these two opponents would end up in conflict. What started as an attempt to safeguard their own position, for both Athens and Sparta, turned into a conflict with very strong ideological overtones. Because of coalitions with one or the other party, large parts of the Greek world were drawn into this war.

Now, warfare was nothing out of the ordinary. Nothing marked the Greek *poleis* as much as their aggressive rivalry: every *polis* wanted to be the best. The most effective way for a *polis* to gather honor, fame, and profit was to acquire hegemony over others. But at the same time, every *polis* was bent on maintaining, or regaining, its independence. Such competitiveness led to endemic warfare. This was in itself quite destructive, but the so-called Peloponnesian War between Athens, Sparta, and their allies, which spanned the best part of the last 30 years of the 5th century (431–404 BC), was a break with the past. For the first time, the Greek world saw warfare on such a scale and of such intensity that one can speak of "total war." Not only did citizen hoplites take part, but also lightly armed troops and cavalry, and not all combatants were citizens: ever more mercenaries were hired. Guerrilla tactics were employed, and this the year round, instead of the ordered battles that took place when the battle season was under way. The fighting became bitter: entire communities were sold into slavery, or slaughtered.

The Spartan land army found it hard to combat Athenian sea power. Led by the clever *strategos* Pericles, the Athenians opted for a defensive strategy: they pulled back behind defendable walls that linked Athens and its harbor Piraeus, the so-called Long Walls. The rest of Attica was abandoned, and all the population crowded behind the walls, where their food supply was ensured from overseas. The fleet meanwhile carried out raids on the coastal areas of the enemy. An epidemic in 430–429 BC killed many Athenians, among them Pericles, but they managed to hold out. Large-scale offensive actions, however, several on the urging of the Athenian politician Alcibiades, ended in disaster, especially the Sicilian Expedition (415–413 BC). This was an attempt by Athens to interfere in the politics of Sicily, turning against Syracuse, daughter city of Corinth, which in its turn was an ally of Sparta. It all ended in a terrible defeat for Athens, in part because of Spartan involvement. Sparta was prompted by Alcibiades, who had fallen out of favor in Athens and now advised the enemy. After this disastrous adventure, Sparta managed to occupy part of Attica on a permanent basis, and many *poleis* subject to Athens now revolted against the Athenian hegemony within the Delian League.

In the end, Sparta won the war with the financial support of Persia, which enabled them to build a fleet of their own. Persia made use of the Peloponnesian War to regain a foothold in the Greek world, by a policy of divide and rule. They had an advisor who knew the weak spots of the Greeks: Alcibiades, who had turned traitor again. The deep crisis Athens found itself in can be gauged from the events in 411 BC, when a group of anti-democratic politicians staged a short-lived revolution. The rights of a large part of the citizen population were severely curtailed. Democracy was, however, restored in the following year, because the *thetes* manning the fleet stood up for their political rights. Meanwhile, Lysander, the commander of the Spartan fleet, with the support of the Persian prince Cyrus II, managed to induce the *poleis* of Asia Minor to abandon Athens. In 405 BC, he crushed the Athenian fleet in a sea battle near the Hellespont. This cut off the Athenian supply of grain from the Black Sea. When Lysander's fleet sailed up to Athens the next year, Athens was forced to capitulate. The Delian League was dissolved, the Athenian fleet had to be surrendered, the walls were demolished, and democracy abolished. Athens was ruled by a repressive oligarchic junta, the Thirty. Sparta was now the only one to wield hegemonic power over the Greek *poleis*, but Persia pulled the strings.

The end of the classical *polis*

Sparta could not enjoy its position as the foremost *polis* for long. It made itself extremely unpopular by its support for undemocratic governments, its recourse to military means to enforce obedience, especially the payment of tribute money, and by not letting its own allies share in any of the profits that its victory brought. Already in 403 BC, after a short civil war, Athens reverted to democracy. New coalitions formed, and *poleis* that had fought against Athens now supported it against Sparta. The most important newcomer was Thebes, in Central Greece, which managed to establish itself as the third major force, next to Athens and Sparta. In Sicily and in southern Italy, Syracuse, now in the hands of the *turannos* Dionysius I, fought a number of wars with other Greek cities and with the Carthaginians, and came out as the paramount force in the region.

The Persians still managed to profit from the divisions among the Greek *poleis*. First, they supported the enemies of Sparta (when they had only just helped it become the biggest power); next, they allied themselves with Sparta in order to enforce a general peace, the King's Peace, so named after the Persian king who, together with Sparta, was its guarantor. All Greek *poleis* were to be independent, except those in Asia Minor, which now returned to Persian rule. Sparta was still the dominant power, but opposing forces developed. In 379 BC, Thebes got embroiled in a conflict with Sparta, and in 378/377 BC Athens created a new league, the so-called Second Athenian League. After a period of confused warfare, interspersed with truces and armistices, 371 BC saw a turning point: in the Battle of Leuctra, the Thebans, led by Epaminondas, put a definitive end to Spartan military superiority. With Sparta defeated, the next year Epaminondas invaded the Peloponnese, which led to the demise of the Peloponnesian League, and to Messenia gaining independence. The

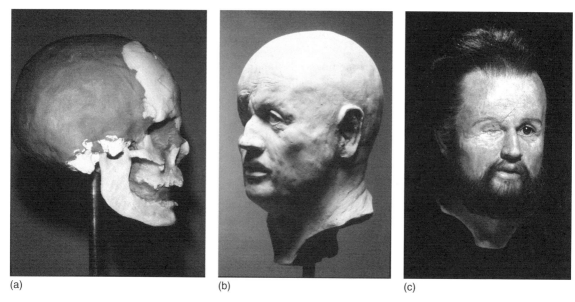

(a)   (b)   (c)

Figure 20   Philip II? Fragments of a skull from Vergina (4th c. BC) and a facial reconstruction based on those fragments. In 1977, archaeologists uncovered some extremely rich 4th-century graves under a huge tumulus in Vergina, Macedonia. In the grave with the most imported finds, known as Tomb 2, the central room contained a golden casket with cremated bones. From the fragments of a skull among these bones, a complete skull was reconstructed (left); on the basis of this skull, a face was reconstructed using forensic techniques (middle); and finally, a makeup artist turned a wax cast of that face into a lifelike image, adding facial hair according to the 4th-century BC Macedonian fashion (right). The result looks like known images of Philip II of Macedon, even though such images usually do not show that Philip had lost his right eye. That we know from written sources: in 354, Philip was hit by an arrow in the head during one of his military campaigns. So have we found the grave of Philip II? Since this reconstruction was presented, it has been shown how difficult it is to interpret cremated bones. Have we been carried away by wishful thinking? Photos: Whitworth Art Gallery, The University of Manchester

traditional Spartan society, already in decline, now collapsed quite rapidly. But neither Athens, nor Thebes, or any other *polis* for that matter, managed to profit in the long run from the disappearance of Spartan power. The *poleis* exhausted themselves in warfare, and the use of mercenaries was an enormous drain on their financial resources. A true general peace was what everyone wanted, but it floundered because of distrust in all directions. The Athenian *rhetor* Isocrates called, in vain, for a Panhellenic unity, for all *poleis* to stand together and confront the archenemy Persia, in order to liberate the Greeks of Asia Minor and conquer lands in the East for Greek settlement.

Meanwhile, in the north, there arose a new power: the kingdom of Macedon. For a long time, the Greek *poleis* had neglected that kingdom, regarding it as an uncivilized outpost of their world. There was truth in this: Macedon was politically and socially backward; it resembled what Greece used to be like long ago, before the *polis* became dominant. But from these half-barbarian lands there descended the troops of King Philip II (359–336 BC), who conquered Thrace and all of Greece. Philippus had created a mighty army, which combined the professionalism of a mercenary force with the loyalty of a citizen army. He recruited his soldiers from among the Macedonian peasantry and paid them with the gold that he got from the Thracian goldmines that he had conquered. In 338 BC, Philip defeated the Athenians and the Thebans in the Battle of Chaeronia in Boeotia. He then forced most *poleis* to join the Corinthian League, which meant that they recognized Philip as their overlord. But Philip had much more ambitious plans: he wanted to put Isocrates' ideas into practice and lead the Greeks against the Persians. In 336 BC, however, Philip was murdered in a palace brawl. It was left to his young son, Alexander, to carry out his father's plans.

In 338 BC, the classical *polis* came to an end: in the future, the Greek world would be dominated by kingdoms, and the majority of *poleis* would lose, at least de facto, their independence. But, of course, Greek cities did not disappear from the map; in fact, their number increased substantially in the period to come. As these cities continued to have local autonomy over their territories—and as we have seen, many classical *poleis* were under the sway of other more powerful *poleis* and did have to make do with local autonomy—we will go on calling these communities *poleis*, even after 338 BC.

Italy and the West

The expansion of the Roman Republic

From the 4th century BC onward, the western Mediterranean witnessed the transformation of Rome from a small city-state in Central Italy into a huge empire. In 510 BC, the Roman Republic was supposed to have come into existence. The date is disputed, because Roman historians made an effort to synchronize the history of Rome with that of Athens. Thus, it is rather suspicious that Rome got rid of its king in exactly the same year that Athens got rid of its *turannos*. But that the Etruscan rule over Rome came to an end, and that in the 5th century Rome operated independently, is a fact. Its survival was no foregone conclusion, though: it had to defend itself against other Latin cities, united with those cities in the Latin league against the Italian peoples who infiltrated into Latium from their mountain strongholds, and against the still very powerful Etruscan cities. Shortly after the start of the 4th century BC, there came on top of all these threats a Celtic invasion.

Around 400 BC, the expansion of Rome took off, with the capture of the Etruscan town of Veji, immediately to the north of the Tiber. The Roman territory doubled in size. The seizure of Rome by the Celts, who from the north penetrated deep into the Italian peninsula, around 390 BC, was a temporary setback. Fifty years on, Rome fought the Samnites in Campania, as an ally of the town of Capua; a bit later, they engaged in battle with the other Latin cities, which rose against the growing power of Rome, but they did so too late. The Latin League was dissolved in 338 BC, and most members were incorporated into Roman territory. Some, however, retained their independent status, officially as allies of Rome, but in reality completely under Roman power. Thus, the small Roman city-state started expanding: its territory, the *ager Romanus*, was steadily enlarged by annexing the territories of defeated cities. The inhabitants of such areas either got full Roman citizenship or a citizenship without political rights; but in both cases, the number of citizens (and the size of the Roman army) was increased. If some territory was not annexed but was granted independence, Rome considered this a favor in return for which the recipient had to show gratitude. This implied obedience: treaties concluded with such communities always stipulated that in matters of foreign policy and warfare, they had to defer to Rome. So Roman power grew along two lines: extension of Roman territory and the number of Roman citizens, and creation of a network of allies who were dependent on Rome.

Internal developments

When the monarchy came to an end, executive power in the Roman state was entrusted to two magistrates, chosen for a period of one year, who came to be called the consuls (they were probably called something else in the 5th century BC). Because the consuls' term of office was limited, the Senate, in which ex-consuls took a seat of honor, remained the most important body of the government. The Senate had a few hundred members: 300 was the number usually given as its traditional size. The popular assembly had only a minor role to play.

The 5th and 4th centuries BC were dominated by the so-called Struggle of the Orders, a conflict between patricians and plebeians. The word "patricians," *patricii*, is derived from *patres*, "fathers," that is, the heads of families. Patricians were family heads that had a seat in the Senate, together with their relatives. It is possible that under the last kings of Rome, the heads of some non-patrician families were admitted to the Senate, and maybe the 5th century BC saw non-patricians in the Senate as well. But by that time, patricians completely dominated the Senate, and also the consulate. They separated themselves from the rest of Roman society by turning the patricians into nobles, a closed caste that one could only belong to by birth. *Plebs* was the designation for all the others. This implies that, other than the patricians, the plebeians were not a homogenous group. Plebeians could be found at any level of Roman society. In the Struggle of the Orders, the plebeians rose against patrician rule, but not every plebeian pursued the same goals. Rich plebeians wanted to access to the Senate and to the consulate and the lesser appointment of *quaestor*, who dealt with public finance and food supply, a function instituted in around 450 BC. Poor plebeians wanted to be relieved of their debts and asked for a redistribution of land. For both parties to succeed, they had to break the power of the patricians. They succeeded in doing so by banding together. They instituted their own assembly, the *concilium plebis*, and chose their own leaders, the ten *tribuni plebis*, tribunes of the people.

By threatening to strike work and refuse military service, the plebeians first managed to have their tribunes recognized as the representatives of the people, who could veto any decision by the magistrates or the Senate, and were themselves inviolable. Next, the patricians were forced to make many further concessions. Over a period of 200 years, the patrician society was slowly dismantled. The recognition of the tribunes was followed by the codification, in 450 BC, of the hitherto unwritten laws of Rome in the Law of the Twelve Tables. Next, the marriage prohibition between patricians and plebeians was removed. At around 420 BC, plebeians became eligible for the function of *quaestor*, and sometime after that for the function of military tribune (around 400 such tribunes often replaced the consuls as the state's leading magistrates), and in 367 BC, plebeians gained access to the consulate itself. In the half century after 367 BC, a new ruling elite came into being, the so-called *nobilitas*, composed of the members of the patrician and the rich and powerful plebeian families. These *nobiles* could, as we have just seen, intermarry; so the elite got bigger. All in all, nothing like democratization occurred in Rome. Early in the 3rd century BC, the Struggle of the Orders was officially ended by the recognition that *plebiscita*, the decisions of the *concilium plebis*, had the force of law, without the Senate having had a say in the matter. However, by that time the *nobiles* could manipulate this plebeian assembly in any direction they wanted.

The poor plebeians got something out of the whole affair as well: their debts were restructured, debt slavery was abolished, their legal rights were guaranteed, and they got land in newly annexed territories. The expansion of Rome provided the funds and the land to give the poor a chance of a better life—as long as it lasted.

Chapter 4.2

The Social Fabric

Economic Life

The Athenian economy: Expenditure

The economy of classical Athens is one of the few complex economies of antiquity about which we have detailed information. Compared to other cities, Athens was an outward-looking *polis*, even extremely so, if one considers Athens' deliberate policy of large-scale imports of food and its central position in a trading network. Many *poleis* were much more introverted, largely agricultural, and strove for self-sufficiency. Sparta, Athens' opposite number, was self-sufficient as far as food was concerned, and it was not much dependent on the outside world for anything else either. One might say that the economic life of Sparta was of a decidedly primitive character when compared to that of Athens. During the period under discussion, the same conclusion applies to Rome. So it seems reasonable to focus on Athens.

Every Athenian had to spend on food, mostly grain: some wheat, but above all barley; on clothing, or on the raw materials for making clothes, which often was done at home; on shelter; on fuel; and on ironmongery, ceramics and the like, products usually provided by specialist craftsmen and not produced in the house. All but the poorest also spent money on a range of products and services to assist in the fulfillment of one's religious duties. Almost every Athenian had to save some money for the occasional bigger outlay, such as investment in one's own or someone else's enterprise, providing one's daughters with a dowry, or paying taxes, if one was wealthy enough to be liable to being taxed.

Under normal circumstances, the ordinary Athenian citizen did not pay any poll taxes; only the wealthy were supposed to contribute the so-called *leitourgiai* (liturgies). A liturgy is taxation in the sense that liturgies were a way to cream off the highest incomes in the Athenian *polis*, but the ideology was different. Whoever took it on himself to pay a liturgy, or rather was compelled to do so, at the most once every two years, presented to his fellow citizens something concrete, such as the defrayment of the costs of a religious festival or the fitting out of a warship. Thus, a liturgy was presented not so much as taxation than as a particular kind of patronage.

Antiquity: Greeks and Romans in Context, First Edition. Frederick G. Naerebout and Henk W. Singor.
© 2014 John Wiley & Sons, Inc. Published 2014 by John Wiley & Sons, Inc.

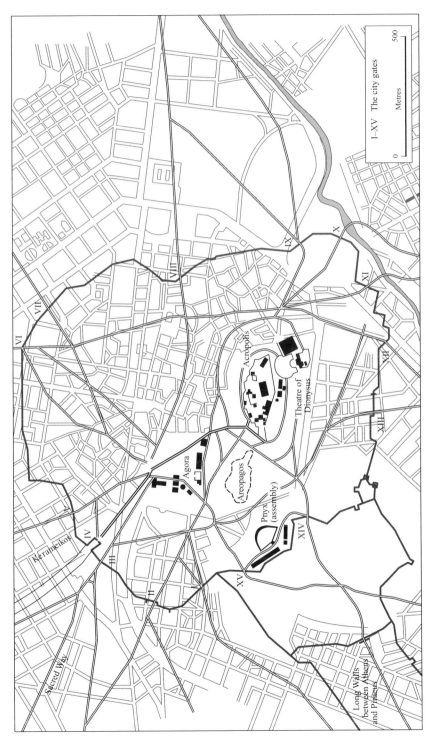

Map 11 Athens, 5th–4th c. BC

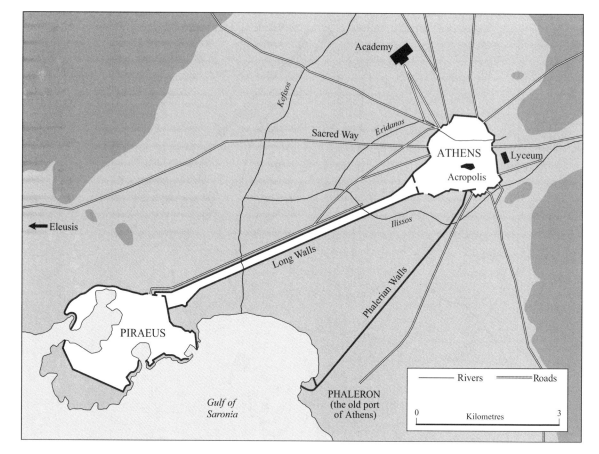

Map 12   The southern half of the Athenian plain

The costs of a so-called common liturgy were a few hundred drachmas, while the so-called extraordinary liturgies, such as the trierarchy, that is, the fitting out and sailing of a *trieres*, caused the generous trierarch to lose at least one talent (a talent is 60 mina, or 6000 drachmas) of his property. Liturgies were imposed upon the small group of wealthy citizens whose property was valued at one talent or over. This group consisted of 2000 people at the most. The even smaller group of those possessing 3 to 4 talents, a half to one percent of the total citizen population, bore the brunt of this system of compulsory gift giving. In return, the liturgists got to pull strings in the political life of Athens. These very few well-to-do individuals were not only notable because they spent so much on liturgies, but also for conspicuous consumption: by spending on luxury goods and services, they displayed their wealth and status.

Of other forms of benevolence by the wealthy, there is not much to tell: they assisted their friends and relatives in times of financial crisis, and made regular small contributions as the patron of a circle of dependents. But charity did not exist. Distributing food certainly was one of the many ways in which the rich let their fellow citizens share in their opulence, to the credit of themselves and their families, but this was never restricted to the needy:

every citizen got his share, including the affluent, who often got a larger share precisely because they were rich and distinguished. Benevolence, whether in the form of a liturgy or an occasional gift, was aimed at the entire community, and not only at the needy members of that community.

The Athenian economy: Income

When considering how Athenians earned an income to meet the aforementioned expenditures, we can look at the productive forces, that is, the natural resources, labor, and capital. Most important of the natural resources was land. In Athens, most arable land was in the hands of private landowners. This ownership was widely distributed: a majority of the citizen population owned at least some land. Within Attica, large-scale landownership hardly existed—but it should be noted that several members of the Athenian upper class owned extensive land holdings outside Attica. Within Attica, small farmers working their own plot of land predominated, while many who were not farmers still had small possessions. Of course, those who owned land did not need to exploit it themselves; they could lease out part or all of it.

In the pre-industrial world, labor was very important among the productive forces. Power from sources other than human labor only contributed a relatively small amount of the total power required. In Athens, human labor was not only provided by free laborers, citizens and non-citizens, but also by slaves. Whenever and wherever slaves were introduced, they had to produce a surplus over and above their cost of living; only the richest could afford to have slaves work exclusively in the household in unproductive tasks. In Athens, slaves could be found in agriculture, in trade and industry, in mining and quarrying, and as domestic staff, but definite information about their numbers is lacking.

Capital consists of the raw materials used in producing goods, and also the reusable capital goods. In the ancient world, capital or investment goods were an underdeveloped category. Of course, tools were in general use, and other types of equipment were fairly widespread, but labor was much more important. Athens, however, offers an example of an industry that was both labor- and capital-intensive: the extraction of silver.

On his own property or on leased land, the Attic farmer could produce food for subsistence, primarily grain crops supplemented by a kitchen garden and some animals herded on common land, and some surplus in order to be able to buy on the market what could not possibly be produced within the household. Alternatively, he could concentrate on producing for the market and obtain part of or even all of the food and other necessities of life by selling or bartering his produce. The majority of small farmers, the so-called *autourgoi*, that is, "those who work their own land," had farms that totaled 3.5 to 5.5 hectares. A single hectare (2.47 acres) could feed an average person for a year, after subtracting sowing seed and taking the fallow into account. This means that the *autourgoi* could subsist on their holdings, although it will often have been difficult to generate much of a surplus to sell or to store in view of the inevitable poor harvests still to come. It is doubtful, however, if most smallholders of Attica practiced subsistence farming. It is not unlikely that many had at least part of their land under cash crops, because market gardens, olive groves, and vineyards are quite likely to have been much more profitable per hectare compared to the cultivation of grain. But the prospect of a nice profit will not always have been the decisive factor: the wish to make a profit was counteracted by the desire to be self-sufficient. Self-sufficiency was the unattainable ideal of every household, as it was of the community at large.

A different way of earning an income was investing one's savings in some business venture, for example, the buying of slaves in order to hire them out as laborers, the leasing out of land, the letting of real estate, or the setting up of some enterprise, from a one-man business down to a "factory" (the largest business mentioned in our sources employed over 100 slaves). It was also possible to invest in shipping, either vessels or cargo, but that carried a high risk. It will have been for this reason that only a few Athenian citizens are known to have owned ships or taken part in overseas trade; that sort of thing was left to non-citizens. Citizens preferred to operate as tax farmers of the Athenian harbor duties. The *polis* did not itself collect any taxes or duties, but preferred to farm this out at a fixed price to a syndicate created for this purpose.

Those who wanted to invest in mining leased an existing mine or a plot where a mine could be developed. The lessor was the *polis*: apparently, Athens adhered to the principle of the so-called *Bergregal*, which implies that everything beneath the soil is state property. Those who leased a mine or plot set to work, employing slave labor, with the intention of extracting as much silver ore as possible. Profits could be enormous, but obviously, without any reliable prospecting techniques, mining was a lottery. Investing in the washing and smelting of the silver ore was far less risky, but required a large outlay in amenities and slave labor.

Some Athenians lent out their money at interest to others in order to enable them to set up some business. Indeed, such private financing was the only way to acquire outside capital, as Athenian banks would not, nor were they supposed to, take any risks with their clients' deposits.

We have talked of self-sufficiency and of cash incomes derived from selling at a profit; leasing or letting out land, estate, or slaves; or lending out money. But many inhabitants of the *polis* had hardly any property at all. They could not grow their own food or produce for the market; they had nothing to let, lease, or lend out; no money to invest; nor securities that enabled them to borrow any money. This group had only one thing to earn an income with: their labor. In Athens, to be a wage earner usually meant to be a day laborer. Day laborers could be found in the building trade, in agriculture, manufacturing, and trade, but the biggest employer, at least during part of the year, was the Athenian fleet. One could compare the salaried rowers of the Athenian fleet to mercenaries.

Toward the end of the 5th century, a day's wages for unskilled labor was 3 obols (half a drachma), and for skilled labor 1 drachma. A wage of 3 obols during 350 days adds up to an annual income of 175 drachmas, which is meager. The amount of grain necessary for bare survival costs about 20 to 30 drachmas per head per year. But a laborer earning a daily wage of 1 drachma could generously provide for a family by working for just 300 days. It is enlightening to compare these wages to the daily allowances, to be discussed below, which the *polis* paid to those engaged in political activities. These turn out to be quite comparable.

Figure 21   Ancient terracing in Attica. In ancient agriculture, frequent use was made of terracing, which hugged the contours of the landscape. Terraces helped to avoid erosion of deforested, intensively cultivated slopes. The landscape on this old aerial photograph is now covered by the metropolis Athens. What we see are the western slopes of the Hymettus mountain range, near Trachones, to the south of Athens. The arrows A, B, and C point to ancient terracing, in different states of preservation. Whereas the terraces themselves have largely vanished, one can still see from the air the light colored bands formed by stones that once were part of their retaining walls. Photo ©John Bradford, *Ancient Landscapes*

Exchange

The imports into Athens include luxury products or the raw materials needed for their manufacture, such as ivory and gold. But these goods, intended for a relatively small elite, constituted a very minor part of the total import basket. The main bulk of imports consisted of essential products: wood, metals, and ores (which also had military-strategic importance), slaves, and above all, foodstuffs. Athens was not capable of feeding its own population. How much food had to be imported, we do not know: there are too many unknown factors involved, as we do not know the exact extent of the arable land, how it was farmed, the yields per hectare, and the size of the population. But we can make some rough calculations, and these indicate that food imports must have been quite substantial.

For the 5th century BC (before the Peloponnesian War), the number of citizens has been estimated as 50,000 at the most, and for the 4th century as 30,000. We should multiply this by about 3.5 to include women and children. We have no idea how many slaves and free non-citizens lived in Athens. Estimates put the total population in the 5th century at 350,000 at the most for the whole of Attica, and in the 4th century at 200,000. It is certain that even with 200,000 residents, Athens was the most populous *polis* of the Greek world. The arable land in Athens, even if it was wholly under grain—which it was not—could not have supported a population of that size. Thus, structural imports of foods from elsewhere were an absolute necessity. This was a unique situation: other *poleis* imported food at some stage of their existence, but no *polis* was as dependent on the outside world as was Athens during its heydays.

What exports could balance these imports from regions with an agricultural surplus production, such as the south of Russia? We often hear olives and wine being mentioned, but quite a large part of the total production—about which again we have no precise information—must have been consumed locally. And even if there was a large exportable surplus, where would it be exported to? Almost all *poleis* had olive groves and vineyards of their own. Athens will, however, have exported manufactured products, above all the still-famed Attic ceramics, and raw materials, especially marble and other building stone. But these are all fairly small sectors of the economy. The main export of Athens must have been silver: profits from the empire, in the form of tribute and of harbor duties, and above all income from the silver mines at Laurion in the south of Attica.

Government

The Athenian government did not interfere much in the economic life of its citizens. Even essential imports, such as wood for shipbuilding, seem to the have been left entirely to private initiative, though Athenian sea power in the 5th century must have put effective pressure on traders to carry their goods to Athens instead of elsewhere. But whatever the role of Athenian power, it is still clear that Athens had no economic policies. There was, however, one predictable exception: the import of grain. Only this trade was regularly discussed in the assembly. Grain imports were literally a matter of life or death. In the 5th century, there was a close relationship between imperial power and the grain trade: the Athenian fleet protected the trade routes, and Athens even had special magistrates called *Hellespontofulakes*, "those guarding the Hellespont," who were charged with keeping open that narrow passage through which flowed the grain from the Black Sea region. In the 4th century, Athens had lost much of its power, and safeguarding the grain imports became ever more difficult. The *polis* went to great lengths, pampering rulers from the Black Sea region and promulgating severe laws such as the law that mandated the death sentence for any Athenian citizen who shipped grain to any port other than Athens. The *polis* also took responsibility for the grain after it had arrived in Attica: special officials kept an eye on the grain as it moved from the harbor to the retailers, and made sure that it was offered at "an honest price." If a shortage seemed imminent, the *polis* tried to buy grain in the open market in order to supply Athenians with grain at subsidized prices. For this purpose, the *polis* taxed those who could afford to pay some extra: if food was distributed, whether subsidized or for free, this was always because of gift giving, more or less voluntary, by the wealthy.

The *polis* of Athens got its income, if we leave aside the tribute that the 5th-century empire brought in, mainly from levying taxes. The non-citizens resident in Athens paid a yearly tax, and they and the wealthier citizens paid a special property tax in times of war. For citizens, this was the only direct taxation. They were taxed in this way very infrequently in the 5th century, but in the next century these war taxes increased in number, and there was even a small tax office instituted in order to convince the wealthier citizens to assist the *polis* on a regular basis. Indirect taxes were very common, and levied on everything from the slave trade to brothel keeping. They were usually farmed out to the highest bidder. The most important indirect taxes were market and harbor duties: in 402–401 BC, a syndicate of tax farmers paid the *polis* the enormous sum of 36 talents in order to be allowed to levy a 2% harbor duty on all imports and exports. As they must have expected to make a profit, this points to a huge trade in Piraeus. The *polis* also collected legal costs and fines, and leased out state property, some land, but more importantly mining concessions at Laurion. If income fell short, the *polis* used to borrow money. These often quite substantial sums of money were lend to the *polis* by temple treasuries.

The expenses of the *polis* were as diverse as its sources of income. First, there were the costs of the democracy to bear, the salaries of magistrates and officials on the one hand, and the pay for those actively pursuing their democratic rights on the other. Comparable to the political pay is the *theorikon*, literally "the viewing money." Originally, this was a subsidy that compensated for the loss of a day's wages when one went to the theater in order to see the plays performed that were an integral part of the festival of the Dionysia (to be discussed below). In the 4th century, the *theorika* turned into "festival pay" that was handed out on ever more festive occasions. For many Athenians, such financial support must have been most welcome, but the *theorika* never were intended as relief for the poor: all citizens could claim these benefits. Of the other expenses in peacetime, the largest were the building costs of public buildings, above all, temples. Apart from such building schemes, the *polis* spent but little on public amenities. It was only in Hellenistic days that some outlay on public schools or on a medical doctor employed by the *polis* is seen. The religious duties of the community involved huge expenses, but here we encounter many liturgies. Obviously, military operations were extremely costly: to field an army, the troops had to be paid, whether it was a citizen army, or, as was increasingly the case, an army of mercenaries. In Athens, large sums were involved in the building of warships: only the fitting out of an existing ship was a liturgy, the trierarchy (as mentioned earlier). When a ship was in service, the *polis* had to pay the rowers, although in practice, certainly in the 4th century when money was tighter, the trierarch was supposed to shoulder that considerable burden as well. As in the case of the provision with grain in times of need, in military matters the *polis* tended to dip deep into the pockets of its rich.

Social Hierarchy

The free and the enslaved

Every ancient society was structured along several different lines. Most importantly, those born free were distinguished from slaves and ex-slaves, and citizens from non-citizens.

These dichotomies were crisscrossed by other distinctions: age, sex, wealth, descent, place of residence, occupation, and education; male versus female, rich versus poor, noble versus commoner, town dweller versus rustic, and so on and so forth. In this way, a complicated network was created within which every individual found his or her place.

In the classical period, those born free and "the others" were clearly defined groups. Rome in the 5th and 4th centuries BC still knew debt slavery or debt bondage, but when we speak of slaves here, we mean slaves from outside the community who were bought (and sold). Such slaves were people who were enslaved during warfare, robbed by pirates or other traffickers, abandoned or sold by their parents, or condemned to slavery. If slaves had children, they also became slaves. But such natural propagation of slaves would have been comparatively rare: male slaves always far outnumbered female slaves, and not all slaves were allowed to start families. In classical Athens, there definitely was no systematic "breeding" of slaves. Concurrent with slavery, there existed many other forms of dependent labor and serfdom, often outside the Greco-Roman world in a narrow sense. Examples from Greece proper were the helots in Sparta and groups in Thessaly and on Crete that were in a comparable position.

The existence of "un-free," in whatever form, was taken for granted in all ancient societies (whether there were a large number of un-free present or not). There were a few thinkers (and comedians) who tried to imagine a society without slave labor, but this was never a serious option. Slave labor was indispensable, or was thought to be so. The treatment of slaves was extremely variable. The individual who was condemned to live out his life as a slave in a copper, silver, or sulfur mine was to be pitied indeed, but a slave who was a trusted housekeeper or steward could be in much better circumstances than many free people could ever dream of. Nevertheless, every slave was, from the standpoint of the law in an extremely inferior position: a slave was an object or rather an animal, an animated tool that was the property of its owner, who could freely dispose of it. But then again it turned out to be difficult to keep denying that slaves were fellow human beings: in classical Athens, one was not allowed to kill one's own slave, and a slave who was ill-treated could run away and ask for asylum (which implied being sold to another owner).

An implicit recognition of a slave's humanity lies also at the basis of the fact that a slave could be liberated: a slave could be given his or her freedom or could be bought free, by anyone willing to do so, or by himself. In practice, though not recognized as such in the law, a slave could own property. If a slave could earn and save, he could in due course put up his own price. In the Greek world, only a small minority of the slave population could expect to liberate themselves or be liberated. Liberated slaves and their descendants did not get citizen rights but became free non-citizens. In contrast, in Rome the liberation of slaves became a common occurrence that many slaves could look forward to. And although the *libertus* usually remained tied to his former master, as to a *patronus*, still, he did obtain citizen rights, with only a few political restrictions.

Citizens and non-citizens

A second fundamental distinction is that between the citizens on the one hand, that is the *politai*, that part of the population that can take an active part in politics; and the non-citizens on the other. There exist *poleis* that divide the inhabitants into a group of "true citizens," such as the Spartan *Homoioi*, and into a group of inferior citizens or even serfs or slaves. We are talking about the autochthonous population, not about foreigners or slaves supplied from elsewhere. The alternative is a *polis* that extends citizenship rights to all freeborn men on its territory. Such was the case in Athens. It is only those who came in at a later date who were excluded.

A citizen was a grown-up, freeborn man who satisfied certain criteria. In the Archaic period, mainly economic criteria were used: the amount of property owned and the contribution that one could make to the defense of the *polis*. In the Hellenistic period, there would be in many places a return to such economic criteria. In classical Athens, it was above all one's lineage that decided whether one was a citizen or not. After 451–450 BC, a strict law stipulated that one could claim Athenian citizenship if one was a male born in legal wedlock of a father who was an Athenian citizen and a mother who was the daughter of an Athenian citizen. Also, the father had to recognize the child as a member of his *oikos*, his household, and it had to be registered with the *polis*. As long as they were minors, the sons of citizens could not exercise any of their citizenship rights, and thus were in a position comparable to that of women, who too could only claim to be related to a citizen. When the son attained majority on his 18th birthday, his citizenship came into effect. In the case of women, this never happened: in the eyes of the Athenians, they remained minors as long as they lived.

The best explanation for the strict rules on Athenian citizenship seems to be that the citizens did not want to dilute the important economic and political privileges that were part and parcel of their citizenship rights, by opening up the citizenship to outsiders. They wanted to restrict these privileges to a relatively small group. Only citizens could own immovable property, both land and a dwelling on one's own land. Non-citizens were not allowed to own any part of the *polis* territory. Only citizens could inherit from other citizens, legally marry a citizen's daughter, lease concessions in the Attic silver mines, be eligible for distributions of money or grain by the *polis*, hold public office and official priesthoods, take an active part in the political life of the *polis*, be a jury member in the courts, and join in the religious life of the *polis* to the full.

The *polis* was home to many free inhabitants who did not match the criteria for citizenship. Athens with its busy harbor was visited by many strangers, *xenoi*, who were passing through: traders, sailors, itinerant craftsmen, tourists, and mercenaries. Also, a large number of scholars came to Athens, which in the 4th century was an important intellectual center. But not everybody was a temporary visitor: there were also many immigrants who came to stay. They had fled poverty, warfare, or personal problems, or had been attracted by the economic potential of Athens. The last-mentioned group, the ones who stayed on, had their own clear juridical status. They were called *metoikoi*, "(im)migrants," anglicized as "metics." The only privilege that the metic status carried with it was the permission to live in Athens. In exchange for that privilege, one had to shoulder several duties: the payment of the *metoikion*, a poll tax or capitation, and serving in the Athenian army. No metic enjoyed the many citizen privileges already mentioned, and in addition metic and citizen were not completely equal before the law.

The rich and the poor

The distinction between the rich and the poor intersects the distinctions between the citizen and the outsider, and between the free and the un-free. The ideology of the *polis* might state that all citizens were equal, but it is obvious enough that in several respects they were not equal at all. The big gap between haves and have-nots was quite conspicuous: in classical Athens, one could meet day laborers who had no property at all, millionaires, and everyone in between. A few philosophers dreamed of an ideal society with all property held in common, but the general opinion was that the difference between rich and poor was a fact of life and quite acceptable. Society at large did not attempt to do away with such differences. The differences in wealth and income were even formalized: as we have seen, ever since the early 6th century, the Athenian citizenry was divided into four classes according to assessable property. In the 4th century BC, the gap between the rich and the poor widened all over the Greek world, as also in democratic Athens, although Athens managed to avoid some of the excesses seen elsewhere. In Sparta, landed property was concentrated in ever fewer hands, and this caused the number of *Homoioi* to decrease, and the number of "lesser citizens," the ones who could no longer afford the compulsory contributions to the *sussition*, to increase. *Perioikoi*, helots, and mercenaries had to replace these demoted citizens in the Spartan army, which started to weaken.

Not only among citizens, but also among metics and slaves we find the entire gamut from extreme poverty to extreme riches. A wealthy slave was much better off than a poor citizen: being free born and having citizenship did not ensure one a comfortable life. The absolute number of rich citizens in Athens was small: the division of property was very much skewed, with a large percentage of total property concentrated in a few hands. Athenians considered as truly *plousioi*, "rich," those who were wealthy enough to be members of a leisure class. These rentiers were the same people who were the benefactors of the *polis* by way of the liturgies, and as we already saw, this was a small group.

Among the rich, we find both old and new money. This implies the existence of upward social and economic mobility, even if the chances of advancement were comparatively slim in 5th and 4th century Athens, where so many lived at or near minimum subsistence level. Some, however, enriched themselves, by way of a windfall profit, a shrewd marriage, a substantial inheritance, or war booty. If one had no citizen's rights, there were even more hurdles to overcome. The richest metics, whether immigrants or liberated slaves, were as wealthy as the richest citizens, but even for them it was difficult to obtain citizenship, certainly after the law regulating citizenship of 451–450 BC. Citizenship could not be conferred by an individual, not even when liberating a slave or adopting an heir. Only the assembly could decide on the naturalization of groups or individuals who had done something special to benefit the *polis*. The most affluent metics could gain goodwill by their willingness to pay taxes and undertake liturgies. By showing themselves to be as loyal to the *polis* as the most loyal citizens, they might hope for naturalization.

Becoming a citizen would not solve all problems: new money was looked down upon, and even the born citizen who had struck it rich was not so easily accepted by the established families. Among the Athenian elite of the 5th and 4th centuries, belonging to the nobility no longer brought any real advantages, even if family trees and ancestors were valued. The noble families of old supplied several of the leading figures of Athenian politics, but these had to share the stage with newcomers. Nevertheless, there was an aristocratic background to many of the ideals of the *polis*. The whole notion of a leisure class originated in the ideology of the nobility, as did the notion that landed property was the best form of property. Nouveaux riches whose property depended upon trade or manufacture could not measure up to such ideals. During the 5th century, they were accepted into wealthy society with bad grace, matters only improving somewhat in the course of the 4th century. Buying land was something in the way of a solution: it was bought with the wrong kind of money, but at least it was the right kind of property. All in all, it was difficult to climb the social ladder in classical Athens. If one made money, there were still political and social hurdles to overcome.

Rome and Roman citizenship

Rome of the 5th century was still a simple society with on the one hand a nobility, the patricians, and on the other "the people," the *plebs*. In the course of the 4th century, this began to change: the people became an ever more heterogeneous group. Strong economic differentiation went hand in hand with the military expansion of Rome. Increased economic power was translated into increased political power: rich plebeians merged with the patricians to form a new elite. The Roman poor could only better themselves at the expense of Rome's neighbors. These developments do not add up to the creation of an Athenian-style "democracy." The new elite monopolized power as much as the patricians had done. Roman citizenship did not give the citizen a true voice in Roman politics. On the other hand, Rome was known for the liberality with which it handed out its citizenship. That was a clever policy, along the principle of "divide and rule," to obtain the allegiance of local elites; it was also a way to rapidly increase the number of Romans, and thus also the number of Roman soldiers. At the same time, the Roman elite could enlarge their own *clientela* because whoever made someone else a Roman citizen became that person's *patronus*. Thus, the hierarchical Roman society with its basic structures in patron–client relationships was strengthened by giving away something that was of relatively little value—at least in political terms. In the Greek *poleis*, which were so egalitarian compared to Rome, citizenship carried with it actual political rights, and thus these communities were at pains to limit their citizenship to a small group of privileged individuals.

Political Organization

Varieties in the forms of political organization

In the ancient world, political life was structured in many different ways: in the East, we encounter monarchies and territorial empires, such as the Persian Empire. In the Greek-speaking world, there were still some monarchs to be found: Macedon, Sparta, and Epirus are the obvious examples. In the peripheral areas of the Mediterranean world, and of course beyond it, there existed many forms of tribal organization. Very prominent in the Mediterranean heartlands were the city-states, which we find in the Greek world, in the Levant, along the African coast (Carthage) and in Italy, among the Etruscans, and the Latins (the Roman Republic being one of them). The role of the citizen body, however that was defined, in governing their community, differed from the one city-state to the next. We find radical democracy, absolute oligarchy, and everything in between. The Athenian democracy was imitated elsewhere in the Greek World, and other *poleis* turned to democracy of their own accord. It was only in the days of Alexander the Great that democracy became the dominant polity among Greek *poleis*. Before that, at least as far as our rather scanty sources allow us to tell, tyrannies, oligarchies, and democracies occurred in more or less equal numbers. Especially outside the Greek motherland, tyrannies remained a common phenomenon even after the end of the Archaic period; as late as the 4th century, their numbers increased. The power of 5th-century and certainly of 4th-century *turannoi* depended on the presence of mercenaries. The rulers of the Hellenistic period were in many respects the heirs of these tyrants.

The Athenian democracy

We can discuss the political life of Athens in greater detail. The basis of the Athenian state lies in the deme: the village or town quarter. The citizens who inhabited a deme gathered in a local assembly to decide on local matters: the organization of a religious festival, public safety, and the management of local finances. The deme also carried out tasks for the central government, such as the selection of candidates for several governing bodies, the maintenance of a kind of registry office (very important for establishing who was a citizen and who was not), and the mobilization of citizen soldiers in case of war. Foreign policy, law making, and jurisdiction were not the responsibility of the deme.

The *ekklesia*, the assembly of all citizens, was literally an assembly that every citizen could take part in: there were no representatives; Athenian democracy was a direct democracy. When the *ekklesiastikon*, assembly pay, was instituted not long after 400 BC, even the poor who could not afford to lose a day's wages were able to participate in governing their *polis*. The assembly had the decisive voice in Athenian policy making. In the 5th century BC, there probably were ten or eleven regular meetings every year, although additional ones could be called for. In the 4th century BC, there were at first 30 days on which the assembly met, which later increased to 40.

It has been estimated that the Pnyx, the hill opposite the Acropolis where the *ekklesia* met, could seat about 6000 men. Apparently, 6000 was deemed sufficient in order to speak of "an assembly of the whole of the Athenian people." Of course, 6000 was a small minority of the total number of citizens, but as we encounter the same figure in the quorum for holding an ostracism and in the total number of jurors, we must conclude that 6000 was seen in Athens as a representative group.

The agenda of the assembly was the responsibility of the *boule*, the Council of 500. The *boule* had to obey certain rules: every year ten assembly meetings, or at least some of them, had to be dedicated to a set of fixed subjects: the grain supply, military matters, and the appointment of magistrates. But otherwise, the *boule* had a free hand. With any item

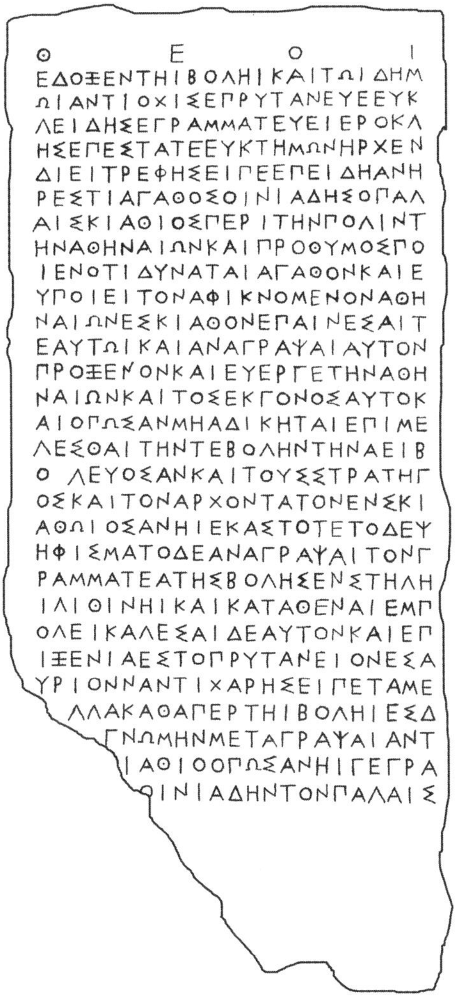

Figure 22 Stele with an Athenian decree (408/407 BC). An Athenian decree honoring one Oiniades of Skiathos, 408/7 BC. Oiniades, an inhabitant of the island of Skiathos (near the Thracian coast on the route from Athens to the north), is praised for the services which he offers to Athenians who pass through Skiathos. The text opens with the following formulaic passage: "Gods. This is a decree of the Council and People of Athens, during the prytany of the *fule* Antiochis, when Eucleides was secretary and Hierocles president. The proposal was made by Euctemon." Next, the proposal is given: it is proposed that Oiniades and his descendants should be allowed to call themselves *proxenos* and benefactor of the Athenians. He will be protected by Athenian power, and on the day after the passing of this decree he will be invited to join the *prutaneis* for a meal held in his honor in their hall on the Athenian Agora. A *proxenos* was a citizen of a *polis* who acted as a kind of honorary consul to the citizens of another *polis*. In the 5th century, the *proxenoi* of Athens played a part in the extension of Athenian power over the members of the Delian League, which explains the fact that Athens extends its protection to Oiniades. The decree also mentions an amendment: it is decided to change Skiathos into Old Skiathos: Oiniades comes from Old Skiathos, lying inland, and not from New Skiathos on the coast. Apparently, the Council liked to be quite precise. It is also decreed that the text of the decree should be inscribed on a marble stele that should be positioned on the Acropolis. That is where this stele was found. Now it is in the Epigraphic Museum in Athens. Drawing © F.G. Naerebout

included in the agenda, they could give advice on how to vote. This advice (*probouleuma*) was not binding, and the assembly could negate it, amend it, or suggest an alternative.

The *boule* counted 500 council members (*bouleutai*). Every citizen 30 years old or over was eligible to be a *bouleutes* for a period of one year. One could be re-appointed just once. The *bouleutai* came from all over Attica: as we have seen in chapter 4.1, this was accomplished by taking 50 men from each of the ten *fulai*. The *fulai* selected their 50 *bouleutai* by the drawing of lots among the demes members. The *boule* met quite often, and the ten groups of 50 *bouleutai* who came from the same *fule* took turns in manning the executive committee that took care of daily business. The 50 members of that committee were called the *prutaneis*; one-third of them were supposed to be on duty for 24 hours. Consequently, any council member had but little time left for his own affairs during his year in office. From the middle of the 5th century or thereabouts, a council member received council pay, the *misthos*, but this *misthos* was less than a proper day's wages. So it does not come as a surprise that among the *bouleutai* whose social background can be traced, the wealthier citizens were overrepresented.

Preparing the meetings of the assembly was the main task of the *boule*. But the council also had to ensure that decisions by the assembly were carried out, and especially to keep a check on third parties hired for certain tasks. The council, or commissions composed of council members, kept an eye on all servants of the *polis*, supervised shipbuilding, the provisioning of the fleet, the tendering and execution of public works, and were involved in the organization of religious rites. The *boule* also functioned as court of the first instance for all cases that had to do with these specific tasks.

The *boule* should not be seen as subservient to the assembly; the probouleutic task gave the *boule* quite a lot of power. The assembly usually followed the council's advice, and when the council refused to put something on the agenda, it was effectively blocked from discussion in the assembly. So, in many respects the *boule* should be seen as the linchpin of Athenian government. This was simply an issue of effectiveness: a group of 500, or 50, will find it easier to discuss a matter thoroughly than an assembly of 6000. The assembly was quite willing to leave the less important decisions to the council. The council also took emergency decisions when there was no time to wait until the next assembly meeting came along. The assembly, however, could reverse such decisions, and always had the final say in any matter. Thus, a strong *boule* never constituted a threat to Athens' radical democracy as it unfolded during the 5th century.

The so-called jury courts that came into being in the 5th century BC, were, in a way, the assembly functioning as a popular court. The jury courts were based on Solon's *Heliaia*, and were also called, now in the plural, *heliaiai*. Now, however, they were courts of the first instance as well, and no longer just courts of appeal, as Solon's *Heliaia* had been. They were also called *dikasteria*, after the *dikastai*, the members of the jury. In fact, the *dikastai* were not quite comparable to jury members, because they were juror and judge at the same time. The presiding magistrate was no judge. The number of *dikastai* could vary from 201 to 2501, depending on how serious the case in hand was judged to be. During the 5th century, the *dikastai* were selected at random from a pool of 6000 citizens of 30 years or over; in the 4th century, every citizen could be a juror. Since the days of Pericles, citizens got paid for this important task. There was no public prosecutor, nor any council: every case was brought forward by a private individual. Possibly a *rhetor* was hired in order to write a rousing speech, but accusation or defense was left to the parties themselves.

In the 4th century BC, everyone who proposed a decree in the *ekklesia* could be brought before a jury court if the decree was considered to be "unlawful," that is to say, "incompatible with the existing laws of the *polis*." If the verdict went against the accused, the proposal and the decree, if the assembly had voted in favor of the proposal, were indeed declared unlawful and the instigator himself was fined. This was intended to avoid the misuse of democratic law making, but of course it could also be a weapon in the hands of rival politicians, subverted more or less in the same way that ostracism (which was no longer in vogue after the end of the 5th century BC) had been.

Magistrates and officials

Athens had many different kinds of magistrates and officials. Officially speaking, they were of different kinds only and not of different rank, even though in real life the positions varied in regard to prestige and political power. The one exception was the military magistrates, where we do find a hierarchy. Most offices, however, were considered to be of equal rank, and in addition one almost always had to share one's position with others: until the middle of the 4th century BC, collegiality was the rule. Any office was shared by several individuals, often ten, in line with the basic decimal structure of Athenian politics. Any citizen 30 years of age or over could aspire to some office; only the *thetes* were excluded. Even during the most radical phase of Athenian democracy, this law remained unchanged, but we get the impression that nobody really bothered to implement it. The positions that were to be filled by drawing lots were de facto open to every citizen, while the positions filled by election, that is the ones for which some special abilities were required, were both by law and in reality the preserve of the most prominent citizens. Apparently, the democratic government was prepared to leave such functions to members of the elite, especially those from old noble families, who had the right kind of education and background. Those leading elements in Athenian politics were never common, inexperienced citizens whom the popular vote suddenly brought to power. The participation of aristocrats and of nouveaux riches shows that nobility or wealth usually did not imply an antidemocratic mindset, despite a number of exceptions that prove the rule. The noble and non-noble wealthy took part, and were always allowed to take part, and in leading roles too, in the political life of the democratic *polis*. We even find them as the instigators of ongoing democratization.

In the *polis*, many tasks, in the fields of religion, finance, public works, defense, jurisdiction, and so on, had to be carried out. These ranged from menial part-time jobs to crucial functions. In the 4th century BC, Athens may have had some 700 magistrates and officials, not counting the lowliest tasks. In the 5th century BC, with an empire to rule, the number of Athenian bureaucrats would have been even larger than that. If one considers the rapid turnover, it is obvious that a great many Athenians, rich and poor, came to occupy some official position, usually for a period of one year.

In the 6th century BC, the *archontes* were the most important magistrates of the *polis*. But after the early 5th century BC, after they were chosen by lot, they lost much of their political power. While the archons remained the titular heads of the *polis*, power shifted to financial and military magistrates, who never were chosen by lot because their job called for specialist knowledge. Especially the ten army commanders, the *strategoi*, came to be the true leaders of the *polis*. In addition to their strictly military tasks, the *strategoi* also supervised the military training of the young citizens, the collection of the war taxes, the liturgies of a more or less military nature (the trierarchy and the gymnasiarchy), and all jurisdiction concerning military and liturgical matters. They also were involved in the sending out of colonists, the distribution of grain, and the conclusion of treaties. They were present at the meetings of the *boule* and enjoyed special privileges during military campaigns. In the 5th century BC, several *strategoi* were among the important *rhetores*, rhetorician-politicians who played a leading role in the political decision making of the *polis*. Pericles is the best known example. In the 4th century BC, when ever more professional soldiers served as *strategoi*, the political importance of the office again diminished.

As we just saw, for an extended period *strategoi* were quite influential in the *polis*. But their influence and power appear to have been strictly limited. A *strategos* had to be chosen; a *strategos* was subject to controls; a *strategos* held his position for one year only (though with the possibility of repeated re-election, in contrast with most offices for which one was chosen by lot); a *strategos* had colleagues; a *strategos* could be removed from office; and a *strategos* was held accountable at the *ekklesia*. For a *strategos* to become a *turannos* was almost impossible. The Athenian constitution safeguarded the balance between the different organs of government. The power of every single constituent part was constrained by every other constituent part. This was not owing to foresight on the part of the founding fathers of Athenian democracy; Athenian government came about as the result of ad hoc politics, but it worked well: despite a few moments of crisis, Athenian democracy kept functioning well into the second half of the 4th century BC. It guaranteed a large measure of stability, and Athens escaped the continuing civil unrest, *stasis*, that was the scourge of many *poleis*.

Chapter 4.3

Daily Life and Mentality

The Individual and Society

Social life

For any Greek *polis*, we can draw a number of concentric circles that demarcate the social fabric within which an inhabitant of that community lives his or her life. If we move from the outside to the inside, we first encounter the *polis* itself; then the large groupings of a military, political, and religious nature; then the family (in the sense of clan or kinfolk); and at the innermost core the *oikos*, the individual household. Not every inhabitant was embedded in society in this way: a slave working in the silver mines had no *oikos*, a slave or a metic often had no family, the non-citizen was excluded from many groups, and so on. On the other hand, everyone could be a member of a religious community and of clubs and associations of many different kinds.

Typical for the *polis* is its community ideal. We encounter this in Sparta, with its *homoioi* in their *sussitia* in a rather extreme form, but it is to be found everywhere. The *politai* felt themselves to be a community, and that community was the essence of their lives: the *polis* consists of its *politai*. In many cases, we can take this quite literally: most *poleis* were face-to-face societies in which all citizens knew one another. With 3000 Spartans, this is easier to achieve than among 30,000 Athenians, but villages and neighborhoods managed to give Athenians a strong sense of community as well.

To be a community implies some kind of self-image, and a self-image implies an image of the "other." The identity of a group is shaped by setting it up in contrast to another group. We have already spoken of the rivalry between *poleis*. *Poleis* were quite different from each other: they had their own dialects, local cults, myths and legends, and peculiar habits. The Athenians were shocked, and fascinated, by the relative freedom enjoyed by Spartan women. That did not fit into the Athenian view of the world. One should not consider Sparta a women's paradise, though. Even if Sparta was definitely "different," it was not that different: non-Spartans will have exaggerated Sparta's peculiarities. Making the others seem as strange as possible is important for establishing one's own identity. The ways of one's own group are seen as absolute: we act normally, others do not. We

Antiquity: Greeks and Romans in Context, First Edition. Frederick G. Naerebout and Henk W. Singor.
© 2014 John Wiley & Sons, Inc. Published 2014 by John Wiley & Sons, Inc.

can easily see this in the arrogance of the Athenians, who considered themselves the most Greek among Greeks, and their judgment of Sparta as "backward." Those who admired Sparta—and the Spartans themselves—did not speak of backwardness, but of purity, of a society that remained unspoiled—as opposed to degenerate Athens. All Greeks, all true Greeks, felt superior to half-barbarous Macedonia.

Despite their mutual rivalry, the Greeks also felt that they had a lot in common. On a higher level, the "other" was not so much the neighboring *polis*, but the non-Greeks out there. Since the 6th century, in Greek eyes the main division between human beings was the one between Greeks on the one hand and barbarians on the other. A *barbaros* was a human being who could not speak Greek and whose uncouth language went like "barbarbarbar." They lacked true civilization. The distinction was one of culture and not of race: one could learn Greek and adopt Greek ways, and thus become civilized and stop being barbarian. In the course of history, many became Greek in this way, and their barbarian origin was not usually held against them. The negative image of the real barbarian, untouched by Greek culture, was supported by the fact that many slaves in the classical period were non-Greeks, from Thrace, from along the Danube, the south of Russia, and Asia Minor. Enslaving fellow Greeks, although rejected by public opinion, was still practiced and in the 5th and 4th centuries became if anything more frequent. However, slavery was associated with the barbarian.

It was under the influence of outside pressure, especially the Persian Wars, that Greeks formulated a Panhellenic idea and developed an ever clearer idea of a Greek identity that was sharply differentiated from a barbarian one. On the other hand, the cultural blossoming of the Greek world in the classical period could not have taken place when Greece would not have been open to outside influences. Greek thinkers tend to celebrate the small size and the localized character of the *polis*, but it is undeniable that contacts between *poleis* and contacts between the Greek world and the "barbarian lands" beyond were of the utmost importance. If one compares the great art and the deep thought of Athens with the stagnation in Sparta, it becomes clear that an open society offers opportunities that are lacking in a closed and xenophobic one.

Athenian citizens were distributed across *fratriai* and *fulai*. In the classical period, the *fratria* had religious responsibilities to fulfill, but more importantly, it also decided on who was to be registered as a citizen. The registration of new citizens by their fathers, once they came of age, was left to the *fratriai*. It is to be expected, though the sources do not tell us, that every Athenian citizen was a member of some *fratria*. Membership of a *fratria* was passed on from father to son. The members, certainly not all relatives, varied in number from tens to hundreds. The four *fulai* (not the Cleisthenic *fulai*, but the older ones) were reduced to a purely religious function in the 5th and 4th centuries BC, and were not important in the life of an Athenian. The new, Cleisthenic *fulai* were, on the other hand, very important for at least military and political life, as we have seen.

In Sparta and some other Dorian *poleis*, we encounter *sussitia* or *andreia*: literally "eating societies" and "male houses," that is, fraternities. These social organizations had a somewhat primitive character: they were supposed to have originated in the male bonding of Indo-European peoples: groups of men who live together and fight together. In Sparta, every grown-up male citizen was incorporated into a *sussition*, quite literally, as he had to put in an appearance at his *sussition* every day and eat there. Until he reached the age of 30, he was also supposed to spend the night there. Comparable to these *sussitia* are the so-called *hetaireiai* (from *hetairos*, "companion"). These *hetaireiai* were aristocratic get-togethers that organized ritualized drinking parties, so-called *sumposia*, for their select membership. *Hetaireiai*, however, were private societies, while *sussitia* were organs of the Spartan state.

Private societies were very common, especially religious ones that came together to celebrate a certain cult. In the life of non-citizens, also slaves, such societies were very important: non-citizens were cut off from quite a large part of the religious life of the *polis*, but here they found an outlet for their religious beliefs. In addition to cult societies, people also formed clubs on the basis of their job or place of origin, though religion always played a large part (as it did in everything). Such clubs organized mutual support, in the way of some kind of insurance, especially concerning burial costs, but some might also have had a guild-like economic function. There is more information about such guilds for a later date: in the Hellenistic period, fraternities or sodalities of all kinds flourished.

In the lives of the Greek citizens, their *oikos* was most important. We cannot translate *oikos* as "family," which will make us think of a nuclear family, that is, a married couple and their children. Most Athenians did indeed live in nuclear families. There might be household slaves living with the family, but not usually an extended family stretching across three or four generations inhabiting the same house. But there is no Greek word for nuclear family; *oikos* conveys a much broader meaning. The word refers to a piece of land with all the immovable and movable property on it, and all living creatures, human and animal, who had their home there. As non-citizens were not allowed to own land in Athens, they obviously could not form a true *oikos*. The people who were part of the *oikos* were mortal, but the *oikos* could be passed on to the next generation. It was something that one had to care for and then hand over undiminished or, if possible, enlarged, to one's heirs. To have a male heir was crucial. Ideally, at the end of one's life, one would have a single grown-up son: in Athens, there was no primogeniture (the right of the firstborn to inherit), so if there was more than one son, the inheritance had to be divided. Either one had to try to become rich enough so that the property could be split up without impoverishing any of the heirs, or one should not have more than one son. But limiting the number of children was a dangerous business: with the death rates as they were, one could easily end up with no heir at all. The only solution left if that were to happen was to adopt a son.

Daughters could not inherit, but they did get a dowry, which was in fact a pre-mortem inheritance. Daughters could pass on property to their sons. If one died childless and had not have the foresight (or the time) to adopt a son, or had only a daughter or daughters, the *oikos* passed into the possession of the nearest male relative. He then merged this *oikos* with his own *oikos*, and in this way the original *oikos* was lost. That was a bad thing: to hand down the *oikos* across the generations was to maintain one's ties with one's ancestors, whose graves were often situated on the land of the *oikos*. Athens was protective of its *oikoi*: they were the foundations of the economic, political, and military life of the *polis*; it was the *oikoi* where the citizens were born, bred, and had their homes.

Socializing

To be able to function within a society, one has to go through a process of socialization. Classical Athens was in many respects a very simple society, based on orality, where youngsters got their education at home and on the streets. Athenian mothers were most likely hardly educated, and could not contribute very much to the schooling of their children; but they did play their part in their early socialization: thus, they undoubtedly were the first to introduce them to myth and legend, not merely children's stories but a serious first introduction to the history, religion, and politics of the community. Depending on the wealth of a household, there might also be slaves who took care of the children: wet nurses, nursemaids, and the *paidagogos*, an elderly slave entrusted with the education of the male children, who would provide basic instruction and accompany a boy who got some kind of schooling outdoors. In Athens, as in other Greek *poleis* (Sparta was the odd one out), education was a private affair. Until after the classical period, all teachers were entrepreneurs in whose business the *polis* did not interfere. There was no compulsory schooling, and how much education one got depended entirely on the wealth of one's parents, who not only had to pay teachers, but also had to dispense with their son's labor. Poorer children would start work at a very early age.

Formal education consisted of three main fields of study: literary, musical, and physical. A literary education implied learning to read and write, and reading the works of Homer and other canonical literature. So, at least part of the population was literate. The plethora of inscriptions, the fact that public announcements were made in writing, and the numerous examples of graffiti, some of which appear to have been authored by inexperienced writers, suggest that a sizable number of Athenians were able to read and write to some degree. Literacy, however, is a difficult concept to define: there any many levels of literacy, and we do not have any reliable numbers. At any rate, written texts did play an important part in Athenian society. Reading, one aspect of literacy, in the ancient world did not usually mean silent reading but reading aloud: in this still largely oral world, written texts were primarily intended to be spoken. Poetry was also supposed to be recited or sung.

This brings us to musical education: children were taught to sing, play instruments, and dance. Perhaps playing instruments was mainly an elite occupation, given the important role of music in the symposia, the drinking parties that were so central to a noble lifestyle. Some singing and dancing was probably taught to a larger section of the population, as it was quite important in the religious life of the *polis*. The dancing and singing chorus was an omnipresent phenomenon. To be a good dancer, one needs to be in good condition, and this is where physical education makes its appearance.

A proper Greek physical education consisted of running, jumping, spear throwing, discus throwing, boxing, and wrestling. Boys and men trained under the supervision of professional trainers at *palaistra*, private institutions, and *gumnasia* provided by the *polis*. *Palaistra* and gymnasiums were not only for sports: they were also important meeting places where citizens would get together. Often, other subjects were also taught there. Although the *polis* profited from having soldiers in good physical condition, physical education does not seem to have had a primarily military function. It appears to have been more important to have well–trained competitors in the games that were a part of many religious rituals.

After having received primary schooling between the ages of 7 and 14, the sons of the rich could go on to "secondary" and "higher" education. These were left to private initiatives as well, and were at first mainly provided by itinerant teachers. At a later stage, we find in Athens a kind of "university" such as the Akademeia run by Plato. Most teachers were designated as sophists. Originally, the name indicated someone with knowledge of a certain subject, an educated person, and a thinker or even a sage. Soon, however, it acquired a negative connotation: still today, sophistry means the use of specious arguments in order to deceive. A sophist was now seen as someone who had a way with words, one who could prove anything and convince anybody, and make wrong seem right; in other words, they were regarded as advocates of nihilism. The background to this negative image was the fact that sophists, especially the ones who were most in the public eye, focused on the relativity of human constructs. Instead of considering society's values and norms as absolute and sanctioned by the gods, they looked at them from all sides, defended, if necessary, the opposite positions, and taught people the value of relativistic thinking. The famous Socrates belongs in these circles. He may have been an individualist who criticized everyone including the sophists, and he may have operated from different principles, but his so-called Socratic questioning had the same impact as the sophists' discourse. At the same time, we should not forget that the main purpose of an ancient education was eminently practical, whether one was taught by a sophist or by some other scholar: to have rhetorical abilities and to be able to convince an audience were prerequisites for a career in ancient politics.

We have been talking about boys; girls were taught by their mothers and possibly by the family slaves. They learned how to run a household, and they knew what comprised the worldview of their society, especially women's role. They were taught music and dance. But hardly any woman could hope for an education that went beyond these basic skills and basic know-how. This simply did not fit into ideas of what a woman would need in life. Also, the early age at which most Greek girls married, 14–15 years of age, made an extended education an impossibility.

Norms, values, and laws

Socialization refers to the initiation of individuals into the norms and values of a particular society. In the Greek world, *themis* (also personified as the goddess Themis) is a basic concept: "the order to be found in the universe, on earth, and in human life," the rules governing human behavior, rules inherent in nature, given by the gods, or formulated by wise ancestors who knew what was best. So *themis*, even if it was often called the divine order of things, was both god-given and human-made. One encountered *themis* in both the unwritten and the written laws of human society. It was only for a handful of thinkers that such notions were rather less clear-cut, at least when theorizing about society. The Greek world was familiar with a long-running debate on the distinction between right and wrong, and good and evil, especially about the issue of whether good and evil are absolute, a question of *fusis*, nature, and thus eternal and universal; or whether the ideas about what is right and what is wrong depend on whose ideas we are speaking of, a question of *nomos*,

Figure 23   Athenian reliefs with two groups of dancers (323 BC). These reliefs, found on the Acropolis and now in the Acropolis Museum, are on two different sides of a base that once carried a statue. The base formed part of a victory monument: a monumental structure with which a *choregos*, the sponsor of one or more dance choruses, commemorated to the gods, his fellow citizens, and future generations that "his" dancers had won the first prize in a contest. On the block to the left, we see seven cloaked dancers, and at their right a female figure, probably a muse; on the right-hand block we see eight armed dancers, and at their left a comparable (or the same) female figure. There is an inscription that reads: "After victory in the *kuklios choros* (the circle dance, a round dance round the altar) [X dedicated this altar]; Atarbos Ly[. . .] has dedicated this after victory in the *purriche* (the pyrrhic, the armed dance). Kefisodoros was archon." The eponymous magistrate in the last line provides us with an absolute date: 323 BC. The dancers in both scenes were not professionals but Athenian citizens who trained in order to dance at a religious festival (in this case, the Panathenaea). The groups of dancers competed with each other: they tried to outperform all others, in order to honor the god, and reap glory for themselves and their *choregos*. Photo: © Acropolis Museum. Photographer: Socratis Mavrommatis

human habits, conventions, norms, and laws. The *nomos* argument of the sophists has already been mentioned earlier.

We know but little about the written laws of the classical period. Athens must have had a large and coherent body of laws, but we have only fragments left. Still, those fragments and accounts of legal proceedings on the basis of the laws give us some information. The scope of Athenian law seems to have been very broad, ranging from civil law concerning property or taxation to criminal law concerning treason and felony. That all this law making was going on does not necessarily imply that the state was expanding its direct control over the life of its subjects. In the ancient world, the state was reluctant to interfere in the private sphere, and also had hardly got the means to do so, and consequently much was left to private individuals. But they had to take recourse to the law. To take the law into one's own hands became progressively less acceptable, and the state's monopoly on power kept on growing.

An interesting example of Athenian lawgiving is the law on *hubris*, "conceit," "self-importance." *Hubris* occurs when one shames another person or violates his or her rights because you happen to be stronger, richer, or more powerful and you think this makes you a superior being. Now Athens was a highly competitive society where people first and foremost sought their own advantage; but it also was a society with a strongly developed sense of honor: a recipe for conflict. The honor of the citizens is maintained by a delicate web of interrelationships that should not become permanently unbalanced, otherwise society would end up in a vicious cycle of revenge and counter-revenge. Here the *polis* stepped in and said that whoever willfully dishonored a fellow citizen could be punished by law in order to maintain, or restore, the precarious balance in this honor economy. The competitive Athenian citizens had to expend their energy in open competitions that could stand the scrutiny of daylight, such as the games held in honor of the city goddess.

As was already said above, *themis* is not necessarily an order that is imposed by the gods. But once there is an ordered human society, the gods do watch over human behavior. Everything that could be considered blasphemous is punished by the gods. Because such divine punishment can affect all of society, including the innocent, for instance when the gods send an infectious disease, there is the possibility of legal proceedings against one who is supposed to be guilty of *asebeia*, "lack of deference toward the gods." In this way, humans can make amends by punishing before the gods do so. Obviously, the accusation of *asebeia* also functions as a corrective for behavior that is considered too unconventional. When Socrates was sentenced to death in 399 BC, it was because he was found guilty of *asebeia* and perverting the youth of Athens. Apparently, there was a fear of a sophistic undermining of the democratic ideal in Athens, and Socrates was thought to be implicated in this and to bear some of the responsibility for the oligarchic intermezzo at the end of the 5th century BC.

The gods also expected people to honor their oaths, not commit perjury, not to kill except in war, and to act honorably toward guests, suppliants, envoys, prisoners of war, and the dead. The gods punish corruption and corruptibility, the misleading of court, council, or assembly, and treason. As people took their oaths in the names of the gods, many of these misdeeds could be classified as *asebeia*. Religion was part and parcel of every aspect of ancient society: to betray the *polis* or one's fellow citizens or a stranger who was at your mercy (and under divine protection) was to betray the gods. To be law-abiding, patriotic, and pious were more or less the same thing.

Men and Women

Gender relationships

The importance of a male heir has already been stressed. Every man or women was supposed to marry, and the main purpose of marriage was to have legitimate children, especially sons who would carry on the *oikos* (and the *polis*). Sexuality was very much thought of in the context of procreation. How men looked at women depended primarily on the female biology: a woman was above all a being that could bear children. Consequently, women were categorized as the young girl who could not yet reproduce, as the nubile virgin, as the sexually active, fertile wife and mother, and as the infertile older woman and mother. Of course, there were women who did not fit into these categories: the unmarried woman who had lost her virginity and the woman who could not bear children (or did not want to: here, we should consider prostitutes who used contraceptives to avoid pregnancy or resorted to abortion). Such women were banished to the margins of society.

So, grown-up women were there to provide heirs; they were mothers of sons (and of daughters who would be the mothers of future sons). But men also saw their marriage partner as an economic partner: a couple was an economic unit. All this implies that a marriage was a marriage of convenience. The father of the bride and the father of the groom, or the father of the bride and the groom himself, drew up a contract. The bride, some 14 years of age, moved in with the groom, who was in his twenties. It is obvious that her position was subordinate from the very start. She could gain authority after she produced an heir and successfully shared the management of the *oikos*, but she would remain subordinate: ancient Greek society was strictly patriarchal. Of course, a marriage of convenience and an asymmetrical power relationship does not rule out love or affection between marriage partners.

A woman's place was in the home. Women went out only for funerals, marriages, and religious ceremonies and festivals. Their religious duties, in particular, gave them some freedom of movement: there were many religious cults in which women actively participated, or where participation was restricted to women. Men went out to work, to take part in the political life of the *polis*, to meet friends, and so on. Women lived on the inside, men on the outside, and their spheres were quite separate. At least, this was the Athenian ideal, an ideal that only the wealthier could fully live up to. The poor had no slaves and needed the labor of their female relatives in order to survive. So there were women out in the fields and on the streets, but they were definitely lower class.

Women were kept away from male strangers, in order to protect the virginity of daughters and to ensure the fidelity of wives, and thus the legitimacy of one's children. Also, the behavior of the women in a household was an index of the honor of the householder: if he could not control his womenfolk, his reputation was at stake. There was a double standard at work here: the women had to be chaste and true to their husbands, while the men were unrestricted in their sexual behavior (except that they should not try to seduce the wife of a fellow citizen). They could have mistresses, consort with prostitutes, had their slaves always at their disposal, and could even have legal concubines, who could bear legitimate free children (who, however, could not be citizens). This was considered perfectly normal, except that squandering one's fortune on sexual pleasures was definitely frowned upon.

Most Greeks were convinced that women were men's inferior, in all possible aspects, starting with the body. Women were seen as frail creatures, the weaker sex. Pregnancies from a young age with all their attendant complications, diseases, being largely confined indoors and not having too much to eat may very well have assured that women were indeed bodily weak. But they were also supposed to be morally unsound: sexually voracious and thus always likely to betray their husbands. Intellectually, women were considered to be backward too. A self-fulfilling prophecy, if what we have said above about the lack of an education is true. Women were seen as inferiors, and were treated as minors. They remained minors throughout their lives: they never really grew up and were not allowed to act independently. They always needed to have a male guardian, their so-called *kurios*. A woman moved from the *kurieia*, the guardianship, of her father to that of her husband, her son, or some other male relative. Freeborn or liberated women who were not Athenians but metics were not bound by such rules and could operate relatively independently. Still, it is unlikely that the wives of Athenian citizens envied such women: undoubtedly they felt proud that only they could give birth to Athenian citizens.

Sexuality

It is nowadays commonly thought that the Greeks, and certainly the Romans, were sexually uninhibited in ways that we can only dream of, or that should fill us with disgust (depending on one's attitude to sexual emancipation in our time). In fact, it is clear enough from our sources that sexual life in the ancient world was as much subject to inhibitions and shame as in more recent times. Sexual acts were seen as something personal that should be kept private. Feelings of shame seem to have become stronger during the classical period, when erotic vase painting, quite popular in Archaic Greece, almost died out. Literary texts became more euphemistic and less explicit. Intercourse was considered to be ritually defiling: it was prohibited in sanctuaries, those who had had intercourse had to refrain for some time from entering sanctuaries or had to cleanse themselves, and sexual abstention was an element in parts of cultic life. A shameless individual was considered to be an untrustworthy individual.

Much imagery with sexual content once belonged in a religious context. Seeing the images in that context does not remove the sexual content, but makes us look at it with different eyes. The ancient world was preoccupied with fertility. This does not come as a surprise, because the fertility of crops, animals, and humans were all of crucial importance for the continued existence of one's community. Also—and this has partly to do with fertility as well—humans were constantly trying to ward off evil. In propagating fertility and warding off evil, some of the same symbols were used, for instance, the phallus, which was easily the most common symbol. The phallus symbolizes fertility, and it also embodies the power that can avert the evil eye.

Of course, sexually explicit images and texts also occurred outside a primarily religious context. These, however, were restricted to very specific occasions, and to very specific genres. At certain venues, such as the symposium and the comedy, it was permitted to speak openly of sexual acts, and display them acted out or put into images, but only on these specific occasions. And here too we find the aforementioned development toward reticence or even prudery. The whole idea of an ancient world that enjoyed unbridled sexual freedom should be rejected. There may not have been such a large gap between a strict morality on the one hand and actual behavior on the other, and ancient society may have been less frustrated about the body and its bodily functions, but they were not uninhibited.

Homosexuality in the ancient world is a difficult subject. First, we should understand homosexuality in those days in terms of sexual acts between people of the same sex, and not as an identity. There is some inkling in the sources of something that approaches a homosexual identity, but this is never very clearly spelled out. Most of the time, homosexuality was about something you do, and not about what you were. Whether homosexuality in the above sense was acceptable to society depended on the social status of the partners involved. Sexual contacts between a citizen and a slave or a free non-citizen were a private affair if—and this is important—the citizen was the active party. How about contacts between citizens? These were, in several places in the ancient world, only acceptable in the shape of *paiderastia*, pederasty, that is the relationship between a young, unmarried man (in his twenties), the *erastes*, and a boy (in his teens, a *pais*), the *eromenos*. The *erastes* was not merely the lover of the boy, but his protector and mentor. Whether there was, in some places, a female variant of this *paiderastia* is much debated. In some *poleis*, pederastic relationships were forbidden, whereas in others, such as Athens, the judgment is ambiguous: the law did not forbid it, but public opinion varied from extremely positive to extremely negative. Other homosexual relationships between citizens were not forbidden by law either, except for prostitution. But they were regarded as dishonorable and were made fun of and worse. This is not to say that such relationships did not exist: of course, we should never forget that the norms of ancient society and the practices of real human beings need not always be identical.

In most Greek communities that accepted pederasty, it seems to have been limited to certain social layers and to certain age groups. In Athens, it must have been relatively marginal, but in the socialization of the sons of the upper crust of Athenian society it would have played an important role. In this way, it most likely formed part of the education of the most important and influential citizens. It must have been for precisely this reason that it is overrepresented in the visual and literary arts of Athens. In Doric societies, such as Sparta, pederasty was institutionalized, a general initiatory and educational rite of passage. In these conservative communities, pederasty was not an aristocratic or elite practice as it was elsewhere, but part of the collective upbringing of young men (but then, all Spartan men were an elite in themselves, as we have seen). It is undoubtedly right to stress the socializing nature of such pederastic relationships, but that is not to say that they were not in fact sexual. Quite a number of Greek men thus went through a phase where their sexual contacts were exclusively homosexual, first as an *eromenos*, then moving on to being an *erastes*, and eventually marrying and having a mainly, though not necessarily exclusively, heterosexual sex life.

Religion, Philosophy, and Scholarship

Greek religion was multiform. In fact, one could say that every Greek community had its own religion. On the other hand, there are enough common denominators among all these local religions to allow us to speak of it in the singular as "Greek religion." We will take a look here at the most important characteristics.

Greek religion was polytheistic: there was supposed to exist an enormous range of supernatural beings, from the Olympians such as Zeus, Athena, or Apollo, to many "lesser" gods and half-gods (the so-called heroes, mortals usually from a mythic or legendary past, who were deified after their death). Also, nature was inhabited by countless nymphs, river gods, and sprites. The Greek lived in a crowded universe. Such a polytheistic pantheon is dynamic: new gods can be added to it, and others can drop out of it. The gods were usually visualized anthropomorphically, and that is also the way they are portrayed in statues or other images. But they can appear in other guises too.

There is no revelation, no Bible or Qu'ran, not even any central texts: of course, every Greek knew the epics by Homer, and these would have influenced people's religious ideas, but they were not sacred texts. Mythology, the stories Greeks told about their prehistory and that were basic to their worldview, had no sacred status either. This means there was no orthodoxy, no teachings that you had to adhere to. One could not deny the existence of the supernatural and had to abide by a number of simple rules of proper human behavior, but otherwise one was free in what exactly to believe and what not to believe—and, apart from social pressure, free to partake in any ritual or not to do so. Thus, ancient Greek religion is flexible and tolerant, but also quite diffuse. We can see in the sources that individual believers had some difficulty in finding their way: for instance, in some specific circumstances, what god to sacrifice and pray to? This was typically one of the questions that individuals, and communities, put to oracles or to other diviners; it was best to ask the supernatural itself. People also turned to the supernatural to learn what mistakes had been made in the past (which had incurred divine displeasure) or what would be the best choice to make in some present or future pursuit. However important oracles might be, they had no official religious authority. Indeed, there was no clear religious authority in the Greek world. There was no priesthood in the sense of a specific caste that possessed unique knowledge and was set apart by some ordination rite, and monopolized all religious rituals. Greek priests and priestesses were usually chosen by lot or by election to fulfill their office for a specific period of time, often a year or some relatively short religious cycle.

Religious rituals consisted of a number of standard elements: the central element was the offering, the giving of gifts to the gods, especially sacrifice, the slaughter of an animal at or on an open air altar, usually cattle, sheep, goats or pigs, and sometimes fowl. In exceptional cases, the entire carcass of the animal was burned, a so-called holocaust, but usually only the shanks or thigh bones; the remainder of the animal was prepared and eaten on the spot, or divided up and taken home as a meal. In this way, a sacrifice implied a common festive meal for those who participate in the sacrifice: a household, a religious sodality, or the whole community. Other offerings were vegetable foodstuff; liquids such as wine, oil, and milk; and perfumes and incense to be deposited, poured out, or burned. Of course, one could also give any other object. This was done according to the principle of reciprocity: you hoped the gods would reward you for your generosity, by fending off evil and promoting your welfare. In a well-known Latin formula, this is expressed as *do ut des* (I give so that you will give to me). In the case of votive offerings, the believer asked the god for some favor first, and promised something in return, a votive gift, because it had been promised beforehand with what in Latin is called a *votum*. A votive gift can consist of arms and armor (possibly the spoils of war), textiles, jewelry or other precious gifts, works of art, land, slaves, cattle, or anything else that was suitable. A special category, which was quite common, comprised representations of the above: miniature weapons, a statuette of an animal, and so on. Some representations carried inscriptions, and some portrayed the believer in the very act of making an offering. Thus there was considerable latitude in gift giving. But the general idea was always the same: humans gave the most they could spare (which might be precious little, but that did not matter), and the gods would reciprocate—maybe not immediately, but in the long run they would help and protect the mortals, who could not survive without this divine goodwill.

When offering something to the god, people prayed: a spoken prayer or a sung hymn. Recitation, song, and stylized movement and gestures are typically heightened forms of communication that are components of rituals the world over. In Greek cults, processions and music and dance were very important parts of the action. Often, these performances were turned into competitions, *agones*: the singers or dancers were divided into different groups who had to compete for the title of the "best." When Greeks could turn something into an *agon*, they did not hesitate. Of course, when everybody was stimulated to outperform the others, the gods were assured of believers who gave them the best they were capable of. We could consider song and dance as offerings as well: one expended one's energy for the gods. This might also hold good for the many other competitions that took place in a religious context: competitions between instrumentalists, elocutionists, authors of dramatic poetry, and of course athletes. Performances and games must have been meant for the gods, otherwise it is difficult to see why they always formed part of a religious festival. Obviously, this did not preclude humans from enjoying them to the full as well. All such competitions, from the grandiose Panhellenic Olympic Games at the sanctuary of Zeus in Olympia to the competitions at a local village festival, drew a crowd. That benefited the sanctuary and the community: an influx of people meant fame and income. It honored the god, as did the competitions themselves.

Rituals largely played out at sanctuaries. A sanctuary was any bit of land set aside for the supernatural. It could be a tiny patch of woodland, or a huge walled area with elaborate architectural features, especially a temple. Temples were no churches, synagogues, or mosques: they were not there for the believers to come together and worship. The temple was where the god lived. You could go there, and depending on the local rules, you could go in, or look inside from the doorway. There would be a statue of the god and offerings and votive gifts. But the action took place somewhere else, or instance, around an altar positioned in front of the temple.

We have to rid ourselves of the image that ruins, neoclassical architecture, history painting, and cinematic reconstructions have implanted in our minds: that ancient sanctuaries were serene places with white marble buildings surrounded by greenery against the backdrop of a blue sea and a blue sky. Ancient Greek architecture was painted in the primary colors, and the statues were colored to look as realistic as possible. The temples were hung with war trophies, floral decorations, and inscribed boards, and surrounded by altars, inscriptions, and votive offerings. There were shelves with the smaller gifts: row upon row of small terra-cotta figurines. The altars smoked, and the soil round them was soaked with blood. People crowded round, their dress as colorful as the sanctuary itself. Here, one fulfilled one's religious duties, but it was also a funfair and a market place. Here there were always things to do and things to see.

Religious festivals

The collective aspect of ancient religion is best demonstrated by the religious calendar. We will take a look at the most important days in the religious year in Athens. But, of course, every community, even a small village, will have had its recurring festivals. The biggest Athenian festival is the Panathenaea. These came round every year in the first month, but once every four years they were held in grand style and were called the Great Panathenaea. The festival was very much about the identity and unity of the *polis* Athens under its tutelary deity, the goddess Athena. All citizens, and to some extent all inhabitants of the *polis*, could take part. There was, for instance, a large procession from the town gate up to the Acropolis that included men and women, the young and the old, citizens and

Figure 24   Inside of an Athenian cup with the god Dionysus as seafarer (c. 530 BC). Here we have the inside of a very famous *kylix*, a black-figure Athenian drinking cup, decorated and signed by Exekias in around 530 BC. It is now in the Staatliche Antikensammlungen in Munich. The decoration is a beautiful image of the god Dionysus as seafarer. It was supposed that every spring Dionysus returned from overseas, when the new wine was opened and the shipping season was about to begin. We see the god reclining with a drinking horn in his hand, while his ship itself finds its way across the sea, symbolized by the dolphins. In the *Homeric Hymn to Dionysus*, we read that a vine laden with grapes grew from the mast and spread to all sides above the sail. That is what the vase painter shows: the god's vine sprouting above the ship that sails on the sea that Homer had already called "wine-dark." In black-figure ceramics, Dionysus and his entourage are one of the most popular subjects, but this is a unique and very striking image. Photo: Staatliche Antikensammlungen und Glyptothek München. Photograph by: Renate Kühling

non-citizens, the free and slaves, and nobles and commoners. Representatives from Athens' colonies joined in, and during the days of Athens' empire, delegations from the *poleis* under Athenian hegemony also participated. The procession and the sacrifice to Athena were the main part of the festivities, but also quite important was a whole set of competitions and games, including dance contests, athletics, and a boat race at Athens' harbor. Participants in these competitions, most of which were open to all Greeks, not only competed for the honor that would accrue to themselves and their cities, but also paid homage to the goddess and to the remarkable *polis* that she favored and protected. In this way, the Panathenaea were a religious ritual, a celebration of Athenian citizenship and a message to the outside world about Athenian power.

In the ninth month, the Dionysia were celebrated, a festival for the god Dionysus, the god of wine, intoxication, ecstasy, and frenzy. Intoxication, ecstasy, and frenzy do not merely point to drunkenness: they also refer to the loss of self in sexual congress. Thus, Dionysus is also the god of the sex drive and of procreation, of humans and animals, the vitality that constitutes the essence of every living creature. But ecstasy and frenzy have also a dark side to them: a loss of self can mean a loss of self-control, going over the edge, losing one's mind. Dionysus is also the god of anomy, madness, destruction, death—which are also part of the human experience. In the worship of Dionysus, we find orgiastic cults that touch upon all these different aspects of the god. The Dionysia are a large-scale festival with all the elements that we by now have come to expect: a big procession, sacrifices, song, and dance. Of special importance are the dramatic performances that took place in the context of the festival. How tragedy, comedy, and the so-called satyr play (a short farcical play that, other than tragedy and comedy, had a traditional Dionysian content, with a chorus of satyrs) came into being and why they belong as an *agon* to the Dionysia are much contested issues. One could suppose that donning a mask and playacting (maybe more than pretending to be someone other than oneself, one *became* the other) has something to do with the characteristics of the god as outlined above.

In the theater of Dionysus on the southern slope of the Acropolis, every year four days of drama were put on. On the first day, five comedies by five different authors were performed. The next three days were dedicated to three tetralogies: three tragedies and a satyr play, each tetralogy by a single author. A jury then selected two winners: one comedy author and one author of a tetralogy. The authors were poet, composer, choreographer, and director in one. It was also a contest between the performers and their "sponsors" (the choregiasts, that is, those who undertake the *choregia*, one of the liturgies that involves paying for a drama performance). The performers were professional actors and a chorus that in the 5th and early 4th centuries BC consisted of non-professional singer-dancers, ordinary Athenian citizens. In the 5th century BC, plays were only performed once. Thus, every year saw 17 completely new plays. Sadly, not much of that production is left to us: we have tragedies by Aeschylus, Sophocles, and Euripides, and comedies by Aristophanes, 44 plays out of the over a thousand that must have been put on during the 5th century BC.

The *polis* organized great shows, to please gods and men, and to impress the world. The norms and values of their society were put on display, and its fame, power, and wealth demonstrated for those at home and abroad. But in religious ritual, the normal order could also be subverted, as when slaves were allowed to be master, or women to command their men. That is a true carnival, the world turned upside down. It was good for blowing off steam, but of course it only lasted for a day. Subverting the order meant re-affirming it: the license to act abnormally ended when the festival ended and there no longer was a religious sanction for such behavior.

Rites of passage

Obviously there is a lot of religious behavior that is not part of some recurrent festival, but which celebrates a unique occurrence. These unique occurrences we might describe as "transitions from the one state to the other," such as birth, coming of age, marriage, death, admission to some community, and other crises in the life of an individual or of society, such as illness and recovery, pregnancy and birth, going abroad and returning home for the purposes of trade, pilgrimage or war, and so on. Such transitions called for some sort of ritual marking, what anthropologists have called "rites of passage."

The ultimate "passage" is death. Despite the efforts of physicians, "medicine men," local healers, and the staff of healing sanctuaries, many diseases obviously were incurable. Some sections of society were especially vulnerable, above all women in labor or new mothers, the newborn, and young children in general. The death of near relatives must have been a very common occurrence. The dead body was either interred or cremated. In 5th- and 4th-century Greece, both practices were common. Everybody would certainly try to ensure that their bodies would be properly taken care of and laid to rest near their place of birth in the company of their ancestors. The graves of the ancestors were a potent symbol of the unity and continuity of the community. Although there was no orthodoxy about life after death, it seems to have been a common conviction that someone who was not buried or cremated with the requisite rituals, and whose grave was not tended, could find no rest.

Death may have been a frequent visitor, but that did not imply any indifference. Rather, it was the other way round: death was fraught with danger and with fear. It was of great concern, as the dead body was seen as a source of ritual pollution. Burial of the body or interment of the ashes took place outside the city walls or outside the built-up area of villages on burial sites or in family tombs situated on estates. If a family could afford it, a grave was marked with a headstone or an even more substantial monument, with an inscription of the dead person's name, and possibly recalling his or her qualities. To live on in the memory of coming generations was something to strive for: fame was important while alive, but not less important after death.

As was stated above, the Greeks had never developed a clear and generally shared idea about life after death. Important in this respect are the mysteries. A mystery cult is a cult in which the individual believer could be initiated, for example, the Mysteries of Eleusis. Eleusis was a sanctuary not too far from Athens, dedicated to Demeter and Kore (or Persephone), two goddesses who originally were closely related to the agricultural cycle. The attraction of an initiation—about which we do not know any details as the secrets of the mysteries were well kept—seems to have depended on the expectations of the next world as it was revealed to the initiates. Outside the mysteries, we encounter the idea that the dead "live on" in their graves, or images of a somber underworld inhabited by shades, or of the Elysian Fields or the Isles of the Blessed at the end of the world. In due course, there arose the idea of an afterlife providing blessings for the good and punishment for the evil. But never did the Greek world develop an image of life after death that was both clearly delineated and commonly accepted.

Everyday religion and magic

"Rites of passage" were associated with unique occurrences, as we just saw. But other religious acts were part of the daily routine. Thus, every meal started with a libation or a small burned sacrifice in one's own hearth, the focal spot of the house and the *oikos*, and personified as a goddess, Hestia. The *polis* also had its *hestia*. The border between this kind of everyday religion and magic, a kind of DIY religion, was constantly shifting: warding off the "evil eye," for example, could be done by appealing to the gods, but also with amulets and incantations. The evil eye was the envious look with which others looked at you, at your relatives, dependents, animals, or other possessions, and which could thereby be destroyed or damaged.

Protecting oneself against the evil eye by magic is an example of apotropaic magic, that is, magic intended to ward off evil. There was also another kind of magic: acts by which the forces of evil were not dispelled, but were called up, in order to intentionally inflict damage on some enemy. From the ancient world, we have many examples of so-called curse tablets or *defixiones*, small sheets of lead that carried the name of the cursed person, with or without some explanatory text. These curses provide us with a very interesting view of the mental life of ancient humans, often common people who otherwise left but few traces in the sources. Often, such curse tablets were rolled, pierced with a nail, and deposited in a grave or some such spot supposed to be near to the forces of the underworld. Again, borders can be seen to be shifting: cursing could be the clandestine procedure just described, but curse tablets have also been found dedicated in temples. Whether something is magic or religion is very much a question of point of view. Most people will have been concerned about things like the evil eye or curses. The philosopher Plato may have rejected the belief in ghosts and black magic, but it seems more than likely that most of his fellow Athenians were quite "superstitious." And Plato too did not doubt the existence of a wide range of divine beings and *daimones*, "spirits."

Religious developments in the 5th and 4th centuries BC

The foregoing description of Greek religion is largely synchronous. This is not intended to imply that Greek religion was static or unchanging. In the 5th and 4th centuries BC, there certainly were changes. People seemed to have become eager for a more personal, internalized religion, and this seems to be related to crises such as the Peloponnesian War. These wishes could partly be fulfilled by the aforementioned mysteries, or by the cult of Dionysus. But also, during the 5th and 4th centuries BC, new gods were introduced, originating in the East and of an ecstatic character, such as the Magna Mater Cybele from Asia Minor and Adonis from Syria. However, such newcomers were usually not introduced in the pantheon of the *polis*: even when new gods were officially introduced into the community, their cult tended to remain a private affair. One Greek god whose cult arose in the 5th century BC was Asclepius, the healing god. Also, Asclepius was a god with whom the believer could get into immediate contact: he was a god of salvation who came to mortals in their dreams. The introduction of new cults did not always go ahead without opposition, and traditional forms of personal or collective devotion were not replaced by something new. But several developments were set in motion that in the subsequent Hellenistic period would profoundly influence the character of Greek religion.

(a)

(b)

Figure 25 Copies of the statue of Athena Parthenos from the Parthenon on the Athenian Acropolis (originally 447–438 BC). To the left, a marble statue of Athena Parthenos, almost life-size, now in the Museum of Fine Arts in Boston. To the right, a small marble statuette found in Athens and now in the Athens National Museum. Both sculptures are 3rd-century AD copies that give us some impression of what the huge statue of Athena Parthenos, Athena the Virgin, in the Parthenon looked like. That statue, made by the famous sculptor Phidias in 447–438 BC, stood 12 m high and consisted of a wooden frame covered with gold and ivory. It has vanished without a trace, and we have to make do with copies like the two here (see also Figure 12). Athena is portrayed as the protector of the city: over a long chiton she wears a short mantle, the *aegis*, made of goatskin and with a frill of live snakes. On the front of the *aegis* is fastened a Gorgon's or Medusa's head. She wears a helmet, has a shield at her side, and carries a lance (according to descriptions of Phidias' statue). In her right hand, she carries a Nike, Victory personified, and inside the shield there is a snake, an animal associated with Athena, and interpreted already in antiquity itself as Erechtheus or Erichtonios, the primordial king of Athens who was (part) snake, and who symbolizes the identity of Athenians as an autochthonous people who from time immemorial inhabited Attica. Photos: a) Museum of Fine Arts, Boston, Massachusetts, USA/Classical Department Exchange Fund/The Bridgeman Art Library; b) Universal Images Group/SuperStock

Philosophy and secularization

As in the discussion of law and normative behavior, we can say that what was no religious problem at all for the average believer could be a serious issue for the philosopher. Thus, the heterogeneity of the pantheon, with any number of, for instance, Aphrodites in as many places or sanctuaries, would be accepted unquestioningly by believers paying homage to those goddesses. Or should that be: that goddess? Struggling with such phenomena, and with the old problem of the theodicy (the moral dilemma caused by the fact that often the good seem to be punished while the wicked prosper), the philosophically minded could come up with ideas ranging from the monotheistic (all these gods are emanations of what is, in fact, a single god or divine power) to the outright atheistic. The Ionic philosopher Anaxagoras (ca. 500–425 BC) developed a materialist vision of the world in which there was but little room for the gods, and Diogenes of Sinope (ca. 400–325 BC) rejected all societal conventions and preached *anaideia*, shamelessness. For this, he was called a *kuon*, a dog, which name his followers took as a sobriquet to carry with pride: the Kunikoi, or the Cynics.

All of this can be seen as part of a process of secularization that affected many aspects of ancient society (without ever approaching the degree of secularization seen in parts of the contemporary world). The 5th-century medical doctor, Hippocrates, was looking for natural, not supernatural, causes of human illness. His contemporary, the historian Thucydides, left no room for divine intervention in the course of history. The sophist Protagoras argued for the relativity of all knowledge (which is the meaning of his famous saying "man is the measure of all things"), and this general skepticism led to an agnostic stance toward the gods, though he does not seem to have contested conventional morality, as some of the other sophists did. The *polis*, however, did not stand by to watch its values being undermined, not even open-minded Athens. Anaxagoras was banished for *asebeia*, and the trial of Socrates has already been mentioned. But the genie was out of the bottle: even when one does not doubt the existence of the gods, still the relationship between god, fate, and individual responsibility is a theme that was discussed widely in the 5th and 4th centuries BC. And even ordinary believers would sometimes be confronted with such questions: they are exactly the conundrums that the authors of Athenian tragedy analyze in their plays.

A representative of rather less radical strands of Greek thought, who did remain within the thought patterns of the *polis*, is Plato. Plato (429–347 BC) rejected the ideas of sophists and cynics. The relativism of the first he opposed with a new idealism, and the individualism of the second he confronted with a new sense of community. Plato's theory of forms or ideas held that the idea was reality, not its inadequate shadow which most people call reality: ideas were eternal and unchanging. Ideas are not to be grasped by our senses, but we can know them by a process of thought. Once we know the ideas, we know the unchanging and absolute norms. Consequently, philosophers, or more specifically Platonic philosophers, are the ones designated to lead humankind in the right direction. Despite his original political aspirations, Plato never came near a position of leadership in the Athenian *polis*. He spent most of his life teaching others his philosophy, in his own school just outside Athens, near the sanctuary of the *heros* Hekademos, hence its name: Akademeia. In his

Politeia and his *Nomoi*, Plato designed an earthly *polis* that came closest to his ideal *polis*. It is a blueprint for a brave new world where the two lower classes of farmer-craftsmen and soldiers are ruled over by an upper class of dictatorial philosopher-magistrates. His *polis* leaves little or no room for dissident voices. Plato tried to interest the tyrant Dionysius II of Syracuse and his successor in putting these ideas into practice, but to no avail.

Aristotle was the most important pupil of Plato's Academy. But although much influenced by Plato, Aristotle's philosophy developed in quite a different direction, without any room for Plato's world of ideas. Aristotle advocated an empirical, inductive way of thinking instead of a deductive one. This time, it is the observable world that occupies the center stage, although Aristotle did not rely exclusively on our senses, but also attributed an important role to the mind. Of Aristotle's oeuvre, we have more strictly philosophical writings, on logic, ethics, and metaphysics, but also a large body of work on zoology, geography, ethnology, history, and some mathematics and astronomy. There was little that this great thinker did not occupy himself with. Aristotle's classifications are still at the basis of our modern scholarship and science, and we constantly use concepts that he introduced, such as premise, conclusion, subject, attribute, matter, and so on.

In Aristotle's work on institutions, one can see his inductive approach at work: he made an inventory of the different political arrangements of his own day, and his ideal *polis* is an eclectic combination of what he thought was best among existing systems of governance. In his *polis*, there is a hierarchy on the basis of wealth and of seniority. Only those whose income ensures that they will have enough spare time can become actively involved in politics, and one's age determines the nature of the role. Aristotle's ideas were never realized either: we do not know of any political influence he may have had in Athens. Aristotle had for a number of years been the educator of the Macedonian prince Alexander, who would become known to all the world as Alexander the Great, but whether we see in Alexander's career anything that can be traced back to Aristotle's teaching is doubtful. Maybe the fact that Alexander thought highly of intellectual pursuits is the only really obvious result of Aristotle's troubles. Aristotle, like Plato, spend much of his life in his own school, at the eastern end of the city of Athens near the sacred grove of Apollo Lukeios and the Muses, hence the Lukeion, or Lyceum. The covered walkways there (the *peripatos*) gave the Aristotelian philosophy the epithet "peripatetic."

Plato and Aristotle had a conservative view of the Greek *polis*, however different their approach may be. Both looked back at the heydays of the *polis* and wondered how, in less prosperous times, the *polis* could be put on a new track. They did not pick up the trends of the 4th century BC, where there was a move in the direction of monarchies. It is true that their ideal *poleis* have elements that favor the idea of a single ruler: although they were combating the sophists, they were both influenced by sophistic ideas, among them the concept of a monarch. These classical Greek philosophers did not have much of an impact on their own world. But the influence of these thinkers, Plato and Aristotle above all others, on the post-antiquity world has been immeasurably large.

PART V

300 BC–1 AD

Chapter 5.1

A Historical Outline

Eurasian Communities

Until far into the 4th century BC, the Persian Empire was the only world empire in Eurasia. The subsequent centuries, however, witnessed the emergence of large empires in all the highly developed regions from China to the Mediterranean. Moreover, these regions became linked to each other by direct and indirect contacts, while at the same time they expanded their respective spheres of influence. Chinese civilization penetrated the peninsula of Korea and initiated centuries of cultural influence on Japan; simultaneously, the sinification of adjacent areas in the south of China continued apace. In India, toward the end of the 4th century BC and in reaction to the short-lived conquest of the northwest of the country by Alexander the Great, for the first time one empire united the Indus and Ganges basins. In the next century, starting from India, Buddhism would expand all over Central Asia. The Persian Empire was destroyed by Alexander the Great (334–323 BC), whose expedition into Asia unleashed countless changes. The Greek states that emerged from his empire after his death would ultimately, one after another, give way to conquering nomadic peoples in Central Asia, to the emergence of the Parthians in Iran, and finally to the expansion of Roman military power in the west. In the 3rd century BC, Rome subjugated the western part of the Mediterranean, in the 2nd century also the eastern part, and in the 1st century BC it would embark on the conquests of large areas of West and Central Europe. Thus, at the end of this period and around the beginnings of our era, three great empires had arisen in Eurasia: the Roman Empire around the Mediterranean, the Parthian Empire in Western Asia, and the Chinese Empire in the east. Commercial routes across land and sea connected these empires as well as India directly or indirectly. Along these routes, artistic influences and religious ideas spread, foremost among them Buddhist ones, although the great age of Buddhist expansion, like that of other major world religions, would continue into the next period.

Antiquity: Greeks and Romans in Context, First Edition. Frederick G. Naerebout and Henk W. Singor.
© 2014 John Wiley & Sons, Inc. Published 2014 by John Wiley & Sons, Inc.

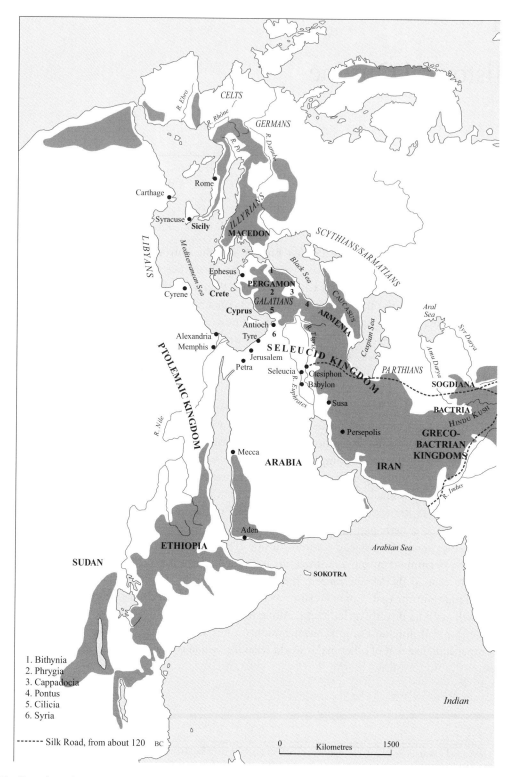

Map 13 Eurasia, 3rd–1st c. BC

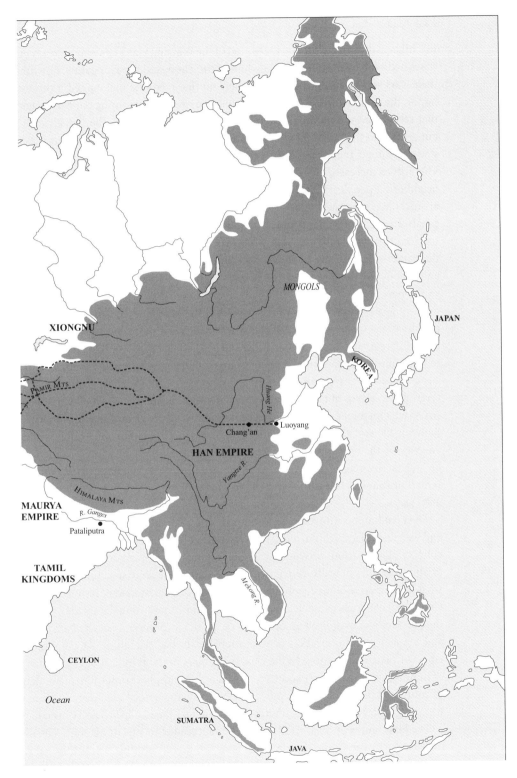

XIONGNU

MONGOLS

JAPAN

KOREA

Pamir Mts.

Huang He

● Luoyang
Chang'an ●

HAN EMPIRE

Yangtze R.

Himalaya Mts.

MAURYA
EMPIRE
R. Ganges
● Pataliputra

TAMIL
KINGDOMS

Mekong R.

CEYLON

Ocean

SUMATRA

JAVA

Map 13 *(Continued)*

East Asia

In China, in the 3rd century BC the period of the Warring States came to a bloody end. These states had evolved from the old kingdom of the Zhou, and for a long time, notwithstanding their wars and rivalries, they had in their mutual relations maintained a certain code of honor, the various princes and their aristocratic vassals constituting one homogeneous elite that recognized the nominal sovereignty of the Zhou dynasty. They fought one another, but seldom to the finish. That had changed already by the 5th and 4th centuries BC: some states absorbed their neighbors, others expanded over hitherto "barbarian" territories. The armies increased in size, both in their mutual wars and in their campaigns against neighboring peoples, thereby inevitably undermining the traditional martial roles of the aristocracy. From the masses of peasants called up for building or repairing dikes and canals, autocratic regimes could also mobilize armies. By the 3rd century BC, cavalry largely replaced the aristocratic chariots, while infantry in large numbers had already begun to fill the battlefields. Warfare between the Chinese states became unmistakably more ruthless and bloody. In the beginning of the 3rd century BC, one state in particular had adapted to the new mode of warfare and had subordinated its entire internal organization to its military goals: western Qin, which protected the heartland of China from incursions by peoples of the western steppes. It is that role that was responsible for the emergence of Qin as a military power. More so than other states, Qin had become militarized—and according to its enemies, "barbarized"—and more than others, it was prepared to disavow traditional customs and codes of conduct and to wage war with all available means. Everything, certainly its system of taxation, and in fact its whole economy, was made to serve that goal. In 256 BC, Qin forces expelled the last representative of the Zhou dynasty from his residence. Between 230 and 221 BC, the remaining six states in China were one by one conquered and annexed by the Qin armies, after which the conqueror had himself proclaimed as *huangdi* or "august sovereign." He would go down into history as the First August Emperor of Qin (Qin Shihuangdi). It was the birth of the Chinese Empire, which was to last for more than 2000 years.

The First Emperor introduced a uniform code of law and ordered standardized measures and weights and a single currency for the whole of his empire. A network of roads was built, connecting the various provincial capitals and their garrisons. Along the northern frontier, existing stretches of walls were now connected into one large structure, the first version of what in the course of time would develop into a complex system of ramparts and walls, the Great Wall of China, as a defense against the Turkish and Mongol nomads of the steppes. A bureaucracy was organized according to the principle of merit instead of aristocratic birth, and a policy of centralization began to replace the old feudalism. At the same time, the emperor mercilessly repressed the class of scholars in the tradition of Confucius: a couple of hundreds of them were executed, while learned and philosophical treatises that seemed to contradict the ideology of legalism—which was the official ideology of Qin in its effort to subjugate everything to the interests of the state—were collected and burned.

The First Emperor died in 210 BC; he was succeeded by one of his sons. The discontent provoked all over China by the policies of the legalistic ministers of Qin led to several rebellions and insurgencies. The Second Emperor reigned only four years over a crumbling empire. In 206 BC, with a rebel army surrounding the capital, his courtiers forced him to commit suicide. That was the end of the Qin dynasty. After a few chaotic years, in 202 BC, the most important rebel commander was recognized everywhere as the new emperor of China, the first of the Han dynasty, residing in a new capital, Chang'an, built next to the ruins of the Qin residence. To some extent, a reaction took place against the rigorous changes that had been so violently pushed through by the first Qin emperor. Feudalism was not completely revived, yet was partially reintroduced, and likewise, legalism was only partly abandoned. The militarization of society was scaled back too. The result was a new stress on duty and a sense of community that did not differ very much from the norms of conduct propagated by Confucius. No wonder, around 100 BC, Confucianism was declared the official philosophy of state; Confucian writings were as far as possible saved from the oblivion to which they had been condemned ever since the book burnings under the First Emperor. The ruler of Qin might have founded the Chinese Empire, but it was the Han dynasty—ruling China, with only a short interruption, for some four centuries—that gave China politically and socially its characteristic features for the following two millennia.

Under the Han dynasty, Chinese expansion steadily continued. Before the end of the 2nd century BC, the border with modern-day Vietnam was reached, while in a northeastern direction the greater part of Korea was brought under the control of the emperor. Roughly at the same time, the Silk Road came to be established, connecting China for a long period to come, albeit with sometimes long interruptions, with Central Asia and indirectly with Parthia and the Greco-Roman world. It had come about as a result of the endeavors of the Han emperors to attack the nomads in their own steppes and to find allies against them among peoples further to the west. A diplomatic mission sent to the west for that purpose around 120 BC for the first time reported to the court at Chang'an on the existence of another world stretching beyond the Pamir mountains to the west. Since then, on the Chinese side caravans were equipped that regularly traveled all the way to the area of the Pamir, where their goods, especially silk, were exchanged against gold, silver, and other valuables brought there by merchants from Bactria, Parthia, and India. Across the Pamir mountains, Chinese silk reached Sogdiana and Bactria, from where some of it was transported further to the west to Parthia, or down the Indus valley to the harbors on the Indian Ocean, where ships from Hellenistic Egypt picked up the coveted material and conveyed it further westward to the countries around the Mediterranean Sea.

India

Until far into the 4th century BC, the north of India remained politically fragmented. In the northwest of the country in the 4th century BC, some influence of the Persian Empire still remained, but politically the power of the Persian king hardly extended to the river Indus and certainly not beyond. Everywhere in Indian society, meanwhile, the rise of the Brahmans could be observed, except where the new movement of Buddhism found many adherents, as was especially the case in the northeast. For the whole of North India, however, suddenly a new era dawned when in 327 BC from across the Hindu Kush, the invading army of Alexander the Great, who in the preceding years had conquered the Persian Empire as far as modern-day Afghanistan and Uzbekistan and had been lured by enticing information to explore this new world, entered the country. Indian rulers in the northern Indus valley and the Punjab voluntarily submitted or were forced into submission. Alexander's army advanced as far as the eastern edge of the Punjab, where the Macedonian soldiers finally persuaded their king to turn back. The invasion then turned south. Partially on ships that Alexander had ordered to be built in the Punjab, the whole expeditionary force moved down the rivers of the "Country of Five Streams" (i.e., the Punjab) and then on and along the Indus river to the ocean. While the fleet sailed from the Indus estuary along the coast of Iran into the Persian Gulf, Alexander's army in 325 BC marched through the desert of southern Iran back to the west. In India only two Macedonian satraps with a small numbers of troops were left behind.

Although the name of Alexander is nowhere mentioned in any written Indian source for this period, his appearance at this juncture of time decisively influenced Indian history. Already during Alexander's lifetime, a political reaction against the foreign invasion set in, especially in the Ganges valley, which Alexander had not reached but where his advance had been feared. A certain Chandragupta Maurya succeeded in a short time in establishing a large, centralized empire with Pataliputra (modern Patna) as its capital. Within a few years after Alexander's death in 323 BC, the Macedonian satrapies of the Punjab and the Lower Indus had been annexed by this Maurya Empire, and before the end of the 4th century Chandragupta had concluded a formal treaty with Seleucus, one of Alexander's generals who had succeeded in uniting large parts of Iran and the Near East under his rule but was still entangled in conflicts with his fellow former generals over the inheritance of Alexander's conquests. By this treaty, the Maurya ruler acquired vast areas west of the Indus in present-day Pakistan and Afghanistan. Thus, the first Indian empire was founded, an empire respected by the Hellenistic kingdoms of western Asia and Egypt, which sent ambassadors to Pataliputra, and that steadily expanded across Central and South India, exerting its influence all over the subcontinent and beyond the Hindu Kush.

The Greeks had left their stamp on India. Alexander himself may have left no traces in the Indian record, but from the 3rd century BC onward, Greeks are mentioned in Indian sources: merchants visiting the harbors of the Indus estuary and, later, those on the west coast of the country; ambassadors calling at Pataliputra; mercenary soldiers entering the service of Indian princes; and finally Greek kings who ruled various larger and smaller kingdoms in Bactria and northwestern India from the 3rd till well into the 1st century BC. But the influence of Greek civilization remained largely limited to a few areas: astronomy and astrology, some medical knowledge, and the use of stone and stucco in sculpture and architecture, and the ways in which human and animal forms were rendered in the plastic arts. Indian civilization, like all great Asian civilizations of the time, was a culture that used wood and sun-baked bricks for building materials, and hence hardly any traces remain of the palaces and other buildings from the period before ca. 300 BC. The absorption of Greek technical and artistic influences was facilitated by a religious and philosophical change in the Maurya Empire in the 3rd century that would have far-reaching consequences.

Around 270 BC, Chandragupta's grandson Ashoka, according to his own account, from sheer aversion to the bloodshed caused by his latest military campaign, converted to Buddhism with its message of nonviolence and world renunciation. As a zealous convert, he started to preach: edicts in the Indian scripts and languages, and a few in Aramaic and Greek announced the desire of the king to bring the *dharma* or the message of the Buddha to his various subject peoples. Until then, Buddhism had been a minority movement in the northeast of India, but Ashoka's propaganda made it the dominant religion of the Maurya Empire, although it did not become a state religion and other creeds were not suppressed. But Buddhism under Ashoka became the first missionary religion in world history, for the idea that one could preach a religion as a message of salvation to, in principle, all people everywhere, instead of only to one's fellow tribesmen or compatriots, and that by sending out missionaries whole new parts of the world could be won for that message, was born in India in this period. Buddhism appeared to be well suited to such dissemination across different cultures. At the same time, its egalitarian character inevitably aroused the resistance of the Brahmans and, to a lesser extent, of the rulers and the warrior caste. This explains the reaction against Buddhism in India that emerged soon after the death of Ashoka. Whereas Buddhist monasteries were built in Bactria, the religion declined in India itself. Eventually, it would nearly disappear from its country of origin but take root in Afghanistan and Central Asia (to remain there until the arrival of Islam) and in the first centuries of our era in China and all over Southeast Asia.

For Indian civilization, the competition between Buddhists and Brahmans, though, yielded an important stimulus, for in the centuries just before and after the beginning of our era India saw a considerable literary production that was mainly religious or philosophical in content. The *Upanishads* as mystical speculations about the essence of the world had evolved from commentaries on the *Vedas* and were now, from the 4th century BC on, gradually put into writing. At the same time, a growing body of Buddhist scriptures was produced in Sanskrit and Pali, the vernacular language of South India. But other subjects too, such as grammar or the traditional laws and customs, were dealt with in systematical and scholarly ways. With all that, the Brahmans in particular became the custodians of learning, which enabled them to make themselves indispensable to the kings. Under the later successors of Chandragupta and certainly under later dynasties after around 200 BC, the association between kings and Brahmans, therefore, became firmer than ever before.

Bactria and Parthia

By conquering the Persian Empire, Alexander the Great had paved the way for further important changes. In the northeast, in Bactria and Sogdiana, he left several garrisons of Macedonians and Greeks behind. Here, in the Iranian heartland, the stiffest resistance had been offered to the conqueror from the west. Bactria comprised the northern parts of modern Afghanistan, separated from the Indus and its tributaries by the mountain range of the Hindu Kush. To the north of Bactria between the rivers Amu Darya and Syr Darya lay Sogdiana, its area largely within modern Uzbekistan. Both Bactria and Sogdiana were in antiquity and far into the Middle Ages fertile and densely populated lands with a mainly Iranian population. But to the north, they provided easy access to invaders from the Central Asian steppes. Nomad horsemen had already for some centuries been the cause of unrest in these regions, and in the 3rd century BC their pressure on the sedentary peoples increased—possibly because the growing power of a unifying China turned the

(a)   (b)   (c)

(d)   (e)   (f)

Figure 26 Coins of Greco-Bactrian and Greco-Indian kings (3rd–2nd c. BC). Around 240 BC, the regions of Bactria and Sogdiana broke away from the Seleucid Empire. The subsequent history of the Greco-Bactrian kingdom and the Greco-Indian communities that came into being is hardly known: textual information is largely lacking, and thus coins are our most important, and often our only, source. We have the names of 37 Greek kings who must have reigned in parts of what are now Afghanistan, Pakistan, and northern India. The quality of their coins is remarkable, and they seem to carry fairly realistic portraits of these rulers. All coins of Greco-Bactrian and Greco-Indian kings shown here are from the British Museum. a) A golden stater of Diodotus I, ca. 250 BC, the first king of an independent Greek Bactria, who is shown wearing the royal diadem. The reverse shows Zeus wielding his thunderbolt. b) Silver tetradrachm of Demetrius I, ca. 190 BC, the king who from Bactria crossed the Hindu Kush and conquered a large area in Gandhara and the Indus basin. He is portrayed with an elephant scalp. The first to have himself depicted in this way, as the conqueror of India, land of elephants, was Alexander the Great, and now Demetrius, invading northern India, shows himself as a new Alexander. The symbolism ultimately derives from Heracles, who donned the skin of the Nemean lion after defeating that animal. c) Silver tetradrachm of Antimachus, ca. 180 BC. This king, possibly the grandson of Diodotus I, ruled Bactria and Sogdiana after the death of Demetrius I. He too crossed the Hindu Kush in order to conquer the lands ruled by the sons of Demetrius. Antimachus, who on other coins calls himself *Theos* ("God"), is depicted here wearing the *kausia*, a traditional Macedonian head covering. From under the *kausia* the ends of his royal diadem are hanging down on his back. The reverse of this coin shows Poseidon, with a palm branch and his trident. d) Silver tetradrachm of Demetrius II, ca. 170 BC, son of Antimachus and conqueror of Gandhara. He too is wearing the *kausia* and the diadem. The reverse shows Zeus with a scepter and a thunderbolt. The inscription is in Kharosthi, one of the Indian scripts of the time. Thus, the coin is also addressing the Indian subjects of Demetrius. e) Silver tetradrachm of Menander, ca. 150 BC, the most famous of the Greco-Indian kings. He is shown with the royal diadem. Menander was a younger son of Demetrius II and ruled a kingdom south of the Hindu Kush that covered a large part of the Indus and Ganges basins (to the north of the Hindu Kush, other Greek kings ruled over Bactria). Of all Greek coins from these regions, the majority have been minted by Menander. Some of these carry Buddhist symbols, such as the wheel of rebirth. f) Silver tetradrachm of Archebius, ca. 100 BC. This king ruled part of Gandhara at a time when Menander's empire had fragmented. He is portrayed as a superhuman warrior, wielding a spear. He wears a royal helmet decorated with the horns and ears of a bull, again over the diadem. The symbolism of the horns goes back to Alexander the Great, who was depicted with the ram's horns of Ammon, his divine father. The bull's horns might point to the god Dionysus, who in the mythic past was supposed to have conquered India. Seleucus I adopted this symbolism, as did the Greco-Bactrian kings before Archebius. Across his left shoulder, the king wears the aegis: gods and heroes who wore the aegis could not be defeated (see also Figure 25). The message of this coin was to no avail: some 50 years after Archebius' reign there were no more independent Greek kings to be found. Photos: © The Trustees of the British Museum nomads' attention more than before to the west. Plundering raids and threatening invasions from the north, therefore, were the dangers confronting Seleucus, Alexander's heir in these regions.

For some time, Seleucus and his successors were successful in defending their northeastern territories, and some Greek cities could even flourish in the region: *gumnasia* and theaters, Greek porticos and Greek-Iranian fortresses, palaces, and sanctuaries arose at the feet of the Hindu Kush amid Iranian and Indo-Iranian populations. In the first half of the 3rd century BC, however, the Iranian Parthians, originating from the steppes around the Aral Sea, penetrated into modern Iran and succeeded in driving a wedge between the Greeks in Bactria and the core regions of the Seleucid Empire in Mesopotamia and Syria. Around 240 BC, the Greek satrap of Bactria declared his independence and minted coins with his own diadem-crowned head. There arose in Bactria a state with a Greek and partially Iranian military upper class, where Greek was the language of government and where Greek culture was in many respects dominant, but where the mass of the population must have been Iranian and Indo-Iranian. The Seleucid kings never succeeded in subduing their former province. The Greek kings of Bactria, on their part, shortly after 200 BC managed to extend their rule across the Hindu Kush and to subjugate large parts of the Indus valley. As a consequence of dynastic infighting and secessions, however, their empire fell apart into several kingdoms on both sides of the Hindu Kush. While the Greeks in Bactria after the middle of the 2nd century BC faced various nomad invaders, the Greeks on the Indian side of the Hindu Kush seem to have flourished for a while. King Menander in the middle of the 2nd century BC extended his rule probably toward the mouth of the Indus and eastward toward Pataliputra, the old capital of the Mauryas. His reign was celebrated as a golden age, and his name lived on in Indian Buddhist literature. In all probability, Menander became a Buddhist and thereby embraced what must have been the religion of a great many of his subjects. In any case, in the 2nd and 1st centuries BC, Buddhism spread across the regions ruled by the Greek kings and after the beginning of our era, Bactria in particular became a region where Buddhist monasteries vied with Iranian, Indian, and syncretic Iranian-Greek-Indian holy places. Here, Greek artists and artistic traditions influenced Indian and especially Buddhist art. Probably, the impulse to carve in sculpture or to depict in painting the Buddha in a human form instead of merely referring to his teachings by certain symbols was due to this Greek influence. The classic Buddha, standing or sitting in meditation with his folded robes, thus owes much to Greek and later Greco-Roman art. In any case, in the region of Gandhara in the northwest of India (now in western Pakistan), from roughly the beginning of our era a characteristic style of Buddhist art would flourish and spread over other parts of India and modern Pakistan and Afghanistan that shows great affinities with Greek art and would last for about five centuries, in its turn influencing Buddhist and Indian art in other regions and later periods.

The kingdom of Menander disintegrated after his death, and around the beginning of our era the last Greek states in the Hindu Kush were absorbed by the empire of the Kushans, originally Iranian nomads who extended their dominion over the Indus valley and northern India as well as Bactria and Sogdiana. It had been at the time when Greek rule in Bactria came to an end and the Kushans first appeared on the scene, around 120 BC, that the Silk Road was established, linking China with Sogdiana and Bactria and hence with the countries farther to the west.

In Iran proper, it was the Parthians who became heirs to the empire of the Achaemenids that had been destroyed by Alexander. For although Seleucus after Alexander's death had succeeded in taking possession of Iran, his and his immediate successors' rule here was always precarious. The Iranian Parthians, in any case, could count on a certain sympathy on the part of the population when they established in around 230 BC their kingdom on the Iranian plateau and from there expanded to the south and the west, annexing after some time the old land of Persis from where the dynasty of the Achaemenids had originated. The Parthians, under their own dynasty of the Arsacids, did not ostensibly forge any links with the Achaemenid past, however, although they adopted the old Persian religion. The latter was not invoked, though, in any reaction against foreign, that is, Greek culture. On the contrary, the Parthians were well disposed toward Greek culture, and Greek-speaking minorities remained in the cities of their empire for a long time, while the kings themselves appreciated Greek art and Greek literature. In the 2nd century BC, the Parthians began their expansion toward the west until the Arsacids had eventually wrested the whole of Mesopotamia from their Seleucid neighbors. The Parthian capital was then transferred to Ctesiphon on the Tigris. In the 1st century BC, the remnant of the Seleucid kingdom was annexed by the Romans. The frontier between the Roman and the Parthian empires henceforth ran through the Syrian desert and along the Upper Euphrates river to the Caucasus mountains, where the kingdom of Armenia would function as a sort of buffer state, in name usually bound to Rome in some form of vassalage. Thus, the Parthian Empire occupied the whole area between Central Asia and the Roman Empire; the Silk Road ran in part through its territory all the way to the harbors on the head of the Persian Gulf or to the Syrian part of the Mediterranean coast. In times of political tension, the Parthians were able to block commercial traffic, but that would happen only rarely.

The Greek World

Already by the 5th and 4th centuries BC, the Greeks had attained great political and military power in the area of the Mediterranean. To a considerable degree, this can be explained by the relative overpopulation of the Greek states and the high level of military participation that characterized Greek communities. In Greece, about half of the free male population was normally available for military enterprises, a much higher percentage than was possible in the Persian Empire with its large but demilitarized population. After Macedon had thrust a form of political unity upon the Greek city-states, a considerable military potential could be mobilized for large-scale wars of conquest. It was Alexander the Great of Macedon who was the first to utilize it. His Macedon army was enlarged by thousands of Greek allies, while other Greeks on an individual basis enrolled as mercenaries in his service. And many thousands more would follow in the tracks of his expedition to the newly conquered regions. Alexander's successors would found their own monarchies in Egypt and western Asia with their armies of Macedonians and Greeks. It was a form of mass migration that would eventually drain the manpower sources of both Macedon and Greece. From roughly 200 BC on, the population of Greece and Macedon must on the whole have declined. At the same time, however, Greek language and Greek culture spread over enormous areas. After Alexander, "the Greek world" was no longer the world of the old *poleis*, which became politically less and less important, but of the states in Egypt and western Asia ruled by Greeks and Macedonians that emerged from the empire of Alexander. With Alexander, therefore, a new epoch began, in Greece and in those other regions, as well as a new phase in Greek civilization. For both, the term "Hellenism" is used. It denotes the period from Alexander up to the beginning of our era as well as Greek civilization during that period, when it had spread, in the wake of Alexander's conquests, as a more or less elite culture over these vast areas outside the regions of the classical Greek world.

Alexander the Great

In 336 BC, King Philip of Macedon was murdered in rather unclear circumstances. Alexander, then 20 years of age, succeeded his father. In a lightning campaign, he crushed rebellions by peoples in the Balkans that his father had subdued. The Greek city of Thebes, which had wished to profit from the situation, was after a short siege razed to the ground. Athens, which had conspired with the Thebans but then speedily offered its submission, was spared. In Corinth, Alexander took over the leadership of the league of Greek states founded by his father. Then, in 334 BC, he was ready to embark on the expedition his father had planned and that he himself was eager to carry through. In the spring of that year, his army of Macedonians, Greek allies, and a mélange of Greek and non-Greek mercenaries marched to the Hellespont, where his transport fleet ferried the troops over into Asia. The satraps of the western satrapies had assembled an army that probably was a little smaller than Alexander's, who had at least 40,000 infantry and some 6,000 cavalry. Its core was made up by the phalanxes of Macedonian pikemen and the heavy Macedonian cavalry, at the head of which Alexander himself was wont to rush headlong into the center of the enemy line. At the small Granikos river in northwestern Asia Minor, the Persians were routed, after which the whole of Asia Minor lay open for the Macedonian advance.

Alexander had crossed into Asia under the slogans of liberation for the Greek cities from Persian dominion and punishment of Persia for the destruction wrought upon mainland Greece 150 years before. That was the official propaganda; other and hardly less official propaganda pointed to Asia Minor as a suitable area for Greek colonization that could relieve the Greek motherland from its burden of overpopulation. Alexander himself, however, was foremost driven by pure, unbridled, and ruthless ambition. He compared his invasion of Asia to the Greek expedition against Troy celebrated in the Homeric epic, which was his favorite poetry, and he would always let his behavior be determined, at least partly, by the heroic ethos of honor, personal courage, and glory. On several occasions, too, he let himself be led by what he called his "longing," an unspecific desire for the new, the unknown, the far-off. He was both a romantic and a political realist, but above all a military genius, a commander who never suffered a defeat and a planner and organizer who managed to feed and transport the largest army of his time over unheard-of distances. His force would increase over the years to eventually 100,000 men, the largest army ever

Figure 27 Building blocks with the dedication of the temple of Athena at Priene (4th c. BC). Building blocks from the wall of the Athena temple in Priene, Asia Minor, now in the British Museum. The block at the top carries an inscription that reads as follows: "King Alexander has dedicated the temple to Athena Polias." The town of Priene was refounded in around the middle of the 4th century BC, and at that time a new temple for the goddess Athena was begun. When Alexander in 334 BC traveled through Asia Minor, the temple was partially finished: enough of it must have been standing for Alexander to be able to dedicate it. Several *poleis* in Asia Minor were granted autonomy and freedom from taxes by Alexander. Priene too was declared free—after submitting to the new ruler, Alexander. The dedication of Priene's temple actually shows how kings disregarded a city's autonomy, and interfered with one of the most central elements of a city's identity, the cult of its protective deity. Nevertheless, Priene seemed proud of Alexander's interest in their temple. Soon, many *poleis* would be competing for the ruler's favors. Photo: © The Trustees of the British Museum

assembled by a European monarch before the age of King Louis XIV. In distances covered, his expedition would be the greatest ever made. When he embarked on his campaign he was 22, and he was not yet 33 when he died, about to embark upon another expedition of discovery and conquest. Both adored by his soldiers and feared by his officers, he had already become a legend in his lifetime, and after his death, myth would overshadow his portrait and his personality.

After the battle of the Granikos, Alexander first marched along the west coast of Asia Minor with its Greek cities. They were ruled by oligarchs or tyrants who were all subservient to the Persian king and in most cases fled before the arrival of the Macedonians. Only Miletus offered some resistance, in vain. Next, the invading army, after subduing the southwest of Asia Minor, advanced along the coast to the east before heading inland toward Central Anatolia. From there, in the following year, the army with some reinforcements progressed to the southeast, meeting no resistance. King Darius III, meanwhile, assembled the imperial Persian army on the plateau of Syria, near the border with present-day Turkey: Iranian (Median, Persian, and Bactrian) cavalry, Persian and Mesopotamian infantry, and Greek mercenary hoplites. In a maneuver that remains a riddle, the Persian king decided to let his army descend into the narrow coastal strip between the sea and the plateau at Issus, in the rear of Alexander, whose army had already passed that spot, although his numerical superiority in cavalry would be useless there. Alexander turned round and managed to create enough room for his Macedonian cavalry to launch an attack on the central spot in the enemy line where Darius himself was, while at the same time holding back his left flank against the advance of the Iranian cavalry. The Persian king did not wait for Alexander to reach his chariot but wheeled around and took flight. That led to the defeat of his whole army. His camp was taken by the victor and with it the king's mother, wife, and daughters fell into Alexander's hands (late summer 333 BC).

Along the coasts of Syria and Phoenicia, the Macedonian army pressed on. Only the city of Tyre on its small island off the coast resisted and forced Alexander into a long and costly siege of about six months. When the city was finally taken, it had been joined to the mainland by a dam built by Alexander's troops. Those of its citizens who had survived the bloody fighting were executed or sold into slavery, and the conquerors moved on, along the coast, to Egypt. The satrap there surrendered without a fight, and in Memphis Alexander was formally recognized as the new ruler of Egypt.

In Egypt, Alexander went on a tour of inspection, visiting first the western arm of the Nile close to where it flows into the sea. Here he selected the terrain for a new city, the first with the name of Alexandria. Several more of these Alexandrias would be founded in the following years in Asia, but none of them would acquire the fame and importance of this first city. From the start, Alexandria was a Greek city that strove to distinguish itself from its Egyptian hinterland and that therefore wished to be called Alexandria "at," not "in" or "of" Egypt. Then, with only a small retinue, Alexander visited the Libyan desert oasis where there was a sanctuary of the god Amun, whom the Greeks identified with Zeus and considered a prestigious oracle-god. What Alexander heard in that sacred spot where he conversed alone with the priests, we will never know, but it is certain that henceforth he proclaimed himself to be the son of Zeus—Amun—and that the Greeks accepted this as something that was not inherently impossible in their religion. In any case, that a young man had in such a short time achieved such huge successes seemed to many of them to point to the involvement of a superhuman agency. Political expediency demanded furthermore that they should henceforth submit to Alexander's demands. For his Macedonian entourage, however, this divinization of their commander already in his lifetime would cause not a few problems in the following years.

In 331 BC, Alexander sought and expected the decisive battle with the Persian king. Darius was in Babylon, where he mustered a new and even larger army, training it in anticipation of the moment that Alexander would turn up and confront him in the heart of his empire. Twice he had offered peace, and he was even prepared to yield all the lands west of the Euphrates to the invader, but Alexander had refused. It was clear by now that the Macedonian claimed the whole of Darius' empire. Marching from Egypt to Syria and then into northern Mesopotamia, Alexander was eager for the final battle. When it took place, in the autumn of 331 BC, at Gaugamela not far from the Tigris in the north of Mesopotamia, it was the largest battle between Greeks (and Macedonians) and Persians in the history of the two peoples. Again, the Persian king did not wait for Alexander's cavalry assault to reach the center of his army where the royal chariot was placed but at the last moment turned round. Successes of the Iranian cavalry elsewhere on the huge battlefield prevented an immediate pursuit. Nevertheless, Alexander's victory was clear. For the second time, Darius had fled, not from cowardice but from the calculation that without his person his empire would disintegrate and his dynasty collapse. Therefore, he hastened eastward across the mountains to Media in order to assemble a new army in the old heartland of Iran. Alexander, meanwhile, advanced along the Tigris River southward, received the capitulation of the satrap of Babylon, then as a young conqueror made his ceremonial entrance into the age-old city.

Thus far, Alexander had had to deal with countries and peoples that were subject to the Persians and that had been either resigned or enthusiastic in accepting him as their new master or their liberator. Beyond Mesopotamia, however, the Iranian territories began, stretching far to the east, first the old land of Elam around the city of Susa, then Persis, the cradle of the Achaemenids, around Parsa or Persepolis, as the Greeks called the royal city. There Alexander had to overcome strong resistance, but the heavy fighting paid off. In both cities, the palaces yielded enormous treasures of gold and silver to the conqueror, solving all financial strains he had been in thus far. Alas, Alexander consigned the famous palace of the Achaemenids in Persepolis to the flames. In the spring of 330 BC, the army marched to Ecbatana in Media, where Darius had taken refuge after Gaugamela. But when Alexander arrived, the Persian king had already moved on toward the east. In Ecbatana, where again a large treasure was taken, the allied troops were sent home to Greece, for the war of revenge against Persia waged by the League of Corinth was now officially over; from then on, the expedition would be an enterprise of King Alexander alone, and on an individual basis the allied soldiers could sign on as his mercenaries. Darius was only a few days ahead, and with a small number of cavalry Alexander pressed on with the pursuit until at last, not far from the Caspian Sea at the roadside, Macedonian cavalrymen discovered the corpse of the last Achaemenid lying in his chariot. The satrap of Bactria and Sogdiana, Bessos, together with a few compatriots from the east of Iran, had slain the failed monarch, and a little later Bessos himself would take the royal tiara and try to re-establish an Iranian monarchy in the northeast. Alexander had the body transferred to Persepolis for a royal burial and continued the pursuit of the murderers. Henceforth, he considered himself the successor of Darius III and the legitimate ruler of the empire that once belonged to the Achaemenids. In his eyes, Bessos was not only a murderer and a traitor but also a usurper.

In the rest of the year 330 BC, Alexander's army covered vast distances, marching through Central Iran eastward in the direction of modern Afghanistan and the Hindu Kush. In various satrapies, new satraps—mostly Macedonians—were appointed, while others were left in office but all were given a Macedonian or sometimes a Greek garrison commander at their side. More and more Alexander behaved as the new king of kings in the tradition of Cyrus and the Achaemenids. This raised tensions within his Macedonian entourage of high officers and friends who had known him since his youth. A conspiracy was detected, and one of his trusted generals was executed as an accomplice. In the following spring, the army moved on and made the crossing over the snowy Hindu Kush from south to north into Bactria. Before long, Bessos was by his frightened co-conspirators delivered into Alexander's hands, who had him tortured and sent to Ecbatana for execution as a king's murderer. Next, he crossed the Amu Darya into Sogdiana and advanced as far as the Syr Darya, the most northern frontier of the former Persian empire. It was the border between two worlds. On the other side of the river, the steppes of Central Asia stretched far and wide, where agriculture and urban living had no place and the territory of the nomads began, that is, the Scythians, as the Greeks called all the peoples roaming the steppes between the Danube in the northwest and the Syr Darya in the northeast. Alexander did not plan any conquests here. In his rear, a dangerous rebellion had broken out among the Iranian nobles of Sogdiana and Bactria that would drag on for two more years. From 329 to 327 BC, Alexander ruthlessly stamped out all resistance. Around that time, new tensions appeared with his entourage of Macedonian friends and officers, which led to more executions, stemming from Alexander's wish—which he soon abandoned—to force Persian court ceremony on the Macedonians and Greeks. In this period too, the conqueror married the daughter of a Sogdian nobleman. Meanwhile, another river frontier of the Persian Empire lured him on: the Indus and the lands beyond.

Before the end of 327 BC, Alexander's army again crossed the Hindu Kush, this time from north to south, and in the spring of the following year his troops descended through the Kabul valley toward the Indus. On the other side of that river, the expedition entered a different world: the world of the tropics in the months of heat just before the monsoon rains. The first princes encountered in the Punjab voluntarily submitted; others, more to the east, resisted in vain. King Poros was, his war elephants notwithstanding, no match for the battle-hardened invaders, but was after his defeat spared by Alexander, who appreciated his courage and martial stature. Worse enemies were the rains that now began and never seemed to stop, the snakes and mosquitoes, the illnesses and the exhaustion, the rumors about more and more lands and warrior peoples ever further to the east. At the eastern rim of the Punjab, Greeks and Macedonians alike began to complain, and their officers conveyed their discontent to the king. After three days of high tension and an impending mutiny, Alexander gave in and announced the start of the journey home. His expedition into the Punjab had illustrated his desire to conquer more than just the Persian Empire, for that had ended at the river Indus, and suggests that he had in mind the subjugation of the whole inhabited world, or at least of the whole civilized world, as far as it was known to the Greeks. In fact, by following the Indus down to the ocean, that goal could in Alexander's eyes still be reached, for the peoples to the east of that river could as well be left alone just as the nomads north of the Syr Darya, for they could be considered to live, so to speak, beyond the pale of civilization.

In 325 BC, the expedition reached the Indus estuary. From there, Alexander marched with most of his army through the coastal regions of modern Pakistan and Iran to the west. The fleet would follow a little later but was much delayed by the prevailing southwestern monsoons. The army, ignorant of the fate of the fleet, wandered through the desert with a huge loss of life, especially among the camp followers who had attached themselves to the army in the preceding years. Exhausted, the troops at last came to Persis, where, just before the end of 325 BC, the fleet also finally arrived. In the following spring, Alexander marched on toward Susa, where he put the administration of his enormous empire in order and started to make plans for new expeditions.

In Susa, Alexander also organized a mass wedding between Macedonians and Persian women. He himself married the eldest daughter of Darius III—his second formal marriage—while on the same day officers and thousands of soldiers formally married their Iranian mistresses or, in the case of the officers, the aristocratic daughters of Iranian princes and noblemen in a huge ceremony paid for by Alexander, who also provided the wedding presents. It was his wish to reconcile the conquerors and the conquered and to create a mixed Macedonian and Iranian elite capable of holding the empire together for a long time to come. Toward that end, he also set up new infantry regiments recruited from young Iranians trained and armed in the Macedonian manner. But when a few months later in Mesopotamia these new Iranian phalanxes would be formally incorporated into the army, while at the same time the Macedonian veterans were released from duty to be sent home, a mutiny broke out among the old soldiers. It was a dangerous moment for the king, but he managed to win them over in an emotional harangue, leading to the dramatic reconciliation between the veterans and Alexander. A huge dinner party was then organized for thousands of his soldiers at which the king openly prayed the gods for concord between Macedonians and Persians in their shared dominion. It was not a prayer that the gods would hear.

The next year (323 BC), Alexander seriously began to prepare his new expedition. This time a fleet setting out from Mesopotamia would circumnavigate Arabia and explore the sea lanes in the Red Sea; in a later phase, the army and the fleet would proceed along the north coast of Africa to the west in order to subdue Carthage and return via southern Europe. Meanwhile, ambassadors from many Greek *poleis* arrived in Babylon to offer Alexander the divine honors that he had in 324 BC formally requested. Ambassadors from states further to the west as well paid homage to the world ruler in Babylon, presumably also from Carthage and Rome, the latter by that time the strongest military power in Central Italy. But when the moment approached for the fleet to sail into the Persian Gulf, Alexander became ill and was immobilized by a persistent fever. His death, two weeks later, has always given rise to rumors but was most probably due to natural causes. Almost immediately, the concord between Macedonians and Persians came to an end: most Persian wives were sent home by the Macedonian officers, and the Iranian phalanxes were disbanded. At the same time, the struggle for possession of the empire broke out among the generals.

The *diadochoi*

In Babylon, the generals first of all canceled Alexander's plans for a new expedition. Then, they deliberated the burial of the deceased, the custody of his son born soon after, and the regency of the empire. But what they decided upon was soon nullified by their near-immediate discord. The history of roughly the first four decades after Alexander's death was a quick succession of wars and shifting alliances between the generals, who seemed determined to prevent one among them from taking over the whole empire that Alexander had conquered. In that period of wars and tensions, Alexander's child and widow would eventually be killed. The generals themselves became the real *diadochoi*, that is, the "successors." Most of them would in the end be killed in battle or by assassination. Their mutual wars sealed the fate of the Greek *poleis* and inaugurated the rule of royal dynasties, for the most important of the *diadochoi* would before the end of the 4th century BC claim royal titles. Thus, in western Asia, Egypt, and southeastern Europe, several kingdoms were founded that were ultimately based on the power of the armies of Macedonian and Greek professional soldiers. The most important of these "successors" were Antigonus and his son Demetrius, Ptolemy, and Seleucus. They were foremost military men and also political realists, not "dreamers" like Alexander, but then, unlike him, they were not geniuses either. Initially, the old Antigonus and his son seemed to have the most success, and they were the first to call themselves kings. But in the end they were defeated by a coalition of Ptolemy, Seleucus, and the temporary ruler of Thrace and Macedon in 301 BC in the decisive battle of Ipsos in Asia Minor. Ptolemy and Seleucus then organized their own kingdoms in Egypt and the greater part of western Asia, respectively. Only in the Aegean region did the struggle for power persist for some time. Eventually, in 277 BC, Antigonus Gonatas, son of Demetrius and grandson of the old Antigonus, ascended the throne of Macedon. Henceforth, three kingdoms competed for dominance in the eastern Mediterranean: Egypt under the Ptolemies, most of the Near East under the Seleucids, and Macedon under the Antigonids.

Greece and Macedon

In Greece, the defeat at Chaeronea in 338 BC and the foundation of the League of Corinth had put an end to the era of political independence of the various *poleis*. Alexander's measures in 336–334 BC only underscored that reality. Whereas on paper the *poleis* might have retained their independence, as members of a league under Macedonian leadership they had in fact become subjects of Macedon. To the Greek cities in Asia Minor, Alexander had in 334 BC brought "freedom and autonomy," but that too meant only local self-government, certainly not the freedom to disobey Alexander. That became clear in 324 BC when Alexander demanded to be recognized as a god by the Greek cities, and these cities, both in Greece and in Asia Minor, dutifully sent their ambassadors to Babylon to convey the divine honors. When after Alexander's death the *diadochoi* waged their near-permanent wars among themselves, the same cities became pawns in the power struggles between the rivals, who especially begrudged each other the old political and cultural centers in Greece.

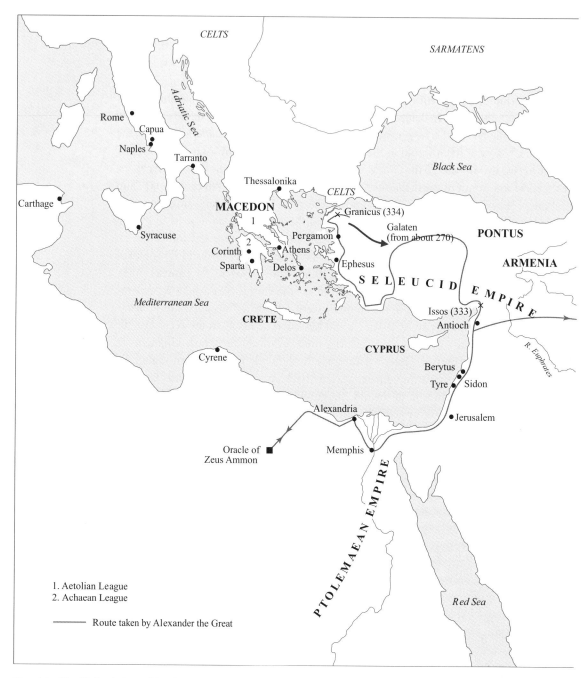

Map 14 The Hellenistic world, 4th–3rd c. BC

CELTS

SARMATENS

Rome

Adriatic Sea

Capua

Naples

Tarranto

Black Sea

Carthage

Thessalonika

CELTS

MACEDON

1

Granicus (334)

Galaten
(from about 270)

PONTUS

Syracuse

Pergamon

Corinth

2

Athens

Sparta

Delos

Ephesus

S E L E U C I D   E M P I R E

ARMENIA

Mediterranean Sea

CRETE

Issos (333)

Antioch

CYPRUS

R. Euphrates

Cyrene

Berytus

Tyre

Sidon

Alexandria

Jerusalem

Oracle of
Zeus Ammon

Memphis

P T O L E M A E A N   E M P I R E

Red Sea

1. Aetolian League
2. Achaean League

———— Route taken by Alexander the Great

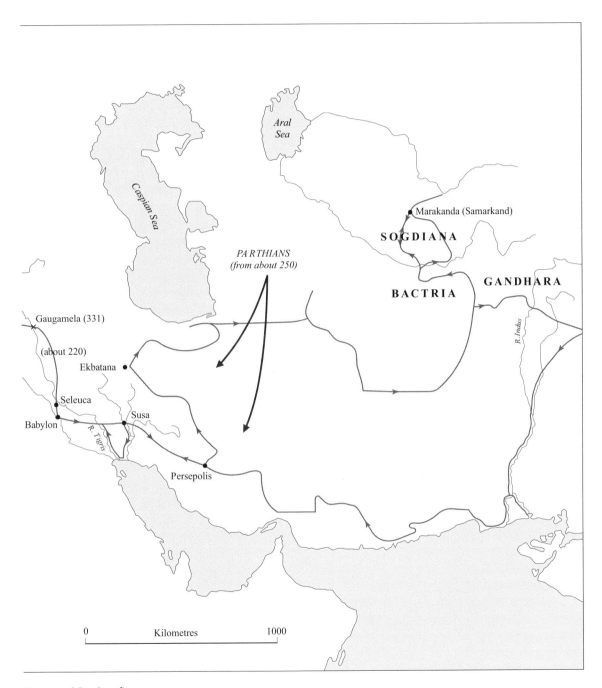

Aral
Sea

Caspian Sea

Marakanda (Samarkand)

SOGDIANA

PARTHIANS
(from about 250)

BACTRIA

GANDHARA

R. Indus

Gaugamela (331)

(about 220)

Ekbatana

Seleuca

Susa

Babylon

R. Tigris

Persepolis

0   Kilometres   1000

Map 14   (*Continued*)

Initially, Athens and several other *poleis* in Greece had reacted to the news of Alexander's death with a rebellion against the vice-regent left by Alexander with plenipotentiary powers in Macedon and Greece. The war did not last long. The Athenian navy was destroyed by the Macedonian fleet in a sea battle, which marked the end of Athens as a maritime power, and the city had to capitulate (323–322 BC). The Macedonian victors abolished the democracy; Athenians belonging to the class of the *thetes* even lost their citizenship. Although a few decades later, the democracy in Athens would be restored for a short period, the year 322 BC was a milestone in the history of Athens and indeed of Greece: the classical period was definitely over, and the time of the territorial monarchies had arrived. In those monarchical states, there was no place anymore for a *polis* democracy, since a people's assembly was unpredictable, often fickle, and less easy to incorporate in the governing plans of a distant monarch than was a small group of oligarchs doing his bidding. That was the reason why the Macedonian kings obstructed democracies in Greece and enforced wherever possible the introduction of oligarchic regimes—the Romans later would do exactly the same. The term democracy, though, often remained in use, but underwent a gradual shift in meaning. It came to denote a "republic," that is, a non-monarchical form of government that had some of the trappings of a democracy, such as an assembly electing the magistrates, but did not allow the assembly any further say in the government, while the persons eligible for office all had to come from the higher propertied classes, making the system in fact an oligarchy, just as Macedon, and Rome later, wished.

After Alexander's death, the Greek cities in Asia Minor fell under the sway of various rival generals and kings in succession: Antigonus, Ptolemy, the rulers of Thrace and Macedon, and after 281 BC for a short while even the Seleucids. But around 270 BC in the west of Asia Minor, a new state seceded from the Seleucid Empire: Pergamon, which was a fortress where one of the former rival kings had lodged much of his treasure. Its ruler managed to extend his realm quickly in the areas surrounding his hill fortress with the help of mercenaries paid for by the treasure of which he had taken possession, and before long most *poleis* in the region acknowledged the king of Pergamon as their sovereign. In European Greece, in the years after the suppression of the anti-Macedonian rebellion in 322 BC, the cities initially had to deal with rival Macedonian vice-regents and kings, a situation that played into the hands of Demetrius, the son of Antigonus, who succeeded in becoming the master of most of southern Greece shortly before the end of the century. The old League of Corinth in which the cities were linked with Macedon had been abolished by then. Eventually, after some more chaotic years, Antigonus, the son of Demetrius, was in 277 BC recognized as the king of Macedon. By then, Athens and the cities of the Peloponnese had regained de facto independence.

Typically for this period, a group of *poleis* in the Peloponnese united to form a political federation, the so-called Achaean League (280–146 BC). Only by pooling their forces could these cities could retain some influence. The league was set up as a military organization, not so much against Macedon as against another league: the Aetolians. The Aetolians in the rather backward northwest of Greece had already founded their league in the 4th century BC and had suddenly emerged as a military power in the 3rd century. They made themselves feared and hated over a wide area by their frequent plundering raids. Their actions contributed to the general impoverishment that came to characterize Greece from the late 3rd century BC as a consequence of mass emigration and population decline. Inevitably, power shifts occurred between the old *poleis*. Athens in the course of the 3rd century BC lost much of its political importance but retained its artistic and intellectual reputation. In Sparta, two kings in succession tried in the second half of the 3rd century to revive its moribund institutions, but just when success seemed within reach, other states became alarmed, and the Spartan experiment was crushed by a coalition of Macedon and the Achaean League in a great battle in northern Laconia in 222 BC. Sparta formally remained independent, just as Athens was, but it was no longer a power of any significance. The new powers in Greece proper were the Achaean and the Aetolian Leagues, and from the economic standpoint, the cities of Corinth and Rhodes, which were both excellently situated for maritime trade. On the whole, in the 3rd century BC, the Greek city-states still managed to play a limited role on the international stage, but in the 2nd century they would quickly succumb to the aggression of Rome. This development was understandable, since in the Hellenistic age warfare had become more and more a matter of large armies and enormous sums of money for mercenaries or battleships: the impoverishment and population decline in Greece, therefore, made the decay of the old *poleis* more or less inevitable.

In Macedon, after nearly half a century of dynastic conflicts and wars, some calm had returned with the accession of Antigonus Gonatas in 277 BC. Macedon was by itself capable of dominating North and Central Greece, but the interventions of other powers, the rise of the Aetolians, and the foundation of the Achaean League prevented the total submission of the whole of Greece that had been achieved by Philip II and Alexander. To the north, meanwhile, Macedon functioned as a bulwark for Greece against the "barbarians" of Central and East Europe. In the early 3rd century BC, it was the Celts who undertook large-scale plundering raids across the Balkans. In 279 BC, they even traversed Macedon and plundered Central Greece, coming close to the rich oracle-sanctuary of Delphi. Pushed back with some difficulty from Greece, these Galatians or "Gauls" crossed over to Asia Minor the next year, where they settled in the heart of the peninsula and eventually would become Hellenized. Sometimes more or less independent, sometimes subject to the Seleucids or the kings of Pergamon, they would in the end share the fate of all states and peoples here and be absorbed into the growing empire of the Romans. Of the great Hellenistic monarchies, Macedon was the first to fall to Rome.

In the 3rd century BC, Rome extended its rule over the whole of Italy, and in two great wars it broke the power of Carthage and brought the western basin of the Mediterranean under its domination. An Aetolian politician toward the end of the century warned his compatriots in vain of the darkening cloud rising in the west. In 200 BC, Rome declared war on Macedon. It was ostensibly a matter of revenge (for King Philip V had assisted Carthage in the last war), but in fact it was sheer imperialism. The ruling Roman aristocracy was always belligerent and after the victory over Carthage in search of new adventures that could provide booty, honor, and glory. The Aetolian Greeks—and later when it was clear the Romans were victorious, the Achaean League—contributed to the Roman invasion force. Philips' army was defeated, and in 196 BC the Romans dictated the conditions for peace. Macedon had to surrender its fleet and to pay a war indemnity, while the Greek cities were all declared to be "free," and Roman garrisons at some strategic points would guarantee their "freedom." In Roman eyes, this meant a "gift" for which the receivers should behave with proper gratitude, and hence be obedient *clientes* toward their new *patronus* Rome. The Greeks did not immediately understand it that way and took their "freedom" rather literally. New tensions would arise between them and Rome.

When Philip's successor seemed after a while busy rearming Macedon, the suspicious Romans declared war on him (171–167 BC). At the battle of Pydna in southern Macedon in 168 BC, the famous Macedonian phalanxes were decisively beaten by the Roman legions. Under the peace treaty, the country was divided into four nominally independent republics. The commercial city of Rhodes was punished by the Romans for its audacity in proposing mediation between the warring parties by the establishment in 166 BC of a free port on Delos, a tiny island in the middle of the Aegean belonging to Athens. A last revival of Macedonian resistance against Rome finally led to its formal annexation in 148 BC as a Roman province (the *provincia* Macedonia).

In the meantime, the actions of the Romans had inspired more resistance to them in the Greek cities, both on the part of those who still dreamed of former glory and of those who turned against the land-owning oligarchies supported by Rome under the slogan of all revolutionaries in antiquity: land distribution and cancellation of debts. The war against Rome in some parts of Greece, therefore, had a socioeconomic aspect to it. The Greeks were mercilessly crushed. The Achaean League was dismantled, and the city of Corinth, the heart of the resistance, was in 146 BC razed to the ground. With these events, the history of independent Greek city-states had come to an end. The country was annexed to the Roman province of Macedonia, except for a few now powerless cities that were still called "free" and "autonomous," such as Athens and Sparta, but which had to resign themselves completely to the wishes of Rome, their official "friend." Exactly 100 years later, in 46 BC, the then Roman dictator Julius Caesar would decide to re-found the city of Corinth as a Roman colony, in large part populated by immigrants from Italy, and in 27 BC South and Central Greece would be united in one *provincia* Achaea. From then on, the country could to some extent recover from the destruction of the past few centuries, but it would never again attain the importance in the Mediterranean area that the Greeks of the classical period and even those of the 3rd century BC had enjoyed.

Western Asia and the Seleucid Empire

In western Asia, Seleucus had emerged from the wars of the *diadochoi* as the strongest of the successor kings. Initially, the center of his empire had been at Babylon, which had also been the seat of Alexander's reign in his last year. But in 310 BC, Seleucus founded on the river Tigris not far from Babylon a new capital, Seleucia, named after himself. It became the center of an empire that stretched all the way to Bactria and Sogdiana. After Antigonus, Seleucus too styled himself "king" (*basileus*). In an expedition to the east, he consolidated his hold on the Iranian regions while conceding to Chandragupta in the treaty already mentioned large tracts of land west of the Indus in exchange for 500 war elephants. These he used to good effect in the final battle against Antigonus in 301 BC, which made him the master of most of Asia Minor and rendered his position nearly unassailable. Syria became henceforth the core of his vast domains, and in 300 BC he founded again a new capital, Antioch, on the Orontes river, named after his son and chosen successor Antiochus. At the

Figure 28 Roman copy of the statue of the goddess Tyche as the city goddess of Antioch (originally c. 300 BC). This statue of the Tuche of Antioch again is a Roman copy of a lost original (see Figure 12). This copy in the Vatican Museum is considered one of the best. The goddess Tyche, Fate personified, was extremely popular in the Hellenistic period, and came to play a part as the city goddess of many communities, symbolizing the fate—that is, of course, the happy fate—of these cities. This all started in Antioch: shortly after the foundation of that city in 300 BC, Seleucus ordered the sculptor Eutychides to produce a statue of Tyche as the goddess of Antioch. Eutychides took several existing elements and combined them into a new concept: Tyche is seated on the mountain Silpios, and her foot rests upon the personified river Orontes; she wears the typical mural crown (a city wall with projecting towers), and in her left hand she carries some ears of wheat as a symbol of prosperity. Soon there would be hardly a place left without such a goddess personifying the city. The theme has remained a popular one to the present day. Photo: Marie-Lan Nguyen/Wikimedia Commons

age of 80, in 181 BC, he led his army in the conquest of the rest of Asia Minor and even crossed over to Europe to annex Macedon, where, however, he was assassinated by a rival claimant for the Macedonian throne.

Whereas Alexander had aimed at a mixed Macedonian-Iranian elite, the ruling elite in the Seleucid Empire, civil as well as military, seems to have been purely Macedonian and Greek, and only at a lower level indigenous aristocrats will have been given some governing posts. This gave the Seleucid Empire in some ways the character of a "colonial" empire, in which the mass of the people was ruled by an ultimately foreign upper class The comparison does not hold completely, for this "colonial" empire had no "motherland," while the Greco-Macedonian elite was not completely closed to persons of Asian descent who had embraced Greek culture and spoke Greek. This meant that Hellenistic culture was not a matter of birth and the prerogative of a certain ethnic group, but could be acquired by learning and adapting. This was important, because the Greco-Macedonian elite would otherwise be too small to hold the vast empire together. Especially, the army would in the course of time increasingly recruit from among the indigenous populations, retaining, however, its Macedonian and Greek character in language, weaponry, and military tactics. The highest echelons in the army as well as in the rest of the government remained, as far as we can tell, in the hands of Greeks and Macedonians and their descendents.

The army of the Seleucids was made up of professional soldiers, initially practically all Greeks and Macedonians, but slowly adopting more and more indigenous recruits who were or would become Hellenized. Whereas the Persian Empire had been sustained by a small standing army of professional soldiers that in time of war could be enlarged by provincial militias, the power of the Seleucids rested solely on their standing army. The gulf between a disarmed population and the royal troops that had existed already in western Asia for a long time became even more marked by the fact that the soldiers now spoke Greek.

The army was concentrated in cities and in large, often fortified, villages. The soldiers there received a house and a piece of land and served as permanent garrisons; sons would follow in their fathers' footsteps when the latter would retire—that at least was the theory to which reality would in varying degrees more or less conform. Such settlements were military strongholds that at the same time functioned as focuses of Hellenistic culture. They were founded by the Seleucid kings at many places. Often, already existing towns or settlements were re-founded as Greek cities with Greek institutions, but also completely new cities were built. Many of them bore the names of kings and queens and were called Seleucia, Antiochia, and so forth. The settlements were from the beginning or after some transitional period organized as Greek *poleis* with a council, magistrates, and assembly of the people, often equipped with a theater, a *gumnasion*, an *agora*, and other amenities of a Greek *polis*. In the case of new foundations, the layout of the city was in the chessboard pattern that differed so markedly from the irregular street plans of western Asian and Indian cities. Indigenous population groups often received a separate legal status apart from the Greek citizenry. This also applied to the Jews, who could be found in many cities in Mesopotamia and Syria and soon in Asia Minor, where they often formed their own communities next to those of the cities they dwelt in. Despite the local autonomy that these cities usually enjoyed, they were not "city-states" such as many of the classical Greek *poleis* had been. But as centers of Hellenistic culture, they were a great success and in the course of time it happened more and more that the ruling elites of long-existing cities, such as for instance in Phoenicia, adopted so much of Hellenistic civilization that they too chose to re-organize their cities as Greek *poleis*.

In order to administer his vast empire, Seleucus entrusted his governors, who bore the Greek title of *strategoi*, on the whole with more authority than the Persian satraps had possessed. As a result, the structure of the empire became rather loose, for the king had to trust the loyalty of his powerful *strategoi*. The enormous distances seemed to justify such a system. It worked well for some time until the problems grew too large, and it became clear that this organization would not be adequate to hold the empire together, apart from the fact that the loyalty of the governors was not always beyond doubt. It was mainly because of the wars that the Seleucids had to wage in the west that they were unable to pay much attention to developments in the east, where first Bactria and then Iran would be lost. Seleucus and his successors had to fight competitors in Asia Minor and the Ptolemies in southern Syria and Judea, areas that the first Ptolemy had seized but were claimed by the Seleucids. Despite several wars fought over them, they would remain in Egyptian hands until the end of the 3rd century. In Asia Minor, soon after the invasion of the Celts, Pergamon emerged as an independent power that would gradually absorb most of western Asia Minor. Shortly after the middle of the 3rd century, there followed the secession of Bactria and the foundation of a Parthian kingdom in northern Iran that cut off the direct link between Seleucid Mesopotamia and the eastern provinces.

In the reign of Antiochus III the Great toward the end of the 3rd century BC, the empire enjoyed a last revival. The king undertook an expedition right through Iran and the Parthian regions to Bactria, as a result of which both the Parthian and the Bactrian kings could retain their royal titles but had to swear allegiance to Antiochus. As a second Alexander—and as the third Macedonian king after Alexander and Seleucus—he then crossed the Hindu Kush and descended into the Kabul valley where he concluded an alliance with an Indian ruler who presented him with more than 100 war elephants. It was an impressive campaign that yielded much prestige, but except for the elephants not much real gains, for the Parthians and the Bactrians hardly paid attention to Antiochus as soon as he had returned to the west. More consequential, on the other hand, was his victory over the army of the Ptolemies in 200 BC, and his subsequent annexation of Judea and southern Syria. After that, it seems that success made him reckless. In 196 BC, he crossed over to Thrace with an army, for his ambitions now seemed aimed at restoring the empire of Alexander including Macedon and Greece. He allowed himself to be invited by the Aetolian League to take the lead in a war of "liberation" of the Greeks against the Macedonians and by implication against the Romans too, for his plans disturbed the peace settlement imposed by Rome in 196 BC. In 192 BC, the king issued a proclamation declaring the Greek cities "free," but one year later the Roman legions landed in Greece, and the Seleucid king was defeated. He withdrew to Asia Minor, where the Romans defeated him again, decisively, in 190 BC. Two years later, peace was signed: Antiochus had to give up his fleet, pay an enormous war indemnity, and recognize the independence of new kingdoms in Asia Minor. It was a turning point in history: the ruler of western Asia was forced to conform to the wishes of a new power in Europe.

A year after the peace treaty with Rome, Antiochus III died, and immediately the areas east of Media fell away from the empire. The Parthians extended their kingdom over practically all of Iran, and at the same time the Greeks of Bactria embarked upon their conquests south of the Hindu Kush and in northwestern India. Then, under king Antiochus IV Epiphanes (which meant the god manifest, an embellishment of the royal name that perfectly suited the ideology of divine kingship inaugurated by Alexander), the Seleucid Empire undertook to settle matters once and for all with its arch enemy Egypt. In 168 BC, Antiochus invaded the country and advanced up to the walls of Alexandria. But again it was Rome that dictated the further course of events. A Roman ambassador appeared in the camp of Antiochus and commanded the divine ruler to withdraw from Egypt at once. That same year in the battle of Pydna, the last king of Macedon had been thoroughly defeated by the Romans, and Antiochus also remembered the defeat of his father in 290 BC. He climbed down and returned to Syria, where a few years later he would be confronted with a rebellion of the Jews.

The Jews in the Hellenistic world

Under the Persian kings, the Jews had on the whole enjoyed a period of calm and prosperity. In more important matters, the high priest of the rebuilt temple at Jerusalem played the role of a secular leader of his people, albeit under the formal authority of the Persian satrap, while lower-ranking priests functioned, for instance, as a judge. On his part, the Persian king acknowledged the validity of the Jewish laws for the internal affairs of the Jews. From the 5th until well into the 2nd century BC, the Jews experienced a period of steady elaboration of their monotheistic faith; it was a period in which several religious prose works were produced, several of which would find their way into the Hebrew Bible. It was also the period in which the synagogue emerged as a place of meeting, prayer, and reading of the holy scriptures, in Judea, Galilee, and among the Jewish communities in the *diaspora*, that is, the "dispersion" of the Jews over foreign lands. Many Jews had remained in Mesopotamia and not returned when the Persian king Cyrus had allowed them to, while others had migrated to Egypt. This situation did not change after Alexander had conquered the Persian Empire. In the 3rd and 2nd centuries BC, Jewish mercenary soldiers would serve both the Ptolemies and the Seleucids, and settle, for instance, in Asia Minor, thus adding to the *diaspora*. After Alexander's death, Ptolemy had taken possession of Judea, and for more than a century it would remain under Ptolemaic rule. During that time, the Jews were treated at least as benignly if not more so than had been the case under the Persian kings, for the Hellenistic kings of Egypt allowed their territories outside Egypt much more autonomy than they granted their Egyptian subjects, while at the same time they extended their favors to the Jews living in Egypt, especially in the new city of Alexandria. In that period, some Greek intellectuals showed an interest in and even some admiration for the Jewish religion. Likewise, among the Jewish elites in Jerusalem and in Alexandria, there were those who admired Hellenistic civilization and tried to adapt to Greek cultural institutions such as the *gumnasion* and the theater. In Jerusalem, such persons were closely connected with the priestly elite. Everywhere in the 3rd and 2nd centuries, the influence of Greek civilization asserted itself, especially in the cities of Phoenicia and Syria, not only through Greek-speaking immigrants but also because members of the local elites adopted Greek customs, by instituting a city council in the Greek manner or practicing sports and gymnastics in the *gumnasion*. For the mass of the population, however, all these things Greek remained alien and often abhorrent, especially so for most Jews in the countryside.

Under the Seleucid kings, those of the priestly elite in Jerusalem who strongly favored Hellenistic civilization went even further on the path of "self-Hellenization," thereby distancing themselves more and more from the mass of the people. Some very pious Jews, the *chassidim*, by their uncompromising adherence to the laws of Moses in all particulars, became in the eyes of the common people a living indictment against the "worldly" priests of Jerusalem and an alternative source of authority. The opposition came to a head when the Jerusalem elite in cooperation with King Antiochus IV began to reorganize Jerusalem as a Greek *polis*. Moreover, the Seleucid king, who was always in financial straits, now eyed the temple treasure in Jerusalem. Suspicion toward the king, the high priest, and the Hellenizing priesthood grew intense. Antiochus reacted by issuing from Antioch in 167 BC edicts that aimed at abolishing the exceptional character of the Jewish religion and bringing it in line with "normal" Hellenized practices. To consider the living king as a god and to place his statue in a temple next to the statue of that temple's god was an accepted way of paying respect to the king in the Hellenistic world. For pious Jews, however, this was blasphemy. The introduction—in all probability—of a statue of Antiochus together with a statue of Zeus Olumpios in the temple of Jerusalem, could in the eyes of pious Jews signify only one thing: that the king was out to destroy their religion. Then followed decrees forbidding circumcision or keeping the Sabbath under penalty of death. Immediately, resistance flared up.

This Jewish resistance to the Seleucid king gave rise to a new phenomenon: the martyr, as the steadfast believer who remains true to the demands of his faith until death, freely choosing death over the smallest infringement of those demands. This, at least, is the image of the Jewish martyr in the *Books of the Maccabees*, which were written partly within a few decades, partly after more than two centuries after the rebellion against the Seleucids. The full "ideology of martyrdom" that would inspire countless others in the course of time most probably developed in later times, but its historical core no doubt goes back to this war of resistance against Antiochus IV. The actual rebellion against the king broke out under the leadership of the Maccabees, the sons of a pious priest in a small village outside Jerusalem. Led by one of them, Judas, they organized a guerilla-like insurgency that the royal troops proved unable to suppress, and in 164 BC they even conquered the city of Jerusalem, except for the fortress with the royal garrison. The temple was solemnly purified of all pagan defilement. The king or his vice-regent—Antiochus was on campaign in Iran where he died in 163 BC—repealed all the decrees against the Jewish religion, but the movement of the Maccabees went on nevertheless, liberating more and more of the countryside. In 161 BC, Judas even concluded a formal treaty of friendship with Rome. A few years later, his brother and successor Jonathan became the high priest of the temple, and in 150 BC he was even appointed *strategos* of Judea by a new Seleucid king. In fact, he now ruled an independent country. Not long after, this independent state was recognized by the Seleucid king, who finally withdrew his garrison from Jerusalem and abolished in Judea the taxes due to him.

In the years that followed, the Seleucid Empire was torn by civil wars between pretenders for the throne and further weakened by Parthian attacks. The little state of the Maccabees or Hashmonaeans (another name for the same family) could in that time consolidate itself. Since the year 104 BC, the reigning Hashmonaeans called themselves kings. This success had a downside, however. During the period of resistance against Antiochus IV, among the pious Jews the hope for a messiah—literally, an anointed one, that is a king—was strongly revived; the messiah from the house of the great king David would according to the prophecies liberate the people of Israel from their enemies and restore them to their former glories—or even bring them greater glories. The only precondition was the return of the people to full obedience to all the laws of Moses; only then could the messiah usher in a Golden Age. For some, that meant a reinvigorated Jewish kingdom, for others the future coming of the messiah was more connected with religious hopes, for instance, that after his rule the dead would be resurrected in order to be rewarded or punished by God in a Last Judgment, after which history would end and a paradise-like Kingdom of God would be initiated. When Judas and his brothers liberated the country, therefore, they did not become kings, for the title of king remained reserved for the messiah who was yet to come. The sheer success of the Maccabees, however, forced those ideas more and more to the background. For with their newly won power, they in their turn began to play power games, internally and externally. Ironically, they even became Hellenized up to a point, as illustrated by the foundation of the Hashmonaean monarchy. During a short period around 100 BC, the new Jewish kingdom was a not insignificant player amid the competing powers in this part of western Asia. Several areas around Judea were "Judaized," sometimes forcibly, and the city of Jerusalem was turned into a near-impregnable fortress. At the same time, many of the ultra-pious Jews, such as the *chassidim*, turned away from the dynasty and the temple. In their eyes, the Hashmonaean kings, Hellenized as they were, could not be the ones who would inaugurate the new time of glory for His people as God had promised, while they saw in the temple, which in their view had become no less "secularized," more of an obstacle to the coming of the messiah than a help. By shunning public life and following the Law as best as they could, these pious ones in their turn strove to bring the promised salvation of the people nearer. That the messiah and with him the Kingdom of God were still to come was for them as well as for most simple believers a certainty. It was these Jewish ideas that would have huge consequences in the centuries to come.

Western Asia: Fragmentation and submission to Rome

The arrival of the first Roman army in Asia Minor in 190 BC in the war between Rome and Antiochus III initiated a period of continuing fragmentation of the area. On the one hand, the kingdom of Pergamon was rewarded for its alliance with the Romans by the extension of its territory over all of western and southwestern Asia Minor. Its capital was embellished by the Pergamene kings and became an important center of Hellenistic civilization, famous for its sculptures and its library. On the other hand, new states arose elsewhere in Asia Minor: the kingdom of Bithynia to the north of Pergamon, that of Cappadocia in the east, beyond the territory of the Galatians (the Celts), and the kingdom of Pontos in the coastal regions of the Black Sea. There, as well as in Cappadocia, strong Iranian influences could still be found. Greek or Hellenized cities were practically everywhere, often royal foundations, while the elites of the various kingdoms were mostly thoroughly Hellenized. Outside the cities, however, Hellenistic culture had not penetrated very deep, and everywhere in the countryside indigenous languages were still spoken. Further to the east, in the Caucasus mountains, the kingdom of Armenia emerged, and like neighboring Cappadocia was under strong Iranian influences. In Iran itself, the kingdom of the Parthians had definitely established itself as the successor to the Seleucids and ultimately to the Achaemenids. In a series of wars, it pushed its frontier further and further to the west. The Seleucid kingdom, consequently, kept shrinking; after the loss of Judea in the 2nd century BC, it was limited in fact to Syria and a part of Mesopotamia that was constantly threatened by the Parthians. Even the coastal cities of Phoenicia regained their independence. Civil wars then weakened the rump state even further.

In the meantime, the influence of Rome expanded. In 168 BC, the new power forced Antiochus IV out of Egypt, and since 161 BC it seemed to protect the Jews against the Seleucids. When in 133 BC the last king of Pergamon died, he left a will in which he bequeathed his kingdom to Rome. The heir eagerly accepted the inheritance, but the population of the kingdom took up arms to defend their independence. Just as in the last war of the Greeks against Rome in 149–146 BC, social and socioeconomic motives played a significant role in the uprising. The rural poor and many of the slaves turned against the city elites that were backed by Rome. Within a few years, the rebellion was crushed, and the former kingdom transformed into the Roman *provincia* Asia. This meant, among other things, that Roman and Italian tax farmers, financiers, and traders entered the province, only to make themselves utterly detested by the population in a very short time.

In the beginning of the 1st century BC, the ambitious king of Pontos, Mithridates, exploited those anti-Roman feelings for his own political ends. In 88 BC, he occupied the province of Asia and had all Romans and Italians living there massacred, then sent his army on to Greece to proclaim, as Antiochus III had done before him, a war of "liberation" of the Greeks. Some Greeks enthusiastically joined the liberators, among them the city of Athens. This decision led to its ruin. For the Roman reaction was predictable: the ambitious and ruthless Roman general Sulla arrived on the scene, and besieged and took the city in 86 BC. Athens, and other cultural centers such as Delphi and Olympia, were plundered by the Roman troops. Mithridates' army in Greece was defeated, and the king had to withdraw from his conquests in Asia Minor. Some years later, when the Seleucid kingdom was threatened by yet another civil war for the throne, Mithridates in alliance with the king of Armenia tried again to expel Roman power from Asia Minor. There followed new Roman expeditions, not always completely successful, until in 66 BC the Roman politician Pompey received a special command to restore order in the east. Mithridates fled before him, and a new Roman province could be organized, the *provincia* Bithynia et Pontus (for, in the meantime, the last king of Bithynia had bequeathed his kingdom to the Romans too). At the same time, in the south of Asia Minor the *provincia* Cilicia was installed. Then, in 64 BC, Pompey formally put an end to the Seleucid kingdom, annexing its remnants as the *provincia* Syria, while the king of Armenia submitted to Rome to become its vassal. In the next year, Pompey advanced on Jerusalem, where a civil war had broken out between two rival Hashmonaean brothers. Pompey recognized one of them as king and the other as high priest, making it clear that Judea, just like Armenia, now had become a vassal state of Rome.

Egypt under the Ptolemies

Of all the *diadochoi*, Ptolemy was probably the luckiest. Already appointed satrap of Egypt by Alexander, he possessed at the time of the king's death a power base that naturally made him one of the most important players in the struggle for supremacy of the period. His prestige was further enhanced by the transfer of Alexander's dead body to Egypt, where he had it interred, eventually, in a special mausoleum in Alexandria. Ptolemy's power rested, like that of his competitors, on a Greco-Macedonian professional army but also on a considerable fleet. The century after Alexander was a period of large warships and mighty sea battles. Ptolemy seized the island of Cyprus and established a maritime dominance in the eastern Mediterranean that would last until far into the 3rd century BC. At the same time, he took possession of Judea and southern Syria and of Cyrene in the west. Like Seleucus, he called himself a king. He founded a dynasty that would be the longest reigning of all the Hellenistic dynasties.

The actual organization of the kingdom was mainly the work of Ptolemy's son, Ptolemy II Philadelphus. Whereas the regions outside Egypt enjoyed a large measure of autonomy, the Nile valley itself was administered as one large royal domain. Apart from Alexandria, the Ptolemies did not found Greek cities, except for Ptolemais in the south. Their rule did not rest on Greek *poleis* but on the age-old exploitation of a powerless Egyptian peasantry by royal bureaucrats. Characteristic of the Ptolemaic kingdom was a far-reaching regulation of all economic life, not only of agriculture—the natural base of its wealth—but also of industrial production and foreign trade. From foreign trade, which since the late 2nd century BC extended as far as India, it was primarily Alexandria that profited. It developed into one of the largest cities in the Mediterranean world. Inhabited by Greeks, Egyptians, and Jews, it was a cosmopolitan metropolis, a center of commerce and culture—with its world-famous Musaeum and library—and at the same time the center of the Ptolemaic government, where all the threads of its bureaucracy converged.

In Egypt, the royal treasury was better filled and the peasant population more thoroughly exploited than anywhere else in the Hellenistic world. The discontent of the indigenous population inspired some to flee their plots and find refuge in the large temples or in the wilderness, and in the 2nd century BC and later, resentment also led to short-lived rebellions. After the first four Ptolemies, reigning in the 3rd century, the kings were in general very weak. In the 2nd and 1st centuries BC, the prestige of the dynasty was also undermined by various civil wars for the throne between close relatives, often incited by ambitious councilors and ministers. The typically Ptolemaic custom of incestuous marriages between brothers and sisters, probably taken over from Egyptian tradition, may have contributed to the fact that most, but not all, members of the dynasty in its later period were completely incompetent. In any case, from 200 BC onward, the kingdom had to acknowledge its inferior position vis-à-vis the Seleucids, and most of its possessions outside Egypt were lost. Since 168 BC, Egypt, in fact, lived under a form of tutelage exercised by Rome. It also lost Cyrene, which shortly after 100 BC became a Roman province. The expedition of Pompey to the east, though, did not touch Egypt, and the country was left alone for a while, as the last surviving Hellenistic monarchy in the Mediterranean world. In the Roman civil war between Pompey and Caesar, however, Egypt got involved. After his defeat against Caesar, Pompey fled to Egypt in 48 BC—only to be murdered there on the orders of the young Ptolemy XIII, who presumed to do the victor a favor. Caesar himself arrived the same year and was seduced by Cleopatra, sister and consort of the king, to choose her side in the struggle for power with her brother. In the fighting that broke out in Alexandria, part of the famous library was destroyed by flames. After Caesar's departure, Cleopatra reigned alone. The next round in the Roman civil wars brought Caesar's general Antony to Egypt. Again, Cleopatra won the Roman commander over to her side. They married and the couple even dreamed of a Roman-Egyptian empire centered on Alexandria. But in 31 BC, in the battle of Actium in western Greece, the Roman-Egyptian navy was defeated by Octavian, Caesar's heir. The famous couple then fled to Egypt, pursued by Octavian. In 30 BC, Antony, and a few days later Cleopatra, committed suicide, and the country became the personal possession of the man who as sole ruler in the whole of the Mediterranean world would be known to posterity as the first Roman emperor.

Italy and the West

During the time that Macedonians and Greeks conquered the Persian Empire and Hellenistic states spread Greek civilization over large parts of western Asia and Egypt, the Roman Republic subjugated Italy and the western basin of the Mediterranean. In the following centuries, it subdued the eastern half of the Mediterranean as well. The rise of Rome, like the Macedonian and Greek expansion to the east, was ultimately made possible by population increase, especially by the growth of a citizenry that saw in military service both a duty and a right. Roman society was, like Greek society and like the societies of Celts and Germans in "barbaric" Europe, a society in which the full citizen or the free member of the community was a man in possession of arms. In this, as has been stated before, these European cultures differed from most of the more developed states in Asia and Egypt, where the mass of the free population was disarmed. Characteristic of Rome, moreover, was the fact that its political organization rather easily allowed the adoption of outsiders into the Roman community. Whereas defeated peoples could be totally exterminated, which rarely occurred, or be completely enslaved, which occurred more often, they could also, usually after a period of transition of one or a few generations, be incorporated into the Roman citizenry, which in Italy became the rule. That meant by definition an enlargement of the military potential of the Roman people. A Greek *polis* could rule as a tyrant over other *poleis*—as democratic Athens had done for some time in the 5th century BC—without adopting the citizens of the latter into her own citizenry. Rome, by contrast, in doing exactly that, could develop into a territorial state in Italy, with an increasing number of Roman towns in its territory. This process had reached a tipping point around 300 BC: since then, none of the other states or peoples in Italy could ever match Rome in military manpower, which made the further subjugation of Italy to Rome a near certainty, unless all the others could permanently unite against her. That did not transpire, and the subjugation of Italy followed in due course during the first decades of the 3rd century BC. With that, Rome could add the manpower of the rest of Italy to her own manpower, which made her at once a formidable power in the wider Mediterranean world. Thanks to this reservoir of manpower, Rome could afford to lose big battles and still go on winning the war. All this does not mean that the Roman expansion was somehow an inevitable process, for apart from the means to carry it out—not only in terms of manpower but also an adequate military and political organization—there also must have been the will to do so. The will, though, was there in more than sufficient measure. The aristocracy that governed Rome was steeped in a militaristic ethos: fame and prestige were actually only military fame and military prestige, and the career of a successful politician invariably included victories on the battlefield. At the same time, however, the enormous successes of Roman expansion would in the end undermine the foundations of the aristocratic republic itself. For while Rome developed into a large territorial empire, her political organization remained for a long time the organization of a city-state. In the 1st century BC, that organization would finally be overhauled with all the violence of a number of civil wars; those wars would in their turn stimulate further territorial expansion until, in 30 BC, the annexation of the last Hellenistic state would coincide with the end of the republic and the beginning of a new monarchy that seemed more suited to the empire that Rome had by that time become.

The Roman conquest of Italy

In 340 BC, an uprising of the Latins provided Rome with the opportunity to establish her power over Latium on a permanent basis. After a brief war, the Latins in 338 BC were forced to accept a peace in which the Latin League was liquidated and replaced by bilateral treaties between Rome and those few Latin cities that were allowed to remain nominally independent; this was the principle of divide and rule in action. Most of the cities of Latium were annexed by Rome, sometimes with full Roman citizenship for their inhabitants, sometimes with a reduced form of citizenship. The latter was in the following years extended to cities in Campania that were allied with Rome, such as Capua. The expansion of Roman influence in Campania brought Rome into conflict with the Samnites, the most numerous of the Italian mountain peoples that were constantly pressing on to the coastal plains and were on the lookout for further expansion toward the Tyrrhenian Sea. In 326 BC, a war broke out that Rome won only with considerable effort. The peace, shortly before 300 BC, brought the whole of Campania and parts of the Apennine mountains into Roman hands. In the meantime and with the requirements of warfare in mind, the Romans had constructed the first of their military roads, the via Appia—named after the *censor* Appius Claudius who had commissioned the work—from Rome to Capua.

In this period, Rome succeeded in largely solving her internal problems as well. Since the consulate and the new magistracies of *praetor* and *censor* had been opened up for plebeians in 367 BC and the following years, a mixed plebeian–patrician elite had emerged: the *nobilitas*. This aristocracy of office continued the policy of territorial expansion, so that by distribution of land in newly acquired areas, the demands of the poorer plebeians could also be met. Thus, there was a clear connection between the winding down of the "Struggle of the Orders" in Rome and Roman expansion in Italy. The political emancipation of the plebeians came to a close with the lex Hortensia of 287 BC, which made decisions of the assembly of the *plebs*—in fact, an alternative assembly of the people—automatically binding for everyone; in other words, a plebiscite henceforth had the force of law. With that, in 287 BC, a period began that has been called the classical Republic, because internal peace was mostly maintained, a period that would last until 133 BC, when civil strife would break out in new and more embittered forms.

Not long after 300 BC, the growing power of Rome resulted in the formation of a grand alliance against her of Samnites, Umbrians, Etruscans, and Gauls. In the battle of Sentinum in Umbria in 295 BC, this coalition, however, was decisively defeated, which sealed the fate of Italy. In the following years, Rome concluded separate treaties with the different peoples involved, after which she was truly the mistress of the whole of Italy from the river Po down to the straits between Italy and Sicily. Only the Greek city of Tarent in the far south retained, with a few allied cities, its independence. To protect itself against Rome, it concluded an alliance with Pyrrhus, the king of Epirus in northwestern Greece, an ambitious monarch who imagined himself to be a second Alexander conquering the west. In 280 BC, he crossed over to Italy. Initially, he managed to beat the Romans twice, but after the second of these hard-won "pyrrhic victories" he offered peace, which Rome rejected. A third battle thereupon ended undecided, after which the king returned to Greece in 275 BC. Three years later, Tarent submitted to Rome. By and large, from 270 BC on, the whole of Italy was under the dominion of Rome. Roughly a quarter of its territory directly belonged to Rome, and the rest belonged to states that were bound to the dominant city in bilateral alliances. By this time, Rome also started to mint her own silver coins and so broke away from a more primitive past in this respect as well. During the war with Tarent and Pyrrhus, Rome concluded treaties with Egypt under king Ptolemy II and with Carthage. The Roman state thus made its entrance into the world of the Hellenistic great powers.

Rome and Carthage

Apart from Rome, there was in the western basin of the Mediterranean after 270 BC another great power: Carthage. This commercial city, once founded by the Phoenicians, had in the 5th and 4th centuries BC largely succeeded in keeping out Greek competitors and exploiting the trade with Etruria and the Iberian peninsula for her own enrichment. With the Greeks of Sicily, especially the city of Syracuse, it waged one war after another, sometimes conquering nearly the whole island, sometimes just holding on to its western tip. In the 3rd century BC, Carthage showed some features of a Hellenistic state with her coins in Greek style and an army of mercenaries after the Greek fashion. At the same time, the cultivation of Carthage's North African hinterland was intensified with the introduction of a new type of large-scale plantation agriculture worked by slaves. Simultaneously, the possibility of recruiting the indigenous Libyan and Berber populations for the Carthaginian army was opened up. In Sicily in the 3rd century BC, Carthage expanded its territory steadily until only Syracuse and its near vicinity was left in Greek hands. Then came the clash with Rome.

Already in antiquity there were debates concerning the reasons and the legal grounds of the wars between Rome and Carthage. In part, that can be explained by the Roman anxiety to assure themselves of the support of the gods in their wars. The wars of the Romans, therefore, had always to be "just" wars, at least in their eyes. It is a fact, however, that in 264 BC, the Roman popular assembly eagerly agreed to a request for help from a band of Italian mercenaries who after the last war between Carthage and Syracuse had seized the town of Messina and called upon the Romans for protection against both Syracuse and Carthage. Offering help to them would entail a great war with Carthage that would not be easy to justify, in view of the recent treaty of friendship. But the war was certainly wished for by

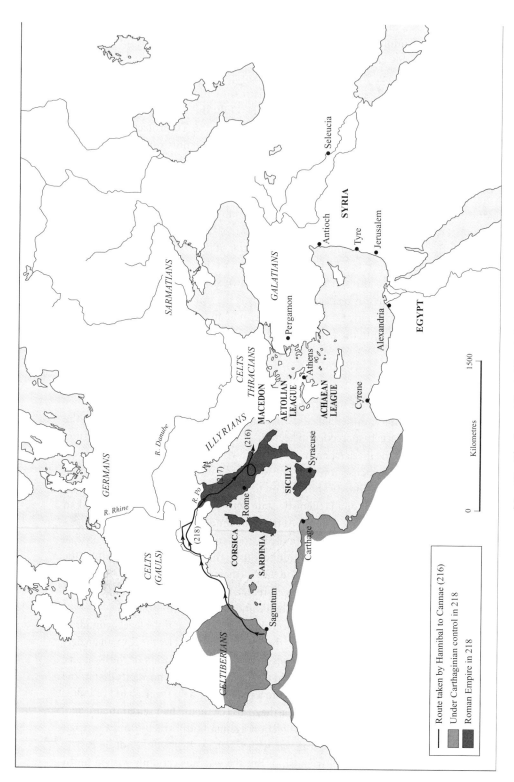

Map 15 The Second Punic War, 218–201 BC

many an ambitious Roman *nobilis*. Thus started the First Punic War (264–241 BC), named after *Puni* or *Poeni*, the Roman name for both Phoenicians and Carthaginians.

In the field, the Roman legions appeared to be unbeatable, but they experienced the greatest difficulties against the Carthaginian fortified towns on the west coast of the island. So the war dragged on, and for a long time the conflict on the sea also hung in the balance. Carthage from the outset possessed a strong navy, but as soon as the war had broken out, Rome began building its own, to be rowed by crews from the allied Greek cities in Italy. Battles between these largest fleets of the time were either won by the Romans, albeit with enormous losses, or remained undecided. Storms destroyed whole fleets on both sides. Never before did the Romans suffer so much loss of life in one war. Finally, in 241 BC, they gained a decisive victory in a large sea battle off the west coast of Sicily. Peace was then concluded on Roman terms.

The peace treaty of 241 BC stipulated a war indemnity, to be paid by Carthage in ten yearly installments, as concrete proof of Carthaginian guilt for the war, and the surrender of the Carthaginian part of Sicily to Rome. Syracuse had been Rome's ally in the war and remained independent; the rest of the island now came directly under Roman rule. Carthage had immediately after the war to deal with a ferocious uprising of her Libyan and mercenary soldiers, who had not been paid for a long time, a situation Rome exploited by forcing Carthage to surrender Sardinia as well, after which the Romans also occupied Corsica. The victor now was presented with the task of administering these newly won territories. During the war, Sicily had always been assigned to one of the two annual consuls, in Roman parlance: Sicily had been his *provincia*. That term remained in use after the war had ended and so came to denote a piece of territory outside Italy directly governed by a Roman magistrate. In 227 BC, it was arranged that henceforth two new *praetores* would be chosen each year to govern the two "provinces" outside Italy, the *provincia* Sicilia and the *provincia* Sardinia et Corsica. With this was created the provincial organization of the Roman Empire. The provincial governor ruled his province as an absolute monarch who did not have to answer to anyone and could only be called to account in Rome after his term of tenure had ended. His primary tasks were maintaining the peace and thus suppressing any stirrings against the new order, and collecting the taxes due to Rome. The inhabitants of the province became neither Roman citizens nor Roman allies, but subjects. The total number of annually chosen praetors had now been raised to four, since apart from the one praetor who was charged with administering civic law in Rome, in the 3rd century a second praetor had been introduced for handling law suits between Roman citizens and non-citizens.

After her defeat, Carthage sought compensation in the west. Hamilcar, the general who had defended the western part of Sicily against the Romans until the very end, now crossed over to Spain with plenipotentiary powers in order to create a new territorial empire for Carthage. He had great success. Many Iberian tribes were subjugated and Carthaginian bases established. His successor concluded a treaty with Rome in which the river Ebro was designated the northern border of the Carthaginian sphere of influence. Rome, in the meantime, subjugated the Celtic tribes in the Po valley and extended the Via Flaminia north of the Apennines toward the Alps.

Figure 29   Carthaginian coins with war elephants (3rd c. BC). These are two Carthaginian coins from the collection of the British Museum. Left, a silver coin (a double shekel) from New Carthage (modern Cartagena) in Spain, with the head of the god Melqart, the Carthaginian Heracles, and like Heracles recognized by his club. It is supposed that Melqart's profile here was modeled on Hamilcar Barcas. Hamilcar, the father of Hannibal, was a Carthaginian general, who after Carthage lost Sicily started building a new empire in Spain. On the reverse side is a war elephant. On the right, another silver double shekel of New Carthage, of a slightly later date. The god Melqart now almost certainly has been given the looks of Hannibal. On the reverse side is another war elephant. The use of elephants in warfare is first attested for India. The Persians were inspired by the Indian example to include some squadrons of war elephants in their army, and next Seleucus I introduced the war elephant in the Hellenistic world. King Pyrrhus of Epirus crossed from Greece to Italy in 280 with an army that included 20 Indian elephants, which at first installed much fear into the Roman troops. After some time, the effect wore off, and the practical use of the elephants in battle turned out to be rather limited. Still, the Carthaginians imitated Pyrrhus; only, their elephants were from North Africa (where the elephant would only become extinct in Roman imperial days). Hannibal took a number of elephants on his journey across the Alps, probably to impress Celtic tribes along his route and thus encourage them to join forces with Carthage. Most elephants did not survive their Alpine adventure. In his first battle against the Romans in 218, Hannibal used his remaining elephants. For another year he had only one elephant left, on which Hannibal himself rode alongside his troops, until this animal succumbed as well, in 217 BC. Photos: © The Trustees of the British Museum

The Second Punic War (218−201 BC) broke out because Rome decided to come to the assistance of a city in Spain south of the Ebro that was besieged by the Carthaginians, on the basis of an alliance that Rome had concluded with that city either before or after the conclusion of the Ebro Treaty with the Carthaginians. The facts of the matter, and thus the questions of "war guilt," are not clear. But it is most likely that Rome, worried by the growing power of Carthage in Spain, was anxious for war. The aristocratic council that governed Carthage probably had wished to avoid war, but the new Carthaginian commander in Spain, Hannibal, the son of Hamilcar, was eager for an opportunity to take revenge for the defeat of his father and the loss of Sicily and the other islands. He had already made his plans for the war that he had seen coming. While Rome in 218 BC sent one of the consuls with an army to Sicily, with the possible intention of attacking North Africa, and the other over land in the direction of Spain, Hannibal was too quick for his Roman opponents. In a surprising maneuver, he marched with his whole army of some 50,000 Spanish and African infantry and 9000 cavalry, as well as a small number of war elephants, to the north. He subdued the tribes on the other side of the Ebro, made his way across the Pyrenees and through the south of Gaul, reaching the river Rhône before consul Scipio on his way to Spain could arrive there. While the latter hastily retreated to the north of Italy, the Carthaginian army moved on toward the Alps. The crossing, made in haste, was disastrous: just about half of the army that had left Spain made it safely to Italy, and most of the war elephants perished.

Hannibal was a brilliant strategist and tactician, and the campaign in which he so unexpectedly invaded Italy from Spain and across the Alps already made his name immortal. That he was able, in the difficult years that followed, to hold an army of such a heterogeneous composition together and stay assured of its loyalty, proves that he must have had the qualities of a great leader as well as considerable charisma. On the battlefield, he was nearly invincible. He was the only commander in antiquity to be compared with Alexander, and as long as he lived his name alone would terrorize the Romans. He descended into northern Italy in 218 BC and there defeated first Scipio and then the other consul who had marched his army all the way from Sicily to the Po valley to try to stop the invasion. The Celtic tribes of the region, only recently subjugated by Rome, now joined Hannibal, bringing welcome reinforcements for his army that had suffered so much and that in the Po valley also lost its few remaining elephants. The following year Hannibal crossed the Apennines and surprised and annihilated a Roman army on the shores of Lake Trasimene. In Rome, now the first panic struck. The senate decided to appoint a *dictator*. He for the rest of the year avoided any contact with the invaders, hoping to wear them out. Meanwhile, another Roman army had arrived in Spain to open a second front against Carthage there. The next year, 216 BC, again two consuls held command in Italy and opinion in Rome shifted back toward an offensive strategy. This, Hannibal exploited to his advantage. At Cannae, in the southeast of the peninsula, he lured the Roman army, more than 70,000 strong, into a huge battle. They were encircled and slaughtered. When night fell, some 40,000 men on the Roman side had been killed, the largest loss in battle on a single day suffered by any European army until the First World War.

After Cannae, there was truly panic in Rome. A new *dictator* immediately raised as many new legions as possible, even slaves being freed for that purpose. At the same time, another strategy was decided upon: an encounter with Hannibal's army had to be avoided at all costs, while all efforts were henceforth directed at maintaining the Roman alliances in Italy and carrying on the war against the Carthaginians in Spain. In the end, this strategy indeed would yield the victory to Rome. For Hannibal's strategy rested on the expectation that the cities and peoples of Italy that were subject to Rome would defect, but even after the crushing defeat at Cannae only very few of Rome's allies were prepared to do so. After 216 BC, Hannibal would traverse Central and South Italy for 13 years, always followed hard on his heels by the Romans, without a pitched battle being fought. In those years, though, large tracts of the countryside, especially in the south, were ravished, but Rome's system of alliances nevertheless held steady. After Cannae, the city of Syracuse imprudently chose Hannibal's side: after a long and hard-fought siege it was taken by the Romans in 212 BC, plundered, and assigned to the province of Sicily. In that period, the Roman army in Spain also booked some successes; after 210 BC, it was led by Publius Cornelius Scipio, the son of the unfortunate consul of 218 BC. A young man who had not yet held any public office, he had been chosen to be proconsul, mainly on the grounds of his prestigious name, by a special popular vote. A proconsul was not a consul but had all the powers of a consul. It seemed as if Rome in these years of crisis needed a strong and charismatic leader.

Thus, Hannibal's success in the years after Cannae slowly melted away. Reinforcements were either not sent or were intercepted and defeated by the Romans. Meanwhile, Rome tapped its reservoir of manpower and raised ever more legions. By 204 BC, Scipio had conquered the whole of Carthaginian Spain and crossed over to North Africa. A little later, Hannibal was called back, now to defend Carthage itself. In 202 BC, his army of veterans and newly mobilized militias confronted Scipio's more numerous and better trained troops and was finally defeated. A year later, in 201 BC, Carthage for the second time concluded a peace treaty with Rome on Roman terms. It had to surrender the remnants of its fleet, pay a huge indemnity in 50 yearly installments and formally give up its possessions in Spain and in North Africa. Hannibal had already fled to the east to escape Roman revenge, and a little later Scipio, now surnamed Africanus, could celebrate his triumph in Rome.

As a result of the Second Punic War, Rome established her dominance in the western Mediterranean. It was a dearly bought victory, for especially southern Italy and Sicily were in many places destroyed and partly depopulated. On the other hand, Spain now became part of the Roman sphere of influence and provided two more provinces: the *provincia Hispania Citerior*, that is "nearer" Spain in the east of the peninsula, and the *provincia Hispania Ulterior*, or "farther" Spain in the south, roughly modern-day Andalusia. These provinces too were governed by *praetores*, so that the number of annual *praetores* was raised to six. Both provinces occupied mainly the coastal areas; the Roman conquest of the whole peninsula would be a long and laborious process lasting almost two centuries.

Rome and the Mediterranean world until 133 BC

The example of Scipio inspired many Roman *nobiles* in the years following his victory over Hannibal to also win fame, glory, and a crowning triumph. For that, the Greek world offered the most seductive theaters of war. King Philip V of Macedon had for a short time been the ally of Hannibal, and this justified in Roman eyes the war that ended with Philip's defeat in 196 BC and Rome's formal declaration to the Greek cities that henceforth they would be "free." This declaration was both shrewd and idealistic. For on the one hand, the Roman senate was not prepared to annex new provinces but yet wanted to extend its political influence, and on the other hand some Roman aristocrats indeed favored a benign policy toward the Greeks, whose achievements in the arts, literature, and philosophy some members of the Roman aristocracy now began to appreciate. The impact of Rome, however, in practice restricted the playing field of other powers in Greece, such as the Aetolian League, while the granting of freedom was in Roman eyes a benefit to which the Greeks should react with due "gratitude" or obedience to Roman wishes. As explained earlier, this was not immediately understood by the Greeks. When in 192 BC the Aetolians invited Antiochus III to liberate the Greeks in his turn, Rome's attitude toward the Greeks hardened. Not only did the Romans defeat Antiochus' army twice and force a humiliating peace on him, they dismantled the Aetolian League as well. Suspicions grew on both the Roman and Greek side. Rumors about the rearmament of Macedon incited the senate to issue another declaration of war (171 BC). After losing the battle of Pydna in 168 BC, the old kingdom was doomed. In 167 BC, it was formally divided into four republics, its king forced to walk as a captive in his victor's triumph. So enormous was the booty that the *tributum*, the tax on landed property that Roman citizens until then had to pay, could be abolished in Italy; since 167 BC, *tributum* would only be levied on property in the provinces, which gave it the connotation of a "tribute."

An uprising of the Macedonians forced the Romans to abolish the four republics and to formally annex the territory as the *provincia* Macedonia in 148 BC. In 146 BC, the last resistance of the Greeks was broken, and most of Greece annexed to the province of Macedonia. In the same year, the end came for Carthage as well. After the peace of 201 BC, the city had made a quick recovery thanks to her commercial network, while the Romans nourished a paranoid fear of a resurgent Punic power. The politician Cato, paragon of Roman discipline and patriotism, used to end every speech in the senate with the remark that "he was further of the opinion that Carthage had to be destroyed." In 148 BC, conflicts between the city and the by then independent Berber princes in Roman eyes offered enough legal grounds for declaring a "just" war. The Third Punic War (149–146 BC) was one long siege of the city, fanatically defended by its inhabitants, who in the end were no match for the Roman army. Carthage was left in ruins, and its territory after a while was organized as the Roman *provincia* Africa. The victorious commander was another Scipio, grandson by adoption of the victor of Hannibal, who went down into history as Scipio Aemilianus Africanus the Younger. He too became a man of enormous prestige, who in his lifetime had no equal among the nobles of the republic.

Roman society was militaristic through and through. In no other important state was the participation of the population in the army as high as it was in Rome in the 2nd century BC. In the first half of the century, the citizens who were liable for military service—a little more than 50% of the citizenry—on average served five years or even longer in the legions. This practice slowly started to take its toll. The campaigns in Spain that dragged on from year to year offered little booty and little glory but the risks of being killed were higher. They were extremely unpopular and created an "un-Roman" sort of war fatigue. Many a soldier discovered on his return to Italy after years of service that his piece of land was neglected, sometimes infringed upon or downright stolen, and that anyway there was not much sense in trying to make a living from it, since with its meager produce he had to face the competition of new landed estates, worked by slaves, that produced on a large scale for the market. It was the nobility that had invested their disproportionately large parts of the flow of war booty from the east in such estates, a new fashion taken over from the Sicilian Greeks and the Carthaginians. Many impoverished peasants and veteran soldiers moved to the towns and cities, to Rome most of all, thus adding to a large unemployed city proletariat. A certain feeling of malaise arose, the sense of a looming crisis. This was the background against which in 133 BC a sudden crisis broke out, which was to lead to a century of internal violence and fundamental changes.

Social changes and internal crisis

The Roman republic with its senate, assembly of the people, and annually chosen magistrates had the political organization of a city-state. But the territory of Rome had by the 2nd century BC grown to an enormous size and would grow even further. Those who did not live in or near Rome would rarely if ever attend the assembly. The lawgiving body of the *comitia tributa* or *concilium plebis* now became dominated more and more by the poorer citizens living in the capital, the proletarians (*proletarii*: literally, those who only have children) and thus became unrepresentative and susceptible to demagogy and corruption. Legislation and elections in these assemblies were corrupted, while the magistrates chosen by the *comitia centuriata* still came from a small group of families that since the 3rd century hardly grew, although the number of citizens had steadily increased. The magistrates and the senate constituted a governing class that considered its right to rule as self-evident. An elite within this elite could be distinguished: the *nobiles* or those who had been consuls or who had consuls as forbears. Nearly everyone was primarily interested in personal power and riches, glory and prestige. Factions within this ruling class coalesced around outstanding personalities but could change rapidly, often hindering an enduring policy. Competition between politicians often stimulated further expansion of Roman territory in the provinces, since victories on the battlefield brought wealth and glory. At the same time, among countless people within the orbit of Roman power, discontent and hatred rose. Impoverished citizens desired, as always, land, or at least low and stable prizes for grain and other commodities; the Italian allies of Rome wanted, in exchange for their constant military service their fair share of the war profits, not just the occasional crumbs; voices were heard amongst Rome's allies, toward the end of the century, that demanded either full Roman citizenship or full independence from Rome; the subject populations in the provinces suffered under extortion and plunder by Roman tax collectors, corrupt provincial governors, and Roman armies passing through; and finally, the masses of slaves on the large estates in Italy and Sicily nursed a despair that could easily lead to rebellion.

That the republican constitution would give way to a monarchy may strictly speaking not have been inevitable, but in retrospect it did seem that way. The republic was in essence the rule of the senate. That rule was gradually undermined by a people's assembly that considered itself more and more the sovereign and by overambitious politicians who further kept that idea alive for their own ends. As long as the Roman army remained an instrument of the state, the senate could neutralize such power-hungry personalities. But toward the end of the 2nd century BC, the role of the army would fundamentally change.

In a certain sense, the Roman Republic perished as a result of its own success. The Hannibalic war and the following expansion had seriously undermined the Italian peasantry; a landless proletariat and the growth of large estates were symptoms of that development. This implied a dangerous weakening of the recruiting base of the Roman army, as long as the principle was maintained that the legions were levied from those who possessed some property in order to pay for their own equipment, as had been the rule until far into the 3rd century. During the war with Hannibal, that property qualification had been lowered, and in the 2nd century it was lowered still further, while at the same time the state provided the recruits with most of their weaponry, but the principle was maintained nevertheless. In theory, two solutions were feasible: either redistribute the land so that enough smallholders would remain to provide the army with the necessary recruits, or abolish the property qualifications altogether and recruit the proletarians for the army as well. Both solutions, however, threatened the powerful position of the senatorial elite.

In 133 BC, the crisis broke out with the actions of the tribune Tiberius Gracchus. In that year, he submitted to the assembly (the *comitia tributa*) a law forbidding citizens to hold more than a certain amount of state-owned land in Italy; what they had occupied above that amount would be distributed among landless citizens. Tiberius Gracchus had reckoned in advance on strong resistance from the senate. Not only were most senators great landowners who stood to lose by his proposal, but also, and primarily, they would be worried that such a huge redistribution of land brought about by one politician would provide that politician with so many *clientes*—the grateful citizens who would owe their existence to him and would henceforth see in him their *patronus*—that with this enormous *clientela* he would tower far too high above all the other aristocrats in the state. That was why Tiberius went with his proposal straight to the people's assembly, thereby violating an unwritten rule of the constitution that gave the senate the opportunity to first deliberate on proposals that would later be submitted to the assembly. This by itself raised senatorial suspicions of the tribune even further. When his proposal looked to be accepted in a following assembly that would after some weeks vote on it, the senate had one of its supporters among the other tribunes nullify the proposal and the vote by his veto. Thereupon Tiberius had the man relieved of his tribunate by the assembly on the spot, after which the people voted in favor of his law. There were no rules in the Roman constitution that explicitly forbade these actions by Tiberius Gracchus and the people, but to depose a magistrate was certainly unlawful—however, it could be argued that a tribune of the people was strictly speaking not a magistrate.

Figure 30   The so-called relief of Domitius Ahenobarbus (1st c. BC) This impressive marble relief of over 6 m in length, dating from the 1st century BC, is now on display in the Louvre Museum in Paris. It probably once formed part of a temple of Neptune in Rome that was dedicated to that god by Domitius Ahenobarbus, after the defeat of some enemies of Octavian in a sea battle. The relief is supposed to show a ritual with which the census, held every five years, was concluded. It seems likely that an actual census was portrayed, the one held in 115 BC by a *censor* who was an ancestor of Domitius Ahenobarbus. In a central position on the frieze is a bull, which is being directed toward an altar. To the left of the bull, a priest (with part of his toga pulled over his head, a sign of respect for the gods) brings a libation at the altar. Behind the bull walk men carrying laurel branches, and servants guiding a sheep and a pig. Those animals will be sacrificed together with the bull: the traditional sacrifice of the *suovetaurilia*, that is, a sacrifice of a pig, a sheep, and a bull. The sacrifice is for the god Mars, who is standing to the left of the altar in the parade armor of a Roman general. To the left of Mars are a lyre and a flute player: music always accompanied a sacrifice. At the far left, we probably see citizens being inscribed into their *tribus*: someone is noting things down on a huge writing tablet. The primary purpose of the census was military, which would be the reason for the presence of soldiers. The relief has, however, also been thought to represent not a census, but a *dilectus*: the occasion when mobilized citizens come forward to be registered as combatants. That ceremony was also concluded with a sacrifice, a *lustratio*: a ritual meant to ensure that the army and the general populace were free of impurity and in divine favor for a period of five years or for the duration of a military campaign. Photo: © RMN-Grand Palais (musée du Louvre)/Hervé Lewandowski

Next, a land distribution committee headed by Tiberius set to work, and some land was indeed distributed among the poor citizens. The senate, however, administered the state's finances and refused to make available the funds needed for the expropriations. Then, news arrived that the last king of Pergamon had died and that his kingdom was bequeathed to Rome. Tiberius Gracchus seized upon this new development and had the assembly of the people not only accept the legacy but also earmark the revenues from the new province for the work of the land distribution committee. With that, the tribune and the assembly clearly encroached upon the prerogatives of the senate to which traditionally belonged the areas of foreign policy and finance. Suspicion, hatred, and fear increased in senatorial circles. On his part, Tiberius Gracchus proclaimed his candidacy for a second tribunate the following year, which again, although not forbidden, went against the spirit of the republican constitution. A band of senators then marched to where Tiberius was addressing his followers; a tumult arose, and the tribune with some of his supporters were lynched on the spot.

"Tiberius Gracchus split the Roman state in two parties," was the judgment of Cicero, nearly 100 years later when those two parties were still in bitter conflict and the Roman Republic was nearing its end. The historical significance of Tiberius Gracchus was indeed that he for the first time showed how one man with an appealing program and the necessary demagogy could use the assembly of the people to outmaneuver the senate. For politicians who wanted to succeed by using the assembly, the term *populares* came into fashion, while those who wanted decisive power to remain with the senate came to be called *boni* (the "good" men, as opposed to the rabble that filled the *comitia*) or *optimates* (the "best" men). Essentially, the *optimates* defended the traditional political order in which the senate wielded supreme authority, whereas the *populares*—who were also senators, but senators in favor of a new political order—promoted the politics of a popular assembly in alliance with strong men.

After the murder of Tiberius Gracchus, the work of the land distribution committee was not halted but brought more and more under the control of the senate and finally sabotaged. The Italian allies had nourished the hope that they too might profit from the redistributions of land, for they had suffered from the wars in Italy and beyond at least as much as Roman citizens had. When it became clear that they were excluded from such redistribution, discontent among them grew. Some of them then pleaded for granting Roman citizenship to all Italians. For most Romans, however, sharing their citizenship with the Italians was a bridge too far. The *nobiles* were against it, because the granting of citizen rights on such a massive scale in one operation was bound again to disturb thoroughly the clientele relations and hence the internal balance of power; the *proletarii* were against it because they did not want the advantages of citizenship—that just now appeared to materialize— to be diluted by the admission of so many newcomers.

Tiberius Gracchus had a younger brother, Gaius, who had the same political aims as his brother but was also driven by a craving for revenge. In 123 BC, he in his turn became a tribune of the people. As an orator and a demagogue who knew how to manipulate the assembly, and he truly frightened the senate. He pushed through a law enabling the proletarians in Rome to buy grain from the state's granaries at a low, fixed price; at the same time, the agrarian law of his brother Tiberius ordering the redistribution of state-owned land was renewed. Other laws infringed on the senatorial monopoly in manning special judicial courts, assigning them to the "knights" (*equites*, the second order of the elite, ranking below the senators). For the allies, he proposed extending Roman citizenship to all the Latins and giving the status of Latins to all the others. Besides, he initiated the foundation of a Roman colony outside Italy, at the very spot where lay the cursed ruins of Carthage. By then, he had provoked more than enough resistance. The senate trumped his colonial proposal by suggesting many more colonies but inside Italy, while at the same time stirring up resentment against granting the citizenship to the allies. Having been already re-elected once, Gracchus' bid for a third tribunate failed. This, the *optimates* in the senate turned to their advantage; in 121 BC, they had the senate declare a state of emergency, which led to a tumultuous fight on the edge of Rome in which Gaius Gracchus and hundreds of his supporters perished.

Although many of his policies failed for the time being, Gaius Gracchus would later prove to have been a politician with foresight. The extension of citizenship to the allies and the foundation of Roman colonies outside Italy would be realized in the following century. The low and fixed price for grain for the city proletariat of Rome would be maintained, and from 58 BC on the grain would even be freely distributed, thanks to other *populares*. In the short run, however, the *optimates* seemed to have won, and the distribution of land in Italy, newly reintroduced by Gaius Gracchus, came to an end a few years later. But the essential problem remained: while the urban proletariat increased, the steady decline of the free peasantry undermined the recruiting base of the Roman army. New wars soon made the problem acute.

Meanwhile, the Roman Empire kept expanding. Pergamon was incorporated as the province of Asia. In 121 BC, a Roman army came to the assistance of the Greek city of Massalia (Latin Massilia, modern Marseille) against neighboring Gallic tribes and a new *provincia* Gallia Narbonensis (named after the provincial capital Narbo, modern Narbonne) was established. In North Africa, war broke out with the most important Berber kingdom in Numidia (northern Algeria). Incompetence and corruption on the side of Roman generals provided the opportunity for an officer of a non-senatorial family, Gaius Marius, to present himself with the help of political friends under the tribunes as savior of the people. In 107 BC, he was elected consul as a *homo novus* (a "new man," since he had no consuls in his family) who would put affairs in North Africa in order. Against senatorial opposition, he would implement an alternative solution to the recruiting problem of the army.

As consul, Marius admitted into the legions which he recruited all suitable volunteers without paying attention to any property qualifications. As a result, his army came to consist for the main part of proletarians. The state provided for their weaponry and other equipment, the costs of which were to be deducted from their pay. As a premium at the end of their period of service, Marius promised them a piece of land. Although Marius' step was in practice less revolutionary than might appear at first sight, because the property qualifications for service in the legions had since the late 3rd century already been lowered considerably at least twice, so that Marius could seem only to take this development to its logical conclusion, his policy nevertheless created in fact a new Roman army. For the promise of land at the conclusion of military service henceforth bound these recruits and soldiers to their commander in the manner of *clientes* bound to their *patronus*. For it was the commander, not the Roman state, that had to fulfill this promise. At the same time, the army distanced itself from the Roman state and from Roman society at large by its near-exclusive proletarian composition. Moreover, to a larger extent than before, it became a professional army because it was expected that it could take some years before the land grants would be realized, and in the meantime the army would be the only provider of a livelihood for the troops. It seems that Marius consciously promoted further professionalization by exercises and harsh discipline.

After a quick conclusion of the war in North Africa, Marius' new army proved its value a few years later against an unexpected enemy from the north. Setting out from present-day Denmark and northern Germany, the Cimbri, a Germanic people reinforced by mixed Germanic-Celtic groups, such as the Teutons, had moved in search of new areas of settlement from Central Europe into Gaul, annihilated a Roman army in a battle at the river Rhône, and then appeared in the north of Italy. Now even more than before, Marius was called upon to be the savior of Rome. In two bloody battles in the south of Gaul and the north of Italy, in 102 and 101 BC, he almost completely annihilated the invaders. In the next year, 100 BC, a tribune of the people and political ally of Marius had the assembly adopt a law that granted land to Marius' veterans, thus fulfilling the promises made at the time of recruitment. With this, an important political precedent was set: a successful commander could now, with the help of a tribune with some rhetorical talent, force his will upon the Roman state.

The beginnings of the civil wars: Marius and Sulla

Marius himself would hardly profit from the political possibilities that were created by his reform. During riots in Rome, he sided with the senate to maintain order in the capital, thus for the time being saving the rule of the *optimates*. But it was not long before a new crisis made itself felt. When for a second time a proposal to extend Roman citizenship to the allies had come to naught by the opposition of the senate, the allies rose en masse against the dominant city. The ensuing Social War (so called after the *socii* or allies), from 91 to 88 BC, was one of the most dangerous wars Rome ever had to fight. Etruscans, Umbrians, and Samnites united and formed a separate state called Italia, which was, in a sense, an imitation of Rome with its own senate and two annually chosen commanders in chief. The war was very bloody. In Rome, the recognition dawned that the war could only be won by promising Roman citizenship to the Italian allies. When that happened, the resistance against Rome rapidly collapsed. In the end, only the Samnites fought on, until they were brought to their knees by the ruthless Cornelius Sulla, one of the outstanding Roman commanders of the time and a convinced supporter of the *optimates*. In 88 BC, Italy was pacified, and the whole area from the river Po down was now united in Roman citizenship.

In the same year, 88 BC, Mithridates of Pontos overran the Roman province of Asia. The senate reacted by ordering the Roman army that had just subdued the Samnites to march east under the command of Sulla. This was a war, everybody believed, that would yield rich booty and much prestige. The political opponents of Sulla and the *optimates*, therefore, begrudged him his command. A tribune of the people and ally of Marius had the assembly relieve Sulla of his position and transfer the command to Marius. Sulla reacted with a march on Rome that unleashed nearly 60 years of civil wars in which the republic itself would perish. That Sulla could make his legions march on Rome was the result of the fundamental change that the Roman army had undergone since Marius' new recruitment. For now, their commander and *patronus* was for the soldiers more important than the will of either the senate or the assembly of the people. In Rome, Sulla had his opponents killed (Marius had fled the city just in time), restored the authority of the senate, and had his command against Mithridates formally renewed. Then he left for the east. One year later, the followers of Marius in their turn seized power in Rome. Political opponents were massacred, and Marius was re-elected consul for 86 BC, in which year he died. The *populares*, who now dominated the state, began on their part to wage war on Mithridates and sent another army to the east, ignoring Sulla. Meanwhile, Sulla had defeated the king's forces in Greece, captured Athens, and crossed over to Asia, where after a few years Mithridates had to give up his short-lived conquests but was allowed to keep his old kingdom, for Sulla was in a hurry to return to Rome. In 83 BC, he landed in Italy.

The party of the *populares* had prepared themselves for Sulla's return but was, as it turned out, no match for him. Some *nobiles* in Italy even recruited their own troops, and then joined Sulla. One of these was the young Pompey (Pompeius), who thereby found favor with Sulla when the latter entered Rome in 82 BC. The senate, dominated again by the *optimates*, installed Sulla as *dictator* for an indefinite period with the task of reorganizing the state. In the three years of his dictatorship—a foretaste of the monarchy that would come later—Sulla had many *populares* and their supporters executed and the position of the senate vis-à-vis the tribunes and the people's assembly considerably strengthened. Proposals to the assembly henceforth first needed the approval of the senate, which in effect ended the independent lawmaking power of the people and rendered the office of the tribunate toothless, the more so since from now on former tribunes would be excluded from a magisterial and senatorial career. The consulate was detached from the command of an army, for in future the consuls had to stay in Rome, while the legions would all be based in the provinces under the command of proconsuls, praetors, or propraetors as provincial governors. This demilitarization of Italy and of the consulate would prove to be one of the enduring measures initiated by Sulla.

In 79 BC, Sulla resigned—one year later he died—and people could see how his constitution would work in practice. Sulla had wished to turn the political clock back in favor of the senate, but in fact his policy was frustrated by the ambitions of individual *nobiles*. Those who wanted more power for themselves than was permitted by the reorganization of Sulla—and that applied to many *nobiles*—soon saw the new constitution as a straitjacket and preferred the full restoration of the tribunate and the people's assembly, because only by means of these institutions could they hope to bypass the senate for their own political ends. Many poorer citizens too, who had set their hopes on further land distribution, looked forward to a restoration of the old constitution. Thus, in the years following 79 BC, there was much agitation against the *optimates* dominating the senate. It was a period of unrest in various respects. After the demise of the great maritime powers of the Hellenistic east and of Carthage in the west, the whole of the Mediterranean was menaced by pirates, making all sea travel and every coast unsafe. It was also in these years that the slaves in Italy rose in a great uprising led by the Thracian Spartacus. It was a veritable war (73–71 BC) that was only ended after two years by Crassus, then the richest man in Rome and one of those politicians who wanted to abolish many of Sulla's reforms that hindered their own careers. The same Pompey who had already made a name for himself in 82 BC and who now returned from Spain, where he had finally put down the remnants of an anti-Sullan movement, joined him in crushing the last bands of the slaves, so that both men, Crassus and Pompey, could pose as saviors of Rome. With their troops in Italy threatening the capital, they were duly elected as consuls for the year 70 BC. In that year, they pushed through the restoration of the tribunate and of the people's assembly to their former powers. Pompey would be the first to reap the fruits thereof.

Pompey, Caesar, and the fall of the republic

In the year 67 BC, the assembly of the people decreed on a proposal by one of the tribunes to grant extraordinary powers to Pompey for the purpose of cleansing the whole Mediterranean of pirates. To that end, he was provided with a fleet and an army and vested with a formal authority (*imperium*) that surpassed the authority of the various provincial governors. In fact, for a limited period, he became the sole ruler of all Roman territory outside Italy. The operations against the pirates were successful, and only one year later and again on a proposal by one of the tribunes, the assembly bestowed another extraordinary command with an *imperium* surpassing that of the governors on Pompey, this time to set the whole of the east, from Asia Minor to Judea, in order. His actions there led, as already mentioned, to the organization of new Roman provinces, such as Syria, that encompassed the remnants of the old Seleucid empire, and the submission of Judea. In 61 BC, Pompey returned to Italy and celebrated a splendid triumph in Rome. He was at the height of his fame and prestige, and it now seemed that the Roman Republic would pass into the hands of one man.

Pompey, however, had made a fatal mistake. After landing in Italy, he had disbanded most of his army with the promise of a speedy distribution of land among his veterans, and had himself gone off to Rome to bask in the glory of his victories. But the lesson to be learnt from Marius and Sulla was that an ambitious politician should keep his army at hand. Now, a majority of the senators seized the moment and refused to approve of Pompey's arrangements in the east and to assign land for his veterans in Italy. Pompey had to look for other means to fulfill his promise to his troops, safeguard his legacy in the east, and preserve his political prestige. Again, the rich Marcus Crassus presented himself, together with a younger, extremely talented, and extremely ambitious politician, Gaius Julius Caesar, a man from an old but impoverished patrician family, who had politically sided with the party of Marius. In 60 BC Pompey, Crassus, and Caesar joined forces to have Caesar elected as consul for the following year in which he would push through the ratification of Pompey's measures, including the grants of land for his veterans; as a proconsul in 58 BC, Caesar would have a province and an army and thus the chance of winning glory and prestige in his turn. Crassus came up with the money needed for the election campaign, and Caesar was chosen as expected. His consulate in 59 BC was spent fulfilling the promises and agreements that the three men had made the year before (the other consul, Caesar's colleague, tried to obstruct his program but was completely ignored): Pompey got what he wanted, and Caesar himself received by vote of the assembly the proconsulate of both the province of Gaul in Italy north of the river Po and of wider Gaul beyond the Alps for a period of five years, starting in 58 BC.

In the end, Caesar would spend nine years, from 58 till 50 BC, in Gaul, systematically conquering the land from the Alps and the river Rhine in the east, to the ocean in the west. Meanwhile in Rome, tribunes of the people with the support of Caesar agitated against the senate and realized by law the free distribution of grain to the urban proletariat. Pompey tried more and more to play a mediating role between the agitated masses and his former friends in the senate. For the time being, he adhered to his alliance with Caesar and Crassus, and at a conference in 56 BC their alliance was even renewed. The three men agreed that Caesar would have again five years in Gaul, starting in 54 BC, to finish his "pacifying" work there, while Pompey and Crassus would hold the consulate together for a second time in 55 BC, after which both would receive a province and an army for their further pursuit of glory and prestige: Spain for Pompey and Syria for Crassus. So it happened, and in 54 BC Crassus departed for the east in the hope of winning as much military glory as his two colleagues already enjoyed by campaigning against the Parthians. His expedition, however, ended in the desert near Carrhae (Harran), where his army, encircled by the Parthian mounted archers, suffered a dreadful defeat and Crassus himself was killed. Pompey, who stayed in Rome and let Spain be governed by his *legati* or representatives, now politically moved to the side of the senate and came to see the *popularis* Caesar as his main political rival.

Riots in Rome between gangs that had connections either with Caesar or with the senate, so it was generally believed, hindered the orderly processes of government. The consular elections for 52 BC were therefore canceled by the senate, and Pompey was for that year to act as *consul sine collega* ("consul without a colleague"). Presumably, Pompey himself enjoyed such a role: seemingly above the conflicting parties, preserving law and order as a *princeps*, a "first man" in the state, in a near-monarchical position. It testifies to their political weakness that most senators were prepared to preserve the republic and with it their own privileged position by such quasi-monarchical means. To those senators belonged the former consul Marcus Tullius Cicero, the greatest orator and one of the most important writers and intellectuals of his time, author of various political and philosophical treatises, who called for concord among the orders (senators, knights, and the common people) with the aim of preserving the republic, a concord that he envisaged in a grand reconciliation presided over by a *princeps*. Others, however, were less conciliatory. Fearful of Caesar's popularity with the populace in Rome and his army in Gaul, they demanded that he lay down his command as soon as his proconsulate ended on the 1st of January 49 BC and come to Rome as a private citizen. Pompey, whose prestige threatened to be outstripped by Caesar's, supported that demand, thus joining in fact the *optimates* against Caesar.

On the 1st of January 49 BC, conflict broke out: the senate rejected Caesar's proposal to leave him only two legions and the proconsulate, so that he could stand for the consulate for the next year. Instead, it ordered Pompey to organize the defense of the republic against the man who now formally acted against the law by keeping his troops and his provinces.

Caesar, who had been in the north of Italy near the southern border of his province, reacted at once by crossing the stream of the Rubicon (near Rimini), which separated his province from Italy. He advanced much more quickly than his opponents had anticipated, and most senators accompanied Pompey in moving to the Balkans, since in Italy they had hardly any Roman troops. Caesar occupied Rome, and then progressed to Spain where in a short campaign he defeated the Pompeian forces and returned to Italy. Pompey, meanwhile, had assembled an army in Greece. In 48 BC, Caesar crossed the Adriatic and at Farsalos in Thessaly the decisive battle was fought. Defeated, Pompey sought refuge in Egypt, where he was murdered on the orders of the king. Caesar went to Egypt and there sided with Cleopatra against her brother and installed her as sole monarch of the country. The next year, in North Africa, the last "republican" army was destroyed, and Caesar returned to Rome in triumph. In the winter and spring of 45 BC, he was again in Spain, and in a final battle defeated the last "Pompeian" army; then back again in Rome he was received with quasi-divine honors.

Caesar's dictatorship: Octavian and Antony

All power in Rome was now in the hands of one man. Formally, however, the republic had not ceased to exist. Magistracies and honors were heaped upon Caesar in the first years, but his position seemed to require a more formal expression. In 46 BC, he became *dictator*, as Sulla had been, first for ten years, then in 45 BC for life. In fact, it was the inauguration of a monarchy, albeit without the name. As *dictator* Caesar reorganized the administration of the provinces and enlarged the senate to 900 men, opening that body to many new families from now totally Roman Italy. The number of recipients of free grain in Rome was brought down to 150,000. For the proletarians and for countless veterans, new Roman colonies were founded outside Italy, the most famous of which were the rebuilt cities of Carthage and Corinth. The Italian towns received a uniform municipal organization. Lastly, the traditional lunar calendar, which had gone wildly wrong (the intercalations required to make the lunar calendar run more or less parallel to the solar year had been neglected for a long time), was replaced by a modernized solar calendar, the work of Alexandrian scholars who improved upon the old Egyptian solar calendar. Caesar's calendar numbering 365 days, divided over 12 months in 3 consecutive years, and 366 days in the fourth year, came into effect on the 1st of January 45 BC and has since then remained the basic calendar in the West and since the last few centuries in the world at large.

   Caesar's position had by 45 BC become that of an absolute ruler. Presumably, he himself wanted to formalize this by instituting a monarchy after the model of Hellenistic kingship. That provoked the bitter resistance of traditionally minded senators, and on the 15th of March 44 BC, when he was entering the assembly of the senate, Caesar was murdered by a small group of senators, among whom Brutus and Cassius were the best known. There immediately ensued a period of political chaos and renewed civil wars. Caesar had in his will made a grandnephew named Octavius his heir, and this young man of 18 years at once presented himself to Caesar's troops and, having assured himself of their loyalty, came to Rome to claim the political heritage of the *dictator* by convincing the senate and the people that Caesar had posthumously adopted him. The senate, which had for a very short time played with the idea of restoring the old republic, was forced to grant the

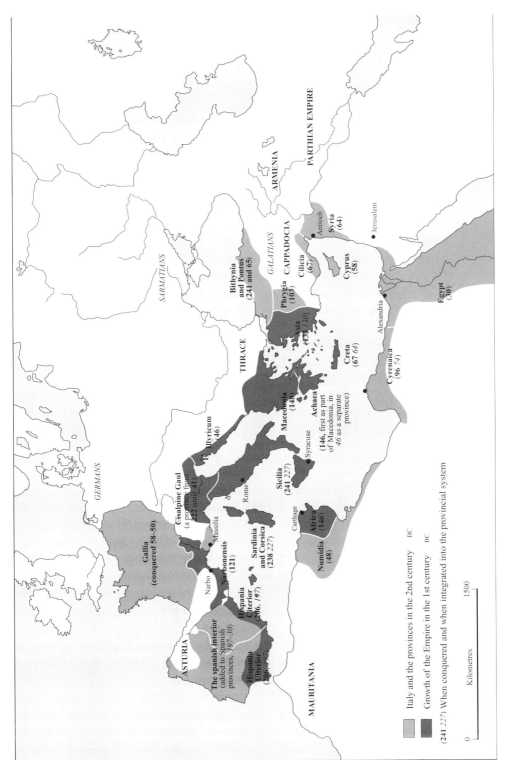

Map 16 The Roman Empire, 3rd–1st c. BC

GERMANS

SARMATIANS

PARTHIAN EMPIRE

ARMENIA

ASTURIA

Gallia
(conquered 58–50)

Narbonensis
(121)

The spanish interior
(added to Spanish
provinces, *197–30*)

Hispania Citerior
206, 197

Massilia

Narbo

Hispania Ulterior
206, 197

MAURITANIA

Cisalpine Gaul
(a province from
222 until –41)

Sardinia
and Corsica
(238 227)

Rome

Carthage

Africa
(146)

Numidia
(48)

Illyricum
(46)

THRACE

Sicilia
(241 227)

Syracuse

Macedonia
(148)

Achaea
(146, first as part
of Macedonia, in
46 **as a separate**
province)

Bithynia
and Pontus
(241 and 65)

GALATIANS

Phrygia
(103)

Asia
133, 130

Creta
(67 64)

Cyrenaica
(96 74)

Alexandria

Egypt
(30)

CAPPADOCIA

Cilicia
(67)

Cyprus
(58)

Antioch

Syria
(64)

Jerusalem

Italy and the provinces in the 2nd century   BC

Growth of the Empire in the 1st century   BC

(241 227) When conquered and when integrated into the provincial system

0   Kilometres   1500

young Caesar Octavianus various powers and soon even the consulship. Allied with Marcus Antonius (Mark Antony), Caesar's most important general, Octavian proved to be a shrewd politician. Together with another general, Lepidus, he and Mark Antony coerced the senate in 43 BC to recognize their triumvirate as a provisional government with plenipotentiary powers to reform the state and punish the murderers of Caesar. These, under the leadership of Brutus and Cassius, had in the meantime assembled an army in the eastern provinces. There, in 42 BC in two consecutive battles at Filippoi in Macedonia, they were defeated and killed, after which Antony remained in the east, while Octavian returned to Rome. Shortly thereafter, they more or less divided the Mediterranean world among themselves: Antony got the eastern provinces, and Octavian the western ones, while Italy remained as a recruiting base for both. In practice, however, Italy fell within the sphere of Octavian, who soon asserted his authority also over Sicily, where a son of Pompey had managed to maintain himself and harass Italy with his fleet. He disarmed Lepidus, and now only Antony was left, who in the meantime had met Cleopatra, married her, and started to reorganize his power around Egypt, dreaming of a Roman-Greco–Egyptian empire centered on Alexandria. Octavian began a propaganda war against his "degenerate" rival, who had been ensnared by an oriental queen, and mobilized opinion in Rome and Italy against the couple. In 32 BC, the final rupture between the rivals occurred. The Roman population of Italy and the western provinces swore an oath of loyalty and obedience to Octavian, who thereafter set out for the east with a huge army and fleet. In 31 BC, the decisive battle took place at sea off the western Greek coast at Actium (Aktion). Antony's fleet was defeated, and he and Cleopatra fled with the Egyptian squadron to Alexandria. Octavian followed with his army, and in 30 BC Antony killed himself. A few days later, Cleopatra, taken prisoner by Octavian, committed suicide too. The state of the Ptolemies was then formally annexed by the victor. The Mediterranean world was now united in one empire under one ruler.

Chapter 5.2

The Social Fabric

Economic Life

In the roughly 300 years from Alexander the Great until the end of the Roman Republic, important changes occurred in the economic life of the Greek and Roman world. They had mainly to do with an enormous increase in scale. Simultaneously, the significance of the market as a stimulus for economic activity considerably increased in comparison with earlier periods. The impulse for these changes ultimately came from the great political events of the time: the conquests of Alexander and the emergence of the Hellenistic kingdoms in the east, and the expansion of the Roman Republic in the west.

Agriculture

The foundation of the economy in the Hellenistic world remained, as always, agricultural, although industry and commerce would become much more important than they had been before. At the level of agrarian techniques and products, in general not much changed. Consequently, production could in fact be enlarged only by bringing more land under cultivation. In some areas, such as Mesopotamia and Egypt, irrigation techniques could accomplish that, but in many places nature itself limited the expansion of land fit for agriculture. The Hellenistic age, though, saw a further spread of wheat cultivation, especially of bread-wheat, which in many areas now became the staple grain, with barley increasingly becoming the food of the poor. At the same time, in the western basin of the Mediterranean, the spread of the cultivated olive and the vine, which had already started in the Archaic period, proceeded at a quicker pace, turning southern Gaul, southern Spain, and northern Africa into important producers of olive oil and wine. Really new agricultural products, such as sugarcane, cotton, or rice, were introduced from India into the Mediterranean world, but they remained curiosities that had no influence on agrarian production at large. The same applied to, more or less, the fruit trees from western Asia that in this period became known in the Greek and later in the Roman world too: the peach, the cherry, and the apricot. Thus, agricultural innovation in the Hellenistic age was not characterized by

Antiquity: Greeks and Romans in Context, First Edition. Frederick G. Naerebout and Henk W. Singor.
© 2014 John Wiley & Sons, Inc. Published 2014 by John Wiley & Sons, Inc.

the introduction of new techniques and only in a minor way by the introduction of new crops or plants. Innovation in agriculture was mainly a matter of organizational change and concerned above all the rise of plantation-like large estates worked by slaves.

In landownership and agricultural labor, in the Hellenistic age, three categories can be clearly discerned: (1) the smallholders who work their own lands, (2) the peasant tenants working parcels of land owned by larger landowners, and (3) the slaves working the fields of their masters. The first category had been characteristic of the Archaic and classical Greek *polis*, which rested, ultimately, on a citizenry of small landowners. In the Hellenistic period too, it remained the norm in Greece and Italy for the free citizen to possess land that he either worked himself or, if he was rich enough, leased out to tenants or had his slaves work for him. In practice, though, this norm was increasingly undermined. Both in Greece and in Italy, inequality in land ownership markedly increased, with the result on the one hand of the growth of a landless proletariat and on the other of a class of very rich large landowners. The latter leased out their lands to tenants, or—which was a new practice—had them worked by slaves. Outside Greece and Italy, the category of free smallholders did exist as well, although circumstances varied from one region to another. The new Greek *poleis* in western Asia naturally adopted the norm of the free citizen as landowner, although there too it was not always easy to maintain. But apart from the Greek cities, in some regions an indigenous class of smallholders had always existed in relatively large numbers, for instance in Syria, Judea, and the Galilee.

Tenant farmers had probably been a very small group in Greece before the Hellenistic age, but not so in many parts of Asia Minor. Traditionally, there the large tracts of land belonging to kings, temples, or rich private landowners had been divided among small tenants. The contracts regulating tenure could vary greatly, from a tenure of a few years to tenures for life. In the latter case, the tenant had in fact become a kind of serf. In many regions, this was the destiny of a large part of the peasant population, bound as they were to the lands of a temple or a king. In Asia Minor, there were ancient and renowned sanctuaries that thrived on extended landed property with large peasant populations tied to the soil. Many Hellenistic kings also, for instance, the Seleucids, had the lands that directly belonged to the crown, worked by un-free tenant farmers who could not leave their lands. Rich city dwellers too, both in the older cities of Asia Minor and in the newly founded cities, often had their landed property worked for them by tenant farmers who in practice could be hard to distinguish from serfs. Thus, the un-free or "half-free" status of a large part of the peasant population in western Asia and Egypt underscored the social and cultural divide between the indigenous countryside and the Hellenized cities. In Egypt, the peasants had been for centuries or more tied to the soil or at least to their village by the state, that is, the king and his functionaries, and treated more or less like serfs. Royal officials inspected the harvests, divided the seed, determined the quota for the next harvest, and oversaw the whole process of production, including the collection for the royal granaries of that part of the harvest that was due to the king—often 50%. The Ptolemies administered Egypt as one large royal domain, worked by an obedient peasant population that was governed by all kinds of directions and rules.

The regulation of agriculture in Egypt under the Ptolemies had much to do with the massive export of grain from the Nile valley to population centers in the Greek world and later to Rome. The Ptolemies organized the economy of their kingdom, especially its agriculture, with an eye on a state-sponsored and state-organized export from which the royal treasury was to primarily profit. Likewise, it was mainly for export to the urban markets that the third category in the organization of land and labor made its appearance: the large private estates worked by slaves.

Apparently, the first more or less systematic "plantation economy" was developed by the Carthaginians in their North African possessions in the 4th century BC. The Greeks in Sicily in the 3rd century adopted the system from their Carthaginian neighbors and also translated theoretical works on the subject. In their turn, rich Roman landowners imitated the large proprietors in Sicily, and thus in the last two centuries of the Roman Republic the form of agricultural organization arose and thrived that is denoted by the Latin terms of *fundus* or *latifundium*.

A *latifundium* was a large landed estate, comparable to a plantation in the 18th or 19th century, where mainly olive oil and wine were produced by slave labor on a much larger scale than was possible for the simple free smallholder. The rise of the *latifundia* was related to the growth of the city of Rome as a consumer market; to the import of great numbers of slaves; and to the partial decline of the free Roman and Italian peasantry in the 2nd century BC—all consequences of the Roman expansion. A *latifundium* or *villa* consisted of a house for the landowner or his steward, central workplaces, storage buildings and stables, and lodgings for the night for the slaves (more often than not low dens in which they slept chained to the walls), surrounded by kitchen gardens, grain fields, vineyards, olive orchards, grassland, and wasteland. In Italy, wine and olive oil were the most important marketable products that could yield the landowner a profit. Since the production of wine, in contrast to that of olive oil or grain, was rather labor intensive, the use of slaves here was certainly profitable. Combined with the relatively easy availability of slaves thanks to the Roman wars of conquest, this may explain why the *latifundium* system was economically feasible and preferred by the large landowners to leasing out their land to tenants. Rich landowners possessed several *latifundia* or *villae* scattered over Italy. The steward or *vilicus*, who managed the domain in the absence of the owner, was as a rule himself a freedman or a slave. Apart from agriculture, considerable tracts of the domain could be set aside for use as grazing grounds for both horses and cattle, while goats, sheep, and pigs could be left roaming the wasteland or forests. This was true especially in southern Italy, in regions that had been devastated by the Hannibalic war, had been made Roman state land after that war, and had come into the hands of rich Roman landowners since. The herdsmen who accompanied the animals—sheep and goats had to be followed for long distances on horseback—were themselves slaves too. The spread of the *latifundia* in Italy after the Second Punic War, attended by an impoverishment and numerical decline of the class of free smallholders—although that class would never completely disappear—literally changed the landscape in many regions and was one of the more important factors in the social and political changes that took place in the late Roman Republic.

Industry and commerce

Industry and commerce received a huge impetus in the Hellenistic period. In part, commerce was, as always, closely related to agricultural production. Whereas around a big city such as Rome horticultural enterprises arose whose products—vegetables, fruit, and flowers—were brought to the city and sold there by the producers themselves, the import of grain from overseas gave rise to a new class of large-scale transporters and traders of grain. At the level of the family business, industry and commerce were traditionally combined, in that the artisan or craftsman himself sold his products from his workshop. This remained largely true, though additional slave labor could sometimes considerably enlarge the workplace. Besides the older crafts such as those of the potter, the bronze worker or ironsmith, the leather worker or shoemaker and the like, new arts and crafts emerged in the big cities of the Hellenistic world and foremost in Rome, specialists for whom there usually had not been enough employment in an earlier period: goldsmiths and silversmiths, furniture makers, tailors and other cloth workers, and so forth. Moreover, completely new professions appeared, such as innkeeper, doctor, schoolmaster, and other more or less intellectual professions, to which, at a higher level, also belonged the lawyer. In the big cities, there were owners of donkeys, mules, and carts to be hired for transport, and also people who in fact had only their manual labor to hire out for a living: dockers and porters in the harbors or at the city gates, laborers in construction projects, and the like. Another category again was made up of those belonging to artistic professions, such as painters, sculptors, mosaicists, or professional musicians and actors, the latter usually moving from city to city in groups that claimed the god Dionysus as their patron. Taken together, the economic life of at least the bigger cities in the Hellenistic world seems to have been richer and more variegated than had been the case in earlier periods. It was not rare for craftsmen and traders from abroad to settle in these cities too; whole streets or neighborhoods could be inhabited by foreigners.

Perhaps the most striking economic characteristic of the Hellenistic age was the emergence of a truly long-distance trade. Compared to the total economic activity of the period, this commerce was probably of minor importance, but the connections that since Alexander the Great had been made between various regions for the first time created an integrated economic space that encompassed the whole of the Mediterranean, West Asia, and parts of Central and South Asia—a space in which not only goods but also ideas could travel. Trade routes crossed both land and sea. On land, the traders dealt primarily in highly valued luxury goods, such as precious stones and pearls from the regions of the Red Sea, the Persian Gulf, and farther away, pepper and other spices from India, incense from South Arabia or Somalia, myrrh and other aromatics from the desert regions of Arabia and Iran, and finally silk from China after the establishment of the Silk Road around 120 BC. These products from countries outside the Hellenistic world were paid for with gold and silver coins or with products of Hellenistic applied art, such as bronze vessels, bronze mirrors, sculptures, glass, and ceramics. Sometimes, the exotic products were processed in the Hellenistic world, such as Chinese silk being dyed in Phoenicia, and could subsequently be re-exported. The merchants in this long-distance trade were mainly Phoenicians, Syrians, Jews, and Arabs, Iranians, and

Indians. Greek and Aramaic were the languages that were commonly understood along the trade routes as far as India. Caravans followed fixed routes touching markets and stopping places and regional or even international commercial centers, such as Petra in the desert of modern Jordan, Antioch, and later Palmyra in Syria, Seleucia, and Ctesiphon on the Tigris in Mesopotamia. In the Mediterranean area itself, it was above all Alexandria in Egypt, a few Phoenician cities, Rhodes, Delos (after 167 BC), Corinth, and Carthage in the west that could be called commercial centers. Much of the caravan trade was intermediate

(a)

Figure 31   Delos and Hatra (2nd–1st c. BC). Delos and Hatra were two important transit centers: the one a seaport, the other a caravan city. The aerial photograph above shows part of the island of Delos in the Aegean sea, and the one overleaf shows Hatra in Northern Iraq, in the desert lands between the Euphrates and the Tigris rivers. Delos, renowned throughout history as the holy island of the god Apollo, in 166 was placed by the Romans under Athenian supervision, to function as a free port for all of the Eastern Mediterranean. The city on the island flourished, attracting traders from far and wide. After about a century, Delos lost its importance again, especially because trade routes tended to be relayed toward Italy. On the photograph here we see from top to bottom (we are looking in a northerly direction): the sacred lake (now dry: the dark circular shape), the agora of the Italian traders, several temples, other agoras and stoas, and then, on the slopes of a low hill, residential quarters. Warehouses lined the seaside. Higher up the hill there are more sanctuaries, also catering to the foreigners in this cosmopolitan community, such as the sanctuaries of the Egyptian Isis and Sarapis and of the Syrian Atargatis. Hatra was a semi-autonomous town in the Parthian Empire. It was founded in the 1st century BC, and it flowered in the first centuries AD until it was captured and destroyed by the Sassanids in 240–245. It was an important trade center on the route from the Persian Gulf to the Mediterranean, and a caravan city where many caravan routes came together (the dark lines leading away from the city in all directions are such caravan routes). We can see an extensive built-up area enclosed by a city wall that was over 6 km in length and strengthened with 160 towers. In the center is a huge sanctuary, walled as well, which housed several temples for both Greek and indigenous gods. It may also have been the seat of the local government. Photos: a) from A.A.M. Van der Heyden *Atlas van de antieke wereld*, Amsterdam 1958 Elsevier; b) Pitt Rivers Museum, University of Oxford, PRM 1998.294.1241

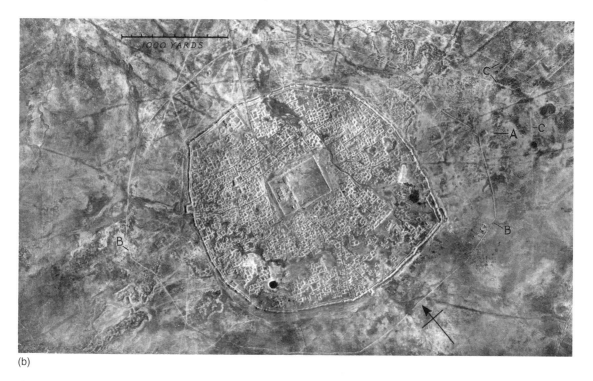

(b)

Figure 31   (*Continued*)

trade: the silk from China, for instance, passed through many hands before it reached the Mediterranean. The same was true, until far into the 2nd century BC, for the overseas trade between Egypt and India: Egyptian ships did not go further than the straits near Aden, where they met Arabian and Indian traders who monopolized the routes up to the west coast of India. The discovery of the monsoon winds toward the end of the 2nd century BC established a direct sea link between Egypt and India, initiating overseas commerce that was modest at first but would greatly increase after Egypt was incorporated into the Roman Empire. The Ptolemies had already at an early stage sent expeditions through the Red Sea to explore the east coast of Africa in search of war elephants, spices, and other exotic valuables. This commerce, as well as the trade with Arabia and India, was heavily regulated by the royal government, for import and export duties on all traded goods provided the royal treasury with a considerable income.

In this way, Egypt was also an exporter of Indian and Arabian goods, apart from its own products such as grain, linen, various vegetable oils, leather, papyrus, and glass. In its turn, the country imported from northern Mediterranean lands timber, metals, wine, and olive oil. On the whole, the balance of trade was very favorable for Egypt, and the royal treasury was usually well-filled. Its income was largely spent on the royal court, the central administration, and on warfare, so that the population at large certainly did not enjoy any increase in prosperity. Thanks to the papyri, relatively much is known of Egypt, but elsewhere, too, the economic innovations of the period cannot have touched the mass of the rural population very much; rather, their position may well have deteriorated both economically and juridically. Those who profited most from economic activities that were more than strictly local were everywhere the rich, both the traditionally rich and the new rich: large landowners; those who in the service of the kings acquired, legally or illegally, enormous fortunes; and a few big merchants. Together, they formed only a very small part of the population, but it was they who offered a market for the luxury goods from the long-distance trade. That market remained small, and thus the trade in luxury goods played only a modest role in the economy of the Hellenistic world. Far more important were the trade movements between various Hellenistic regions dealing in grain, wine, and olive oil. The group of countries that were thus connected with each other gradually increased, which made possible more economic development and growth regionally. That was the case, for instance, in the Black Sea region in the 3rd century BC, where the Greek cities experienced growing prosperity as a result of the grain trade. Above all, the orbit of the Hellenistic economy expanded in a western direction: here, the Roman conquests brought about the unification of Italy, where the import and export of agrarian products led to an economic flourishing, while the elite, grown rich on war booty, offered a strong consumer market.

All that commercial traffic required, among other things, harbor facilities. In the Hellenistic period, new and artificial harbors were constructed that were provided with quays, piers, docks, arsenals, and light towers, foremost at Alexandria but hardly less impressively at Carthage, Rhodes, Delos, and a few other Greek cities (Athens and the Piraeus in comparison lost much of their significance).

Money circulation

Commerce in the Hellenistic world was stimulated by a circulation of money that went deeper and farther than in earlier times. When Alexander had taken possession of the treasures of the Persian king in Susa, Persepolis, and Ekbatana, he had much of the gold and silver coined, and this money was brought into circulation by way of payments to his troops. Successors such as Antigonus and Seleucus would do the same with what was left of the treasures. This sudden and huge increase in the money supply, hardly balanced by any increase in the production of goods, caused serious inflation in the Hellenistic world. At the same time, the now monetized economy of western Asia was connected with that of the Greek world proper, creating one large, integrated economic system. Formally, there was no question of a monetary union, though, for the Greek cities and the new Hellenistic kingdoms had their own currencies in the form of bronze and silver coins, while since the time of Philip and Alexander some cities and all the kingdoms also minted gold coins. But the coins were easily interchanged, the silver and gold coins deriving their value essentially from their weight in precious metal. The most important unit was the silver *drachme*, usually modeled on the Attic standard, and the silver tetradrachms (four drachmas) minted by Alexander and the Hellenistic kings dominated international trade. Toward the end of the 3rd century BC, Roman coins were added to the international currency: the silver *denarius* and *sestertius* (one fourth of a *denarius*), and since the 1st century BC, golden Roman *aurei* would be irregularly issued. Understandably, the money changer became a familiar figure in the big Hellenistic cities.

The evolution from money changer to banker had already started in the 4th century BC. In the classical *poleis*, temples had functioned as places where individuals and states could leave their valuables as deposits, for safekeeping. States could also borrow from the temples, in which case the temple lent from its own property, not from the deposits stored in it. Thus, the temples did not function as rudimentary "banks" in the modern sense. In the 4th century BC, however, in Athens and the Piraeus, the money changer, taking over the role of "deposit banks" from the temples, at least for private citizens, did assume some functions of the modern banker. One could deposit money with the moneychanger or money dealer without receiving any interest, but the dealer was obligated to make the money available at any given moment or to pay the money to a third party after a written order to that effect was issued. In that way, a rudimentary credit system could develop. Cicero could transfer money from Rome to his son in Athens by writing to his banker without having to send, literally, a heap of coins overseas. The banker, in his turn, could try to make more money for himself with the sums entrusted to him by investing in certain economic activities, such as giving a loan to merchants against an interest that could vary from 10% to 30%, usually with the ship and/or its cargo as security. It seems that in some places, such as commercially important Delos, the temples could also act in such a banking capacity. No doubt all this favored international trade in the Hellenistic world. Yet, both the budding banking activities and the international trade itself remained hemmed in by various limitations inherited from the previous period that prevented commerce and banking from flourishing as in the early modern age. Loans and commercial activities in antiquity were essentially ad hoc activities, aimed at a specific transaction. Merchants pooled their money—either their own or borrowed from a third party such as a "banker"—for one commercial enterprise at the time, not for a business or "company" that would endure. In the prevailing juridical systems, which acknowledged only individual accountability, the creation of a company or firm together with partners was virtually impossible.

Apart from the usual unavailability of interest on money deposited, this simple "banking system" had another weakness: it catered exclusively to the very rich. For the common people, it was impossible not only to borrow but also to deposit money and thus to save. "Saving" money in antiquity meant safekeeping, and often in a primitive way by literally hiding money in a pot in the ground. As a result, only the very rich made use of "bankers" or indulged in a little "banking" themselves by giving loans, often against exorbitant interest rates, to merchants for commercial activities or to cities for paying their tributes to kings or states—to the Roman state, in particular. Especially, rich Romans of the equestrian order or "knights" (the elite ranking just below the senatorial class) in the 2nd and 1st centuries BC often used their wealth in that way. United in a sort of consortium, they rented the tax for one year that a given province had to pay to Rome, the amount of which had been fixed in advance, by simply paying that amount of money into the Roman treasury first and collecting, or rather extorting, the actual tax in the province concerned afterward, with a considerable surplus, amounting to 100% of the taxes due, as a reward for themselves. The practice was regularly lamented by the provincials, who, however, were mostly powerless, since the governor would protect the tax collectors with his troops, and would usually receive a fair share of the profits. These persons, known as *publicani* (since it was public transactions that they leased from the Roman government), were understandably hated. It could also happen that when the Romans imposed on a province an extra amount of tribute by way of punishment, the cities there had to borrow the full amount from a group of *publicani*, who then proceeded to collect their money with exorbitant interest in annual installments for the next few years. In this way, in the last two centuries of the Roman Republic, enormous amounts of money, that is, coins in silver and in gold, ended up in Roman hands, part of a general process of shifting wealth and economic prosperity from the eastern Mediterranean to Italy, as a result of the expansion of Rome.

The slave trade

The period initiated by Alexander the Great can, from an economic point of view, be seen as one of increasing interaction and even interdependence between various regions around the Mediterranean. More than before, goods were produced for the market, the products themselves still being mainly agrarian, and only in a minority of cases goods from industry or long-distance trade. "Industry," of course, was mostly not associated with mass production. The term usually referred to, as we have seen, the activities of artisans and craftsmen working in small family businesses. Only in a few potteries and brick-making facilities and in state-owned workplaces that produced weaponry for the army could one speak of mass production with a certain division of labor. One commercial "product", at the same time an important part of the labor force, however, needs some special treatment here: the slaves.

The slave trade had already existed in classical Greece, but presumably not yet on any large scale. Certainly, in the Hellenistic age, this trade assumed large proportions. In part, it was fed by the purchasing of slaves in "barbaric" regions, especially on the northern coast of the Black Sea, where chieftains sold their war captives and parents sometimes their own children to the slave traders coming from the Hellenistic cities. The enormous rise in the supply of slaves in this period, however, was clearly connected with the many wars between the Hellenistic states. The custom of selling war prisoners into slavery had already existed in classical Greece and was maintained in the Hellenistic world, although sometimes voices were raised against the practice, at least among the Greek states. Those voices did not prevent the "marketing" of countless numbers of prisoners of both Greek and other ethnic backgrounds. Especially, the expansion of Rome brought ever more human merchandise onto the market—and directed the flow increasingly toward Italy where the buying power was concentrated. Sometimes the prisoners were sold on the spot in a Roman army camp as slaves to their new owners, sometimes they were sold to slave traders following the army, who would bring them to the slave markets in, for instance, Delos, since 167 BC a duty-free commercial center for all kinds of international trade. The island owed that status to Rome, which thereby deliberately wanted to harm the commercial interests of Rhodes, which after 167 BC indeed rapidly declined. Delos became a natural center for the slave trade, which was soon also fed by the developing piracy all over the Mediterranean

(a)

(b)

Figure 32 Slaves in Hellenistic art (3rd–1st c. BC). Slaves were omnipresent in most ancient societies and have been frequently depicted In Hellenistic art. In general, one can say that Hellenistic art had a penchant for portraying humans who did not answer to the common aesthetic ideals of Greek art: the elderly, the crippled, dwarfs, and people from other ethnic backgrounds. Such portrayals ranged from realistic to caricature. On the left, we see a black African boy. This delicate bronze statue was found in the north of France, and is now in the Bibliothèque Nationale in Paris. It has been dated to the 2nd-1st century BC. This boy represents a category of slaves that had a relatively secure existence, compared to their fellow slaves working in chain gangs on landed estates or in mines (the kind of slave that rarely made it to a work of art). He appears to be a singer or musician; he most likely carried a harp, which he held in his right hand, letting it rest on his right shoulder and playing it with his left hand. He seems himself carried away by his song. Among the large slave population of Hellenistic days, slaves from sub-Saharan Africa must have been a small minority. But that, of course, made them even more conspicuous and a popular subject in ancient art. The terra-cotta statuette on the right shows us a different aspect of slavery. The statuette, dubbed "the old pedagogue," dates to the 3rd century BC; now housed in the Louvre, it probably was made in Athens. The *paidagogos* was a slave, usually a man of advanced age, who looked after the young master, accompanied him on his way to school, and supervised and assisted in his upbringing and schooling. The *paidagogos* was, accordingly, a slave who was valued for his learning and his reliability. But he was a slave nevertheless; he had to carry the writing equipment and playthings for his young charge. This old man is carrying a couple of bags containing knuckle bones. Photos: a) © RMN-Grand Palais (musée du Louvre)/Hervé Lewandowski; b) © BnF, Dist. RMN-Grand Palais/image BnF

Sea, practiced foremost by the inhabitants of the coastal areas of Cilicia in southern Asia Minor. Kidnapping people at sea or in shore raids and selling them at the slave markets was a practice that had been held in check by Rhodes until 167 BC and partially by Carthage until 146 BC, as long as these cities possessed some maritime power, but that went totally unchecked later in the 2nd century and the beginning of the 1st century BC. Only in 67 BC would Pompey largely put an end to the practice. Slaves were employed in considerable numbers in the households of the rich but also, in lesser numbers, in those of many middle-income citizens; and on the large private estates or *latifundia* that were dependent on slave labor. The latter were mainly found in Italy and Sicily, and it was there where since roughly 200 BC the largest numbers of slaves ended up.

Government actions and the economy

The Hellenistic kingdoms and republican Rome hardly pursued any economic policy. An exception was Ptolemaic Egypt, where the government tried to manage the country as one large estate, or, perhaps, oligarchic Carthage, which strove by force to turn the trade in vast tracts of the western Mediterranean into a monopoly for its own merchants. But, in general, governments hardly if ever took measures aimed directly at some economic purpose—apart, of course, from levying tributes or taxes. What Rome did in 167 BC—deliberately hurting the commerce of Rhodes and favoring Delos by making the latter an international port of free trade—was, as far as we know, unique. The main reason for this was no doubt the lack of sufficient knowledge of the laws of economics. Yet, government actions, both in times of war and of peace, often did have great economic effects. For instance, the payment of soldiers in the Hellenistic kingdoms and in Rome, constituted a regular monetary "injection" into the economy. Coins frequently were minted by the states solely for the purpose of paying the troops and in that way coins were brought into circulation; an increase in all sorts of small-scale commercial activities as well as inflation was often the result. Warfare always meant devastation and plundering. It was in the form of war booty—especially gold and silver, works of art and other valuables, and slaves—that a large part of the wealth of Greek cities and Hellenistic kingdoms was transferred to Rome and Italy. Presumably, war was the most important factor in transferring wealth from one region to another. To a much lesser degree, war was a creator of wealth, for instance, by state contracts for the manufacture of weapons, tents, and so on, or the commissioning of warships—presumably, much of the industry here, such as smithies, was set up by the state and connected with state arsenals.

The equivalent of plunder was in times of peace the levying of tribute or taxes. All the Hellenistic kingdoms and Rome practiced direct taxation on property, either in the form of a fixed amount related to the size of the property or of a certain percentage of the income thereof. Here too, Roman expansion brought about a redirection of capital flow toward Italy, as when after the annexation of regions outside Italy as provinces, the direct taxation that their inhabitants used to pay to their own rulers—10% of the yield in Sicily, which became the norm in many other provinces—now went to Rome. The regular income from the provinces grew so large that since 167 BC, when an exceptionally large but one-time amount of booty was obtained from Macedon, the levying of taxes on Roman citizens in Italy was discontinued. Moreover, several states had owned properties, foremost mines, which, leased out to tenants or directly exploited by state-owned slaves, provided considerable income. As the conqueror, Rome took over these from the defeated cities or kings. Finally, everywhere in the Mediterranean world indirect taxes yielded another source of income for the state. They appeared in various forms. Omnipresent were tolls and custom duties at harbors and frontiers. A common tariff was 2% of the value of all imported and exported goods. That Rhodes until 167 BC managed to cash in 50,000,000 drachmas annually in this manner tells us something about the volume of trade there was in that period. The income from tolls and custom duties in Alexandria and the Red Sea ports of Egypt together certainly cannot have not been less than that sum. Other indirect taxes were special duties on particular transactions, in Rome, for instance, a 1% levy on the value of manumitted slaves.

All that income was also spent by the states, in the first place on near-endless wars. Armies and navies always swallowed up a large part of the state budgets, in time of peace alone already 50% or more. In time of war, income had, if possible, to be supplemented by plunder, and in the case of Roman wars very often also by "war indemnities" imposed on the defeated parties as soon as peace was concluded. Because the costs of warfare in these centuries hardly constituted economically sound investments that could create new wealth, they ultimately hindered economic growth. In contrast, the final annexation of all lands around the Mediterranean into the one empire of Rome would initiate a period of general peace and hence of growing prosperity, especially in the Greek-speaking east. Further state expenditure was on building projects, both harbors and roads for military and commercial purposes and luxury buildings in the big cities. Initially, only Hellenistic centers such as Alexandria, Antioch, Pergamon, and Rhodes could boast large and imposing works of architecture, but in the 2nd century BC Rome too, relatively late, started a series of public works, such as multipurpose public halls or basilicas, aqueducts, stoas, and temples, although a renovation and re-urbanization on a grand scale in Rome would only begin under Caesar, Augustus and the emperors succeeding him. Other state expenses were purely consumptive, for instance, the distribution of grain in Rome to the poorer citizens. Only in states with some level of bureaucracy, such as Egypt, the apparatus of government itself was a serious expense item, hardly if at all in states with a city-state government structure, such as the Greek *poleis* or Rome.

We may conclude that state actions in the Hellenistic period deeply affected the economy but seldom as a result of a conscious policy. Economic thinking did not rise above a simple level. Wealth was considered as something static, something people possessed or not, to be acquired only by taking it away from the possessor, so that the enrichment of one party implied the impoverishment of another. Economic reality, with its small elite of the very rich, seemed to confirm this thinking, as did political reality with the rise of Rome and the consequent enormous transfer of riches to Italy.

The Social Hierarchy

In the Hellenistic period, essentially three different regions came into permanent contact with one another: western Asia and Egypt, the Greek cities, and Roman Italy, each with its own characteristic social organizations and structures. In very broad terms, these could

Figure 33   Relief in situ at the Horus temple at Edfu, in Greek Apollonopolis Magna, from about 130 BC. The relief shows the coronation of Ptolemy VIII Euergetes II by Nechbet (to the right) and Wadjet (to the left), the goddesses of Upper and Lower Egypt. Ptolemy, the Greek king, here appears in a traditional Egyptian idiom as the pharaoh who unites all of Egypt: his crown is the double crown that is a combination of the two crowns worn by the two goddesses. We can also distinguish the royal false beard attached to his chin, the Uraeus snake on his forehead, and the bull's tail hanging from the pharaoh's kilt. These are all royal emblems. The two cartouches immediately above the head of Ptolemy show his own name and the throne name that he took at his accession. In Hellenistic Egypt, it was usual to show the Greek-Macedonian rulers in either Greek or Egyptian guise. Even though the two might have been, and most likely often will have confronted each other, a combination of amalgamation of styles within a single image was only rarely seen (see also Figure 37). Photo: Merten/Mauritius/SuperStock

be summarized as follows: in the Greek cities, a relatively large measure of equality, both socioeconomic and political; in Roman-Italian society, a relatively large measure of inequality and a stress on vertical social ties; in Egypt, a clear and steep hierarchy of the rich and powerful on the one hand and a dependent, mostly poor and usually un-free peasant population on the other; with local variations and exceptions, the latter pattern applied also to Asia Minor and the Near East. The establishment of the Hellenistic kingdoms and the expansion of Rome to some extent led to an intermingling of these different types of society, creating more categories and groups, socioeconomic as well as political, and entrenching various social positions more deeply than ever. The rich on the whole became richer, the powerful even more powerful, and the poor usually became poorer. Between the extremes, new categories appeared, sometimes in an ambiguous position (for instance, rich but not powerful, or not so rich but politically influential). In the end, in a patchwork of various juridical and political statuses, the hierarchical model of society became predominant all over the Mediterranean lands that were united in the Roman Empire, even in the Greek cities, where it largely repressed the old notion of equality among the citizens.

Political and juridical hierarchies

Everywhere, anyone's status in society could be defined in more or less precise juridical or political terms. First of all, there was the separation between citizens and non-citizens. The classical Greek *polis* had been built on this separation, and in the Hellenistic period too, it was still formally maintained, both in the Greek motherland and in the new Greek cities in Egypt and western Asia. But certainly in the latter, the distinction began to fade away. In several Asian communities founded by Hellenistic kings, more Asians than Greeks were resident; while only Greeks—not invariably *all* Greeks in the city—enjoyed full citizenship as *politai*. Other ethnic groups, such as the omnipresent Jews, often had their own communities with forms of self-government, so that the *polis* strictly speaking was not identical with the city. For the Greek population, it was not always possible to maintain its privileged position, and thus, certainly in everyday life, *politai* and other groups to some degree merged into one amalgam. In the Greek motherland, it was a little easier to hold on to the old delimitations of the citizenship, although it is striking that in the Hellenistic period, in various *poleis*, citizenship was granted to foreigners much more often than would have been possible in the Classical age—sometimes even collectively to all the citizens of a friendly city in treaties of "equal citizenship" between two *poleis*. This suggests that citizenship was no longer considered such an exclusive prerogative, presumably because in real life it had lost part of its significance. On the whole, this was true of Rome also.

Until far into the 4th century BC, Rome was a city-state with a limited territory. When the Roman expansion began, however, since 340 BC, Roman citizenship proved to be a much more flexible institution than citizenship in a Greek *polis* was. With relative ease, the Romans granted their citizenship to subdued cities and peoples in Italy, thereby considerably increasing the number of Roman citizens. They also created intermediate forms of citizenship, such as a citizenship without voting rights that was given to a number of cities and that after one or two generations was invariably converted into full citizenship. The privilege of citizens of allied Latin cities that allowed them to move to Rome individually, where they then would receive Roman citizenship, can also be seen as an extended promise of Roman citizenship to these cities. On the other hand, though, the Romans also created a separate category of Roman citizenship, that of the freedmen who—in contrast to Greek cities, where freed slaves became free residents but not citizens—received Roman citizenship with certain limitations, such as voting rights only in the four urban *tribus* or districts and no right to be elected for any magisterial function. In Roman society, it seems, possessing Roman citizenship meant less for a person's status than the possession of citizenship had meant for the *polites* of the Classical Greek *polis*, and looked more like the possession of the somewhat devalued citizenship of contemporary

Greek cities. In Rome, this was naturally related to the much greater significance of the social hierarchy. Here, someone's status was above all determined by whether he belonged to the super-elite of the *nobiles*, or to the wider group of the senators, or to the *equites* or "knights," or to which of the five official property classes of the citizenry, or whether he even fell below the latter and belonged simply to the *proletarii*; and further, whether he belonged to the *clientes* of a distinguished *patronus*, to the *amici* of a powerful man, and so forth.

The stress on social hierarchy in Rome was doubtless already well established but seems in the period of Roman expansion to have increased even more. It was in the 4th and early 3rd centuries BC that citizens were classified into five property classes. The assignment of the individual citizen—after an assessment of his property by the *censores*—to one of these classes was officially related to the requirements made of the citizens concerning their military equipment, since only citizens of these property classes served in the army. But in the course of time, the variations in weaponry and equipment between the citizens disappeared, but the five classes remained. This organization, then, primarily served not the needs of the army but the voting procedure in the *comitia centuriata*. There, among the common citizens, those of the first class cast their votes first, then those of the second class next, and so on, giving the wealthier citizens a disproportionate influence on the outcome of the voting. Likewise, it was in this period that the special categories of citizenship without voting rights and the limited citizenship of freedmen were created. Next, within the Roman elite in the late 3rd century BC, a formal delimitation was introduced by a law of 218 BC that forbade senators from owning seagoing ships, thus making it impossible for them to engage personally in overseas trade. As a consequence, the senators were now distinguished from the rest of the wealthy elite in that they followed some special rules. About 100 years later, the senators were formally no longer considered as "knights with a seat in the senate," but as a separate *ordo*, the members of which no longer received money for the upkeep of a warhorse from the state, as the real "knights" or *equites* did, and who in the assembly of the *comitia centuriata* no longer voted together with the *equites* in one block of 18 *centuriae*, but were now classified under the citizens of the first property class. As a result of this, there were now two *ordines* within the wealthy elite: the senators and the *equites*. The latter possessed property yielding at least 400,000 *sestertii* annually, served in their younger years in the army in various officer ranks, and received for their horse a state subsidy. Thus, the *ordo senatorius*, to which membership of the senate was limited, was set apart from the *ordo equester*, a much larger group of several thousand persons whose members could be officers but not army commanders—since only senators were magistrates and commanders in the field—and enjoyed greater freedom in regard to economic activities, such as participating in a consortium of *publicani*, but could not follow a political career. Those with political ambitions had to give up all commercial activities and try to get elected into one of the lower magistracies, thus becoming senators, after which they could try by befriending senators and nobles to climb higher, although it was very exceptional for a newcomer to reach as high as the consulate. Most members of the equestrian order did not have such ambitions and were satisfied with managing their landed property. It was they whom politicians such as Gaius Gracchus and later *populares* tried to mobilize against the senate, with limited success. After the establishment of the monarchy, though, the equestrian order would serve as the most important reservoir of candidates for officer posts and various other functions in the service of the emperors.

Thus, the expansion of the Roman state brought about a further development and refinement of the social hierarchy. Various formalized categories arose for Roman citizens and for non-citizens within the state. Among those who possessed Roman citizenship, a distinction was made between the elites of the two *ordines* and the rest; between the five property classes and the *proletarii* (who until the time of Marius were largely excluded from the army); between the freeborn and the freedmen. Outside the orbit of the *civitas Romana*, the allies with Latin status were distinguished from the other allies in Italy, where the former had more privileges and could on an individual basis rather easily acquire Roman citizenship. Officially, all allies counted as *peregrini*, foreigners, and they had to serve in their own contingents in the Roman army. Only after the Social War in 89 BC would they receive full Roman citizenship. Outside Italy, the inhabitants of the Roman provinces were subjects who had to pay their tribute and stay quiet, disarmed and powerless in the face of the governor and his troops. The inhabitants of the so-called free and autonomous cities that had concluded treaties of friendship with Rome were considered free *peregrini*. Of course, they had in fact lost their independence, but their autonomy guaranteed them freedom from Roman taxes and Roman jurisdiction. Beginning in the time of Caesar, more and more citizens of provincial towns and cities, autonomous or not, would receive Roman citizenship on a personal basis. As to the slaves, they were evidently non-citizens as well, but those belonging to Roman masters could hope one day to be freed and thereby become Roman citizens in their turn.

The Greek cities lacked the formal hierarchies of Rome. Here, the traditional tripartite division between citizens, slaves, and foreign residents was still in force. Former slaves in these cities became foreign residents, not citizens as in Rome. Within the citizenry, there were no formal "classes" or ranks. However, as stated before, the value of the citizenship must have decreased, especially since practically everywhere the democracies had given way to oligarchies and the growing divide between rich and poor became the new hierarchy. In the Greek cities in Asia, moreover, the indigenous population constituted a fourth category, living either as separate groups in the cities themselves, or in the surrounding countryside. They were mostly tenants working the lands owned by the citizens, and were sometimes near-serfs. Although not without some rights, they were certainly excluded from the assemblies and the magistracies and could not be considered citizens. Other tenants or serfs in western Asia worked the lands owned by large temples or exceptionally rich individuals, such as ministers of the crown. The picture here was further complicated by the existence in Syria, Judea, and elsewhere of free peasants or farmers who owned their lands and lived together in villages or small towns under the direct authority of the king, his satrap or, later, the Roman governor. They often remained largely outside the influence of Hellenistic culture, although subject to the kings and later to Rome. In Egypt too, there were free farmers on lands granted to them by the king, originally Macedonians and Greeks, later also native Egyptians. But the mass of the people here were dependent tenant-farmers or peasants working the lands of the king, of temples or of rich ministers or courtiers, and living in villages together, under constant supervision, in serf-like status. Here, the chasm separating a factually un-free peasant population and the Greek citizens of Alexandria, not to mention the courtiers and functionaries around the king, was wider than anywhere else between the inhabitants of one state in the Hellenistic and Roman world.

Socioeconomic hierarchies

Among the inhabitants of the Hellenistic states, the socioeconomic distinctions were no doubt sharper than they had been in the classical Greek cities. That had everything to do with the enormous expansion of Greeks and Macedonians to the east and the new possibilities, and the concomitant opportunities for some to become extremely rich. It had also to do with the rather sudden and deep inflation that struck the Greek world on the return of thousands of Alexander's veterans with their newly minted gold and silver, an inflation that hit those who had only their labor to sell the hardest. Finally, it had also to do with the loss of democracy in many Greek *poleis*, which only deepened the gulf between rich and poor citizens. In the Greek motherland, we hear in this period of an emerging large landownership and a growing landless debt-ridden agrarian proletariat. The Macedonian kings, and later the Romans, wholeheartedly supported the rich landowners against possible revolutionary changes. The few such attempts, in the uprisings in Greece in 146 BC and in the kingdom of Pergamon in 133 BC, were repressed by Rome with brute force. The unrest here involved Greek citizens as well as groups of slaves, as in Pergamon. Elsewhere in Asia, the poor were primarily the non-Greek inhabitants of the countryside, who were political outsiders with no tradition of pushing through reforms by institutional means. We do not hear of any rebelliousness on their part, except where the discontent and the resentment could be channeled by religious conviction, as in the messianic movements among the Jews. Elsewhere, resistance was mostly passive, for instance in Egypt, where it sometimes took the form of a flight into the wilderness outside the Nile Valley, or to the temples, which offered asylum. Apart from the traditional rural poverty, in this period in some big cities an urban proletariat appeared, which was probably a new phenomenon. Essentially, the urban poor had to try to maintain themselves by begging or by casual labor for more wealthy "entrepreneurs" or the government—for instance, in construction work. In fact, we do not know very much about the employment of the poor citizens in cities such as Alexandria or Rome, except that charity on the part of rich citizens and the government must have played an important role. In the Greek cities, wealthy citizens could on certain occasions, whether in times of general scarcity or when some public festivities were to be celebrated, help their poor fellow citizens with food or grain, thereby winning gratitude and prestige and at the same time helping the poor earn their livelihood. In Rome since Gaius Gracchus, the state took care of the grain supply for the *proletarii* by offering cheap grain imported from Sicily, later also from North Africa and Egypt; Julius Caesar gifted 150,000 poor citizens free grain, a number that would be raised to 200,000 under the first emperor.

We hardly know more about the middle-income groups that mainly must have been living in the cities than we know about the very poor. The latter are often estimated, in analogy with cities in Early Renaissance Italy, about which we know more, at one-third of the citizenry. The groups "in the middle," from the almost poor to the almost rich, then, should have formed nearly two-thirds, for the elite from which councilors and magistrates were selected was always small, a few percentage points at most. The various professions in the Hellenistic cities, mentioned earlier, must nearly all have been practiced by representatives of these groups "in the middle." These practitioners, though, certainly were not all of them citizens of the cities where they lived, but in not a few cases foreign residents, freedmen, or sometimes even slaves who ran their own businesses and shared the profit with their masters. In any case, the "middle groups" must have been rather diverse, certainly in the bigger cities where much ethnic diversity could be found.

Slaves and freedmen

Slaves and freedmen were a prominent feature of cities such as Rome in this period. Their numbers are difficult to estimate but must have been considerable—in Italy in the last century BC, there could have been as many as 2 million out of a total population of about 7 million. Italy and Sicily were at that time probably the regions with the highest numbers of slaves, since it was there that the landed property of the Roman elite was concentrated. In the Greek east, slaves presumably were a little less numerous. There, slavery was predominantly an urban phenomenon, whereas in the west it was both an urban and a rural phenomenon as a consequence of the use of slave labor on the *latifundia*. In the Hellenistic cities and in Rome, slaves were found in the households of the elite and were a luxury; they were present in many "middle-income" households as well, though in much fewer numbers. Also, slaves could be put to work outside the household, working alongside free laborers or practicing their crafts in workshops of their own (a situation also known from classical Athens); in both cases, they had to hand over part of their wages or their profits to their owner, for whom the slaves' activities could thus be an attractive investment. For the slaves themselves, this arrangement could be profitable as well, since in this way they were often able to save some money, enabling them after some years to buy their own freedom. Greek and Roman law considered the slave as strictly speaking a "thing" and not as a person with certain rights, but in practice the money that a slave accumulated for himself was acknowledged as his own, so that he could use it in buying his freedom. The slave-owner could, of course, refuse the deal, but deliberately postponing it for years was generally frowned upon. Of their own accord, slave-owners very often freed their slaves, both male and female, either after some years during their own lifetime or else by a will and testament after their death. Various motivations played a role in this, ranging from the altruistic—the wish to reward a slave for years of service—to the egoistic, for the freed slave often had to go on paying his former master from the profits he earned, without the master having to pay for his livelihood; besides, the freedman generally stood to his former master (or his heir) as a *cliens* to his *patronus*, obliged to pay him respect and to help him materially or otherwise. In general, the more freedmen one had, the more prestige accrued, for their presence—sometimes literally following the patron whenever he appeared in public—lent some luster to their former owner, while their number testified to his wealth and magnanimity.

In Roman society, the freedmen were presumably more numerous, proportionately, than elsewhere. The freedman or *libertus* was automatically a Roman citizen. At the same time, he remained subservient to his former master, as indeed a *cliens* to his *patronus*, as long as the latter lived and sometimes this relationship extended to his patron's heir. A patron could thus materially profit from his freedmen but more important was the general renown and prestige derived from the act of manumission and the dedication the freedmen would subsequently show him. In the Greek world, such notions seem to have been less developed. There, the freed slaves did not automatically become citizens, and their presence did not lend their former owner the same measure of prestige as was normally the case in Rome. But it could be said that everywhere the presence of freedmen complicated social relations; for on the one hand, an ex-slave might attain considerable wealth, but on the other hand he remained a foreign resident in Greek eyes, or a citizen with less than full citizenship rights in Roman eyes, not to mention the "stain" of having once been un-free. Thus, the position of the freedmen was always ambiguous to some extent, and subject to social restrictions, irrespective of the wealth that some of them acquired. Only their sons, if born after their fathers' manumission, could in Roman society exercise full citizenship rights and rise to local magistracies or even be admitted into the equestrian order, although formally that was only allowed for the grandsons of freedmen. In this manner, the institution of slavery coupled with the practice of manumission provided an important route for social mobility in the otherwise rather static society of the Roman world.

Household slaves in the cities could entertain the hope of more or less humane treatment coupled with a chance of manumission later on—although we should not forget that many of them were never freed and that the treatment even of slaves in daily contact with their master or mistress was often brutal, with whippings and torture being normal punishment. For their fellow slaves outside the cities, however, there was in general little hope of escaping their dismal fate. In the Hellenistic east, slaves were probably not much used in agriculture, since tenant-farmers and seasonal free laborers usually provided the workforce there. But slaves were put to work, chained like convicted criminals, in mines and quarries; especially notorious were those in Ptolemaic Egypt. Treated barbarously, the slaves often succumbed after a couple of years. In Italy and Sicily, it was the system of *latifundia* where a real "slave economy" developed. This type of agricultural organization was built on slave labor and was in most cases was probably profitable. It flourished in the 2nd and 1st centuries BC when the supply of slaves was abundant. They were treated hardly better than cattle, while the prospect of manumission was small; in fact, it was limited to those few individuals who were singled out to become overseers of groups of slaves or stewards of an entire *villa* (hence *vilicus*). It was the concentration of large numbers of slaves on these *latifundia* in the 2nd and 1st centuries BC, combined with the fact that many of them came from the same ethnic background—Syrians, Thracians, Gauls—that explains the three unexpectedly large-scale and serious slave uprisings or slave wars that occurred during the late republic.

Rebelliousness among slaves was not uncommon in antiquity, but it had always been local, short-lived, limited in scope, and therefore not a threat to the existing order. That was certainly not true of the three massive uprisings in the years 135–71 BC. The first two rebellions took place in Sicily, and involved large numbers of slaves, mostly originating from Syria and Asia Minor, both times led by charismatic leaders who for a while had great success and in both cases managed to subdue much of the island, inaugurating short-lived kingdoms of ex-slaves. In the end, though, Roman armies entered the scene and crushed these "slave kingdoms." Typically, the rebels lacked any form of "ideology" that demanded an end to slavery; on the contrary, when they briefly enjoyed the upper hand, they in their turn enslaved their former masters or the population of cities overrun by them. The movements clearly originated with the desperate elements among the slaves, mostly those toiling at the *latifundia*; the household slaves in the cities were hardly involved, and certainly there was no fraternizing with the very poor but free proletariat. The third rebellion was the one already mentioned before, led by Spartacus in Italy in the years 73–71 BC. It showed in essence the same characteristics as the earlier rebellions, and broke out in a school for gladiators in Capua—for in this period, that too was a possible fate for slaves in the Roman world: to be sold or hired out to a gladiator school. The rebellion was led by the Thracian Spartacus. He turned out to be a leader with strategic insight who frequently defeated the Roman army corps sent out against him. In the end, however, he was no match for the armies of the ambitious Crassus and Pompey. The survivors of the last battle in the south of the peninsula were all crucified along the Via Appia, the traditional punishment for rebellious slaves. Since then, no more uprisings on such a scale occurred. That may have been the consequence of a deliberate policy of the large landowners to avoid grouping slaves of the same ethnic origin together, as they had become well aware of the risks; it certainly was in the end also a consequence of the gradually diminishing importance of the *latifundia* system, which in the 1st and 2nd centuries AD would slowly give way to a system of leasing out parcels of land to tenant-farmers.

Wealth and social elites

The social hierarchy of this period can thus be briefly sketched as follows: At the bottom, there were the slaves in the countryside in Italy and Sicily, or those condemned to mines and quarries; only just a little higher stood the peasant populations in Egypt, the Near East, and Asia Minor, the agrarian proletariat in the Hellenistic world; a little above these, the urban proletariat in the big Hellenistic cities and Rome; above them, the middle-income groups of smallholders and free farmers in the countryside and various professionals in the cities, in which may be included also the freedmen and foreign residents there; above all of these, finally, a small elite of the rich and super rich. Representatives of these elites wielded political power everywhere, for they produced the councilors and magistrates, the generals and governors. Their riches were in the main traditionally agrarian, for they were large landowners who had their lands outside the cities worked for them by tenants or slaves. Only a few among them supplemented their agrarian wealth by commercial activities, and only a very few owed their riches solely to commerce. Presumably, the latter could only be found in some cities in the east, such as in Phoenicia, and rarely elsewhere. In case someone had become rich by commerce, he as a rule invested his capital as soon as possible in landed property, for in the Greco-Roman world only that was considered respectable. The Roman law of 218 BC even formally stipulated that the senatorial elite were not to concern themselves with overseas trade. Whenever a Roman senator wished to engage in commerce, he used intermediaries or straw men: freedmen could be very useful for this purpose. By such roundabout means, senators could even be involved in the ceramic industry or in brick works, but this was probably rare. Senators who really traded in most cases sold the produce of their estates, and in practice this was handled by their stewards. The ideal of being a respectable landowner was so strong that even most of the Roman "knights," who were not barred by law from going into commerce, preferred to lead the traditional life of the large landowner.

The sources of this wealth in land could vary: for some, it was the result of lucky inheritances and/or profitable marriages, coupled with some successful transactions; for others, it was the investment of capital acquired elsewhere; for most, however, these riches were the fruit of political power. In the Hellenistic kingdoms, all the land was in theory the property of the king, who could and did give away parts of it to ministers and generals, officials and favorites. Vast estates in western Asia and in Egypt had thus come into private hands. In Italy, the expansion of Rome had been accompanied by the acquisition of land that was regularly distributed among poor citizens as well as among the Roman elite. The latter also occupied much of the state lands, which after the war with Hannibal had become so extensive that the old rules limiting their use were no longer applied, so that rich senators and *equites* took possession of large tracts for their *latifundia* and grazing grounds. Next, the Roman rich and powerful acquired new possessions in the provinces or bought more land with capital derived from war booty or the extortion of non-Romans. In this way, the wealth of the elite grew apace with the political successes of the state. The rise of Rome led to an accumulation of riches in the hands of the Roman elite as had never been seen before, and the gulf between this elite and those at the bottom of society, the slaves and proletarians, was deeper and wider than ever.

Between the social and economic realities of the Hellenistic world and the traditional political norms of the city-state, especially of the Greek *polis* with its notion of a certain degree of equality of all citizens, there was a growing rift. In this period, a new phenomenon (but related to the liturgies of the Classical Period) emerges that can be seen as an attempt to bridge it: euergetism, literally, "doing good" for the community, "giving" on a large scale, on the part of the rich and powerful (a phenomenon that would come to flourish in the first centuries AD). Euergetism involved the gift to the citizen population of articles such as grain (not only in times of need but also sometimes on festive occasions), and the financing of festivals, theater shows, sacrifices, and games, and public works. That the rich were prepared to do this had everything to do with the old ideal of *time* (honor), for their euergetism was invariably rewarded with public praise, taking the shape of honorary inscriptions or even statues. Thus, in some way the elite and the mass of the citizens needed and supplemented each other: in exchange for honor and public praise, which would translate into election for magistracies and councils—in other words, into political power—the elite was prepared to dip deep into its purses. On the other hand, by receiving all those benefits, the poor citizens could still believe that they belonged to a *polis* community, the leaders of which they gladly recognized as their benefactors.

Social mobility

Social mobility in Hellenistic and Roman societies could come about in different ways, but was always a relatively rare occurrence. In practice, climbing the social ladder was a process that spanned generations. For the individual to rise socially, there were only three possible routes. Those who had acquired riches in commerce or industry could invest these in land and settle down as respectable landowners in the city; they themselves or their offspring would become citizens and after a while could even join the elite. Examples of such social mobility, however, are very scarce. Yet, such social climbing could not be ruled out, especially in the big cities of western Asia, but in all probability it must have been rare indeed. Another form of social mobility was provided by the armies of the period. In the Hellenistic kingdoms, professional soldiers and officers, usually of Greek or Macedonian origin, could in the royal service be promoted to high commands, be endowed with great riches, and end up as members of the landowning elite in Egypt or in one of the many new *poleis* in western Asia. In Rome too, the army offered to some degree a possible career for those with talent; common soldiers could sometimes and with some luck acquire enough booty to buy some land in Italy, or they could be promoted to the rank of subaltern officers. The rank of *centurio* was for them the highest achievable rank, and during the Roman Republic, this was infact almost unattainable, because most of the *centuriones* then were men of the equestrian order. In the late republic, the Roman army had become an army of mostly proletarians led by aristocratic officers; as long as the *optimates* dominated politics, there was not much room for social mobility. Under Caesar and Octavian, however, subalterns from the equestrian class were much more easily promoted to higher commands, a trend that would continue during the empire, while the possibilities for common soldiers to reach the centuriate would also be much enlarged. Finally, a last route for social mobility, paradoxically, passed through the stages of slavery and manumission. This route was especially of importance in Roman society, since the freedmen here became Roman citizens. Slavery was a massive phenomenon in the Roman world, and manumission of urban slaves occurred on a large scale. Many of those freed reinforced the ranks of the various middle groups in the city, but not a few also reached, albeit usually after two or three generations, the ranks of the elite. Numbers and percentages are, as usual, unknown, but it is likely that this third form of social mobility was in the late republic as well as in the early empire the most important of the three.

Political Organization

In political organization too, in the Hellenistic and Roman worlds mainly three different regions can be distinguished: those of the Greek *poleis*, the Hellenistic kingdoms, and Rome.

The Greek *poleis*

In the Hellenistic period, the political independence of the Greek *poleis* disappeared, while their internal organization took on new forms. Everywhere, the trend was toward oligarchy, as also in the Greek cities in Asia Minor that had been liberated from the Persians by Alexander the Great and officially declared "democracies." The abolishment of the democracy in Athens by the Macedonians in 322 BC was a milestone. "Democracy" everywhere from now on meant nothing more than a republican constitution with an assembly of the people that was allowed to elect the magistrates. Those magistrates always belonged to the rich elite, a requirement that was more and more formalized by the introduction of property qualifications for candidates. Before and after their term as magistrates, they sat on the city council or *boule*, the members of which—the *bouleutai*—as a rule were members for life. In fact, the *bouleutai* governed the cities, with a handful of elite families usually dominating the *boule*. The magistracies were few in number, from two to eight, while the number of councilors could vary from a few dozen to five or six hundred. The scope of government remained limited and amateurish, although it regularly encompassed a few more tasks than in earlier times. Apart from the traditional judiciary, now it also included the policing of the city and its surrounding territory, and apart from supervising the markets, the *gumnasia* and public education, now often there was also a rudimentary healthcare with a doctor in the service of the city. The rest of the citizens acquiesced in the rule of the elite—at least, we know very little of any significant resistance—and appreciated the gifts and benefits of the rich, their euergetism, which became an ingrained part of city politics and was expected of all office holders and even from those rich who happened not to hold any office. This euergetism, as said before, emerged in the 3rd and 2nd centuries BC; for many, it no doubt mitigated to some degree the loss of actual democracy.

In their external relations, the Greek *poleis* could be divided into two categories: those under the sovereignty of a Hellenistic king, and those who had managed to preserve something of an independent policy. The first group only enjoyed some internal autonomy and were on the whole subject to a king to whom they usually had to pay taxes as well, albeit sometimes under the fiction of a voluntary contribution; often, they had even to allow a garrison of the king's troops to be stationed within their walls. Cities belonging to the second group always had to navigate between the main powers and were ultimately at the mercy of the vicissitudes of grand politics. Some favorably situated cities kept their independence for a relatively long time, such as Rhodes; others sought refuge in a federation of cities, such as the Achaean League. In the end, all had to give in to the rising power of Rome. Most Greek cities, having belonged to defeated Hellenistic kingdoms, became part of the new Roman provinces under the supervision of Roman governors. But a few cities, such as Athens and Sparta, were acknowledged by Rome as "free," "autonomous," and "friend of the Roman people." Surrounded by Roman provincial territory, they remained autonomous enclaves where the citizens did not have to pay tribute to Rome and were not submitted to Roman jurisdiction. Although they had in fact lost their independence, their position was often envied by other Greeks.

The Hellenistic kingdoms

In comparison with the *poleis*, the Hellenistic kingdoms in Greek eyes embodied two new principles in the organization of a state: they were territorial states comprising the areas of several cities and peoples, and they were monarchies. The territories were to a lesser or higher degree patchworks of cities, regions, and ethnic groups, often with diverse political and juridical statuses. They were held together by the person of the king. The monarchies thus lent these states their raison d'être, for without the kings they would disintegrate. The authority with which the king ruled was not offered to him in any form "from below," but rested on the simple right of the conqueror. The Macedonians and Greeks spoke of "with the spear acquired" land and meant by this that the sovereignty over the lands in western Asia and Egypt had fallen to the victor: to Alexander the Great at first, and then to the *diadochoi*, his successor. In this view, all authority flowed automatically from the conqueror-king downward, and all inhabitants of his lands were by definition his subjects, part of the booty that had been won by his victory or the victory of his forbears. Greek political theoreticians could declare, therefore, that all legislation in these kingdoms was purely a matter of the royal will, for the king was "the law incarnate" and lower functionaries derived their authority from him. This, however, was the political theory. In practice, the Antigonids and the Seleucids especially had to reckon with all sorts of existing power centers and were often forced to cede considerable independent powers to their satraps and governors. In fact, these kings lacked the bureaucracy and the apparatus of a state that would enable them to rule as the absolute monarchs that they claimed to be. Greek cities within their realms retained much of their internal autonomy; temple-states in Asia Minor and elsewhere, such as in Judea around the temple at Jerusalem, were practically small autonomous states within the boundaries of the great Seleucid kingdom. Egypt, in contrast, was much more homogeneous; the regulation of economic life from above was deeply rooted there, so that the Ptolemies could build on pre-existing traditions. They succeeded in creating the most extensive and for the peasant population the most repressive bureaucracy in antiquity.

The central position of the Hellenistic kings also explains the phenomenon of the ruler cult. It was mainly a Greek notion, this official identification of the ruling king with a godhead. In the Greek cities, this cult initially was a largely spontaneous expression of gratitude for the benefits granted by the monarch; that was, so to say, the religious part of it. The political part was added a little later. After his return to Babylon in 324 BC and shortly before his death, Alexander had ordered the cities in the Greek motherland to officially pay him divine honors. It made his position nearly unassailable and gave him an authority above any other secular power. Such an official cult of the living ruler thereafter became normal in the kingdoms of the Ptolemies and the Seleucids, and later in Pergamon. Political calculation thus certainly played a role in this, for the divinization of the kings was part of the propaganda aimed at making the rule of these monarchs acceptable to their Greco-Macedonian and Hellenized subjects (what the native Egyptian and Asian populations thought of it mattered less).

Rome

As a city-state, Rome had first subjugated Central Italy, next the rest of the peninsula, and then had added more and more provinces. Its constitution, however, remained for a very long time that of a city-state, so that the growing empire consisted of roughly three areas inhabited respectively by citizens, allies, and subjects. For a while, this architecture seemed to work reasonably well, but the continuing expansion in the course of the 2nd century seriously undermined the whole structure, and in the next century the republic gave way to the rule of one man.

In the period from the end of the Struggle of the Orders until the tribunate of Tiberius Gracchus (287–133 BC), the organs of the city-state in Rome functioned in such a way that Rome could be said to be governed by aristocratic consensus. The assemblies of the people, the magistracies, and the senate to some extent balanced each other out, although the senate clearly retained a preponderance of power. In the traditional *comitia centuriata*, the voting was organized in *centuriae* combined with the property classes, which gave the most political clout to the citizens of the first two property classes and the *equites*, who together were far from a majority in the population but did have a majority of the 193 *centuriae* or voting blocks that made up the assembly. This assembly mainly functioned as an electoral assembly for the election of the higher magistracies—*praetores, consules*, and *censores*—and also as the people's assembly that voted on a very few important decisions regarding subjects such as war and peace. The *comitia tributa* had a simpler organization and voting procedure. Here, the citizens were divided over the 35 *tribus* or "districts" in which they were registered. They cast their votes in a one-man-one-vote procedure, so that a majority vote decided the vote of each *tribus*, after which a simple majority of the *tribus* was enough to determine the final outcome. This assembly elected the lesser magistrates such as the *quaestores* and *aediles* and was regularly convened for all sorts of legislation. In practice, it hardly differed from the *concilium plebis*, the assembly of the *plebs*, which elected the tribunes of the people and was always presided over by tribunes. Clearly, the patricians had no access to that assembly, but they were just a handful of families in this period, and since its decisions or *plebiscita* had the force of law, the tribunes could convene the *concilium plebis* to suggest a *plebiscitum* or else turn to the *comitia tributa* (where patricians could participate) and initiate a law (*lex*). The *comitia tributa* was clearly more democratic than the traditional *comitia centuriata*, and in the later republic it had become the most important legislative body. Those who introduced the legislative proposals often were tribunes who had already deliberated these proposals in advance in the senate—the tribunes had in fact become lower members of the senate—so that the legislation actually was decided in the senate, after which some tribunes ensured that the assembly of the people sanctioned these decisions by giving them the formal status of law. As long as the tribunes of the people cooperated with the senate in this way, an image of harmony and concord prevailed. In the course of the 2nd century BC, however, that image began to disintegrate, until in 133 BC Tiberius Gracchus ended this cooperation, and a century of political crises began.

The magistracies of the Roman Republic in this period (287–133 BC) grew together into a balanced system in which politicians could make a career. The *cursus honorum* was the series of magistracies that a successful politician had to occupy in a predetermined order. The lower magistracies with which one had to begin were those of *quaestor* (usually in charge of finances, such as the sums to be paid for the army, and general assistants of the consuls when on campaign), tribune of the people (although strictly speaking, a tribune of the *plebs* was not serving the whole people or *populus* and therefore was not a magistrate), and *aedilis* (mainly in charge of supervising the markets and public order). The higher magistrates were in possession of *imperium*, the highest military authority. They were the *praetores* (two of whom acted as judges in Rome; the others went to the provinces as governors) and the two *consules*. The office of *censor*, held every five years by two men for the duration of 18 months, counted as the most honorable. The *censores* were responsible for holding the census every five years, with the ensuing assignment of the citizens to their various property classes and the admission of members to the orders of *equites* and senators; they also commissioned public works and government activities, for instance, leasing out the tax collection in certain provinces to the *publicani*. Various rules determined the minimum age at which one was allowed to hold these magistracies (for the consulate, it was fixed at 42) and the period that had to elapse between two magistracies. Holding the same magistracy twice was a very rare occurrence, except for the consulate. Here, the law laid down that between two consulates there should be an interval of at least ten years. Of all the magistracies, the consulate was the most sought after, bringing the most power and the most opportunities to acquire glory and prestige. Therefore, eligibility for this office was regulated by certain rules that made it very difficult for newcomers and those who had held the lower magistracies but had no consul in their families to reach the consulate. In the classical republic of 287 to 133 BC, it was only a few dozen families, both patrician and plebeian, that time and again produced the consuls. They were the *nobiles*, literally the "known" or "renowned" ones, an aristocracy of office that ruled Rome. Someone not belonging to their circle who yet became *consul*—a rarity—was called a "newcomer" (*homo novus*). The Roman nobility tried to keep its own circle as far as possible an exclusive one, which explains why the number of *consules* was not enlarged and the number of *praetores* remained for a very long time limited to six. Where there was a need for more persons with the same constitutional powers, ex-consuls were retained with the title of proconsul—or, exceptionally, someone was made a proconsul who had not yet been a consul. In the late republic, the proconsuls would be a normal feature, while *propraetores* could also be appointed. The rules of the *cursus honorum* were not always strictly observed, though; especially, some very powerful *nobiles* managed in times of war or other tension to become consul at a much younger age, or to hold a second consulship within ten years, if not immediately after the first. In the extraordinary position of such persons—one could think of Scipio Africanus the Elder, of Scipio Aemilianus Africanus the Younger—already something can be discerned of the things to come: the accumulation of magistracies and competences in one person, accompanied by the necessary bending of the rules in that person's favor.

The office of *quaestor* allowed its holder immediate entry into the senate, so that this council came to consist of all acting magistrates and all former magistrates. Within the ranks of the senate, the former consuls and former censors were the most respectable members. Thus, of the roughly 300 senators, a minority of *nobiles* set the tone. When it came to voting, younger and lower-ranking senators hardly dared to vote differently from the members who had acquired so much *dignitas* (prestige) and *auctoritas* (authority). As long as there was consensus among the rather small circle of *nobiles*, decisions could be made quickly. Lower senators often were connected with more powerful colleagues in a sort of *clientela*: the term more often used was *amicitia*, "friendship," but it was an unequal "friendship." Among themselves, the higher *nobiles* could also form ties of friendship and cooperation in a *factio*, a political faction on a temporary basis. Mutual jealousies usually stimulated the emergence of counter factions to prevent too much power, glory, and prestige from accruing to one faction or to just a few noble names. Politics in the Roman senate could as a result of this become a game of rather subtle and complex maneuvering, that in itself could sometimes hinder decision making. Ultimately, this contributed to a certain powerlessness of the senate in the face of the large problems that arose in the wake of the Roman expansion.

The apparatus of government of the Roman Republic was very small. There were some slaves in public service, for instance as scribes, but they certainly were not numerous. The spirit of the republic was that of a city-state with all the amateurism that went with it. Offices of state were honorary positions that did not pay any salary. If a magistrate needed any assistance, he was supposed to use his own slaves and freedmen for the bureaucratic work involved; if he needed advice, then he consulted his own friends. All this was possible as long as Rome considered itself to be a city-state and meddled with the internal affairs of its allies and provincials as little as possible.

The area of Rome itself, the *ager Romanus*, since 270 BC comprised about one-quarter of the territory of Italy south of the river Po. It consisted mainly of the city of Rome with the territories of Latium and Campania. Within these territories, several towns were located that had the status of *municipia*. A *municipium* was a town or community inhabited by Roman citizens outside the city of Rome, who paid taxes and served in the legions like other Roman citizens. Otherwise, the *ager Romanus* was made up of a number of *coloniae Romanae* (Roman colonies), generally rather small but fortified towns founded at various spots along the coasts for strategic reasons. About three-quarters of Italy outside the *ager Romanus* was nominally independent and connected with Rome by a system of alliances. In Roman eyes, these allies were a sort of *clientes* who had to be grateful to Rome, and therefore be subservient to it, because Rome had allowed them after their final defeats to maintain their autonomy. There were two such categories. The first consisted of Latins (*Latini*): the inhabitants of a few ancient cities in Latium that had retained their independence after 338 BC. The other category consisted of the so-called *coloniae Latinae*. These were new and relatively large settlements founded by the Romans all over Italy in areas that were suitable for agriculture and also had strategic importance. The colonists were partly of Italian, partly of Roman origin, the latter having lost their Roman citizenship by settling in such a colony, for officially, the Latin colonies were allies of Rome with internal autonomy and Latin rights, which meant that they had the same status as the old Latin cities in Latium. Their magistrates could on an individual basis freely move to Rome and automatically become Roman citizens. By far the most numerous of the Italian allies were the peoples who had been subdued in the decades around 300 BC, such as the Etruscans, Umbrians, Samnites, and Greeks. As the *socii* ("allies"), they were collectively distinguished from the *Latini*. They too enjoyed internal autonomy, but they had always to follow Rome's lead in external policy matters and provide troops for the Roman armies. Their contingents were put under the command of Roman officers and organized as legions under the name of "wings" (*alae*), since on the battlefield they would be posted on both sides of the Roman legions. They also provided the Romans with most of their cavalry in the field. In this way, Rome held Italy in submission without the need to interfere much in the affairs of the various tribes, cities, and peoples, while having at its disposal all the manpower of the peninsula. The latter was used abundantly, leading to bitter discontent on the part of these allies, since they had to bear much of the burden of the Roman wars but did not share equally in their profits, for all of the tributes, indemnities, extortions, and most of the war booty ultimately went to the Roman masters.

The provinces, meanwhile, were treated by Rome in a completely different way than Italy. The people here were deprived of most of their rights. They were subjects of Rome, who had to pay their tribute and be obedient to the governors that were sent from Rome to rule over them. Initially, for the governorships new *praetores* were elected, but after 197 BC, the number of praetors remained fixed at six. Henceforth, new provinces were governed by *proconsules* or *propraetores*. The collection of taxes due to Rome was sometimes in the hands of local dignitaries, sometimes in those of Roman *publicani*. Especially in the latter case, the tax collection went hand in hand with much extortion and corruption. Rome treated its provinces as mere sources of income that could be squeezed to the utmost, not as parts of an empire for which it felt responsibility. Such notions would only emerge later, when the republic had given way to the monarchy.

The transition from republic to monarchy is the overriding theme of Roman history from 133 BC to 30 BC. It was Roman expansion itself that undermined the republic. The wars outside Italy created an impoverished but still free peasantry and stimulated at the same time the rise of the large landowners, senators as well as *equites*. In the city of Rome, the proletarians dominated the *comitia tributa*, the main legislative assembly (since impoverished peasants who moved to Rome remained registered in their rural *tribus*, all the *tribus* became more or less "proletarianized"). Whatever their motives, politicians such as the Gracchi brothers paved the way for a politics of demagogy, from which in the end only various "strong men" would profit. The proletarianized army, Marius' creation, handed ambitious *nobiles* the tools with which to pressure the senate or the people to do their bidding, so that the competition between power-hungry *nobiles* became a deadly danger for the state. At the same time, the discontent of the Italian allies at last found expression in the Social War that ended with all of Italy south of the Po as *ager Romanus*, inhabited by Roman citizens and where a great number of towns now became Roman *municipia*. Rome seemed inevitably to move in the direction of a territorial state ruled by a monarch in the manner of the Hellenistic kingdoms. Individual Roman potentates in this century already foreshadowed the coming regime: Marius, elected six times *consul* in the short period 107–100 BC; Sulla, *dictator* for three years (82–79 BC); and Pompey, *consul* without a colleague in 52 BC. It was Sulla who also transformed the consulate into a more or less civilian office in a demilitarized Italy, placing the legions in the provinces under the command of *proconsules* and *propraetores*, in essence the arrangement of the later empire. That empire, after a first attempt by Julius Caesar, was finally established by Octavian. Whether it was really inevitable is a theoretical question; that the traditional republican constitution no longer fited the new circumstances was obvious. Still, the new monarchy would for a long time to come preserve some republican memories both in the façade behind which much of the one-man's rule would be hidden, and in the federalist character of that empire, based as it was on a large number of internally autonomous cities. The latter feature, a remnant of the republican organization, would for a long time prevent the development of a Roman imperial bureaucracy, such as had existed in Ptolemaic Egypt and still existed in contemporary China of the Han dynasty.

Chapter 5.3

Daily Life and Mentality

The Individual and Society

Ever since the 19th century, when the concept of Hellenism was introduced to designate and characterize an era, it has repeatedly been maintained that Hellenism stood for the conscious or unconscious dissemination of Greek culture. However, it remains debatable whether there was in fact more to it than mere geographical expansion. It is true that Greek *poleis* were founded for the disbanded mercenaries of Alexander and his successors in a vast territory extending from the Mediterranean to Uzbekistan and Kashmir, but these *poleis* were no more than islets of Greek culture in an ocean of indigenous cultures. Because of a distinct sense of superiority, the Greek inhabitants of these islets were not particularly desirous to share their Greek city culture with the surrounding "barbarians"; on the other hand, the indigenous population was not always keen to embrace the culture of the conquerors either. The development of law in the Hellenistic period may serve as an illustration. This period had four types of law functioning side by side: local Greek law, which was specific for every Greek *polis*; a somewhat loosely defined "general Greek law" applied to Greeks wandering outside the *polis*; an increasing amount of royal Greek law; and indigenous law, which varied from region to region and was hardly influenced by Greek law. This judicial patchwork existed throughout the Hellenistic period; naturally, the various judicial forms evolved and changed, but separately. Only the Greek language in its Hellenistic form, the so-called *koine*, spread widely among non-Greeks, and became the lingua franca in many parts of the Hellenistic world, a general means of communication that was used by members of the many different language groups. In the Near East, however, it never completely ousted the regional lingua franca, Aramaic. Many indigenous languages and dialects never developed a culture of writing and have disappeared without a trace, but this does not mean they did not exist. We may presume that regional differences were considerable, and it is therefore dangerous to generalize; in regions such as Asia Minor, the use of Greek was widespread, but in other parts the Greek language was not nearly as influential.

Naturally, in certain regions, members of the indigenous elite wanted to "Hellenize," for opportunistic reasons, and sometimes perhaps because they were genuinely enthusiastic.

Antiquity: Greeks and Romans in Context, First Edition. Frederick G. Naerebout and Henk W. Singor.
© 2014 John Wiley & Sons, Inc. Published 2014 by John Wiley & Sons, Inc.

Some of them gradually found their way into the world of the Macedonian and Greek elite. We find that Romans who migrated to the newly conquered territories in the East likewise became part of the local elite. This degree of assimilation, however, only concerns a handful of people. Greek culture was only adopted by larger groups in regions with a strong Greek presence, such as Asia Minor and parts of the Balkans where it had been promoted for centuries by Hellenistic princes and later, too, by the Roman authorities. For the most part, Greek and indigenous culture existed side by side. Egypt, with on the one hand Greek Alexandria and its court for the Greek rulers, and on the other hand the rural areas where these foreign conquerors continued to be viewed with aversion and distrust, is a good example of this. However, for Greeks and Egyptians at the lower end of the social scale it was difficult to live separate lives. But this did not lead to Hellenization either; on

Figure 34   Sculptures from the Buddhist monastery at Tepe Shotor, Afghanistan (3rd–4th c. AD). These photographs show sculptures decorating two chapels of the Buddhist monastery of Tepe Shotor, at Hadda in southern Afghanistan. They date from the 3rd or 4th century AD, and although the Hephtalites destroyed all Buddhist monasteries in the area in the 5th century AD, these sculptures survived, only to fall prey to the iconoclasm of the Taliban in the very recent past. The sculptures are in stucco, a technique developed to a high standard in Hellenistic Alexandria and subsequently exported to the East, as far as Afghanistan. But in an important Buddhist center such as Hadda, it was not merely the technique that was copied: one of the companions of the Buddha, seen seated to the left of the Buddha in the picture above, has the looks and attributes of Heracles, while another Buddha is accompanied by someone, detailed in the picture overleaf, who looks like Alexander the Great. Gandhara, in the 2nd century BC had been part of the kingdom of the Greek king Menander, and in the first centuries AD appears as an important center of art inspired by Greek examples. Photos: © Catherine Jarrige

Figure 34 (*Continued*)

the contrary, the poorer Greeks, a minority among their Egyptian neighbors, tended to gradually assimilate with the indigenous population. On the periphery of the Hellenistic world, it was not just the humblest people who adapted to the local situation, but in the long run the whole of society did so. This holds true, for instance, for the Greeks in the remotest eastern regions.

Even though Greeks in the East assimilated to their surroundings, for instance by turning Buddhist, local culture did not remain completely unaffected; Buddhist art, for example, shows strong Greek influence. Thus, one should not think simplistically about Hellenization, nor, for that matter, about its counterpart "orientalization." The key concept is acculturation. When two cultures meet, in whatever manner, we will find acculturation processes: changes set in motion by the contact. Acculturation is reciprocal, although it does not necessarily concern the same cultural aspects and may not be of equivalent scope. This is not about the mere "adoption" of goods and patterns; changes on both sides are generally much more subtle. For instance, stressing one's own cultural identity as a reaction to the other's presence is also an expression of acculturation. Members of the Ptolemaic dynasty played the role of pharaoh for their Egyptian subjects, but this should not be seen as an example of the merging of two cultures or an assimilation of the Greeks with the Egyptian context. It was, indeed, no more than a recurring "performance," and in this way almost the opposite of merging or assimilating. All the same, it *was* an expression of acculturation. At the same time, playing the role of pharaoh influenced Greek conceptions of monarchical rule: as a result of the acculturation process, Greek culture itself also changed.

The situation described above, in which Greek and non-Greek inevitably influenced each other but deliberate assimilation was mostly avoided, has one big exception: Rome. Here, cultural as well as political relationships were different. Greek influence on Rome, especially in the area of religion, dates from long before the Roman conquest of the Greek East, but it was this very conquest that gave momentum to the acculturation process. Although the Romans were the military victors, they had to admit that the Greeks were their cultural superiors, and, significantly, had no problems in doing so. They were not uncritical toward the Greeks: although they felt almost unlimited admiration for the Greek cultural heritage, they were largely contemptuous of their Greek contemporaries, whom they called *Graeculi*, "little Greeks." The Greeks, in their turn, generally saw the Romans as "barbarians," which strengthened Rome's ambivalent attitude to Greece. Despite all this, the Romans, as military and political masters, could afford to be open to Greek influence: this was Rome's own choice. The Hellenization of Rome was profound; it is hard to overestimate Greek influence on all aspects of Roman civilization. There were some protesters who favored "old Roman values," but they were incapable of turning the Greek tide. However, again, we should not think simplistically about this process: the Greek influence did not make Rome "Greek." Rome remained Roman, but the definition of "Roman" was subject to constant change, and the Greek heritage, adapted or not, became part of "Romanness."

The *polis*

In the various Hellenistic societies, the *polis* was the natural environment for Greeks wherever they lived, just as it had been in the Classical period. Now, however, *poleis* were part of large monarchies, and they were subsequently incorporated in a single empire of unprecedented dimensions. In any case, they had de facto lost their political independence, which is illustrated, for example, by the fact that everywhere royal law functioned alongside local law. At times, central power temporarily disappeared, and *poleis* were again able to take control for a while, but the coming of Rome spelt the definitive end of any form of political independence. In the old days, for instance, the citizens of the polis were also its soldiers, even if they saw little action. Rome effectively demilitarized the *poleis*: waging war was a job for Roman legions. In the centuries following Alexander, *poleis* increasingly turned inward, and policy came to mean local policy.

Apart from political independence, there was another loss: *koinonia*, the citizens' sense of community, gradually disappeared during the first two centuries of the Hellenistic period. The transition to authoritarian forms of government, a process of oligarchization, and an ever-widening gap between rich and poor may be held responsible for this development. External politics, but also internal *koinonia*, became rather make-believe than actual independent policy making, seen for instance in the continual rivalry between *poleis*, all seeking to be the biggest and the best, and the accompanying expressions of pride where one's own *polis* was concerned. The puffed-up sense of identity of the Hellenistic city dwellers was on the one hand a moving spirit, but on the other hand no more than a futile pose in a world that had changed fundamentally. Local chauvinism was indisputably genuine, but it was of a different order from the sense of superiority shared by a citizenship that is truly united. Philosophy presented some new alternatives for the role of the *polites*, particularly the Stoa's *kosmopolites* or "citizen of the world," but this was hardly a serious alternative for the average city dweller.

There were, however, viable alternatives to *koinonia*. To begin with, *poleis* housed a multitude of clubs, societies, and "guilds." Every *polis* had its *gumnasion* as an important center of Greek cultural identity: a school for the sons, and sometimes the daughters, of the elite, which also functioned as a cultural community center. The many private societies that flourished as never before and where everyone could feel secure were of even greater importance for creating a sense of community. There was some form of association for every segment of society, every professional group, and every religious denomination. Many of these clubs, both the societies dedicated to the cult of a particular deity and the associations that were not explicitly religious, had social objectives, such as mutual funeral insurance. The expanding membership of these private associations may be interpreted as a turning away from public life in favor of privacy. Such particularism seems to have been a general social phenomenon. This may also be deduced from the increasing importance of family life.

Paradoxically, this movement from the public toward the private in due course offered a new way to structure public life: public life became modeled on private life. One could also say that in the course of the Hellenistic period, public life was increasingly absorbed by private life. That is to say, the private life of a small group within the various communities, the family life of the urban elite, was important enough to encompass all of the *polis*. The result was a paternalistic system in which the *polis*' inhabitants were seen as the children and the members of the elite as their fathers and mothers. In exchange for respect and obedience, these "parents" offered protection. At the state level, the paternalism of the urban elite may be compared to the role of the Hellenistic monarchs and that of the prominent leaders of the late Roman Republic.

Euergetism

Euergetein is Greek for "to be beneficent", in particular toward one's community, by distributing food, providing funds for festivities, granting loans to the city, financing public building and infrastructure, or performing public services, for instance acting as an envoy, without requiring payment. The mechanisms of benefaction in the Hellenistic *polis* may be compared to what has been said before about Athenian benefactors, the liturgists, who could likewise afford to be big spenders: one flaunted one's riches for fellow nabobs and fellow citizens. The difference is that the Hellenistic elites were pulling the strings without any control from below and were much wealthier than the average liturgist in Classical Athens.

As the power and wealth of these *euergetai* became larger, so did their generosity. Up to about 150 BC, their riches benefited their fellow citizens, and they were supposed to act for the greater good of the *polis*; after that time, however, members of the elite increasingly supported their own "children-subjects" and, characteristically, little difference was made between citizens and non-citizens when, for example, food was distributed. The *polis* still profited from their donations, but these came to be seen as favors instead of expressions of civic duty. The generous no longer acted for the benefit of the *polis*, but for their own benefit and that of their family. Even the statue erected by the city to honor its benefactor was likely to be paid for by the laureate. On a city level, *euergetai* behaved as if they were Hellenistic monarchs, with corresponding results: in several instances, *euergetai* and their families were worshipped.

Municipal benefaction included sums determined by the donor as well as liturgies on the basis of certain fixed rates. The system of liturgies flourished as never before and was even expanded; in Classical Athens, for instance, public building projects had been paid for by the city treasury. The boundaries between office holding and benefaction became blurred. In Classical Athens, liturgy and office had been very different matters (holding an office had been something for which one *received* money); for the magistrates of the Hellenistic period, benefaction increasingly became part of their office, until, predictably, it had become a condition for holding office, and holding office had become a privilege of the rich.

The regular sources of income of most cities were definitely not sufficient to maintain a city life that met the standards of the elite and kept "the population at large" reasonably content. This, naturally, also resulted from the fact that the elite did not pay normal taxes, but opted for a limited redistribution of means through euergetism. And, much more than just paying taxes, euergetism contributed to the honor and glory of the benefactors and their families. As a result of all this, however, benefaction became ever more a necessity. This should not be underestimated: given the laissez-faire economy of the Hellenistic period, with its painful contrast between vast wealth and dire poverty, it is hard to imagine how the elite could have acted otherwise. The munificence of the elite served to buy off social unrest. The restive urban proletariat demanded "bread and circuses." These included religious spectacles of every kind; large-scale festivities and other community events were an everyday occurrence. The larger the city, the wealthier the local powers, and the more grandiose the entertainment that was put on. Nowhere more so than in the royal capital—where the king was supposed to show his munificence.

During the Hellenistic period, education and health care gradually became part of the responsibilities of local authorities, and here, too, the basis was formed by liturgies and gifts. Cities established schools: the *gumnasion*, which used to offer a combination of physical and artistic training, developed into an all-round institute for lower and secondary education. Cities also appointed municipal physicians to make sure there was at least some medical care; possibly the destitute received free treatment. In this way, fields that in earlier periods had been strictly private became a matter of collective organization. However, the fact that benefaction was mandatory does not imply that the elite were reluctant benefactors. This was a win-win situation: they reaped fame—directly as individuals as well as indirectly because of the reputation of their city—and they continuously strengthened their position by binding their fellow townsmen.

Hellenistic urban development

The foregoing discussion necessitates a more detailed look at the Hellenistic city; this is where the results of the munificence of the elite were most apparent. An increase in scale led to the development of real metro*polis*es, cities with thousands, sometimes hundreds of thousands, of inhabitants. Such cities offered every form of modern convenience, although, of course, not every dwelling was comfortable! Smaller towns, too, were fitted out with an *agora* with stoas and prestigious public buildings, wide streets with arcades, fine sanctuaries, a water supply system, bathhouses, and—the pride of every town—city walls with towers,

Figure 35   A model of the acropolis of Pergamon as it looked in the first half of the 2nd c. BC. In the Staatliche Museen in Berlin, one can find a large-scale model of the acropolis of Pergamon, illustrated here. In 282 BC, the stadtholder of Pergamon rejected Seleucid rule and founded his own royal dynasty, the Attalids. In the 2nd century BC, large parts of Asia Minor came under Pergamene rule. In this period, the embellishment of the acropolis of Pergamon was taken in hand, and it was developed into an impressive, monumental ensemble. The Pergamene acropolis is a hill that rises 274 m above the surrounding plain. From the south and the west, it slopes upward, and on the northern and eastern sides it has sheer cliffs. On the model, we look up the slope, from the southwest (above) and from the southeast (overleaf): at the bottom left, there is a rectangular agora partly surrounded by stoas; from there, a staircase leads to the next rectangular terrace, which carries the enormous altar of Zeus, a masterpiece of Hellenistic architecture (now in Berlin). To its left, along the western flank of the acropolis, the huge so-called theater terrace, with a Dionysus temple at its far end, and the theater behind it. To its right, at the eastern rim of the acropolis, there is the *heroon*, the sanctuary of the deified members of the Attalid dynasty. Above the Altar of Zeus stands the temple of Athena, patron goddess of the city; it is surrounded by huge stoas. Above that there is another temple: it was built in Roman days for the deified emperor Trajan, so it is an anachronistic element in this reconstruction of the Hellenistic layout. Between the two temples stands what was probably the library. The other buildings crowding the eastern half of the slope are part of the palace complex, while the top of the hill is occupied by military barracks and arsenals. Photos: a) Christa Begall. © 2013. Photo Scala, Florence/BPK, Bildagentur für Kunst, Kultur und Geschichte, Berlin; b) © 2013. Photo Scala, Florence/BPK, Bildagentur für Kunst, Kultur und Geschichte, Berlin

Figure 35   (*Continued*)

all this at the expense of the rich. Many of the newly founded cities were built according to the Hippodamic system, the checkerboard pattern that was at the time associated with the 5th-century architect Hippodamus of Miletus although the concept was much older (it had already been applied at the time of the Archaic colonization). For the first time, urban public space was treated as a valuable entity in its own right: main streets were clearly distinguished from narrower side streets, and the *agora* became a purely representative area in the center of town, so that separate marketplaces had to be created for commercial activities. All subsequent European urban planning derives from these developments, especially that of the Romans, who perfected Hellenistic ideas about town building.

The erection of an impressive urban façade fitted the oligarchic context. A concentration of public buildings around a central square lined with monuments mainly dedicated to the local elite was exactly the right stage setting for the exertion of power by that same elite. The power of the monarch could be expressed in the same way; at the residences of Hellenistic princes, such as Alexandria or Pergamon, temples, altars, theater, *odeion* (the hall for music and recitation), *mouseion* ("sanctuary of the muses"), library, *gumnasion*, and *agora* with public buildings were centered around, or even integrated into, the royal palace. In Alexandria, even the hippodrome, the track for chariot races, was situated in the city center and closely associated with the palace. In this way, the monarch presented himself as the protector of religion, maecenas toward scholarship and art, provider of public entertainment, and, of course, administrator. This ideology was an incentive for elites and princes to energetically embark on major construction works, and cities competed with each other in architectural tours de force. The monumentalism of Hellenistic cities often resulted in architectural ensembles that met certain esthetic standards. On the other hand, cities ran the risk of being no more than theatrical backdrops for the rule of the elite, another sign that the days of the Classical *polis* were gone.

Men and Women

Women in a changing male-dominated society

As has been briefly mentioned before, the demise of the traditional Greek *polis* culture (or, at least, of its political aspects) was connected to a re-evaluation of personal relationships: part of the effort that used to be directed at the outside world now went into private life. As far as marriage was concerned, there was a definite shift from contract to personal feelings, but whether this resulted in an improvement of the legal position of women is debatable. An ideology that advocates private life, romantic love, marriage, and the family is one thing, and genuine social change is another. However, most probably there was more to it than just ideology. It is highly likely that the powerful emotions expressed on gravestones for children and spouses were not just platitudes.

Because of this re-evaluation of marriage, women were much more visible within city life—this, at any rate, holds true for the women of the elite. Girls received a certain measure of education and were taken into account when cities established schools. But it is hard to say how fundamental such changes were. A few examples from Egypt (because of the papyri, most of our information on legal matters comes from Egypt) should not tempt us into speaking of a reversal of the social and legal position of women. As has been pointed out before, given its geographical dimensions and its time frame, it is dangerous to generalize about the Hellenistic period. Looking back to Classical times, we see an unmistakable continuity: the *kurios* was still a general phenomenon. In Egypt and elsewhere in the East, for instance, in Jewish circles, women acted independently, as they had always done in accordance with indigenous law. In these same areas, however, Greek women were still supposed to follow a *kurios* according to Greek rules of law.

The public activities of women from the elite have often been seen as an indication of fundamental change. Not only were they mentioned and honored together with their husbands, they also acted independently as benefactresses in religious positions, and, from the 1st century BC, also in non-religious ones. In the first three centuries of the Christian era, the number of women who held public positions and the variety of offices held by women would increase markedly. But what does this mean? It turns out that many of the offices held by women from the elite were of a ceremonial nature or were only nominally held by them. We do not find them in positions that involved "real" political authority, such as overseer of a market or ambassador, let alone member of the local council. What mattered most in all cases was the money they brought along: benefiting the community was the essence of every office held by a woman. This does imply, however, that the women in question had their own property at their disposal. Or should we say: were allowed to dispose of their property?

These developments are probably closely linked to a social structure in which the elite played an increasingly paternalistic role. Such paternalism presupposes maternalism: bringing the female members of local dynasties on to the stage is a natural consequence of thinking in terms of hereditary power and wealth. It does not mean they are a structural part of this power. This also holds true for Hellenistic princesses, who are said to have been role models for the ladies of the elite. The intriguing role women from the upper classes were allowed to play in public life meant they were more visible and had some freedom of movement. This is something new. But there was no genuine "emancipation of women" or a significant role for "women" in public life: in the Hellenistic period, most women remained as mute and powerless as before.

The sources present us with a very comparable image of Roman women. During the Republican period, Roman women, too, were completely subject to the authority of their fathers, their nearest male relatives, or their husbands. It is a Roman characteristic that in many cases the husband had considerably less authority over his wife than the woman's father or her other male relatives, because in certain types of marriage the woman did not become part of her husband's family. It has often been stated that as a result, these women achieved a certain measure of independence; this, however, is hard to determine. We find that in the 2nd century BC, women from the elite, the so-called *matronae*, moved more freely, because they could make use of the possibilities offered by the growing wealth of their families and by their own properties. In this respect, they undoubtedly followed the example of upper-class women in the Hellenistic cities and even that of Hellenistic princesses. Practical considerations also played a role: as the male members of the elite were frequently and for lengthy periods of time engaged in political and military activities abroad, women entered the public stage as representatives of their families. But in this case, too, this did not mean "emancipation," not for the women of the elite, and certainly not for women from the lower classes. Behind the scenes, every woman, in her own way, may have had great influence; seen from the outside, she always remained in a dependent position.

Sexuality and reproduction

As far as sexual mores are concerned, the Hellenistic period does not show dramatic changes, though a more romantic view of sexuality is evident. This is probably the result of the re-evaluation of marriage and the family mentioned earlier. A more refined eroticism—"soft porn" products for public consumption—replaced the often crude sexuality of images and texts from the Archaic and Classical Greek world closely related to the *sumposion*. It is significant that large-scale sculptural representation of the female nude, especially statues and figurines representing the goddess Aphrodite, seems to have started in the middle of the 4th century BC. That writers and artists showed less interest in homosexuality also fits the new mood. Some scholars are of the opinion that this change in tone reflected, or caused, a change in behavior. Romanticism, eroticism, and even idealized family life would have been no more than a cover-up for a society in which hedonism flourished and in which, compared to earlier periods, heterosexual intercourse was more and more detached from reproduction. In this context, it is often pointed out that during the Hellenistic period the number of children per family was reduced dramatically due to contraception (some effective methods were probably known), abortion, infanticide, or the abandonment of newborn babies. Naturally, this piece of information influences the way we look at sexual life, but we lack proof for this or most other statements concerning actual behavior. Abandoning infants was a standard solution in the ancient world, where many lived below what we would now call the poverty line. There is no firm evidence for an increase in this kind of behavior in the Hellenistic period.

Because of what has been said before about the demography of the ancient world, it will be clear that a marked reduction in family size must have resulted in a decreasing population. Sure enough, sources speak of a decline, especially in Greece. A drop in the number of landowning citizens, recorded for a number of places, notably in Sparta, does not, however, seem to have had primarily demographical causes, but social ones: in a society replete with mercenary armies, communities no longer see the need of maintaining the citizens' army to the required standard. This opens up possibilities for the elite to enlarge its territory at the expense of others. In fact, our knowledge of demographical developments during the Hellenistic period is extremely limited. Migration patterns are the only matter about which we can make informed guesses, although, of course, there are no figures. Many Greeks moved either east or to Egypt, as mercenaries or in the wake of military conquest. Over a long period, a powerful countercurrent of both Greeks (sometimes second-generation migrants) and non-Greeks (especially Jews and Syrians) moved from the East to the West. The size of the population leaving Greece and Macedonia should, therefore, not be exaggerated. In addition, we should not forget to include slaves when mentioning patterns of migration: large-scale warfare during the whole of the period led to the enslavement and subsequent transfer of vast numbers of people.

Religion, Philosophy, and Scholarship

Hellenistic religion in the Greek *poleis*

"*The* Hellenistic religion" does not exist: differences in time and place are simply too large. Armed with this warning we can, nonetheless, mention a number of features that were characteristic of religious life in the last three centuries before the beginning of the Christian era. The following will be discussed below: syncretism; henotheistic tendencies; hierarchization of the relationship between deity and worshipper, but, paradoxically also the reduction of the distance between the two; belief and unbelief, both an expression of the fact that the self-evident *polis* religion had disappeared; an increase in the heroization and deification of mortals; a greater prevalence of belief in miracles, epiphany, private devotion, confession, astrology, and magic. None of these developments is really new; we can find a pre-Hellenistic example for all of them. But the extent to which they thrived was unprecedented.

As has been stressed earlier, in the Hellenistic context near-complete assimilation was rare. In the field of religion, however, we find a merging of elements of the Greek heritage

(a)

(b)

Figure 36   Stele from Petra with the goddess Atargatis (1st c. AD) and the head of an Atargatis statue from Armenia Minor (2nd c. BC). To the left is the goddess Atargatis as depicted in Petra, in the Jordanian desert, and to the right is Atargatis in her Greek guise. The stele from Petra, now in the museum of Amman, combines a purely aniconic South Arabian style, where the goddess al-Ozza (in Petra known by her Syrian name Atargatis) is represented by an undecorated block of stone, with Hellenistic anthropomorphism. Its inscription says: "The goddess of Hayyan, son of Nibat" and is written in a Nabatean script of the 1st century AD. The bronze head on the right was found in Armenia Minor, just to the west of the upper reaches of the Euphrates river. It is dated to the 2nd century BC and is now in the British Museum. We again have Atargatis, or Anahita as she may have been called in Asia Minor, but now looking exactly like the Greek Aphrodite. Al-Ozza, Atargatis, Anahita, and Aphrodite were considered one and the same goddess. But she was given the iconography people were most familiar with or considered most appropriate. Photos: a) Jürgen Liepe; b) © The Trustees of the British Museum

on the one hand and Eastern elements on the other: this phenomenon is usually called religious syncretism. Syncretism implies both continuity and discontinuity: on the one hand there are long-lived traditions, and on the other new "imports." Syncretism itself was a continuously evolving process, and both the traditional ingredients and the new combinations changed. At a certain stage, old and new, Greek and non-Greek, can hardly be distinguished: something original has emerged, and this we can only call Hellenistic. Usually, the Greeks were at the receiving end: the rather formless Greek polytheism had always been open to foreign influences; the intensifying contacts and the spiritual needs of the age meant an even greater openness. In general, the more exclusive religions of the East went no further than borrowing forms of Greek anthropomorphism and the concept of the immortal soul. Nevertheless, even these religions did not remain unchanged; acculturation is, after all, mutual, and evolution continued within the new context. Even a rejection of Greek influence resulted in a reshaping of the domestic religious traditions, especially when, in the process, one came to make use of forms and arguments taken from the "adversary," which was often the case. This is most obvious for Judaism (and later Christianity), where Greek influence is unmistakable, but the unique identity is not lost.

All of this does not mean, however, that in the Greek *poleis*, including the newly founded ones in far-away territories, old forms and concepts were discarded. *Poleis* continued to honor the gods of the traditional pantheon with traditional cults: they named the months after the old gods, the cities' coins carried their images, their temples continued to occupy a central place, their festivals were celebrated in a grand manner, and so on. This is a perfect illustration of the fact that the much-changed and ever-changing *polis* life was deeply rooted in the past. Again we find a blend of continuity and discontinuity: Hellenistic culture had meant the end of the classical *polis*, but the classical *polis* was nonetheless the basis on which Hellenistic culture rested and from which it continued to evolve. And there was even change within continuity: temples became bigger, festivities more opulent, and inscriptions longer. Outward appearances became ever more important and very often served some political aim, which is hardly surprising in the light of what has been said earlier. We should not jump to the conclusion that people no longer believed in the ancient pantheon, but, nevertheless, public ritual often seems to have been rather hollow. This of course does not tell us anything about individual religiosity.

Within the whole of religious life, the relative importance of the old gods did diminish, but not, as we just saw, as a result of neglect but because of growing competition from non-Greek gods and their cults. Very often these cults had an ecstatic character, and many of the gods involved were savior gods, *soteres* (the ancient gods were sometimes also designated with this epithet, for example, Zeus Soter). It is evident that such gods and cults were in demand: similar Greek cults likewise flourished, especially the cult of Dionysus, and often took the form of mystery cults. In fact, all mystery cults thrived, including the one at Eleusis. It was the heyday of the cult of Asclepius. Before being introduced into the religious life of the *polis*, however, foreign gods and cults were adapted to Greek taste. For the Greeks, they were only attractive in their syncretistic forms. This could be done through identification, for instance, the Egyptian god Ammon or the Syrian Ba'al would be presented as Zeus. It also happened that the deity kept its own name and appearance, but in a Hellenized form, as happened to a sizeable number of Near Eastern gods. These new gods (and also the old gods in new attire) typically had a cosmopolitan character. They were not tied to a specific *polis*, but belonged to the whole world.

The most important example of a deity whose cult gained momentum on the waves of syncretism is the Egyptian goddess Isis, partly identified with Demeter for the Greek public. In her case, we could speak of deliberate syncretism, because the Ptolemaic rulers promoted the Hellenized cult of Isis and her son Serapis. But Isis would have made it even without the Ptolemaic dynasty: she was worshipped everywhere as the greatest of goddesses, whose praises were sung in so-called aretologies (enumerations of *aretai*, virtues and miraculous deeds). She is a clear example of Hellenistic henotheism: the tendency to look upon one god as more important than all the others—a god one could really convert to, a god about whom one wished to (or felt the duty to) spread the word. This was a kind of zeal that was alien to Greek polytheism. Being drawn to one particular god, however, did not mean one had to renounce the others. Total exclusivism was limited to genuine monotheists (Jews) and dualists (Persians). Hierarchization of the relationship between deity and believer is highly characteristic of, though not limited to, henotheism: the gods were addressed as kings and queens; the believers were their subjects, even their servants or slaves. Paradoxically, the distance between gods and worshippers simultaneously diminished: deity and believer entered upon a personal relationship. Within this relationship, the believer could seek the attention of the god through special devotion or confession; as a token of his presence the god could perform miracles or appear to the devotee, something known as "epiphany."

The special attraction of Isis was that, according to her worshippers, she was more powerful than fate. The idea that all mortals are subject to fate is typical for Hellenism. There was, therefore, a growing interest in Tyche, a goddess who personified blind fate, as well as in astrology and oracles. These could be of help in knowing the future. But here one is confronted with the problem of predestination: if the future can be known, can it be changed if one does not like it? During the Hellenistic era, much thought was given to this dilemma: the most exalted of the gods, such as Isis, were supposed to help cut this Gordian knot. Magic also presented a solution. Magic is religion, albeit a form of religion in which one does not ask for the favors of the gods, but attempts to wrest from the gods what one desires: perform the right ritual, and one may be sure of success. Magic may be used to break the power of fate and in this way enable humans to bend its course. Under the influence of Mesopotamian, Syrian, and Egyptian examples, magic, and astrology, too, grew into a substantial business. "Business" is certainly not a misnomer for the ever-growing army of healers, seers, magicians, and miracle workers who came to offer their supernatural services.

Heroization, and even deification, of mortals was not unknown in the Greek world. There had always been heroes, and for the deification of a living man we may cite the late-5th-century example of General Lysander. Now, however, this evolved into a veritable cult of the divine ruler: Alexander the Great and his successors were honored with temples, sacrifices, priests, and festivities, at first mainly (but not exclusively) when they died, later already during the kings' and queens' lifetimes. The deification of the members of the Ptolemaic and Seleucid dynasties knew, of course, pharaonic and Eastern precedents, but nevertheless had its own character. The Ptolemies, for instance, were not divine *because* they were pharaohs. They were, as a matter of fact, twice divine: on the one hand they were (Greek) gods in their own right, on the other, as pharaohs, they were incarnations of Horus, and after their deaths, of Osiris. The fact that they were put on the same level as Horus and Osiris was of a different order than their elevation to the status of Greek god: the latter did not imply equation with, for instance, Zeus or Apollo. Apparently, the divine ruler was "a lesser kind of god," dependent on higher powers: the various dynasties all had a tutelary deity from the traditional pantheon, and prayers for the rulers were addressed to other gods.

The background to the cult of the divine ruler was in the first place a political one. These new public cults were started deliberately; the rulers were newcomers, and needed to be legitimized. But, naturally, this can only work when at least some of the subjects believe in the divinity of their rulers. When we think of politics and religion as incompatible, we tend to see a merging of the two as mere politics. This is erroneous: in most of these cases, no force was needed to establish the cult. Sometimes the initiative was taken by the subjects themselves. The cult of the divine ruler tied in with the popularity of the savior gods: the ruler, too, was a *soter*, a savior. We see here the pattern of patronage and euergetism, but on a truly royal scale. The cult of the divine ruler and the hierarchization of religious life mentioned earlier illustrate that a new social order of princes and oligarchs also implies a new religious order. This is not to say, however, that political changes constitute the only plausible explanation for the religious changes that took place during the Hellenistic period: reality was many times more complicated, and monocausal explanations are usually inadequate.

Religion in Rome

Hellenistic syncretism was not only found in the East, but also in the West: in Rome. Here, the Greeks, and also the Etruscans, were the "donors" and the Romans the "recipients"—this can also be observed outside the field of religion. In Rome, anthropomorphism seems to have been the result of acculturation, as was the interpretation of omens; the preferential treatment reserved for the god Jupiter within the Roman pantheon has an Etruscan background, and "typically Roman" phenomena, such as gladiatorial combats and triumphal processions, were likewise borrowed from the Etruscans. Already in the 5th century, temples were built in Rome for the Greek gods, such as Apollo. It is hard to say on what native trunk these Greek and Etruscan shoots were grafted: we know very little about the earliest stages of Roman religion. Written sources mainly date to the 1st century BC and later. With Roman conservatism in mind, we may, of course, try to reconstruct something of Rome's earliest religious images and customs. But we should be aware that we then look through the eyes of authors from much later times who possibly, or even probably, also reconstructed their own past without sufficient knowledge of the facts. In that case, our reconstructions would be just as unreliable as the Roman reconstructions on which they are based. Archaeological finds cannot always provide a definite answer to specific questions, but they clearly demonstrate that a quest for the "genuine," "pure" or "original" Roman religion is doomed to fail: even at the earliest stages, we find Greek and Etruscan elements. We may therefore cautiously conclude that from the beginning Roman religion was an amalgam of many ingredients, including Greek ones. This may be the reason it was such an excellent breeding ground for further Greek influence.

The way the early Romans looked at their gods is comparable to what has been said earlier about the Greeks: they feared their gods, especially their anger toward those whose piety fell short, because the gods could decide to strike at the wrongdoer's environment. People tried to maintain a good relationship with the gods (the *pax deorum*) through ritual, mainly sacrifices and votive gifts. In Roman religion, ritual (the *cultus deorum*) was an even more important element than in Greek religion. This is apparent from the central position held by religious specialists: *pontifices* (priests) and *augures* (interpreters of omens). The Roman pantheon was very open, even more so than the Greek one: the inclusion of foreign gods was institutionalized in the form of the *evocatio*, a ritual in which the god of an adversary was invited, through prayer and votive gifts, to leave his own people and move to Rome. We find foreign influences at a very early stage, but from the early 3rd century such influences increased significantly, not only in number but also in power. The result was a profound Hellenization of Roman religion. "Indigenous gods," such as Janus, Venus, or Vesta, did not, however, disappear from the pantheon: they received an anthropomorphic form and were in some cases identified with Greek gods; rituals such as *lustratio* (ritual purification) and augury, divination by observing the flight of birds, continued to be performed. From time to time, we even see revivals of "genuine Roman" elements; quite often, however, these were no more than newly invented "ancient customs of our fathers."

The Hellenization process of the 3rd and 2nd centuries was much advanced by the great changes (and crises) Roman society underwent at that time. As the Athenians had done earlier, the Romans, too, imported savior gods and ecstatic cults from the East, especially Asclepius and Cybele. From the late 2nd century BC, the number of imported gods grew: Isis, Osiris, and Serapis arrived in Italy—more will be said about their history later on. And, just as had happened in Greece, there was opposition to the new developments from those who sought to protect the ancestral religion and prevent a supposed threat to the public order. In Rome, too, the opposition had little permanent success. Sometimes, however, it was possible to keep out certain elements of a new cult or make it illegal for Romans to take on its priesthood, even after the god had been officially accepted.

All of the foregoing may be described as Hellenization, because even non-Greek deities came to Rome via the Greek world, in an adapted form that was recognizable to the already strongly Hellenized Romans. When cults were taken directly from an alien culture—those of Celtic gods, for instance—these were first adapted to the Greco-Roman system through anthropomorphism and identification with the gods one was familiar with. This specifically Roman variant of Hellenistic syncretism is known as the *interpretatio Romana*. This not only concerns deities who became part of the state cult in Rome, but also many of the gods from the provinces of the Roman Empire who were not, or not immediately, honored in this way. The latter, too, were usually accepted by the Romans who lived there.

Greek philosophy also gained a foothold in Rome, including its skepticism concerning the traditional religious order. This skepticism, however, was not inappropriate given the crisis the Roman Republic faced at the time. Part of this crisis was a politicizing of religion, in the sense that religion was increasingly manipulated to serve political aims; mortals even came to usurp divine power. Caesar may serve as an example: he was a member of the *gens* Julia, who claimed descent from Venus via Aeneas, and it was only a small step to contend that the great man himself was more than a mere mortal. Although influence from the Hellenistic East no doubt played a role in these developments, they were mostly indigenous: they were a reaction to social changes and found support in certain aspects of Roman religion, notably the ancestral cult.

Non-Greek Hellenistic religions

It has been mentioned earlier that the religions of the East were usually more exclusive than the Greco-Roman religions. This does not mean that these religions were not

Figure 37 Stele of a Cretan dream interpreter from Sakkara in Egypt (3rd–2nd c. BC). This limestone stele with polychrome paint from Sakkara (Memphis) in Egypt, now in the Egyptian Museum in Cairo, is a very well-known object: it is interesting because of the content of the text it carries, and because of its decoration and shape. The stele is dated to around 200 BC, and appears to be the "street sign" of a dream interpreter: "I interpret dreams, as ordered by the god. May you have good luck. The interpreter is a Cretan." The god is probably the god Sarapis: the stele was found near a Sarapis sanctuary, and the painting on the stele shows the god Apis, appearing as the sacred Apis bull, in front of an altar. Apis, who originated as a fertility god, had by this time developed into a god of the Underworld: he was called "the Apis who had become Osiris," that is, Osiris–Apis, and in its Greek variant, Sarapis. This is a Greek-looking stele, carrying a Greek text; but the two columns framing the text and the caryatids crowning these columns are clearly in an Egyptian idiom. Photo: INTERFOTO/Alamy

affected by Hellenism: as was said before, acculturation is a mutual process. Syncretistic phenomena also occur in Eastern religions, particularly where the representation of gods is concerned: Greek anthropomorphism was of great influence here, even if it often tied in with indigenous traditions. With respect to the substance of religious traditions, influences are much harder to discern; if they were there at all, they often met with fierce resistance. The clearest example of this is Judaism, which in this period already was a fundamentally exclusive monotheistic religion. The Maccabean (or Hasmonean) rebellion had many causes, religious-nationalistic ones, but also causes of an economic and political nature. It is typical that the religious component was afterward cited as the main cause, because, whatever the backgrounds to this insurrection may have been, opposition to Hellenization was from that time on a thread in Jewish history. This not only concerned external influence, but also the Hellenized group within its own ranks. Be that as it may, for many Jews, particularly for those outside Palestine, orthodoxy was a relative matter. In Alexandria, for instance, the Jewish community underwent a rather strong Hellenization as a result of which it became necessary to translate the Jewish Bible, the Tanakh, into Greek: the so-called Septuagint. However, all in all, Hellenization did not touch the heart of Jewish monotheism.

We saw that monotheists had a strong tendency to be exclusive, to isolate themselves from those who were not fellow believers. This was also true of the Jews. Polytheists, whose cults were an intrinsic part of the whole of social life, often looked upon Jewish exclusivism with aversion. This requires some attention because these feelings of aversion constitute the roots of anti-Semitism. In the ancient world, friction between the various religions was, in the first instance, not a matter of lofty ideology, but of day-to-day reality on a local level. On the one hand Jewish communities isolated themselves for religious reasons, and on the other they wished to take full part in city life and even demanded citizens' rights. In some cases, under very specific circumstances, this led to clashes between Jews and non-Jews. In this story, Alexandria plays the main part. Egypt already had an anti-Jewish movement because Jewish tradition, as laid down in the Torah, had given the Egyptians the role of the villain. Anti-Jewish feelings became even stronger under the rule of the Ptolemies, since they employed many Jews as mercenaries and tax collectors. Alexandria was a city with a large Jewish community that had managed to gain an exceptional, but disputed, position. Within this specific context, hatred against the Jews also spread to the Greeks. Similar developments took place in other cities, either inspired by the Alexandrian example or as a parallel development.

Examples of local aggression stand in contrast to several instances in which we see Jews living peacefully together with their non-Jewish fellow citizens, from which we may conclude that this was not impossible. Nevertheless, the Hellenistic situation produced something that looks much like an ideology, something that may be called anti-Judaism—a term that is to be preferred to "anti-Semitism" with its modern associations. The Egyptian and Greek defamatory pamphlets against the Jews, combined with anti-Jewish propaganda from the side of the Seleucids in the wake of the Maccabean rebellion, led to a change in the way part of the intelligentsia looked at the Jews. Initially, there had been a certain admiration for Jewish monotheism; during the Hellenistic period, however, attitudes turned increasingly negative, and Jews came to be seen as "misanthropic," "inhuman," and "a-social." The anti-Jewish stories from the propaganda mentioned above were reproduced again and again. But although the influence of these negative opinions on actual behavior seems to have been minor, they are not unimportant because they formed the breeding ground for the later Christian rejection of Judaism. Christian anti-Judaism had its own face, because it was founded on theology, but from the continuity between antique ideas and early-Christian thought it is evident that Hellenism, especially Ptolemaic Egypt, contributed to the emergence of anti-Jewish stereotypes.

We are rather well-informed about Judaism. Thanks to papyri and inscriptions, we are also able to reconstruct the development of the Egyptian religion; here, Hellenization played only a minor role. As was the case with the Jews, in Egypt, too, opposition against "the oppressor" (first the Persians, subsequently the Greeks, and finally the Romans) was of considerable significance in the acculturation process. Time-honored common religious systems had for centuries provided both political as well as a certain religious unity; for the Egyptian masses, these systems now gradually lost their meaning. The disappearance of an independent Egyptian state resulted in a fragmentation of religious life in which local ideas and customs gained importance, but this localized religiosity looked back to Egyptian tradition.

We know very little about specific religious developments elsewhere in the Near East between the rise of the Persian Empire and the beginning of the Roman imperial period. In the Seleucid kingdom—soon to be largely a part of Parthian territory—we find Greek gods, Greek anthropomorphism, and Greek religious architecture, not only within but also without the Greek community. Still, Greek influence is only one among many. The whole vast area from Syria to Iran was teeming with gods: Syrian gods, Arab gods, Greek and Mesopotamian gods. . . This was syncretism on an enormous scale. We can do little more than try to distinguish the various local pantheons; trying to figure out what is specifically Hellenistic and what seems a continuation of previous stages is extremely difficult. In Mesopotamia itself, some temples continued to function during the Hellenistic period; in Iran, Iranian dualism survived. This dualism is said to have influenced other religions, for instance, Judaism, but we know next to nothing about its development in the Hellenistic period. One thing is certain: the trend toward universal religious systems that was characteristic for the Classical era ended in fragmentation. The sluices were opened, and every region, settlement, and individual was inundated with choices.

Philosophy

Apart from a kaleidoscope of beliefs, the Hellenistic world also knew unbelief. Both can be seen as an expression of the fact that there no longer was a *polis* religion that could be taken for granted. Euhemerus (c. 300 BC) contended that the gods had once been human. Others saw the gods as abstractions or allegories. Developments that had begun in the course of the 5th or during the 4th century reached a high point in the philosophy of the Hellenistic era. Rational criticism carried through to such lengths was, however, rare: most philosophers accepted the existence of the divine, albeit in an abstracted form. Nevertheless, even the religious ideas of less radical philosophers reflect the disappearance of old borders and certainties. This mainly concerns the skeptics and the cynics, who were thriving, and two new currents: the Epicureans and the Stoics. The Aristotelian and Platonic schools also continued to exist; during the Hellenistic period, the latter went through a Skeptic phase. Typical of Hellenistic thought is a tendency toward escapism: all schools, however different, teach how to be detached, how to avoid suffering, and how to be free even if, practically speaking, one is not free.

The Skeptics could boast a long tradition: the founder of the school, Pyrrho of Elis, a contemporary of Alexander, invoked the example of Socrates. Central to Skepticism is the denial of all forms of knowledge, whether based on observation or on rational thought. This leads to a rejection of judgment, so that one may reach an ideal state of complete detachment (*ataraxia*) through indifference. Cynicism, which likewise saw Socrates as its predecessor, opted for anti-culture: man is free when he rejects all physical needs and social conventions. The cynic is anti-everything and pro-nothing.

In late-4th-century Athens, Epicurus developed a philosophy that built on Democritus' theory of atoms and taught that natural and human life obey fixed laws and processes, that the gods exist but are incapable and unwilling to intervene in the course of things, and that there is no life after death. Happiness is only for those who manage to reach *ataraxia*, the state of being without desires. The best thing to do is to leave the world and keep aloof from everything. These ideas were later reduced to a simple "seize the day" message by enemies of Epicurean philosophy.

The Stoa was named after the Stoa Poikile, the "Painted Colonnade" where its founder Zeno (c. 300) conducted his teaching. The school contended that man has the duty to aspire after a virtuous life, in harmony with nature. Nature is governed by *logos*, reason (to be identified with God, in the singular). Sensory observation and rational thinking will lead to the required knowledge of *logos*. The inner self of the person who has attained this knowledge will be unmoved, because he sees that all is in accordance with nature and *logos*; he will then freely and happily accept everything that life has in store for him. Although the teachings of the Stoa are individualistic in character, they did not advocate aloofness but an active role within the world; in this respect, Stoics differed from Epicureans. According to the Stoics, the world and its various manifestations of authority and property did not require change. Since they saw everyone as part of nature and therefore part of *logos*, the Stoic doctrine had the potential to be critical of the existing social order or even to become a-social. In practice, however, Stoicism did not attack the social order, because the essence of Stoic thinking is acceptance: the sage relies on his inner self, and freedom is inner freedom. The ideas of the Stoa were particularly popular with the Romans. The concept of unmoved acceptance within the fullness of life fitted in with their norms and values, whereas the aloofness of the Skeptics and Epicureans did not.

Traces of the escapism of Hellenistic philosophy may also be found in literature in the form of exoticism, the theme of the noble savage, pastoral poetry, and utopian writings. Some of the foregoing religious phenomena can also be seen against this background. All of this reflects feelings of unrest, nurtured by the loss of *koinonia* (especially the ever-increasing social inequality) and insecurity brought about by the political changes. This, however, did not result in attempts to change society. The Utopians, like the philosophers, did not preach a rejection of social inequality or slavery; they offered a way to deal with one's poverty or one's servitude. The Hellenistic period did not produce any social alternatives. The very few traveling cynic philosophers were a-social loners with hardly any measurable influence. Skeptics, Epicureans, and Stoics at a certain point recoiled from the consequences that might come from their long-running debates about individuality and freedom.

Alexandrian science and scholarship

During the Hellenistic period, science, in our sense of the word, for the first time detached itself from philosophy. We even see a physical separation: philosophy remained primarily an Athenian concern, while science flourished at the courts of the various dynasties, especially in Pergamon and Alexandria. We should also mention Syracuse, mainly because of one man, Archimedes (c. 250 BC), and his accomplishments in the fields of geometry, optics, (hydro)statics, astronomy, and engineering. The cultural and intellectual flourishing of Hellenistic cities was mostly (but not entirely) owing to the patronage of the princes and the elite. As a result, intellectual culture was an affair of the elite; on the one hand they invested vast sums of money in the arts and sciences, leading to developments of an unprecedented magnitude; on the other, however, art and learning increasingly took place outside the range of vision of the average city dweller.

Alexandria, in particular, became famous as a center of pagan and Jewish scholarship. Thanks to Ptolemaic patronage, the Alexandrian Mouseion, the "sanctuary of the Muses," grew into the largest conglomerate of art and scholarship in the whole of antiquity: a large-scale continuation of Plato's Academy and Aristotle's Lyceum. The Mouseion was unprecedented in its scope, the result of euergetism on an enormous scale, which was much to the honor of the Ptolemies. Apart from prestige, there was a practical side to it: the Mouseion's librarian was also responsible for the education of the heir to the throne. At the Mouseion, scholars and artists lived together in a pleasant intellectual atmosphere, somewhat in the style of an Oxbridge college. They met in the corridors and gardens or in the dining hall, and a unique library with a large number of titles (precisely how many, unfortunately, remains unknown) was available to them. Here, a considerable amount of research was carried out, especially in the field of philology and literary studies: that many of the Greek "classics," including Homer's epics, have come down to us is ultimately the fruit of Alexandrian exertions.

But there was more than textual criticism: Alexandrian astronomy and geography of the 3rd century could flourish thanks to Euclid's systematization of current mathematics (c. 300 BC). The most appealing example is Eratosthenes' fairly exact calculation of the circumference of Earth. It is remarkable that, despite all this theoretical activity, factual knowledge of the world remained limited. One is inclined to think that curiosity about the world at large would be bound to grow in a period in which the Greeks were founding cities in a good part of Eurasia and in which, because of Rome, the western Mediterranean became part of the horizon. But the Greek sense of superiority put a spoke in the wheel. The world was divided between Greeks and barbarians, and what was alien merely served to set off what was familiar: it could never be interesting for its own sake. A colorful story fitted this world view better than factual information, so not much effort was made to obtain such information. Long-distance commerce yielded little knowledge: there were hardly any traders who personally transported goods from the area of origin to the destination. Instead, there were fixed trade routes along which goods were passed from hand to hand. The reports of a few rare long-distance travelers did not alter this picture: Megasthenes, who had been sent to Chandragupta by Seleucus I, wrote a report about India that was in many instances reliable, but little credence was given to his observations. Pytheas (c. 300 BC), an astronomer and mathematic, may have been one of the few who left his home for scientific reasons rather than economic or political ones. He probably reached the Faeroe Islands, Norway, or Iceland, but nobody took his stories seriously.

Divisions between theoretical knowledge and empirical knowledge in the field of geography have their counterpart in the equally striking gap between technical knowledge and technology. This includes medicine. Medical studies made great progress, especially in Alexandria, not least because of the systematic application of dissection, as a result of which anatomical knowledge advanced by leaps and bounds. We do not find, however, that this led to an improvement of medical care. The same holds true for mechanics: much was gained on the theoretical side, but this did not result in a wealth of technological applications. Existing appliances, such as pumps and water clocks, were improved, and some new ones introduced, for instance, the simple but revolutionary screw supposedly invented by Archimedes. Much progress was made in the field of military technology, for example, with artillery and siege engines: princes did want to see some practical results from their patronage. But despite theoretical progress and some new applications, there was no technological breakthrough. In Alexandria, scientists experimented with complicated hydraulic systems and even with steam propulsion, which resulted in a fully operational miniature "steam engine," but there was no subsequent Industrial Revolution. Insufficient knowledge of materials, limited engineering ability, and the low price of labor have all been mentioned as possible reasons. A conservative attitude may have been more decisive: developing theories could be seen as a proper pursuit, but engineering was manual work and therefore unworthy of a member of the elite.

Second, and perhaps more important, theoretical research was hampered by adverse currents; Hellenistic empirical rationalism was, in the end, no match for movements we would call "unscientific" or even "anti-scientific." The roads of philosophy and science may have parted, but it was philosophy that set the limits. Empirical thinking never found sufficient support, and the ideas of skepticism, for instance, were of course fatal for the development of science. In addition, astrological practices and the like increasingly became part of philosophy, instead of being opposed by it as had initially been the case. Even the Stoa, an eminent example of materialistic philosophy, at a certain point maintained that astrology had great value. Science followed suit and consequently was no longer science in our sense of the word.

PART VI

1 AD–500 AD

Chapter 6.1

A Historical Outline

Eurasian Communities

China

During the first two centuries of the Christian era, the Chinese Empire flourished. After a difficult period at the beginning of the 1st century, the Han dynasty managed to consolidate its power, and from 25 until 220 AD China was governed by the so-called Later Han, also known as the Eastern Han because the capital was moved from Chang'an to Luoyang. During the turbulent first two decades of the 1st century AD, the territories that had been conquered around 100 BC were lost: Vietnam in the south, Korea in the north, and also large parts of Central Asia, especially the Gobi Desert and the Tarim Basin. However, the Han immediately and with great energy set about reconquering what had been lost, and by around 100 AD everything was again more or less under control. During this period, trade with the West was thriving. The overland route was the so-called Silk Road, in fact a string of routes running from the Huanghe via a chain of oases through Sogdiana, Bactria, Iran, Mesopotamia, and Syria to the Mediterranean. Because the Roman Empire preferred direct trade, the seaway to India became more important than the overland route. India also supplied Chinese silk, as well as many other interesting products. From the start of Rome's imperial era, sea traffic between Egypt and India was more intensive than before. But China not only exported its silk, and the other products it had to offer, to the West: Han China was conducting trade with the whole of Asia.

Apart from nomadic intruders at the northern borders, populous China was relatively peaceful and orderly under a centralized administration with a vast number of officials. Culture was flourishing and so was technology: the wheelbarrow, the watermill, paper, the glazing of pottery, cast iron—these were all Chinese inventions from this period. Experiments were conducted that would result in the production of porcelain, and the manufacture of textiles, especially silk fabrics, was highly advanced. The regime, however, began to show internal weaknesses. Powerful clans, notably those of the court eunuchs and of the empresses and their relatives, vied with each other and with the bureaucrats, the Confucian officials. The central government weakened and there were

Antiquity: Greeks and Romans in Context, First Edition. Frederick G. Naerebout and Henk W. Singor.
© 2014 John Wiley & Sons, Inc. Published 2014 by John Wiley & Sons, Inc.

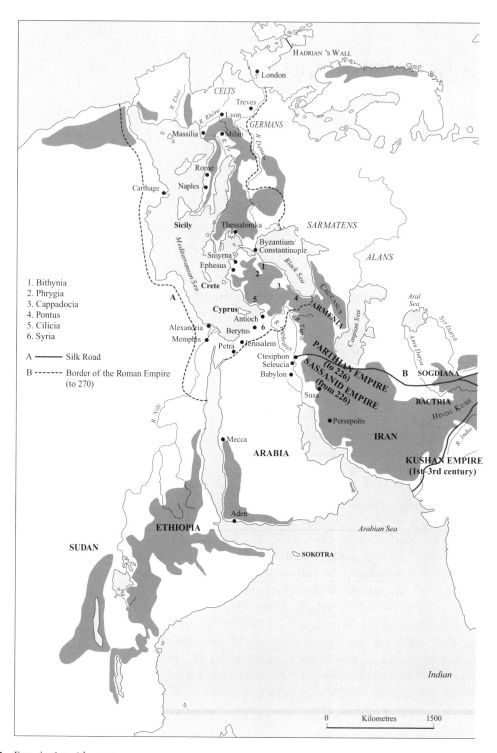

1. Bithynia
2. Phrygia
3. Cappadocia
4. Pontus
5. Cilicia
6. Syria

A ——— Silk Road

B - - - - - Border of the Roman Empire
(to 270)

Map 17   Eurasia, 1st–6th c. AD

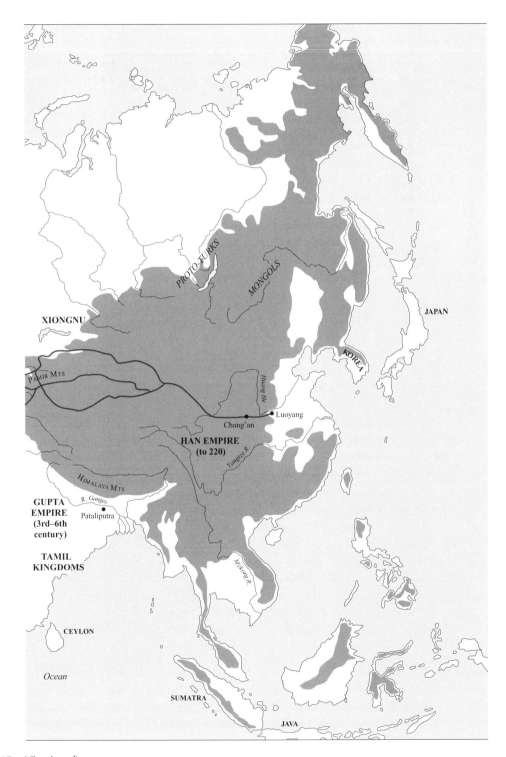

XIONGNU

PROTO-TURKS

MONGOLS

JAPAN

PAMIR MTS

KOREA

Huang He

Chang'an • • Luoyang

HAN EMPIRE
(to 220)

Yangtze R.

HIMALAYA MTS

GUPTA
EMPIRE
(3rd–6th
century)

R. Ganges
• Pataliputra

TAMIL
KINGDOMS

Mekong R.

CEYLON

Ocean

SUMATRA

JAVA

Map 17   (*Continued*)

re-feudalizing tendencies. Large-scale landownership increased, and small independent farmers were no match for large estates farmed by tenants: they gradually became the serfs of a small group of rich and powerful landowners. Those at the lower end of the social scale were increasingly worse off. The central government was harassed by rising internal unrest and by financial problems resulting from a decrease in tax revenues because of the decline of the peasantry. Apart from unruly peasants, usurping generals, and warlords who tried to take advantage of waning central authority, there was increasing pressure at the borders. The policy to establish "barbarians" as auxiliary troops within the borders proved to be a danger rather than a safety measure.

The period between 200 and 600 AD has been called the Chinese "middle ages." After 220 AD, the Han Empire broke up into three states: Wei in the north, Shu-Han in Sichuan, and Wu on the lower reaches of the Yangzi and in the south. Attempts to restore the Han Empire resulted in war between the three new realms, but these attempts in the end were unsuccessful. Even internally, the new states showed very little effective unity. The ensuing chaos, a succession of civil wars, and usurpations of power are reminiscent of the end of the feudal era in the 4th and 3rd century BC. It is remarkable that, now as then, cultural vigor went hand in hand with political decline. The northern and western borders lay open to "barbaric" invaders, proto-Tibetans and nomadic tribes of various cultural backgrounds who spoke Turkish and Mongol languages. Up to the Sichuan mountain range and the Yangzi, everything descended into disorder and fragmentation, a jumble of small "barbaric" states that were usually short-lived. Nevertheless, there was no significant cultural rupture: invaders were absorbed by China in an ongoing process of acculturation. The newcomers even continued the expansionist policies of the Han Empire. However, as has been mentioned before, acculturation is always a two-way development, and this was also the case in this period. China itself was deeply influenced by the "barbarians" within its borders. During the so-called Epoch of the Six Dynasties (3rd to 6th centuries AD), in the southern regions one weak dynasty replaced another, but not one was able to restore internal order, let alone reconquer the north. But in this case, too, expansionist policies were not completely abandoned and the sinification of southern China continued.

During the Eastern Han, Buddhism reached China via Central Asia. With it came elements of Iranian and Hellenistic culture: even Japanese Buddhist sculpture of the 7th and 8th centuries still shows traces of Western influence. A flourishing of Buddhism came only during the 3rd and 4th centuries. In that period, there was also direct overseas contact with the Indian subcontinent and with Sri Lanka. This was part of the commercial activities that were instrumental in spreading both Buddhism and Hinduism to Southeast Asia and the Indonesian archipelago. Buddhism, and the Indian scholarship that came in its wake, left a significant mark on China. Both further developed in China and from there found their way to Japan and Korea. The period from the 4th through the 9th century AD has been called the Buddhist era of Asian history.

Kushan, Central Asia, and the Indian subcontinent

The empire of Kushan flourished in the 1st through 3rd centuries AD in region of present North India, Pakistan, Afghanistan, and the Central Asian republics. Its center lay between

Gandhara and the upper reaches of the Ganges. Kushan, a descendant of the Mauryan Empire, was most probably a Tocharian realm. The Tocharians, the most eastern Indo-Europeans, had been evicted from Chinese Turkestan by the Xiongnu, a conglomerate of nomadic tribes that controlled most of the steppes north and northwest of China. The name Xiongnu is usually translated as "Huns," but whether the Xiongnu may indeed be equated with the Huns who appeared in Europe during the 4th century is uncertain. The Kushan Empire was of great importance as a crossroads of cultures: it was one of the regions influenced by Irano-Hellenistic culture and served as a bridge between India and China. It played a significant role in the dissemination of the Hellenistic heritage in South- and Southeast Asia and of Buddhism in Central Asia and China. The Indo-Scythian Empire of the Sakas and other indigenous realms were located south of the Kushan region. Around 240 AD, Kushan came under Sassanid (i.e., New Persian) influence; in the 4th century, it became part of the territory of the Hephthalites or White Huns, who were formally Sassanid vassals. The same century saw the emergence of a new empire in northern India: the Gupta Empire, whose center was the middle Ganges region. This empire subsequently expanded in all directions. After a brief period of intense bloom, the Gupta Empire broke up into an eastern and a western part in the 5th century AD; at its northern borders, it was threatened by the White Huns. During the 6th century, new Hindu empires came upon the scene, and also, in Afghanistan and Central Asia, the Turks.

Persia under the Parthians and the Sassanids

During the first two centuries of the Christian era, Iran was Parthian territory. The Parthian Empire was internally unstable and, moreover, came into regular conflict with Rome, usually as a result of aggressive Roman provocation. Periods of war alternated with periods of armed peace. The Romans tried to profit from the differences between, on the one hand, the Parthian rulers and, on the other, the Parthian and Iranian aristocracy. This necessitated a complex and subtle diplomacy. Rome was ceaselessly trying to expand, and some Roman emperors, deliberately emulating Alexander the Great, aimed specifically at enlarging the empire in the East. The emperor Trajan, most notably, established the provinces of Armenia, Assyria, and Mesopotamia after having beaten the Parthians. His successor Hadrian, however, gave up these newly gained territories in exchange for a peace treaty, and the Euphrates again became the border. Later, during the 2nd century, the Parthians in their turn invaded the Roman Empire. They were driven back, but peace did not return; there was a decennia-long situation of conflict with varying tactical chances. At the same time, the Parthians were fighting the Sakas and Kushan on the eastern borders of their territory. It was this warfare on two fronts and internal unrest that brought about the decline of the Parthian Empire. At the end of the 2nd century, the emperor Septimius Severus managed to conquer a large area beyond the Euphrates that, as the province of Mesopotamia, would be part of the Roman Empire until 336 AD, with only some minor interruptions.

In around 230 AD, the role of the Parthians was taken over by the New Persian Empire of the Sassanids. The Sassanid Empire began as a rebellion against Parthian authority led by a Parthian vassal and developed into a deliberate attempt to restore the former Achaemenid Empire. This, as has been noted, had also been the aim of the Parthian kings, but they had never been able to realize their ideal. The Sassanids were more energetic. Their often obdurate attitude toward the minorities in their territories was inspired by a return to a strict Zoroastrianism. The Greeks, who under the tolerant and syncretistically minded Parthians had known flourishing communities, were among the victims of these new policies. A more aggressive position toward the outside world also fits this image. For the Romans, the fall of the Parthian Empire meant a worsening of the situation: unlike the Parthians, the Sassanids did manage to establish a strong centralized state. Right from the beginning, they were a serious threat to the eastern borders of the Roman Empire. For centuries the Sassanids stood their ground and inflicted defeats on Romans as well as Hephthalites. The New Persian Empire lasted until 642 AD.

The Roman Empire and its neighbors

At the end of the 1st century BC, with the restoration of the republic as a pretext, the Roman state was transformed into a monarchy with monocratic power in the hands of what we call emperors. In 31 BC, Octavian, the adoptive son of Caesar, defeated what remained of his enemies; in 27 BC he received the name of Augustus. By that time the new political order had been largely established. The first two centuries of the Christian era were the heyday of the Roman Empire. At the end of the 2nd century AD, after almost 200 years of relative peace and order, Germanic tribes began to put pressure on the northern borders of the empire. During the 3rd century AD, the empire descended into internal anarchy as a result of never-ending disputes over the imperial throne. Provincial armies, harassed by intruders and dissatisfied with central power, advanced their commanders as candidates for succession. The ensuing civil wars took away troops needed for defending the borders. As a result, the mainly Germanic invaders could no longer be stopped: a vicious circle. By the end of the 3rd century AD, however, the implementation of a kind of permanent "state of emergency" led to a vigorous restoration of the empire. For its weak Western part, this proved only a temporary reprieve: during the 4th and 5th centuries AD, Germanic presence—both unauthorized, and authorized in the form of auxiliary troops—was increasingly felt and eventually led to the formation of a number of de facto independent states. The invasions of the 4th and 5th centuries AD and the pressure on the borders of the Chinese Empire in the same period may be partly ascribed to the same developments: the expansionist forces in Central Asia, especially the Huns and related peoples.

The Roman Empire

The Pax Romana: 1st and 2nd centuries

From January of the year 27 BC, the first Roman emperor Gaius Julius Caesar Octavianus, known as Augustus, set about restoring order following the civil wars of the 1st century BC. In complete accordance with prevailing Roman conservatism, this was presented as the restoration of the Roman Republic, but there was a monarchy behind the republican

Figure 38 The so-called Lyon Tabulae inscribed with a speech by the emperor Claudius (1st c. AD). This is a very famous inscription, engraved on two bronze tables, found in the 16th century in Lyon, and now in the Gallo-Roman museum there; hence, its name: the Tabulae Lugdunenses, the Lyon tabulae. The text, alas incompletely preserved, is that of a speech of the emperor Claudius, held for the senate in Rome in the year 48. In his speech, Claudius advocated, of course with success, that the senate admit to high office and to its own ranks inhabitants of the province Gallia Lugdunensis. It is for this reason that an inscription documenting this important step toward full integration of Gaul into the empire was put up in Lyon: they were the beneficiaries. From the rather digressive speech, we can see Claudius' love of history, which is also known from other sources: much of the speech is about precedent. The importance of this text lies in the fact that the historian Tacitus discusses in his *Annals* 11.24 the same speech: now we can compare what will have been, more or less, the emperor's own words with what an ancient historian made out of them. It appears that Tacitus gives a reliable account of what the speech was about, but shortened and rewrote it considerably. Photo: De Agostini/SuperStock

façade. The attempts to hide this monarchy were not all equally convincing; in fact, it became ever more blatant as time went by. During this monarchical regime—which had, of course, been prepared by the developments of the late republic—the old social system that belonged to a city-state was replaced by a new one that befitted an empire. The first three centuries of this new order, from 31 BC until 284 AD, are known as the Principate, after Augustus' constitutional arrangements in which he and his successors held the position of *princeps*, "first citizen." In this way, Octavian/Augustus had managed to fix a new course. In order

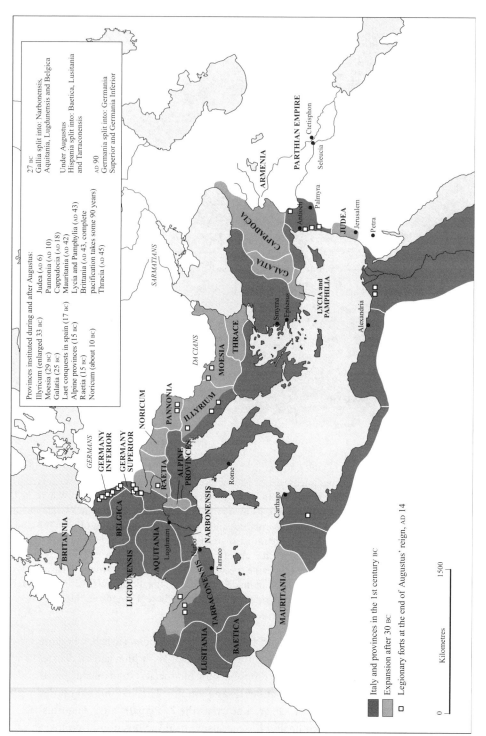

Map 18 The Roman Empire, 1st c. AD

Provinces instituted during and after Augustus:

Illyricum (enlarged 33 BC)
Moesia (29 BC)
Galatia (25 BC)
Laet conquests in spain (17 BC)
Alpine provinces (15 BC)
Raetia (15 BC)
Noricum (about 10 BC)

Judea (AD 6)
Pannonia (AD 10)
Cappadocia (AD 18)
Mauritania (AD 42)
Lycia and Pamphylia (AD 43)
Brittania (AD 43, complete
pacification takes some 90 years)
Thracia (AD 45)

27 BC
Gallia split into: Narbonensis,
Aquitania, Lugdunensis and Belgica

Under Augustus
Hispania split into: Baetica, Lusitania
and Tarraconensis

AD 90
Germania split into: Germania
Superior and Germania Inferior

Italy and provinces in the 1st century BC

Expansion after 30 BC

Legionary forts at the end of Augustus' reign, AD 14

0   Kilometres   1500

to make this very clear to everyone, he initiated a large-scale propaganda offensive: an impressive building program, a propagandist imagery that permeated the public sphere from monuments to coins, and the engagement of poets who had to sing the praises of the new order, most prominently Horace and Vergil. We cannot yet call them "court poets"; nevertheless, the *princeps* was their *patronus*. In Horace's poetry, the praises of Augustus should be read between the lines. Vergil, on the other hand, wrote an epos, the *Aeneid*, which shows rather obvious parallels between the mythical past of its hero, Aeneas, and the Principate. In addition, Aeneas was supposed to have been an ancestor of the Julii, Augustus' adoptive *gens*. The historian Livy was in the meantime working on an extensive survey of Roman history, a success story that provisionally culminated in the glorious present.

Augustus' first successors were Tiberius, Caligula, Claudius, and Nero; together they formed the Julio-Claudian dynasty from 27 BC to 68 AD. The relationship between *princeps* and the Senate was of crucial importance for the internal situation. The Senate was a bastion of republican ideals; would the monarchs manage to steer clear of its sensitivities by playing the game of the "restored republic," or would they risk a confrontation by being openly autocratic? A lack of acceptance from the side of the elite could even be an impediment for a de facto dictator. Caligula and Nero seem to have been rather unstable personalities. Still, we need not believe all of the horror stories told about these emperors. Such stories can be traced back to a senatorial revulsion against their being too autocratic or too philhellenic, or simply against their behavior, which was seen as unsuitable for a member of the Roman elite. But even capable administrators, such as Tiberius and Claudius, did not have a harmonious relationship with the Senate. Tiberius was an introverted figure; Claudius antagonized the Senate because of his reliance on his personal slaves and freedmen and his attempts to admit Gallic nobles to the ranks of the senators.

The major expansion of the empire came to an end with the reign of Augustus. After the annexation of Egypt, the pacification of the Spanish interior, and the shifting of the northern border from the Alps to the Danube, the dimensions of the empire did not change significantly. Augustus himself seems to have had plans to conquer the whole of Eurasia, although he did not have the slightest notion of its actual dimensions. However, his very first attempt to move the border from the Rhine to the Elbe floundered when it met Germanic resistance. In practice, offensive policies were replaced by defensive ones, except for those cases where the Romans saw a rare belated opportunity for expansion, such as the conquest of England and Wales under Claudius, which resulted in the addition of the province of Britannia. It is still a matter of debate whether this conquest served certain strategic and economic interests or was mainly an attempt by Claudius to boost his feeble reputation by following in the footsteps of Julius Caesar and coming up with a military success. A second major enlargement of the empire was the annexation of Dacia (roughly present-day Rumania), north of the Danube, under Emperor Trajan at the beginning of the 2nd century AD. Attempts to gain a foothold east of the Euphrates have already been mentioned.

Despite the conquest of Britannia, an enterprise that had cost much time and money, on the whole during the 1st century AD priority was given to the consolidation and pacification of territories that had been annexed at an earlier stage. This policy was not without success:

the 1st and 2nd centuries AD have been designated the era of the Pax Romana, a situation of peace and quiet under Roman authority. However, we should not idealize this; at the grassroots level, violence and insecurity were common. Everywhere, have-nots were subjected to systematic aggression from the side of the haves. Sometimes the have-nots turned the tables on the haves: in the rural parts of this immense empire, little was done to maintain public order, and encounters with robbers were rightly feared. Nevertheless, the overall image is one of long-standing internal peace. There were regular wars at the borders, but for the time being no serious threats to the integrity of the empire.

The most important crisis of the period took place in the late sixties. Nero's suicide, provoked by an army rebellion, meant the end of the Julio-Claudian house. The "year of the four emperors" that followed, 68–69 AD, presents a crisis of succession that may be seen as a shadow cast by future events. The background is as follows: the Roman monarchy did not rest on constitutional foundations, hidden as it was behind a republican façade. For this reason, there was no system to ensure regular succession by a legitimate heir. During the 1st and 2nd centuries AD, this generally did not pose a problem as sons or adoptive sons were put forward who enjoyed the goodwill of the army. But in 68–69 AD, this proved impossible, and the various army units each advanced their own candidate for emperor. The result was civil war.

Two major rebellions can be considered a side effect of the civil war of 68–69 AD. In the area of the Rhine and Moselle the Batavian Rebellion erupted, and in Judea the Jewish War, which had begun during Nero's reign, escalated. Both rebellions were quelled with considerable trouble, especially the one in Judea, which had not only been fired by political and economic unrest, but also by strong religious and nationalistic sentiments. The Jewish territories had been restless even before the rebellion and continued to be so afterward. We may place the conviction and subsequent crucifixion of a supposed Galilean rebel named Jeshu or Jehoshua (Jesus), a carpenter-builder from Nazareth, about 40 years before, against this same background of continuing unrest fired by anti-Roman messianism. The followers of this Jesus called him the Messiah (in Greek, the Christos). Their movement detached itself from Judaism during the fifties and sixties and gained support throughout the empire. In due course, these Christians would make a name for themselves.

What do these rebellions tell us about the maintenance of order within the Roman Empire? Was the Pax Romana threatened by internal unrest with a socioeconomic or, more importantly, ideological background, because subject peoples were waiting for the first opportunity to throw off the Roman yoke? This is a relative matter: apart from the Jews, who, inspired by very specific messianic ideas, entered upon the unequal struggle with Rome several times, there are not many examples of rebelliousness. As a result of their incorporation into the Roman Empire and the social and economic changes that came in its wake, there were rising tensions in some traditional societies on the northern borders that at times exploded in armed rebellion. This was, for instance, the case on the British Isles in 60–61 and along the Rhine and Moselle in 69–70 AD.

At the end of the "Year of the Four Emperors," provincial governor Vespasian emerged victorious. Vespasian, founder of the Flavian dynasty (69–96 AD), used military means to bring about the pacification of the empire. In order to obtain enduring peace, he made every effort to better integrate its various parts. His policies were definitely successful. Vespasian's successors, Titus and Domitian, were good administrators, too, but this did not prevent them from getting embroiled in conflicts with senatorial circles. In the case of the very autocratic, not to say tyrannical, Domitian, this conflict ended in bloodshed; first, the blood of several senators and subsequently that of Domitian himself, who was killed by his own Praetorian Guard. Another succession crisis was averted by diplomatic action: Nerva, an old *nobilis*, proved to be an acceptable transitional figure, even more so when he adopted Trajan, who had the confidence of the army, as his son and heir. This became a set pattern; the following period is therefore named the era of the adoptive emperors (96–180 AD). Interestingly, Trajan was the scion of a Roman family from Spain; for the first time, the emperor himself had been born outside Italy.

Trajan took an expansionist line: he established the province of Dacia on the northern borders and managed to repel the Parthians in the East. By the time of his successor Hadrian, however, the empire was running out of money, and Hadrian returned to a policy of consolidation. Hadrian's Wall in the north of England may serve as a symbol of these developments (even though since the time of Domitian no attempts had been made to subject Scotland to Roman rule): the border zone of the empire was marked with coast-to-coast fortifications. The term used for this phenomenon is *limes*: a defendable (and defended) border. Over time, such fortified borders appeared in various forms on all sides of the Roman Empire. The *limites* were, however, never meant to effectively seal off the empire from the outside world; the *limes* should be seen as a contact zone that allowed the regulation of border traffic—and which could function as a line of defence if necessary. Unlike Trajan, Hadrian was not popular with the senatorial elite, despite his sound administration: he was a philhellene and a restless man, always on the road.

Antoninus Pius, another transitional figure, was succeeded by Marcus Aurelius, who was a follower of the Stoa: a philosophical diary to which he committed his inner life has come down to us. During his reign, there was a significant change in the fortunes of the Roman Empire. Under Marcus Aurelius, pressure on the borders built up to breaking point, not because he was unfit to be an emperor, but because of demographic developments over which Rome had no influence whatsoever. These brought about an unstoppable drift of northern tribes toward the south. Population growth in the central Germanic area on the Baltic resulted in migrations that set in motion the whole of the Germanic world. The Danube border was held, and there were even some successes in the East, but this required considerable effort. Pax Romana began to lose its luster.

Crisis and restoration: The 3rd and 4th centuries

Augustus' Roman Empire flourished until about 160 AD. After that, there was continuous unrest at the northern and eastern borders; enemies even managed to invade the empire. At the end of the 2nd century AD, there were additional internal problems: the era of the adoptive emperors ended with the succession of the son, not the adopted son, of Marcus Aurelius, Commodus: alas, he proved a failure. The emperor's megalomania, his violent death, and the ensuing struggle for power brought the 2nd century to an ominous close.

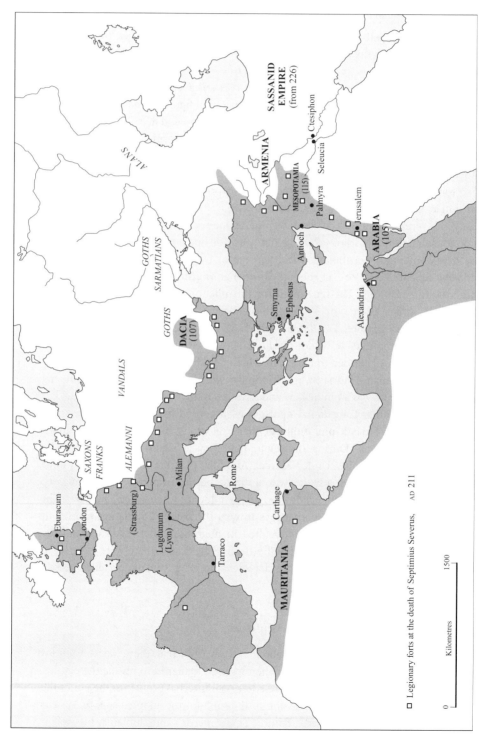

Map 19 The Roman Empire, 2nd–3rd c. AD

□ Legionary forts at the death of Septimius Severus, AD 211

ALANS

GOTHS

SARMATIANS

GOTHS

SAXONS

FRANKS

ALEMANNI

VANDALS

DACIA
(107)

ARMENIA

MESOPOTAMIA
(115)

SASSANID
EMPIRE
(from 226)

Ctesiphon

Seleucia

Palmyra

Jerusalem

ARABIA
(105)

Antioch

Smyrna

Ephesus

Alexandria

Eburacum

London

(Strassburg)

Lugdunum
(Lyon)

Milan

Rome

Tarraco

Carthage

MAURITANIA

0   1500

Kilometres

Initially, order was restored through the intervention of Septimius Severus, who had been a legate on the Danube. Septimius Severus, a forceful personality and capable soldier, was born in North Africa and was the first truly provincial emperor. He seemed to be able to turn both the internal and the external tide. His in-laws, however, were power-mad Syrians who were preoccupied by their own interests. His son Caracalla (211–217 AD) was an unstable and murderous man. After Caracalla was assassinated, chaos and anarchy increased, at first under members of the Severan dynasty. After Alexander Severus was murdered in 235 AD, the Thracian commander Maximinus was proclaimed successor by his troops. This brought dynastic rule to an end, and what followed was a long succession of usurpers, the so-called soldier emperors.

Army units advanced one imperial candidate after another; over a period of 50 years there were 25 emperors, not one of whom died in his bed. There was permanent civil war, and society was totally militarized. The economy collapsed because of inflation and impoverishment, partly caused by increasing fiscal pressure. Economic stagnation, or decline, went hand in hand with banditry. The population was ravaged by epidemics. Parts of the empire seceded, notably the so-called Imperium Galliarum (which comprised Gaul, Germania, Britannia, and Spain) and also Palmyra in the East. Goths, Alamanni, and Franks seized the opportunity and crossed the mostly undefended borders. The strong and aggressive Sassanids took over the role of the Parthians. Shortly after the middle of the century, the emperor Decius was killed in a battle against the Goths at Moesia near the mouth of the Danube; somewhat later, the Sassanids conquered Armenia, the Franks invaded Gaul and Spain, the Alamanni and Marcomanni threatened the Danube frontier, the Alamanni managed to reach Italy, the Goths overran Macedonia and the area of the Black Sea, and finally the Sassanids occupied Mesopotamia and Syria.

The empire showed signs of decline; that much is certain. One often speaks of "the crisis of the 3rd century," but both the exact beginning and the nature of this crisis are debatable. It is also highly uncertain to what extent contemporaries felt they were living through "a crisis." In any case, there was no question of defeatism; a seemingly unshakable confidence in its own strength and power undoubtedly contributed to the empire's chances of survival. Nevertheless, the problems were considerable. Feelings of desperation were perhaps reflected in the rise of religious fervor aimed at personal salvation. In this period religions that preach such salvation as one of their main tenets, such as Christianity, blossom. There was also an increasing involvement of the state in the beliefs of its subjects, something we not only find in the Roman Empire, but also with the Sassanids. One example of such state interference is the large-scale persecution of the Christians, which was probably elicited by the rather sudden increase in their numbers. With their exclusivist monotheism, the Christians were the ideal scapegoat for the problems afflicting the empire.

The 50 years following the death of Alexander Severus were not only a low point in the history of the Roman Empire, but also a turning point. That the empire did not fall, but managed to make a strong recovery shows us how resilient it actually was. Recovery, however, was not possible without substantial reforms. These reforms were, in fact, so fundamental that Greco-Roman culture, the product of a millennium-long evolution, was completely rebuilt within a few centuries. For this rebuilding process, the existing foundations were used; despite profound change there was undeniable continuity, and many of the reforms had their roots in the developments of the 3rd century AD. But there were also striking discontinuities. A new society was emerging, what we call Late Antiquity, which was in many respects different from what went before and may be seen as a prelude to the Middle Ages. Some of these discontinuities are highly dramatic, such as the eventual collapse of part of the empire and the ascendancy and victory of a new religion, Christianity.

As the 3rd century AD progressed, forceful figures entered the stage, who, through autocratic rule, managed to restore a modicum of order. These are the so-called Illyrian emperors, military die-hards from the Balkans. This development culminated in the reign of Diocletian, the architect of the aforementioned recovery. The era of recovery is therefore usually said to begin with his accession in 284 AD. The new social order is known as the Dominate; the emperor who had previously been the alleged *princeps*, was now openly called *dominus*, the absolute sovereign. The *dominus* ruled with divine authority and was surrounded by court ceremonial inspired by that of Eastern monarchs. The absolutism of the *dominus* is only one aspect of the totalitarian character of the new society. This is exactly as negative as it sounds: totalitarianism, even if never fully realized, was the high price that had to be paid for restoration of the internal order and the ability to defend the empire against external enemies. Its totalitarian features also formed the great weakness of the Dominate: in retrospect, for the Western half of the empire, the recovery of the late 3rd century was only a stay of execution. But it was a considerable stay; the West managed to keep its head above water for another century, now with and now without its Eastern counterpart. After that came a wave of "barbaric" invasions from the north that swept all away. The Eastern part of the empire proved more resilient; here, the reforms of the late 3rd and early 4th centuries were the foundation for another millennium of imperial history.

Diocletian's recipe for the restoration of internal order and the reconstruction of border defenses was: more soldiers, more bureaucracy, and, consequently, more taxes. The latter could only be effected by even more bureaucracy. A new social and state order emerged that, as has been pointed out, built on 3rd-century developments: these were now formalized. The *reparatio* ascribed to Diocletian, the "second Augustus," was therefore a relative matter, just as the first Augustus' restoration had been. Diocletian did not restore, he transformed. All his reforms, later continued by the emperor Constantine, had a military background that, nonetheless, affected the whole of society. Government and succession took a new form: a separate *Augustus* was appointed for the Western and Eastern halves of the empire. This was soon replaced by the so-called tetrarchy (system of four rulers): next to the two *Augusti* there were two *Caesares*, who were the designated successors of the *Augusti* and, like them, responsible for part of the territory. The provinces were subdivided into smaller units, which were regrouped into 12 so-called dioceses. Border defense was strengthened, and mobile field armies were set up. Increasingly, Germans from across the borders were enlisted: as a matter of fact, the army underwent a process of "barbarization," which would be of crucial importance for future developments. These reforms were financed thanks to the *annona*, a system of payments in kind (not to be confused with the wheat provision for the city of Rome of the same name) that had developed in the course of the 3rd century AD and was expanded into a regular tax system for the whole empire. In connection with this, attempts were made to completely regulate economic life and fix every individual's social status not only for the present, but also for future generations. The state that resulted from these measures was totalitarian in concept, but never in practice, for the simple reason that it lacked the necessary practical and logistic means to control everybody and everything.

Diocletian's arrangements for succession did not work: dynastic forces proved too powerful. After another civil war, Constantine, son of the *Caesar*, and later *Augustus*, of the Western half of the empire, became the absolute ruler in 324 AD. Constantine rejected Diocletian's system of succession, but in other respects continued his policies. He even kept a token tetrarchy: he divided the empire into four prefectures and raised three sons and a nephew to the rank of *Caesar*. Through his reform of the coinage system and introduction of the golden *solidus*, he managed to bring about the recovery of the monetary economy that Diocletian had unsuccessfully pursued. As a symbol of the new order, Constantine founded a new capital at the location of the *polis* Buzantion (Byzantium): Konstantinoupolis (Constantinople), a second Rome. But, unlike Rome, the new capital was Greek, and Christian!

The fact that Constantine, for unknown reasons, converted to Christianity, is of crucial importance for its development from minority religion to dominant religion to state religion. It is possible that Constantine appealed to the Christian god in his struggle for the emperorship, most particularly before the battle of the Milvian Bridge just north of Rome, in 312 AD. Here Constantine beat his rival Maxentius, and he may have ascribed his victory to the interference of the god of the Christians. Despite his conversion, however, he remained tolerant toward heathendom for a long time. In the course of the 3rd century, Christianity had expanded: it has been suggested above that there may be a relationship with the situation of crisis within the empire. In the context of Diocletian's reforms, persecution of the Christians was taken up again: Christian monotheism could not be reconciled with a new order under divine authority. But the anti-Christian mood was flagging. Constantine's conversion meant that Christianity was no longer a counterculture: it would become the religion of the rulers and, as a result, undergo profound change.

There was another side to being "the religion of the rulers": Constantine immediately attempted to subject the church to his authority, even where doctrine was concerned. It is clear that in the Christian empire the emperor remained the *dominus*. He could no longer be worshipped, but as he was in direct contact with the Christian god, he was definitely on a higher plane than an ordinary mortal. Because of its association with secular power, Christianity expanded even more. In 391–392, Theodosius the Great banned all pagan cults, and in this way Christianity effectively became the state religion. In the years before Theodosius' measure, a firm line had been taken with internal dissidents in order to establish a uniform orthodoxy. Now it was the turn of the pagans. Over a period of 100 years, the persecuted Christians had turned into persecutors.

After Constantine, the Eastern and Western part of the empire grew ever more apart. He had been unable to arrange succession, and the resulting civil wars affected the West more than the East. Two or three emperors continuously fought each other. Rome no longer had the power to stop the advancing Germanic peoples. These had been set adrift as a result of local (lack of food in the Germanic territories) as well as Eurasian (the westward movement of the Huns across the Central Asian steppes) developments. At the beginning of the final quarter of the 4th century, the Huns invaded the territory of the Ostrogoths in southern Russia and caused the Visigoths to flee to the other side of the Danube. Once permitted to remain inside the empire, the Visigoths rebelled: in the battle of Hadrianopolis (378 AD), they won a sweeping victory over Emperor Valens, who was killed with many of his troops. General Theodosius, who was proclaimed emperor and was subsequently known as Theodosius the Great, managed to temporarily pacify the Visigoths. Theodosius was the last emperor to rule over a united empire, but only for five months. After his death in 395 AD, the empire was divided between his two sons, and this partition turned out to be definitive. The formal division between East and West became a fact.

The Greek East and the Latin West

The distinctive character of the East of the empire

The East of the empire was Greek. The Greek language held a special position among the empire's many other languages, for instance, the Celtic languages of the West. Rome was aware of this fact: ever since the emperor Claudius, there was a Latin and a Greek chancellery. Of course, Rome did not simply adopt everything from the Greek world. In every acculturation process, influences move in every direction, and in the East, too, there were changes because of the Roman presence. There were, for example, organizational measures that enabled the Eastern territories to function within the imperial administration. In other fields, Roman culture was likewise enthusiastically embraced. Compared to what happened in the West of the empire, however, these changes were limited in extent and character. It may even be maintained that Rome continued the Hellenization of the East and promoted it by founding Greek *poleis* and supporting the Greek (and not the Roman) way of life.

The East was of great importance for the empire. At the beginning of the imperial period, the Roman territories between the Danube and the Euphrates were a patchwork of provinces and client states. Between the reigns of Augustus and Domitian, this region underwent a halting process of "provincialization." After all the client states had become provinces, Trajan, Marcus Aurelius, and Septimius Severus made attempts to incorporate territories east of the Euphrates; Rome also tried to move the southern frontier in the direction of the Arab Peninsula. In this way, it would seem, Rome attempted to create a buffer zone to protect the Eastern provinces, because these—and North Africa, which belonged to the Latin-speaking part of the empire—were clearly the center of the empire. These territories were more urbanized (or would become so during the 1st and 2nd centuries AD) and more densely populated than the provinces in the north and west of the empire, and had a stronger economy. With the rise of the dangerous empire of the

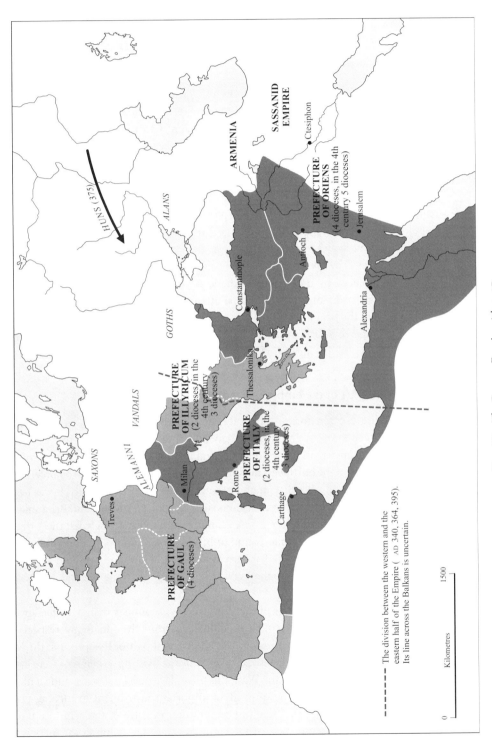

Map 20 The Roman Empire, 4th c. AD

PREFECTURE OF GAUL (4 dioceses)

PREFECTURE OF ILLYRICUM (2 dioceses, in the 4th century 3 dioceses)

PREFECTURE OF ITALY (2 dioceses, in the 4th century 3 dioceses)

PREFECTURE OF ORIENS (4 dioceses, in the 4th century 5 dioceses)

SAXONS

ALEMANNI

VANDALS

GOTHS

ALANS

HUNS (375)

ARMENIA

SASSANID EMPIRE

Treves

Milan

Rome

Carthage

Thessalonica

Constantinople

Antioch

Jerusalem

Alexandria

Ctesiphon

- - - - - The division between the western and the eastern half of the Empire (AD 340, 364, 395). Its line across the Balkans is uncertain.

0   1500

Kilometres

Sassanids, the defense of the Euphrates frontier would be more important to Rome than the defense of the Rhine.

The East after 395 AD

After some trouble with unruly Visigoths and various candidates for the imperial throne at the beginning of the 5th century, the East entered somewhat smoother waters during the first half of that century. The East had hastened to the aid of the West in fighting the Germanic Vandals, who had crossed from Spain to North Africa, but this ended in heavy defeats. Nevertheless, it managed to keep the Persians and the Libyan nomads at bay. The Huns were an even more redoubtable adversary, but they could in several instances be bought off. In the north and on the Balkans Visigoths and Huns had inflicted much damage, but Asia-Minor, Syria, and Egypt were intact. The empire was still wealthy and populous enough to supply both taxes and troops. The latter was especially important: it meant that, unlike the West, the East was not dependent on the support of unreliable Germanic "allies." What remained of the Germanic troops could in the course of the 5th century be replaced by indigenous soldiers. A period of internal chaos, in which—also thanks to Eastern diplomacy—Germanic attention was mostly turned toward the West, was followed at the beginning of the 6th century by a forceful restoration of the old order. Under the emperor Justinian, attempts were even made to recapture the West from the hands of the Germanic kings who had divided it among themselves.

The Western part of the empire

The Mediterranean territories, especially the eastern Mediterranean and North Africa, remained the center of the empire. But, generally speaking, all coastal areas and Italy were of greater importance than the more peripheral regions. The so-called "decline of Italy" in favor of provinces in the northwest during the 1st and 2nd centuries is debatable. Seen from Rome, these provinces were distant and of minor interest. Paradoxically, it was because of the somewhat marginal character of regions such as Gaul, Germania, and Britannia that the consequences of being part of the Roman Empire were more strongly felt there than in the Greek East. All in all, the Roman conquest brought many more fundamental changes to the West than to the East. In the East, tax systems, local law, and even old administrative units often remained intact; in the West, the coming of Rome was far more often an occasion for renewal.

The Celtic-Germanic societies of the West were less complex than Mediterranean societies, and were therefore wide open to influences from the—in many respects—more developed outside world. Urbanization was an essential part of this process: the Mediterranean world was, after all, characterized by city culture. Existing settlements were upgraded, and new cities were founded. In the West, this took place on a large scale, and all these cities were Latin cities. The army, too, proved an important instrument in turning provincial recruits into Roman citizens. Urbanization and the presence of the army were of prime importance for the dissemination of the Latin language and culture. But there was more than just Latin influence: there were influences from all over the empire. For this reason the

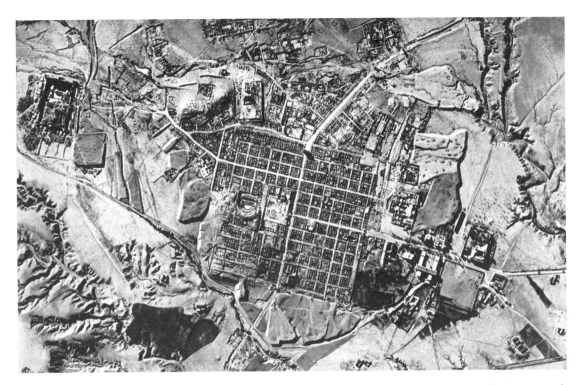

Figure 39 The Roman city of Timgad in Algeria (2nd–4th c. AD). Timgad was a Roman town in Numidia, in present-day Algeria. It is a good example of a Roman provincial town in the western parts of the empire. Such towns were built on a square ground plan with a regular grid, based on the layout of a Roman army camp, usually on virgin territory. Thus, these towns were new centers of Roman city life. Nevertheless, Timgad took its name from a local village, Thamugadi. After its foundation in 100 AD, the town was officially known as colonia Marciana Traiana Thamugadi (Marciana Traiana after the reigning emperor Trajan and his sister Marcia). The town had all the trappings of a Roman imperial town: a forum, a theater, triumphal arches, temples, market halls, bath complexes, dwellings for the elite with wall paintings and mosaics, and apartment buildings for the less well to do. In the photograph, one can see the city as it was laid out in the 2nd century AD, and a couple of "suburbs" of the 2nd, early 3rd centuries. The number of inhabitants is not known, but in its heyday (late 2nd and 3rd centuries), it will not have housed over 10,000. In the late 3rd and 4th centuries, Timgad was an important Christian center. Photo: from A.A.M. van der Heyden, *Atlas van de antieke wereld*, Amsterdam 1958 Elsevier

word Romanization is not used here; the term is too one-sided. Not everyone in the empire "became Roman," but every individual was an inhabitant of the empire and thus was affected by the process of acculturation. Most fundamental in this respect were the economic and accompanying social changes: economies that had always been self-supporting became part of the monetary market economy of the empire.

All this should, however, not lead to the conclusion that the Western part of the empire turned into an area with a homogenous Mediterranean city culture in no time. Rome did not have the slightest intention to exert direct authority and direct influence at all levels. Local elites and their networks of patronage were absorbed into the empire's interrelationships, but for many others little changed. Acculturation is two-way traffic: despite "empire-wide" unifying elements, regional differences continued and thrived. There are only a few instances of opposition against change; one example is the Batavian Rebellion. Such rebellions may be seen as so-called nativist movements in which, within a context of acculturation, the subordinate party reacts against the dominant one by emphasizing its own identity. In fact, rebellions of this kind are usually an indication that changes have already taken place. As far as the Roman Empire is concerned, the (temporarily) successful rebellions characteristically owed their success to the extent to which their leaders had become integrated in the empire and were able to fight the Romans with Roman organization and technology.

The West after 395

After the division of the empire, the weakest, Western part had few chances of survival. This is obvious from its previous history. When expansionist policies were replaced by a striving for consolidation, there was this long Western border zone where traffic had to be controlled and the unauthorized entry of large groups had to be prevented. Through military superiority and diplomacy (which often meant buying the loyalty of Germanic leaders), stability was maintained until the 3rd century, when the internal weakening of the empire opened the floodgates. Some attempts to turn the Germanic tide were temporarily successful, but in the course of the 4th century the frequency and intensity of the Germanic invasions increased, and it was ever harder to cope with the situation. In the late 4th century, a solution seemed to present itself: the Germanic intruders were given a place where they could live under their own leadership, as allies (*foederati*), and they were also given the opportunity to enter the Roman army to assist in keeping their Germanic brothers outside the empire. This solution offered few guarantees: the Germanic troops were unreliable. In the West (as in the East), Germans and Huns were regularly played off against other Germans and Huns, but the Germans were always well aware of their own interests. Over time, Germanic enclaves emerged that were de facto independent. Apart from outside pressure, there was continuing internal decline: recruitment and taxation were increasingly problematic, which resulted in ever more frenetic administrative measures. It was in this context that the elite turned away from the empire in a final attempt to secure its own wealth and power. In the 5th century, the Western senatorial elite was no longer inclined to comply with the central authorities' wishes; its hostile attitude rendered effective civic administration and taxation impossible.

After 395, the West had little to expect from the East. The imperial throne was continuously contested, and behind that throne stood Germanic generals, for instance, the Vandal Stilicho, who at the beginning of the 5th century de facto controlled the West. Stilicho, for that matter, was extremely competent, both as a soldier and as a diplomat, and Emperor Honorius' decision to remove him from power was disastrous. To begin with, the Visigoths and their king, Alaric, could no longer be controlled: in 410, the Visigoths captured and sacked Rome. The military significance of the raid was small, but its symbolic value was enormous. The fall of Rome came as an immense shock to all inhabitants of the empire. After Italy had been thoroughly plundered, and Alaric had died, the Visigoths moved to Gaul, which was at the time in a state of complete anarchy. Their kingdom in the southwest of France lasted until the beginning of the 6th century. In the meantime, Vandals, Alans, Suevi, and Burgundians had broken the Rhine frontier. They managed to reach central France and Spain. In 429, the Vandals crossed to North Africa, where they established a kingdom that lasted for more than a century. Their fleet controlled the western Mediterranean, and in 455 they even carried out an expedition against the city of Rome. The infiltration by the Franks, a conglomerate of Germanic tribes, was more gradual. From the 4th century, they had slowly penetrated the northern provinces, and during the 5th and early 6th centuries they, by degrees, conquered the whole of Gaul. The defense of Britannia had been given up at the beginning of the 5th century, and in the course of that century it was taken over by Saxons, Angles, and Jutes.

In the middle of the 5th century, both Romans and Germans were threatened by the Huns, who, under their king Attila, put pressure on the Balkans, Gaul, and Italy from the Hungarian plains. The danger was averted with military might and vast sums of money. Attila's death and the subsequent collapse of his realm put an unexpected end to the threat; it had been a narrow escape. Nevertheless, at that time the Western part of the empire could actually no longer be saved: from Scotland to Carthage, it consisted of independent Germanic kingdoms and some, equally self-governing, Roman enclaves, all under the completely nominal authority of the emperor. But not for long: in 476 the German mercenary Odoacer deposed the child emperor Romulus Augustulus and proclaimed himself king of the Germans in Italy. Was this the fall of the Roman Empire? Yes, because the fall of its Western part meant the definitive end of the empire's political unity. No, because nothing changed: the transition from what we call antiquity to the Middle Ages had been long under way and would continue for centuries. For those who lived through it, this was not a dramatic moment: Odoacer and his successors recognized the Eastern emperor; the Germanic kingdoms saw themselves as a continuation of the Roman Empire; the Christian, Latin culture of late antiquity did not disappear, but would form the basis of what was to come.

Chapter 6.2

The Social Fabric

Economic Life

The transition from the republican era to the era of the emperors did not involve dramatic changes in economic life. There were some new elements, such as the great economic power of the emperor and the ever-increasing financial needs of the state, which had to pay for the army, the bureaucracy, and the court—all conducted on an imperial scale. The wars of the late republican period had resulted in an economic depression in many (but not all) parts of the empire. The end of these wars meant recovery and sometimes considerably more than that. However, the fact that in some places the economy was booming should not tempt us into jumping to conclusions about the economic state of the empire. It is probable, however, that there was economic growth all over. The favorable conditions of the Pax Romana meant the population was growing, which implies an increase in economic demand. Productivity also probably increased: more land was used for agriculture, and this land was developed more effectively; we can also discern an expansion of non-agrarian activities. The productivity per capita may likewise have increased, not because of technical innovation, which was almost non-existent, but as a result of specialization or social stimulus. Whether this indeed happened is uncertain. The relative order and integration of the first two centuries of the imperial era certainly favored regional and inter-regional exchange. Governmental transports of tax goods and the like should not, however, be seen as a commercial activity but as redistribution.

Wherever there was growth, there was a rise in the level of prosperity, but not everyone profited to the same extent. During the 1st and 2nd centuries AD, the rich became richer, most of the poor remained poor, and the state also wanted its share. If agriculture did indeed generate a surplus, it was creamed off by the tax collectors. Some of the tax money went back to the agricultural regions in the form of soldiers' pay and other governmental expenditures, but how much was plowed back is debatable. All in all, apart from an increase in scale, there was little that distinguished the new era from the previous one. The empire remained an underdeveloped area where most of the population lived around the subsistence level on an income derived from agriculture. The rich elite made no

Antiquity: Greeks and Romans in Context, First Edition. Frederick G. Naerebout and Henk W. Singor.
© 2014 John Wiley & Sons, Inc. Published 2014 by John Wiley & Sons, Inc.

attempts to stimulate the economy; it was interested in consumption, not in investment. The emperors had no economic policy in our sense of the word. Needless to say, the imperial administration often concerned itself with economic matters, such as food supply and the balancing of tax revenues and government expenditure. But none of the emperors or their personnel made deliberate attempts to direct the economy. They merely tried to have enough in the government coffers.

Before going into details, it must be pointed out that it is almost impossible to give an overall picture of the imperial economy because of a shortage of data, especially figures. We cannot quantify essential matters such as production, trade, or taxes. In addition, we must ask ourselves whether drawing large chronological lines (indicating periods of high or low, for instance) or presenting rough geographical indications (East versus West, the situation in the various provinces) will result in something we can rely on. We are gradually coming to the conclusion that the character of the economy as well as the speed and direction of its development was characterized by considerable regional differences. For instance, evidence for the situation in the north of Italy does not necessarily hold good for its middle or south. Armed with this warning, we shall now, nonetheless, take a look at some general characteristics and trends.

Integration and disintegration

The integration of the provinces in the Roman economy is a characteristic of the imperial era. Although the provinces would continue to carry the heaviest burdens (which is not so strange in view of their economic potential), the dichotomy between Italy as the center of production and the provinces as the milch cow that was being milked for the welfare of Italy was on its way out. For Italy, provincial integration meant leveling out: from an economic (and also, as we shall see, from a political and social) point of view, Italy increasingly came to resemble other parts of the empire. Whether this indicates the decline of Italy is open to question: archaeological data seem to indicate a certain growth in the provinces and stagnation in Italy. If there was a decline, it took place during the 3rd century AD when cities (though not every city) all over the empire showed signs of crisis: Italy was no exception. Integration in the Roman economy meant that the provinces became part of an economic network that covered the whole of the empire. Paradoxically, this boost for the provincial economies (especially the ones in the West, which were extremely underdeveloped) spawned various processes of independent development, which affected this same network in a negative way. In the 3rd century and later, integration was therefore followed by disintegration, although in the meantime all economies had been raised to a higher level.

Integration of the provinces in the state economy also meant their entry into a monetary economy. This was stimulated by the use of money for collecting taxes and paying soldiers. The use of money spread both horizontally (all over the empire) and vertically (at all levels of society). Money was meant to be used in ordinary market transactions, but, apparently, it was not always available. Because of these temporary shortages of ready money, during the whole imperial period payments were just as likely to be made in kind. The extent to which every regional economic network was genuinely part of the monetary economy is therefore relative. These unintended shortages are an illustration of the lack of some form of monetary policy: one kept an eye on the circulation of coins, but there was no macroeconomic view of the flow of money. It seems that the Roman authorities saw money, with its evident propagandistic possibilities, as a political rather than an economic instrument. In general, however, monetizing tendencies had been so profound that even the deep recession of the 3rd century AD was only temporary.

This recession was partly the result of the depreciation of coins. During the first two centuries, imperial coinage had a very stable standard (which was changed only once, under Nero) with gold, silver, and bronze or copper coins in fixed relations. In many places, especially in the East, local coins were in use alongside those of the empire. The gold and silver coins, which were the prerogative of the emperor, had an intrinsic value. This meant that the amount of coins was directly related to the amount of gold and silver, a structural weakness of the Greco-Roman economies. During the 3rd century AD, when emperors were constantly short of money, there was a continuous depreciation of the coinage: at a certain point there was hardly any silver left in the "silver" coins. This is a fatal development for a monetary economy based on intrinsic value. In large parts of the empire, the monetary economy was abandoned. In addition, there was strong price inflation. There had been only little inflation during the first two centuries: a price rise of no more than 200% over 200 years. During the 3rd century, however, inflation rapidly increased. During the 4th century, the monetary system was reformed, which allowed a return to a monetary economy. The further history of the financial system is replete with uncertainties. For the emperors, it must have remained a matter of concern: we find that there were several reforms during the 4th century alone.

Agriculture, industry, and trade

As in the past, agriculture was the most important sector within the economy. There were still many independent peasant farmers, but there was also large-scale landownership. Landowners included the emperor and members of the *ordines*, but also other well-to-do individuals such as wealthy freedmen. Their land would be either cultivated by slaves or be given to tenants, *coloni*. It should be noted that landownership did not always imply large rural estates (*latifundia*); that was only one possibility. Often, however, the property consisted of a number of scattered plots of land. During the imperial era, landownership and the employment of tenants increased, especially in Italy and Sicily, in Africa, Spain and Gaul, and in the Balkans. In the 2nd century, most of the land of the empire was on lease, but the peasant farmer never completely disappeared and neither did the tiller-slave. It is certain that these various types of farmers and landowners encountered changes in agricultural production. Production became more market-oriented, even for those for whom self-sufficiency had been the norm. This was caused by the necessity to meet the needs of the army and the cities, and to have ready money at one's disposal in order to participate in the monetary economy, including the payment of taxes.

The manufacture of non-agrarian products mostly remained small scale, despite the fact that here, too, market-oriented production became the norm. There were some exceptions, however, such as imperial enterprises that worked for the army, the army's own production

Figure 40 Stamps on *terra sigillata*, naming producers, and a *terra sigillata* plate inscribed with the oven load of a pottery (1st–2nd c. AD). The four images on the left show stamps on *terra sigillata*, a popular kind of red earthenware. The four stamps read: Eros, Gaius Tigranus, Officina Bilicati (from the workshop of Bilicatus), and Grati manu (by the hand of Gratus)—quite heavily abbreviated, as is common in Latin inscriptions. These are the names of the owners of the potteries, not of individual potters or of mold makers—as we can judge from some surviving accounts. Eros and Gaius Tigranus were active at the start of the 1st century AD, in Puteoli (near Naples) and in Lyon; Gratus should be placed in the first half of the 2nd century, and was based in Vichy (Central France); Bilicatus' active life is dated to 30–50 AD, and his home was La Graufesenque, in the south of France. All stamps are taken from *terra sigillata* items found in the Netherlands; indeed, *terra sigillata* was exported all over the empire and beyond: *terra sigillata* produced in La Graufesenque was found in Sudan, Poland, and the south of Russia. The stamps are an important source for establishing patterns of long-distance trade. The image on the right is of a *terra sigillata* plate from La Graufesenque carrying a graffito text. The first two lines are Celtic and mention the numbers of the oven and the oven load. Next, we have a list of potters' names. Each name is accompanied by the type and the number of ceramics contributed by that potter to the oven load. We do not understand everything in the text, but some lines can be translated unambiguously, such as the fourth line from the bottom: "Felix Scota, plates 5200," and in the last line: "Masuetos, sauce bowls, 9500." When we compute the total number of items in this single oven load, we reach the staggering figure of 27,945 items. This was production on a truly industrial scale. Photos: a-d) © Rijksmuseum van Oudheden, Leiden, NL; e) Musée Fenaille, Rodez, France/Giraudon/The Bridgeman Art Library

centers, and some enterprises (for instance, potteries and brick works) where something like industrial-scale production took place. Market orientation means there was trade in manufactured goods. This trade, and the sale of agricultural products, was stimulated by the unity of the empire and the infrastructure that belonged to it. New roads (and some canals) came to serve as trade routes, although they often were constructed for a different reason, for instance, to emphasize the power and authority of Rome, or to facilitate the transfer of

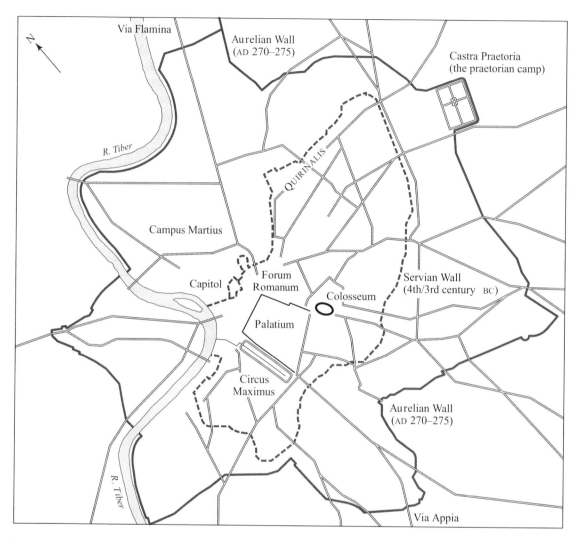

Map 21   Rome, 1st–2nd c. AD

troops, the provision of the army, and the imperial mail. Nevertheless, traders were free to use them, which they did, mainly for local trade over a relatively short distance. For long-distance transport, especially of bulk goods, ships were generally used, and there was inland shipping as well as overseas transport. The average tonnage of seagoing vessels was a mere 100–150 tons, but in the imperial period there were bigger ships (300–500 tons), too. The largest ship described in the sources was about 1200 tons, which is comparable to the 17th-century vessels of the Dutch East India Company. All ships with a larger than average tonnage were used for transporting grain from areas with a surplus to army locations, and especially to the big cities.

Cities held a special position in economic life. The Roman Empire had more large cities than were seen in Europe in any period before and long after. There were some cities with

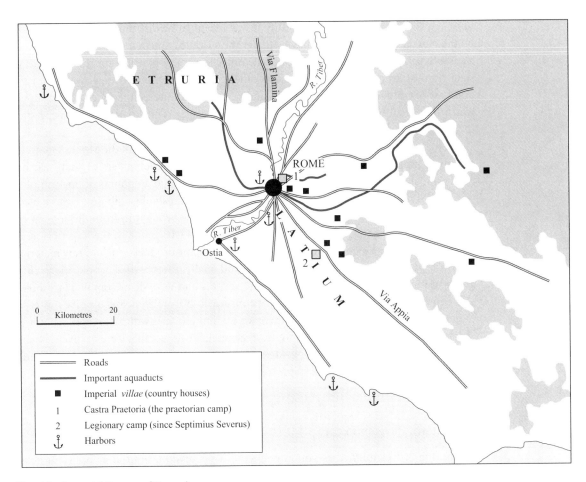

Map 22   Imperial Rome and its environs

populations of more than 100,000, such as Carthage, Alexandria, Antioch, Rome of course, and later Constantinople. And there were many where some tens of thousands of people lived, several of which were located in the Western part of the empire, for instance, Cologne, Treves, and Lyon. Providing food for these cities determined the main trade currents. All large cities were either located near the sea or, like Rome, near waterways that were easily accessible from the sea. It could not be otherwise; a metropolis could not be supported by its own hinterland. Rome is an extreme example about which we have some details because of the bread provided by the emperors to go with the circuses. At the time of Augustus, the number of people eligible to receive free grain (later free bread) was probably 200,000. There were some later modifications, but the number of recipients remained fixed. These 200,000 were men over the age of 10 (most probably), in possession of full civil rights, registered residents of Rome. If we add the younger boys, women and girls, slaves, and all others who for various reasons were not eligible, we can try to calculate the total population. This, it has been suggested, may have been about 1 million. This figure is uncertain, as are all numerical data concerning antiquity. It is clear, however, that Rome needed an almost unimaginable amount of grain, whether it was meant to be distributed or to be brought on the market. A separate bureaucracy under the so-called *praefectus annonae* took care of a smooth turnover of the grain supplies. Its officials were responsible for the transport of state grain to Rome for distributions and other governmental purposes, as well as for the purchase of grain in case of shortages. In addition, they monitored the general grain supply which they tried to control by granting certain privileges. This led to an increasing state involvement in the food supply of the city of Rome.

But man does not live by bread alone: on the basis of the material of the Monte Testaccio, a rubbish heap on the Tiber with roughly half a million cubic meters of shards, it has been estimated that at a certain point Rome imported 55,000 amphoras of Spanish olive oil, about 4 million kilos, per annum. And this is just Spanish olive oil: Rome was a black hole that absorbed vast quantities of food that had to be brought in from distant centers of production. And this, in proportion of course, holds true for all of the larger cities. In addition, there was an enormous need for primary-sector products, such as raw materials for textile production and building materials. And finally, cities needed people. Many cities in the pre-industrial world knew a mortality surplus and were demographic black holes. The empire's cities did not produce; they consumed. Naturally, a sizeable city's internal economy also generates income. And there were definitely cities with an exceptionally large export-oriented manufacturing economy. In general, however, cities were passive elements in the economic life of the empire, centers of consumption, which reflects the fact that the possessors of power, wealth, and status were city dwellers. Social inequality was at the basis of the cities' role as parasites.

Late antique developments

During the 3rd century, the economy entered a depression, both at a local and at an empire-wide level, although its degree showed regional differences. Production and trade diminished, and the depreciation of the coinage and accompanying inflation mentioned above led to demonetization. Large-scale hoarding of precious metals, mentioned in written sources and confirmed by archaeological finds, was both a cause and a result of this development. The authorities did their best to maintain tax revenues at a sufficient level, because both the civil wars and the frontier wars had to be paid for. Nevertheless, the incomes of cities and the state fell steadily, because of the general reduction of economic activity and the tendency to evade taxes. Attempts to control developments, for instance by increasing the amount of currency through further depreciation, or by enlarging the relevant bureaucratic institutions, were counterproductive and deepened the crisis.

People of all classes tried to avoid falling into the hands of the money-hungry state. In the West of the empire, the elite turned its back on the cities and withdrew to its estates. A career in the imperial government also offered a way out. It was no longer attractive to be a member of the city council and to do good. Beneficence had become a heavy burden, as one was not only supposed to give but also to stand security for tax revenues. There was therefore a trend toward autarchy. This trend was characterized by large agricultural estates with fortified *villae*, where the landowner knew himself to be ensured of food and further basic products and could keep tax collectors at bay. De-urbanization was a logical consequence: without the elite, city life went into a decline. Because of fiscal pressure, many farmers and craftsmen were forced to give up their independence and seek refuge with a powerful lord. They were welcomed, but kept in a dependent position and forced to perform services for their master. In time, this late-antique form of exploitation made it hard to distinguish between *coloni* and slaves. On the other hand, it also happened that dissatisfied *coloni* ran away. A radical way of escaping dire circumstances for both farmers and city dwellers was banditry: from the 3rd century onward there were many, sometimes large, groups of drifters ransacking the countryside. In the 4th century, the Christian church began to offer a safe haven for those who wish to escape from society and its burdens, in the form of monastic life or a career among the clergy.

The state opted for coercion. The aim of this policy of coercion was to find sufficient means to pay for the large, and ever-growing, amount of unproductive elements in the army and the administration. Initiatives toward this policy can be found at an early stage, but it was fully developed under Diocletian and Constantine. The system of coercion was exemplified by the so-called price edict issued by Diocletian, which was an attempt to control the prices of goods, services, and transport. We also increasingly find that social groups were tied to their profession (initially this was limited to crucial professions such as bakers or skippers, but it gradually spread to other professions), to their position in the administration (members of city councils and officials), or to the soil (*coloni*). The exchange of goods between producers on the one hand and the army and bureaucracy on the other was no longer left to the free market but strictly regulated, as was the wheat supply of Rome, Constantinople, and some other major cities. Diocletian also introduced a new tax system, the *annona*, a direct levy based on the number of inhabitants and the surface area.

All of this was ineffective: the coercive measures only led to a further decline of the economic network, because people tried to find ways around the rules and regulations. This is also reflected by the formation of estates that were, in effect, small states within the state, where officials were no longer welcome. The economy of the Western part of the empire became regionalized and shrank because of the decline of production and trade; tax revenues fell accordingly. Although all of this contributed to the fall of the West, the Roman economy itself survived the collapse of the empire. In several places, people reverted to self-sufficiency or underdeveloped market systems; nevertheless, despite general decline and deterioration, the church and the Germanic states retained elements of antique economic life, for instance, the villa system and the monetary economy.

Social Hierarchy

The Ordines

The transition from republic to Principate showed as little revolutionary change in social structures as there was in economic life. The fact that the social pyramid was now crowned by the person of the emperor was, of course, significant, and led to adaptations of many kinds. But the social relationships between "high" and "low" remained essentially the same. During the first three centuries of the imperial period, the top of the social pyramid consisted of three classes. These had emerged in earlier times, but were further formalized at the beginning of the imperial era. To begin with, there was the *ordo senatorius*, which Augustus and his successors distinctly separated from the second class, the *ordo equester*. In order to belong to the *ordo senatorius*, one had to possess a minimum property of 1 million *sestertii* and be well born (or obtain an imperial edict that banished the obstacles of a humble origin). Members of this class were supposed to comply with certain rules of conduct: they were not allowed to fight in the arena, for instance, or to marry their liberated female slaves. Sons of senators were automatically admitted into the *ordo*, but they had to satisfy all the qualifications: this aristocracy was not just based on birth. Members of the *ordo senatorius* typically went through the following *cursus honorum* (administrative career): first, some minor official functions in Rome, followed by a term as an officer in the field; subsequently the lower magistratures (beginning with the function of *quaestor*, which involved inclusion in the Senate), and then the *praetor*-ship and perhaps the consulate, which could both lead to the position of provincial governor, either in the service of the emperor or of the Senate.

During the imperial period, the Senate on average consisted of 600 members; the *ordo* of about 2000. Despite its very limited numbers, the *ordo* knew a certain internal stratification: *nobiles* who had consular ancestors formed a separate class. On the other hand, there were newcomers: families belonging to the *ordo senatorius* had a remarkable tendency to die out (possibly because their members deliberately limited the number of children, had no children at all, or remained unmarried). This necessitated the admission of these so-called *homines novi*. Initially the "new blood" came from Italy, later increasingly from the provinces. The recruitment was, however, selective; during most of the 1st century, only Roman citizens from Latinized provinces were eligible. In due course, very sparingly, a few Greek-speaking individuals were admitted. And not every speaker of Latin could pass muster: despite the intervention of Emperor Claudius, only very few Gauls were admitted to the Senate during the 1st century. It was only by the early 3rd century that the *ordo senatorius* and the *ordo equester* mainly consisted of non-Italians.

The *ordo equester* was the second class. Its membership required a minimum property of 400,000 *sestertii*, three generations of free birth, and registration in a membership register. Formally, one's origins did not play any role, but in practice membership became hereditary. This *ordo* likewise involved established rules of conduct and probably had some tens of thousands of members. It was a rather heterogeneous group, so there was definitely an internal stratification. A small elite of central government officials increasingly set itself apart. The fact that only a minority of the *equites* had an administrative career explains the smallness of this group. Such a career, or *cursus*, usually passed through the following stages: one began as an army officer, after which one might become *procurator* (the financial assistant of a provincial governor, or the governor of a small province). A few were subsequently promoted to one of the so-called "major prefectures": *preafectus vigilum*, *praefectus annonae*, *praefectus Aegypti*, and *praefectus praetorio*, respectively, head of the fire brigade and police in Rome, head of the grain supply in Rome, governor of Egypt, and commander of the Praetorian Guard, the imperial elite forces. The *ordo equester* was a reservoir of new senators: we have just mentioned the *ordo senatorius*' need for fresh blood. The *ordo equester* itself was supplemented by members of the city elites and also from the ranks of the army. This was especially the case after the 2nd century, when there was increasing social mobility within the lower classes.

The *ordines decurionum* made up the third class. Every city had its own *ordo*, which consisted of the members of the city council, the *curia* or *boule*—hence the name *decuriones* or *curiales*, and in the East, *bouleutai*. All in all, these *ordines decurionum* were a very heterogeneous group. If we assume that there were about 2000 cities in the empire, there must have been more than 200,000 *decuriones*, and, of course, the elite of *metropoleis* such as Ephesus, Antioch, or Carthage cannot be compared to that of some insignificant provincial town. The second and third class to a certain extent overlap: *equites* were, as a matter of course, often *decuriones*, but *decuriones* were not usually *equites*. Members of the *ordo* had to be of good birth, which in practice meant that freedmen (but not their sons) were excluded; they had to be wealthy (we have criteria that vary from 20,000 to 100,000 *sestertii*), and they had to be morally acceptable (no record of convictions, an honorable profession). Wealth was by far the most important criterion, but being born into a decurial family was, at least de facto, a great help. The importance of property should be seen in the light of euergetism: *decuriones* were supposed to be the beneficiaries of their community. What has been said about euergetism in the chapters on Hellenistic city life holds good here as well. It may even be said that euergetism rose to unprecedented heights; during the first centuries of the imperial period, the (partly institutionalized) munificence of its elites kept cities afloat. The wealthiest individual in the empire, the emperor, naturally surpassed the members of the elite as a large-scale *euergetes* within the city of Rome, but also outside of it.

The general population

Together the three *ordines* made up a very small minority: women and children included possibly between a half and one percent of the total population. From the 2nd century, the division between this group and the rest of the population acquired a legal basis: the *honestiores* against the *humiliores*. But the fact that the dividing line between the elite and "the rest" was of prime importance does not mean that the 99% who made up "the rest" were a homogenous group. There were several other legal and economic dividing lines. The difference between citizen (*civis*) and non-citizen (*peregrinus*) still had a certain importance at the beginning of the imperial era, but when every inhabitant of the empire became the subject of a single monarch, this legal distinction gradually lost much of its significance. Roman citizenship used to have some attraction for the provincial elite, possibly more for ideological than for practical reasons, but as it became more common it could no longer function as a bait. The final outcome of this development was the so-called *constitutio Antoniniana* of 212, which conferred Roman citizenship on all (or almost all) free inhabitants of the empire. By then, however, citizenship had very little meaning: in practice, only the *honestiores* enjoyed the privileges that came with Roman citizenship, and the rest of the population had been reduced to the legal level of *peregrini* or slaves.

In addition, it should be mentioned that in the Greek East, citizenship had never been granted on the same scale as in the West. The division between the Greeks and the Hellenized on the one hand, and the "oriental" population of the inlands of Syria, Palestine, and Egypt on the other, was something Rome inherited from the Hellenistic era. The first

Figure 41   Grave stele of Regina, from South Shields on Hadrian's Wall (2nd–3rd c. AD). This gravestone was discovered at South Shields, on Hadrian's Wall, and is preserved in the Roman Fort Museum there. This stone, from the 2nd or 3rd century AD, is a perfect illustration of the cosmopolitanism of the Roman Empire. The epitaph reads as follows: "To the spirits of the departed. Barates from Palmyra [put up this stone] for his freedwoman and wife Regina, a Catuvellaunian. She was 30 years of age." The text goes on, in Palmyrene: "Regina, freedwoman of Barates. Alas!" Regina, who has a Roman name, is a member of the Celtic tribe of the Catuvellauni, who were based in Hertfordshire, immediately to the north of London. She was the slave of Barates from Palmyra, in the far east of the empire. At some stage, Barates gave her freedom, and married her. On her gravestone, she is portrayed as a wealthy lady: she has risen in the world. Barates is far from home, but he is not the only one hailing from Palmyra on Hadrian's Wall: we have the gravestone of a Barates from Corbridge. That is nearby, and it may be the same Barates, but the name was quite common in Palmyra. And there must have a Palmyrene stone mason at hand: the style of Regina's grave marker is Palmyrene, and of course there is the Palmyrene text. Photo: © Tyne & Wear Archives & Museums/The Bridgeman Art Library

two groups were eligible for Roman citizenship, whereas the others were not. But the Greeks and similar groups were not given citizenship as readily as comparable individuals and communities in the West.

The distinction between the free-born (*ingenui*), the slaves (*servi*), and the freedmen (*liberti*) was and remained more important than the one between citizens and non-citizens. Slavery was normal during the whole of the imperial period, although we have no figures. For some towns or regions, the argument can be made that about one-third of the population was un-free. On the other hand, in several parts of the empire there were no large communities of slaves; this phenomenon was confined to Italy and parts of North Africa, and some places in the Greek East where there were concentrations of slaves. Slavery never disappeared, but the number of slaves may have fallen during the imperial period. The virtually unlimited influx of slaves that had been characteristic of the 2nd and 1st century BC came to an end when Roman expansion was halted, but the external sources never ran completely dry because war and the capture of people continued. It is unclear whether the decline in external supplies may have been compensated for by the birth of slaves within households (as children of slaves), or by a supply of free individuals who sold themselves or were sold by their destitute parents. Slaves who were private property were probably well treated during the imperial period (a trend that is also reflected by legislation) and could hope for liberation (*manumissio*). Prisoners of war and convicts who were forced to work in the mines, however, led a hopeless (and probably rather short) life. On the other side of the spectrum were the slaves and freedmen who belonged to the imperial court, the so-called *familia Caesaris*. Several among them became so wealthy and powerfull that they cannot possibly be equated to the general mass of deprived and powerless slaves.

The free, too, could be in a dependent position; we have clear examples of this from Egypt, Gaul, and Asia Minor. Dependence could take many forms, ranging from slavery resulting from debt to the relative freedom of certain groups of tenants. As has been mentioned above, after the 2nd century, patron–client relationships between the rural population and the landowning elite developed into a kind of serfdom. This is another example of a leveling trend (compare what has been said about citizenship earlier): slave and free man came to resemble each other.

In most cases, freedmen invisibly merged with the free, even when bonds of patronage often tied them to their former masters. The wealthy *liberti* held a special position: they fell between two stools, because their status of former slave and their social position as rich individuals could not easily be reconciled. The number of wealthy individuals among the *liberti* was, in fact, somewhat out of proportion: we should be aware that these might have been people who had gained experience (and property) as the slaves of merchants, bankers, and entrepreneurs. Once free, a freedman often bought land, and it was only his origins that prevented him from joining the ranks of the *decuriones*. Sometimes the rule that *decuriones* should be born free was disregarded: the *liberti*'s money was welcome. Usually, however, members of this group were given a special function, that of *Augustalis*, which on the one hand set them apart and on the other hand enabled them to benefit the city with their wealth. The *Augustales*, sometimes even explicitly designated *ordo* (the *ordo Augustalium*), formed a college that directed the city's imperial cult. In this way, rich freedmen could be involved in the city's euergetism.

In this discussion about slaves and freedmen, much has been said about the contrast between the rich and the poor. The existence of wealthy freedmen, and even of wealthy slaves, makes it clear that the distinction between the rich and the poor did not correspond with the distinction between the elite and the masses. The members of the three *ordines* may have been rich or very rich, but not every man of means belonged to the *ordines*. Disregarding their position in the official order, the rich could also be termed *potentes*, in Greek *dunamenoi*, "magnates," those who, within a network of patronage, manage to ensure a maximum number of clients. Some of those below the level of the *ordines* may have been (relatively) rich; the majority of the empire's population was poor or very poor. But they, likewise, were not a homogenous group, even though during the imperial period homogeneity increased as the gap between the rich and the poor widened. There was especially a large ideological difference between the poor city dwellers and the equally poor rural population. The city dwellers, a very small part of the total population, felt nothing but disdain for "those stupid yokels." *Rusticitas*, "rusticity," also stands for a lack of culture; *urbanitas*, "urbanity," is almost synonymous with culture and refinement.

In this discussion about the contrast between the rich and the poor, we should also examine the extreme un-equalizing tendencies that characterized the Roman world. Sources tell us about properties of hundreds of millions of *sestertii* (hundreds of times what was required for membership of the highest *ordo*), but on the other hand poverty could be dire: in Egypt, tax collectors apparently considered it worth the trouble to register the ownership of one-tenth of a house or one-sixth of an olive tree. This also was true for incomes from government office: in the 1st century, a common legionary earned 900 *sestertii* a year; his officer, the *centurio*, made 15,000; the highest-ranking *centurio* 60,000; the *legatus Augusti* 200,000; the *proconsul* of the province of Asia pocketed 1 million *sestertii* a year.

Within the agrarian community that was the Roman Empire, property meant above all land. The unequal access to landownership was the basis of economic and social inequality, and it was maintained through heredity. Although we definitely find social mobility (both upward and downward), there were many insurmountable obstacles on the road to wealth. The groups that best managed to penetrate the ranks of the elite were often freedmen and, as their position gained importance in the course of the imperial period, soldiers and officers.

Late antique developments

During the 3rd century, citizenship, free birth, and an Italian or other geographically central background lost their significance. Power, status, wealth, and membership of an *ordo*, which at one time were almost synonymous, became disconnected. As a result, the social underclass became more homogenized (and poorer), whereas the upper classes became more differentiated. Despite all differences between them, both town and country presented the image of large groups of destitute and oppressed people without any rights. The *coloni* may serve as an illustration: legally, they were free individuals with a right to property, but in fact they were serfs and, since Diocletian, bound to the soil, obliged to perform services for their lords, and to marry within their class. Imperial legislation openly recognized the fact that their position was no different from that of slaves. The elite, on the other hand, came to consist of rich, but as a group powerless, senators, powerful *equites* and military men, and locally important *decuriones*, who were increasingly exploited by the state. Apart from origins and property, political loyalty, legal education, and especially military talent now were avenues toward bettering one's situation.

The reforms of the late 3rd century resulted in a formalization of the changes that had occurred earlier. Senators and *equites* merged into one single *ordo*: a new *ordo senatorius*. During the late 4th century, this new *ordo* saw the introduction of a hierarchy, from *clarissimi* via *spectabiles* to *illustres*, which was related to specific official functions. This constitutes the formalization of a hierarchical order that had been in the making for a long time. Heredity was now of little importance: whoever attained the rank of *clarissimus*, either in the army or in the bureaucracy, became a member of the senatorial class. The *illustres* were a select group: they were the ones who were genuinely rich and educated, former consuls and distinguished (former) ministers, who increasingly came to dominate the senates of Rome and Constantinople. Below the *ordo*, but still within the elite, were the bureaucrats (*officiales*) and the lower-ranking officers. Dignitaries of the church fell outside the official ranking, but should of course be considered as members of the elite. And finally there are the *curiales*, who more generally used to be called *decuriones*. Despite the fact that they were still mostly large landowners, it is doubtful whether they could still be seen as belonging to the elite; more than any other of the groups that have just been mentioned, they had fallen victim to the central government's coercive policies. They certainly no longer belonged to the *potentes*; in the 4th century, this term was only used for members of the Senate, high-ranking civil administrators, and military commanders.

Political Organization

Imperial power and imperial bureaucracy

In the foregoing, it has been argued that the transition from republic to Principate brought no dramatic changes for the larger economic and social structures. The transition was, however, of great significance for the political structures of society, even though the changes had been long developing. An autocrat managed to concentrate central authority in himself. The modern German word *Kaiser* ("emperor") points at the monarchy behind the republican façade of Augustus' new order; it was derived from the personal name Caesar that was adopted by all Roman emperors. In Latin, however, there was no equivalent for "emperor" or *Kaiser*: Caesar was a personal name; *imperator* was a title that indicated the power of *imperium* and military victories; Augustus ("Exalted One") was a quasi-religious title for a great patron who has everybody as his client—it also became a personal name for emperors. The term *princeps* did not belong to the official titles; it means "the first citizen," the first of the senators, the person at the top of the social pyramid. In the ordinary parlance of the East of the empire, the term *basileus* (king) was used, but never in official documents. This obscure terminology was introduced by Augustus because of the sensitivities of the elite: Caesar's luck had turned when he had adopted the title of *rex* (king). This time the elite had to be humored, on the one hand to definitely end the period of civil war and on the other hand to involve the members of the elite in the new system that aimed to guarantee peace and regulated governance. As a result hereditary succession could not be formally arranged, which led to many problems.

The constitutional foundation of the Principate was very limited and concerned two derivatives of republican offices, the first of which was the *tribunicia potestas*, the "authority of tribune of the people." This gave the emperor personal immunity, the right of veto, the right to summon the Senate and *concilium plebis*, and the right of initiative. The *tribunicia potestas* also had ideological significance: it presented the emperor as the "protector of the people." Second, the emperor was able to control the empire through his *imperium proconsulare*. This *imperium* is called "proconsular" because the *princeps* possessed *imperium* without actively taking office as *consul*; it implied the governorship of part of the provinces, the so-called imperial provinces, especially border provinces, which in practice meant the emperor was the commander of most of the army. But the emperor could also intervene in provinces of which he was not the governor, and we do, indeed, find that he was not only involved in the administration of the imperial provinces but also meddled in that of the senatorial ones. In addition, every inhabitant of the empire, whether citizen or not, could appeal to the emperor against legal sentences, which may be seen as a broad interpretation of his *imperium proconsulare*. There is much uncertainty about the precise legal basis of the *imperium*, but, in any case, it is the central element of imperial authority: the reign of an emperor commences with the granting of the *imperium*.

Sometimes Augustus and his successors took on the consulate or the office of *censor*, but this was not a structural element of their position. The office of high priest, however, was: every emperor was *pontifex maximus*. This did not have great political importance; its significance was ideological. Finally, the Senate granted the emperor additional authorities on a regular basis (although the emperor, of course, often acted without legal authority): this concerns matters such as coinage, declarations of war and peace, the granting of citizenship, the founding of colonies, and the nomination of magistrates. After the abolishment of the popular assembly in the 1st century, the emperor habitually nominated the most important magistrates.

In reality, the power of the emperors was based on the army, not on the rather laborious and contrived fitting in of regal authority in antiquated republican molds. The emperor was the *patronus* of soldiers and veterans. Under the first emperors, the Roman army underwent radical changes: military service disappeared (although it was never formally abolished and was resorted to in cases of emergency) and the Roman army became a professional one, manned by volunteers who "signed up" for a long term. These "professionals" formed a powerful *clientela* that guaranteed the position of the emperor (but at the same time also threatened it). Another essential element was the wealth of the imperial house: loyalty may be bought—not just the soldiers' loyalty, but also that of the population of the city of Rome, which, because of its size and its proximity to the imperial court, was a significant factor. Every inhabitant was bound to the emperor through euergetism on an imperial scale: regular and special gifts, and "bread and circuses." The support of the army and his position as the most important *patronus* of the empire lend the person of the emperor *auctoritas*, unsurpassable personal prestige. It was to be expected that at a certain point the republican façade would crumble, and that gradually one would cease to pretend. In due course, a autocratic emperorship emerged, including the deification of the monarch.

There was no other authority functioning alongside that of the *princeps*. The Senate was divested of most of its power, as were the various popular assemblies, who saw their small share in the administration shrink even further. From the beginning, imperial decrees, edicts, and constitutions had the same authority as senatorial decrees, plebiscites, and laws, although this was only formalized under the Flavian emperors. Offices, too, lost their real power, with the exception of some lower-ranking magistratures of a technical character. The consulship became an honorary function and was every year fulfilled by several pairs of consuls, the duties of the praetors were reduced to the organization of circuses in Rome, and so on. But although the Senate was no longer a powerful factor, individual senators could still play an important role: the emperors had to use this group to fill the most important administrative positions. The *legati Augusti pro praetore* (the provincial governors to whom the emperor delegated his proconsular duties), for instance, were former consuls or former praetors (and so, of course, were the proconsuls who ruled the senatorial provinces).

The distinction between the imperial and the senatorial provinces reflects a dichotomy that characterized the entire administrative apparatus. On the one hand there was the new imperial bureaucracy, and on the hand republican offices continued to function. From a constitutional point of view, the imperial bureaucracy was made up of individuals in the emperor's personal service. In fact, this new administrative machinery was better suited to the ruling of an empire than the old republican city-state administration, and, over time, completely replaced it. The disparity between the imperial household and the vestiges of the republican state is very much apparent in fiscal developments: the old state coffers (the *aerarium*) lagged far behind the imperial treasury (the *fiscus Caesaris*). The imperial bureaucracy not only engaged senators, but also *equites*. In the 2nd and 3rd centuries, these even became the "real" bureaucrats. In addition, slaves and freedman were engaged for clerical work in Rome; something we might call "ministries" developed around the imperial court. It should be kept in mind, however, that this new imperial bureaucracy, despite its many responsibilities, was much smaller than that of modern states. During the first two centuries of the imperial period, it was tiny when seen in relation to the size of the empire: the whole civil and military bureaucracy consisted of no more than a few hundred people; so few, in fact, that they could all personally report to the emperor. It has been estimated that the number of officials in Han China, to give an example of a contemporaneous state with a complex bureaucracy, was 20 times higher. The aims of the Roman bureaucracy were, therefore, modest: maintaining peace and order and collecting taxes. This was mainly achieved by leaving existing bureaucratic structures within the empire intact or reinforcing them, and covering them with a thin veneer of Roman administration. In China, by contrast, the aim was a truly centralized government.

Provinces and cities

The empire was divided into provinces. Initially there was a distinction between senatorial and imperial provinces, but by the second half of the 3rd century this had disappeared. At the edges of the empire (and sometimes as an enclave within it), there was a decreasing number of client states. Italy held an exceptional position: it was not considered a province and, therefore did not pay direct taxes. Moreover, it was governed from Rome by the Senate and by Roman magistrates. But in Italy, too, there was increasing imperial interference, until Diocletian definitively abolished Italy's special status. Another special case was Egypt, which was an imperial province with a somewhat different character. Because it was essential for the empire's food supply, emperors scrupulously shielded it from the Senate.

Senators had to ask permission to enter Egyptian territory and, despite its size and wealth, its administration was in the hands of an *eques*, the *praefectus Aegypti* mentioned earlier, and not in those of a senator.

In the provinces, the Roman administrative veneer was indeed thin: below the level of the provincial governor, local government was left to the local elites. The upper echelons of the local elites met at provincial diets, but these meetings were mainly organized for the maintenance of the imperial cult, the exchange of tokens of honor, and the promotion of local interests in relation to Rome. These diets were not administrative institutions: in essence, administration was a local matter. This implies that the Roman Empire was a very mixed conglomerate of various constitutional forms: although taxation was everywhere well organized, it was without a uniform empire-wide system for a long time. Rome simply lacked the funds and the manpower to fill every level of provincial government with Roman magistrates and officials. Moreover, leaving existing structures intact was also a very effective solution.

This does not mean, however, that Rome left matters to take their own course: the East knew a venerable administrative structure based on the cities, but in most of the West of the empire this urban administrative structure had to be created—which was done accordingly, because the city was the basis of Roman administration. In North Africa, Spain, Gaul, and other northern provinces, Rome actively promoted the founding of cities. In imitation, or on the instigation, of Rome, a network emerged that consisted of *coloniae, municipia*, as well as urban communities that enjoyed neither Roman nor Latin rights, the *civitates peregrinae*. In the West of the empire, such cities probably mostly had a constitution based on Roman examples, as well as Roman jurisdiction: because in the case of the *coloniae* and *municipia* adaptation to Roman practice must have been obligatory, the *civitates* most likely voluntarily decided it was best to follow suit.

Everywhere within the cities of the West we find comparable structures, although sometimes local names were used for the various administrative organs. These structures were of a timocratic–oligarchic character. What remained of the popular assemblies in the East lost its significance during the 1st and 2nd centuries so that, here too, we find only oligarchies. The process of oligarchization, which was already fully under way in the Hellenistic period, was now completed. Both in the East and in the West, authority lay with the city council, the *boule* or *curia*. These councils consisted of members of the socioeconomic elite, who were appointed for life. Alongside the council, there were a number of magistratures.

Late antique developments

Late antiquity saw the creation of a semi-totalitarian system of governance called the Dominate, after the title *dominus* ("lord") assumed by a now openly autocratic emperor. Legal theorists helped prop up this autocracy with the proposition that the sovereignty of the people had passed to the emperor. Diocletian, systematic as he was, also systematized the divine character of the emperorship, in order to provide further support for the Dominate: the tetrarchs were now presented as a divine family, whom the citizens had to approach (if they approached them at all) with religious reverence. Around this new system, a court ceremonial developed that was partly based on Greco-Roman traditions and partly on a Sassanid model. Naturally, the Christian emperors could not be gods, but they remained *sacer* and thus superhuman beings. Late antique court life and everything it involved would survive into the Byzantine period.

The Dominate also required a new administrative organization, which involved four important developments. First, the imperial bureaucracy took over all duties. The idea of a separate republican, senatorial administration was discarded; the emperor became the sole source of law. In due course, the distinction between the emperor as a ruler and the emperor as a private person became blurred: *fiscus* and imperial domains merged. The emperor ruled with the assistance of an imperial council, the *sacrum consistorium* directed by the "*quaestor* of the holy palace," but the grand chamberlain (a eunuch) was sometimes the most powerful person in the imperial household. Second, the military and civil administrations were strictly separated. Magistrates, such as provincial governors, were no longer allowed any form of involvement in the military; non-professional officers, whose term in the army was part of their *cursus*, disappeared. On the other hand, soldiers and *centuriones* did sometimes perform civilian duties, especially those related to the *annona*. Third—and this seems to contradict the second point—the civil administration (and, in a certain sense, the whole of society) was militarized; the growing "army" of bureaucrats was reorganized along military lines. Officials now performed their duties as *militia*. Four, urban and provincial institutions were made uniform. The aim was to replicate the same administrative structures all over the empire; even Italy was divided into provinces. In this context, one might speak of decentralization: the empire was seen as a whole without a clear center, that could subsequently be divided into more or less equal administrative–military units, without paying attention to socioeconomic realities. All this happened under Diocletian's tetrarchy and under his successors.

The aim of Diocletian's tetrarchy (his appointment of a co-emperor and two *Caesares* as the assistants and successors of the *Augusti*) had been to strengthen his control over the empire and secure the succession. The *Caesares* were subordinate to the *Augusti*, and one of the *Augusti* could issue laws for the whole of the empire. So, formally the empire was still unified, as had been the case in earlier periods, with co-regents. Two administrative layers were established between the tetrarchs and the provinces, newly divided into smaller units: the empire was divided into 12 dioceses, each directed by a *vicarius*, and into two prefectures, each directed by a praetorian prefect (since the beginning of the 3rd century, the praetorian prefect had developed into a kind of minister of justice and internal affairs). As we saw, the tetrarchy lasted for only one generation, but Constantine did not do away with his predecessor's initiatives. The number of prefectures was extended to four, although with the abolishment of the Praetorian Guard at the beginning of the 4th century, the prefects no longer had a military task. These four prefectures more or less corresponded with the four official parts of the tetrarchy. The *vicarii*, who directed the (now 13) dioceses, as well as the governors of the more than 100 provinces, were completely dependent on the prefects. In this way, Diocletian's four-part division was continued. This four-part division in principle meant a quadrupling of the imperial bureaucracy. This and an expansion of the army in the same period led to enormous financial pressure and was the cause of late antique fiscalism.

Border troops maintained the *limes* that had been strengthened under Diocletian. These troops no longer came under the command of the provincial governor but were led by *duces*. Apart from the border troops, there was the *comitatus*, the (imperial) "escort." This was a mobile field army that had developed during the 3rd century and subsequently gained importance. This field army had its own *magistri* and did not fall under the command of the *duces*. The most important unit within the *comitatus* was a heavily armed cavalry; after all, the empire had to be able to fight mounted adversaries on every frontier. This does not mean, however, that under Constantine and his successors there was no role for the *limitanei*, as the border troops came to be called during the 4th century; they were of great importance for the empire's defense. But as the 4th century progressed, their position unmistakably weakened, and during the 5th century the borders were demilitarized, especially in the West, with obvious results.

Finally, there were the *foederati*, individuals who came from beyond the borders and fought on the side of the Romans as (paid!) allies. Initially, they were employed for single campaigns, after which they went back to where they came from, but from the late 4th century, larger and smaller groups of *foederati* permanently settled in the empire. The employment of *foederati* may be seen as a symptom of a slow but steady "barbarization" (mostly "Germanification") of army units. At first, Germans were engaged as high officers, but gradually their number among ordinary soldiers grew. During the 4th century, about one-third of the Roman army consisted of soldiers with a Germanic background; the army was then very much an instrument to make Roman soldiers out of Germanic warriors. This changed after the battle of Hadrianopolis: in the 5th century, the Western army mainly consisted of Germanic troops, and at that point the balance of power shifted fundamentally.

Chapter 6.3

Daily Life and Mentality

The Individual and Society

Societies and other associations

In the world of the Roman Empire, some social organizations dating from an earlier period slowly began to lose their significance, while new ones appeared. The *fulai* in the Greek cities, for instance, were not formally abolished, but being organizations of the citizen community in a period in which that community had lost much of its political significance, they became largely devoid of meaning. Institutions such as the Greek *efebeia* had already in the Hellenistic period become "clubs" for the youth of the more well-to-do families and retained that elitist character during the empire. The same could be said of the societies of young men in the Latin-speaking cities, the so-called *iuventus* or *collegia iuvenum*, in which the sons of the elite could prepare themselves for officer posts in the army, or for a career in local politics. In general, however, during the empire, associations with an apolitical character grew in importance, a development that had already begun in the Hellenistic age. Societies of a more private nature could have various aims. A common term used was *collegia*, a Latin term, because in Roman law, and especially during the empire, the legal status of such societies, even those in the Greek world, was defined with some accuracy. A *collegium* could consist of members who shared the same profession, or it could have been founded to worship a specific deity, or its aim could solely be to provide a decent burial for its members. But apart from the stated aims, companionship and conviviality always played a major role, with common meals often the most important activity. In republican Rome, the founding of a *collegium* had in principle been free; its members could devise their own rules as long as no laws were infringed. Gradually, however, the government intensified its supervision, and the senate assumed the authority to dissolve *collegia* that it deemed a threat to public order. For the same reason, Julius Caesar and the first emperors ruled that in order to start a *collegium*, the formal permission of the senate had to be acquired in advance. That permission was as a rule given, certainly for *collegia* of the *tenuiores* or "little men," but one imperial order or senatorial decree was enough to dissolve an "illegal" association. At the same time, during the empire the government increasingly granted

Antiquity: Greeks and Romans in Context, First Edition. Frederick G. Naerebout and Henk W. Singor.
© 2014 John Wiley & Sons, Inc. Published 2014 by John Wiley & Sons, Inc.

various *collegia* a semi-official status and began to employ their members for various public tasks in the cities. The later trend of making certain professions compulsory was linked to that development.

Education

Rome and other cities of the Roman Empire possessed an educational system that was mainly derived from the Greek cities of the Hellenistic age. Schools were private institutions for the children of parents who could afford the probably modest tuition fees. The "primary school" for children of about seven to twelve was often run by a freedman; the school itself was often part of a public space that was temporarily partitioned off, for instance, by curtains hung between the columns of a *stoa* or *basilica*. Reading, writing, and counting were the subjects taught. The pupils wrote with a sharp pencil or *stilus* on wax tablets; since books were expensive, much had to be learned by heart. We do not know how many children in the cities on average attended such classes, and so we do not know what percentage of the city population was able to read and write and thus how widespread literacy was (among the mass of the population in the countryside, in any case, it must have been very much lower than in the cities).

"Secondary education" was in the Roman world the domain of the *grammaticus*, also often a freedman but with a somewhat higher status than the schoolmaster. He was supposed to teach Latin and Greek grammar, which in practice meant reading the famous classical authors with some explanations regarding mythological and historical persons or episodes. This sort of general education by the *grammaticus* in the west was given in the same corners of public spaces as the "primary schools," in the Greek cities often a part of the *gumnasion* was marked out for it. Girls could attend these schools as well as boys, at least in the west, but their participation in public education at the secondary level must have been very small, if it existed at all. The daughters of the elite, however, regularly received all sorts of private lessons at home, as did upper-class boys. In Roman society, the "secondary" education was practically limited to the teachings of the *grammaticus*, but in the Greek cities the old traditions of education in music and gymnastics lived on. There, traditionally, a certain degree of supervision by the city government was normal, and the *gumnasiarchos* who supervised the *gumnasia* was an important official. Thus, the *gumnasia* in the Greek cities were not only places for bodily exercises but also for literary education.

In the *gumnasia* as well as in the theaters, for a substantial fee, itinerant *literati* or rhetors (professional orators) sometimes performed, declaiming their show speeches for the educated and snobbish part of the city population. That high esteem for rhetoric was typical of the education and of the literature of the empire. Words should have their maximum effect, to be achieved by various means: not only by rhetorical tricks and techniques and stylistic artifices, but also by a show of learning and speaking a "pure" language. In Greek, the latter meant the language of the great authors in the Attic dialect of the 5th and 4th centuries BC; in Latin, it was the language of Cicero and the poets of the age of Augustus. Their language had become the norm; theirs was the "classical" Greek and Latin taught by the *grammaticus* and imitated by the rhetor. Meanwhile, the language in everyday use had distanced itself more and more from these norms. As a result, rhetoric,

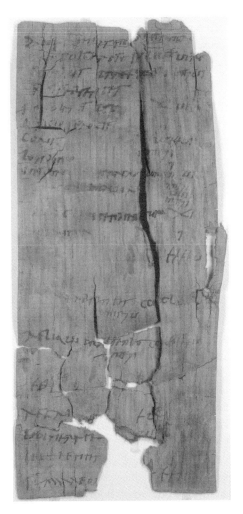

Figure 42 A wooden tablet from the Roman fort at Vindolanda, containing an army strength report (2nd c. BC). This is one of the so-called Tabulae Vindolandenses: hundreds of very thin slices of wood, written on with ink, that were found on the rubbish dump of the Roman fort of Vindolanda, just behind Hadrian's Wall. These texts give a unique insight into the life of a Roman army camp in the 2nd century, and also underscore the important part that writing seems to have played in that life. The camp was administered in writing down to the smallest detail, such as individual soldiers asking for a day's leave, but there is also private correspondence of many different kinds. Even the lower ranks appear to have been able to read, and probably to write. We cannot conclude from this that Roman Britain was a literate society: the army was in many respects a world apart. But still, it changes our view of ancient literacy. The text partially illustrated here is a strength report: "May the 18th, total number in the First Cohors of the Tungri, commanded by the prefect Iulius Verecundus: 752, of whom 6 *centuriones*. Absent: body guards of the governor 46; in Coria 337, including two *centuriones*; in Londinium 1 *centurio*; [illegible passage]. Total absent: 456, including 5 *centuriones*. Present: 296, including one *centurio*. Of these ill: 15; injured: 6; down with an inflammation of the eyes: 10, in total 31. Fit for active service: 265, among whom 1 *centurio*." Photo: © The Trustees of the British Museum

literature in general—for most authors on a variety of subjects tried to write in a "classical" mode—and already the teaching of the *grammaticus* were something strange to the world in which the mass of the population lived and spoke. The literary culture of the empire thus mirrored the gulf in society between the elite and the masses: the latter did not participate in the learned and dignified, artificial, and often not a little sterile "letters" that for the educated elite constituted higher culture.

Finally, "higher education" in organized form hardly existed. In the Latin-speaking parts of the empire, in Rome and a few other cities and provincial capitals such as Carthage, it was limited to the activities of some professors teaching Latin and Greek rhetoric or literature. Any education in philosophy and the sciences took place only in small circles coming together in the house of some scholar or in that of his wealthy patron. In that way, some "schools" could for a while exist, but they were all short-lived. Next to this form of higher education, in the Greek east there were still a few centers of learning where scholars could be active on a more or less permanent basis. Athens still had its Platonic Academy, where the writings of the master were studied besides astronomy and mathematics, but literary subjects were neglected. In Alexandria, where the Musaeum had been a center of learning under the Ptolemies, during the empire the scientific activities were continued on a reduced scale: mathematics, astronomy, and geography were the fields in which scholars there worked in the tradition of Aristotle and the Peripatetic school. The diffusion of all sorts of pseudo-science such as astrology and alchemy was marked, which in a mix with religion and magic exerted wide influence. Also new was the fact that the Christian community in Alexandria took over some parts of the scholarly tradition. Since about 200 AD, Alexandria became a center of theological learning that not only inspired theological speculation but also more practical expertise in the fields of textual criticism and chronological studies. Later in the 3rd century, Caesarea in Palestine and Antioch in Syria became centers of Christian learning as well. Then, not long before 300 AD, another type of higher education made its appearance in the east in the form of the law school, where jurists and prospective officials in the service of the emperor could be educated. The most important was established in Berytus (Beirut), and later another one would flourish in Constantinople.

Law and public order

One of the most important legacies of Rome was a comprehensive corpus of civil law. Other states in antiquity, of course, had at least some laws and regulations in this area too, but in Rome civil law reached a level of systematization and refinement that was unknown elsewhere. The process had started already in the early republic and reached its peak in the late 2nd and early 3rd centuries AD. Since the republic, the collection of laws and legal rules had been constantly commented on and refined by professional jurists. The first emperor Augustus gave these jurists the official authority to explain the law, their interpretation to be used by judges in their verdicts. These jurists, then, exerted a great influence on the development of private law, the more so because since the 2nd century members of the emperor's council and high officials in imperial service came to be increasingly recruited from among jurists. Shortly after the middle of that century the jurist Gaius wrote his *Institutiones*, a textbook for aspiring jurists that thanks to its lucid formulations of existing law became decisive for many centuries. With the growth of imperial government and the extension of Roman citizenship to more and more free inhabitants of the empire, subjecting a growing number of people to the rules of Roman law, the role of imperial officials in explaining, applying, and extending the law became more and more important. Since about 200 AD, the highest officials, who also acted as judges, the *praefecti praetorio*, were often jurists themselves, whose sentences and collections of valid law in their turn became new sources of jurisprudence. The most important of them was the great jurist Ulpian in the 20s and 30s of the 3rd century AD.

In the field of criminal law, such an imposing edifice was never erected: here, rather, chaos and simplification ruled. In the last century of the republic, for Roman citizens there had emerged a system of jurisdiction by panels of jurors, with different courts for different crimes, where the accused could have a lawyer to speak in his defense, and where in general punishments were rather mild (often, exile was the severest punishment instead of execution, and there was no torture during interrogation). Such court cases were for Roman citizens considered the "normal" procedures, all other procedures being "abnormal." First, the jurisdiction that a Roman magistrate exercised on the basis of his *imperium* belonged to the latter category—there was no separation of powers between a governor or magistrate and a judge. Unhampered by a panel of jurors or by procedural rules, the magistrate had great freedom of action. In that way, Roman magistrates and their delegates judged their subjects in the provinces as well as non-Romans and Romans of low status in Italy and Rome itself. This made the "abnormal" jurisdiction normal. During the early empire, the system of juror panels for Roman citizens would gradually disappear, and only senators would long preserve the privilege of being judged solely by their fellow senators. The "abnormal" but quick and efficient jurisdiction (*cognitio extraordinaria*), therefore, became the norm throughout the empire. Roman citizens in the provinces could appeal to the emperor in Rome against judicial verdicts until well into the 2nd century; in the course of the 2nd and 3rd centuries, however, more and more criminal jurisdiction was taken over by the Praetorian Prefects, from whose sentences there was no appeal.

In most criminal cases, it was the rule that the injured party himself or someone on his behalf should bring an accusation and personally convince the judge of the guilt of the accused. This was the accusatorial process, in which there was no public prosecutor and in which the accuser ran the risk, in case the accused was acquitted, of being himself punished for calumny with the punishment due for the crime of which he had wrongly accused the other. In fact, this was a remnant of archaic times in which self-help had been the rule in criminal cases. During the empire, though, another procedure was established: the inquisitorial process. Now it was the magistrate-judge himself taking the initiative and acting as prosecutor and as judge at the same time. In doing so, he was hardly bound by any rules, letting third parties raise accusations as well and shifting the burden of proof onto the accused, who had to prove his innocence. Such procedures were especially applied in cases of *maiestas*, a broad and dangerously vague category of activities that could be interpreted as high treason or conspiracy against the emperor. In course of time, this inquisitorial procedure became more common, but never fully replaced the accusatorial procedure. This went hand in hand with a coarsening of jurisdiction by simplifying the rules and regularly applying torture, even for witnesses. During the empire, especially in the 3rd and 4th centuries, torture in the juridical process became widespread, while death penalties became more frequent and were meted out for an increasing number of crimes in the form of crucifixion, being thrown to a wild beast in an arena, or burning at the stake. At the same time, especially in the field of criminal jurisdiction, a distinction was made between the more honorable (*honestiores*) and the more humble (*humiliores*) members of society. What had been the rights of all Roman citizens during the republic were now limited to the more honorable ones: they should not be tortured when interrogated, and in case of capital punishment they should be "honorably" beheaded or sent into exile, while the more humble people should always be tortured first and as a capital punishment suffer the spectacular executions already mentioned. In practice, though, the privileges of the *honestiores* were often infringed upon, mainly in cases of conspiracy against the emperor. The *honestiores* comprised the elites of senators, *equites*, city councilors, and veteran legionary soldiers, together probably less than 2% of the population; all the others were *humiliores*. Thus, the divide in society between the high-placed and the lowly that characterized the empire probably more than earlier periods and that came to surpass all other social distinctions, became very much visible in the field of criminal jurisdiction.

Organized forms of collective entertainment: The games

The imperial period saw a peak of activity in various organized forms of public entertainment, games, and shows. In this, the euergetism of the period was expressed. The local benefactors provided the populations of their cities not only with distributions of food or with contributions to public works but also, and often primarily, with all kinds of entertainment. That was true above all of the greatest living benefactor, the Roman emperor himself. For the emperor, the slogan "bread and circuses" was a necessary political program. The masses of the metropolis Rome had to be fed and entertained, and thus kept content with the regime. A contented populace would cheer the emperor and confirm his power, and also be favorably disposed toward the senatorial elite. But discontented masses were always unpredictable and therefore potentially dangerous.

Public entertainment during the empire took many forms, most of which already had a long history. Traditional were the games of the Greek type—running, boxing, wrestling, and the like—of which the Olympic Games were still the most famous, although in the big cities of the empire many more had been introduced in imitation of the Olympics, especially in the Greek east. Since the Hellenistic age, the participants were all professional athletes, so that the games provided the public with passive entertainment. Chariot racing was often a part of such games but was also held on other occasions, especially in the west. Its popularity grew immensely during the empire. In the big cities, races were organized on a regular basis with the passionately engaged public divided into several supporters associations. The most spectacular ones were held in Rome in the hippodrome of the Circus Maximus at the foot of the Palatine hill on which the palaces of the emperors rose. The close connection between imperial palace and racetrack was typical of the later empire: the emperors were only too aware that in order to "relate to" the people, they had to attend the races as often as they could. In the new imperial residences of the late 3rd and early

Figure 43 Graffito of a gladiator from Pompeii (before 79 AD) and gravestone of the gladiator Apollonius, from Asia Minor (late imperial period). The graffito on the left was found on a wall in Pompeii (regio I, insula VI) and dates from sometime before 79 AD. We see a gladiator, a *Samnis* or *secutor*, that is, a swordsman, armed with a short sword, a helmet with visor, a shield, and a single arm guard and a single shin guard. According to the accompanying text, his name is Oceanus, he is a *libertus* (a freedman), and he has been victorious 13 times. Graffiti with texts about and images of gladiators are found on several Pompeian walls and illustrate the huge popularity of this "sport." To the right is the gravestone of one Apollonius from Asia Minor, now in the Museum of Antiquities in Leiden. It dates back to the late imperial times. The inscription says: "Apollonius [has] 48 victories [to his name]. Zosime, his wife [put this up] to honor his memory." Apollonius, portrayed on the small relief as a *retiarius*, the gladiator armed with a net and a trident, is the "top scorer" among all gladiators of whom we know the number of victories. Whether Apollonius died in his bed or was killed in his last fight, we will never know. The fact that this gravestone is from Asia Minor should remind us of the enormous popularity of these bloody Roman games in the Greek east. Drawing: from *Corpus Inscriptionum Latinarum*, volume IV, 8055a; Photo: © Rijksmuseum van Oudheden, Leiden, NL

4th centuries, palace and racetrack (the *circus*) were always built adjoining each other, for instance, the grand palace and the hippodrome in Constantinople.

The stone amphitheaters were a largely new phenomenon in the empire, replacing the wooden and often temporary constructions of the late republican period. They were meant for animal shows and gladiatorial games. The shows with animals originated in the period of the classical republic and had become very popular. Different, often exotic animals were incited to fight each other or were chased and killed by human hunters. The more animals from exotic places were offered up to be killed, the more prestige accrued to the organizer of the games. During the empire, convicted criminals also could be sent into the *arena* (that is, literally, the "sand" in the middle of the amphitheater) with only token weapons, or no weapons at all, sometimes even tied to a pole, to be mauled or torn up by the beasts. Sometimes, mythological stories about heroes and ferocious animals could thus be re-enacted. These shows were extremely expensive, for the animals often had to be imported from far away. Hardly less popular were the gladiatorial games. Among the stone amphitheaters built for these shows since the last days of the republic, the one nick-named the Colosseum in Rome, built under Vespasian and Titus, was the largest and most famous. It could hold 50,000 spectators. The gladiatorial games also originated in the time of the classical republic, and in the 1st century AD they became popular all over the empire. Originally, the gladiators had been war captives who were forced in ritual combats to fight to the death as a kind of funeral sacrifice for a deceased nobleman, but soon their combats had become pure entertainment. The fighters were originally prisoners of war, slaves, or convicted criminals, but during the empire, when it had been forbidden to send slaves as gladiators into the arena, more and more volunteers chose this profession. Their training, their equipment, and the staging of the combats themselves were again very costly, so that holding gladiatorial games was always a hugely expensive affair. This explains why not all the gladiators got killed, not even if they were defeated in combat, for they were too expensive to die. Many sought this profession, for the winner could earn considerable prize money. Nevertheless, death certainly was an occupational hazard, and the lives of many gladiators were at some point rudely cut short. The men themselves were often admired for their courage and skill but at the same time despised for throwing away their lives. It was the local rich who in the provinces provided the shows on a relatively modest scale; in Rome, the *quaestores* had to celebrate their magistracies by holding gladiatorial games at their own costs, although often the emperor would subsidize the poorer among them. But the most frequent and the most expensive shows in Rome were held by the emperor himself. There were special schools for gladiators in Rome, as well as a whole menagerie of animals that were fed and constantly replenished at imperial expense. Altogether, the costs for the amphitheater shows in Rome must have swallowed up a considerable part of the imperial budget, probably the second largest part after the costs for the military.

Apart from the bloody shows in the amphitheater, there were other performances in the theaters. Classical drama, however, lost much of its appeal during the empire and was gradually replaced by mime and pantomime, in which music and dance played major roles. When in the course of the 4th century the Roman Empire became largely Christian and various elements of urban life began to change or to disappear altogether, the shows and games too decayed, both as a result of constant protests by the church against these forms of entertainment and because of a lack of funds. The Greek-style games disappeared altogether shortly after the last Olympic Games were held in 393 AD. Gladiatorial games outside Italy disappeared in the course of the 4th century, and in Italy itself shortly after 400 AD. Animal shows continued longer, but they were increasingly limited to shows with "local" animals, again because of the costs involved and the breakdown of long-distance trade in much of the empire in the 5th century. Mime shows, however, were still staged in Constantinople in the 6th century, while chariot racing would continue for even longer, albeit on a much reduced and less costly scale.

Men and Women

Marriage and sexuality

The Roman Empire was a patchwork of peoples and cultures, ranks and classes, which makes it difficult to speak in general terms about a topic such as marriage and sexuality. Nevertheless, a few broad outlines can be drawn. There was, first, the "civic" obligation, already referred to before, to marry and beget lawful offspring. In this world, infant mortality was so high that every community had foremost to take care to maintain itself numerically. Whoever shirked his duty in this respect could count on general disapproval. Further, as far as we know, monogamous marriage was the rule everywhere, although some features could vary from region to region. In Egypt, for instance, marriages between brothers and sisters were a common phenomenon, especially among the peasant population, but these were seen as barbarous in Roman eyes and later, with the spread of Roman law, mostly repressed. About the marriage customs and sexual habits of the masses of the population, though, our knowledge is very limited. Where we have some information, especially concerning the upper classes, no big changes are seen over the years in comparison with earlier periods. Neither in the Greek cities, nor in Italy and Rome, did ideas and practices regarding marriage and sexuality differ very much from those of the Hellenistic or even the Classical periods. Opinions on the roles of men and women and the purpose of marriage were too deeply rooted to undergo radical changes. Everywhere, marriages were more or less (usually more) arranged by parents or relations; almost everywhere, the bride was as young as possible, from 12 to about 16 years of age, in order to ensure as long a period of childbearing as possible; everywhere, however, maternal death during labor was frequent, and infant mortality was high. Views on sexuality were traditional. The wife had to be faithful to her husband, but for the man a high degree of sexual freedom was normal, especially regarding slave girls or boys. The social position of women did not change very much during the empire. At the most, a certain trend from the Hellenistic period was continued, allowing elite women to make more of a public appearance as "benefactresses" of their cities or even as titular magistrates, without actually being on par with the men of their class. Still, during the empire some changes made themselves gradually felt that would ultimately have a great influence on the development of a "Western" morality regarding marriage and sexuality.

Among the upper classes in the Greco-Roman world of the empire, a certain measure of idealization of marriage and the family can be discerned. To some extent, a degree of prudishness went hand in hand with it. Philosophers recommended sexual abstinence, certainly outside marriage, and sometimes went as far as to recommend sex only for the purpose of begetting a child. Some inscriptions set up in memory of a deceased spouse now have a tone of intimacy and refer to the happiness of marriage, in a way that was lacking in earlier periods. It is difficult, however, to ascertain how widespread such feelings and ideas were. Christian morality, which limited sex to married couples and preached a more or less equal relationship between man and wife in terms of mutual fidelity, may have been influenced by some notions that were already prevalent among at least part of the elites in the Roman world. The Christian message that the man too had to be faithful to his wife corresponded with most Jewish moral precepts as well as with the new prudishness of many philosophers. Among the latter, some even recommended total continence and an ascetic life. Such notions were related to the idea of an immaterial and immortal soul that should ultimately be freed from its bodily ties, a liberation for which the suppression of sexual activity was deemed a prerequisite. Among pagans and Jews, such ideas were not received well—they seemed to contradict the requirements of society and the commands of the Jewish God. But Christians took over the notion of a soul that was threatened by and had to be protected against the forces of sexuality. In the 3rd and 4th centuries, this gave rise to a Christian asceticism. In its most extreme form this came to be represented by hermits and a little later by monks and to a lesser degree nuns, who completely broke with the norms of ancient society by deliberately choosing a life of absolute celibacy. It is hard to tell whether or not the phenomenon of thousands of celibates in late antiquity did indeed have a demographic effect, but the Christian stress on celibacy was felt outside the monastic sphere too, especially by women: Christian widows did not remarry—whereas that was normal in the pagan world, as long as the woman was of childbearing age—and Christian upper-class girls were often pressed not to marry at all but to devote their lives to the Church as pious deaconesses. Taken together, these ascetic trends may well have had some negative demographic consequences in the late antique world, but in the absence of hard quantitative data this must remain hypothetical.

Demographics

The demography of the Roman Empire is a much debated subject. A lack of sources prevents any "hard" conclusions. The many funerary inscriptions, for example, do not lend themselves to any reconstruction of the age structure of the population, because the ages mentioned on the stones are not always accurate and the inscriptions are not representative of the population at large. We have to make do, therefore, for the overall population of the empire, with comparisons with other pre-modern societies. Much uncertainty notwithstanding, we may assume that the picture of a pyramid with a very broad base and only a narrow peak reaching the higher ages—the result of high infant and child mortality—was valid for the empire just as it had been for earlier periods in antiquity. Likewise, the question of the total number of inhabitants of the empire and its fluctuations can only be answered by more or less informed guesses. For cities and provinces, estimates can be made, but the sum total of all estimates has necessarily a high measure of uncertainty. Thus, the calculations or estimates of the number of inhabitants of the Roman Empire in the 1st century AD vary from 50 to 80 million, and those of the city of Rome from 400,000 to well over 1 million. Rome was no doubt a unique metropolis; other large cities such as Alexandria, Antioch, and Carthage in all probability did not surpass the 300,000 mark, or even the 200,000 mark. A very few cities might have had about 100,000 inhabitants, a handful others between 25,000 and 100,000, but the vast majority of the more than 1000 towns and cities of the empire had between 5,000 and 20,000 inhabitants. When it comes to the population of the countryside, our uncertainties only increase. It is more than probable that there must have been fluctuations in the numbers of inhabitants in various regions.

In general, the population of the empire seems to have reached its highest peak in the 2nd century. In the 3rd century, there must have been a decline in population, especially in the western half, but certainly not everywhere, while toward the end of the century and in the following 4th and 5th centuries the population in the eastern half must have recovered and even increased, while in the west the population levels of the 2nd century would not be reached again for many centuries.

The factors that could explain long-term changes in the size of the population are not always clear. Wars and epidemics generally seem not always to have played a decisive role, since the population losses caused by these calamities tended to be made up for within a few generations. That said, the catastrophes that struck the empire in the 2nd and 3rd centuries AD—a severe epidemic after 166 AD that probably introduced smallpox into the Roman world, another epidemic around the middle of the 3rd century, perhaps measles, not to mention near-constant wars and foreign invasions—were of such a nature that they must have led to a population decline that in most of the western half of the empire was simply too serious to allow for a speedy recovery. In the eastern half, however, as stated, the population seems not only to have recovered in the later 3rd and 4th centuries but to even have increased somewhat. A more important factor than mortality for population increase or decrease is, in general, the prevailing fertility rate. Changes brought about in the rate of fertility by changes in diet, health, society, mentality or religion, inevitably have their effects in the form of an increase or decrease of population. The Christianization of the Roman Empire and the accompanying diffusion of certain ascetic ideals might therefore, as was already suggested, have had some negative consequences for the overall size of the population. However, not only must this remain a presupposition, it is also a fact that asceticism was in the 4th and 5th centuries AD stronger in the east than in the west of the empire, which suggests that this factor can at most have played a secondary role. So we must conclude that epidemics and social and political upheavals were more important (in the 6th century the east would be ravaged by invasions and an epidemic and then in its turn suffer a population decline).

Religion, Philosophy, and Scholarship

The Roman Empire was not only a patchwork of peoples and cultures, it was also a melting pot of traditions and ideas in the fields of scholarship, pseudo-science, and religion. From this, new religious movements and developments arose, but in science and scholarship it was more a matter of collecting and summarizing of what had been achieved in an earlier age: innovation and increase of knowledge were, with some important exceptions, lacking, so that knowledge became rigid and in late antiquity prone to decay.

Scholarship and literature

In many respects, the figure of Pliny (Plinius) the Elder, in the 1st century AD was typical of the state of science and scholarship in the early empire. He wrote the bulky *Naturalis Historia* or *Natural History* (that is, research into all things in nature),

Figure 44   Altars for the goddess Nehalennia, from the Scheldt river in the Netherlands (3rd c. AD). Two votive altars, both dedicated to the goddess Nehalennia, both dredged up in 1970 from the Scheldt river together with numerous others, and now in the Museum of Antiquities in Leiden. These altars (in fact altar-shaped steles) had been standing around a Nehelennia temple that at the end of the 3rd or in the early 4th century disappeared into the river when it changed its course. Nehalennia was an indigenous goddess, apparently of the type of Fortuna, who was especially venerated by seafarers (there was another sanctuary of her on the Dutch coast, at Domburg). Although an indigenous goddess, she is portrayed in a Roman manner on Roman-style dedications with Latin inscriptions. Apart from such religious aspects, these dedications are interesting for the light they throw on the trade between the Continent and the British Isles in the first half of the 3rd century AD. Several of the inscriptions mention traders, their home towns, and their cargo. The inscription of the altar on the left reads as follows: "To the goddess Nehalennia Marcus Exgingius Agricola from the *civitas* of the Treveri [Treves and surrounding territory on the Moselle river], salt trader in Cologne, has fulfilled his vow, willingly and for good reason." And the one on the left reads "To the goddess Nehalennia Placidus, son of Viducus, from the *civitas* of the Veliocasses [Rouen and territory, in France], trader on Britain, has fulfilled his vow, willingly and for good reason." Photos: © Rijksmuseum van Oudheden, Leiden, NL

in which he mostly uncritically dealt with a range of subjects, from all sorts of natural phenomena to superstitious practices, together an encyclopedia of received knowledge, scholarly opinion, and much pseudo-science. Independent research or scientific innovation is indeed scarce in his work. One science Pliny was interested in was geography, and here during the empire some real progress was made. In the time of Augustus, the Greek Strabo had written a geographic and ethnographic summary of the known world, describing the lands and peoples of the Roman Empire and adjacent regions in Asia as far as India. Since Strabo, knowledge had increased, both as a result of the overseas trade along the coasts of East Africa, India, and in the waters of Southeast Asia, and of the overland trade along the Silk Road across Central Asia. The results of this increase in knowledge were in the middle of the 2nd century collected by the great Alexandrian scholar Ptolemy (Claudius Ptolemaeus) in a comprehensive geographical description of the world. For the precise locations of various places on his map, Ptolemy used a system of meridians and parallels that had been tentatively developed in the Hellenistic age. Ptolemy's world reached from Ireland to Java and China, It supposed the existence of an overland connection far away in the Southern Hemisphere between the south of Africa and the southeast of Asia that turned the Indian Ocean into an immense "lake." Despite such misconceptions, this work was the height of ancient geographical knowledge, and it would remain the decisive work in its field until the age of the great European discoveries began in the later 15th century AD (a period in which many explorers would also search for Ptolemy's unknown "Southland" or *terra australis*). Ptolemy's geography was linked to his cosmology or astronomy, which built on the work of predecessors, describing among other things the positions of more than 800 stars with their coordinates. In Ptolemy's view of the universe, which was a summary of previous cosmological designs, the spherical earth was in the middle of everything, encircled by the seven spheres of the planets and an eighth sphere of the so-called fixed stars. Each of the planets—among which the sun and the moon were also included—moved in smaller circles or epicycles on its imaginary circle around the earth. This was a construction meant to reconcile the apparently erratic movements of the planets as observed in the sky with the presupposition that being perfect they should move in perfect circles around Earth. Holding on to that Platonic and Aristotelian dogma required more and more epicycles and complex constructions in the course of time, until at last in the 16th century Copernicus would suggest that the planets did not move around Earth but around the sun, and a little later Kepler proved that their orbits were not circles at all. After nearly 1400 years, the end of the Ptolemaic universe had arrived.

In the field of medical knowledge, the physician Galen (Galenus) in the second half of the 2nd century AD played a role comparable with that of Ptolemy in astronomy and geography: he summarized all the medical knowledge of his predecessors and contemporaries. He, however, supplemented it with numerous observations and diagnoses of his own. His copious writings would remain the authoritative textbooks in medicine until far into the 18th century. Yet, compared with the achievements of Alexandrian medical science in the Hellenistic world, the work of Galen shows some regression: there was no place in Galen's view for experiments and for dissection of the human body, but there was plenty of prejudice and all sorts of pseudo-scientific reasoning. The latter more and more characterized all "science" during the empire, in which pseudo-sciences like alchemy and astrology flourished. This and the rise of Christianity with its own mythical worldview would in large measure put an end to science as a form of rational inquiry during the later empire.

Technical inventions were in the empire certainly still made, especially in military machinery (such as the field artillery of small torsion crossbows) and in architecture. In the latter, some mathematical knowledge was still required, for instance, in the construction of domes, but the military machines were mainly the product of practical knowledge and experience, not of a direct link between science and technique.

Literature and learning, such as historiography and jurisprudence, during the empire bore the stamp of the hierarchical order of society, for they were the domain of the elite, and the artificial, unnatural but "classical" Greek and Latin in which they were expressed guaranteed that they would remain so. The literary style was heavily influenced by rhetoric in various styles. Much of what was written has been lost, but one of the monuments of Latin literature and historiography was certainly the work of Tacitus (early 2nd century AD), large parts of which have been preserved. In two masterly works, he dealt with the history of the Roman emperors after Augustus until the reign of Nerva (14–96 AD). A Greek contemporary of Tacitus was Plutarch, a learned and well-read author of numerous works, among them biographies of many famous Greeks and Romans and religious treatises. For modern historians, Plutarch is a valuable source for many aspects of ancient history. Later in the early 3rd century, the Greek-speaking senator Cassius Dio produced an important history of Rome from the beginning until his own time, of which considerable portions have been preserved, while in the 4th century Ammianus Marcellinus wrote the last important Latin history of Rome, among which the books dealing with his own times have been preserved. During the empire, the novel became a typical form of entertainment literature for a reading public that was probably wider than just the elite. A high literary level was reached by Petronius with his *Satyrica*, a picaresque novel written in the time of Nero, as well as by Apuleius in his fantastic novel *Lucius or the Golden Ass* (2nd century). Greek novels were more numerous but on the whole of a lesser literary quality than the two Latin ones just mentioned. They were invariably sensational and often sentimental. In the 2nd and 3rd centuries, in Christian circles edifying stories about the apostles were produced, which could be seen as Christian counterparts to the novel. The lives of the saints, which would be written starting in the 4th century, continued that genre in some ways. In the 4th century, Christian prose and poetry began increasingly to replace pagan literature.

Religions in and outside the Roman Empire

When it came to religion, the world of the Roman Empire witnessed a mix of old and new, tradition and innovation. In the Archaic and Classical periods, religion had largely been a matter of the community or the state, but in the Hellenistic period at the latest various forms of a more personal religiosity and more private religious organizations blossomed besides the traditional state cults. That development continued during the empire, so that apart from the cults maintained everywhere by the Roman state or by the various cities and provincial councils, private religious organizations and private religiosity flourished.

The traditional cults persisted until well into the 4th century AD. Inscriptions and votive offerings testify to the ongoing worship of Jupiter or Zeus, of Hercules, Apollo, Dionysus, and many other representatives of the classical pantheon. But it is clear that these deities could no longer monopolize the attention of their worshipers, for they were often overshadowed by other divine figures and other cults that promised a more intense contact with their worshippers.

In the Hellenistic period, the need for a more intimate relation between man and deity as well as between the worshippers of one and the same deity themselves had given rise to the spread of various cult associations and the worship of particular deities that seemed to meet that need. Typical of the age was the syncretistic character of many of these gods and cults, where elements of different origin merged into one divine figure or into one complex of myths and rituals. Moreover, often the worshipers of Isis, Asclepius, or other deities considered their god the greatest, the mightiest, or the highest. In henotheism, one god or goddess was seen as standing above all others, ruling all the others as his subordinates, or even comprising all the others as aspects of himself. During the empire, private cult associations and the phenomenon of henotheism spread even more widely. That could also be said of the worship of, or at least the anxious reverence for, the divinized powers of Luck or Fortune (Latin: Fortuna) and Fate or Destiny (Latin: Fatum). The latter was often linked with astrology, since the stars and the planets in the opinion of nearly everybody in principle determined the destiny of men and states. At the same time, practically all people attempted to influence gods and planets in order to change their fate. This explains to a large extent the wide diffusion of all sorts of magical practices. In the same category belonged the extraordinary powers that were attributed to certain people: wise or holy persons who had a special relationship with the divine world and were therefore able to perform miracles and overcome the decrees of fate. With these acts, they proved that they had been chosen by a higher power or even that a divine being resided in their human body. Such ideas too had emerged in the Hellenistic period but spread more widely during the empire.

The religious picture of the Roman Empire in the first three centuries can thus be sketched in a few broad strokes. In the first place, local cults proliferated everywhere, which as a result of contact with Greco-Roman culture had often been hellenized or romanized to various degrees. Many Celtic deities, for example, had in the process of *interpretatio Romana* been identified with gods such as Mercury (Mercurius, Greek Hermes), Apollo, Mars, or Hercules, while in Asia Minor, to mention another example, many local gods and goddesses were identified with the Greek Zeus, Artemis, Aphrodite, and others. This syncretism was a natural part of a wider process of acculturation. In the larger cities of the empire and in the old core lands of Greece and Italy, the traditional deities still possessed their temples and cults paid for by the city or the state.

But besides the traditional cults, various more recent cults of non-Greek or non-Roman origin had appeared, often in the form of private cult associations. Since the Hellenistic period and well into the 3rd and 4th centuries AD Isis and the Anatolian goddess Cybele were extremely popular; since the early empire, it was, among others, the god Mithras, whose cult acquired numerous adherents. The followers of Mithras were mainly found among government officials, officers, and soldiers, and his cult places, Mithraea, along the military roads and adjacent to the camps at the frontiers, as well as in Rome and Ostia. Mithras was a god with a Persian name who in the Roman Empire by a syncretistic process had been assembled from elements of other cults and deities. For instance, he could easily be equated to the sun god. His worship flourished especially during the 3rd century, together with that of Sol Invictus, the Unconquerable Sun, who was then promoted by some of the emperors as the special protector of the empire and of their own persons. At the same time, the cult of Mithras was closely connected with astrology and with the notion of an immortal soul that came from a realm of light beyond the stars where, after death, she would return by ascending through the various spheres of the planets with the help of Mithras, who would protect her against the planet gods.

Such ideas about a journey of the soul to heaven were also known outside the circles of the worshipers of Mithras. They corresponded with the prevailing view of the universe of many intellectuals and with the belief in an immortal but immaterial soul that was held by most philosophers. As far as we know, the large majority of inhabitants of the Roman Empire did not have any strong beliefs regarding the afterlife. The numerous funerary inscriptions testify mostly to a pessimistic resignation: the grave is literally the last resting place, and death the end of life. Some of the deceased, who had not been buried properly, were believed to roam Earth as ghosts haunting the living, but that was not an enviable fate and certainly no solace for their relatives. Some special cults, such as the old mysteries of the goddesses of Earth and the grain at Eleusis in Attica, and also more recent ones such as those of Isis and Mithras, promised some form of existence of the soul after death for their worshipers who had undergone initiation. But we know little more about the messages preached by these so-called mystery cults (from *musterion*, initiation), since they required their adherents to keep silent about what they heard and saw. Certainly, the notion of an afterlife for the soul was spread by some philosophical schools that based themselves on the teachings of Pythagoras and Plato and had become rather popular during the empire. According to them, human souls originated in a realm of light and pure spirit somewhere between the stars or even beyond; through the spheres of the planets they had invisibly descended on Earth and entered into human bodies (either at conception or at birth); after death, in the vast majority of cases they moved to another body, human or animal, but the souls of those who had disassociated themselves from material greed and immorality and had led an ethically pure life dedicated to philosophical contemplation would ascend again, escape from Earth and find rest in the heaven of their origin. Such ideas lived on among relatively small groups, but they were important because of their influence on Christians and related groups, as well as on the philosophical school of Neoplatonism that was prevalent in late antiquity. In Neoplatonism, Plato's doctrine of the ultimate reality of ideas was revived in decidedly religious form that tended toward mysticism. Its founder in the 3rd century was Plotinus, who studied in Alexandria and then moved to Rome, where he founded his own school. His followers would dominate the last centuries of pagan philosophy until the final closure of the Platonic Academy in Athens in the 6th century AD.

In the Roman world, belief in miracles, in miracle workers and in "divine" humans was widespread. A "divine" man—or a "human" god—was also the Roman emperor himself. The Hellenistic tradition of the ruler cult had been effortlessly transferred to Octavian/Augustus. After the civil wars had been brought to an end and after the chaos, plundering, and extortions, especially in the east of the empire, a period of reconstruction had begun, and the divine worship that many Greek cities paid to the man who had become sole ruler was largely spontaneous and honest. "Savior" and "Benefactor" were the most common names with which he was addressed; altars, statues, and temples were the material expressions of this cult. In Rome and in Italy, Augustus and most of his successors mitigated this cult somewhat, because an all too official divinization did not sit well with the fiction of the emperor as *princeps* among his fellow senators, who had restored "the republic" and since then maintained it. But also in Rome, it was clear to everyone that the emperor was not an ordinary human being. After his death he was officially declared a *divus*, that is a god, by the senate and was supposed to take his place among the other gods; in Rome, his statue would be placed in a temple of his own or in the temple of another *divus* or another god, while outside Italy his statues were usually already in his lifetime placed in such sanctuaries. Likewise, various attributes of the emperor and the very name Augustus itself already suggested a near-divine status for the living ruler. Some emperors commended to be given divine honors in Rome as well—for instance, Caligula and Domitian—but because of their despotic rule, the senate in their case refused them posthumous divinization (cursing and erasing their memory, instead). Meanwhile, the cult of the living emperor spread also to the western provinces. Already under Augustus it was organized, closely connected with the cult of the goddess Roma, in the two regional centers Tarragona in Spain and Lugdunum (Lyons) in Gaul. At annual festivals and fairs, sacrifices were brought and games celebrated that together took on the character of a show of loyalty of the provinces to the emperor and to Rome. Comparable provincial organizations of the emperor cult appeared in the east, especially in Asia Minor. There, the office of provincial high priest for the cult of the emperor was much sought after by the local aristocrats. With all that, the emperor cult assumed a clearly political element as an expression of loyalty and solidarity. Still, sincere religious emotions did certainly play a role in this worship of this mighty figure who was so far away in Rome and yet so powerful that he could only be conceived of as a god. Gradually, such ideas spread also in Rome and Italy. When the emperors came to behave more and more as absolute rulers, divinization during their lifetime was accepted in Rome as well. During the troubles of the 3rd century, some of the so-called soldier-emperors tried to make their position unassailable for would-be rebels and pretenders by presenting themselves as the special companions or favorites of a mighty god, usually the Unconquerable Sun, and thus enhancing their own divine status. Some of them called themselves openly "Lord and God" (*dominus et deus*): some of Aurelian's coins carried the message "Born Lord and God."

The Jews

The emperor cult formed part of the polytheism that was the religion of the Roman world. In that world, only the Jews and the Christians stood apart because of their monotheistic and exclusive beliefs that did not admit any other worship than that of their sole deity. The Christians, therefore, would for more than 200 years be seen as opposed to the gods of the empire and sometimes even be persecuted, but the Jews were recognized as a separate nation with their own and very old traditions, who enjoyed a special and exceptional status in the empire. Jewish communities in the diaspora could already in the Hellenistic period be found in many Greek cities and before the beginning of our era also in Rome and some other towns in Italy; during the empire, they also migrated to the western provinces. Everywhere, the Jews were entitled to build their synagogues, to collect money for the temple in Jerusalem, and to live according to their own religious customs, while they were not obliged to participate in the pagan cults of their surroundings or in the emperor worship. After Judea in the beginning of the 1st century AD had become a Roman province, the Roman authorities were sometimes confronted with the more militant expressions of

Figure 45   A wall painting from the synagogue at Dura Europos (245 AD). This wall painting is one of a whole series decorating the inside of the synagogue in Dura Europos. Dura Europos on the Euphrates was founded by Seleucus I as a military base; it always remained a garrison town. In the 2nd century BC, it became part of the Parthian Empire; in 167 AD the Roman Empire took over and made it an outpost of Roman Syria, until the Sassanids overwhelmed and destroyed it in 256. Several wall paintings in buildings that shortly before the Sassanid takeover had been incorporated into the defenses of the town, their spaces filled up with bricks, survived the 3rd-century destruction. Together they provide us with a unique insight into the art of painting in the Near East in the Hellenistic and Roman eras. An important characteristic of this art seems to have been the convention of portraying individuals in full frontal view, their faces too directed straight toward the viewer. Dura is interesting from the perspective of the history of religions as well: there are sanctuaries for Syrian gods, but also a large and rich Jewish synagogue and a small, poor Christian meeting place. Obviously, Judaism was far more important here in the 3rd century than up-and-coming Christianity. In the synagogue, we have several wall paintings from the years 244/245. In spite of the Biblical injunction not to portray humans, these wall paintings show many people, and among them important individuals from the Jewish Biblical tradition, such as David and Solomon. Also, there seem to be quite some non-Jewish elements present, in content and in execution. The wall segment in the illustration above shows the story of the childhood of Moses: a naked slave girl has stepped into the river Nile and has retrieved the child Moses from a casket that is now drifting empty upon the waters. Immediately above, we see how the daughter of the pharaoh hands the child, unknowingly, to the mother of Moses to nurse it. Several girls stand in attendance. To combine two phases of the same story into a single image is a common way of telling it—and saving space. Those already familiar with the story shall have no trouble "reading" the image. Photo: www.BibleLandPictures.com/Alamy

the Jewish religion in the form of messianic movements, that by preaching and often by guerrilla-like violence as well tried to prepare the people for the arrival of the messiah as foretold by the ancient prophets. In circumstances that are not very clear to us but in which clumsy actions by the Roman governors of Judea must have played a considerable role, some of that messianic fervor was released in a massive revolt against the empire in the years 66–70. It was brutally crushed by the Romans under Vespasian and his son Titus, when Jerusalem after a long and hard-fought siege was taken and destroyed in 70 AD. In the vicinity of the Dead Sea, pockets of Jewish resistance would hold out till 73. The Jerusalem temple, focus of the Jewish religion, was destroyed as well.

Remarkably, Jews outside Judea hardly suffered from the rebellion of their co-religionists. Henceforth, the money that they used to send to the temple in Jerusalem had to be paid as a tax to Rome, but in other respects their special status was unaffected. In Judea and Galilee, rabbis or teachers of the holy scriptures became more important, since with the destruction of the temple the old priesthood no longer had a function. A group of rabbis was generally acknowledged as authoritative in judging matters that had to do with the Jewish religion. That amounted to interpretation and explanation of the law, and so it was in the century or so after 70 AD that the *Mishnah* (literally: "repetition" or "instruction"), a corpus of commentaries and refinements of the Mosaic Law, took its form. Messianic expectations, meanwhile, had not completely disappeared after 70 AD. In the years 115–117, under the emperor Trajan, serious revolts broke out among the large Jewish communities in Egypt, Cyrene, Cyprus, and northern Syria. These too, however, were repressed with much slaughter. In Alexandria and in Cyprus, for instance, the Jewish communities were completely wiped out. Finally, in 132–135 a last revolt against the Romans broke out in Judea, again to be crushed, this time by the emperor Hadrian. After these failed uprisings, the period of instant messianic expectations was over, and the history of Judaism could enter a new phase.

After 135 AD, the rabbis were the undisputed leaders of the Jewish people. The temple in Jerusalem could not be rebuilt, and even the city itself was declared forbidden for Jews by the emperor Hadrian, while the province of Judea was now renamed Palestina (after the ancient people of the Philistines that had inhabited the coast) in order to deprive the Jews of a "territorial" identity. As a religious and ethnic group, however, they were free to live everywhere, except for the city of Jerusalem, now named Aelia after the family name of Hadrian. That emperor also had forbidden the practice of circumcision, which could be seen as a direct attack on the religious identity of the Jews, but that measure was revoked by his successor for the sons of Jews, though not for outsiders who wished to become Jews. This meant that henceforth Judaism was limited to the Jewish people and that conversions to Judaism were no longer allowed. As a result, the Jews remained an ethnic group or separate nation, whereas the Christians developed into a multi-ethnic movement. Thanks to the rabbis, the Jews both in Palestine and in the diaspora preserved their religious traditions and often impressed outsiders by their severe monotheism and ethical way of life. The rabbis accumulated a large corpus of additions, refinements, and casuistic interpretations of the law. All that learning eventually found its way into the two collections of the *Talmud* (that is: "study," a bulky commentary on the earlier *Mishnah*) that between the 2nd and the 7th centuries AD was compiled in Babylon and in Jerusalem (the latter and shorter one, finished in the 4th century, came to be eclipsed by the longer Babylonian one). Babylon had been a center of Jewish life since the destruction of the first temple in 587 BC and would remain so till far into the Middle Ages. Elsewhere outside the Roman Empire, Jewish communities emerged in Iran and India and along the Silk Road as far as, eventually, China.

Religious developments in Asia

The spread of Jewish communities in Asia can be seen as part of a wider phenomenon of movements of people, cultural influences, and cultural exchanges in the vast regions between the Greco-Roman world, the Near East, Iran, and Central Asia. The eastern border of the Roman Empire was only a political frontier, for the peoples living under Parthian and later Sassanid rule shared many religious ideas and traditions with, for instance, the indigenous inhabitants of Roman Syria and eastern Asia Minor. Just as Judaism had attracted non-Jewish adherents in the Roman Empire, it likewise found sympathy and, doubtless, converts in Asia, while it also influenced other religions, giving birth to sometimes remarkable religious hybrids, for example, the Mandaeans in the south of present-day Iraq. Likewise, Christian groups would spread in the wake of Jewish communities far to the east. At the same time, the lands east of the Roman Empire in the first centuries AD experienced a strong religious revival. Thus, in Iran the traditional religion of Zoroastrianism with its fire worship and eschatological message (i.e., about the end of the world and the final rewards and punishments of humankind) re-emerged under the Sassanids, even to become the state religion. This renewed Zoroastrianism, with its sharp distinction between good and evil, light and darkness, God and Satan, made strong ethical demands of its followers and became more and more intolerant and exclusive. Its revival under the Sassanid kings was not unrelated to their aggressive policies toward Rome and the intermittent suppression of religious minorities within Iran.

Farther into Asia, Buddhism in this period flourished and steadily expanded. In the Hellenistic age, the area of northern Pakistan and modern-day Afghanistan had become a stronghold of Buddhism, from where in the first centuries AD it spread along the Silk Road into China. By that time, the main branch of Buddhism here had become the Mahayana ("the great vehicle") that in some important ways distinguished itself from the older, so-called Hinayana ("the small vehicle") or Theravada ("the old faith") Buddhism, in that it stressed far less the rigorous asceticism of the individual as a path to salvation—for in that way, real salvation or enlightenment could only be attained by a very small group of steadfast ascetics. Instead, it preached a message of possible salvation for the mass of the common people with the help of the Buddha in his various divine manifestations and of the bodhisattvas, those altruistic spirits who had voluntarily postponed their own ultimate salvation in order to assist, with the spiritual merit they had themselves already assembled, all those poor souls who needed help and mercy. These bodhisattvas and Buddha manifestations formed a veritable pantheon of Buddhist "deities," and sometimes local deities would be admitted to it as new bodhisattvas. This was the form of Buddhism that in the 2nd century AD reached China and in the 6th century Japan. It was as the message of Buddha's compassion with suffering humankind that this Mahayana Buddhism acquired a large following, while the older form was more or less preserved in Sri Lanka (from where it would be dispersed to Southeast Asia in the 10th century).

There are some remarkable parallels between Mahayana Buddhism on the one hand and some religious movements in the Greco-Roman world on the other, especially in a shared longing for redemption or salvation from an earthly existence that was seen as fundamentally miserable, and in the concomitant worship of a divine Savior or Redeemer who from sheer goodness and compassion concerned Himself with the fate of humankind. Thus, there are some obvious similarities with early Christianity as well. There is, however, no reason to think of any influence from one on the other beyond the possibility of some stories and story-motives traveling from east to west, and perhaps vice versa. Rather, the similarities seem to point to an underlying pattern, a religious need for personal salvation, that in this form could come to the surface after many traditional sociopolitical and religious links and associations had been severed by the establishment of large multi-ethnic and multinational states and empires in the wake of Alexander's conquests.

Western Asia and Iran in the time of the Roman Empire constituted a region in which perhaps the most numerous and the most diverse religious movements ever came into contact with each other. Besides the numerous and ancient local cults and the national religion of Iran that Zoroastrianism had become, there was a Buddhist presence in the east of Iran, there were many Jewish communities and syncretistic groups such as the Mandaeans already referred to, and since the 2nd century also Christian communities. In this environment in the 3rd century AD, a new, syncretistic world religion appeared, constructed from elements of all the aforementioned religious movements. This was Manichaenism, named after its founder Mani. He was a visionary preacher and religious organizer who was expelled from the Jewish sect to which his parents in Mesopotamia belonged for his claim of having received special revelations ordering him to preach as an apostle of Christ a completely new message. He presented himself as the last in a line of historical prophets or apostles—among whom he included Zoroaster, Buddha, and Christ—who had come to save humankind. His religion was extremely dualistic, teaching a sharp division between light and darkness, good and evil, in the Zoroastrian tradition. The human soul was originally part of the world of pure light among the stars and had as a result of an extremely complicated sequence of fateful events become imprisoned in human bodies, just as other particles of the divine light had been swallowed up by plants. Only by an extremely ascetic life, practicing celibacy and vegetarianism, could an elite among the faithful—the elect—hope after death to return to the realm of light. Other believers, who had to maintain the elect in this life, could hope to be reborn among the elect and thus in a following generation be redeemed themselves. All others, the unbelievers constituting the rest of humanity, were doomed: they would in the end, when good and evil, light and darkness, would be forever separated, burn to nothingness together with the material world. Mani modeled his movement after the Christian Church and sent out 12 apostles to various regions. He had much success and Manichaean communities sprang up in the Roman Empire, Iran, and Central Asia. There, it was the second missionary religion, after Buddhism, that spread along the Silk Road and in the early Middle Ages even reached China. Mani's creation thus became a truly universal religion. But it provoked resistance too, mainly because of its radical asceticism and rejection of the existing order. In Iran, already in the 3rd century the Manichaeans were persecuted (Mani himself died in prison), and in around 300 the Roman emperor Diocletian outlawed them under punishment of being condemned to the stake. The Christian emperors of the 4th century and later continued that policy, with the result that in the 6th century the Manichaeans practically disappeared from the west, although some later Christian heretical movements probably continued in their footsteps. In Central Asia, they vanished as a result of the expansion of Islam in the Middle Ages; only in China they would linger on until about the 16th century.

Origin and early spread of Christianity

Christianity arose within Judaism in the first half of the 1st century AD. About the historical Jesus of Nazareth, not very much is known with any degree of certainty, since the sources (the Gospels and the letters by the apostle Paul) leave room for different interpretations and reconstructions of his person and his message. In all probability, he was convinced that God had entrusted him with a decisive role in the establishment of the promised messianic "Kingdom of God" on earth. His preaching worried the official Jewish priesthood as well as the Roman authorities, and after a relatively short career as a messianic prophet he was crucified as a rebel by the Roman governor. His closest followers interpreted Jesus' death as an event with far-reaching consequences, although from the very beginning there must have been various interpretations of the meaning of his death. In most of these, though, he was seen as the promised messiah, the "anointed one" (in Greek, Christos) whose death had not been real, since he was thought to have risen from the grave and ascended to heaven. His resurrection and ascent to heaven for many followed from the divine nature of his person, since he was seen as the Son of God. In Jewish tradition, that was probably not much more than a metaphor for someone exceptionally loved or favored by God, but according to Greek ideas he must have been in a supernatural way really the "son" of God and therefore a divine being himself, who proved his divinity by his resurrection. According to the apostle Paul, though, who had not himself known Jesus but had converted to the early Christian movement, Jesus' death had been a redeeming sacrifice that had averted God's justifiable punishment from falling on humanity. All human beings deserved the punishment of death because of their sins, but Jesus had taken that punishment over onto himself and thus saved those of humankind who believed in him. This interpretation was probably not the prevailing one amongst early Christians but would become so gradually in the 4th century and later. For most of the early Christians, Jesus Christ was primarily the wise teacher who had shown humankind the true religion of the one and only God and who defeated the devil, who had wanted to silence him on the cross, by his resurrection and ascent to heaven. All Christians believed that "at the end of time" Christ would come back to Earth to usher in the Kingdom of God, in which the redeemed would live forever, whereas the sinners who had rejected his message would forever burn in hell.

Among the Jews in Judea and Galilee, the idea that Jesus of Nazareth had been the promised messiah or Christ was mostly not favorably received, but among the Jews in the diaspora and pagan sympathizers with Judaism it found more support. Under the influence of the apostle Paul, who was one of the strongest characters among the first generation of "Christians," as they came to be called, those who accepted Jesus as the messiah or Christ did not have to follow the traditional Jewish customs, such as circumcision, since Christ was now presented as the Son of God who had come to save all people, not only the Jews. Instead, the Christians developed their own rituals and rules, such as baptism, which Paul expressly presented as a substitute for circumcision. As a result, the followers of Paul and other apostles now more and more set themselves apart from the Jews and began to form an independent movement. Some Christian groups, though, followed Jewish customs and considered themselves as "Jews" who believed that the promised messiah had indeed come in the person of Jesus of Nazareth. But these "Judeo-Christians" would eventually disappear, and the boundaries between Judaism and Christianity as two separate religions would gradually harden in the course of the first centuries AD. Within Christianity, it would eventually be the line of Paul and his interpretation of Jesus and his death as a redeeming act for all humankind that would become the most widespread (or "catholic," "righteous," or "orthodox") form of Christianity.

Paul was a man with a mission, someone who wandered from city to city to preach his message to the Jewish communities and their pagan sympathizers in Asia Minor, Greece and finally in Rome. The Christian movement that sprang up as a result of his preaching and that of other apostles was an urban phenomenon. For a considerable time to come, Christianity would remain urban, hardly touching the masses of the people in the countryside. In the cities, the Christian communities constituted small groups of people from practically all ranks and classes of the population, with the exception, generally, of the elites. They assembled on Sundays in the morning and the evening in the houses of well-to-do members of the community. In general, Christians seem to have led a life withdrawn as much as possible from "the world," which they saw as sinful, expecting instead a speedy return of Christ, who would usher in the end of the existing world and the establishment of "God's Kingdom". But gradually they came to realize that the second coming of Christ would probably not occur in the immediate future, and they increasingly accepted the world as it was, especially the Roman Empire, which they believed God had created in order that the Christian message might spread easily among the nations. Only the worship of the many gods and divine powers of polytheism was unacceptable. From their Jewish heritage, the Christians had revived as their core conviction that the True and Only God abhorred the worship, especially in the form of bloody sacrifices, of all other so-called gods. For Christians and non-Christians alike, the refusal to sacrifice was the defining characteristic of being a Christian. Polytheism was therefore for Christians the stumbling block. As long as they remained small groups, the Christians distanced themselves as much as possible from pagan festivities with their processions, sacrifices, common meals, and games. Consequently, in the eyes of the rest of the population the Christians were seen as anti-social and "atheist," for they did not honor the gods and thereby risked provoking the wrath of the gods that could affect the whole community. In the first two centuries, the enmity of the Jews also played a role, since in Jewish eyes the Christians were apostates from Judaism, blasphemous, and at the same time dangerous competitors for the adherence of those pagans who had some sympathy for the monotheistic ideas and moral standards of both groups.

The conflict between Christianity and the Roman authorities: Growth of the church

Initially, the Roman authorities had viewed the Christians as Jews, but after a while they realized that they formed a separate group that was not entitled to the privileges of the Jewish nation, and was a group with a diffuse character that by its rejection of the religion and much of the prevailing morals of the empire constituted a danger to the Roman order. That, in any case, was the conclusion reached in Rome when in 64 AD the Christians of the city were accused of having started the great fire in which a large part of Rome had been destroyed. On the orders of Nero, Christians had been arrested, interrogated, and convicted of what the historian Tacitus called "hatred of humanity." Probably, that should be understood as a reference to the Christians' rejection of pagan society and their triumphant prediction—maybe repeated while Rome was burning—that this world would end in flames to be replaced by a new one in which only those saved by Christ would live. A "large number" of Christians in Rome, again according to Tacitus, was then crucified, burned at the stake, or thrown to wild beasts. Since Nero's massacre, Christians in the view of the Roman authorities were people who rightly deserved the death penalty as long as they embraced the convictions that could apparently inspire them to horrible crimes. Rather soon, however, it was discovered that in fact they did not commit the crimes they were accused of. Nevertheless, being a Christian remained a capital offense, for the simple reason that the Christians' "anti-social" and "atheist" behavior in itself threatened the well-being of society; brought before a magistrate who ordered him to sacrifice, a Christian's refusal to do so, moreover, challenged the authority of Rome and fully justified the death sentence. If, however, a Christian in such circumstances did offer sacrifice, he thereby proved that he was no longer a Christian or not a "real" Christian, consequently of no danger to society or the state, and was therefore acquitted. Whether or not a Christian was willing to sacrifice was thus the sole criterion used to condemn or to acquit an accused Christian. This was the basis for the direction that the emperor Trajan (ca. 112 AD) gave to his governors. It was of no importance if the accused had never committed a crime, but neither was it important if he or she had been a Christian for a long time: as soon as the accused offered sacrifice, he or she was acquitted, but the death sentence was inescapable if he or she refused the magistrate's order to sacrifice. The government, though, should according to Trajan not actively search for Christians but only act when someone brought in a formal accusation and appeared in person with the accused before the magistrate (as was the normal procedure in many other criminal cases). If the accused then proved to be innocent by offering sacrifice, he or she had to be acquitted but the accuser punished for "calumny."

If only Trajan's direction had been invariably followed, presumably only a very few Christians would have been convicted and executed. But the idea that the Christians as "atheists" were a danger to the community was widespread, and that sometimes caused spontaneous outbursts of hatred toward them in the larger cities, especially in times of a great pagan festival or after some calamity had struck. The Roman governor, in his wish to maintain order, often reacted by arresting Christians as the source of all unrest, sometimes even searching for them, and placating the public with the spectacle of their death, often on the occasion of games in the amphitheater. Another element usually played a role here as well: the wish on the part of some Christians to die as martyrs. Most Christians were convinced that those who died as Christians had to "sleep" in their graves until the day after the Lord returned, when all the dead would be resurrected; only the martyrs did not have to wait so long, because their souls had gone straight to heaven at the moment of their death (and would return with Christ on Earth in the future, to be reconnected with a new body). In heaven, the martyr could intercede with God Himself for the faithful on Earth, which was the reason why the latter started venerating the martyr-saints. Moreover, in early Christianity the ritual of baptism was taken very seriously, for in principle one who was baptized could count on being saved—unless some grave sin was committed after baptism, for instance, the sin of offering sacrifice to an "idol." In such cases, no forgiveness was possible, and eternal hell fire would be the inevitable outcome. Only dying as a martyr could wash away such a deadly sin, making as it were, the martyr's blood a second baptism. That must have been a reason for some Christians to provoke the authorities and actively to seek martyrdom, while others might simply have been driven by the wish to be assured of salvation in the afterlife. Other Christians again, saw in these events the signs that the time could no longer be far off that Christ himself would return.

Still, the scope of the persecutions should not be exaggerated. Until the middle of the 3rd century they were always local and never lasted more than a few days. In fact, we know only of a handful of persecutions in a few cities, the largest number of victims being 48. Most Christians in the first three centuries AD never experienced a persecution and heard about it only from hearsay. These persecutions by no means hampered the further spread of the church. The Christian expansion over the empire went from east to west, and for a long time the center of gravity of the religion would remain in the Greek-speaking east. The diffusion into the countryside in Egypt, Syria, and Asia Minor started in the 3rd century, in the west a century later. Socially, the church in the 2nd and 3rd centuries reached the upper classes, although among senators she would long remain a tiny minority. This implied that the church numbered a growing number of educated members, foremost in the Greek-speaking east. As a result, there appeared Christian writings and a Christian theology was created. This was mainly the work of the so-called Apologists, Christian writers who in their treatises or "open letters" tried to defend their faith against the objections of pagan society and the anti-Christian laws of the emperors. In doing so, they assured their readers of Christians' loyalty to the empire and the emperor, who in their view had received his authority from God. They also tried to reconcile the Christian faith with the main tenets of Greek and Roman philosophy, especially Platonism and Stoicism, and presented Christianity as in fact the most perfect "philosophy," since, among other things, it was also the most ancient, going back to Adam, the patriarchs and the Israelites, whose position of "chosen people" had been taken over by the Christians, "the true Israel." All good things in ancient philosophy, in this view, were plagiarized from the scriptures of Moses and the prophets. Not many pagans can have been convinced by all that, but it was clear that the church began to abandon her initial total rejection of the world; instead, she started to look forward to the time that the empire might become Christian itself. At the same time, the Jews were more than ever rejected by Christians, because they had refused to listen to the message of Christ and his apostles and because "they" had been the murderers of Christ. Their favored place with God had now been assumed by the church. Consequently, the books of the Hebrew Bible, in which according to the Christians the coming of Christ, his death, and resurrection were frequently foretold, were appropriated by the Christians as their so-called Old Testament. They were placed besides the books of the so-called New Testament, in which four gospels (describing Jesus' actions and teachings), letters under the names of Paul and a few other apostles, a history of the early spread of Christianity (the so-called Acts of the Apostles), and the Apocalypse of John (a revelation about future catastrophes and the end of time) were combined. All these writings, brought together since roughly the 3rd century AD, formed the Christian Bible.

In the first two centuries, Christianity was far from homogeneous; instead, there existed a bewildering multiplicity of sects and subgroups. There were some sects that appealed to direct inspiration by the Holy Spirit and therefore rejected or at least questioned the authority of the traditional scriptures and the established leaders of the Christian communities. Other groups moved along the edges of Christianity, stressing not so much faith but an inner "knowledge" (Greek: *gnosis*, hence "Gnostics"), which brought them close to philosophical speculation about the nature of the soul and of the universe. For these Gnostics, salvation was not brought about by the redeeming work of Christ and in particular by his death on the cross, but by the inner knowledge that some men and women possessed, knowledge about the origin of the souls and human destiny. In this, they resembled somewhat those pagan intellectuals who believed in an origin of the soul in a special realm of light among the stars. The Gnostic view, however, was dualistic, positing a realm of pure spirit beyond the evil and material world. For many of them, Christ's mission had been an esoteric one: to reveal that "knowledge" to those of humankind who would understand, for the vast majority would remain ignorant, doomed to perish with this world of evil. Such ideas were hardly Christian, and the church did her utmost to combat them—eventually with success, for in the 4th century most of the Gnostic groups would disappear. In their opposition to the gnostics, the more "orthodox" Christians had been forced to formulate the core of their own beliefs more clearly and succinctly and at the same time to strengthen the authority of the bishops, their community leaders.

The organization of the Christian communities took shape in the same first three centuries. In essence, each Christian community was autonomous and had a clergy of several ranks, the most important and ubiquitous being those of the "elders" or priests and the deacons. Everywhere, there was one leader at the top of the clerical hierarchy: the bishop (from Greek *episkopos* or "overseer"), who enjoyed an absolute authority in spiritual matters but also supervised the material assets of the community. He had the power to excommunicate the unforgivable sinner from the community. The church as a whole was a kind of confederation of bishoprics, for in the 3rd century there was not yet one overall authority, although the bishop of Rome was honored by the others as the most respectable of all, the successor of the apostles Peter and Paul and the leader of the largest and richest community. How many Christians there were in the 3rd century, we do not know, but their numbers certainly varied from one region to another, being on average much higher in the east than in the west. Estimates for the empire as a whole in the year 300 mostly vary from 5% to 10%. The 3rd century was a period of crises for the empire, caused among other things by the invasions of foreign enemies. In that situation, the emperors, who also stressed their own divine nature, more than before appealed to the gods for help and protection. That brought them into conflict with the church.

In 249, the emperor Decius issued an edict ordering all the inhabitants of the empire to offer sacrifice to the traditional gods. It was like a religious mobilization in which the combined piety of all citizens would propitiate the gods. Christians who refused to participate were automatically suspected of being hostile to the well-being of the empire. This entailed the first empire-wide persecution of Christians on the orders of the imperial government. The number of martyrs is unknown, but in the tradition of the Church the emperor Decius would figure as one of her bitterest enemies. Probably, there were a couple of hundred victims all over the empire, since many Christians fled, or had others sacrifice in their place, or bought special certificates stating, falsely, that they had sacrificed, or indeed complied. What to do with the latter two categories would become a vexed question in the church for some years to come. In 251, the persecution stopped when Decius was killed in battle against the Goths, but in 257 another emperor, Valerian, launched another empire-wide persecution. He put pressure on the clergy, forcing them to sacrifice and thus to prove their loyalty and solidarity, in the expectation that the rest of the Christians would follow the examples of their leaders. But again, most clergy went into hiding or fled, and the number of martyrs was probably not very high. In 260, the emperor was taken prisoner by the Persians. His son distanced himself from his father's policies and immediately ended the persecution, even restoring confiscated property to the church. That meant that the Roman state recognized the church as a legal organization, and thus the period of persecutions ended, or so it seemed.

In the years following 260, the numbers of Christians must have grown considerably, and Christianity now also spread to the countryside of provinces in the east. Perhaps it was this development that worried some influential pagans. In around 300, the emperor Diocletian, a man who was convinced that only the cults of the traditional gods could guarantee the survival of the empire and who had presented himself and his colleague-emperors of the tetrarchy as the close companions and earthly representatives of Jupiter and Hercules, outlawed in an edict the new sect of the Manichaeans as a threat to the Roman order. Similar reasoning probably inspired him a little later to take measures against the Christians. In four edicts in the years 303 and 304, he attacked first the clergy, then all the Christians, by ordering them to sacrifice, apparently expecting to force many Christians to renounce their faith and push the rest back to the margins of society. That started the so-called Great Persecution, which would last a few years. Diocletian's colleague-emperors in the west, however, cooperated only half-heartedly, and the persecution was soon limited to Egypt and the eastern provinces. There, especially in Egypt, probably hundreds of Christians, if not more, died as martyrs. But the numbers of Christians in the east had by then grown already so large that these martyrdoms rather enhanced the prestige of the church. When Diocletian resigned in 305, the persecution in the east was still going on, albeit at a reduced level. His successor there, Galerius, continued half-heartedly with the anti-Christian policy, whereas in the west in 306 Christians everywhere regained their freedom of worship. At last in 311, on this deathbed, Galerius issued the edict of toleration that declared Christianity a legal religion. The Christians were ordered to pray to their god for the well-being of the state and of the emperor—but that they had always been wont to do. In the eastern provinces, persecution would be resumed for a while in 312, but in 313 it finally stopped. An epoch ended, and about the same time a new one began with the conversion to Christianity of the first emperor.

Constantine and the Christianization of the empire

At the time when Galerius ended the persecution in the east, Constantine ruled the far western provinces. Since he had come to power there in 306, he had formally revoked the persecution edicts and restored the property of the church. The ruling emperor in

(a)

Figure 46 The Nag-Hammadi Codices (4th c. AD). In 1945, a large sealed vessel was found near Nag Hammadi, in Egypt, on the middle reaches of the Nile. The vessel contained several codices, that is: books (as opposed to scrolls). After many vicissitudes, the books ended up in the Coptic Museum in Cairo. They contain Coptic (Egyptian written in a Greek alphabet) translations of Greek texts of a Gnostic nature. The original texts and translations date to the 2nd and 3rd centuries AD, and the codices were compiled in the second half of the 4th century. This discovery dramatically enlarged our knowledge of Gnostic literature: of the 52 individual works contained in the codices, 40 were completely unknown before the Nag Hammadi find. Those 52 works are a very mixed bag, with strong syncretic tendencies. But nevertheless, it is clear that the codices must have belonged to Christians. The area around Nag Hammadi was inhabited by Christian communities: shortly before the codices were written, Pachomius founded the first monasteries there. Possibly the codices were hidden when Orthodox Christians toward the end of the 4th century attacked their Gnostic brethren. Overleaf is illustrated a page from Codex I, with the end of the Gospel of the Truth, a Gnostic meditation on Christ, and the beginning of the tract "On resurrection," which defends an unorthodox position on life after death. Except for their contents, the codices are also interesting because they are an example of how Christians changed over from papyrus scrolls to papyrus leaves gathered into books with pages. In the case of the Nag Hammadi codices, the papyrus leaves are gathered in a kind of leather envelopes, among the oldest "bookbindings" known to us. Photos: a) Z. Radovan/BibleLandPictures.com; b) Institute for Antiquity and Christianity, Claremont, California

(b)

Figure 46 (*Continued*)

Italy, Maxentius, in 306 had done the same. In 312, Constantine invaded Italy, defeated his competitor Maxentius, and took Rome. He thereby became the Augustus or supreme ruler of the western half of the empire and at the same time revealed himself as a Christian. Later legend told of a miraculous conversion just before the final battle against Maxentius, but in reality Constantine had already turned to the Christian God at the beginning of his campaign, employing a military standard with the abbreviation of the name "Christos," and after his final victory he must have felt convinced that he had made the right choice. Why he had turned to the Christian God in the first place, we do not know. But the pagan gods were certainly discredited by the failure of the recent persecutions, while probably there were Christians in Constantine's family, among whom possibly his mother. In any case, immediately after his victory over Maxentius he took various measures in favor of the church and gave enormous sums of money for the building of new and imposing churches in Rome and elsewhere. In 324, after a short civil war, Constantine annexed the east and became sole ruler of the whole of the Roman Empire. His pro-Christian policy was immediately extended to the eastern provinces. At the same time, various manifestations of paganism were repressed, although being a pagan was not prohibited. The wealth and privileges bestowed upon the church, though, transformed her into the richest and most powerful institution in society next to the emperor. Social pressure, opportunism, and conformism brought about a rapid growth of the number of Christians. In the second half of the 4th century, the urban population must already have been over 50% Christian. Since Constantine, the church was in alliance with the state. This considerably enhanced the prestige and power of the church, while the emperor's position was sanctified in Christian terms, ruling henceforth "by the grace of God."

On the one hand, Constantine and his immediate successors forbade certain pagan practices, limited others, confiscated temple treasures, and finally banned the offering of sacrifices, and on the other hand they greatly favored and patronized the Catholic Church. The clergy received various rights and privileges, the property of the church was exempted from taxation, and large sums of money and vast estates were transferred to her for the building and maintenance of new churches. Her newly acquired wealth enabled the church to practice charity on a grand scale, which in its turn ensured the conversion of the numerous urban poor. Gradually, daily life was Christianized. Sunday was made an official holiday by Constantine. Slowly, the whole complex of pagan urban life with its euergetism, pagan education, and pagan entertainment was forced out. The cities started to change in character and appearance—a process that would continue during the 4th century and would largely be completed in the 5th: public space in the shape of *gumnasia*, theaters and amphitheaters, public baths, basilicas, stoas, and market squares shrank. In their stead there was a shift to a more private life and to the church: private houses, closed to the outside world, often on narrow streets and alleys now filled the spaces of former squares and avenues, and sometimes even former public buildings. The main public space that remained was the church, towering above the private houses. When the custom to erect churches over or near graves outside the city by the 6th century led to burying inside the church or next to it in a "churchyard" within the city walls, this marked the end of the ancient city and the beginning of the medieval town.

In the 4th century, bishops and some missionary preachers energetically undertook the Christianization of the countryside. But various pagan practices and beliefs would live on for centuries more, secretly and time and again repressed, or openly in "Christianized" forms (Christian saints, for example, replacing pagan spirits or deities in rituals that essentially remained the same). In the cities, paganism in the 4th century was heavily discriminated against and finally, in 380 and the following few years, formally forbidden by the emperor Theodosius I, who closed the temples and issued various edicts banning all sorts of sacrifices and pagan worship. In 381, the same emperor made Catholic Christianity the state religion of the empire.

Rise of asceticism and monasticism: Ecclesiastical disputes and schisms

During the 4th century, some important developments had changed the character of Christianity. An ascetic movement originating in the east in the previous century now exercised a wide appeal. For a long time Christianity had known an ascetic undercurrent preaching celibacy, but since the later 3rd century hermits (literally, "people in the wilderness") had made their appearance in Egypt, who saw in voluntary solitude and self-mortification an imitation of Christ and a way to salvation. When persecution had stopped after 260 and finally after 313, martyrdom as a direct way to salvation (and sainthood) was no longer feasible, and this may have given an extra impulse to the movement into the desert, where the recluses strove to overcome the demons of their desires, freeing themselves from all but the barest needs and thus attaining a near-saintly status. In around 320 in Egypt, the first communities of monks appeared, men who at the edge of the desert lived their ascetic lives collectively under severe rules prescribing from hour to hour what they had to do and how they had to concentrate their minds on the divine. Such monasteries were led by an abbot, who in Egypt and soon elsewhere in the east was supervised by the local bishop. The monasteries attracted thousands of men (others, fewer in number, were for nuns) and grew into a very important social phenomenon. In the second half of the 4th century, the movement reached Rome and soon Gaul. There, in the 4th and 5th centuries, the foundations were laid for the monasticism of the European Middle Ages. This monasticism was part of a broader ascetic movement, already referred to, within Christianity in praise of celibacy, forbidding widows to remarry, propagating an unmarried status for some girls, and trying to allow sex only for the purpose of procreation within a lawful marriage. The unmarried women were usually supposed to assist the church in her caring for the very poor or the sick.

Christian learning and theology flourished in the same period as the ascetic movement spread. Eusebios, the bishop of Caesarea in Palestina, was the writer of the first history of the church, a world chronicle, and various treatises in which the whole of history, from the Creation to the time of Constantine was presented as a meaningful process, led by God, with the Christian empire as its glorious outcome. Other theologians devoted much ingenuity to dogmatic questions. Because of the intertwining of church and state since Constantine, dogmatic questions leading to ecclesiastical conflicts and schisms were always also of political importance. In the 4th century, the main question concerned the relationship between God the Father and Christ the Son who was also God. The followers of the Egyptian priest Arius (Areios) were of the opinion that the Son could not be co-eternal with God the Father; as soon as He, Christ, was there He was also God, but there logically must have been a "time" (if one could speak of "time" before the creation of the world) in which He was not, hence He was "lesser" than the Father. This view caused great consternation among all those who saw Christ as equally, not "lesser" divine. Arius was excommunicated by the bishop of Alexandria but received much support elsewhere in the east. When Constantine had conquered the eastern half of the empire in 324, he was immediately confronted by this dispute that had grown very bitter. He convened a council of bishops in 325 in Nicaea, near the Bosporus, where more than 200 bishops should decide the matter. Constantine himself often attended the sessions, eager for a formal unity of the church, for which he as emperor felt responsible. The bishops decreed that the Father and the Son were "of the same essence," a verdict that nearly all bishops could subscribe to and that became orthodoxy. Nevertheless, the dispute went on for years, for the formula of Nicaea was rather vague. In the end, though, the emperor Theodosius convened a council in Constantinople in 381, where the dogma of Nicaea was reaffirmed and extended with the Holy Spirit: these three "persons" of the one God were deemed to be of the same "essence." That was the dogma of the Holy Trinity. Those who thought otherwise were now heretics, as were various other Christian subgroups, all of which were outside the "Catholic" church and faced increasing discrimination, and even persecution. This dispute, which after 381 died out in the empire, was historically important because it forced the emperors to intervene in the church, it exacerbated a growing rift between the Greek-speaking east (where the question of the trinity was fervently debated) and the Latin-speaking west (where many were hardly aware of the problem and hence a bit suspicious of the Greeks), and because it widened the gulf between the inhabitants of the Roman Empire and the Germanic invaders settling there in the 5th century, who had in the meantime been converted to the Arian form of Christianity.

In the Latin-speaking west, a Christian literature flourished in the 4th and 5th centuries. It reached its height in the works of Augustine, bishop of Hippo in North Africa (modern Algeria). In a sense, Augustine closed the period of Christian antiquity and opened that of the Christian Middle Ages. His main work, apart from numerous treatises on various theological subjects, was the *City of God* (*de Civitate Dei*), written under the impact of the decline of the empire in the west, especially after the plundering of Rome by the Visigoths in 410. Augustine's message was that this event had been less catastrophic than many other calamities that had struck Rome in the past, but that, eventually, it was not important in the greater scheme of things. For the empire was, after all, of no significance in the light of eternity. In opposition to the earthly "city" of the empire and to everything made by men, he placed the "City of God," peopled by all the faithful and existing for all eternity, the world of heaven and the spirit against the imperfect material world.

The ecclesiastical conflicts had another political dimension in that the positions of the great bishoprics came into play here. In the 4th century, the bishops of the provincial capitals had as metropolitan bishops acquired a certain authority and supervision over the other bishops of their province; likewise, the bishops of some important supra-provincial centers such as Alexandria, Antioch, Constantinople, and others claimed an even higher authority over the bishops in regions such as Egypt, Syria, etc. At Nicaea in 325, the bishop of Rome was recognized as the highest ranked of all the bishops, but in the Greek east the patriarchs of Alexandria, Antioch, and Constantinople vied for the second place. The council of 381 formally assigned that second place in the church to the bishop of Constantinople, which inspired the patriarchs of Alexandria to make some attempts at securing their own independence from the new imperial city. This was part of the background to a new dogmatic conflict that divided the church in the 5th and 6th centuries. This time it was about the nature of Jesus Christ and the question of the relationship between the human and the divine in his person. Nestorius, the patriarch of Constantinople, stressed the human character of Jesus, who had in his view only become divine by his resurrection and ascent to heaven; the patriarch of Alexandria defended the fully divine character of Jesus, starting from his miraculous conception and birth. In a first round in 428, Nestorius was condemned by most of his fellow bishops, deposed, and sent into exile to Egypt by the emperor (since Constantine, the emperors automatically supported the decisions of a council and banished bishops who had been deposed). Nestorius' followers, however, spread his interpretation among the by then already numerous Christians in the Sassanid Empire. Next, the patriarch of Egypt overplayed his hand by trying to force through an extreme view of the nature of Jesus, the doctrine of Monophysitism (stating that in Jesus there actually was only one *physis* or "nature," that is, his divine nature), which aroused much opposition. In 451, at the council of Chalcedon (on the Bosporus opposite Constantinople) it was decided, following a written statement of the bishop of Rome to that effect, that in the one person of Jesus there were two natures mysteriously combined, a human and a divine nature. This time the patriarch of Alexandria had to go into exile, while the pope, as we may now call the bishop of Rome, had established his authority in the wider church.

When Eusebius of Caesarea wrote his history of the church, the church for him was practically confined to the Greco-Roman world. Christianity outside the Roman Empire, as in Asia, gets only minimal attention in his work. In Sassanid Persia, Christianity was reinforced by war prisoners taken in Syria and Asia Minor by the Persian kings during their incursions into the Roman Empire in the 3rd century and settled in Mesopotamia. Until the 4th century, the Christians here were more or less left undisturbed, but in the 4th and 5th centuries they were sporadically persecuted. The influence of Christianity and Gnosticism on the religion of Mani is obvious. Not long after 300, probably between 310 and 320, the king of Armenia became a Christian and ordered his people to convert likewise. After 428, as mentioned above, the adherents of Nestorius made their appearance among the Christians in the Persian Empire and won most of the communities there over to their doctrine. The Nestorians then organized themselves as a separate church under their own bishops and patriarch, independent of Constantinople or Rome. This church exhibited a strong missionary zeal: the Nestorians became enthusiastic promoters of their religion, which made it the third missionary religion after Buddhism and the Manichaenism, and Nestorianism spread along the Silk Road as far as China.

PART VII

AFTER 500 AD

Chapter 7

The 6th Century and Later

Eurasian Communities

The period of the 5th, 6th, and 7th centuries was in nearly the whole of Eurasia a time of conquests and migrations of peoples, of old empires falling and new ones rising. China was, after a period of political disruption and fragmentation following the demise of the Han dynasty in 220 CE, in the 4th century split into a part south of the Yangzi river under a Chinese dynasty, and a part north of that river that in its turn was divided among various Chinese and foreign rulers. In the end, the north, reunited in the later 6th century, in 588 reconquered the south under the short-lived dynasty of the Sui. In 618, the dynasty of the Tang replaced the Sui, initiating a period that in many respects would be the height of premodern Chinese history: roughly three centuries during which the emperors from their capital at Chang'an ruled a colossal empire and Chinese civilization flourished in many areas as it had never flourished before. The radiation of Chinese culture over East and Southeast Asia in this period was particularly marked, although even in the time after the fall of the Han dynasty such cultural radiation had never wholly disappeared. In the 4th, 5th, and 6th centuries, Chinese civilization deeply influenced Korea and Japan. Korea had been subject to Chinese influences already during the Han dynasty, when it had even been partially annexed by China, but thereafter some independent Korean kingdoms had emerged that incorporated several elements of Chinese culture, among them Mahayana Buddhism. Via Korea, Buddhism reached Japan with the arrival there of some monks in 552. Initially patronized by the emperors, Buddhism quickly became the second religion in the country, next to the indigenous Shintoism. During the Tang dynasty, the Chinese influence on Japan would be immense, covering nearly all sectors of life, from a centralized state organization to a preference for Chinese poetry among the elite.

To the south, Chinese cultural influences penetrated deep into modern-day Vietnam, where they encountered the equally strong cultural influences from India. Indian traders, Brahmans, and Buddhist monks from the 2nd to the 8th centuries spread Indian political and religious ideas, literature, and art in the wake of overseas trade from India to Southeast Asia. There, indigenous rulers adopted many of these ideas and developed an Indian-inspired divine kingship, such as in the emerging kingdom of the Khmer. In general, the

Antiquity: Greeks and Romans in Context, First Edition. Frederick G. Naerebout and Henk W. Singor.
© 2014 John Wiley & Sons, Inc. Published 2014 by John Wiley & Sons, Inc.

Figure 47 Sculpture of a foreigner on horseback, China (7th–9th c. AD). A large terra-cotta sculpture of a foreigner on horseback, dating to the Tang Dynasty (7th–8th c. AD). The foreigner is characterized as such by his facial features, beard, and dress; more specifically, we can recognize him as a horseman from some nomadic tribe in Central Asia. Other such sculptures portray people from Western Asia and sub-Saharan Africans. All images of foreigners, whether horsemen or riding and leading camels, symbolize the cosmopolitan trade along the Silk Road. The court and aristocrats of Tang China were interested as never before in the exotic. According to the sources for the period, ivory, precious woods, tropical animals, spices, and perfumes were imported into China from the south; horses, leather, furs, and weapons from the north; and textiles, glass, precious stones and ores, and dancing girls from the west. Together with all these objects also traveled ideas and customs: Manichaenism, Tocharian music, and Turkish dress were among the many things that caught the fancy of Chang'an, the Tang capital, the highpoint of cosmopolitanism, home to foreigners from all directions of the compass. Photo: The Granger Collection/TopFoto

ruling elite in Southeast Asia incorporated much of Hinduism into its literature and art, while Mahayana Buddhism also found many adherents, especially in parts of Sumatra and Java (after the 12th century both Hinduism and Mahayana Buddhism would in many places give way to Theravada Buddhism).

The Indian subcontinent itself experienced a cultural efflorescence, especially since the 4th century in the Gupta Empire in the Ganges valley. It was, among other things, the golden age of Sanskrit literature, both secular and religious. Buddhism still flourished in some parts of the country, and the places associated with the life of the Buddha attracted thousands of pilgrims and students from various countries. At the same time, the Brahmanical reaction against Buddhism gathered strength. After the fall of the Gupta Empire in around 500 and during the political fragmentation of the 6th and 7th centuries, the Brahmans everywhere got the upper hand, and Buddhism was reduced to an ever-shrinking minority in the country of its origin. From this restored Brahmanism classical Hinduism arose, covering a wide spectrum from polymorphous polytheism to competing mystical and philosophical schools. It was at the same time a period of rich artistic development in which Indian sculpture and architecture would become the examples for the art of South and Southeast Asia for many centuries to come.

To the north of India, in around 600 AD, the Tibetans established an empire across the Himalayas and large parts of modern-day western China, partly based on aggressive raiding of its neighbors. It came under the influences of both Chinese and Indian culture and in the 8th and 9th centuries, when it had already shrunk in size and become politically weakened, developed its own peculiar form of Buddhism. Farther to the north, in the broad strip of land that constituted the various routes of the Silk Road and in the adjacent northerly steppes, in the period from the 4th to the 9th centuries, great changes took place. These were caused by the movements and migrations of nomad peoples, especially the loose agglomerations of tribes and peoples of a proto-Turkish language group: Huns, Avars, and others. The Hephtalites or White Huns in the 4th and 5th centuries infiltrated the areas of Sogdiana and Bactria, from where they maintained a constant pressure on the Gupta Empire in northern India as well as on Sassanid Iran. Another group of Huns appearing in the plains north of the Black Sea in 375 was pushed westward by the expansion of the Avars from what is now Mongolia. In the 5th century, these Huns established a large but loosely structured political organization bent on raiding and extracting tribute from neighboring peoples under their king Attila. Centered on modern-day Hungary, they threatened the Roman Empire for a while. After Attila's death, his "empire" fell apart, and the Huns, scattered from Hungary to the Caucasus, were mostly absorbed by the Avars, who in their turn had migrated from the eastern steppes to the area around the Caspian and Black Seas in the 5th and 6th centuries. In the 6th, 7th, and 8th centuries, they sometimes threatened the eastern Roman Empire and its capital Constantinople and invaded Central Europe. Pushed back by the Frankish expansion in the 8th century, they would eventually disappear, absorbed by new waves of migrating peoples from the east. Another proto-Turkish empire of the steppes had arisen in Mongolia in the 6th century, pressuring the Avars to the west, and thereafter expanding over a wide area from the Amur river to the Aral Sea. It fell apart in its turn in the 8th century, when the Muslim conquerors from the southwest and the armies of Tang China from the east divided Central Asia among themselves.

In western Asia, Iran and Mesopotamia were ruled by the Sassanid kings until well into the 7th century. Dominated by an Iranian aristocracy and a Zoroastrian priesthood, this state hardly inspired its various subjects to a sense of solidarity. The Zoroastrian priests sometimes incited the kings to persecute minority groups such as the Manichaeans and the Christians. Nevertheless, the Christians especially greatly increased in number. Since the middle of the 5th century, most Christian communities here were Nestorian. The city of Nisibis in northern Mesopotamia, which had been wrested from the Romans in the 4th century, in the late 5th century became a center of Nestorian theology and learning, where

Christian treatises and ancient Greek philosophical and scientific works were translated into Syriac (after the Muslim conquests, its scholars and translators would play a considerable role in transferring ancient learning to the Arabs). The Sassanids waged several wars in the 4th century with the Roman Empire, and again in the 6th (during the 5th century, they were mainly engaged in fighting the Hephtalites in the east). These Roman-Iranian wars on the whole did not yield any permanent gains for either of the two contestants (with the exception of Nisibis), but in the early 7th century a decisive about-turn seemed to occur, when the Sassanids succeeded in overrunning Syria and Palestine, invaded Egypt, and penetrated deep into Asia Minor. For the Christian Roman Empire, the loss of the relic of the holy cross, triumphantly taken away from Jerusalem by the Persians, was an especially hard blow. The reaction took the shape of a grim campaign of retribution, exercised with great skill and energy by the emperor Heraclius (Herakleios), culminating in the siege of Nineveh in 627, in a sense the first crusade in history, since religious fervor was the main motivating force. It symbolized the end of the ancient world and the beginning of a new, medieval world—visualized, as it were, in the icons of the Mother of God that were carried in Heraclius' army, just as the legionary eagles had been in a former age. The expedition was a great success: the Sassanid king was decisively defeated—and shortly after murdered by his own followers—all lost territory recovered, and the holy cross in a great ceremony brought back to Jerusalem. However, these campaigns had seriously weakened both parties. Only a few years later, the Arabs began their invasions of the eastern Roman and the Iranian Empire. The latter collapsed after a few battles: around 650, the whole region between the Mediterranean Sea and Sogdiana was conquered by the Arabs, who in the following century would penetrate India and proceed as far as the western borders of the Tang Empire in Central Asia. With the Muslim conquests, the process of Islamization began at once: Christians, Jews, and to some extent Zoroastrians were tolerated by the conquerors as second-rate subjects without many rights, and all others were forced to embrace Islam or were reduced to slavery. After a few generations, even of the "tolerated" religions, the believers would be reduced to a minority.

In this period, the Roman Empire, the most westerly of the Eurasian empires, lost its western half when in the 5th century the provinces there gave way to various Germanic kingdoms. The eastern Roman Empire, on the other hand, proved itself strong enough to survive the migrations of the 5th century and even to reconquer parts of the west in the 6th. Here, the period between 395 and the reign of Heraclius in the early 7th century was in many respects one long transition from antiquity to the Middle Ages, from the Roman to the Byzantine Empire. In 395, the empire was still Roman in a late antique form, that is, strongly bureaucratic and officially Christian; under Heraclius the organization of government began to take on a new character, initiating a trend toward feudalism that would characterize medieval Byzantium. At the same time, and as a result of the loss of Egypt, Palestine, Syria, and eastern Asia Minor to the Arab conquerors in first half of the 7th century, the empire became smaller and more homogeneous in that it was now more or less uniformly Greek and Orthodox Christian. With that transformation, the history of the Byzantine empire proper began, and was to last until 1453.

The western Roman Empire had formally come to an end in 476—although the emperors in Constantinople would long maintain their claim to the sovereignty of the western part.

There, a new world emerged from a mixture of Roman and Germanic traditions. The church played a crucial role in preserving elements of the ancient civilization and as a unifying force that brought the new states together in a certain common Christian sentiment, first within the boundaries of the old empire, soon also beyond these by the conversions of the Irish and Scots in the west and the Germans in Central Europe in the period of the 5th to the 8th centuries. Medieval Europe thus continued the split between a western half—Latin and Germanic—and an eastern half, which became Byzantine and since the later 6th century also Slavonic. Whereas the Germanic peoples of Central Europe, and later those of Scandinavia as well, were converted to Roman Catholic Christianity and thereby became absorbed into the Latin west, most of the Slavonic peoples of eastern Europe would receive Christianity from Byzantium, and adopt with it not only their own script but also various political and cultural traditions and as a result find themselves to some extent in opposition to the Latin west.

The Germanic West

The Germans had entered the Roman Empire in small groups, of some tens of thousands at the most. The tribes that had settled within the borders of the empire, from the British Isles to the northern coast of Africa, were usually small minorities among the large majority of the original population. Nevertheless, they managed to hang on for some time to their own identities, as Burgundians, Visigoths, and so on, and create their own kingdoms, by a self-imposed isolation. This isolation from the local population can be clearly seen from their religion: they were adherents of Arianism (except for the Franks, who were Catholics, and the Anglo-Saxons, who were not Christian at all). In around 600, all Germans went over to orthodox Catholicism, and in due course they were all assimilated into the underlying population.

The German elite in their newly conquered territories were no enemies of Roman culture: in fact, they all wanted to preserve Roman culture and considered themselves still as part of Romania, the Roman world. That they did not want to cut the ties that bound them to a Roman past is obvious from the codification of Germanic laws. In the late empire, laws had always been territorial: they applied to everyone living within a particular area. Now whether you fell under Roman or some Germanic body of law came to depend on your descent. German princes codified the laws that applied to their Roman subjects in *leges Romanae*, and the laws that applied to their German subjects in *leges barbarorum*, "laws of/for the barbarians." The very fact that Germanic common law was codified, and in Latin too, clearly shows the eagerness to remain part of a Roman legal tradition, not to make a clean break with it.

As already stated, the Anglo-Saxons are a different case. They were no Christians, but pagans, and their kingdoms were in Britain, which had always been a peripheral part of the empire. Roman culture and the Latin language had less chances of survival there than on the Continent. How much survived is much debated: some see quite some continuity after all, because the Roman Empire had struck deeper roots than one might expect, and others think that the British Isles rapidly reverted to pre-Roman Iron Age culture, because Roman culture had never been more than a thin veneer. However

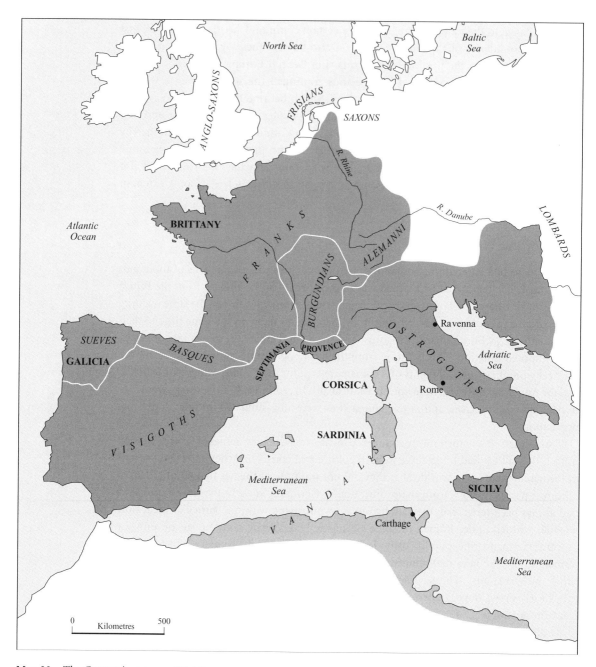

Map 23 The Germanic states, c. 525 AD

Map 24   The Germanic states, c. 575 AD

that may be, from the early 7th century, when a re-Christianization of the British Isles gets under way, they are brought again within the pale of Latin culture—if they had ever been outside of it, as Christianization did not only come from the south, but also from the north. When the Anglo-Saxons conquered most of Britain, Celtic Christianity saved itself in the border regions, especially in Wales. In the 5th century, it was a Welshman, Patrick, who drove the Christianization of Ireland, which had already commenced at an earlier date, rapidly forward. This all grew into a specific Celtic Christian culture that expanded between 550 and 650 to Scotland, England, and subsequently to the Continent, as far as the Alps.

For most people little changed now that they had Germanic overlords. Many local elite families adapted to the new power structure, whereas the small farmers and *coloni* simply remained on the land. Towns continued to exist, and the *civitates* became the model for the new bishoprics. Still, the complexity of society decreased, which applied to the government as well. Germanic princes were quite willing to keep up the governmental apparatus, including taxation, but they did not really have the means to do so. Attempts to preserve central government by a hierarchy of magistrates, such as *dux*, "duke", and *comes*, "count" or "margrave", in due course only led to further fragmentation. The process toward a much weakened central power that had already set in the late empire continued inexorably.

The expansion of the Franks was mainly the work of Chlodovech, better known as Clovis. In 481, Clovis took over from his father, Childeric, who was the son of Merovech, the semi-mythical ruler after whom the dynasty of the Merovingians was named. Clovis conquered large parts of Gaul, battling other Franks, other Germanic tribes, and Romans. His conversion to Catholicism—and that of many of his followers—was an important factor in his success: the church, quite powerful in Gaul, henceforth gave him its support. In 536, all of present-day France, except for Septimania (the region between the Rhône river and the Pyrenees) and Brittany, and sizeable parts of present-day Germany were in Frankish hands.

Italy had become the prize of the Ostrogoth Theodoric at the end of the 5th century when the emperor at Constantinople recognized him as king. Theodoric is as important a figure as Clovis: he considered himself an heir to Rome and strove after hegemony in what had been the western half of the empire. By a clever marriage policy, he managed to realize some of his ambitions, until the new emperor Justinian interfered. Justinian had wanted to implement the idea that the emperor in Constantinople ruled all of the Roman Empire ever since 476, when imperial power in the west came to an end. He conquered Italy and the coastal areas all around the Mediterranean. But what seemed another revival of Roman power was in fact only a final spasm before it passed away forever. When the plague hit the empire in 542–543, its reserves were depleted. It became clear that the Germans had come to stay. The Ostrogoths had been removed from power, but in 568 the Avars, a nomadic tribe in Central Asia, pushed the German Longobards or Lombards out of Pannonia (present-day Hungary) and into Italy. First employed by the Byzantines as *foederati*, they rapidly become the sole rulers. Byzantium could not put up any effective resistance: they had to fight Avars, Bulgarians, and Berbers on their many borders. And, momentously, in Mecca, Mohammed was born. The West was now truly independent and would have to fend for itself.

The successes of the Franks have already been mentioned. They too were a small minority, and thus their Merovingian Empire was very Gallo-Roman in nature. Nevertheless, there were some specific Germanic traits. Most importantly, there was no concept of empire. The Frankish territories were not considered a *res publica*, but as the private property of the Merovingian rulers. Division among heirs split up Clovis' empire into a number of kingdoms, the rulers of which went after each other with a bloodthirstiness so extreme that sometimes unity was restored only because all competition had been killed off. While these Merovingian power struggles were under way, two important developments took place: first, the so-called Mayor of the Palace, the *majordomus* of the Merovingian courts, steadily increased his power. Especially the Mayors who belonged to the family of the Carolingians became very prominent: they were destined to become the next ruling dynasty. And second, the Christianization in the 7th and 8th centuries of areas to the north of the Merovingian Empire, the present-day Netherlands and bits of western Germany, prepared the way for a new round of Frankish expansion.

The Visigoths had been forced back by the Franks into Spain. There, a Visigothic kingdom survived for two centuries, with a flourishing culture, but often chaotic politics. In 711, Arabic forces crossed at Gibraltar: the Visigoths, weakened by internal strife and by strained relations between the Goths and the Ibero-Romans, hardly put up any serious resistance. Already in 717–718, Arabic armies crossed the Pyrenees. In 732, the Franks defeated the Arabs in the Battle of Poitiers, but the Iberian peninsula would remain in Arabic hands for quite some time to come.

In 751, the Mayor of the Palace, Pepin the Short, deposed the last Merovingian king, and ascended the throne himself. His heir was Charlemagne, who ruled from 768 to 814. The real Charlemagne has become mostly obscured by myth and legend, but one thing that we can say about him is that he was extremely effective as a commander on the battlefield. He battled successfully with the Arabs south of the Pyrenees; he fought in Italy, Germany, and Denmark; and he defeated the Slavs who had moved from the East up to the Elbe, and the Avars in the Hungarian plain. It was probably the idea of Pope Leo III to crown this conqueror emperor in Rome in 800. Byzantium refused to recognize this new emperor as an equal of its own emperor, but Charlemagne did not need Byzantium's approval. His being crowned emperor was a crucial moment in the emancipation of the west.

After 840, the Carolingian unity was lost again. Altogether, the 9th and 10th centuries were a period of crisis for large parts of Europe. Its borders were under attack by Norsemen, Arabs, and since the end of the 9th century, Magyars (Hungarians). Central government collapsed, especially in the West-Frankish kingdom. Only the kings of the East-Frankish kingdom managed to keep some order, defeat Norsemen, Slavs, and Magyars, and even expand their kingdom toward the east. Beginning in 962, the East Frankish kings were crowned emperor. Otto III, at the end of the 10th century, son of a German king and a Byzantine princess, considered his imperial title to no longer indicate his supremacy in the west, but to stand for the *renovatio imperii romanorum*: the revival of the Roman Empire. This idea of a renewal of the Roman Empire would survive for many centuries, in the notion of a Holy Roman Empire. So five centuries after the end of Roman rule, not only was Rome still remembered, but it was reinvented—in the west, while Byzantium with its emperor still existed.

The Byzantine East

While the western empire fell, the eastern empire persisted. Many explanations can be given for this difference. Always, the eastern half of the empire had been more urbanized than the western half, while commerce and money circulation too had taken deeper root there. The apparatus of government in the east too was more developed and better controlled, centrally, than was the case in the west. It was made up largely of persons of relatively low social backgrounds who owed their position to the emperor, whereas in the west the senatorial aristocracy monopolized the higher government posts and thereby was in a position to weaken or even to sabotage imperial policies, such as tax collection. As a consequence, the government in the east could impose its will on the great landed magnates much more effectively than was possible in the west, where the large landowners of the senatorial class practically ignored the central government and hardly if at all paid taxes. The emperors in Constantinople, therefore, had a fuller treasury than their western colleagues and that enabled them, especially in the 5th century, to pay off the Huns with large sums of gold not to invade their territory and to hire considerable numbers of Germanic mercenaries. The latter, however, could pose a risk to the internal security of the state. In the course of the 5th century, the eastern emperors purged their armies of Germans and began to recruit instead from the warlike populations of Asia Minor, their own subjects. The creation of an indigenous army that was only reinforced by mercenaries, together with the very strong strategic position of Constantinople, protected since the early 5th century by huge walls, gave the eastern empire such an advantage that it would be able to survive many military setbacks and remain the undisputed center of an empire for many more centuries. The weaker west, meanwhile, had to cope with the main thrust of the Germanic invasions from across the Rhine and the Upper Danube.

Although the eastern Roman Empire after 395 largely remained intact, it unmistakably changed in many ways. The Christianization of society brought about the disappearance or transformation of many elements of ancient civilization, such as the games and shows in the amphitheaters and theaters, or the public baths and the *gumnasia*, or the studying and teaching of the sciences and pseudo-sciences of antiquity, not to mention the various pagan cults, which had all been forbidden by the emperor Theodosius I near the end of the 4th century. Churches, monasteries, and the fortified mansions of great landowners now presented another picture of the city and the countryside. The high esteem in which ascetic ideals were held led to a narrow view of sexuality, a glorifying of virginity and celibacy, and the rise of a numerous population of monks, nuns, and hermits. At the same time, the imperial government for a long period upheld the political structure and the political ideology of the old Roman Empire. It maintained the essentials of Diocletian's and Constantine's organization of the empire with its prefectures, dioceses, and provinces and its separation between military and civilian powers. Also, until nearly the end of the 6th century, it kept up the old pretension that the empire was in fact co-extensive with the civilized world, and that other states, if they could not be subdued, still had to acknowledge the higher sovereignty of the emperor in Constantinople, the more so since he was now a Christian, anointed in God's name and His deputy on Earth. From that standpoint, it became politically expedient to convert other peoples to Christianity and bring them thus

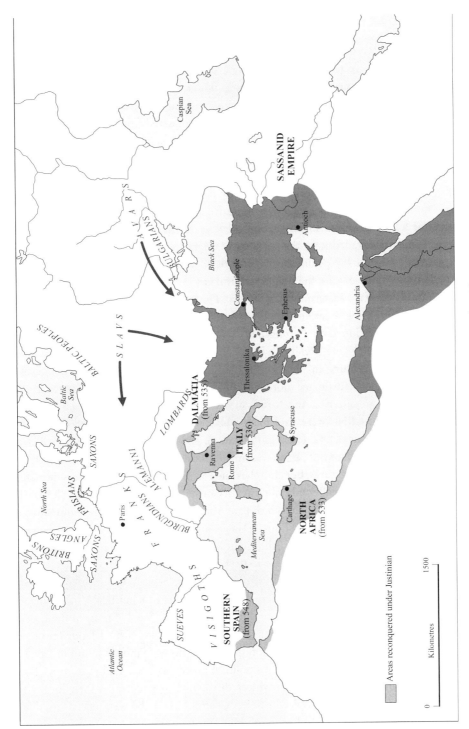

Map 25 The Eastern Roman Empire, 6th c. AD

to some form of recognition of the authority of the emperor; hence, the officially organized missions to Nubia and Ethiopia in the 6th century and to the Slavs in the 7th and 8th centuries.

In the 6th century, the eastern Roman Empire under the reign of Justinian seriously tried to live up to its claims of being a universal empire with a stubborn effort to bring the western basin of the Mediterranean under the direct rule of Constantinople. Around 540, North Africa was taken from the Vandals and annexed; thereupon, in the 40s and 50s of the century, Italy was with great effort reconquered from the Ostrogoths; both regions were as new prefectures added to the empire. Finally, in the 50s, some coastal areas of southeastern Spain were conquered from the Visigoths. All these successes, which spelled the end of two Germanic kingdoms, had only been achieved with the utmost exertion. Italy and the city of Rome were largely destroyed in the process. The weakened empire proved unable to offer effective resistance against new dangers presenting themselves in the following years. Already in 568, three years after Justinian's death, the Longobards or Lombards invaded Italy, the last wave of migrating Germanic peoples to enter the empire; soon, most of the peninsula that had been won at so high a cost was definitely lost for Constantinople. Still, the reign of Justinian (527–565) was generally seen by posterity as the height of the eastern Roman Empire. This emperor, the last ruler whose native language was Latin in this Greek environment, lived on in history as the great codifier of Roman law, who commissioned the *Corpus Iuris Civilis*, a collection of the then still valid laws and legal rules, and their interpretations by the great Roman *jurisprudentes*. Its later introduction, in the 10th century, in Western Europe would profoundly influence the development of civil law there. Justinian, moreover, one of the greatest builders in ancient history, had churches, monasteries, and fortifications erected all over his empire. Typically, most of these constructions were paid for by the state, because the cities under his rule had lost their independent financial administration, and with it most of their ancient autonomy. Likewise, typical for this period was the specific character of all that architecture: no theaters or other civic structures, but churches and fortifications, as if to buttress the defenses of the empire both spiritually and militarily. In Constantinople itself, Justinian left the largest and most impressive domed church of Late Antiquity as an enduring monument to his reign: the Church of the Holy Wisdom or Hagia Sophia (now the Aya Sofia mosque in Istanbul).

Justinian's efforts to restore the old unity of the Roman Empire were seriously hampered by the great theological and ecclesiastical disputes of the time. First, as we saw, the adherents of Nestorius had been driven out of the church; next, the council of Chalcedon in 451 had created a deep rift between those who held to a mystical duality of human and divine natures in the one person of Jesus Christ—the view of most of the Greek-speaking Orthodox and of the Latin-speaking Catholics—and those who defended the overall divine nature of Christ: the so-called Monophysites, who were mostly found in Egypt and Syria. This lent the conflict a dangerous political aspect. The Monophysite convictions of most Christians in those eastern provinces threatened to undermine their loyalty toward the emperor in Constantinople. Justinian's conquests in the west raised the dilemma how to reconcile Catholics and Monophysites in one unified empire and one church. Neither imperial decrees nor a new council convened by Justinian in Constantinople solved the question. When Justinian died after nearly 40 years of rule, tensions in Syria and Egypt still ran high.

The last decades of the 6th century and the first decades of the 7th brought a deep crisis for the East Roman Empire, a crisis from which it would emerge transformed into another sort of state. Seriously weakened by Justinian's war efforts in the west as well as by the economic and demographic consequences of a severe epidemic that raged in 542 and following years (probably the first occurrence of bubonic plague in Europe), the empire in the second half of the 6th century had to deal with large-scale incursions of the Slavs from across the Lower Danube. These migrations caused a comprehensive ethnic transformation in the Balkans, where practically all of the mainland, with the exception of Constantinople and heavily fortified cities such as Thessalonica, became inhabited by Slavonic peoples, the ancestors of modern-day Croats, Serbs, and other so-called South Slavs, while in the 7th century, another people, the Bulgars, also crossed the Danube. The core of that people were descendents of the Huns who had settled near the Volga river. In their new habitats in the Balkans they adopted a Slavonic dialect. As a result, the government in Constantinople during most of the 7th century had lost practically all authority in the Balkans. Only in the course of the 8th and 9th centuries would the mainland of Greece be slowly re-hellenized, the rest of the Balkans with the exception of Albania (the land of the ancient Illyrians) remaining Slavonic. The Slavs of the Balkans, however, would all accept Orthodox Christianity from Byzantium.

The crisis in the Balkans in the beginning of the 7th century was accompanied by another crisis in the Asian parts of the empire. The enormous and unexpected successes of the Sassanids, already mentioned before, rocked the empire to its foundations. In 610, a coup d'état gave the throne to the energetic Heraclius; the religiously inspired war that followed ended in a great victory for Constantinople and a serious weakening of the Persian Empire. Heraclius witnessed the greatest triumph and the deepest humiliation of the empire. For in the 30s and 40s of the 7th century, the Islamic Arabs broke out from the Arabian peninsula in a serious of lightning campaigns, inspired by their newly won religion, and in a few years conquered Palestine and Syria. By the time Heraclius died in 641, Arab armies had entered Armenia and were approaching the walls of Alexandria in Egypt. A few years later, Egypt and the coast of Libya were in Arab hands, and Arab fleets harassed the Aegean. The old East Roman Empire shrank to western and central Asia Minor, a few coastal areas in the Balkans with the cities of Constantinople and Thessalonica, the Aegean islands, and a few outlying areas such as Sicily and the region around Ravenna in Italy—all the rest of Justinian's empire had now fallen to Arabs, Slavs, and Lombards.

The shrunken empire in the 7th century again changed in character. Although its people stubbornly kept calling themselves "Romans," the name "Roman Empire" was in fact no longer fitting; since the 17th century historians used the name Byzantine Empire instead. There was a transformation in many areas. In the political organization of his realm, Heraclius definitely took leave of Diocletian's and Constantine's heritage: new offices and new titles appeared and the beginnings of a new provincial organization were set up in which the separation between military and civilian powers was largely abolished and a trend to feudalism initiated. The language of the government was now invariably Greek; already under Justinian, new laws had been issued in Greek, but Heraclius went a step further: the traditional Latin title of the emperor was replaced by the sole Greek term *basileus* (king or emperor). The empire had become considerably smaller but at the same time more homogeneous, from the religious point of view too. With the loss of Syria and Egypt, the adherents of Monophysitism were no longer subjects of the emperor, and so the necessity to persuade them to agree to subtle theological compromises with the Orthodox and Catholic populations elsewhere in the empire had disappeared. As a Greek and Orthodox state, the empire would survive the deep crises of the late 7th and early 8th centuries—when the capital Constantinople itself was twice threatened by Arab armies and fleets—and in the 9th and 10th centuries even reconquer all of the Balkans, Asia Minor, and parts of Syria, to dominate the eastern Mediterranean again, for the last time. The arrival of Turkish peoples in western Asia in the 11th century would introduce its slow and inexorable decline and fragmentation, until the Ottoman Turks, by finally taking Constantinople in 1453, would seal the end of this last remnant of the Roman Empire.

The Christian Church

From the world of antiquity, more than one new world emerged. In the west, it was the Latin and Germanic states, assembled in the Catholic Church under the leadership of Rome; next, it was the Byzantine Empire in the Balkans and Asia Minor, which through the Orthodox Church brought various peoples in eastern Europe under its influence; and finally, Christians in Africa and Asia. The last-mentioned were, from the 7th century, under Islamic domination, gradually became a minority, and in the course of the Middle Ages at various places would disappear altogether. Islam itself to a degree took over the role of heir to the ancient world—to a degree, because Islam consciously positioned itself as the antithesis of Greco-Roman culture, creating completely new structures in many fields, while deliberately destroying the old.

Perhaps the most obvious heir to the Roman Empire was the Roman Catholic Church, led by the pope in Rome as in earlier days the empire had been by the emperor. In her organization in bishoprics and archbishoprics, the Catholic Church preserved the political organization in *civitates* and *provinciae* of the Roman Empire. The bishop of Rome acquired his position as head of the church thanks to the prestige that automatically accrued to the Christian community of Rome as the largest and richest of all communities, which was both the "imperial" city and refounded as a Christian city by the apostles Peter and Paul, whose funerary monuments outside the city were venerated by the faithful. Unlike the Greek east, the Latin west of the empire did not have large and prestigious episcopal sees that could compete with Rome. The authority of the bishop of Rome was in the 4th century formally accepted in the church at large, but as a result of the growing rift between the two halves of the empire it was in practice mostly limited to the west. The absence of an emperor in the west after 476 contributed to the establishment of papal authority over western Christendom—again in contrast to the Greek east. Gradually, the popes developed their authority in liturgical and doctrinal matters. Here, popes Leo I (middle of the 5th century) and Gregory I (around 600) may be mentioned. Just like many bishops in the

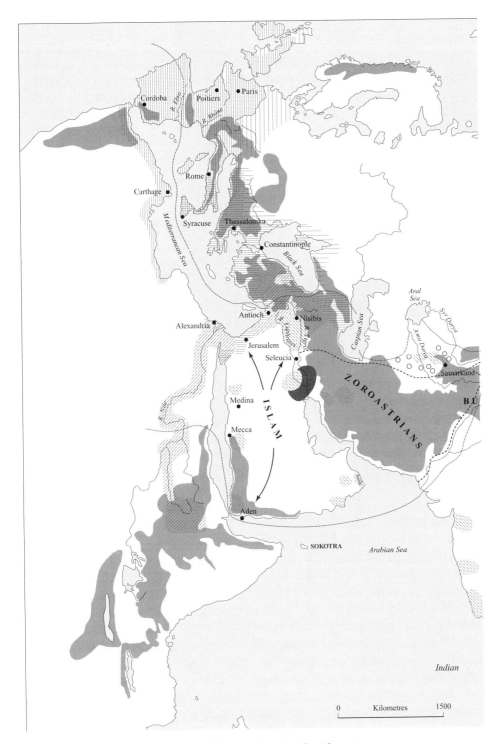

Map 26 Religions in Eurasia, 7th–8th c. AD

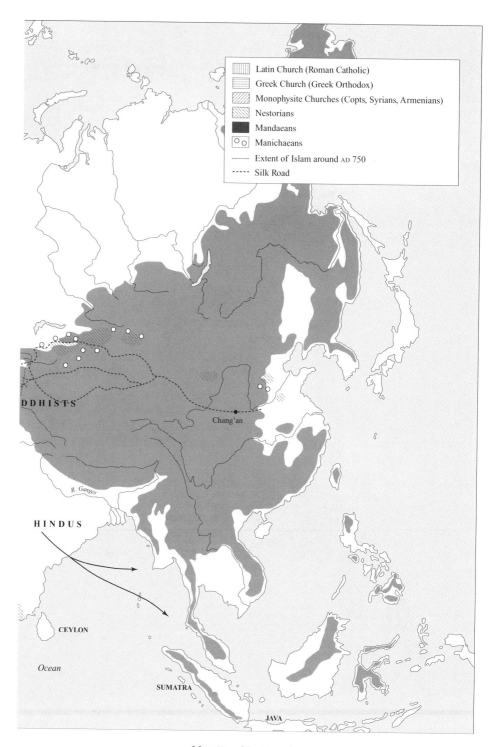

Map 26 *(Continued)*

Figure 48 Mosaic from Ravenna with the Emperor Justinian (6th c. AD). In 525 the building of the cathedral of Ravenna, dedicated to St Vitalis, started. Twenty-three years later, it was finished. In the meantime, Ravenna had been conquered by Justinian. Now, the choir of the church was embellished with mosaics that showed, on the one side, the emperor Justinian and his courtiers, and on the other side the empress Theodora with her companions. These mosaics are among the very best that early Byzantine art has to offer. Justinian is in the center, dressed in a purple robe (purple was a color that only the emperor was allowed to wear), with bejeweled slippers and crowned with a heavy diadem decorated with gems and pearls. From this late antique diadem, the medieval imperial crown would develop. The face of the emperor is thought, as also that of Theodora, to be a true likeness: Justinian had his portrait sent to all provinces; and this mosaic is supposed to have been made by artists from Constantinople, not by local ones, unlike other mosaics in the church. The emperor holds a golden bowl, his present to the new church. On his right we have the emperor's court represented by two courtiers dressed in white. The purple squares on their dress are meant to cover their hands whenever they take something from the emperor, or give him something. The bearded courtier has been tentatively identified as Belisarius, the general who initiated the conquest of Italy. Next to the courtiers, we see the palace guard, their shields decorated with the christogram, the Chi Rho, which goes back to Constantine. On Justinian's left-hand side stand one other courtier, toward the back, and the ecclesiastical powers: first Maximianus, archbishop of Ravenna, holding a cross; and next, two priests, one with a costly codex, the other with an incense burner. The background of the mosaic is all heavenly gold, from which the emperor's head is set off by a nimbus that distinguishes him from mere mortals. Photo: The Art Archive/Alamy

west, the popes also functioned as de facto rulers of their city, a dominion they in the 8th century managed with the help of the Frankish kings to enlarge to much of Central Italy (the so-called Papal States).

The church in the west was on the whole remarkably uniform. This was not only the result of a single leadership, but also because of the use of Latin as the language of the liturgy. While spoken Latin in the early Middle Ages more and more distanced itself from the written language—to give rise, in the 7th to 9th centuries, to the various Romance languages—the continued use of Latin in the church guaranteed the survival of the written language and consequently of the link with ancient Latin literature. In this way, the church maintained a considerable measure of continuity with the past, notwithstanding the loss of much of ancient literature. On her part, the church inspired a new Latin literature, both in prose and in poetry.

Toward the end of the 4th century, the new phenomenon of hermits and monks also reached the west. The first monasteries in Gaul were modeled after those in the Greek east. In the 6th century, the Italian Benedict founded on the Monte Cassino in southern Italy the first monastery of a new type, for which he had written the rules. Apart from prayer and contemplation, in the new rules much time was reserved for work. That work could take different forms, but intellectual work, such as the copying of manuscripts, was seen as important. Thus, the so-called Benedictine order would be of great significance for the intellectual history of Europe. Monasteries became centers where to some extent books and an ideal of learning would always be preserved, even when, in the 6th to 10th centuries, illiteracy would be prevalent throughout most of western Europe.

The Latin Church had no tradition of missionary work among the heathen until around 600, when Pope Gregory the Great (Gregory I) sent his missionaries to England with the express purpose of converting the Anglo-Saxons. Since then, missionary endeavors, stimulated by the popes, became more normal, although the missionaries often required the support and protection of secular potentates. Here, the Franks offered their help, especially the Carolingian kings, with the result that an intimate cooperation arose between the papacy and Frankish monarchy. The successes of the missions in Germany, Poland, and Scandinavia considerably enlarged the domain of the Catholic Church up to the beginning of the 11th century, while at the same time enhancing the prestige of the papacy.

Compared to the rather independent Latin Church, the Greek Church in the eastern Roman Empire since the 4th and 5th centuries was in a clearly weaker position. Various patriarchs competed for second place after Constantinople—or, as in the case of Alexandria, for a virtually equal place. The patriarch of Constantinople was recognized as the highest in rank, but his independence was regularly infringed upon by the emperor, whose wishes in ecclesiastical matters too had the force of law. It would be wrong, though, to speak of "Caesaropapism" (that is: the emperor as head of the church), since by far most of the emperors in the eastern Roman or Byzantine Empire followed their bishops and synods in theological matters. Still, conflicts between the emperor and the patriarch were not rare, and this must have helped to prevent the emergence of a single and fully independent ecclesiastical authority in the eastern church that could be compared with the papacy in the west. Moreover, the split between Orthodox and Monophysites in the 5th century had no parallel in the western church. Also, in the east the liturgy was often rendered in the vernacular. This led to Coptic, Syriac, and Armenian liturgies and separate churches (mostly Monophysite), and a little later in the 8th through 10th centuries to Bulgar, Serbian, and Russian liturgies and churches (all Orthodox) under the umbrella of Constantinople.

Monasticism had originated in the eastern Roman Empire, and monks and monasteries would always play an important social and sometimes political role there. On the whole, monastic life in the east had a different character from that in the west. Since the introduction of a monastic rule by the bishop and theologian Basil of Caesarea in Cappadocia toward the end of the 4th century, all monasteries in the eastern empire followed his regulations. These provided ample time for contemplation and for the liturgy and relatively little for work (and no time, or very little, for intellectual work). As a consequence, the Greek Orthodox monasteries became centers of prayer and mysticism, not places of intellectual life. Copying of manuscripts happened in the east too, but not as regularly and on such a scale as in the west. All the monasteries in the east were under the authority of the local bishops, and all of them belonged to the order of Basil, whereas the monasteries in the west were mostly independent of the bishops—thus constituting a rival authority—and would since the 11th century belong to various often competing monastic orders, further splitting ecclesiastical authority.

In their missionary work also, the Greek and Latin churches differed from each other. After the missions in Nubia and among the Slavonic peoples, Constantinople made little effort to bring "barbarian" peoples into the church. Thus, the Orthodox Church, by continuing the classical Greco-Roman attitude that saw the "barbarians" beyond the borders as essentially uninteresting, unimportant, if not contemptible, identified herself more or less with the empire and with "the civilized world."

The Monophysites of Syria and Egypt, meanwhile, organized themselves in the 6th and 7th centuries in separate churches that became practically independent of Constantinople. After the Arab conquests, that separation became permanent. In the following centuries, the Monophysite churches steadily shrank, although the Coptic Church still represents about 10% of the population of modern-day Egypt. In Syria, they have become a very tiny minority. The older Nestorian Church, on the other hand, flourished, especially in Central Asia, and won adherents as far as China. But in western Asia they were harassed by the Muslim conquerors, and in Central Asia after about 1300 they were persecuted by the Islamic Mongol rulers, which led to their rapid decline.

Islam

The history of Islam in its earliest phases is based on written sources that date from the 8th century or later. These sources look back at earliest Islam from a very specific religious and political point of view, and may well distort history in a serious way. Scholarship on the 6th and 7th centuries seems to be divided between those who support a view of early developments within Islam that is more or less close to Islamic orthodoxy, and those who argue for an Islam that only took shape during the period of conquests outside the Arabian peninsula and that only created an identity of its own toward the end of the 7th or the

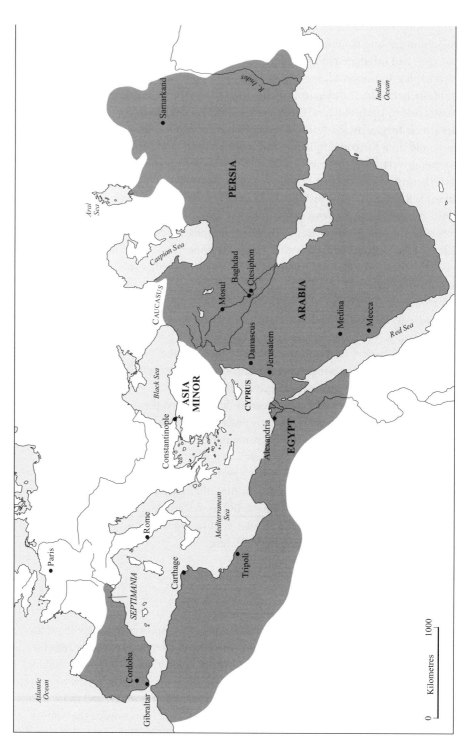

Map 27 The Islamic world, c. 750 AD

beginning of the 8th century. Here, we stick to a traditional account—but it should be noted that neither this, nor any other account, is supported by independent evidence.

The joining together of many Arabic tribes in a single community, the *umma*, is usually explained by pointing at the pressure put on the Arabian peninsula by Byzantium, Sassanid Persia, and Ethiopia. Ethiopia conquered the south of the peninsula in the 6th century. There had been a period when kingdoms to the north and south, such as Nabatea, Petra, Palmyra, and Yemen had brought about some political and economic integration of the Arabian peninsula, but now the area was fragmented. Under attack from Greeks, Sassanids, and Ethiopians, there was little that it could do, as it lacked a political center from where resistance could be organized. Also, its adversaries all had an exclusivist religion that strengthened their identities, the monotheism of Christians and Jews and the dualist Zoroastrianism of Persia. The religions of the Arabic tribes did not—and could not—fulfill the same function. The only common element was the town of Mecca, an important trade hub, but also housing a central sanctuary, the Ka'ba. But Mecca was also affected by the 6th-century troubles.

Here enters Mohammed (Muhammad), scion of a Meccan family. He was a man with an interest in religion, who from 610, when he was about 40 years of age, followed his calling as a prophet. For many years, God is supposed to have revealed His words to Mohammed, with the archangel Gabriel as an intermediary. This revelation was later written down in *Al-Qur'an*, the Qur'an (probably, "what is recited"). On the basis of these visions, Mohammed preached a monotheism that was close to the Jewish monotheistic tradition. His success was quite limited at first, and the animosity of many Meccans made Mohammed leave for Madina (Medina): the *hijra* ("the migration") of 622—the year that became the base year of the Islamic calendar. In Madina, the *umma* of Mohammed and his followers separated from the Jews and Christians, and, at least so we are told, at that moment a new monotheistic religion came into being: Islam ("Surrender to God").

Mohammed not only advocated monotheism, but also Arabic unity. Diplomacy and force did indeed bring this unity about, but Mohammed's death in 632 threatened to undo everything, especially because of the question who would take over Mohammed's leadership role. This was solved by the institution of the caliphate. A *khalifa* is a successor, or a stadtholder or vicaris. First, there was talk of a *khalifa rasul Allah*: a successor to the prophet of God, and later we also hear of a *khalifa Allah*: a stadtholder of God on Earth. Between 632 and 661 there ruled four orthodox caliphs, all from the direct circle of Mohammed. Between 661 and 750, the caliphs belonged to the dynasty of the Umayyads. It was in this period that the incredibly rapid expansion of Islam took place.

Immediately after the death of Mohammed, all Arabic tribes were once and for all incorporated into an Arabic unity. A combination of martial traditions, a longing for plunder and booty and the religious duty to fight a *jihad*, a holy war, against the infidels, brought Arabic armies to Damascus in 636, to Ctesiphon in 637, to Jerusalem in 638, Mosul in 641, and Alexandria and Tripolis in 643. Between 640 and 660, all of Iran and parts of Afghanistan were conquered; between 643 and 711, all of Northern Africa; and after 711, Spain. In 720, not even a century after the death of Mohammed, Islam ruled from the Indus to the Pyrenees. Only Byzantium withstood the Arabic onslaught: in 674–678 and in 717–718 the Arabs tried to take Constantinople, but to no avail.

It is remarkable how the Arabs managed to resist assimilation. Usually, when nomadic tribes from the periphery invade central powers, as happened in China and with the Roman Empire, the newcomers are rapidly absorbed. Not so the Arabs, who rather put their stamp on the territories they conquered. The explanation should lie in the fact that they had their own extremely powerful and exclusive set of norms and values based on their religion. In the Near East, the Arabs at first had a purely fiscal relationship with the local populations, which remained in majority non-Islamic for at least two centuries after they had been conquered.

The rapid expansion went together with internal troubles: already in the 7th century, the Islamic Arabs fought their first civil war. This ended with the murder in 661 of the fourth caliph 'Ali, a most traumatic event that led to the permanent division between the adherents of 'Ali and his descendants—the Shi'a—and those who recognized the Umayyad dynasty as the legitimate caliphs—the Sunna. The Umayyads tried to bring political stability, which did not return after 661, by attempting to centralize government, not so much around the person of the caliph but around a state. Part of this policy was to diminish the Arab character of the government, for instance, by replacing Arabs in the army by Syrians. The capital was transferred from Medina to Damascus. But Arabic remained the lingua franca. When the Byzantine and Sassanid bureaucracies, which the Arabs had taken over intact, were turned into an Umayyad bureaucracy, Greek and Persian were replaced by Arabic.

The years between 730 and 750 were a period of profound crisis: heavy setbacks were suffered on battlefields from the Amu Darya to France, from Northern Africa to Anatolia, and political and religious unrest were rife. The Umayyads were removed from power by a new dynasty, the 'Abbasids, who continued the Umayyad policy of building an Islamic, not an Arabic, empire. The Arabic *umma* was now replaced once and for all by an Islamic *umma*. The symbol of this new Islamic Empire was the newly founded Baghdad, a cosmopolitan capital city that in the 9th century grew to become the largest city in the world outside China. The shift from Damascus to Baghdad turned Islam from being essentially Mediterranean into a successor to Sassanid Persia. But the glorious days of the 'Abbasids were short-lived. In the 9th and 10th centuries, their Islamic Empire began to fall apart in smaller states. Sometimes this was merely the recognition of an existing state of affairs: thus, Spain had been autonomous since the mid-8th century. Political fragmentation meant economic regression. But although the Islamic imperium was never to return, still strong cultural ties continued to exist between the lands that once had been part of it, fostered by a shared religion.

The Ancient Heritage

When we speak of the heritage of the Greco-Roman world, we usually give pride of place to "*the* Renaissance," the "rebirth" that is supposed to have taken place in Italy in the 14th and 15th centuries and of which the rediscovery of the classical world was one of the main components. "Renaissance" is an 18th century concept that was popularized in the 19th century: the sequence of antiquity, Middle Ages, and Renaissance implied a cultural cycle: flowering, decline and fall, a dark intermediate period, and a revival. In the

19th century, however, we also find a renewed interest in the Middle Ages, and this inspired scholars to go and look for the medieval roots of what happened in 14th and 15th century Italy in order to "debunk" the Renaissance. The debate has continued ever since. Even if it cannot be denied that great changes occurred during the period commonly designated as the Renaissance, and that the speed and intensity of these changes increased, the debate has made it clear that these changes had been prepared for by developments taking place over many centuries. Hence, we now speak of "the Renaissance of the 12th century" and of "the Carolingian Renaissance."

But by distinguishing other "renaissances," the whole concept of "*the* Renaissance" has become rather hollow: in fact, the break with the past that is implied in the word "rebirth" never happened. What we call "Western culture" builds on a Greco-Roman heritage (including Christianity, even though that is only in part of Greco-Roman origin). Indeed, one can speak of a single cultural complex comprising Greek and Roman culture and what came after, and that one can distinguish from, for instance, the East Asian cultural complex. This is not to deny that besides Greece and Rome, other "genetic material" contributed to the forms and contents of "Western culture"; but the Greco-Roman heritage has been dominant in many respects or for long stretches of time.

The foregoing is not a plea to accord a special status to Greco-Roman antiquity because that is where our roots lie. It is simply the establishment of a blood relationship. The heritage left by the ancient world has been continuously (re-)interpreted, adopted, adapted, and (re-)appropriated. It is not a static entity, but very much living and changing all the time—and as the heritage changes, our image of the legators changes with it. It is the nature of this reception ("reception" is the word often used to cover this whole process of (re-)appropriation, and so on), or rather of these receptions, each within its own context, that merits our attention, not the mere fact that some things have come down to us. And we can also turn this round: the Greco-Roman world is interesting for its own sake, and not because it can be seen as a forerunner of our own world. We might add to the foregoing that the amount of heritage is changing as well: the material and nonmaterial heritage keeps growing. In the Middle Ages, texts that had been forgotten were rediscovered. In the Renaissance, this continued, but archaeology (*avant la lettre*) also came to play a part, and in the centuries to follow archaeology expanded hugely in scope. Epigraphy and papyrology contributed and contribute a steady stream of new documents. Our knowledge of the ancient world and the size of the ancient heritage increases every day.

We have to distinguish between instances of continuity and of rediscovery. Some aspects of the ancient world knew a continued existence in some part of what once was the Greek or Roman world, or even outside of it. The one element survived here, the other there, and subsequently, by transmission or diffusion, they could spread again. But there is also discontinuity: much was forgotten in the course of time. Some of it was rediscovered. Often, rediscovery took place in the context of, or was occasioned by, a desire to recreate the ancient world. Although this has always been, and will always remain, an impossibility, we should distinguish between say, neoclassical architecture, which has produced buildings that, if they are not imitations, still approach ancient architectural ideals, and the opera, which began as a revival of Greek drama, but developed into something that has but very little to do with ancient drama—as far as we know what that actually looked like.

The continuity is embodied by the Romania: a world that was in many ways a continuation of the late Roman Empire, and which was felt to be that. The Germanic successor states were part of that Romania, and carried the Roman heritage in their constitutions and laws, and in their nascent state ideology. They also were, or rapidly became, Christian communities. Christianity was the main force that safeguarded continuity in the transition to the Middle Ages. The church was itself an institution from late antiquity that became the main repository of ancient culture, ancient learning, and the Greek and Latin languages. Monasteries played an important role here, and also in the Christianization of large areas, inside but also outside the old borders of the Roman Empire.

In the east, Byzantium and eastern Christianity took care of the ancient heritage. Continuity is evident, in the case of Constantinople–Byzantium, but it is also part of their self-image: the Byzantine Empire called itself the Roman Empire. They were also part of the Romania, albeit an increasingly exclusively Greek Romania, in the same way in which the west became almost exclusively Latin. The crisis between the death of Justinian and the first quarter of the 7th century resulted in a purely Greek Byzantium that did not any longer look primarily to the west. Religious differences between east and west slowly became an unbridgeable divide.

And then there was Islam. As already said, the Arabs put their mark on the territories they conquered. But, of course, according to the laws of acculturation, they themselves did not remain unaffected. This was not anything new: thanks to the caravan routes, large parts of the Arabic world had been in close contact with the Hellenistic kingdoms and the Roman Empire. These contacts persisted into late antiquity, especially by missionaries spreading Christianity. But now the contacts became more intense than ever: the first Arabic conquests put them in possession of thoroughly Hellenized areas: Syria, Egypt, and the western part of the Sassanid Empire. Under the orthodox caliphs and the Umayyad dynasty, we see Arabs distancing themselves from Greek culture and language, which were associated with paganism, but nevertheless this period already sees some translations from Greek and Syrian into Arabic in the fields of alchemy and medicine.

The 'Abbasids, who moved away from the Greek world, from Damascus to Baghdad, were quite self-assured, and thus less defensive about their own religion, language, and culture. There were ever more translation from Greek and Syrian, but also Indian languages and Persian, into Arabic, mostly done by polyglot Jews and Christians. This was still done for practical reasons: the Islamic world was eager to acquire knowledge from the sciences and pseudo-sciences of the Greco-Roman world. But theology became important too: Christians had access to a lot of ancient philosophy, and Islam followed suit. Also, Mohammed was supposed to have stressed the importance of learning in religion and all of human life, so study was deemed important.

In the 8th and 9th centuries, there came into being a specific Islamic culture based in large part on the ancient heritage, especially in its late antique manifestations. This has also been called a renaissance. The Islamic world, with its specific culture, and its large numbers of Jews and Christians, can certainly be called part of the Romania—but in this instance, that was not an ideology shared by that Islamic world itself.

The west (re)discovered much Greek philosophy and scholarship, the knowledge of which had been lost, or which in some cases might never have been known at all, by way

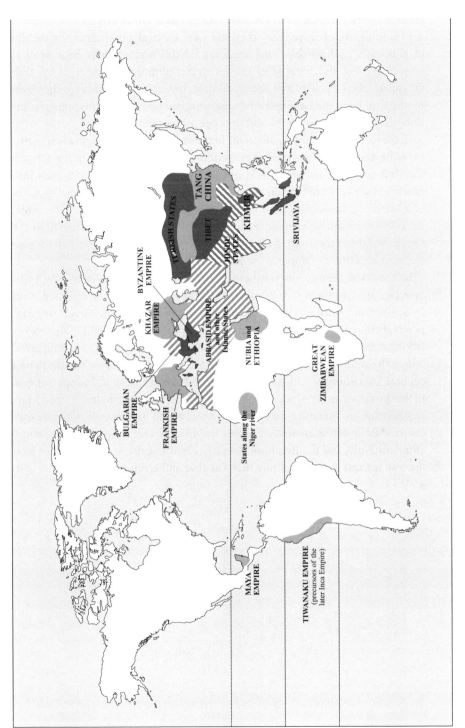

Map 28   The world, c. 800 AD

of the Islamic world, especially through contacts in Spain and on Sicily, usually by way of Latin or Hebrew translations of Arabic translations of Greek originals. But however indirect the transmission of these texts, they still were of great importance for the development of philosophy, scholarship, and science. And this was not only because of the ancient knowledge, but also because of the important additions made to it by Arab scholars. Of course, the Crusades also meant contact, but culturally speaking they were not very productive. Even the conquest of Constantinople by western crusaders resulted in more Christian relics than Greek manuscripts being brought to the west.

In the west, we can see two moments in time when interest in the ancient heritage peaked: the aforementioned Carolingian renaissance and the Renaissance of the 12th century. But the 10th and 11th century should not be supposed to be devoid of such interest. How much was actually known about the ancient world during the Middle Ages, the meaning of a "medieval humanism" and what they actually made of it all, are the subject of lively debate. We can say with certainty that almost all knowledge was restricted to Latin texts or Greek thought as transmitted in Arab sources. Aristotle's *Logic* (in a Latin translation) was the most important example of the latter category.

In the 14th century, in northern Italy, we enter a completely new phase: ancient manuscripts, Latin and Greek ones, started to be systematically collected. Contacts with Byzantium not only produced texts, but also teachers of the Greek language. Ancient poetry, fictional prose, and drama came to be appreciated, something that earlier had been lacking outside of Byzantium. The availability, soon by way of the printing press, of a huge body of forgotten texts was one of the foundations of what we now call the Renaissance, the cultural flourishing of 15th-century northern Italy, radiating to Europe north of the Alps. In this Renaissance, a re-creation of the ancient heritage was undertaken on a large scale: in architecture, art, literature, and music, the goal was to overcome existing discontinuities by consciously imitating ancient examples. In 1453, the year Constantinople was taken by the Ottoman Turks and the Byzantine Empire ceased to exist, Greeks who fled to Italy found there an interest in Greek culture that was alive and kicking.

Appendices

Note: Greek names are given in their Latinized version, or the shortened version thereof that is generally used in the Anglophone world. Between brackets, there is a transcription of the original Greek—if different. For names in the main text not included in the appendices, the reader can turn to the index, where the appropriate transcription of every Latinized version of a Greek name is given.

Antiquity: Greeks and Romans in Context, First Edition. Frederick G. Naerebout and Henk W. Singor.
© 2014 John Wiley & Sons, Inc. Published 2014 by John Wiley & Sons, Inc.

CLASSICAL ATHENS

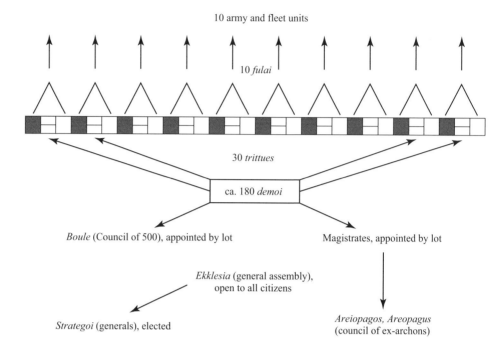

10 army and fleet units

10 *fulai*

30 *trittues*

ca. 180 *demoi*

Boule (Council of 500), appointed by lot

Magistrates, appointed by lot

Ekklesia (general assembly),
open to all citizens

Strategoi (generals), elected

Areiopagos, Areopagus
(council of ex-archons)

THE CLASSICAL ROMAN REPUBLIC

Populus Romanus
has two assemblies:

comitia tributa (or *concilium plebis*) where the *populus* gathers distributed across 35 *tribus* (districts). Every citizen has access to the *comitia tributa*–only plebeians if *concilium plebis*. Voting is by *tribus*; within his *tribus* every citizen has one vote.

comitia centuriata, where the *populus* gathers distributed across 193 *centuriae* (centuries), divided among 5 classes.
Voting is by century and by class, starting with the first class and the *equites*.
Voting is stopped when a majority is reached—which means that classes IV and V seldom or never voted. The *proletarii* make up a single century in the 5th class.

Gathers in the Forum or on the Capitol.

Gathers in the Campus Martius.

Presided over usually by a *tribunus plebis*, always by a tribune if *concilium plebis*.

Presided over by a magistrate in possession of *imperium* (*consul* or *praetor*).

Functions as a legislative assembly (with increasing power)

Decides specific cases, such as matters of war and peace.

Chooses the tribunes when assembled as *concilium plebis*, and lower magistrates (*quaestor* and *aedilis*) when assembled as *comitia tributa*.

Chooses consuls, *praetores* and, every five years, a *censor*.

All magistrates and tribunes become members of the senate (for life) immediately upon assuming office. Within the senate, the *nobiles* (ex-consuls and their descendants) form an elite within this elite.

IMPERIAL ROME: THE PRINCIPATE

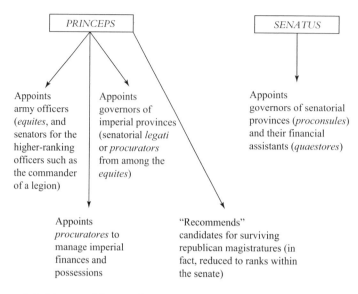

Inhabitants of the empire:

1 Roman citizens (*cives Romani*) in Italy and in many communities outside Italy (the number of individuals with citizenship steadily increased until 212 when all free inhabitants of the empire, with the possible exception of category 3 below, obtained citizenship).

2 The free inhabitants of the provinces or of so-called "autonomous" towns, who do not have the Roman citizenship (*peregrini*).

3 "Serfs" or other types of farmers bound to the soil or to their place of residence in Egypt and Asia Minor.

4 Slaves. Freedmen are *cives Romani* if freed by a Roman *patronus*; otherwise, they are included with the *peregrini*.

IMPERIAL ROME: THE DOMINATE

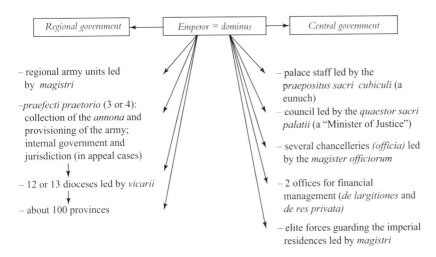

The inhabitants of the empire are all *cives Romani*, except:

1 slaves;
2 *foederati* settled within Roman territory (starting with the Visigoths in the Balkan in 382).

HELLENISTIC RULERS

Ptolemies

305–283 BC	Ptolemy I Soter (Ptolemaios I Soter)
283–247	Ptolemy II Philadelphus (Ptolemaios II Filadelfos)
247–221	Ptolemy III Euergetes (Ptolemaios III Euergetes)
221–204	Ptolemy IV Philopator (Ptolemaios IV Filopator)
204–181	Ptolemy V Epiphanes (Ptolemaios V Epifanes)
181–145	Ptolemy VI Philometor (Ptolemaios VI Filometor)
145	Ptolemy VII Neos Philopator (Ptolemaios VII Neos Filopator)
145–116	Ptolemy VIII Euergetes II (Ptolemaios VIIII Euergetes II)
116–107	Ptolemy IX Soter II (Ptolemaios IX Soter II)
107–88	Ptolemy X Alexander (Ptolemaios X Alexandros)
88–80	Ptolemy IX Soter II (Ptolemaios IX Soter II)
80	Ptolemy XI Alexander II (Ptolemaios XI Alexandros II)
80–51	Ptolemy XII Auletes (Ptolemaios XII Auletes)
51–48	Ptolemy XIII Philopator II Philadelphus (Ptolemaios XIII Filopator II Filadelfos)
48–30	Cleopatra (Kleopatra VII)

Antigonids

306–301 BC	Antigonus Monophthalmus (Antigonos Monofthalmos)
301–283	Demetrius Poliorcetes (Demetrios Poliorketes)
283–239	Antigonus II Gonatas (Antigonos II Gonatas)
239–229	Demetrius II (Demetrios II)
229–221	Antigonus III Doson (Antigonos III Doson)
221–179	Philip V (Filippos V)
179–168	Perseus

Attalids

283–263 BC	Philetaerus (Filetairos)
263–241	Eumenes I
241–197	Attalus I (Attalos I)
197–159	Eumenes II
159–138	Attalus II (Attalos II)
138–133	Attalus III (Attalos III)

Seleucids

305–280 BC	Seleucus I Nicator (Seleukos I Nikator)
280–261	Antiochus I Soter (Antiochos I Soter)
261–246	Antiochus II Theos (Antiochos II Theos)
246–226	Seleucus II Callinicus (Seleukos II Kallinikos)
226–223	Seleucus III Soter (Seleukos III Soter)

223–187	Antiochus III Megas (Antiochos III Megas)
187–175	Seleucus IV Philopator (Seleukos IV Filopator)
175–163	Antiochus IV Epiphanes (Antiochos IV Epifanes)
163–162	Antiochus V Eupator (Antiochos V Eupator)
162–150	Demetrius I Soter (Demetrios I Soter)
150–145	Alexander Balas (Alexandros Balas)
145–139	Demetrius II Nicator (Demetrios II Nikator)
	Antiochus VI Epiphanes II (Antiochos VI Epifanes II)
139–129	Antiochus VII Sidetes (Antiochos VII Sidetes)
129–125	Demetrius II Nicator (Demetrios II Nikator)
125–121	Cleopatra Thea (Kleopatra Thea)
121–95	Antiochus VIII Grypus (Antiochos VIII Grupos)
	Antiochus IX Cyzicenus (Antiochos IX Kuzikenos)
95–83	Philip I Philadelphus (Filippos I Filadelfos)
	Antiochus X Philopator (Antiochos X Filopator)
	Antiochus XI Philadelphus (Antiochos XI Filadelfos)
	Antiochus XII Dionysus (Antiochos XII Dionusios)
	Antiochus XIII Asiaticus (Antiochos XIII Asiatikos)
83–69	(Interregnum of Tigranes of Armenia)
69–64	Antiochus XIII Asiaticus (Antiochos XIII Asiatikos)
	Philip II Philoromaeus (Filippos Filoromaios)

ROMAN EMPERORS

27 BC–14 AD	Augustus		
14–37	Tiberius	306–337	Constantinus
37–41	Gaius (Caligula)	307–324	Licinius (East)
41–54	Claudius	337–361	Constantius II
54–68	Nero	337–340	Constantinus II (West)
68–69	Galba, Otho, Vitellius	340–353	Constans (West)
69–79	Vespasianus	361–363	Julianus Apostata
79–81	Titus	363–364	Jovianus
81–96	Domitianus	364–375	Valentinianus I (West)
96–98	Nerva	364–378	Valens (East)
98–117	Trajanus	375–383	Gratianus (West)
117–138	Hadrianus	379–395	Theodosius I (the Great)
138–161	Antoninus Pius	383–392	Valentinianus II (West)
161–180	Marcus Aurelius	395–408	Arcadius (East)
180–192	Commodus	395–425	Honorius (West)
192–193	Pertinax	408–450	Theodosius II (East)
193	Didius Julianus	425–455	Valentinianus III (West)
193–211	Septimius Severus	450–457	Marcianus (East)
211–212	Caracalla and Geta	455	Petronius Maximus (West)
212–217	Caracalla	455–456	Avitus (West)
217–218	Macrinus	457–461	Maiorianus (West)
218–222	Elagabalus	461–465	Severus (West)
222–235	Alexander Severus	467—472	Anthemius (West)
235–238	Maximinus Thrax	472	Olybrius (West)
238—244	Gordianus iii	473–474	Glycerius (West)
244–249	Philippus Arabs	474–475	Julius Nepos (West)
249–251	Decius	475–476	Romulus Augustulus (West)
251–253	Trebonianus Gallus	457–474	Leo I (East)
253–260	Valerianus	473–474	Leo II (East)
260–268	Gallienus	474–491	Zeno (Zenon) (East)
268–270	Claudius II Gothicus	491–518	Anastasius
270–275	Aurelianus	518–527	Justinus
275–276	Tacitus	527–565	Justinianus
276–282	Probus	565–578	Justinus II (Ioustinos II)
282–284	Carus, Carinus, Numerianus	578–582	Tiberius II Constantinus (Tiberios II Konstantinos)
284–305	Diocletianus	582–602	Mauricius (Maurikios)
285–305	Maximianus (West)	602–610	Phokas (Fokas)
305–311	Galerius	610–641	Heraclius (Heraklios)

PHILOSOPHERS

Pre-Socratics:

Thales of Milete (1st half of the 6th c. BC)
Anaximander (Anaximandros) of Milete (6th c. BC)
Anaximenes of Milete (6th c. BC)
Heraclitus (Herakleitos) of Ephesus (ca. 500 BC)
Xenophanes (Xenofanes) of Colophon (2nd half of the 6th c. BC)
Parmenides, active in Elea, Italy (ca. 500 BC)
Zeno (Zenon) of Elea (5th c. BC)
Pythagoras (Puthagoras) of Samos, active in Italy (2nd half of the 6th c. BC)
Philolaos (Filolaos) of Croton (2nd half of the 5th c. BC)
Empedocles (Empedokles) of Akragas (5th c. BC)
Leucippus (Leukippos) of Milete (5th c. BC)
Democritus (Demokritos) of Abdera (2nd half of the 5th c. BC)
Anaxagoras of Clazomenae (2nd half of the 5th c. BC)

Sophists:

Protagoras of Abdera (5th c. BC)
Prodicus (Prodikos) of Ceos (2nd half of the 5th c. BC)
Gorgias of Leontini (2nd half of the 5th c. BC)
Hippias of Elis (2nd half of the 5th c. BC)

Classical philosophers:

Socrates (Sokrates) of Athens (2nd half of the 5th c. BC)
Plato (Platon) of Athens, founder of the Academy in Athens (4th c. BC)
Antisthenes of Athens (1st half of the 4th c. BC)
Diogenes of Sinope, known as Kunikos (Cynicus, the Cynic) (4th c. BC)
Aristippus (Aristippos) of Cyrene (4th c. BC)
Aristotle = Aristoteles of Stageira, founder of the Lyceum in Athens (4th c. BC)
Theophrastus (Theofrastos) of Eresus, second head of the Lyceum (ca. 300 BC)
Speusippus (Speusippos), second head of the Academy (2nd half of the 4th c. BC)
Xenocrates (Xenokrates), third head of the Academy (ca. 300 BC)

Hellenistic and Roman philosophers:

— Stoics:
Zeno (Zenon) of Cition, founder of the Stoa in Athens (ca. 300 BC)
Cleanthes (Kleanthes), second head of the Stoa (1st half of the 3rd c. BC)
Chrysippus (Chrusippos), third head of the Stoa (2nd half of the 3rd c. BC)
Panaetius (Panaitios) of Rhodes (2nd c. BC)

Posidonius (Poseidonios) of Apamea (ca. 100 BC)

Seneca (1st half of the 1st c. BC)

Epictetus (Epiktetos) (ca. 100 BC)

Marcus Aurelius (Roman emperor 161–180 BC)

— Epicureans:

Epicurus (Epikouros) of Samos, active in Athens (ca. 300 BC)

Lucretius (1st c. BC)

— Skeptics:

Pyrrho (Purrhon) of Elis (2nd half of the 4th c. BC)

Sextus Empiricus (2nd c. AD)

— Platonists and Eclectics:

Carneades (Karneades) of Cyrene (1st half of the 2nd c. BC)

Cicero (1st c. BC)

— Jewish Platonic philosophers:

Philo (Filon) of Alexandria (1st half of the 1st c. AD)

— Neopythagoreans:

Numenius (Noumenios) of Apamea (2nd half of the 2nd c. AD)

— Neo-Platonists:

Plotinys (Plotinos) of Alexandria (3rd c. AD)

Porphyrius (Porfurios) of Tyre (2nd half of the 3rd c. AD)

Iamblichus (Iamblichos) (ca. 300 AD)

Chalcidius (4th c. AD)

Macrobius (ca. 400 AD)

Boëthius (6th c. AD)

Proclus (Proklos), head of the Academy (5th c. AD)

Damascius (Damaskios), head of the Academy (2nd half of the 5th c. AD)

Simplicius (Simplikios), head of the Academy (1st half of the 6th c. AD)

Hypatia (Hupatia) of Alexandria (ca. 400 AD)

John Philoponus (Ioannes Filoponos) of Alexandria (1st half of the 6th c. AD)

SCHOLARS AND SCIENTISTS

Late Archaic and Classical Greece:

Hekataeus (Hekataios) of Milete (ca. 500 BC), geographer, ethnographer
Alcmaeon (Alkmaion) of Croton (1st half of the 5th c. BC), medical doctor
Hippocrates (Hippokrates) of Cos (2nd half of the 5th c. BC), medical doctor
Herodotus (Herodotos) of Halicarnassus (5th c. BC), historian
Thucydides (Thoukudides) of Athens (2nd half of the 5th c. BC), historian
Archytas (Archutas) of Tarente (ca. 400 BC), mathematician
Xenophon (Xenofon) of Athens (1st half of the 4th c. BC), historian
Eudoxus (Eudoxos) of Cnidus, active in Athens (4th c. BC), mathematician, geographer, astronomer
Ephorus (Eforos) of Cymae (4th c. BC), historian
Aristotle = Aristoteles of Stageira, active in Athens (4th c. BC), polymath and philosopher
Timaeus (Timaios) of Tauromenion (2nd half of the 4th c. BC), historian

The Hellenistic world:

Theophrastus (Theofrastos) of Eresus, active in Athens (ca. 300 BC), botanist
Euclid = Euclides (Eukleides), active in Alexandria (ca. 300 BC), mathematician
Aristarchus (Aristarchos) of Samos, active in Alexandria (1st half of the 3rd c. BC), astronomer
Herophilus (Herofilos) of Chalcedon, active in Alexandria (1st half of the 3rd c. BC), medical doctor
Eratosthenes of Cyrene, active in Alexandrië (2nd half of the 3rd c. BC), geographer
Archimedes of Syracuse (2nd half of the 3rd c. BC), physicist
Polybius (Polubios) of Megalopolis, active in Rome (2nd c. BC), historian
Hipparchus (Hipparchos) of Nicaea (2nd half of the 2nd c. BC), astronomer
Philo (Filon) of Byzantium (2nd half of the 2nd c. BC), physicist, engineer
Posidonius (Poseidonios) of Apamea (ca. 100 BC), ethnographer, geographer, philosopher
Hero (Heron) of Alexandria (end of the 1st c. BC?), physicist
Diodorus (Diodoros) of Sicily (2nd half of the 1st c. BC), historian

The Roman world (Late Republic and Imperial period):

Cato Maior ("the Elder") (2nd c. BC), historian, agriculturalist
Mucius Scaevola (2nd half of the 2nd c. BC), jurist
Varro (1st half of the 1st c. BC), linguist, antiquarian, agriculturalist
Caesar = Gaius Julius Caesar (1st half of the 1st c. BC), historian
Sallust = Sallustius (1st c. BC), historian
Vitruvius (2nd half of the 1st c. BC), architect, engineer
Nicolaus (Nikolaos) of Damascus (end of the 1st c. BC), historian
Dionysius (Dionusios) of Halicarnassus (early 1st c. AD), historian

Strabo (Strabon) (end of the 1st c. BC), geographer

Livy = Titus Livius (end of the 1st c. BC, early 1st c. AD), historian

Cornelius Nepos (1st half of the 1st c. AD), historian

Pompeius Trogus (end of the 1st c. BC, early 1st c. AD), historian

Valerius Maximus (1st half of the 1st c. AD), historian

Velleius Paterculus (1st half of the 1st c. AD), historian

Pomponius Mela (1st half of the 1st c. AD), geographer

Curtius Rufus (1st c. AD), historian

Pliny = Plinius Maior ("the Elder") (1st c. AD), encyclopedist

Frontinus (2nd half of the 1st c. AD), engineer, military theoretician

Flavius Josephus (Flavios Josefos) (1st half of the 1st c. AD), historian

Tacitus = Cornelius Tacitus (ca. 100 AD), historian

Suetonius (1st half of the 2nd c. AD), historian

Plutarch = Plutarchus (Ploutarchos) of Chaeronea (1st half of the 2nd c. AD), historian

Arrianus (Arrianos) (1st half of the 2nd c. AD), historian

Appianus (Appianos) (1st half of the 2nd c. AD), historian

Ptolemy = Claudius Ptolemaeus (Klaudios Ptolemaios) of Alexandria (2nd c. AD), astronomer, geographer

Pausanias (2nd c. AD), travel writer

Galen = Galenus (Galenos) of Pergamon (2nd c. AD), medical doctor

Gaius (2nd c. AD), jurist

Cassius Dio (Kassios Dion) (ca. 200 AD), historian

Herodianus (Herodianos) (1st half of the 3rd c. AD), historian

Papinianus (1st half of the 3rd c. AD), jurist

Ulpian = Ulpianus (1st half of the 3rd c. AD), jurist

Diophantus (Diofantos) of Alexandria (2nd half of the 3rd c. AD), mathematician

Pappus (Pappos) of Alexandria (ca. 300 AD), mathematician

Ammianus Marcellinus (4th c. AD), historian

Anonymus author of the Historia Augusta (2nd half of the 4th c. AD), historian

Vegetius (2nd half of the 4th c. AD), military theoretician

Cassiodorus (6th c. AD), encyclopedist

Jordanes (6th c. AD), historian

Procopius (Prokopios) (6th c. AD), historian

Agathias (6th c. AD), historian

POETS AND PROSE WRITERS

Archaic Greece:

— Epic poetry
[Homer = Homerus (Homeros)], *Iliad*
[Homer = Homerus (Homeros)], *Odyssey*
Homeric Hymns
Hesiod = Hesiodus (Hesiodos) (ca. 700 BC)

— Lyric poetry
Archilochus (Archilochos) of Paros (7th c. BC)
Callinus (Kallinos) of Ephesus (7th c. BC)
Tyrtaeus (Turtaios) of Sparta (7th c. BC)
Alcman (Alkman) of Sparta (ca. 600 BC)
Mimnermus (Mimnermos) of Colophon (ca. 600 BC)
Alcaeus (Alkaios) of Lesbos (ca. 600 BC)
Sappho (Sapfo) of Lesbos (ca. 600 BC)
Solon of Athens (1st half of the 6th c. BC)
Theognis of Megara (1st half of the 6th c. BC)
Stesichorus (Stesichoros) of Himera (6th c. BC)
Anacreon (Anakreon) of Teos (6th c. BC)
Ibycus (Ibukos) of Rhegion (2nd half of the 6th c. BC)
Bacchylides (Bakchulides) of Ceos (ca. 500 BC)
Simonides of Ceos (1st half of the 5th c. BC)
Pindar = Pindarus (Pindaros) of Thebes (5th c. BC)

Classical Greece:

— Drama
Aeschylus (Aischulos) of Athens (1st half of the 5th c. BC)
Sophocles (Sofokles) of Athens (5th c. BC)
Euripides of Athens (2nd half of the 5th c. BC)
Aristophanes (Aristofanes) of Athens (2nd half of the 5th c. BC)

— Rhetoric
Andocides (Andokides) of Athens (2nd half of the 5th c. BC)
Lysias (Lusias) of Athens (1st half of the 4th c. BC)
Isaeus (Isaios) of Athens (1st half of the 4th c. BC)
Isocrates (Isokrates) of Athens (4th c. BC)
Aeschines (Aischines) of Athens (4th c. BC)
Demosthenes of Athens (4th c. BC)

Hellenistic and Roman world:

— Drama
Menander (Menandros) of Athens (ca. 300 BC)
Plautus (1st half of the 2nd c. BC)
Terence = Terentius (1st half of the 2nd c. BC)

− Rhetoric

Cicero (1st c. BC)

Dio Chrysostom (Dio Chrusostomos) of Prusa (ca. 100 AD)

Aelius Aristides (Ailios Aristeides) (2nd c. AD)

Libanius (Libanios) of Antioch (4th c. AD)

− Prose

Quintilianus (1st c. AD)

Petronius Arbiter (1st half of the 1st c. AD)

Pliny = Plinius (Minor, "The Younger") (ca. 100 AD)

Apuleius (2nd c. AD)

Aulus Gellius (2nd c. AD)

Athenaeus (Athenaios) (2nd c. AD)

Lucian = Lucianus (Loukianos) of Samosata (2nd half of the 2nd c. AD)

Aelianus (Ailianos) (ca. 200 AD)

Philostratus (Filostratos) (1st half of the 3rd c. AD)

Longus (Longos) (2nd c. AD)

− Poetry

Theocritus (Theokritos), active in Alexandria (3rd c. BC)

Apollonius Rhodius (Apollonios Rhodios) (3rd c. BC)

Herondas of Alexandria (3rd c. BC)

Callimachus (Kallimachos), active in Alexandria (3rd c. BC)

Livius Andronicus, active in Rome (2nd half of the 3rd c. BC)

Naevius, active in Rome (ca. 200 BC)

Ennius, active in Rome (ca. 200 BC)

Menippus (Menippos) of Gadara (2nd c. BC)

Lucilius, active in Rome (2nd half of the 2nd c. BC)

Lucretius, active in Rome (1st half of the 1st c. BC)

Catullus, active in Rome (1st half of the 1st c. BC)

Vergil = Vergilius (2nd half of the 1st c. BC)

Ovid = Ovidius (2nd half of the 1st c. BC)

Horace = Horatius (end of the 1st c. BC)

Tibullus (end of the 1st c. BC)

Propertius (end of the 1st c. BC)

Phaedrus (early 1st c. AD)

Lucanus (1st half of the 1st c. AD)

Statius (2nd half of the 1st c. AD)

Martial = Martialis (2nd half of the 1st c. AD)

Juvenal = Juvenalis (ca. 100 AD)

Ausonius (2nd half of the 4th c. AD)

Claudius Claudianus (ca. 400 AD)

Rutilius Namatianus (1st half of the 5th c. AD)

Nonnus (Nonnos) (1st half of the 6th c. AD)

CHRISTIAN AUTHORS

Before 200:

Paul = Paulus (Paulos), Apostle, author of *Epistles* (mid 1st c.)
Marc = Marcus (Markos), Apostle, evangelist (2nd half of the 1st c.)
Matthew = Mattheus (Matthaios), Apostle, evangelist (2nd half of the 1st c.)
Luke = Lucas (Loukas), Apostle, evangelist and author of *Acts* (2nd half of the 1st c.)
[John = Iohannes (Ioannes)], *Book of Revelation (Apocalypse)* (end 1st c.)
Anon., Pseudepigraphic letters in the *New Testament* (end 1st, begin 2nd c.)
Ignace = Ignatius (Ignatios) of Antioch (early 2nd c.)
Polycarp = Polycarpus (Polukarpos) of Smyrna (1st half of the 2nd c.)
Hermas of Rome (1st half of the 2nd c.)
Anon., *Epistle of Barnabas* (1st half of the 2nd c.)
Marcion (Markion) of Sinope (2nd c.)
Basilides (Basileides) of Alexandria (2nd c.)
Valentinus of Rome (2nd c.)
Athenagoras of Athens (2nd c.)
Melitto (Melitton) of Sardes (2nd c.)
Justin = Justinus (Ioustinos) (2nd c.)
Anon., Apocryph Gospels and Acts of Apostles (2nd half of the 2nd c.)
Clemens (Klemens) of Alexandria (2nd half of the 2nd c.)
Irenaeus (Irenaios) of Lyon (2nd half of the 2nd c.)
Tatian = Tatianus (Tatianos) (2nd half of the 2nd c.)

Greek authors from ca. 200:

Hippolytus (Hippolutos) of Rome (early 3rd c.)
Origenes of Alexandria, active in Caesarea (1st half of the 3rd c.)
Dionysius (Dionusios) of Alexandria (3rd c.)
Eusebius (Eusebios) of Caesarea (ca. 300)
Athanasius (Athanasios) of Alexandria (1st half of the 4th c.)
Basil = Basilius (Basileios) of Caesarea in Cappadocia (2nd half of the 4th c.)
Gregory = Gregorius (Gregorios) of Nazianze (2nd half of the 4th c.)
Gregory = Gregorius (Gregorios) of Nyssa (2nd half of the 4th c.)
Didymus (Didumos) of Alexandria (2nd half of the 4th c.)
Apollinaris of Laodicea (2nd half of the 4th c.)
Synesius (Sunesios) of Cyrene (ca. 400)
Diodorus (Diodoros) of Tarsus (ca. 400)
Theodorus (Theodoros) of Mopsuestia (ca. 400)
John Chrysostom = Iohannes Chrysostomus (Ioannes Chrusostomos) of Antioch and Constantinople (ca. 400)
Theodoretus (Theodoretos) of Cyrrhus (1st half of the 5th c.)
Cyril = Cyrilus (Kourillos) of Alexandria (1st half of the 5th c.)
Evagrius Ponticus (Euagrios Pontikos) (1st half of the 5th c.)

Palladius (Palladios) (1st half of the 5th c.)
Pseudo-Dionysus the Areopagite (Dionusios Areopagites) (2nd half of the 5th c.)

Latin authors from ca. 200:

Minucius Felix (ca. 200)
Tertullian = Tertullianus of Carthage (ca. 200)
Cyprian = Cyprianus of Carthage (1st half of the 3rd c.)
Novatianus (2nd half of the 3rd c.)
Commodianus (2nd half of the 3rd c.?)
Arnobius (ca. 300)
Lactantius (1st half of the 3rd c.)
Firmicus Maternus (4th c.)
Marius Victorinus (4th c.)
Juvencus (4th c.)
Prudentius (4th c.)
Jerome = Hiëronymus (2nd half of the 4th c.)
Ambrose = Ambrosius (2nd half of the 4th c.)
Paulinus of Nola (2nd half of the 4th c.)
Sulpicius Severus (ca. 400)
Pelagius (ca. 400)
Augustine = Augustinus (ca. 400)
Salvianus (1st half of the 5th c.)

CHRONOLOGY

Antiquity: Greeks and Romans in Context, First Edition. Frederick G. Naerebout and Henk W. Singor.
© 2014 John Wiley & Sons, Inc. Published 2014 by John Wiley & Sons, Inc.

	Italy and the western Mediterranean	Aegean/Greek world	Egypt
2000		Bronze Age on Crete, the Cyclades and the Greek mainland; Minoan culture on Crete (Knossos)	ca. 2100 Middle Kingdom (Thebes)
1900	Bronze Age in Italy "Italic peoples" come to Italy		
			Decline of the Middle Kingdom
1800			
1700			
	Bronze Age in Western Europe		
			The Hyksos invade Egypt
			New Kingdom; the Hyksos driven out; 18th dynasty (Thebes)
		Mycenaean culture on the Greek mainland	
1600			Egyptian conquests in Nubia and in Palestine/Syria
		Decline of the Cycladic and Minoan cultures	
1500		Mycenaean Greeks invade Crete	
1400		Highpoint of the Mycenaean culture (Mycenae, Pylos)	
1300			
			Attacks by Sea Peoples; Egypt stands firm
1200		Disruptions in Greece (invasions by the Sea Peoples?); end of the Mycenaean culture	

	Near East	Central-Asia and India	China
2000	Independent Sumerian city-states in decline; invasions by mountain tribes; rise of Babylon	Indus culture in present-day Pakistan	Neolithic; first states form around the Yellow River
1900			
1800	Hammurabi rules over Babylon		
1700		Arrival of the Indo-Aryans	
	Invasions by Hittites and Mitanni, decline of Babylon, and rise of Assyria		
	Hittite empire in Asia Minor and Syria; Palestine under Egyptian rule		Shang dynasty; Bronze Age
1600			
1500			
1400		Indo-Aryan states at the Indus and the Ganges	
1300	Fall of the Hittite empire; Aramaeans and Hebrews (Israelites) in Palestine, Syria, and Mesopotamia		
1200	Italy and the western Mediterranean	Aegean/Greek world	Egypt ca. 2100 Middle Kingdom (Thebes)

	Italy and the western Mediterranean	Aegean/Greek world	Egypt
1100			
1000		Dorian migration	End of the New Kingdom Libyan and Ethiopian dynasties
	Hallstatt culture in Central Europe	Ionian and Aeolian migrations	
900			
	Etruscan culture in Italy; foundation of Carthage		
800		Revival of Greek culture; rise of the *polis*, renewed contact with the Near East; start of the so-called archaic colonization	
	Greek settlement in Southern Italy and on Sicily		
700	Etruscan expansion; Rome an Etruscan city		Conquest by Assyria
			Egypt quickly regains independence under the 26th dynasty (Saïs)
600		Codification of laws in the Greek *poleis*; Solon in Athens; rise of the Spartan social model	
	Latène culture in Western Europe		525 conquest by Cambyses; Egypt part of the Persian Empire
	Etruscans removed from Rome, creation of the Roman Republic	Persian Wars: 490 Marathon, 480 Salamis; creation of the Delian League (First Athenian Empire); Peloponnesian War	
500			
400		Rise of Macedon	
	Rome expands across Latium	338 Battle of Chaeronea	
		336–323 Alexander the Great	332/1 Alexander the Great in in Egypt, foundation of Alexandria; the Ptolemies; Ptolemies and Seleucids fight over Syria
300	Rome conquers Italy to the south of the Po river		
	264–241 First Punic War		
	218–201 Second Punic War		
	Rome starts expanding in Spain and in Greece		Egypt loses control of Palestine (217)
200			
	146 Rome conquers Carthage	148 Rome conquers Macedon	
		146 Destruction of Corinth, Greece turned into a Roman province	
100			

	Near East	Central-Asia and India	China
1100			Zhou dynasty; Chinese culture expands to West and South
	Israelite kings: David, Salomo		
1000	Israelite kingdom split into Judea and Israel; Phoenician states flourish; Assyria begins a renewed expansion		
900			
800			770 Luoyang capital of the
	721 Fall of Samaria		Eastern Zhou
700	The Assyrian Empire reaches its largest extension		
			Political fragmentation Of China
	612 Fall of Nineveh, demise of Assyria		
600	587 Fall of Jerusalem; New-Babylonian Empire 539 Babylon conquered by the Persians		
500	Persian Empire		Warring States Period
400			
	334–323 Alexander the Great conquers the Persian Empire the Seleucid dynasty is Alexander's heir		
		327-325 Alexander the Great in India 305 Treaty between Chandragupta and Seleucus I; Maurya dynasty (Pataliputra)	
300			
	ca. 250 Greek Bactria independent; rise of the Parthians in Iran; rise of Pergamon in Asia Minor		
			221 Political unification under the Qin dynasty 206 The Han dynasty; expansion in
200		190–100 Indo-Greek kings	ca. 120 Opening up of the Silk Road Chang'an becomes the capital
		A Kushan Empire created on the Indus and in Afghanistan	
100			

	Italy and the western Mediterranean	Aegean/Greek world	Egypt
	64 Syria part of the Roman Empire; 30 Egypt part of the Roman Empire; end of the Roman Republic; Augustus (27 bc–14 ad) first emperor	46 Corinth re-founded; creation of the province of Achaea	30 Egypt incorporated
			into the Roman Empire
1			
	Growth of the Roman Empire		
100			
	German tribes and Persians attack Rome Civil war		
200			
	Loss of Dacia Diocletian		
300			
	312 Constantine the Great: reformer and Christian 395 Death of Theodosius I: Roman Empire split in Eastern and Western part		
400		330 Foundation of Constantinople	
	476 Fall of the Western Empire	ca. 440 Invasion of the Visigoths	
500	German successor states in Gaul, Spain, and North-Africa		
		Slavic invasions	
600			ca. 640 Conquest of Egypt by the Arabs

	Near East	Central-Asia and India	China
1			
	64 Remains of Seleucid Empire incorporated by Rome; Euphrates border between Romans and Parthians; Greek states in Afghanistan and India cease to exist		
			"Eastern Han," capital Luoyang; expansion toward the west and into Korea
100			
200			
			220 End of the Han dynasty; Three Kingdoms Period
	226 Parthians displaced by the New-Persian dynasty of the Sassanids		
		ca. 250 Creation of the Gupta empire in the Ganges basin Invasions by the Heftalites in northwestern India	
300			
			Political fragmentation; Nomad invasions in the north
400			
		End of the Gupta Empire	
500			
600			581 China reunited under the Sui dynasty 618 The Tang dynasty
	ca. 640/50 The Sassanid Empire overrun by Arabs		

Suggestions for Further Reading

This list of titles is highly selective: its purpose is merely to direct the readers of the present book who want to delve deeper into any of the many subjects discussed here to works of reference and some recent overviews. We have limited ourselves almost exclusively to publications in English.

The list is subdivided as follows:

1   Sources

    1.1   Written sources
    1.2   Unwritten sources
    1.3   Source criticism

2   Reference

    2.1   General
    2.2   Geography
    2.3   Chronology
    2.4   Biography, prosopography
    2.5   Periods, areas

        2.5.1   Prehistory
        2.5.2   Egypt
        2.5.3   Ancient Near East
        2.5.4   Greek world
        2.5.5   Roman world
        2.5.6   Late Antiquity
        2.5.7   Further afield

    2.6   Religion
    2.7   Philosophy/science
    2.8   Law
    2.9   Language/script

Antiquity: Greeks and Romans in Context, First Edition. Frederick G. Naerebout and Henk W. Singor.
© 2014 John Wiley & Sons, Inc. Published 2014 by John Wiley & Sons, Inc.

2.10   Literature/performing arts
2.11   Architecture/representational arts
2.12   Socioeconomic history
2.13   Reception(s) of the ancient world

3   Bibliographic tools

3.1   General
3.2   Specific
3.3   Internet portals

1   Sources

1.1   Written sources

Guides to the editions of Greek and Latin literary texts:

Berkowitz, L. and K.A. Squitier, *Thesaurus Linguae Graecae: Canon of Greek Authors and Works*, New York 1986 (online version: wwww.tlg.uci.edu).

Conte, G.B., *Latin Literature*, Baltimore 1994.

Translations:

The Loeb Classical Library (Greek/Latin and translations on the facing page).

Penguin Classics.

Inscriptions:

Bérard, F. et al., *Guide de l'épigraphiste. Bibliographie choisie des épigraphies antiques et médiévales*, Paris ⁴2010 (fundamental bibliography of epigraphical literature; annual supplements are published online: http://www.antiquite.ens.fr/ressources/ publications-aux-p-e-n-s/guide-de-l-epigraphiste/article/presentation).

Papyri:

Bagnall, R.S. (ed.), *The Oxford Handbook of Papyrology*, Oxford 2009.

Anthologies:

Adkins, A.W.H. and P. White, *The Greek Polis*, Chicago 1986.

Arnaoutoglou, I., *Ancient Greek Laws: A Sourcebook*, London 1998.

Austin, M.M., *The Hellenistic World from Alexander to the Roman Conquest*: A Selection of Ancient Sources in Translation, Cambridge 1981.

Bagnall, R.S. and P. Derow (eds.), *The Hellenistic Period: Historical Sources in Translation*, Oxford 2008.

Barker, E., *From Alexander to Constantine: Passages and Documents Illustrating the History of Social and Political Ideas, 336 B.C.-A.D. 337*, Lanham, MD ²1985.

Beard, M., J. North, and S. Price, *Religions of Rome, vol. 2 : A 11 Sourcebook*, Cambridge 1998.

Braund, D., *Augustus to Nero: A Sourcebook on Roman History 31 B.C.-A.D. 68*, London 1985.

Burstein, S.M., *The Hellenistic Age from The Battle of Ipsos to the Death of Kleopatra VII*, Cambridge 1985.

Campbell, B., *The Roman Army, 31 B.C.-A.D. 337: A Sourcebook*, London 1994.

Campbell, B., *Greek and Roman Military Writers*: Selected Readings, London 2004.

Champion, C.B., *Roman Imperialism: Readings and Sources*, Oxford 2003.

Chavalas, M.W., *The Ancient Near East:Historical Sources in Translation*,Oxford 2006.

Chisholm, K. and J. Ferguson, *Rome: The Augustan Age*, Oxford 1981.

Cooley, A.E. and M.G.L. Cooley, *Pompeii A Source Book*, London, 2004.

Cotter, W., *Miracles in Greco-Roman Antiquity: A Sourcebook*, London 1999.

Crawford, M.H. and D. Whitehead, *A Selection of Ancient Sources in Translation*, Cambridge 1983.

Dalley, S. (ed.), *Myths From Mesopotamia: Creation, The Flood, Gilgamesh, and Others*, Oxford 1991.

De Bary, T. and I. Bloom, *Sources of Chinese Tradition vol. 1*, New York ²2000.

Dillon, M. and L. Garland, *Ancient Greece: Social and Historical Documents from Archaic Times to the Death of Socrates*, London 1999.

Dillon, M. and L. Garland, *Ancient Rome from the Early Republic to the Assassination of Julius Caesar*, London 2005.

Dodgeon, M.H.D. and S.N.C. Lieu, *The Roman Eastern Frontier and the Persian Wars: A Documentary History. [Pt. I]: A.D. 226–363*, London 1991; G. Greatrex and S.N.C. Lieu, *The Roman Eastern Frontier and The Persian Wars: A Documentary History. Pt. II: A.D. 363–630*, London 2002.

Ehrman, B.D. and A.S. Jacobs, *Christianity in Late Antiquity: 300–450 C.E. A Reader*, New York 2004.

Feldman, L.H. and M. Reinhold, *Jewish Life and Thought among Greeks and Romans: Primary Readings*, Edinburgh 1996.

Ferguson, J., *Greek and Roman Religion. A Source Book*, Park Ridge, NJ 1980.

Fornara, C.W., *Archaic Times to the End of the Peloponnesian War*, Baltimore 1977.

Foster, J.L., *Ancient Egyptian Literature: An Anthology*, Austin 2001.

Foster, J.L. and S.T. Hollis, *Hymns, Prayers, and Songs: An Anthology of Ancient Egyptian Lyrical Poetry*, Atlanta 1995.

Futrell, A., *The Roman Games: A Sourcebook*, Oxford 2006.

Gardner, J.F. and T. Wiedemann, *The Roman Household: A Sourcebook*, London 1991.

Garland, L. and M. Dillon, *Ancient Greece: Social and Historical Documents from Archaic Times to the Death of Socrates*, London 1994.

Greenidge, A.H.J. and A.M. Clay, *Sources for Roman History*, 133–70 *B.C.*, Oxford ²1986.

Grubbs, J.E., *Women and the Law in the Roman Empire: A Sourcebook on Marriage, Divorce and Widowhood*, London 2002.

Jacobsen, T., *The Harps That Once . . . Sumerian Poetry in Translation*, New Haven ²1997.

Harding, P., *From the End of the Peloponnesian War to the Battle of Ipsus*, Cambridge 1985.

Hoffner, H.A., Jr., and G.M. Beckman, *Hittite Myths*, Atlanta ²1998.

Hubbard, T.K., *Homosexuality in Greece and Rome: A Source Book of Basic Documents*, Berkeley, CA 2003.

Humphrey, J.W., J.P. Oleson, and A.N. Sherwood, *Greek and Roman Technology: A Sourcebook*, London 1998.

Irby-Massie, G.L. and P.T. Keyser, *Greek Science of the Hellenistic Era: A Sourcebook*, London 2002.

Johnson, M. and T. Ryan, *Sexuality in Greek and Roman Literature and Society: A Sourcebook*, London 2005.

Kaegi, W.E., Jr., and P. White, *Rome: Late Republic and Principate*, Chicago 1986.

Kearns, E., *Ancient Greek Religion: A Sourcebook* , Chichester 2010.

Kraemer, R.S., *Women's Religions in the Greco-Roman World: A Sourcebook*, Oxford 2004.

Lee, A.D., *Pagans and Christians in Late Antiquity: A Sourcebook*, London 2000.

Lefkowitz, M.R. and M.B. Fant, *Women's Life in Greece and Rome*, Baltimore ³2005.

Levick, B., *The Government of the Roman Empire: A Sourcebook*, London 1985.

Lewis, N. and M. Reinhold, *Roman Civilization: Selected Readings*, New York ³1990.

Lichtheim, M., *Ancient Egyptian Literature: A Book of Readings*, Berkeley 1973–1980.

Lieu, S.N.C. and D. Montserrat, *From Constantine to Julian, Pagan and Byzantine Views: A Source History*, London 1996.

Lindenberger, J.M. and K.H. Richards, *Ancient Aramaic and Hebrew Letters*, Atlanta ²2003.

Lomas, K., *Roman Italy, 338 B.C.-A.D. 200: A Sourcebook*, London 1996.

Longrigg, J., *Greek Medicine from the Heroic to the Hellenistic Age: A Sourcebook*, London 1998.

Maas, M., *Readings in Late Antiquity: A Sourcebook*, London 2000.

McClure, L.K., *Sexuality and Gender in the Classical World: Readings and Sources*, Oxford 2002.

Macmullen, R. and E.N. Lane, *Paganism and Christianity, 100–425 C.E. A Sourcebook*, Minneapolis 1992.

Meijer, F. and O. van Nijf, *Trade, Transport and Society in the Ancient World*, London 1992.

Miller, S.G., *Arete: Greek Sports from Ancient Sources*, Berkeley ²1991.

Minford, J. and J.S.M. Lau, Classical Chinese Literature: An Anthology of Translations, *vol. 1: From Antiquity to the Tang Dynasty*, New York 2002.

Morrison, K.F., *The Church in the Roman Empire*, Chicago 1986.

Ogden, D., *Magic, Witchcraft, and Ghosts in Greek and Roman Worlds: A Sourcebook*, Oxford 2002.

Parker, S.B., *Ugaritic Narrative Poetry*, Atlanta 1997.

Parkin, T. and A. Pomeroy, *Roman Social History: A Sourcebook*, London 2007.

Pollitt, J.J., *The Art of Ancient Greece: Sources and Documents*, Cambridge 1990.

Pollitt, J.J., *The Art of Rome C.753 B.C.-337 A.D. Sources and Documents*, Englewood Cliffs, NJ 1966.

Pritchard, J.B., *The Ancient Near East in Pictures Relating to the Old Testament*, Princeton 1954.

Pritchard, J.B., *The Ancient Near East: An Anthology of Texts and Pictures*, Princeton 1958.

Pritchard, J.B., *Ancient Near Eastern Texts Relating to the Old Testament*, Princeton ³1969.

Pritchard, J.B., *The Ancient Near East: Supplementary Texts and Pictures*, Princeton 1969.

Rhodes, P.J., *The Greek City States: A Source Book*, London 1986.

Rhodes, P.J. and R. Osborne, *Greek Historical Inscriptions*, 404–323 B.C., Oxford *166*2003.

Rice, D.G. and J.E. Stambaugh, *Sources for the Study of Greek Religion*, Atlanta, GA ²2009.

Robinson, E.W., *Ancient Greek Democracy: Readings and Sources*, Oxford 2004.

Roth, M.T., H.A. Hoffner, Jr., and P. Michalowski, *Law Collections from Mesopotamia and Asia Minor*, Atlanta 1995.

Rowlandson, J., *Women and Society in Greek and Roman Egypt: A Sourcebook*, Cambridge 1998.

Sabben-Clare, J., *Caesar and Roman Politics 60–50 B.C.*, London 1971.

Sage, M.M., *Warfare in Ancient Greece: A Sourcebook*, London 1996.

Shaw, B.D., *Spartacus and the Slave Wars: A Brief History with Documents*, Boston 2001.

Shelton, J.A., *As the Romans Did: A Sourcebook in Roman Social History*, New York ²1997.

Sherk, R.K., *The Roman Empire: Augustus to Hadrian*, Cambridge 2001.

Sherk, R.K., *Rome and The Greek East to the Death of Augustus*, Cambridge 1984.

Stanton, G.R., *Athenian Politics, C.800-500: A Sourcebook*, London 1990.

Stern, M., *Greek and Latin Authors on Jews and Judaism*, Jerusalem 1974–1984.

Stevenson, J., *A New Eusebius: Documents Illustrative of the History of the Church to A.D. 337*, London 1957.

Stevenson, J., *Creeds, Councils and Controversies: Documents Illustrative of the History of the Church*, A.D. 337–461, London ²1972.

Stockton, D.L., *From the Gracchi to Sulla: Sources for Roman History*, 133–80 B.C., London 1981.

Sweet, W.E., *Sport and Recreation in Ancient Greece*: A Sourcebook with Translations, New York 1987.

Trapp, M., *Greek and Latin Letters: An Anthology with Translation*, Cambridge 2005.

Wente, E.F. and E.S. Meltzer, *Letters from Ancient Egypt*, Atlanta 1990.

Whittaker, M., *Jews and Christians: Greco-Roman Views*, Cambridge 1984.

Wiedemann, T., *Greek and Roman Slavery: A Sourcebook*, London 1981.

Williams, M.H., *The Jews among the Greeks and Romans: A Diasporan Sourcebook*, London 1998.

Yavetz, Z., *Slaves and Slavery in Ancient Rome*, New Brunswick 1990.

There also are series dedicated to publishing anthologies of translated texts, such as:

Library of Early Christianity, Philadelphia 1986–1987.

New Documents Illustrating Early Christianity, North Ryde/Grand Rapids, MI 1981-.

1.2   Unwritten Sources

There are countless publications of archaeological artifacts. Here we can only refer to some of the titles listed under 2.11 below.

See also:

Alcock, S. and R. Osborne (eds.), *Classical Archaeology*, Chichester 2012.

Bintliff, J., *The Complete Archaeology of Greece: From Hunter-Gatherers to the 20th Century A.D.*, Chichester 2012.

Matthews, R., *The Archaeology of Mesopotamia: Theories and Approaches*, London 2003.

Wendrich, W. (ed.), *Egyptian Archaeology*, Chichester 2010.

1.3   Source criticism

Bagnall, R.S., *Reading Papyri, Writing Ancient History*, London 1995.

Bagnall, R.S., *Everyday Writing in the Graeco-Roman East*, Berkeley 2011.

Biers, W.R., *Art, Artefacts and Chronology in Classical Archaeology*, London 1992.

Bodel, J., (ed.), *Epigraphic Evidence: Ancient History from Inscriptions*. London 2001.

Cooley, A.E., *The Cambridge Manual of Latin Epigraphy*, Cambridge 2012.

Crawford, M. (ed.), *Sources for Ancient History*, Cambridge 1983.

Finley, M.I., *Ancient History: Evidence and Models*, London 1985.

Howgego, C., *Ancient History from Coins*, London 1995.

Keppie, L.J.F., *Understanding Roman Inscriptions*, Baltimore 1991.

McLean, B.H., *An Introduction to Greek Epigraphy of the Hellenistic and Roman Periods from Alexander the Great Down to the Reign of Constantine (323 B.C.-A.D. 337)*, Ann Arbor 2002.

Marincola, J. (ed.), *A Companion to Greek and Roman Historiography*, Oxford 2007.

Metcalf, W.E. (ed.), *The Oxford Handbook of Greek and Roman Coinage*, Oxford 2012.

Pelling, C.B.R., *Literary Texts and The Greek Historian*, London 2000.

Pestman, P.W., *The New Papyrological Primer*, Leiden [2]1994.

Potter, D.S., *Literary Texts and the Roman Historian*, London 1999.

Van De Mieroop, M., *Cuneiform Texts and the Writing of History*, London 1999.

2   Reference

2.1   General

Encyclopedic, multi-volume:

Baumann, B. et al. (eds.), *The New Pauly*, Stuttgart 1996–2003.

Bagnall, R.S. et al. (eds.), *The Encyclopedia of Ancient History*, Boston 2012.

Still important are the older (French and German) reference works:

Daremberg, Ch. and E. Saglio (eds.), *Dictionnaire des antiquités grecques et romains d'après les textes et les monuments*, Paris 1873–1919 (online: http://dagr.univ-tlse2.fr/sdx/dagr/rechercher.xsp).

Wissowa, G. and W. Kroll (eds.), *Paulys Realencyclopädie der classischen Altertumswissenschaft (PW, RE),* Stuttgart, etc. 1894–1978 (the largest reference work; with many supplement volumes; there also exist index volumes).

Ziegler, K. and W. Sontheimer (eds.), *Der Kleine Pauly: Lexikon der Antike*, Munich 1964–1975.

Encyclopedic, single volume:

Hornblower, S. and A. Spawforth (eds.), *The Oxford Classical Dictionary (OCD)*, Oxford [4]2012.

Shipley, G. et al. (eds.), *The Cambridge Dictionary of Classical Civilization*, Cambridge 2006.

Textbooks:

Edwards, I.E.S. et al. (eds.), *The Cambridge Ancient History (CAH)*, Cambridge [3]1961- (the most authoritative series of text books).

Boardman, J., J. Griffin and O. Murray (eds.), *The Oxford History of the Classical World*, Oxford 1986.

Erskine, A. (ed.), *A Companion to Ancient History*, Oxford 2008.

Grant, M. and R. Kitzinger (eds.), *Civilization of the Ancient Mediterranean: Greece and Rome*, New York 1988.

Lane Fox, R., *The Classical World : An Epic History of Greece and Rome*, London 2006.

Starr, G.C., *A History of the Ancient World*, New York [2]1974.

2.2   Geography

Bell, R.E., *Place Names in Classical Mythology: Greece*, Santa Barbara 1989.

Branigan, K. et al. (eds.), *Lexicon of The Greek and Roman Cities and Place Names in Antiquity, ca 1500 B.C.-ca A.D. 500*, Amsterdam 1992-.

Grant, M., *A Guide to the Ancient World: A Dictionary of Classical Place Names*, New York 1986.

Hansen, M.H. and T.H. Nielsen (eds.), *An Inventory of Archaic and Classical Poleis*, Oxford 2004.

Stillwell, R., (ed.), *The Princeton Encyclopedia of Classical Sites*, Princeton 1976.

Atlases:

Baines, J. and J. Málek, *Atlas of Ancient Egypt*, Oxford 1980.

Barraclough, G. (ed.), *The Times Atlas of World History*, London [4]1993.

Beek, M.A., *Atlas of Mesopotamia: A Survey of the History and Civilisation of Mesopotamia from the Stone Age to the Fall of Babylon*, London 1962.

Branigan, K., *Atlas of Ancient Civilizations*, London 1976.

Cornell, T. and J. Matthews, *Atlas of The Roman World*, Oxford 1982.

Fagg, C. and F. Halton, *Atlas of The Ancient World*, London 1979.

Grant, M., *Ancient History Atlas, 1700 B.C.–A.D. 565*, London 1989.

Grollenberg, L.H., *Atlas of the Bible*, London [2]1957.

Hammond, N.G.L., *Atlas of the Greek and Roman World in Antiquity*, Park Ridge, NJ 1981.

Heyden, A.A.M. van der and H.H. Scullard, *Atlas of the Classical World*, London 1959.

Haywood, J. et al. (eds.), *Cassell Atlas of World History, vol. 1: The Ancient and Classical Worlds*, London 2000.

Kinder, H.et al., *The Penguin Atlas of World History, vol. 1*, Harmondsworth 1974.

Levi, P., *Atlas of The Greek World*, Oxford 1980.

McEvedy, C., *The Penguin Atlas of Ancient History*, Harmondsworth 1967.

Meer, F. van der and Chr. Mohrmann, *Atlas of the Early Christian World*, London 1959.

Talbert, R.J.A., *Atlas of Classical History*, London 1985.

Talbert, R.J.A. (ed.), *Barrington Atlas of The Greek and Roman World*, Princeton 2000 (the topographical standard).

2.3   Chronology

Bickerman, E.J., *Chronology of the Ancient World*, London 1968.

Kienast, D., *Römische Kaisertabelle: Grundzüge einer römischen Kaiserchronologie*, Darmstadt ²1996 (fundamental overview of the reigns of the Roman emperors).

Mellersh, H.E.L., *Chronology of the Ancient World, 10,000 B.C. To A.D. 799*, London 1976.

Samuel, A.E., *Greek and Roman Chronology: Calendars and Years in Classical Antiquity*, Munich 1972.

2.4   Biography, Prosopography

Davies, J.K., *Athenian Propertied Families* 600–300 B.C., Oxford 1971.

Fossey, John M., *The Study of Ancient Greek Prosopography*, Chicago 1991.

Grant, M., *Greek and Latin Authors 800 B.C.-A.D. 1000*, New York 1980.

Grant, M., *The Roman Emperors: A Biographical Guide to the Rulers of Imperial Rome, 31 B.C.-A.D. 476*, London 1985.

Hafner, G., *Bildlexikon Antiker Personen*, Zürich 1993 (a 'facebook' of ancient individuals).

Hazel, J., *Who's Who in The Greek World*, London 2000.

Heckel, W., *Who's Who in The Age of Alexander The Great: Prosopography of Alexander's Empire*, Oxford 2006.

Jones, A.H.M., J.R. Martindale and J. Morris, *The Prosopography of The Later Roman Empire (PLRE)*, Cambridge 1971–1992.

Leick, G., *Who's Who in The Ancient Near East*, London 1999.

Lightman, M. and B. Lightman, *Biographical Dictionary of Greek and Roman Women*, New York 2000.

Rice, M., *Who's Who in Ancient Egypt*, London 2002.

Rice, M., *Personennamen Der Antike (PAN)*, Wiesbaden 1993 (a lexicon that gives all variant spellings of ancient names)

2.5   Periods and Areas

2.5.1   Prehistory

Cunliffe, B., *The Oxford Illustrated Prehistory of Europe*, Oxford 1994.

Dickinson, O., *The Aegean Bronze Age*, Cambridge 1994.

Gamble, C., *The Palaeolithic Societies of Europe*, Cambridge ²1999.

Harding, A.F., *European Societies in the Bronze Age*, Cambridge 2000.

Kohl, P.L., *The Making of Bronze Age Eurasia*, Cambridge 2007.

Renfrew, C. and P.G. Bahn (eds.), *The Cambridge World Prehistory*, Cambridge 2013.

Whittle, A.W. R., *Europe in The Neolithic*: The Creation of New Worlds, Cambridge 1996.

2.5.2   Egypt

Bagnall, R.S. and D.W. Rathbone (eds.), *Egypt from Alexander to the Early Christians: An Archaeological and Historical Guide*, Los Angeles 2004.

Bard, K.A., *Encyclopedia of the Archaeology of Ancient Egypt*, London 1999.

Bunson, M., *The Encyclopedia of Ancient Egypt*, New York ²1999.

Helck, W., E. Otto and W. Westendorf (eds.), *Lexikon der Ägyptologie*, Wiesbaden 1972–1992 (the most comprehensive reference work).

Kemp, B.J., *Ancient Egypt. Anatomy of a Civilization*, London 1994.

Riggs, C. (ed.), *The Oxford Handbook of Roman Egypt*, Oxford 2012.

Shaw, I. and P. Nicholson (eds.), *British Museum Dictionary of Ancient Egypt*, London 1996.

Wengrow, D., *The Archaeology of Early Egypt: Social Transformations in North-East Africa, c. 10,000 to 2,650 B.C.*, Cambridge 2006.

2.5.3   Ancient Near East

Akkermans, P.M.M.G. and Schwartz, G.M., *The Archaeology of Syria. From Complex Hunter-Gatherers to Early Urban Societies (c.16,000–300 B.C.)*, Cambridge 2004.
Arberry, A.J. et al. (eds.), *The Cambridge History of Iran*, Cambridge 1968–1991.
Bienkowski, P. and A. Millard (eds.), *British Museum Dictionary of the Ancient Near East*, London 2000.
Encyclopaedia Iranica, London 1982-.
Kuhrt, A., *The Ancient Near East*: *c.* 3000–330 B.C., London 1995.
Postgate, N., *Early Mesopotamia. Society and Economy at the Dawn of History*, London 1994.
Reallexikon der Assyriologie, Berlin 1928- (the most comprehensive reference work).
Snell, D. (ed.), *A Companion to the Ancient Near East*, Oxford 2005.
Van De Mieroop, M., *A History of the Ancient Near-East c.*3000–323 B.C., Oxford [2]2007.

For Judaism see:
Collins, J.J. and D.C. Harlow (eds.), *The Eerdmans Dictionary of Early Judaism*, Grand Rapids 2010.
Davies, W.D. and L. Finkelstein (eds.), *The Cambridge History of Judaism*, Cambridge 1984-.
Goodman, M., J. Cohen and D. Sorkin (eds.), *The Oxford Handbook of Jewish Studies*, Oxford 2002.
Schürer, E., *The History of The Jewish People in the Age of Jesus Christ (175 B.C.–A.D. 135)*, Edinburgh 1973–1986.
Werblowsky, R.J.Z. and G. Wigoder (eds.), *Oxford Dictionary of Jewish Religion*, New York 1997.

2.5.4   Greek World

Bugh, G.R. (ed.), *The Cambridge Companion to the Hellenistic World*, Cambridge 2006.
Cartledge, P., *Ancient Greece: A History in Eleven Cities*, Oxford 2009.
Errington, R.M., *A History of the Hellenistic World 232–30 B.C.*, Oxford 2008.
Erskine, A. (ed.), *A Companion to the Hellenistic World*, Oxford 2003.
Green, P., *Alexander to Actium: The Historical Evolution of the Hellenistic Age*, Berkeley 1993.
Hall, J., *A History of the Archaic Greek World*, Oxford 2006.
Hornblower, S., *The Greek World, 479–323 B.C.*, London 2002.
Kinzl, K.H. (ed.), *A Companion to the Classical Greek World*, Oxford 2006.
Osborne, R., *Greece in the Making, 1200–479 B.C.*, London 1996.
Osborne, R. (ed.), *The World of Athens: An Introduction to Classical Athenian Culture*, Cambridge 2012.
Raaflaub, K. and H. Van Wees (eds.), *A Companion to Archaic Greece*, Oxford 2008.
Rhodes, P.J., *A History of the Classical Greek World*, Oxford 2005.
Samons, L.J., II, (ed.), *The Cambridge Companion to the Age of Pericles*, Cambridge 2007.
Shapiro, H.A. (ed.), *The Cambridge Companion to Archaic Greece*, Cambridge 2007.
Shipley, G., *The Greek World after Alexander, 323–30 B.C.*, London 2000.

2.5.5   Roman World

Bispham, Edward (ed.), *Roman Europe*, Oxford 2008.
Bunson, M., *Encyclopedia of The 20Roman Empire*, New York 1994.
Cornell, T.J., *The Beginnings of Rome: Italy and Rome from the Bronze Age to the Punic Wars (c.1000-264 B.C.)*, London 1995.

Flower, H.I. (ed.), *The Cambridge Companion to the Roman Republic*, Cambridge 2004.

Forsyth, G., *A Critical History of Early Rome: From Prehistory to the First Punic War*, Berkeley 2005.

Potter, D.S. (ed.), *A Companion to the Roman Empire*, Oxford 2005.

Potter, D.S., *The Roman Empire at Bay, A.D. 180–395*, London 2004.

Rosenstein, N.S. and R. Morstein-Marx (eds.), *A Companion to the Roman Republic*, Oxford 2006.

Temporini, H. and W. Haase (eds.), *Aufstieg und Niedergang der Römischen Welt*, Berlin 1972- (a huge series of volumes on all aspects of the Roman world, mostly in the imperial period; multilingual).

Woolf, G., *Rome: An Empire's Story*, New York 2012.

2.5.6   Late Antiquity

Atiya, A.S. (ed.), *Coptic Encyclopedia*, New York 1991.

Bowersock, G.W., P. Brown and O. Grabar (eds.), *Late Antiquity: A Guide to the Postclassical World*, Cambridge, MA 1999.

Cameron, A., *The Mediterranean World in Late Antiquity, A.D. 395–600*, London 1993.

Di Berardino, A. (ed.), *Encyclopedia of the Early Church*, New York 1992.

Esler, P.F. (ed.), *The Early Christian World*, London 2000.

Ferguson, E. (ed.), *Encyclopedia of Early Christianity*, New York 1999.

Frend, W.H.C., *The Rise of Christianity*, Philadelphia 1985.

Galinsky, K. (ed.), *The Cambridge Companion to the Age of Augustus*, Cambridge 2005.

Gregory, T., *A History of Byzantium*, Oxford 2005.

Jeffreys, E., J. Haldon, and R. Cormack (eds.), *The Oxford Handbook of Byzantine Studies*, Oxford 2008.

Johnson, S.F. (ed.), *The Oxford Handbook of Late Antiquity*, Oxford 2012.

Lenski, N. (ed.), *The Cambridge Companion to the Age of Constantine*, Cambridge 2005.

Parry, K. et al. (eds.), *The Blackwell Dictionary of Eastern Christianity*, Oxford 2000.

Kazhdan, A.P. et al. (eds.), *The Oxford Dictionary of Byzantium*, Oxford 1991.

Klauser, T. et al. (eds.), *Reallexikon für Antike und Christentum*, Leipzig/Stuttgart 1941- (a fundamental work of reference for early Christianity and its roots in the pagan world).

Maas, M. (ed.), *The Cambridge Companion to the Age of Justinian*, Cambridge 2005.

Mitchell, S., *A History of the Later Roman Empire, A.D. 284–641*, Oxford 2006.

Rousseau, P. and J. Raithel (eds.), *A Companion to Late Antiquity*, Malden 2012.

Treadgold, W., *A History of the Byzantine State and Society*, Stanford 1997.

For Islam, the most important works of reference are:

Encyclopaedia of Islam, Leiden ^{5}1960–2006.

Encyclopaedia of The Qur'ān, Leiden 2001–2006.

2.5.7   Further Afield

Allchin, B. and R. Allchin, *The Rise of Civilization in India and Pakistan*, Cambridge 1988.

Haywood, J. and B. Cunliffe, *The Historical Atlas of the Celtic World*, London 2009.

Kulke, H. and D. Rothermund, *A History of India*, London ^{5}2010.

Lewis, M.E., *The Early Chinese Empires: Qin and Han*, Cambridge, MA 2007.

Lewis, M.E., *China's Cosmopolitan Empire: The Tang Dynasty*, Cambridge, MA 2009.

Lewis, M.E., *China Between Empires: The Northern and Southern Dynasties*, Cambridge, MA 2009.

Loewe, M. and E.L. Shaughnessy (eds.), *The Cambridge History of Ancient China: From the Origins of Civilization to 221 B.C.*, Cambridge 1999.

Nylan, M. and M. Loewe (eds.), *China's Early Empires: A Re-Appraisal*, Cambridge 2010.

Sinor, D. (ed.), *The Cambridge History of Early Inner Asia*, Cambridge 1990.

Tarling, N. (ed.), *The Cambridge History of Southeast Asia, Vol. 1: From Early Times To C. 1800*, Cambridge 1992.

Twitchett, D. and M. Loewe (eds.), *The Cambridge History of China, Vol. 1: The Ch'in and Han Empires, 221 B.C.-A.D. 220*, Cambridge 1986.

2.6   Religion

Bellah, R.N., *Religion in Human Evolution from the Paleolithic to the Axial Age*, Cambridge, MA 2011.

Burkert, W., *Greek Religion*: Archaic and Classical, London 1985.

Beard, M., J. North and S. Price, *Religions of Rome*, Cambridge 1998.

Hart, G., *A Dictionary of Egyptian Gods and Goddesses*, London 2005.

Johnston, S.I. (ed.), *Religions of the Ancient World. A Guide*, Cambridge, MA 2004.

Kindt, J., *Rethinking Greek Religion*, Cambridge 2012.

North, J.A., *Roman Religion*, Oxford 2000.

Ogden, D. (ed.), *A Companion to Greek Religion*, Oxford 2007.

Parker, R., *On Greek Religion*, Ithaca 2011.

Price, S. and E. Kearns, *The Oxford Dictionary of Classical Myth and Religion*, Oxford 2003.

Rüpke, J. (ed.), *A Companion to Roman Religion*, Oxford 2007.

Toorn, K. van der, B. Becking, and P.W. van der Horst (eds.), *Dictionary of Deities and Demons in The Bible*, Leiden/Grand Rapids 1999.

Two very important works of reference, multi-volume, multilingual, the first dedicated to religious iconography, the second to ritual:

Lexicon Iconographicum Mythologiae Classicae (LIMC), Zürich 1981–1999.

Thesaurus Cultus Et Rituum Antiquorum (ThesCRA), Los Angeles 2004–2012.

Judaism: see 2.5.3 above.

Early Christianity and Islam: see 2.5.6 above.

2.7   Philosophy, Science

Brunschwig, J. and G.E.R. Lloyd (eds.), *Greek Thought: A Guide*, Cambridge, MA 2000.

Cartledge, P., *Ancient Greek Political Thought in Practice*, Cambridge 2009.

Gill, M.L. and P. Pellegrin (eds.), *A Companion to Ancient Philosophy*, Oxford 2006.

Guthrie, W.K.C., *A History of Greek Philosophy*, Cambridge 1962–1981.

Johansen, K.F., *A History of Ancient Philosophy, from the Beginning to Augustine*, London 1998.

Lang, P., *Science: Antiquity and Its Legacy*, London 2014.

Zeyl, D. (ed.), *Encyclopedia of Classical Philosophy*, Westport, CT 1997.

See also the Sciences in Antiquity series (Routledge).

2.8   Law

Berger, A., *Encyclopedic Dictionary of Roman Law*, Philadelphia 1953.

Gagarin, M. and D. Cohen (eds.), *The Cambridge Companion to Ancient Greek Law*, Cambridge 2005.

Kunkel, W., *An Introduction to Roman Legal and Constitutional History*, Oxford ²1973.

Nicholas, B., *An Introduction to Roman Law*, Oxford 1975.

Robinson, O.F., *The Sources of Roman Law*: Problems and Methods for Ancient Historians, London 1997.

2.9   Language, Script

Bonfante, L. et al., *Reading the Past: Ancient Writing from Cuneiform to the Alphabet*, London 1990.

Christidis, A.-F. (ed.), *A History of Ancient Greek, from the Beginnings to Late Antiquity*, Cambridge 2007.

Janson, T., *A Natural History of Latin*, Oxford 2004.

Woodard, R.D. (ed.), *The Cambridge Encyclopedia of the World's Ancient Languages*, Cambridge 2004.
    See also 1.3.

2.10   Literature, Performing Arts

Easterling, P.E. and E.J. Kenney (eds.), *The Cambridge History of Classical Literature*, Cambridge 1982–1985.

Finkelberg, M. (ed.), *The Homer Encyclopedia*, Boston/Oxford 2011.

Gregory, J. (ed.), *A Companion to Greek Tragedy*, Oxford 2005.

Michaelides, S., *The Music of Ancient Greece:An Encyclopedia*, London 1978.

Naerebout, F.G., *Attractive Performances*: Ancient Greek Dance, Amsterdam 1997.

Wille, G., *Musica Romana. Die Bedeutung der Musik im Leben der Römer*, Amsterdam 1967 (the only comprehensive study of music in Roman life).

Young, F., L. Ayres, and A. Louth (eds.), *The Cambridge History of Early Christian Literature*, Cambridge 2004.

2.11   Architecture, Representational Arts

Arnold, D., *The Encyclopedia of Ancient Egyptian Architecture*, Princeton 2003.

Boardman, J., *The Diffusion of Classical Art in Antiquity*, London 1994.

Boardman, J. (ed.), *The Oxford History of Classical Art*, Oxford 2001.

Campbell, G. (ed.), *The Grove Encyclopedia of Classical Art and Architecture*, New York 2007.

Pollitt, J.J., *Art in the Hellenistic Age*, Cambridge 1990.

Preston, P., *Lexikon Antiker Bildmotive*, Stuttgart 1997 (an iconographical dictionary).

Robertson, M., *A History of Greek Art*, Cambridge 1975.

Robertson, M., *A Shorter History of Greek Art*, Cambridge 1985.

Sparkes, B.A., *Greek Art*, Oxford 1991.

Stewart, P., *Roman Art*, Oxford 2004.

A very important multi-volume reference work (for those who read Italian) is:

Enciclopedia dell'arte antica: classica e orientale, Rome 1958-.

Two important series not dedicated exclusively to the arts of the ancient world, but containing several relevant volumes:

The Oxford History of Art

Thames and Hudson World of Art

For religious iconography, see 2.6.

2.12   Socioeconomic History

Alföldy, G., *The Social History of Rome*, Baltimore 1988.

Bradley, Keith R. and P. Cartledge (eds.), *The Cambridge World History of Slavery, Volume 1, The Ancient Mediterranean World*, Cambridge 2011.

Dalby, A., *Food in the Ancient World from A to Z*, London 2003.

Gschnitzer, F., *Griechische Sozialgeschichte von der mykenischen bis Zum Ausgang der Klassischen Zeit*, Wiesbaden 1981 (important social history of Greece, translated into several languages—but alas not into English).

Golden, M., *Sport in the Ancient World from A to Z*, London 2004.

Harris, W.V. (ed.), *The Monetary Systems of the Greeks and Romans*, Oxford 2010.

Hin, S., *The Demography of Roman Italy: Population Dynamics in an Ancient Conquest Society 201 BCE-14 CE*, Cambridge 2013.

Horden, P. and N. Purcell, *The Mediterranean World*: Man and Environment in Antiquity and the Middle Ages, Oxford 1987.

McCormick, M., *Origins of the European Economy. Communications and Commerce, A.D. 300–900*, Cambridge 2001.

Oleson, J.P. (ed.), *The Handbook of Engineering and Technology in the Ancient World*, Oxford 2008.

Parkin, T.G., *Demography and Roman Society*, Baltimore 1992.

Sabin, P., H. van Wees, and M. Whitby (eds.), *The Cambridge History of Ancient Warfare*, Cambridge 2007.

Sallares, S., *The Ecology of the Ancient Greek World*, London 1991.

Scheidel, W., *Debating Roman Demography*, Leiden 2001.

Scheidel, W., I. Morris, and R.P. Saller (eds.), *The Cambridge Economic History of the Greco-Roman World*, Cambridge 2008.

Younger, J., *Sex in the Ancient World from A to Z*, London 2004.

2.13   Reception(s) of the Ancient World

Grafton, A., G.W. Most, and S. Settis (eds.), *The Classical Tradition*, Cambridge MA 2010.

Hardwick, L., *Reception Studies*, Cambridge 2003.

Hardwick, L. and C. Stray (eds.), *A Companion to Classical Receptions*, Chichester 2011.

Kallendorf, C.W. (ed.), *A Companion to the Classical Tradition*, Chichester 2010.

Martindale, C. and R.F. Thomas (eds.), *Classics and the Uses of Reception*, Malden 2006.

3   Bibliographic tools

3.1   General

Marouzeau, J. et al., *L'Année Philologique (APh)*, 1924- (the most important bibliographic tool for classical studies; online: www.annee-philologique.com/).

Schaps, D.M., *Handbook for Classical Research*, London 2010.

Online:

TOCS-IN = Tables of Contents of Journals of Interest to Classicists: projects.chass.utoronto.ca/amphoras/tocs.html

Online Reviews:

Bryn Mawr Classical Review: bmcr.brynmawr.edu/

Gnomon Online: http://www.gnomon.ku-eichstaett.de/Gnomon/en/

3.2   Specific

Annual Egyptological Bibliography 1947-.

Archäologische Bibliographie des Jahrbuchs des Deutschen Archäologischen Instituts, 1932–1993 (main archaeological bibliography, continued as an online publication).

Archiv für Orientforschung (journal that publishes an annual bibliography for the Ancient Near East)).

Bulletin Analytique d'histoire Romaine (BAHR) 1962- (online: http://www2i.misha.fr/flora/).

Byzantinische Zeitschrift (journal that carries an annual bibliography for Byzantium; in addition, it publishes since 1994 a separate Supplementum Bibliographicum).

Christ, K., *Römische Geschichte. Einführung, Quellenkunde, Bibliographie*, Darmstadt ³1980 (large bibliography for Roman history in all its aspects).

Revue d'Histoire Ecclésiastique (journal that publishes an annual bibliography that has good coverage of publications concerning Late Antiquity and Early Christianity).

Souček, V. and J. Siegelová, *Systematische Bibliographie der Hethitologie 1915–1995*, Prague 1996 (Hittitological bibliography).

Weiler, I., *Griechische Geschichte. Einführung, Quellenkunde, Bibliographie*, Darmstadt ²1988 (the Greek counterpart of the Christ volume on Rome mentioned above).

Subject bibliographies:

Alföldy, G. (ed.), *Bibliographie zur römischen Sozialgeschichte*, Stuttgart 1992–1998 (comprehensive bibliography of Roman social history titles, arranged thematically).

Decker, W., Jahresbibliographie zum Sport im Altertum (annual bibliography of publications on sport, games, dance, in the journal *Nikephoros*).

Flach, D., P. Kehne, and S. Link, *Bibliographie zur römischen Agrargeschichte*, Paderborn 1991 (bibliography for Roman agricultural history).

Goodwater, L., *Women in Antiquity: An Annotated Bibliography*, New York 1975.

Mor, M. and U. Rappaport, *Bibliography of Works on Jewish History in the Hellenistic and Roman Periods*, Jerusalem 1976-.

Motte, A. et al. (eds.), *Mentor: Guide bibliographique de la religion grecque/Bibliographical Survey of Greek Religion*, Liège 1992.

Motte, A. et al. (eds.), *Mentor 2: Guide bibliographique de la religion grecque/Bibliographical Survey of Greek Religion (1986–1990)*, Liège 1998.

Robinson, T.A., *The Early Church: An Annotated Bibliography of Literature in English*, Metuchen 1993.

Scanlon, T.F., *Greek and Roman Athletics: A Bibliography*, Chicago 1984.

Suder, W., *Geras. Old Age in Greco-Roman Antiquity: A Classified Bibliography*, Wroclaw 1991.

White, K.D., *A Bibliography of Roman Farming*, London 1970.

3.3   Internet Portals (as of September 2013)

ABZU. Guide to networked open access data relevant to the study and public presentation of the Ancient Near East and the Ancient Mediterranean world: www.etana.org/abzubib

Bibliotheca Classica Selecta: bcs.fltr.ucl.ac.be/default.htm

Electronic Resources for Classicists: www.tlg.uci.edu/index/resources.html

Internet Ancient History Source Book: www.fordham.edu/halsall/ancient/asbook.html

Internet Resources for the Study of Judaism and Christianity: ccat.sas.upenn.edu/~jtreat/rs/resources.html).

KIRKE = Katalog der Internetressourcen für die Klassische Philologie aus Erlangen: www.kirke.hu-berlin.de/ressourc/ressourc.html).

Lacus Curtius: into the Roman world: penelope.uchicago.edu/Thayer/E/Roman/home.html

North American Patristics Society. Internet resources: Patristics.org/resources/other-resources-and-guides/

Oraculum. Datenquellen zur Antike: www.medicamina.bplaced.net/initium/index.php

Oxford University Centre for the Study of Ancient Documents: www.csad.ox.ac.uk/CSAD/

Papyrology Home Page: www.users.drew.edu/~jmuccigr/papyrology/

Perseus Digital Library: www.perseus.tufts.edu/ (not just a portal, but a huge digital library)

Rassegna degli strumenti informatici per lo studio dell'Antichità classica: www.rassegna.unibo.it/ (a great portal; alas not updated after 2007).

Resource Pages for Biblical Studies: www.torreys.org/bible/

Society for Late Antiquity WEB Page: www.sc.edu/ltantsoc/

Voice of the shuttle. Website for humanities research: vos.ucsb.edu/

Index

References to figures and information in captions to figures are indicated as, for example, 311f.

A
'Abbasid dynasty, 390, 392
abortion, 22, 175, 279
Abraham, 69
Academy *see* Akademeia
acculteration, 134–5, 271–2,
        281–7, 296, 308–12, 347,
        392. *see also*
        Hellenization;
        Romanization;
        sinification
accusatorial process, 337, 356
Achaean League, 210–11, 212,
        263
Achaemenid Empire, 70, 71,
        136, 200
acropolis, 275–6
    Acropolis, 105, 141, 153–4,
        165f, 174f, 180, 182,
        185f
Actium, Battle of, 221, 240
administration, 167–8,
        213–14, 222, 225, 262–3,
        265–7, 327–32
Adoptive Emperors, 303
Adrianopolis *see*
        Hadrianopolis
aedilis, 265, 397

aegis, 185f, 198f
Aeneas, 284, 301
Aeneid, 301
Aeolians, 56f, 72
aerarium, 329
Aeschylus, 182
Aetolis, Aetolian League, 211,
        228
Afghanistan, 195–9, 205, 270f,
        296–7, 352, 389
Africa, 14, 34, 250f, 311f, 380
afterlife, 120, 183, 347–8, 357
age class society, 100, 114–15
ager Romanus, 149, 267–8
agon see contests (games)
agora, 214, 245f, 275–6
    Agora, 153, 165f
agriculture, 13–20, 57–8,
        93–4, 155–6, 259, 316,
        317
    irrigation systems, 17, 20,
        36, 41, 51, 67, 131, 135,
        241
    and population growth,
        13–14
    rise of, 14–17, 32–4
    terracing, 157f
Ahriman, 122

Ahura Mazda, 122
Akademeia, 173, 186–7, 336,
        348
Akkad, Akkadians, 42, 47
Akragas, 76
Alamanni, 305
Alans, 312
Alaric, 312
Albania, 381
Alcibiades, 146–7
Alexander Severus, 305
Alexander the Great, 187,
        195–6, 198f, 200–7
Alexandria, 217–18, 220, 221,
        240, 252, 276–7, 288–90,
        336, 364, 386
'Ali, 390
alphabets, 68–9, 73, 91, 92f,
        113
Alps, 32, 65, 138, 225–7, 237
Altamira, 31
Amazons, 124–5
Americas, 12, 14, 35, 61, 393
amicitia, 266
Ammianus Marcellinus, 346
Ammon, Amun, 198f, 203,
        208, 281
Amorites, 42, 47, 48–50

amphitheaters, 339–40
Amu Darya, 197, 205–6
anaideia, 186
Analects see *Lunyu*
Anatolia, 35, 42
Anaxagoras, 186
Anaximander, 125–6
Anaximenes, 126
ancestor worship, 40
andreia, 170–1
Anglo-Saxons, 373–6
animal husbandry, 15f, 17,
    33–4, 94
    and human health, 32f,
        33–4
animal shows (games), 339–40
annona (distribution of grain),
    257, 319–20, 322
annona (taxation), 306, 321,
    331, 399
anthropomorphism, 121,
    122–3
anti-Christian persecutions,
    355, 356–7
anti-Judaism, 286
anti-Semitism, 286
Antigonids, 207, 264, 400
Antigonus Gonatas, 207,
    210–11
Antigonus Monophtalmos,
    207, 210, 212, 247
Antimachus, 198f
Antioch, 212–13, 364
Antiochus I Soter, 226
Antiochus III Megas, 215, 228
Antiochus IV Epiphanes,
    215–16, 217, 219
Antoninus Pius, 303
Antony (Marcus Antonius),
    221, 240
Anyang, 39f
Apennines, 86, 222, 225, 227
Aphrodite, 117, 186, 278, 280f,
    347
Apis, 285f
Apollo, 85, 119
Apuleius, 346
aquaducts, 319

Arabia, Arabs, 371, 372, 381,
    387–90, 392
Aramaeans, 42, 66, 68
archaeology, 3–10, 391
Archebius, 198f
Archimedes, 289, 290
archon, 79, 145, 153, 396
aretology, 281
Argos, Argolis, 76
Arianism, 363–4, 373
aristocracy, 72, 74–6, 77–8,
    90, 105–6, 150–1, 163,
    231, 232, 266–7, 321–2,
    323
Aristogiton, 81f
Aristophanes, 182
Aristotle, 187, 287, 336
Arius (Areios), 363
Armenia, 365
arms and armor, 54–5, 66, 76,
    107–9, 124f, 139f, 179,
    221, 230, 233
army
    cavalry, 194, 201, 203, 267
    hoplites, 81, 82, 88, 141, 146,
        262
    Macedonia, 148–9, 201–3,
        206, 212
    mercenaries, 71, 84, 146, 211
    and politics, 107–8, 328
    Rome, 90–1, 212, 225, 229,
        230–4, 262, 267–8,
        305, 306–7, 310, 328,
        331–2, 335f, 372
    Seleucid Empire, 214
    war elephants, 226
    warrior classes, 107–8, 112
Arsacids, 200
art, 31, 53, 96, 118f, 119, 270f,
    271, 370f, 385f
Artemis, 119, 347
asceticism, 23, 353–4, 362–5,
    386
Asclepius, 184
asebeia, 175, 186
Ashoka, 196–7
Asia, 124–5
Asia Minor

Archaic period, 83–4
    Hellenistic period, 201–3,
        210, 218–19, 233,
        234–5, 264
    Roman Imperial period,
        351–2
assembly, 72, 74, 79, 83,
    89–90, 97, 104–7,
    210–14, 262 *see also*
    comitia; *concilium*;
    ekklesia
Assur, 68
Assurbanipal, 67f–8
Assyria, 8, 67–8
astrology, 136, 196, 279, 282,
    290, 336, 345, 347
astronomy, 48, 126, 135, 196,
    289, 336, 345
ataraxia, 288
Atargatis, 245f, 280f
atheism, 186, 287, 355–6
Athena, 180–1, 185f
Athens
    Archaic period, 75f, 76,
        78–82, 84, 104–6
    army, 396
    Classical period, 139–41,
        142–8, 152–63, 396
    democracy, 79, 82, 100,
        104–6, 142–5, 164–8,
        210, 262
    economy, 152–8
    education, 172–3, 336
    empire *see* Delian League
    Hellenistic period, 201, 219,
        262, 263
    laws, 173–5
    navy, 141, 145, 210, 396
    political organization, 396
    religion, 81f, 180–2
    Roman Imperial period, 336
    social organization, 115,
        116–17
Attalids, 275, 400
Attica, 55, 74–6, 80, 93,
    141–7, 155–8, 185f
Attila, 313
auctoritas, 266

augury, 283–4
Augustales, 325
Augusti, 306, 331
Augustine, Saint, 364
Augustus, 221, 238–40, 262,
    298–302, 319, 327–9,
    336, 348–9
Aurelian, 318, 349
Australopithecus, 27
autarchy, 152, 156, 316, 320
autourgoi, 155
auxilia, auxiliaries, 296, 298
Avars, 376

B
Ba'al, 281
Babylonia
    Archaic period, 67, 68,
        70–1, 114
    Bronze Age, 48–50
    Hellenistic period, 204,
        206–7
    Roman Imperial period,
        351–2
Bactria, 197–200, 204–5, 215,
    371
Baghdad, 390
Balkans, 34, 37, 42, 45, 201,
    211, 238, 270, 306, 310,
    313, 316, 381–2
Baltic, 45, 303
banking, 248–9 *see also* money
barbaroi, barbarians, 123–4,
    162
Basil, Saint, 387
basileus, 72, 83, 103–4 *see also*
    kings
Basque, 45, 138
Batavian Rebellion, 302, 312
Belisarius, 385f
Benedict, Saint, 386
Benjamin, 70
Bessos, 204–5
bishops, bishoprics, 358,
    362–5, 376, 382, 386–7
Bithynia, Bithynia et Pontus,
    219
black-figure pottery, 96, 181f

Black Sea, 76, 96, 99, 114, 123,
    137, 147, 158, 218, 247,
    249, 305, 371
body armor, 54–5
Boeotia, 55, 83
bog bodies, 21f, 32f
boni see *optimates*
Book of the Dead, 51
books, 334, 360f, 386
    codex, codices, 360f
    scrolls, 69, 113, 360f
boule, bouleutai, 214, 216, 263,
    320–3, 330
    Athens, 142–5, 164–6, 168,
        396
brahmana, 135
Brahmanism, 134–5, 195, 197
Brahmaputra, 13
Britain, Britannia, 5f, 301, 302,
    313, 344f, 373–6 *see also*
    England
Brittany, 376bronze working,
    37, 58, 73
Brutus, 238, 240
Bucchero ware, 92f
Buddha, Buddhism, 135–6,
    196–7, 198f, 199, 270f,
    271, 296, 352–3, 369–71
Bulgars, Bulgarians, 376, 379,
    381, 393
bull cults, 35, 53
bureaucracy, 51, 194, 220, 252,
    264, 282, 306, 316,
    319–20, 321, 327–32,
    390
Burgundians, 312, 373
Byblos, 68, 69
Byzantium, 372, 376, 377,
    378–82, 392, 394

C
Caesar *see* Julius Caesar
Caesarea, 336
Caesares, 306, 331
calendars, 7–9, 48, 50–1, 240
Caligula, 301, 349
caliphate, 389
Cambyses, 71

Campania, 88, 91, 149, 222,
    267
Campus Martius, 397
Canaanites, 68
Cannae, Battle of, 227
Capitol, 397
Cappadocia, 218
Capua, 149, 222, 260
Caracalla, 305
Carolingians, 377, 386, 391,
    394
Carrhae, Battle of, 237
carrying capacity, 13–14,
    16–17, 20, 30–1, 113–14
Carthage, 66, 92, 103, 137, 141,
    223–8, 251
Caspian Sea, 42, 136–7, 371
Cassius, 238, 240
Cassius Dio, 346
caste system, 64, 103, 135, 197
Catholicism, 380, 382–6 *see
    also* Christianity
Cato the Elder, 229
cattle, 33, 94
Caucasus, 42, 200, 218, 371
cavalry, 194, 201, 203, 267
    war elephants, 226
cave paintings, 31
celibacy, 23, 342, 378
Celts, 65, 66, 138, 211
    Christianity, 376
censor, 222, 231f, 255, 265–6,
    328, 371, 397
census, 101, 231f, 266
Central Asia, 12, 14, 15, 41, 45,
    65, 197, 199, 371
    chronology, 413, 415, 417
centuriae, 255, 265, 397 see also
    comitia centuriata
centurio, 262, 326, 331, 335f
ceramics, 4, 31, 35, 37, 53, 66,
    72–3, 77, 85, 88, 95–6,
    152, 158, 181f, 244, 293,
    317f
Chaeronea, Battle of , 149
Chalcedon, Council of, 364,
    380

Chandragupta Maurya, 196–7, 212, 289
Chang'an, 196
chariots, 42, 52, 55, 138
    racing, 338–9
Charlemagne, 377
chassidim, 216–18
Childeric, 376
children, 22, 114, 279, 342
    legal status, 161, 171
    see also education
China
    agriculture and climate, 12, 14, 34, 38
    Archaic period, 61–4, 102–3
    chronology, 413, 415, 417
    Classical period, 131–4
    Hellenistic period, 194–5
    influence on other cultures, 40, 131, 369
    kings and emperors, 102–3
    late antiquity, 369, 370f
    Roman Imperial period, 293, 296, 329
    society, 39–40, 195, 293, 296, 370f
    technology, 38–40, 45
Chios, 72–3
Chlodovech see Clovis
choregia, 182
Christ, Christos, 302, 354, 361
Christianity, 7, 8–9, 302, 305, 307, 321, 336, 341–2, 346, 354–65, 371–2, 373, 376, 378, 380–1, 382–7, 392
    apologetics and literature, 409–10
    persecution of, 356–7, 359–60, 365
christianization, 343, 360–2, 373, 376–8, 392
christogram, 361, 385f
chronology, 7–10, 48, 50–1, 91, 240, 411–17
Cicero, Marcus Tullius, 232, 237
Cilicia, 219

Cimbri, 234
Circus Maximus, 318, 338
cities
    Archaic period, 74–8, 86–7, 114
    Classical period, 152–63
    early civilizations, 36–7, 45, 47
    food supply, 157–8, 318–20
    Hellenistic period, 213–14, 229, 257–60, 273–7
    local gods, 202f, 213f
    planning and development, 275–7
    population, 21, 114, 229, 318–19, 320, 342–3
    Roman Imperial period, 310–13, 318–21, 330
citizenship, 160–1, 162–3, 221, 232, 234, 254–7, 258–9, 323–4, 338, 398–9
city council see *boule, bouletai*; *curia, curiales*
City of God, The (Augustine), 364
cives see citizenship
civil wars, 220–1, 234–40, 302–3, 305, 307–8
civilizations, core-periphery relations, 40–1
civitates, 330, 376, 382
clarissimi, 327
class
    age classes, 100, 114–15
    Archaic period, 74–6, 77–8, 94, 97–101
    aristocracy, 72, 74–6, 77–8, 90, 105–6, 150–1, 163, 231, 232, 260–1, 266–7, 321–2, 323
    caste system, 64, 135
    citizenship, 160–1, 162–3, 221, 232, 258–9, 323–4, 338
    Classical period, 138, 145, 150–1, 159–63
decuriones, 323, 325, 327

egalitarianism, 100
freedmen, 254, 258–9, 324, 325–6
fulai (tribes), 99–100
Hellenistic period, 229–34, 252–62
and land ownership, 19–20, 77, 94, 230–4, 260–1, 320–1, 326
property classes, 79, 101, 150–1, 162–3, 230–1, 247, 248–9, 255–6, 266, 322–3
Roman Imperial period, 320–7
serfs, 98–9, 256–7, 320–1, 324, 325
slaves, 77, 97–8, 99, 159–60, 170, 249–51, 256, 258, 259–60, 320–1, 324–6, 398–9
social mobility, 261–2
warrior classes, 107–8, 112
Claudius, 299f, 301
Cleisthenes, 81–2, 142–4, 170
Cleopatra, 220–1, 240
clergy, 321, 358–9, 362, 385f
    see also bishops and bishoprics; priesthood (non-Christian)
climate change, 11–13, 32
Clovis, 376
codex, codices, 360f
coinage see money
collegia, 333–4
Cologne, 319
coloni, 316, 321, 326, 376
coloniae, 267, 330
colonies, colonization, 72–3, 76–7, 83–4, 137, 164, 197–200, 201–3, 213–16, 218–19, 256, 263–4
Colosseum, 318, 340
comedy, 119, 177, 182
comes, 376
comitatus, 332

comitia, 89–90, 150–1, 222, 229–38, 255, 265, 268, 327–8, 397

comitia centuriata, 230, 255, 265, 397

comitia tributa, 230, 265, 268, 397

Commodus, 303

concilium plebis, 150–1, 230, 265, 327, 397

Confucius, Confucianism, 131–4

conspicuous consumption, 19, 77, 83, 94, 96, 101, 154, 244, 258

Constantine, 306–7, 321, 331–2, 360–4

Constantinople, 339, 364, 372, 378, 382, 386–7, 394

Constantinople, Council of, 380–1

constitutio Antoniniana, 323, 398

consuls, 397

contests (games), 85, 111–12, 172, 179–80, 328, 338–40

copper, 37–8, 55

core-periphery relations, 40–1

Corinth, 201, 212

Corinthian League, 149, 201, 206, 207, 210

Corpus Iuris Civilis, 380

Corsica, 83, 138, 225

cosmology, 126

cosmopolitanism, 220, 245, 273, 281, 324f, 370, 390

Council of 500 *see boule*, *bouletai*

councils *see boule*, *bouletai*; *curia, curiales*

crafts and industry, 19–20, 95, 155, 156, 244, 316–17

Crassus, Marcus Licinius, 236, 237

Crete, 53, 77

crime and punishment, 49, 259, 260, 337–8, 339–40, 356

Croesus, 84

Ctesiphon, 200

culture *see* society

cuneiform script, 42, 47–8

curia, curiales, 323, 327, 330

curse tablets, 184

cursus honorum, 265–6, 322, 331

Cybele, 347

Cycladic culture, 53

Cyme, Battle of, 139f, 141

Cynics, 186, 288

Cyprus, 72–3

Cypselus, 78

Cyrus, 70, 71, 84, 136

Cyrus II, 147

D

Dacia, 301

daily life, 109–28, 169–87, 269–90, 333–65

dairy products, 15

Damascus, 68, 390

dancing, 172, 174f

Danube, 34, 303, 305, 308, 378, 381

dao, 134

Daodejing, 134

Darius I, 71, 136, 137, 139–41

Darius III, 203, 204–5, 206

Dark Age (Greek), 71–3, 85, 94–5, 101, 103, 106–7, 110, 120, 123, 125

dasa, 135

dating, 7–10, 48, 50–1, 91, 240

David, 69, 217, 350f

de-urbanization, 320–1

death, life after death, 120, 183, 347–8, 357

Decius, 359

decuriones, 323, 325–7

defixio see curse tablets

Delian League, 145–6, 147

Delos, 245f, 249–51

Delphi, 85, 119

demes, 144, 396

Demeter, 119, 183, 281

Demetrius I, 198f

Demetrius II, 198f

Demetrius Poliorketes, 207, 210

democracy, 79, 82, 100, 104–6, 142–5, 164–8, 262–3

Democritus, 288

demography, 20–3, 72–3, 76, 113–15, 200–1, 211, 221–2, 229, 277–8, 320, 342–3

demos, 105–6, 142–3, 144–5

dendrochronology, 9–10

Denmark, 21f, 32, 234, 377

desertification, 13, 17, 34, 37

diadochoi, 207, 219–20

diaspora, 216–18, 349–52, 354–5

dictator, 227, 235, 238, 268, 301

diffusion, 18, 336, 347, 391

dignitas, 266

dikastai, 166–7

dilectus, 231f

diocese, 306, 309, 331, 378, 399

Diocletian, 8, 306–7, 321, 329, 330–2, 359

Diodotus I, 198f

Diogenes of Sinope, 186

Dionysia, 159, 182

Dionysius, 8

Dionysius I, 147

Dionysius II, 187

Dionysus, 159, 181f, 182, 281

Dipylon vase, 75f

disease, 20–2, 33–4, 183, 381 *see also* health

distribution of land, 78, 212, 232, 235

divination, 4, 40, 85, 88, 95, 113, 119, 122, 179, 203, 282, 284, 349

divus, 349

documents *see* written sources

domestication, 14–15, 17, 33–4

Dominate, 306, 330–1, 399

dominus, 306–7, 330, 349, 399

Domitian, 303

Domitius Ahenobarbus, 231f

Dorian Greeks, 57, 77
dowry, 94, 115–16, 152, 171
drachma, 154, 156, 198f,
     247–8, 252
Dracon, 78
draft animals, 94
drama *see* theater
Dravidians, Dravidian
     languages, 132, 135
dualism, 136, 282, 287, 353,
     358, 380, 389
dunamenoi, 325–6
Dura Europos, 350f
dux, 376

E
Ebro, 225–6
Ecbatana, 204
ecology, 11–23, 32, 33
economy
     agriculture, 13–20, 93–4,
          156–7, 241–3
     Archaic period, 80, 93–7
     Bronze Age, 53
     Classical period, 136,
          145–6, 152–8
     Hellenistic period, 195, 196,
          200, 229, 241–52,
          260–1
     inflation, 316
     late antiquity, 320–1
     mining, 18, 155, 156, 259
     money, 19, 85, 198f, 247–9,
          251, 315–16
     and politics, 251–2, 316,
          320–1
     prehistory, 13–20, 30
     Roman Imperial period, 18,
          293, 305, 306–7,
          314–21
     tariffs, 252
     taxation, 152, 154, 159, 229,
          248–9, 251–2, 274,
          306–7, 314, 320–1
     trade and exchange
          networks, 18, 53,
          55–6f, 80, 95–6,
          157–8, 195, 196, 200,

     244–51, 252, 260–1,
          293, 317–18, 344f,
          370f, 371
     tribute, 136, 145–6, 249
ecstatic cults, 182, 184, 281,
     284
education, 100, 112, 113,
     172–3, 274, 334–6
efebeia, 333
egalitarianism, 100
Egypt
     Archaic period, 68, 102–3
     chronology, 412, 414, 416
     economy, 15, 245–7,
          329–30
     Hellenistic period, 203–4,
          219–20, 238, 240,
          245–7, 253f, 256–7,
          277
     late antiquity, 380–1
     pharaohs, 38, 50–2, 102–3,
          219–20, 246–7, 253f,
          264, 271–2, 282, 400
     prehistory and early
          dynasties, 37–8, 50–2
     religion, 38, 50–1, 68, 121,
          203–4, 286–7, 359,
          362–3, 380–1
     Roman Imperial period,
          329–30
     social class, 99, 256–7
     wars, 70–1, 215–16, 220–1,
          238, 240
ekklesia, 158, 162, 166–7, 175,
     396
ekklesiastikon, 145, 164
Elam, Elamites, 50
Elbe, 301, 377
electrum, *elektron*, 85
elephants, 198f, 215, 226
Eleusius, 183, 281, 348
elite(s)
     aristocracy, 72, 74–6, 77–8,
          90, 105–6, 150–1, 163,
          231, 232, 260–1,
          266–7, 321–2, 323
     caste system, 64, 135
     decuriones, 323, 325, 327

     property classes, 79, 101,
          150–1, 162–3, 230–1,
          247, 248–9, 255–6,
          266, 322–3
     and social mobility, 261–2
     warrior classes, 107–8, 112
     see also kings
emperors, 327–32, 348–9, 377
England, 5f, 32, 301, 303, 376,
     386 *see also* Britain,
     Britannia
entertainment, 85, 109–13,
     328, 338–40
Epaminondas, 147
Ephesus, 73, 76, 85, 323
epic poetry, 4, 73–4, 94, 95,
     104, 109–10, 112–13,
     117, 120, 123, 178, 201,
     289, 407
Epicurism, 287, 288, 404
Epicurus, 288
epigraphic sources
     (inscriptions), 4, 75f, 92f
Epirus, 163, 223, 226f
eponymy, eponymics, 8, 104,
     174f
equality, 100
eques, equites, 248–9, 255–6,
     259, 262, 322–3, 330
era, 8
Eratosthenes, 289
ethics, 121–2, 134, 175, 352
     and sexuality, 177–8, 341–2
     see also religion
Ethiopia, 68, 125, 380, 389
Etruria, Etruscans
     Archaic period, 66, 86–8,
          90–1, 98–9
     Classical period, 139f, 141,
          149
     prehistory, 91f, 92f
Euboea, 73, 92f
Euclid, 289
euergetes, euergetism, 261,
     273–7, 328
Euhemerus, 287

Euphrates, 13, 17, 36, 49, 66, 200, 204, 245f, 280f, 297, 301, 308, 310, 350f
Euripides, 182
Eusebius, bishop of Caesarea, 363, 365
evocation, 284

F
factio, 266
familia Caesaris, 325
family, 67f, 89, 114–17, 171, 175–6, 277–9, 341–2
fasces, 91
Fatum, 347
Fertile Crescent, 33–4, 37, 46f
fertility cults, 23, 35, 177
fertility rates, 22–3, 113–15, 175, 279, 343
festivals, religious, 8, 48, 78, 80, 85, 99–100, 111, 113, 116–19, 123, 152, 159, 164, 174f, 176, 180–2, 261, 281, 349, 356
feudalism, 194–5, 296, 372, 381
fides, 89
fiscus, fiscus Caesaris, 329, 331
Flavii, Flavian emperors, 302
foederati, 332, 399
food supply, 157–8, 318–20, 329–30
Fortuna, 344f, 347
forum, 311f
Forum Romanum, 90, 318, 397
Franks, 304, 305, 313, 371, 373, 376, 377, 386, 393
fraternities, 170–1
fratria, 170
freedmen, 254, 258–9, 324, 325–6, 398
fulai (tribes), 99–100, 142–5, 170, 396
fusis, 173

G
Gaius, emperor *see* Caligula
Gaius, jurist, 336–7
Galatians, 211, 218

Galen, 345
Galerius, 359
Galilee, 216, 242, 351, 354
Gallia, 234, 237, 239f, 300 *see also* Gaul
  Gallia Cisalpina, 239f
  Gallia Lugdunensis, 299f
  Gallia Narbonensis, 233
games, 85, 111–12, 172, 179–80, 328, 338–40
Gandhara, 198–9, 270f, 297
Ganges valley, 40, 64, 135, 196
Gaugamela, Battle of, 204
Gaul, 226, 233, 234, 237, 239f, 241, 259, 299f, 300, 305, 310, 312–13, 316, 322, 325, 330, 363, 376, 386
Gefolgschaft, 138
gens, 89
geography, 124–5, 289, 344–5
geological change, 11–12
Germania, 300, 305, 310
Germanic peoples, 234, 303, 306, 308, 310–13, 332
  western kingdoms, 372–7
gerousia, 105
gladiatorial games, 339f, 340
gnosis, Gnosticism, 358, 360f–1f
goats, 33, 94
Gobi Desert, 293
gods, 31, 40, 47–8, 50–1, 57, 69–70, 85, 88, 103, 113, 117–23, 127, 135, 139f, 173–5, 178–81, 184, 186, 202f, 213, 223, 244–5, 281–8, 331, 346–9, 355, 359, 361
gold, 55, 149, 157, 195, 204, 244, 247–8, 251, 257, 307, 316, 378
Gospels, 354, 358
Goths, 304–5, 308–12, 359, 364, 373, 376–7, 380, 399
governance, 167–8, 213–14, 222, 225, 262–3, 265–7, 327–32, 396–9

Gracchus, Gaius, 232–3, 265, 268
Gracchus, Tiberius, 231–2, 265, 268
grain, distribution of *see annona* (distribution of grain)
grain trade, 157–8, 318–20
grammaticus, 334
Granikos, Battle of, 201
gravestones, 324f
Greece
  Archaic period, 71, 73–85, 93–101, 103–8, 123–4
  art, 73, 96, 118f, 119, 270f, 271
  Bronze Age, 42, 45, 52–7
  chronology, 8, 412, 414, 416
  citizenship, 254, 256–7
  Classical period, 139–49, 152–87
  colonies, 72–3, 76–7, 83–4, 137, 164, 201–3, 218–19, 223, 256, 263–4
  cultural identity, 169–70, 173–5, 269–73
  daily life, 109–20, 122–8, 169–87
  Dark Age, 71–3
  economy, 152–8
  education, 172–3, 334–6
  Hellenistic period, 200–12, 228–9, 254, 256, 261, 262–3, 269–83, 287–90
  influence on other cultures, 122–3, 216–17, 269–72, 308–10, 311, 390–4
  language and scripts, 42, 53–7, 72, 91f, 113, 123, 170, 199, 200–1, 214, 269, 308, 322, 334, 345, 364, 380–2, 392, 394
  literature, 4, 72, 73–4, 112–13, 346, 407–8, 409–10

Greece (*continued*)
 philosophy, 125–7, 173,
  186–7, 284, 403–6
 poleis, 74–85, 97–101,
  103–6, 261, 262–3,
  272–3
 politics, 163–8, 205, 206,
  207–16, 228–9, 254,
  256–7, 262–4
 population, 72–3, 76,
  113–15, 200–1, 211,
  279
 religion, 117–23, 178–86,
  279–82
 slavery, 77, 97–8, 159–60,
  170
 trade and exchange
  networks, 77, 96
 wars, 124f, 139–41, 146–9,
  200–16, 228–9
Greek (language), 42, 53–7,
  72, 91f, 113, 123, 170,
  199, 200–1, 214, 269, 308,
  322, 334, 345, 364, 380–2,
  392, 394
gumnasiarchos, 168, 334
gumnasion (gymnasium), 111,
  172, 274, 334
Gupta Empire, 297, 370–1

H
Hadda, 270f
Hades, 120
Hadrian, 297, 303, 351
Hadrianopolis, 308, 332
Hallstatt culture, 65–6,
  138
Hamilcar, 225
Hamitic languages, 42
Hammurabi, 48–50
Han dynasty, 195, 293, 296,
  329
Hannibal, 226–8
Hanno, 137
Harmodius, 81f
Hashmonaeans (Maccabees),
  217–19, 285–6
Hatra, 245f–6f

health, 20–1, 32f, 33–4
 life expectancy and fertility,
  22–3, 342–3
 medicine, 274, 290, 345
Hebrew, 69, 216, 394
Hecataeus, 124–5
Heliaia, 166
heliaiai see jury courts
Helladic culture, 54–7
Hellenism, definition, 201
Hellenization, 122–3, 211,
  214, 216–17, 218, 242,
  264, 269–72, 281–7, 308,
  323–4, 347, 381, 392
Hellespont, 55, 147, 201
Hellespontofulakes, 158
helmets, 139f
helots, 82, 98, 110, 141, 160,
  162
henotheism, 281–2
Hephtalites, 270f, 297–8,
  371–2
Heracles, 198f, 226f, 270f
Heraclitus, 126–7
Heraclius (Herakleios), 372,
  381–2
Herculaneum, 12
hermits, 362–3, 386 *see also*
  monasticism
Herodotus, 142
heroes, hero-cult, 120, 178,
  279, 282
Hesiod, 112–13
hestia, Hestia, 184
hetaireiai, 171
Hiëro (Hieron), 139f
hieroglyphs, 37
hijra, 389
Himalayas, 12, 13, 371
Himera, Battle of, 139f, 141
Hinayana, 352
Hindu Kush, 195–6, 197–200,
  205, 215, 296–7
Hinduism, 135–6
hippeis, 79, 101
Hippias, 80, 81f, 91, 106
Hippocrates, 186
Hippodamus, 276

hippodrome, 276, 318,
  338–9
Hispania, 225–8, 377, 380
Hittites, 52, 66
Holy Roman Empire, 377
Homer, 73–4, 109–10, 112,
  120
Homo erectus, 27
Homo habilis, 27
homo novus, 233, 266
Homo sapiens, 27–30
homoioi, 82–3, 100, 161, 162,
  179
homosexuality, 115, 177–8,
  278
honestiores, 323, 338
Honorius, 313
hoplites, 81, 82, 88, 141, 146
Horace, 301
horses, 38–9, 42, 45, 52, 54–5,
  65, 72, 94, 138
 chariot racing, 338–9
 domestication, 33, 42
Horus, 102f, 282
hostis, 123
Huangdi, 194
Huanghe, 14, 36, 38–40, 45,
  293
hubris, 174–5
humanity, origins, 27–30
humiliores, 323, 338
Huns, 297, 312, 313, 371
hunter-gatherers, 13, 17, 30–3,
  34
Hyksos, 51
Hyperboreans, 125

I
Iberia, 138, 223, 225, 377
Ice Ages, 31
Iliad, 73
illustres, 327
Illyrian emperors, 306
Illyrians, 66, 381
imperator, 327
imperial cult, 330–1, 348–9,
  359

imperium, 236, 265, 327–8, 337
 imperium proconsulare, 328
Imperium Galliarum, 305
India, 215
 Archaic period, 64, 103
 chronology, 413, 415, 417
 Classical period, 134–6
 climate and vegetation, 13
 Hellenistic period, 195–7, 205–6, 246
 late antiquity, 369–71
 literature, 197
 politics, 103, 196, 369–70
 religion, 23, 135–6, 195, 196–7, 369–71
 Roman Imperial period, 296–7
Indo-Aryans, 38, 40, 45, 134–5
Indo-European language group, 42–5, 57–8
Indo-Iranians, 45
Indus, 38, 196, 199–200, 205–6
 influence on other cultures, 40
industrial production systems, 317
inequality, 65–6, 94, 97–101, 138, 150–1, 252–62, 302, 325–6
infant mortality, 22, 342
infanticide, 22, 279
inflation, 316
ingenui, 324
inheritance rights, 94, 97, 116, 161, 171
initiation, 115, 119, 183, 348
innovation, technological *see* invention
inquisitorial process, 337
inscriptions, 4, 75f, 92f
insignia, 91
Institutiones, 336
interpretatio Romana, 284, 347
invention, 19–20, 290, 345
 spread of metallurgy, 37, 58, 73, 86

Ionia, 72, 73, 76, 83–4, 126
Ionian Revolt (500–494 BC), 84
Ipsos, Battle of, 207
Iran, 200, 204–5, 206, 218–19, 353–4, 371–2
Iraq, 33, 36–7, 245f, 352
Ireland, 345, 376
iron, 65–6, 73, 86
irrigation, 17, 20, 36, 41, 51, 67, 131, 135, 241
Isaac, 69
Isis, 281–2, 347
Islam, 371, 372, 381, 387–90, 392
Isocrates, 148
Israel, 68–70
Israelites, 69–70, 103, 120 *see also* Judaism
Issus, Battle of, 203
Italic peoples, 45, 57, 86, 88, 93, 98–9, 106, 107, 114, 122–3, 138
Italy, Italia
 Archaic period, 86–91, 114, 122–3
 chronology, 412, 414, 416
 Classical period, 138, 149–51
 Hellenistic period, 221–3, 226–8, 232–3, 256, 267–8
 late antiquity, 376, 380
 prehistory, 45, 57–8
 Roman Imperial period, 315, 329
 see also Rome
iuventus, 333–4

J
Jacob, 69
Janus, 284
Japan, 35, 61, 131, 191, 296, 352, 369
Jehoshua (Jeshu) *see* Jesus of Nazareth
Jerusalem, 70–1, 121, 216–19, 264

Jesus of Nazareth, 302, 354–5, 380
Jewish War, 302
jihad, 389
Jonathan (Maccabaeus), 217
Judah, Kingdom of, 69–70, 103
Judaism, 69–70, 121, 216–17, 285–6, 302, 349–52
Judas Maccabaeus, 217–18
Judea, 216–18, 285–6, 302, 349–51
Julian calendar, 8
Julio-Claudian dynasty, 301
Julius Caesar, 8, 212, 220–1, 236–40, 262, 268, 284
Jupiter, 90–1, 123, 283, 346, 359
jurists, 336–7
jury courts, 145, 161, 166–7
Justinian, 376, 380–1, 385f–6
Jutes, 313

K
Ka'ba, 389
Kabul, 125, 205, 215
Karkemish, 46, 66
Kashmir, 269
khalifa see caliphate
Kharosthi, 198f
Khmer, 369, 393
kings, 55, 83, 106–7, 263–4, 271–2
 deification, 47, 50–1, 102–3, 282–3, 284, 328, 330–1, 348–9
klerouchia, 145–6
Knossos, 53
koine, 269
koinonia, 272–3, 288
Kongfuzi, Kongzi *see* Confucius, Confucianism
Konstantinoupolis *see* Constantinople
korai, 118–19
Koran *see* Qur'an
Kore *see* Persephone
Korea, 191, 195, 293, 296, 369

kouroi, 118–19
kshatriya, 135
Kunikoi *see* Cynics
kureia, kurios, 176, 277
Kushan empire, 296–7

L
La Graufesenque, 317f
Laconia, 55, 76, 211
Lagash, 47
land ownership, 19–20, 51, 77, 94, 230–4, 320–1, 326
languages, 42–5, 66, 86, 134–5, 334–6
Laozi, 134
Lascaux, 31
Latène culture, 138
latifundia, 259
Latin (language), 88, 308, 310, 322, 334, 345, 380, 392
Latin League, 149, 222
Latins, Latini (people), 88–9, 149, 222, 232–3, 256, 267
Latium, 86, 88, 91, 149, 222, 267
Laurion, 158
laws
    Code of Hammurabi, 48–50
    Draconian constitution, 78
    Germanic kingdoms, 373
    Greece, 116–17, 161, 166–8, 171, 173–5, 258, 269, 277–8
    magistrates and officials, 167–8, 213–14, 222, 225, 262–3, 265–7, 327–9, 336–8
    Rome, 150–1, 222, 230–3, 258, 265, 266, 327–9, 333–4, 336–8, 356
Lebanon, 68
Legalism, 134
legati, 237
    legati Augusti pro-praetore, 326, 329, 398
leges barbarorum, 373
leges Romanae, 373

legiones, 90–1, 212, 225, 229, 230–4
leitourgia see liturgy
Leo I, pope, 382
Leo III, pope, 377
Leonidas, 141
Lepidus, 240
Lesbos, 72
Leuctra, Battle of, 147
lex Hortensia, 222
liberti, 324–5, 398 *see also* freedmen
Libya, 52, 68, 76, 203, 223, 310, 381
lictores, 91
life expectancy, 22–3, 342–3
Liguria, Ligurians, 138
limes, 303, 332
limitanei, 332
Linear A script, 53
Linear B script, 53, 55, 57
lingua franca, 66, 136, 269, 390
literacy, 112–13, 172, 335f
literature, 4, 72, 73–4, 112–13, 346, 407–10
liturgy, 152, 154–5, 159, 162, 168, 182, 273–4
Livy, 301
logos, 288
Longobards, Lombards, 376, 380
Lukeion, 187
Lunyu, 131
Luoyang, 61
lustratio, 231f
luxuries, 19, 77, 83, 94, 96, 101, 154, 244, 258
Lyceum *see* Lukeion
Lydia, 85
Lyon, 319, 349
Lyon Tabulae, 299f
lyric poetry, 112, 113, 407
Lysander, 147, 282

M
Maccabees, 217–18, 285–6

Macedon, 83, 148–9, 187, 195–6, 200–12, 228–9, 251
    colonies, 197–200, 212–16
Madina, 389
magic, 31, 183–4, 279, 282, 336, 347
magister officiorum, 399
magistrates, 167–8, 213–14, 222, 225, 262–3, 265–7, 337–8, 396–9
Magna Mater, 184
Magyar, 377
Mahayana, 352–3, 369–70
maiestas, 337
Mandaeans, 352–3, 384
Mandate of Heaven, 40, 102–3
Mani, 353
Manichaenism, 353–4, 359, 365, 370–1, 384
manumission, 3, 259, 262, 325 *see also* freedmen; *liberti*
Marathon, Battle of, 141
Marc Antony *see* Antony
Marcomanni, 305
Marcus Aurelius, 303
Mari, 49, 53
Marius, 233–5, 236, 268
marriage, 22, 30, 94, 114–17, 175–6, 182, 220, 277–9, 341–2, 363
Mars, 231f
martyrdom, 357, 359
Massalia, 76, 92f, 233
mathematics, 128, 289
matronae, 278
Maurya dynasty, 135, 196–7
Maxentius, 307
Maximinus Thrax, 305
Maya, 393
Mecca, 376, 389
Medes, 70, 71
medicine, 128, 159, 183, 186, 196, 274, 290, 345, 392
Mediterranean climate, 12–13
megalithic cultures, 35
Megasthenes, 289
Memphis, 50, 203

Menander, 198f, 199

Mencius, 134

Mengzi *see* Mencius

mercenaries, 68, 71, 78–80, 85, 96, 106, 114, 138, 146, 148, 156, 159, 161–2, 164, 196, 200–4, 210, 211, 216, 223, 225, 269, 279, 286, 313

Mercurius, 347

Merovech, 376

Merovingians, 376

Mesolithic era, 31

Mesopotamia
    Archaic period, 67–8, 103, 121
    early civilizations, 36–7, 42, 45–50
    Hellenistic period, 204
    influence on other cultures, 40–1, 117
    languages, 42
    late antiquity, 371–2
    Roman Imperial period, 352–4

Messenia, 55, 76, 82–3, 147

messiah, 217–18, 302, 351, 354–5

Messina, 223

metallurgy, 37, 58, 73, 86 *see also* copper, gold, iron, silver

methodology, 3–10, 16–17

metoikion, 161

metoikoi, metics, 161–2, 169, 176

Middle Ages, influence of Greco-Roman culture on, 390–4

migration, 38, 41–5, 54, 55–7, 86, 352, 381
    Greek colonies, 72–3, 76–7, 83–4, 137

Miletus, 73, 76, 84–5, 203

Miletus, Battle of, 84

militia, 331

Milvian Bridge, Battle of the, 307

mina, 154

mining, 18, 155, 156, 259

Minoans, 52–3

Minos, 53

Mishnah, 351

misthos, 166

Mitanni, 50, 52

Mithras, 347–8

Mithridates, 219

Moesia, 300, 305

Mohammed, 376

monarchy, 47, 78, 80, 102–3, 106–8, 137, 163, 187, 200, 210, 218, 222, 230, 235, 237–8, 263–4, 268, 272–3, 276, 298–9, 302, 306, 323, 327

monasticism, 363, 378, 386, 387

money, 19, 85, 198f, 226f, 247–9, 251, 315–16

Mongols, 15, 45, 65, 194, 296, 387

monitization, 85, 316, 320

Monophysitism, 364–5, 380–1, 386, 387

monotheism, 69–70, 121, 282, 285–6, 305, 307, 349

Monte Testaccio, 320

Mosaic law, 70, 216, 218, 351

Moselle, 302

Moses, 69–70, 350f, 357 *see also* Mosaic law

Mosul, 389

Mouseion (Musaeum), 289, 336

mummification, 51

municipia, 238, 267–8, 330

music, 172, 250f

Muslims, 371, 372, 381, 387–90, 392

Mycenae, 54–5

Mycenaeans, Mycenaean culture, 54–7, 66, 72

mystery cults, 183, 281–2, 346–8

mysticism, 64

mythology, 41, 73, 88, 117, 119, 122, 125–7, 169, 172, 178, 334, 340, 345, 347

N

Nabataea, 280f, 389

Nag-Hammadi Codices, 360f–1f

Narbo (Narbonne), 233

Narmer Palette, 102f

navy, 84, 141, 210, 225 *see also* ships

Neanderthal, 30

Neapolis, 76

Near East
    Archaic period, 66–71, 102–3
    chronology, 413, 415, 417
    Hellenistic period, 216–18
    prehistory, 14, 15, 32–5, 45, 52
    Roman Imperial period, 349–52

Nebuchadnezzar, 71

Nehalennia, 344f

Neo-Babylonian Empire, 70–1, 103

Neolithic era, 32–5

Neoplatonism, 348, 404

Neptune, 231f

Nero, 302, 356

Nerva, 303

Nestorians, 365, 371–2, 387

Nestorius, 364–5, 371–2, 380

New Carthage (Cartagena), 226f

New Guinea, 14

New Persian Empire *see* Sassanid Empire

New Testament, 358

Nicaea, Council of, 363–4

Nike, 185f

Nile, 13, 17, 36, 37–8, 40, 50, 51, 68, 102f, 220, 242–3, 257, 350f, 360f

Nineveh, 67f–8, 70, 95

Nisibis, 371–2

nobiles, nobilitas, 397

nomads, nomadism, 14, 15, 41, 65, 197, 199, 371
nomos, 173–4
Norsemen, 377
novels, 346, 408
Nubia, 50, 68, 380, 387
Numidia, 233, 311f

O
obol, 157
Octavius *see* Octavianus
Octavianus, Gaius Julius Caesar (Augustus), 221, 238–40, 262, 298–302, 319, 327–9, 336, 348–9
odeion, 276
Odoacer, 313
Odyssey, 73
officiales, 327
officium, officia, 399
oikos, 171
Old Testament, 69, 308
oligarchy, 106, 164, 210, 262–3
olive oil, 80, 320
Olympia, 8, 85, 95, 111, 139f, 219
Olympiads, Olympic Games, 8, 85, 111, 119, 122, 123, 180, 338
optimates, 232–8, 262
oracles, 40, 85, 95, 113, 119, 122, 179, 203–4
orality, 172
ordines, 321–3
    ordo Augustalium, 325
    ordo decuriones, 323, 325–7
    ordo equester, 248–9, 255–6, 259, 262, 322–3, 330
    ordo senatorius, 231–3, 237–8, 255, 260–1, 266–7, 268, 301, 303, 312, 322, 326–7, 329–30, 337, 338, 357, 378
Ormuzd, 122
Orontes, 213
Orpheus, 122
Orphics, 122, 127

Orthodox Christianity, 380, 386–7 *see also* Christianity
Osiris, 282
Ostia, 19, 347
ostraca, 142f, 144–5
ostracism, 142, 144, 164, 167
Ostrogoths, 376, 380
Otto III, emperor, 377
Ottomans, 382, 394

P
Pachomius, 360f
paidagogos, 250f
paiderastia, 115, 177–8
Pakistan, 14–15, 71, 135, 196–9, 206, 296, 352
palace economies, 53, 55
palaistra, 172
Palatine, Palatium, 90, 338
paleoclimatology, 11–13
Paleolithic era, 27–31
Palestina, Palestine, 42, 50, 52, 97, 103, 323, 351, 372, 381
Pali, 197
Palmyra, 245, 305, 324f, 389
Pamir, 195–7
Panathenaea, 81f, 111, 174f, 180–1
Panhellenism, 85, 111, 119, 123, 148, 170
Pannonia, 376
paper, 4, 293
papyrus, papyri, 4, 69, 96, 246, 360f
parchment, 4
Parthenon, 185f
Parthia, 199, 200, 215, 218–19, 237, 297–8
Pataliputra, 196, 199
paterfamilias, 89–90, 150
patres, 89, 90, 150
patriarchs, Christian, 364–5, 386–7
patriarchs, Jewish, 69, 357
patriarchy, 61–2, 116, 176
patricians, 90, 150–1, 163, 222, 265–6

Patrick, Saint, 376
patronage, 138, 152, 154–5, 160, 163, 212, 231, 233–4, 235, 244, 255, 258–9, 283, 289–90, 301, 311, 325–6, 327–8, 336, 362
patronus, 99, 398
Paul, Saint, 354, 355, 358, 382
Pausanias, 141
pax deorum, 283
pax Romana, 302
peasants, 18, 39–40, 51, 52–3, 67–8, 79, 89, 93–4, 98–9, 103, 107, 108, 148–9, 194, 220, 229–30, 233, 242–3, 253–4, 256–7, 260, 264, 268, 296, 316, 341
pederasty *see* paiderastia
Peloponnese, 52–3, 72, 76, 83, 141, 147, 210
Peloponnesian League, 83, 140, 147
Peloponnesian War, 146–7
pentakosiomedimnoi, 79
Pepin the Short, 377
Pergamon, 210, 218, 219, 232, 275f–6f
Periander, 78
Pericles, 146
perioikoi, 83, 162
Persephone, 183
Persepolis, 136, 204–5
Persia
    Archaic period, 70, 71, 84, 124f
    Classical period, 136–7, 139–41, 147–8
    Hellenistic period, 201, 204, 206–7
Persian Gulf, 38, 196, 200, 206, 244, 245f
Persian Wars, 145, 170
Persis, 200, 204, 206
Peter, Saint, 358, 382
Petra, 245, 280f, 389
Petronius, 346
Phaistos, 53

phalanx, 76, 88, 90, 101, 141, 201, 212

pharaohs, 38, 50–2, 102–3, 219–20, 246–7, 253f, 264, 271–2, 282, 400

Philip II of Macedon, 148–9

Philip V of Macedon, 211, 228

Philistines, 68

philosophy, 125–8, 186–7, 284, 287–90, 403–6
   Christian apologists, 357, 409–10
   Confucianism, 131–4
   Legalism, 134
   peripatetics, 187, 336
   pre-Socratics, 126, 403
   science, 126, 288–90, 343–5, 405–6
   sophists, 173, 403
   Stoics, 288, 357, 403–4
   Taoism, 134

Phoenicia, Phoenicians, 66, 68, 103, 137

Phrygia, Phrygians, 66

physical geography, 11–13

piracy, 56f, 95, 160, 235–6, 249

Piraeus, 146, 154, 159, 247

Pisistratus, 79–80

Platae, Battle of, 141

Plato, 173, 184, 186–7, 287, 348, 357

plebeians, *plebeii, plebs*, 150–1

plebiscitum, 151, 222, 265, 328

Pliny the Elder (Plinius), 343–4

Plotinus, 348

plousioi, 162

Plutarch, 346

Pnyx, 153, 164

poetry, 4, 73–4, 94, 95, 104, 109–10, 112–13, 117, 120, 123, 178, 201, 289, 407

Poitiers, Battle of, 377

Poland, 317f, 386

polis
   Archaic period, 74–85, 97–101, 103–6

Classical period, 142–9

Hellenistic period, 261, 262–3, 272–3

politai, 105, 112, 160–1, 169–70, 254 *see also* citizenship

politics
   Archaic period, 74–85, 90–1, 102–8
   Bronze Age, 51–2
   and citizenship, 160–1, 162–3, 221, 232, 234, 254–7, 323–4
   Classical period, 142–9, 150–1, 163–8, 396–7
   democracy, 79, 82, 100, 104–6, 142–5, 164–8, 262–3
   and the economy, 251–2, 316, 320–1
   feudalism, 194–5, 296, 372, 381
   Hellenistic period, 204–5, 206–16, 254–7, 262–8, 277–8
   late antiquity, 369–70, 373–82
   military influences on, 107–8, 112, 328
   oligarchy, 106, 164, 210, 262–3
   and religion, 47, 50–1, 68, 69–70, 102–3, 119, 202f, 216–18, 231f, 264, 282–3, 348–9, 351, 364–5, 386–7
   Roman Imperial period, 293–313, 327–32, 397–9
   voting procedures, 255, 265, 397

pollution, 17–18

polyculture, 15, 16

Polynesia, 30

polytheism, 120, 121, 349, 355

Pompeii, 12, 339f

Pompey, 219, 220, 236–8, 251

pontifex, pontifex maximus, 328

Pontos, 218, 219

populares, 232–5, 255

population growth, 13–14, 113–15 *see also* demography

populus Romanus, 397

Poseidon, 198f

potentes, 325–6, 327

pottery *see also* ceramics
   black-figure and red-figure, 96, 110f, 124f
   Bucchero ware, 92f
   Dipylon vase, 75f
   prehistoric forms, 35

poverty, 94, 101, 154–5, 156, 230, 256–7, 325–6

praefectus
   praefectus Aegypti, 322, 330
   praefectus annonae, 320, 321, 322
   praefectus praetorio, 322, 337, 399

praepositus sacri cubiculi, 399

praetor, 397

Praetorian Guard, 303, 322, 331

pre-Socratics, 126, 403

prehistory, 27–35

Priene, 202f

priesthood (non-Christian), 47, 64, 68, 76, 89, 103–4, 106, 117–19, 135, 161, 179, 216–19, 231f, 283–4, 328, 349, 351, 371 *see also* clergy

primary sources, 3–4

princeps, 237, 299–301, 306, 327–8, 348, 398

Principate, 299–301, 321–30, 398

prisoners of war, enslavement, 249, 340, 365

probouleuma, 166

proconsul, 227, 235, 236–7, 266, 268, 326, 329, 398

procurator, 322, 398

proletarii, 230, 232–3, 234, 237, 238, 242, 255, 256, 257, 260, 262, 268, 274, 397

property classes, 150–1, 230–1, 247, 248–9, 255–6, 266, 322–3

property law, 49

prophets, 69, 70, 351, 353, 357

prostitution, 175–6, 178

Protagoras, 186

provincia, province, 399

proxenos, 165f

prutaneia, prutaneis, 165–6

psyche, 122, 126–7

Ptolemy (Claudius Ptolemy), 345

Ptolemy Euergetes II, 253f

Ptolemy I, 207, 210, 215–16, 219–20

Ptolemy II Philadelphus, 220, 223

Ptolemy VIII Euergetes II, 253–4

Ptolemy XIII, 220, 238

publicani, 248–9, 255, 266, 268

Puni *see* Phoenicia, Phoenicians

Punic Wars, 223–8

Punjab, 13, 196, 205–6

purple, 83, 95–6, 385f

Pydna, Battle of, 212, 216, 228

Pylos, 55, 72

pyramids, 35, 50–1

Pyrenees, 226, 376, 377, 389

Pyrrho of Elis, 287

Pyrrhus, 223

Pythagoras, Pythagoreans, 127–8, 348

Pytheas, 289

Q

Qin dynasty, 194–5

Qin Shihuangdi, 194

quaestor, 397–8

quaestor sacri palatii, 331, 399

Quirinalis, 90

Qur'an, 389

R

rabbinic Judaism, 351

racing, 338–9

radiocarbon dating, 9–10

rationalism, 134, 290

Ravenna, 385f–6

Re (Ra), 50–1, 103 *see also* Ammon, Amun

red-figure pottery, 96, 110f, 124f

Red Sea, 125, 136, 206, 244, 246, 252

reincarnation, 127

relics, 394

religion, 57, 117–23, 175, 178–86, 279–87, 346–65

  ancestor worship, 40

  anthropomorphism, 121, 122–3

  and art, 31, 53

  asceticism, 23, 64, 353–4, 362–5, 386

  Buddhism, 135–6, 196–7, 198f, 199, 270f, 271, 296, 352–3, 369–71

  bull cults, 35, 53

  Christianity, 8, 302, 305, 307, 321, 336, 341–2, 346, 354–65, 373, 376, 378, 380–1, 382–7, 392

    persecution of, 356–7

  and competitive games, 111, 123, 172, 179–80

  death and the afterlife, 120, 183, 347–8, 357

  fertility cults, 23, 35, 177

  festivals, 8, 48, 78, 80, 85, 99–100, 111, 113, 116–19, 123, 152, 159, 164, 174f, 176, 180–2, 261, 281, 349, 356

  henotheism, 281–2

  Hinduism, 135

  hunting magic, 31

  imperial cult, 328, 330–1, 348–9, 359

  initiation rituals, 183, 348

  Islam, 371, 372, 381, 387–90, 392

  Judaism, 69–70, 121, 216–17, 285–6, 302, 349–52

  and kingship, 47, 50–1, 102–3, 328, 330–1, 348–9

  local gods, 202f, 213f, 344f

  and magic, 184

  Manichaenism, 353–4, 365

  Monophysitism, 380–1, 386, 387

  mystery cults, 183, 281–2, 346–8

  oracles, 85, 119, 179, 203–4

  and politics, 64, 68, 69–70, 119, 202f, 216–18, 223, 231f, 282–3, 348–9, 351, 364–5, 386–7

    kings, 47, 50–1, 102–3, 264, 284

  polytheism, 120, 121, 349, 355

  prehistory, 30–1

  reincarnation, 127

  role in banking, 248

  sacrifice, 39f, 48, 117, 179, 231f, 356, 359

  and scripts, 47–8

  Shintoism, 369

  syncretism, 279–81, 284–5, 287, 346–7, 365

  Taoism, 134

  Zoroastrianism, 122, 136, 298, 352, 353, 371

Remus, 89

Renaissance, definition, 390–1, 394

renaissances, 391, 394

renovatio, 377

reparatio, 306–7

Republic, 91, 107, 138, 149–51, 164, 221–2, 228–38, 251, 262, 264–8, 273, 278, 289, 298–301

res privata, 399

revolts (slave revolts), 235–6, 259–60
rhetoric, 334–6, 407, 408
Rhine, 34, 237, 301, 302, 312–13, 378
Rhodes, 212, 249, 251, 252
Rhône, 378
rites of passage, 31, 178, 182–3
roads, 5f, 222, 225, 260, 318–19
Romance languages, 386
Romanization, 310–13, 373–6, 390–4
Rome
    Archaic period, 88–91, 100
    army, 90–1, 212, 225, 229, 230–4, 262, 267–8, 305, 306–7, 310, 328, 331–2, 335f, 372
    chronology, 8, 91
    citizenship, 221, 232, 234, 254–6
    Classical period, 138, 149–51, 163, 397
    economy, 18, 19, 248–9, 251–2, 314–21
    education, 334–6
    Greek influence on, 272, 283–4
    Hellenistic period, 211–12, 221–40, 248–9, 251–2, 254–6, 264–8, 272
    Imperial period, 298–313, 314–65, 398–9, 402
        Eastern empire, 308–10, 325, 329–30, 359, 361–2
        Western empire, 310–13, 329, 330, 332, 360–2
    influence on other cultures, 310–13, 373–6, 390–4
    kings, 90–1
    language and literature, 88, 91, 301, 346, 364, 407, 408, 410
    late antiquity, 320–1, 326–7, 330–2, 372–3, 382–6

philosophers, 404, 405–6
politics, 90–1, 106–7, 150–1, 163, 215–16, 229–40, 254–6, 264–8, 298–313, 327–32, 364–5, 397–9
civil wars, 220–1, 234–40, 298, 305, 307–8
population, 221–2, 229, 318–19, 320, 342–3
religion, 122–3, 231f, 283–4, 346–65
roads, 5f, 222, 317
social class and inequality, 89–90, 99, 163, 229–34, 250f, 320–7
territorial expansion, 149–50, 211–12, 218–19, 221–2, 233–4, 237, 238, 239f, 240, 251–2, 268, 301, 303
wars, 211–12, 218–19, 221–9, 233–40, 251–2, 302–3, 305, 307–8, 372
see also Byzantium
Romulus, 89
Romulus Augustulus, 313
Rubicon, 238
rulers, 55, 83, 106–7, 263–4, 271–2
deification, 47, 50–1, 102–3, 282–3, 284, 328, 330–1, 348–9
Rumania, 301
Russia, 33, 42, 71, 77, 158, 170, 308, 317f, 387
rusticitas, 326

S
sacer, 331
sacrifice, 39f, 48, 117, 119, 179, 231f, 356, 359
sacrum consistorium, 331
Sahara, 13, 34
sainthood, 346, 357, 362–3 *see also* martyrdom
Sais, 68

Sakas, 297
Salamis, Battle of, 141
salinization, 17
Samaria, 417
Samnites, 88, 149, 222–3, 234
Samos, 72, 74, 76
Sanskrit, 197, 370
Santorini *see* Thera
Sarapis, 285f
Sardinia, Sardinia et Corsica, 57, 86, 92, 137, 225
Sargon, 47
Sarmatians, 137
Sassanid Empire, 297–8, 364, 371–2, 381, 390
satyr play, 182
Saxons, 313
Scandinavia, 58, 138, 373, 386
science, 126, 288–90, 343–5, 405–6
Scipio, Publius Cornelius, 226–7
Scipio, Publius Cornelius Aemilianus Africanus Numantinus (Scipio Africanus the Younger), 266
Scipio, Publius Cornelius Africanus, 227–8, 266
Scotland, 14, 303, 313, 376
scripts
    alphabets, 68–9, 73, 91, 92f, 113, 135
    Chinese characters, 40
    cuneiform, 42, 47–8
    hieroglyphic script, 37
    invention of, 37, 40, 47–8
    Linear A script, 53
    Linear B script, 53, 55, 57
    religious importance, 48
    syllabic scripts, 48, 53, 136
    see also literacy; literature
scrolls, 69, 113, 360f
Scylax, 125
Scythians, 71, 137
sea levels, 11, 32
Sea Peoples, 56f, 57

sea transport, 141, 317–18 *see also* navy
secondary products revolution, 15
secondary sources, 3–4
secularization, 186–7
sedentary societies 15, 31–4
    population density, 13–14
    relationship with nomads, 41, 65, 97, 197, 199
Seleucia, 212, 214, 245
Seleucid Empire, 8, 199–200, 212–16, 218–19, 287, 400–1
Seleucus, 196, 199, 200, 207, 212–14
Semites, 42, 47, 66, 104 *see also* Israelites
Senate, senators, 231–3, 237–8, 255, 260–1, 266–7, 268, 301, 303, 312, 321–2, 326–7, 329–30, 337, 338, 357, 378
senatus (Senate), 90, 397
Sentinum, Battle of, 223
Septimania, 378
Septimius Severus, 297, 305
Septuagint, 286
serfs, serfdom, 45, 82–3, 86, 93–4, 97–9, 107, 160–1, 242, 256–7, 296, 320–1, 325–6, 398
servi, 324
Servius Tullius, 91
sestertius, 248
Severi, Severan dynasty, 305
sexuality, 175–8, 278–9, 341–2
    celibacy, 23, 342, 378
    homosexuality, 115, 177–8, 278
shamanism, 31, 65
Shamash, 49f
Shang dynasty, 38–40
sheep, 33, 94
Shi'a, 390
shifting cultivation, 17, 41
Shintoism, 369

ships, 141, 317–18
Shu-Han, 296
shudra, 135
Siberia, 12
Sichuan, 296
Sicily, Sicilia, 259–60 *see also* Syracuse
Siddharta Gautama *see* Buddha, Buddhism
Sidon, 68
silk, 4, 40, 195, 244, 246, 293
Silk Road, 195, 200, 202f, 244–6, 293, 370f, 371
silver, 18, 66, 141, 155–6, 158, 161, 195, 204, 247, 251, 257, 316 *see also* coinage
Sinai, 37, 50, 69
sinification, 40, 191, 296
skepticism, 284, 287–8, 290, 404
slavery, 77, 97–8, 99, 115, 159–60, 170, 236, 249–51, 256, 258, 259–60, 320–1, 324–6, 398–9
Slavs, Slavonic peoples, 373, 381, 387
Social War, 234, 256, 268
society
    age classes, 100, 114–15
    Archaic period, 72–3, 74, 82, 93–128
    Bronze Age, 36–58
    Classical period, 152–87
    core-periphery relations, 40–1
    daily life, 109–28, 169–87, 269–90, 333–65
    Hellenistic period, 216–17, 229–34, 241–68, 269–90
    initiation rituals, 115, 119
    late antiquity, 378–82
    prehistory, 30, 33–5
    Roman Imperial period, 305–6, 314–65
social class *see* class
women *see* women

socii, 234, 267–8
Socrates, 173, 287–8
Sogdiana, 197, 198f, 204–5, 371
Sol (Invictus), 347
solidus, 307
Solomon, 69, 350f
Solon, 79, 99, 166
sophists, 173, 403
Sophocles, 182
soter, 281, 283
soul, 51, 122, 127–8, 134, 281, 342, 347–8, 353, 357–8
sources, 3–7, 346
South Asia, early civilizations, 38
South East Asia, 344–5, 353
Southeast Asia, 12, 13, 15, 34, 35, 37, 38, 45, 116, 134, 197, 296, 297, 369–70, 371
Spain, 225–8, 377, 380
Sparta
    Archaic period, 76, 77, 80, 82–3, 84, 98, 100, 104, 110
    Classical period, 141, 146–8, 160, 162
    Hellenistic period, 211
    social organization, 114–15, 116, 170–1
Spartacus, 236, 260
spectabiles, 327
sports, 85, 110, 111–12, 172
Sri Lanka, 13, 296, 353
Srivijaya, 393
stasis, 168
stater, 198f
steppe nomads, 14, 15, 41, 65, 197, 199, 371 *see also* nomadism
Stilicho, 312
stoa, 245f, 252, 275, 288, 334, 362
Stoa (Stoics), 288, 357, 403–4
Strabo, 344–5
strategoi, 146, 168, 396
stratigraphy, 7

Struggle of the Orders, 150–1, 222
Sudan, 40, 317f
Suevi, 312
Sui dynasty, 369
Sulla, 219, 234–5, 268
Sumer, Sumeria, 15f, 42, 45, 47
sumposion, symposium, 112, 116–17, 171
sun, sun god, 49f, 50–1, 103, 347, 349
Sunna, 390
suovetaurilia, 231f
Susa, 206
sussitia, 100–1, 110, 162, 170–1
syllabary, syllabic script, 48, 53, 136
synagogues, 216, 349–50
syncretism, 279–81, 284–5, 287, 346–7, 365
Syr Darya, 197, 205–6
Syracuse, 146, 223–5, 227, 289
Syria, 15, 52, 215–18, 350f, 380–1

T
Tabulae Vindolandenses, 335f
Tacitus, 299f, 346, 356
talents, 154
Talmud, 351–2
Tanakh, 286
Tang dynasty, 369, 370f
Taoism, 134
Tarent, 223
tariffs, 252
Tarim Basin, 293
Tarquinius, 90
Tarquinius Superbus, 91
taxation, 152, 154, 159, 229, 248–9, 251–2, 274, 306–7, 314, 320–1
technology, 19–20, 290, 345
spread of metallurgy, 37, 58, 73, 86
temples, 35, 38, 47–50, 85, 90–1, 117, 120, 159, 180, 202f, 245f, 248, 257, 264,

275f, 281, 283, 287, 311f, 344f, 348, 349, 362
Temple (Jerusalem), 70, 216–17, 264, 349, 351–2
terra sigillata, 317f
Thales of Miletus, 126
Thamagudi *see* Timgad
theater, 119, 182, 340, 407–8
Thebes (Egypt), 83
Thebes (Greece), 55, 76, 147–8, 201
themis, Themis, 173, 175
Themistocles, 141–2
Theodora, empress, 385f
Theodoric, 376
Theodosius I the Great, 307, 363–4
theorika, 159
Thera (Santorini), 12, 53
Theravada, 352, 370
thermoluminescence, 10
Thermopylae, Battle of, 141
Thessalonika, 381
Thessaly, 52, 55, 83, 98, 114, 160
thetes, 104, 145–7, 167
Thrace, Thracians, 137, 139f, 141, 148–9, 170, 207, 210, 215, 259
Thucydides, 186
Tiahuanaco *see* Tiwanaku Empire
Tiber, 88, 149, 318–20
Tiberius, 301
Tibet, 371
Tigris, 13, 17, 36, 40, 50, 67, 204
tile stamps, 317f
Timgad, 311f
timocracy, 330
Tiryns, 55–7
Titus, 303
Tiwanaku Empire, 393
Tocharians, 44, 297
Torah, 286
torture, 259, 337–8

town council *see boule, bouletai; curia, curiales*
trade
Archaic period, 80, 95–6
Classical period, 157–8
Hellenistic period, 195, 196, 200, 244–51, 252
late antiquity, 370f, 371
prehistory, 19, 53, 55
Roman Imperial period, 293, 317–18, 344f
slave trade, 249–51
tariffs, 252
transport costs, 20
tragedy, 119, 182, 186
Trajan, 297, 301, 303, 351, 356
transport, 5f, 20, 222, 244, 317–20
Trasimene Lake, Battle of, 227
tree-ring dating (dendrochronology), 9–10
Treves, 319
tribune of the people (*tribunus plebis*), 150, 231–7, 265, 397
tribunicia potestas, 327–8
tribunus (army), 90
tribute, *tributum,* 136, 145–6, 249
trierarchy, 154, 159, 168
Tripolis, 389
triremes, *trieres,* 141
trittues, 143–4, 396
triumphus, 91
Troy, 55
turannoi, turannis, 78–82, 84, 106, 164
turannoktonoi see tyrannicides
Turkestan, 297
Turks, 15, 45, 65, 194, 295–7, 371, 382, 394
Tyche, 213f, 282
tyrannicides, 81f, 106
Tyre, 203

U

Ulpian, 337
Umayyad dynasty, 389–90, 392
Umbria, Umbrians, 86, 223, 234, 267
umma, 389
Upanishads, 197
Ur, 47
Urartu, 68
urbanism, urbanization, 37–8, 42, 61, 65–6, 86, 131, 275–6, 308, 310, 320, 326, 330, 340, 378
urbanitas, 326
Uruk, 47
Utopianism, 288
Uzbekistan, 195, 197, 269

V

vaishya, 135
Valens, 308
Valerian, 359
Vandals, 310, 312–13
varna, 135
Vedas, 64
vegetation zones, 12–13, 32
Venus, 284
Venus-figures, 31, 35
Vergil, 301
Vespasian, 302–3
Vesta, 284
veto, right of, 150, 327
via Appia, 222, 260, 318–19
via Flamina, 225, 318–19
vicarius, 331, 399

Vietnam, 195, 293, 369
vilicus, 243, 259
villa, 243, 259, 319–21
Vindolanda tablets, 335f
Visigoths, 310, 312, 377, 380
voting procedures, 255, 265, 397
votives, 119, 179–80, 283–4, 344f, 346

W

wages, 156–7
Wales, 5f, 301, 376
war
    Archaic period, 67–8, 70–1, 76, 82–3, 84, 88, 124f
    Bronze Age, 51–2, 55–7
    Classical period, 139–41, 146–9
    Hellenistic period, 200–16, 218–19, 220–9, 233–40, 249–51, 252, 267–8
    late antiquity, 371–2, 376, 377, 381, 390
    Roman Imperial period, 302–3, 307–8
Wei, 296
White Huns *see* Hephtalites
women
    Archaic period, 67f, 89, 95, 114–17
    Classical period, 161, 169, 175–6, 178
    education, 334
    Hellenistic period, 277–9

    legal status, 116–17, 161, 171, 178, 277–8, 341
    pregnancy and childbirth, 22–3, 113–15, 175–6, 278–9, 343
    prostitution, 175–6, 178
    Roman Imperial period, 334, 341–2
Works and Days, 113
written sources, 3–4, 69–70, 142f, 165f, 299f, 335f, 346
    see also scripts
Wu, 296

X

Xenophanes, 127
xenos, 161
Xerxes, 141
Xiongnu, 297

Y

Yahweh, 120 *see also* Judaism
Yangzi, 296, 369
Yellow River *see* Huanghe

Z

zeugitai, 79, 81–2, 142
Zeus, 85, 111, 123, 139f, 178, 180, 198f, 203, 217, 275, 281–2, 346–7
Zhou dynasty, 61–4, 194
ziggurat, 48
Zimbabwe, 393
Zoroaster, 122, 136, 353
Zoroastrianism, 122, 136, 298, 352, 353, 371